1969

This book may be kept

THE POEMS OF ALEXANDER POPE

VOLUME V

THE DUNCIAD

The Twickenham Edition of the Poems of Alexander Pope

★

GENERAL EDITOR: JOHN BUTT

VOLUME I

PASTORAL POETRY and THE ESSAY ON CRITICISM.
E. Audra, Directeur de l'Office National des Universités, Paris.

VOLUME II

THE RAPE OF THE LOCK and other poems. Geoffrey Tillotson, Professor of English, Birkbeck College, University of London.

VOLUME III—i

AN ESSAY ON MAN. Maynard Mack, Professor of English and Fellow of Davenport College, Yale University.

VOLUME III—ii

EPISTLES TO SEVERAL PERSONS (MORAL ESSAYS). F. W. Bateson, Lecturer in English, Corpus Christi College, Oxford.

VOLUME IV

IMITATIONS OF HORACE and AN EPISTLE TO DR ARBUTHNOT and THE EPILOGUE TO THE SATIRES. John Butt, Professor of English, University of Durham, King's College, Newcastle upon Tyne.

VOLUME V

THE DUNCIAD. James Sutherland, Professor of English, University College, London.

VOLUME VI

MINOR POEMS. Norman Ault and John Butt.

THE

DUNCIAD,

VARIORVM.

WITH THE

PROLEGOMENA of *SCRIBLERUS.*

DEFEROR IN VICVM

VENDENTEM THVS ET ODORES

LONDON.

Printed for A. DOD. 1729.

ALEXANDER POPE

THE DUNCIAD

★

Edited by
JAMES SUTHERLAND

LONDON : METHUEN & CO. LTD
NEW HAVEN : YALE UNIVERSITY PRESS

First published October 21st 1943
Second Edition, revised, 1953
Third Edition, revised, 1963
Reprinted 1965

3.2
CATALOGUE NO. 02/4770/35 [METHUEN]

PRINTED IN GREAT BRITAIN BY
BUTLER AND TANNER LTD, FROME AND LONDON

PREFACE
TO THE FIRST EDITION

ONLY a very naïve reader would care to maintain that all poetry should be immediately self-evident, and that the poet should not presume upon any knowledge that is not "common knowledge." On the other hand, a poet's references are sometimes so recondite that even to his contemporaries much of his meaning is lost, or, if not lost, found only with the help of footnotes which he or his editor has been compelled to supply. With the passage of time, too, what was once common knowledge may cease to be generally known; and this is a misfortune which is particularly liable to overtake that kind of satire which is built of contemporary human material. All Pope's poems make a considerable demand upon the modern reader, but none more than the *Dunciad*. The reader whom Pope had in view was one who possessed the intellectual background of a well-read amateur of letters in the early eighteenth century. This ideal reader would have a lively recollection of at least the more familiar classical authors, and would therefore be quick to respond to the classic phrase in a modern context, the deliberate echo, the epic turn, the *double entendre*; he would have an intimate acquaintance with the London life of his day, and more particularly with the leisured world of wits and beaux and men of letters; and he would be easily familiar with the political and domestic history of the period. So equipped, an intelligent reader of 1728 would respond to the *Dunciad* with the immediate awareness of a contemporary and the discrimination natural to one of the initiated.

Compared with readers such as these, the twentieth-century reader is necessarily at a disadvantage. Pope's allusions—and, if need be, his jokes—may be explained by his editor; but explanation is not the same thing as immediate recognition, and to one who had actually known Dennis and Cibber and Curll how much more telling some of Pope's thrusts must have appeared. Yet much remains. If personal satire is bound to date, it is a policy of despair for later generations to give it up as unintelligible or inoperative. Much of the social background may still be acquired, in the pleasantest way imaginable, by reading the *Tatler* and *Spectator* and other works of the period, and the well-informed reader can at least walk down a Grub Street of his own imagining. The effort must be made; the reward is to watch with discernment one of the great masters of satire at his chosen task. And with the fading of the personalities a purely aesthetic enjoyment of the poem is easier to-day than it was in 1728. The indignation of Pope's victims has cooled, the heat of the controversy has departed; but the whole grotesque structure of

v

the *Dunciad* survives in a complication of monstrous and frozen beauty,

> And on th' impassive Ice the Lightnings play.

In the preparation of this edition I have had much generous assistance from my colleagues at University College and Birkbeck College. In particular I have to thank Professor H. E. Butler and Professor E. H. Warmington for helping me to trace a number of classical quotations and references, and to the former for enlisting the help of Mr E. H. Blakeney when all else failed. For other information not specifically acknowledged in the notes I am indebted to Sir E. K. Chambers, Mr Warren R. Dawson, Miss Helen L. Gardner, Mr H. G. Pollard, Professor G. Sherburn, Professor D. Nichol Smith, Mr Basil Willey (for a commentary on Book IV, ll. 459–500), Mr Harold Williams, Mr E. S. de Beer, and to my fellow editors, Mr Norman Ault and Mr Geoffrey Tillotson. Finally, Mr John Butt has taken more trouble with this volume than one has any right to expect of a general editor; his criticism and assistance have been invaluable, and his patience inexhaustible.   J. S.

PREFACE
TO THE SECOND EDITION

FOR this "Second Edition, with Some Additional Notes" I have corrected a few mis-statements and misprints, reconsidered two passages in the Introduction, and supplied some additional annotation. Most of the new notes come from an article contributed by the late Mr George G. Loane to *Notes and Queries*, vol. 186 (1944), pp. 36–7. The late Canon F. E. Hutchinson, whose kindness and scholarship it is a pleasure to remember, also sent me some valuable suggestions and queries, and corrected a number of errors "as well committed as unamended" by Pope's editor or printer. The notes which I owe to those two scholars will be found on pp. 477–84, and are indicated by the initials: G.G.L. and F.E.H. For other suggestions and corrections I am indebted to Mr Norman Callan, Mr Ian Jack, Mr J. C. Maxwell, Mr Robert Manson Myers, Mr James M. Osborn, Professor Robert W. Rogers, and Professor George Sherburn. I have also profited from reviews of the first edition of this volume by Professor Louis I. Bredvold and Professor R. H. Griffith.   J. S.

University College, London.

1952

PREFACE
TO THE THIRD EDITION

IN preparing this edition I have made use of a considerable number of comments on the poem which have been published since the previous edition, or which have been communicated to me privately. A few corrections have been made in the text of the poem and the notes, and a few minor changes or additions incorporated in the notes where those could be made without unduly disturbing the type; but the bulk of new editorial matter will be found at the end of the volume. To re-set the entire volume would not only be a costly procedure, but would lead to a change in the pagination, and that, in turn, would lead to confusion and exasperation among scholars who would have to cope with a double system of reference. For the convenience of the reader the notes added to this edition have been conflated with those added to the second edition: the additional notes will therefore be found to run consecutively from the Introduction to the Biographical Appendix.

In conclusion, I may be allowed to add that though I cannot agree with the Rev. William Wotton that the commentary on a poem requires "more Fineness of Thought, and Happiness of Invention, than perhaps Twenty such volumes as those were upon which these very Criticisms were made", I am beginning to see why he said it.

J. S.

CONTENTS

Frontispiece: The title page of the first edition, in quarto, of *The Dunciad Variorum,* 1729.

INTRODUCTION[1]

I

THE publication of the *Dunciad* in May 1728 marked a turning point in Pope's literary career. For the past fifteen years he had been engaged in such heavy labours as the translation of Homer, and the dull duties of an editor; but by March 1725 he had got Shakespeare off his hands, and in June of the following year the last volume of the *Odyssey* appeared. Pope was a free man again, free to write what he pleased. That he was already beginning as early as 1725 to plan for the future seems to be indicated by a letter which he wrote to Swift on September 15. "Your Travels I hear much of; my own, I promise you, shall never more be in a strange land, but a diligent, I hope useful, investigation of my own territories. I mean no more translations, but something domestic, fit for my own country, and for my own time." Those words, it is true, might fit almost everything that Pope published after 1728, and one is hardly justified in reading into them a provisional forecast of the *Dunciad*. A month later, however, he wrote to Swift again, and this time he mentions "the conclusion of one of my Satires, where, having endeavoured to correct the taste of the town in wit and criticism, I end thus:

> But what avails to lay down rules for sense?
> In George's reign these fruitless lines were writ,
> When Ambrose Philips was preferred for wit!"

Later in the same letter he assures Swift that he has certain designs in his head, but he will tell him what those are when Swift comes to visit him. "Then you shall have no reason to complain of me for want of a generous disdain of the world . . ." And finally, in the same letter still: "My name is as bad an one as yours, and hated by all bad poets, from Hopkins and Sternhold to Gildon and Cibber." In view of later developments, it is reasonable to see in this name-

---

1. Throughout this edition *Dunciad* A, or simply A, is used in referring to *The Dunciad, Variorum* of 1729, the text of which will be found on pp. 1 to 245. *Dunciad* B, or B, is *The Dunciad, in Four Books*, 1743 (pp. 247 to 426 of this edition).

less satire in which Pope had endeavoured "to correct the taste of the town in wit and criticism" the germ of the poem that afterwards became the *Dunciad*. His reference to "one of my Satires" suggests that he had a number of satirical poems at Twickenham still in manuscript. Those may have included some of the short poems that afterwards appeared in the *Miscellanies*, but others may have been worked into the scheme of the *Dunciad*, when that scheme was finally evolved. The line on Philips, at least, was not wasted; it was incorporated in the third book (A iii 322), and, if not actually the conclusion of the poem, forms part of the pessimistic summing up of contemporary wit and taste.

By 1725 Pope had received more than enough provocation from his literary contemporaries to justify some sort of answer. He had been attacked for being a papist, for being deformed, for being a Tory, for daring to translate Homer, for presuming to meddle with Shakespeare merely to make money, for blasphemy and obscenity, for ingratitude, and dishonesty, and disaffection to the government of his country.[1] With Dennis and one or two others Pope may have been the aggressor; but for the most part he had been wantonly attacked. Such attacks were a commonplace in the world of politics, but Pope was not a professional politician. More often than not he had been abused for nothing more than being successful; his poems were read and praised, those of his detractors were not. In 1716, provoked by Edmund Curll, he had made an unpleasant reply to an unpleasant person, and he had allowed himself some incidental flicks at a number of Curll's authors; but, on the whole, his claim that he had been patient is justified:

> Yet then did *Gildon* draw his venal quill;
> I wish'd the man a dinner, and sate still . . .

But if Pope was silent, he was not unmoved by the malice of his enemies. How keenly he felt their petty, and usually anonymous, attacks on his reputation may be seen from a letter he wrote to Swift on December 14, 1725. It was not, he said, the great ones of the world that made him angry. "My spleen is at the little rogues

---

1. This list of his supposed crimes might be considerably extended. Before 1727 the two favourite ways of baiting Pope in the newspapers were to ridicule his translation of Homer and his edition of Shakespeare, and to suggest that both were merely jobs undertaken for the printers by a mercenary man of letters.

of it; it would vex one more to be knocked on the head with a piss-pot than by a thunderbolt . . . But to be squirted to death, as poor Wycherley said to me on his death-bed, by apothecaries' apprentices, by the understrappers of under-secretaries to secretaries who were no secretaries—this would provoke as dull a dog as Philips himself." By 1725 he was certainly contemplating an effective and final retort to those "fools and scoundrels" who had been annoying him for so many years. "This poem," he wrote of the *Dunciad* on March 23, 1728, "will rid me of these insects." He no longer felt inclined to follow his own earlier policy and let them "die of themselves."

Of the various exasperating circumstances that may have induced Pope to change his tactics, the appearance in 1726 of Lewis Theobald's *Shakespeare Restored*[1] probably weighed most heavily with him. To one as sensitive as Pope, the publication of this volume must have caused intense annoyance and some acute mental suffering. His reputation, of course, would stand or fall on his poetry, not on his editing; but he was unwilling to think that something he had toiled at so hard was done badly, and certainly not as badly as Theobald's book made out. Here was an exposure of his incompetence as an editor, all the more galling for being in the main justified. Theobald made matters worse, too, by keeping his eyes fixed on Shakespeare, for whose writings he confessed to " a Veneration almost rising to Idolatry," and not on Pope, whose presence in this field he looked upon as incidental and unfortunate. After a decent tribute to Pope's own achievements as a poet, he proceeded in the pages that followed to treat him as nothing more than the editor of another man's work, and a poor one at that. Pope had dismounted from his Pegasus and chosen to go on foot; he must be prepared for any hard knocks that came his way. Had Theobald shown more malice, Pope might have found him easier to answer; but Theobald stuck to his Shakespeare, occasionally throwing out an impersonal comment, "Correct, therefore, as common sense requires," and calling attention to Pope's blunders or omissions only to emphasize the need for editorial accuracy.

---

1. *Shakespeare restored: Or, A Specimen of the Many Errors, As Well Committed, as Unamended, by Mr Pope in his Late Edition of this Poet* . . .

But what Theobald himself was usually too good-natured or too magnanimous to do, there were others ready enough to undertake; and soon after the publication of *Shakespeare Restored* letters began to appear in the newspapers, pointing out what a wretched bargain the subscribers to Pope's *Shakespeare* had made, and suggesting that the task of editing the dramatist should be handed over to a competent scholar. In *Shakespeare Restored* Theobald had concentrated upon an examination of *Hamlet*, but he promised— or, as Pope must have felt, threatened—to turn his attention to the other plays. Having staked out his claim in 1726, he continued to interest himself in Shakespeare, and in the course of the next two years the results of his work on the text were more than once given to the newspapers. If this interest in Shakespeare persisted (as it seemed likely to do), there would never be an end to those damaging exposures. Theobald, in fact, however amiably, was levying a sort of intellectual blackmail on Pope; the thought of him continuing to "crucify poor Shakespear once a week" in the public journals must have been highly disturbing to the man who had just edited the plays. Till Theobald was discredited he remained a persistent source of irritation; the best defence in this case was an attack so devastating that his reputation would be ruined. But Pope could not hope to destroy Theobald with his own weapons: the pedantic critic had exposed the amateurishness and insufficiencies of the poet turned editor, and if Pope was to reply it must be as a poet, not as a scholar. The reply came at last in the *Dunciad*. If it is objected that Theobald occupies a comparatively small space in the poem, it should be remembered that Pope's ridicule overflowed in 1729 into the notes. One or two of those are recognizable parodies of Theobald's own notes in *Shakespeare.Restored*, and the whole ponderous apparatus is intended to burlesque the labours of learned commentators and textual critics.

The importance of Theobald in the genesis of the *Dunciad* was adequately—perhaps too fully—recognized by his friends. A writer in *Mist's Journal*, June 8, 1728,[1] was willing to see in the exposure of Pope's *Shakespeare* the sole reason for the poem; and

---

1. The article is signed "W.A." In *1729a* (Appendix II) Pope attributed it to "*Dennis, Theobald*, and others." Later he assigned it to "some or other of the Club of Theobald, Dennis, Moore, Concanen, Cooke, who for some time held constant weekly meetings for these kind of performances." See p. 211n.

"Orator" Henley, writing some years after its appearance,[1] still took the same line.

Mr *Theobald* in his *Shakespear Restor'd*, convicted Mr *Pope* of Ignorance, both of Shakespear, which He pretended to publish, and of the *English Tongue*, in numerous Instances. Mr *Pope*'s little Bag of Choler burst within him on his *sinking* in Reputation, by that Attack of Mr. *Theobald*, and he wrote a *Dunciad* to blacken all that knew he was prov'd an *Ignoramus*, that is, all Mankind.

But important as *Shakespeare Restored* is in any discussion of the origins of the *Dunciad*, it must not be made to account for everything. If, as has been suggested, the beginnings of the poem may be traced to a date earlier than 1726, Theobald cannot be held solely responsible for Pope's satire. Before that date Theobald had given too little offence to Pope, and had himself been too little in the public eye, to be celebrated as King of the Dunces. If some version of the *Dunciad* existed as early as 1725, the poem in that earlier form had almost certainly some other hero.

In March 1726 Swift came to England, and spent the next few months with Pope at Twickenham. Swift's connection with the *Dunciad* is important. If we are to believe his own account,[2] it was he who "put Mr Pope on writing the poem, called the Dunciad." Pope's version of what had occurred is rather different. He nowhere admits that it was Swift who gave him the idea of writing such a poem, but he willingly allows Swift much of the credit for the poem that he eventually wrote. "Without you," he tells him, "it had never been"[3]; and in a note added to the *Dunciad* in 1729 he is more specific.

Dr *Swift* . . . may be said in a sort to be Author of the Poem: For when He, together with Mr *Pope* . . . determin'd to own the most trifling pieces in which they had any hand, and to destroy all that remain'd in their power, the first sketch of this poem was snatch'd from the fire by Dr *Swift*, who persuaded his friend to proceed in it, and to him it was therefore Inscribed.[4]

1. *The Hyp Doctor*, No. 29, June 22-29, 1731.
2. *Correspondence*, ed. F. E. Ball, iv 330.
3. EC vii 139.   4. See p. 201.

The anecdote sounds a little too dramatic; but there is no reason
to doubt that Swift persuaded his friend to persevere with a poem
which up till then had shown little promise of success, and it is
possible that Swift not only saved the manuscript but indicated
to Pope how the poem itself might be saved. It has been suggested,
in fact,[1] that what Swift snatched from the flames was a poem
satirizing the choice of a city poet and thus satirizing dullness
in poetry. The action of the *Dunciad* takes place on Lord Mayor's
day, 1719. Why 1719? "A possible hypothesis—and nothing more
—is that the poem originated in the choice of a city poet (who
'functioned' on Lord Mayor's Day) in burlesque of the recent
choice of a laureate (December, 1718)."[2] The fairly extensive
references to Settle, who, as Pope notes,[3] was poet to the City of
London, and whose office it was "to compose yearly panegyricks
upon the Lord Mayors, and Verses to be spoken in the Pageants,"
give further support to this conjecture. Settle died in 1724, and,
in Pope's words, "upon Settle's demise, there was no successor
to that place." Why not re-write the poem (Swift may have
suggested) providing a successor to Settle, a new candidate to
the throne of Dullness? Swift was staying with Pope when
Theobald's book came out, and if Pope was annoyed by Theobald's
criticisms no one would know it better than Swift. The idea, therefore, of making Theobald the hero of the poem may have come
from Swift, and it may have been just this happy suggestion that
persuaded the dissatisfied author to try again. Now, at one stroke,
Theobald was to supply the poet with a hero for his poem, and the
editor of Shakespeare with the sort of revenge that he was best
fitted to take. The poem, which had originally been a satire on
dull poets, would now satirize dull critics as well: it would thus
be a typical production of the Scriblerus Club.

Swift made another visit to his friends in England in April
1727, and again spent part of the summer with Pope at Twickenham. In some verses written about this time, he describes how he
would sit "plodding on a book," being too deaf for conversation,

---

1. By Professor George Sherburn in *The Best of Pope*, New York, 1929.
What follows in this paragraph is a précis of the very plausible conjecture
tentatively put forward by Professor Sherburn.

2. Sherburn, op. cit., p. 450.   3. A i 88.

while Pope, who was now hard at work on the *Dunciad*, would walk to and fro courting his Muse.

> Now Backs of Letters, though design'd
> For those who more will need 'em,
> Are fill'd with Hints, and interlin'd,
> Himself can hardly read 'em.[1]

The poem was rapidly taking shape in the summer of 1727, and no doubt Swift, who was always fond of throwing out hints for others to develop, was kept well informed of the progress being made, and contributed some suggestions which Pope was glad to improve. When the poem was completed it was Pope's intention to publish it along with other pieces of his own and of Swift's in a volume of *Miscellanies*.[2] On June 30, however, he wrote to the publisher, Benjamin Motte, and informed him that it would make "three sheets at least," and that he intended to "take time till winter to finish it." The poem had clearly grown beyond his original conception, for he went on to say: "It may then be published, singly first if proper. I'm sure it will be advantageous so to do—but say not a word of it to any man."

When the third volume of the *Miscellanies* appeared at last in March, 1728, the poem on which Pope had been working was not included. Instead, he had sent to Motte the prose treatise, *Peri Bathous: Or the Art of Sinking in Poetry*, a work to which several members of the Scriblerus Club may have contributed—Arbuthnot in particular—but which in its final form was almost wholly the work of Pope. "I have entirely methodized, and in a manner written it all," he told Swift. "The doctor grew quite indolent in it, for something newer, I know not what."[3] The *Peri Bathous* was not thrust into the third volume of *Miscellanies* merely as a stopgap; it was not so much a substitute for the *Dunciad* as a prelude to it. In rewriting the treatise Pope was making it serve his own purpose; and it is possible that Arbuthnot's indolence was due to a distaste for the highly personal twist that Pope was now giving

---

1. "*Dr.* Sw— *to Mr.* P—e, *While he was writing the* Dunciad."—*The Poems of Jonathan Swift*, ed. Harold Williams, 1937, ii 406.

2. Two volumes of Pope's and Swift's *Miscellanies* in prose were published by Motte in June, 1727. This third volume was to consist of their miscellaneous pieces in verse.

3. EC vii 110.

to it. In one of the attacks upon Pope which the *Dunciad* provoked there is an apparently well-informed reference to the *Peri Bathous.* Swift, it is asserted, never saw the treatise until after it was published, and Arbuthnot

> who originally sketch'd the Design of it, desired that the Initial Letters of Names of the Gentlemen abused might not be inserted, that they might be *A* or *B*, or *Do* or *Ro*, or any thing of that Nature, which would make this Satire a general one upon any dull Writers in any Age: This was refused by *Pope.*[1]

At all events, the treatise as it left the hands of Pope contained numerous examples of bathos drawn from the writings of such men as Blackmore, Dennis, Theobald, Welsted, and Philips; and in the notorious sixth chapter these and other authors were classified in a ludicrous fashion as birds, fishes, reptiles, etc., and distinguished quite clearly by the initial letters of their names. Pope afterwards tried to maintain that the initials had been inserted at random, and that there were so many bad poets about that "some one or other took every letter to himself."[2] The initials, however, had been chosen deliberately, and no intelligent reader in 1728 could have been in any doubt that the "J.D.," "C.G.," and "J.O." cited as porpoises were John Dennis, Charles Gildon, and John Oldmixon. The *Peri Bathous*, in fact, was to serve as a sort of ground-bait for the subsequent sport of the *Dunciad.* Pope was counting on a bitter reply from the various authors whom he had provoked in this treatise; and then, after a suitable interval had elapsed, he could publish his poem. The *Dunciad*, whether published anonymously or acknowledged by the author, would be ostensibly a defence of Alexander Pope, a just retribution on those who had abused him.[3] It would appear, too,

---

1. Leonard Welsted and James Moore Smythe, *One Epistle to Mr A. Pope* (1730), pp. vi–vii.

2. In a note from *1735a* onwards to "The Publisher to the Reader." See p. 201*n.* The words first appeared in the Dedication to Savage's *Collection of Pieces in Verse and Prose,* 1732—"commonly supposed to have been written by Pope" (Griffith, vol. i, pt. i, p. 203). See Johnson, *Lives,* iii 147.

3. This, at any rate, was the impression which he tried to give in the Preface to the *Dunciad* of 1728, where the reader is reminded that "every week for these two Months past, the town has been persecuted with Pamphlets, Ad-

at a most advantageous moment, when Pope's quarrel with his critics had already been well advertised by their pamphlets and their angry letters in the newspapers.

Pope had hitherto taken some trouble to keep his poem a secret; but the news of what he was doing was beginning to spread beyond the circle of his closest friends. Writing on February 5 1728, the poet Young told Thomas Tickell:

> Mr Pope is finishing a Burlesque Heroick on Writers, & yᵉ modern Diversions of the Town, it alludes to Homer & Virgil throughout. The 5th Book of Virgil is burlesqued into Games in which Booksellers run for the Authors & p-ss for Author-esses etc., as is likewise Part of the 6th by a Vision of Heroes in Dullness etc. 'tis near done & what is done is very correct.[1]

Young had obviously seen the poem in manuscript, and if Young could tell Tickell, Tickell could—and no doubt did—tell some one else. The first reference to the poem in the newspapers appeared just one week before the date of publication, when a letter (which Pope afterwards ascribed to Dennis) was published in the *Daily Journal* of May 11, stating that Pope was now writing The Progress of Dulness—a progress, the writer added, that had begun in *Windsor Forest, The Temple of Fame,* and so on.[2] At last, on May 18, the poem was published, but the publication was wrapped in mystery.

On the title-page of the first edition there appeared the imprint:

DUBLIN, Printed, LONDON Reprinted for A. DODD, 1728.

The date is correct, but probably nothing else. For a long time nineteenth-century book collectors used to keep a sharp eye on

---

vertisements, Letters and weekly Essays, not only against the Wit and Writings, but against the Character and Person of Mr. Pope." The anonymous author of the *Dunciad* was the only man who had appeared in his defence. On the other hand, in the facetious assertion that the poem was "the labour of full six years" the prefacer contradicts himself.

1. R. E. Tickell, *Thomas Tickell and the Eighteenth Century Poets*, p. 143.

2. Until shortly before its publication the *Dunciad* was always referred to by Pope and his friends as the "Dulness." The change to "Dunciad" was announced by Pope in a letter to Swift, dated March 23, 1728. No doubt Pope felt that the original title offered too easy a mark for the critics.

the market for an *editio princeps* published in Dublin; but the only Dublin edition of 1728 that has ever come to light is that bearing the imprint: "London: Printed, and Dublin Re-printed by and for G. Faulkner. . . . and T. Benson." It is now generally believed that the words "Dublin, Printed" were simply intended to mislead the public, by suggesting that the poem was the work of some Irish wit, and so to conceal for the time being the real author. Nor, in all probability, was the poem printed "for A. Dodd." Mrs Anne Dodd, widow of Nathaniel Dodd, was a retailer of newspapers and pamphlets who had in recent years become a publisher as well.[1] If she was the publisher of the *Dunciad*, she was entitled to have her copyright secured by entering it, or having it entered, in the Stationers' Register. On May 30 James Bettenham, a printer, entered a claim for the copyright of "The Dunciad an Heroic Poem in three Books" in the Register, and deposited with the Company the nine copies that the act of 8 Anne required.[2] The name of the author, usually given with such entries, was not divulged. Bettenham might conceivably have been acting on behalf of Mrs Dodd, and Mrs Dodd on behalf of Pope; but there are good reasons for believing that the circumstances were very different. When in 1729 Lawton Gilliver filed a bill in Chancery to restrain certain booksellers from publishing a pirated edition of the *Dunciad*, the Court had to consider, among other matters, Mrs Dodd's connection with the poem.[3] Commenting on the fact that the name "A. Dod" appeared on the title-page of the quarto of 1729, the four defendants state that they take this person to be

> Anne Dodd a publisher who lives without Temple Bar And these Defts are well informed and do believe that the sd Ann Dodd neither then had nor now hath any right or Title to the said Copy nor any Share whatsoever in the property thereof and that her name was put to the said Quarto Edition of the said Book without her Privity Knowledge or Consent and that she never Sold or Disposed of the said Books.

An affidavit sworn to by Mrs Dodd herself confirms this statement. If she had no right to the copy of the 1729 *Dunciad*, it is

---

1. I have given some facts about her in the Biographical Appendix.
2. "The Dunciad of 1729": *Modern Language Review*, xxxi (1936), 347–8.
3. *Ibid.*, p. 351. (P.R.O. C 11/2581/36.)

unlikely that she had any to that of 1728; otherwise she would have been entitled—until she had disposed of her interest to some one else—to go on republishing the poem in its original form, though she might have had no right to include in her editions the notes and other matter added in 1729. Such a state of affairs would have been intolerable to Lawton Gilliver, to whom, in fact, the poem was eventually assigned in the autumn of 1729.[1] It is a safe guess, therefore, that Mrs Dodd was never in any sense the publisher of the poem; and in making use of this woman's name Pope's intention was probably to suggest that the publication of the poem was unauthorized. "How I became possest of it is of no concern to the Reader," Mrs Dodd is made to say. ". . . . If it provoke the Author to give us a more perfect edition, I have my end. Who he is, I cannot say, and (which is great pity) there is certainly nothing in his style and manner of writing, which can distinguish, or discover him." In fact, Mrs Dodd is telling the world that she has got hold of the copy and means to publish it, though she has received no authority from the author to do so and does not even know who he is. In later years Pope referred to the editions of 1728 as "imperfect," or even "surreptitious" (A i 104n.), and the inference intended is that they were published without his consent.[2] The first "perfect" edition was the quarto of 1729; but Pope, who instructed his printer to put "Printed for A. Dod" on the title-page of this edition too, was not even then prepared to acknowledge his authorship.

Was Bettenham, then, the original publisher of the poem? He was certainly the printer of the 1728 *Dunciad*.[3] Sixty five years later Daniel Prince, the Oxford bookseller, recalled how he was "the apprentice trusted to go to the Author with the proofs in great secrecy. I had the wit to keep the sheets with some of his marks to correct."[4] Bettenham, however, was a printer rather than a publisher. It is unlikely that at any time he held the copyright of the poem, and his entry in the Register was most probably made

1. *Ibid.*, p. 351. (P.R.O. C 11/549/39.) See pp. 460 ff.
2. In the "Letter to the Publisher" Cleland suggests that the author would not have omitted a commentary in the 1728 editions "had he approv'd of the first appearance of this Poem." See p. 11.
3. "The Dunciad of 1729": *Modern Language Review*, xxxi 347; Griffith, vol. i, pt. ii, p. 578.   4. J. Nichols, *Literary Anecdotes*, iii 705.

on behalf of the real owner, Pope himself, in the hope that it might
discourage piracy.[1] It must have been a slender hope, for the Act
of 8 Anne required that the name of the author should be stated,
and this Bettenham had omitted to do.

Pope's motives for anonymous publication are reasonably
clear. Until January 1728, if not later, it was his intention to
include in the poem the inscription to Swift, and if this did not
actually brand Pope as the author it narrowed the field to one of
Swift's intimate friends. The decision to omit the inscription may
not have been taken till almost the last moment; for on June 1
Swift was writing from Ireland: "The doctor told me your secret
about the Dunciad, which does not please me, because it defers
gratifying my vanity in the most tender point, and perhaps may
wholly disappoint it." The secret must surely have been Pope's
decision not to own the poem for the present, and perhaps, as the
last clause suggests, never to own it at all if circumstances proved
unfavourable. As the day of publication drew near, Pope's nerve
may have failed him, and the fear of legal or other reprisals may
have induced him to change his plans.[2] It has even been suggested[3] that his original intention was to publish the poem with
notes on the duces; if that is so, then his nervousness would have
had more justification. At all events, the contention of the Publisher
of 1728 that the author of the poem must have been peculiarly
intimate with Pope "from the knowledge he manifests of the most
private Authors of all the anonymous pieces against him" has
much more application to the annotated Dunciad of 1729 than to
the 1728 poem, in which the names of some duces are left
entirely blank and others more or less effectually concealed by an
initial letter.[4] It may be, however, that Pope's reasons for pub-

---

1. At least one contemporary journalist hinted that Pope himself was the
publisher of the poem. Cf. *The Daily Journal*, Sept. 9, 1728: "The Bookseller
is obliged to the incensed Writers of the Town . . . or rather the *Author,* if it be
true, as is said, that he makes a little Profit by the *retailing* of it."

2. It was the opinion of at least one of his victims that he was "liable by the
Laws of the Land to be punish'd when he shall be discovered," and that he
had therefore refrained from acknowledging his authorship.—*Pope Alexander's
Supremacy . . . examined,* (1729), p. 3.

3. *Notes and Queries,* I Ser. x 198.

4. e.g. "Breval, Besaleel, Bond, the Varlets caught" (A ii 118) reads in
1728a "**, **, and **, the wretches caught."

lishing the *Dunciad* as he did were due less to nervousness than to the vanity of authors. He may, in fact, have yielded to the impatience of Swift and allowed the poem to be published before he was fully satisfied with it.[1] Pope laboured carefully at all his poems, but he said himself that the *Dunciad* cost him as much pains as anything he ever wrote.[2] Nor was it his habit to publish in a hurry.[3] It *was* his habit, on the other hand, when he had anything "better than ordinary to say, and yet too bold," to reserve it for a second or third edition, when "nobody took any notice of it."[4] Such considerations may have been at work here. It was one thing, no doubt, to authorize the publication of a libel, and quite another to leave it lying about so that some rascally person got hold of it and published it. When the excitement had died down, the author could come forward with the usual plea that his poem had crept into print "without the last corrections from the author's hand," and that he was now compelled, in justice to himself and the public, to publish a more "correct" edition.

Whatever may have been Pope's reasons for anonymity, there seems to have been little doubt from the first that he was the author. "Who is the Author of the *Dunciad*?" Dr William Stratford was writing on May 25 to the Earl of Oxford; but he added immediately, "Is it not Pope?"[5] Some natural doubts may have arisen from the fact that the poem which had just appeared was not called "The Progress of Dulness," and further uncertainty must have been caused by the fact that the first duodecimo edition carried an announcement, which was repeated in newspaper advertisements of the poem: "Speedily will be Published, The Progress of Dulness, an Historical Poem. By an Eminent Hand.

---

1. And if the poem was to be a reply to Theobald and those others who had been writing against him since the publication of the *Peri Bathous* it would have to appear soon, or else it would be out of date.

2. Spence, p. 142.

3. "My *Essay on Criticism*," he told Spence, "was written in 1709; and published in 1711; which is as little time as ever I let anything of mine lay by me." (Spence, p. 170.)

4. Richard Porson, *Tracts and Miscellaneous Criticisms*, 1815, pp. 323-4.

5. *MSS. of the Duke of Portland* (H.M.C.), vol. vii, p. 464.

Price 1s. 6d." It is now generally believed that this announcement was a further move in Pope's process of misleading the
public, and was intended to convey the impression that the poem
of that title which Pope was believed to have been writing had
not yet been published. At this point Edmund Curll seems to
have stepped in. Realizing, no doubt, that no poem by the
"eminent hand" would be forthcoming, he decided to supply
one. In the *Daily Journal*, June 12, 1728, he advertised "The
Progress of Dulness. A Poem. By an Eminent Hand. . . . Price 1s."
On July 5 he advertised it again, with the significant addition:
"The True Copy, no other Piece, under this Title, being intended
to be publish'd."[1] Those last words would scarcely have been
added if Curll had been responsible for the original advertisements of "The Progress." It will be noted, too, that his poem sold
at one shilling; in spite of some prose additions he had not been
able to pad it out to a one-and-sixpenny pamphlet.

"The Beggar's Opera has knocked down Gulliver," Swift
wrote to Gay on March 28. "I hope to see Pope's Dulness knock
down the Beggar's Opera." Swift's hopes were fulfilled. If Savage's
account of the excitement on publication day is not just imaginary,
the effect of Pope's satire on Grub Street was startling enough.

> On the Day the Book was first vended, a Crowd of Authors
> besieg'd the Shop; Entreaties, Advices, Threats of Law, and
> Battery, nay Cries of Treason were all employ'd, to hinder the
> coming out of the *Dunciad*: On the other Side, the Booksellers
> and Hawkers made as great Efforts to procure it . . .[2]

---

1. Griffith, vol. i, pt. ii, pp. 580–2.
2. *A Collection of Pieces in Verse and Prose . . . By Mr. Savage*, 1732, p. vi. How far
Pope went in physical danger on account of the *Dunciad* it is difficult to say.
The son of John Dennis is said to have arrived one night at Lord Bathurst's
villa, where Pope was dining, and to have sent in a message for Pope to say that
he was outside with his sword (EC viii 237). Dennis himself is responsible
for a statement that after the *Dunciad* was published Pope did not dare to appear without a tall Irishman attending him (*Remarks upon the Dunciad*, 1729,
p. 12). The legend was varied by saying that he became "a prisoner in his own
house" (*Pope Alexander's Supremacy*, 1729, p. 11). Against such assertions one
must place the far more reliable evidence of the poet's sister, Mrs Racket:
"My brother does not seem to know what fear is. When some of the people
that he had put into his Dunciad, were so much enraged against him, and
threatened him so highly: he loved to walk out alone, and particularly went

As edition followed edition, there was a renewed outburst of anti-Pope satire and comment from those whom he had ridiculed, and from others who joined in the scrap of their own free will. Facetious reports of this literary war kept on appearing in the *Daily Journal*, the *London Evening-Post*, and *Mist's Journal*: the *Dunciad* was more than a poem, it was an event. Its effect on the reputation of the duncesis difficult to assess, and no doubt it would be easy to exaggerate the damage they suffered. In a facetious piece, *The Legal Tryal and Conviction of Mr Alexander Pope of Dulness and Scandal*,[1] "the plaintiff, John [*i.e.* James?] Ralphe," claims heavy damages from Pope because

> The Fame and Reputation of the said *John* hath greatly suffer'd with his Booksellers, Printers, and Hawkers, by the false and malicious Aspersion aforesaid.

More serious, perhaps, is the suggestion of another pamphleteer[2] that by setting Theobald "in a very ridiculous Point of Light" Pope had prevented many people from subscribing to his edition of Shakespeare. "I was desired, a great while ago, to subscribe to *Shakespear*. I thought the Gentleman mad that ask'd me, and refused him. Such was the Prejudice Mr *Pope* had given me against *Theobald*."

II

It was not long before the public began to feel the need of some sort of key to the dunces. The Earl of Oxford wrote on May 27 to say that many of his friends had been asking for one, and three weeks later Pope was able to tell him that the curiosity of George II had been sufficiently aroused for him to make a similar demand. Writing from Ireland on July 16, Swift took the opportunity of reminding Pope that "twenty miles from London nobody understands hints, initial letters, or town facts and passages; and in a

---

often to Mr Fortescue's at Richmond. Only he would take Bounce [his large Danish dog] with him; and for some time carried pistols in his pocket." (Spence, pp. 267–8.) Pope himself told Spence that he would not go a step out of his way to avoid those who threatened him, for "he thought it better to die, than to live in fear of such rascals." (*Ibid.*, p. 268.)

1. See Giles Jacob's *The Mirrour*, 1733, pp. 77–8.

2. *A Dialogue Concerning Mr Pope and His Writings*, pp. 54–5. (Included by Curll in his miscellany, *Post Office Intelligence*, 1736.)

few years not even those who live in London." Long before this,
however, Edmund Curll had gone some way towards satisfying
the curiosity of the London reader by publishing, on May 29, *A
Compleat Key to the Dunciad.*[1] It was followed before long by a
second, and a third, edition. At least one other printed Key was
on sale about the same time, though this, like Curll's, was clearly
unauthorized.[2] Curll also refers[3] to a manuscript Key which was
on view at the shop of Lewis the bookseller, and there may have
been others. As early as June, and perhaps earlier, Pope himself
was hard at work on the annotation of his poem. "The Dunciad
is going to be printed in all pomp," he told Swift on June 28.

> . . . It will be attended with *Proeme, Prolegomena, Testimonia
> Scriptorum, Index Authorum* and *Notes Variorum.* As to the latter, I
> desire you to read over the text, and make a few in any way you
> like best, whether dry raillery, upon the style and way of com-
> menting of trivial critics; or humorous, upon the authors in
> the poem; or historical, of persons, places, times; or explana-
> tory; or collecting the parallel passages of the ancients.[4]

In later years Pope was in the habit of asserting that he was no
more than the author of the poem, and that the rest of the book was
the work of two or three of his friends.[5] This is certainly an

1. It was advertised by him as "Explaining all the Passages, Pieces, and
Persons Libelled, in that scurrilous, obscene, and impious Satire."—*The Evening-
Post,* June 1–4, 1728. Mrs Dodd, the "publisher" of the poem was one of those
from whom this *Key* was to be had.

2. Cf. *Mist's Journal,* June 8, 1728: "Order'd that Mr C—k [i.e. Thomas
Cooke] do compose the said *Key* to the *Dunciad.*" This can hardly refer to
Curll's *Key* which had been on sale for some days. This other *Key* may be that
described by Professor Griffith in *The Cambridge Bibliography of English Literature,*
vol. ii, p. 298, and referred to in the notes to this edition as ANONYMOUS KEY.

3. *The Progress of Dulness,* p. 34. See also Curll's *Key* (3rd ed.), p. vi.

4. A still earlier indication of Pope's intentions is to be found in his letter to
Lord Oxford, June 13, 1728, where he asks (apparently for the second time)
for "the extract out of Caxton's preface, how he came by Virgil. I want it
speedily . . ." This extract was to appear as Appendix III to the *Dunciad
Variorum.* Did Oxford's compliance with this request qualify him for being
styled one of the "authors of the notes"?

5. In the Advertisement to the *Dunciad Variorum* the publisher is made to
state that the commentary was sent to him "from several hands." Writing to
Sheridan, October 12, 1728, Pope stated: "Some very good epigrams on the
gentlemen of the Dunciad have been sent me from Oxford, and others of the

exaggeration. Swift may have sent some hints, but he had little first-hand knowledge of the Grub Street of 1728. Nor had Arbuthnot much liking for the extremely personal satire in which the *Dunciad* abounds; his taste in wit is more likely to have found expression in the "Virgilius Restauratus," and this piece has, in fact, been claimed for him with some confidence.[1] Of Pope's other friends, Gay was probably too indolent to contribute much, and Bolingbroke, like Swift, knew too little about the dunces to write notes about them. There remain two others to be considered: William Cleland and Richard Savage.

Cleland was not, as has sometimes been supposed, a complete phantom; yet the "Letter to the Publisher" which bears his name has all the marks of Pope's style. It is clear from three letters which Pope wrote to the Earl of Oxford in July, 1728, that Oxford's amanuensis was then copying out Cleland's letter and the notes variorum for the press. Pope, of course, could have hired a scrivener if he had so wished; his motive in making use of the Earl's may have been economy, but was more probably secrecy. If Cleland had really written (and not merely signed) his Letter, it could surely have gone to the printer in his hand; if Pope wrote it, he would naturally wish that only some one who was perfectly discreet should see that it was in his handwriting.[2] Beyond lending his name to it, Cleland had probably not much more to do with writing the Letter than Mrs Anne Dodd had with publishing it.

Richard Savage, on the other hand, had almost certainly a good deal to do with the *Dunciad Variorum*. He was at this time on friendly terms with Pope, and was probably his chief link with Grub Street. Pope's lofty contempt for the lives of the dunces may have been largely assumed; but he was bound to rely upon others for much of his information about them. At all events, it was

London authors." One or two of these may have found their way into the editions of 1729.

1. E.g. by Lester M. Beattie, *John Arbuthnot*, p. 284. In the "Advertisement to the Reader" of *1743a* Warburton refers to the notes "written by Mr Cleland, Dr Arbuthnot, and others." See also Pope's letter to Warburton, Nov. 27, 1742 (EC ix 225).

2. It should perhaps be added that in the summer of 1728 Pope was writing with considerable difficulty owing to an accident to his hand when he was pitched out of Lord Bolingbroke's coach and cut by flying glass.

widely believed among Pope's victims that Savage was the chief informant, or, as they preferred to put it, informer. In Cooke's revised *Battle of the Poets* (1729) he appears among the combatants as a spy. In the *Hyp Doctor*, April 29, 1735, Henley expressed the general opinion with his usual violence:

> *Richard Savage*, Esq; was the *Jack-all* of *that Ass* in a *Lyon's Skin*, he was his *Provider*: Like *Montmaur*, the *Parasite* of *Paris*, he rambled about to gather up *Scraps of Scandal*, as a Price for his *Twickenham Ordinary*; no Purchase no Pay; no Tittle-tattle, no Dinner: Hence arose those *Utopian* Tales of Persons, Characters and Things, that rais'd, by the *clean Hands* of this *Heliconian Scavenger*, the *Dunghil of the Dunciad*.

One is probably safe in assuming that when Norton Defoe is said to be writing a Life of Colonel Chartres (A ii 383), or when Ralph is said to have "smiled and reply'd, *Shakespear writ without rules*" (A iii 159), the information came from Savage.[1]

When allowance has been made for all such assistance, there still seems good reason to believe that Pope wrote the greater part of the notes himself, compiled the Testimonies of Authors, the List of Books and Papers, the Parallel of the Characters of Mr Dryden and Mr Pope, and the Index of Things (including Authors). For one thing, he was the only person likely to have in his possession the information on which many of the statements were based. For years he had been carefully collecting the various printed attacks upon him. He had even got Tonson to bind them together in six volumes, labelled "Curll and Company," "Libels on Pope," etc. The volumes are still in existence[2]; and it is significant that Pope had underlined and occasionally annotated the more outrageous statements of Dennis, Curll, and the rest, as if he intended to make some reply. Some of the *Dunciad* notes, too, relate to matters which only the injured author himself would

---

1. See also Johnson, *Lives*, ii 362. Apparently Savage had been moved to write a satire on the same lines as Pope's. In the *Grub-Street Journal*, May 28 1730, Gilliver announced "The Gentlemen of the Dunciad. A Poem. By Mr. Savage, with a Preface." It never appeared. Savage may have been the link between Pope and Mrs Dodd. His *Wanderer*, advertised in the *Daily Journal*, January 31, 1729, was "Printed for J. Walthoe, and sold by A. Dodd." (*Notes and Queries*, I Ser. x 217.)

2. In the British Museum, C 116 b 1–4, and Victoria and Albert Museum.

think worth recalling. There seems to be no escaping the conclusion, therefore, that when Pope decided to publish the *Dunciad*
with Notes Variorum it was he himself (with Savage acting,
perhaps, as a sort of secretary) who worked through his four
volumes of Libels, Jacob's *Poetical Register*, Winstanley's *Lives of
the Poets*, and other works of reference or abuse. The purely
personal aspect of the *Dunciad* was Pope's own business; he could
hardly expect his friends to manifest a very lively concern over
what Dennis had written or Philips spoken against him a dozen
or fifteen years ago. But it is just from such trivialities that the notes
to the *Dunciad* are often constructed.

The publication of the *Dunciad Variorum* was attended by delays
and mystifications similar to those of 1728. The same secrecy was
observed in the printing: Pope still refrained from handing his
poem over to a publisher, but sent the copy direct to the printer.
According to Dennis,[1] the poem of 1729 was

> printed by one *Wr-t*, who was formerly Operator to Alderman
> *B-*, and who lives in a Place call'd *Peter's Hill* . . . Does not
> half the Town know, that honest *J.W.* was the only Dunce
> that was persecuted and plagu'd by this Impression? that
> Twenty times the Rhapsodist alter'd every thing that he gave
> the Printer? and that Twenty times, *W.* in his Rage and in
> Fury, threaten'd to turn the Rhapsody back upon the Rhapso-
> dist's Hands?

Dennis's "honest J.W." is J. Wright, who was printing for Lawton
Gilliver in 1733, and perhaps earlier. He was sending Pope proofs
by October, 1728, but Pope took his time over them; he was in an
unusually wretched state of health, and his mother was having
one of her last illnesses. He was clearly worried, too, about the
trouble which might be in store for him. If it had been desirable
to proceed cautiously in 1727-8, it was still more necessary now,
when the names of the dunces were to be printed in full, and their
careers set forth in a succession of satirical notes. Pope did not,
in fact, publicly admit that he was the author of the *Dunciad*
until it was published in vol. ii of his *Works* in 1735; but Cleland's "Letter to the Publisher" in the quarto of 1729 had made
no secret of the fact that the poem was by Pope.

---

1. *Remarks upon . . . the Dunciad*, 1729, pp. 7-8.

On March 12, 1729, the *Dunciad Variorum* was presented to
George II by the hand of Sir Robert Walpole.[1] It did not reach the
booksellers until some date early in April, and when it did it was
by the consent of three noblemen to whom Pope had meanwhile
assigned the copyright, the Earl of Oxford, the Earl of Burlington,
and Lord Bathurst. For some time the three lords had been dis-
posing of copies privately to their friends and acquaintances; and
this form of private publication, while not exposing the author to
an action for libel, was no doubt providing him with an advance
publicity for his poem.[2] Pope, in fact, was sheltering behind his
three noble friends, who were unlikely to be brought into court
by the Concanens and Welsteds whom he had attacked. Meanwhile he had found a bookseller willing to relieve the three noblemen of their responsibilities.[3] On April 10, 1729, Lawton Gilliver
was advertising in the *Daily Post:*

> This Day is publish'd, in a Beautiful Letter in Quarto, A Com-
> pleat and correct Edition of the DUNCIAD . . . Printed for
> Lawton Gilliver against St. Dunstan's Church, in Fleetstreet,
> and A. Dodd without Temple Bar. Price 6s. 6d.

Gilliver was forced to mention Mrs Dodd in his advertisement, for
her name appeared on the title-page, and not his own. It appeared
again on the title-page of the octavo edition, which was also put on
sale early in April; but thereafter it disappears for good from the
bibliography of the *Dunciad*. On April 17 Gilliver was selling this
same octavo with a cancelled title page: "Printed for Lawton
Gilliver at Homer's Head . . ." A few days later he found himself

---

1. *Dunciad* A 1 *in.* The King, having read the poem, declared that Mr Pope
was "a very honest man."—Swift, *Correspondence*, iv 73.

2. "The new Edition of the *Dunciad* in Quarto, mention'd in our last, is in
the Hands of some of the Nobility."—*The Flying Post; or, The Weekly Medley*,
March 29, 1729. Cf. *Pope Alexander's Supremacy . . . examin'd*, 1729, pp. 9–10.

3. In the suit which Pope brought against Lintot in Chancery, 1743
(C11/549) it was stated that "some time" in 1728 Gilliver "did print and publish
an Edition or Impression of the said Book or Poem"—a statement which is
almost certainly untrue. It was further stated that Gilliver's copyright was due
to expire in December 1742. If this second statement is accurate, Gilliver must
have secured the copyright in December 1728, i.e. fourteen years previously.
But see "The Dunciad of 1729" in *Modern Language Review*, vol. xxxi, p. 347,
where evidence is adduced that Gilliver was buying the quarto of 1729 like any
other member of the booksellers' trade. See also p. 462 below.

competing with a pirated edition in octavo, "Printed for A. Dob."
A lively advertising contest followed in the newspapers, Gilliver
warning the public against the imposture, and the Dob publishers
retorting that "the Pompous Quarto Edition" was far too ex-
pensive. "The Publick," they insisted, "is now insulted, for having
paid so great a Price as 6s. 6d. for that Edition" when the Dob one
was selling at two shillings.[1] Two separate Dublin editions in 1729
afford some evidence of the poem's popularity; and finally, on
November 24, Gilliver published "The Second Edition, with some
Additional Notes." The demand was now temporarily exhausted,
and no further edition appeared until the poem was reprinted in
the *Works*, vol. ii, 1735. The war with the dunces, however, was
carried on with unabated liveliness in the pages of the *Grub-Street
Journal*. What part Pope took in this journal is not certainly
known; but though Henley, who called it "The Dunciad trans-
prosed," may have been wrong in stating that Pope founded it and
"intended it to continue his *Dunciad*," he almost certainly gave it
his support.[2]

III

For the next thirteen years Pope was content with making only
a few minor changes in his poem. Subsequent editions up to 1742
saw one or two names altered, a few notes expanded or modified,
and one addition to the apparatus, the black-letter "By the
Author A Declaration," first included in the *Works*, 1735. But no
substantial addition was made to the poem itself until the publication, in March 1742,[3] of an entire new book: *The New Dunciad: As
it was Found in the Year 1741*. In this fourth book the prophecies of
Book III were at length fulfilled; the reign of dullness, only
threatened in 1728, had really begun. Now the Great Mother

> bids Britannia sleep,
> And pours her Spirit o'er the Land and Deep.

The satire of 1742 goes far beyond the pedantries of Theobald,
who (though he was still alive) is not even mentioned. Pope is

---

1. *The Daily Journal*, *The Daily Post*, April 27, 1729 etc.

2. *Why How now, Gossip Pope* (2nd ed.), 1743, p. 5; *The Hyp Doctor*, No. 48,
Nov. 2–9, 1731. See also vol. iv, pp. 124–5n.

3. March 20 (Griffith, vol. i, pt. ii, p. 440). The entry in the Stationers'
Register (by John Wright) is dated March 18.

looking critically at contemporary England after twenty years of Walpole's administration, and exposing the nation's follies and stupidities one after another: the decay of the theatres, of the schools and universities, of the aristocracy, of the arts and sciences, of the Church, of public and private morality, of liberty; the growth of luxury, of free thinking, of political corruption; the follies of virtuosi, of young peers who patronize the Opera or who make the Grand Tour, of pedantic scholars, of gourmets, of freemasons . . . The tone is graver, the satire (with one or two notable exceptions) less purely personal in its application. Like almost all his later work, it shows clearly his sharpened interest in politics.

By 1740 Pope had the advantage, if it was an advantage, of having met Warburton; and Warburton seems to have been to the fourth book what Swift had been to the first three. He "concerted the plan" of the fourth book with Pope,[1] and the poem proceeded, if not under his guidance, at any rate with his constant encouragement and advice. On November 12, 1741, Pope, who was then staying with Ralph Allen near Bath, invited Warburton to come and spend a few weeks there. "Your exhortations," he told Warburton, "may be most effectual to make me resume the studies I have almost laid aside." If Warburton would "unbend to the idle amusement of commenting upon a poet, who has no other merit than that of aiming by his moral strokes to merit some regard from such men as advance truth and virtue," the unfinished poem might be completed. Warburton accepted the invitation, and his visit no doubt gave Pope the encouragement, advice, and even some of the information, that he needed.

The poem upon which Pope was now engaged—the last of his works—had developed out of a project which he never realized. On March 25, 1736, he outlined to Swift the plan for four epistles "which naturally follow the Essay on Man. 1. Of the extent and limits of human reason and science. 2. A view of the useful and therefore attainable, and of the un-useful and therefore unattainable, arts. 3. Of the nature, ends, application, and use of different capacities. 4. Of the use of learning, of the science of the world, and of wit. It will conclude with a satire against the misapplication of all these, exemplified by pictures, characters, and examples."

1. EC ix 222n.

Fragments from all four epistles may have found their way into the *New Dunciad*, and the projected conclusion in particular seems to cover much of the same ground. In a rather different account of those four epistles which he gave to Spence,[1] Pope explained that "the second would have been on knowledge and its limits:— here would have come in an Essay on Education; part of which I have inserted in the Dunciad." The section of the poem dealing with education runs to just over two hundred lines (B iv 135-336); and there are other episodes, such as the contest between the florist and the butterfly collector with its satirical reflections on Queen Caroline (who had died in 1737), which are almost certainly fragments of the earlier scheme.

In taking Warburton into his counsels, and making him to some extent a collaborator in a poem satirizing dullness, Pope was naturalizing to the realm of wit one of the Queen's own subjects. It would be idle to speculate on Warburton's contribution to the *New Dunciad*; but his heavy hand can be felt at times in the poem itself,[2] and still more in the commentary. On April 23, 1742, about a month after the publication of the poem, Pope was thanking him for the zeal he had shown "for that piece of my idleness, which was literally written only to keep *me* from sleeping in a dull winter, and perhaps to make others sleep unless awakened by my commentator."[3] The poet seems here to be giving his friend the credit for the commentary which accompanied the new book; but in his edition of 1751 Warburton distinguishes the notes which had appeared in 1742 with the letters "P.W." to indicate that they were jointly composed by the poet and his editor.

From the first, readers of the *New Dunciad* complained of its obscurity. A writer in *The Universal Spectator*, April 3, 1742, recorded the opinion of the town critics:

> The Censure they pass is, That the *Satire* is too *allegorical*, and the *Characters* he has drawn are too *conceal'd:* That *real Names* should have been inserted instead of *fictitious* ones.

---

1. Spence, p. 315. Cf. also p. 289.

2. Courthope is almost certainly right in his suggestion that the metaphysical part of the *New Dunciad* was "largely inspired by Warburton."—EC v 337. It probably owed a good deal, however, to Bolingbroke too.

3. Cf. *Dunciad*, A i 92.

2

Characters like Mummius and Paridel puzzled Pope's contemporaries, and have never been satisfactorily identified; the satire on the type is effective enough, but the reader is piqued by his failure to discover the individual. A still more hostile critic complained that "the want of Perspicuity is so notorious, that . . . it is *a Darkness to be felt* in ev'ry *Line* by ev'ry *Reader*."[1] In his opinion the plan, the grammar, the sense, the stories, the allusions, and the characters were all obscure. This is going much too far; but the fourth book does sometimes lean too heavily on the explanatory notes to make it intelligible, and more knowledge is often assumed in the reader than could fairly be expected, even in 1742. Perhaps the *New Dunciad* suffers from having been talked over too fully with Warburton: Pope may sometimes have failed to realize that what, after due explanation, was crystal clear to his friend, might not be readily intelligible to the general public who had not Warburton's advantage.[2]

IV

The final step was taken in 1743, and Pope had still one surprise left for the public. During the winter of 1742-3 he was hard at work revising all four books, and when at last, in October 1743,[3] *The Dunciad, In Four Books* was published, it had a new hero: Theobald had been dethroned, and Colley Cibber crowned in his place. Theobald's name survives in only two lines of the poem, though there are occasional references to him in the notes. The official account of what had happened was given by Warburton.

1. *A Letter to Mr C–b–r, On his Letter to Mr P——*, 1742, pp. 8–9.

2. Even Gray, who was himself blamed by his contemporaries for obscurity, found some lines "hardly intelligible." (*Correspondence*, ed. P. Toynbee, 1915, vol. ii, p. 22.) "The Metaphysician's part," he told West, "is to me the worst" —the very part, as has been suggested, where Pope probably followed most faithfully the suggestions of Warburton. According to Ruffhead (*Life of Alexander Pope*, p. 394) the fourth book "was esteemed obscure . . . and but a faint imitation by some common hand, of the other three. He [Pope] had himself the malicious pleasure of hearing this judgement passed on his favourite work, by several of his acquaintance."

3. October 29 (Griffith, vol. i, pt. ii, pp. 461–2). The entry in the Stationers' Register (by Mary Cooper) is dated October 28—George II's birthday was on Oct. 30: the *Dunciad* of 1743 was therefore, as Professor Sherburn has suggested to me, "almost a birthday present for the King."

"A ridiculous book," he explained, had been published against Pope, "full of Personal Reflections, which furnished him with a lucky opportunity of improving This Poem, by giving it the only thing it wanted, a more considerable Hero."[1] The "ridiculous book" was Cibber's celebrated pamphlet, *A Letter from Mr Cibber, to Mr Pope*, published in the summer of 1742. Pope had certainly reason to be angry with Cibber, for the old actor had raked together some ludicrous and discreditable incidents of Pope's youth, and set them out in his pamphlet with a droll impudence that was undeniably effective. Cibber himself claimed that he had made the poet "as uneasy as a Rat in a hot Kettle for a Twelvemonth together,"[2] and it is true that the *Letter* made a considerable impression on the Town and was the subject of comment in almost all the literary periodicals. Cibber, a man without dignity, had done his best to strip Pope as naked as himself.

But no one has ever explained why Cibber, who had borne Pope's sneers with good nature for so many years, should at length in 1742 allow himself to be provoked into a reply. The only line in the *New Dunciad* that could have annoyed him was that which described how he reposed in the lap of Dullness:

> Soft on her lap her Laureat son reclines.

This may, of course, have been for Cibber the last straw[3]; but it is possible that his *Letter* was not so much a protest against past offences as a warning to Pope not to go any further. Cibber, in fact, may have heard—and Pope may have taken steps to ensure that he did hear—of the project to revise the *Dunciad* and make the laureate the new hero. The *Peri Bathous* had stirred up the dunces in 1728, and similarly in 1742 Pope may have wished to startle

---

1. "Advertisement to the Reader," 1743. In a letter to Warburton, Sept. 20, 1741, Pope wrote: "If I can prevail on myself to complete the Dunciad [i.e. *The New Dunciad*] it will be published at the same time with a general edition of all my Verses." This seems to indicate that Pope had not yet thought of revising the whole poem or giving it a new hero.

2. *Another Occasional Letter from Mr Cibber to Mr Pope*, 1744, p. 15. Cibber's "Tom Tit" story was made the subject of a cartoon, in which Pope appeared perched on the whore's lap. See "A Letter from Mr T–ph–s C—r," *The Universal Spectator*, Oct. 16, 1742.

3. The anecdote about Pope perched on the lap of the whore looks like a direct retort to his gibe at Cibber reclining on the lap of Dullness.

Cibber into some abusive retort that would justify his enthrone-
ment in the *Dunciad*, and incidentally advertise the forthcoming
poem in its new form. This is no more than speculation; but at
some time in 1742 or 1743 Pope played a characteristic trick on
Cibber, and arranged that a spurious proof sheet of the revised
Dunciad should be "stolen" from the printer's and sent to him. The
account of this in Spence's *Anecdotes*[1] tells us less than enough to
reconstruct the incident satisfactorily:

> The false leaf of the Dunciad sent to Cibber, as stolen from
> the printer's by a friend, mentions the story about Mr Pope in
> Cibber's letter, and insinuates that Gay was one of the party,
> and that Cibber, breaking in upon Mr Gay's privacy, found
> him in company with his own daughter, and therefore pulled
> him away.

It is natural to assume that the false leaf was sent to Cibber after
the publication of his letter with its account of the "Tom Tit"
episode, but it is just possible that it came to Cibber's hands before
he had written his *Letter* at all, and that this unsavoury joke at his
daughter's expense was the very reason why he wrote it. In a four-
page pamphlet,[2] dated Feb. 13, 1742 (i.e. 1743), Cibber states,
"There is lately come to my Hands an undoubted Copy of some new
Lines, which in the next Edition of your *Dunciad*, now in the Press,
you intend to honour my Name with." The lines, however, refer to
"Cibber's brazen, brainless brothers" (B i 32), and no mention is
made of his daughter or of the incident with which her name had
been connected. Either Cibber chose to remain silent, or else the
information on which this pamphlet was based did not come from
the "false leaf of the Dunciad" mentioned in Spence's *Anecdotes*.

In a suit in Chancery which Pope brought against Henry Lintot
in 1743,[3] he stated that Lawton Gilliver knew and had often been
told that his right in the *Dunciad* was for fourteen years only, and
that when the copyright expired Pope intended to call in the

---

1. Op. cit. p. 348. It is to this incident that Pope seems to be referring in a
letter to Warburton, March 24, 1743. "You guessed right as to the verses sent
that silly fellow. It was done by a friend of mine who had your opinion of his
impenetrability . . ."

2. *A Second Letter from Mr Cibber to Mr Pope*, 1743. B.M. 1890 c. (13).

3. P.R.O. C. 11/549/39.

original copy and "to reprint and publish the said book or Poem with diverse Alterations Additions and Improvements thereto." If Pope was considering an extensive revision of his poem before 1742 he can scarcely have avoided thinking of Cibber as a possible hero; and if he had not thought of him as King of the Dunces, others certainly had. In a burlesque of Cibber's birthday ode for 1732 Dullness bids him ascend the throne, and the notion that Cibber was the supreme poetical dunce was widespread among the wits of the day.[1] The satirizing of the laureate and the burlesquing of his wretched odes had become a literary game. Pope himself had already contributed a few couplets to the satirical canon; but now, in this more splendid baiting of the revised *Dunciad*, he was once again to outstrip all his contemporaries, and once more take his place as the acknowledged leader of the wits. But though Pope may have had Cibber marked down for some time before 1743, he had to wait until the copyright of the *Dunciad* expired in December 1742 before republishing his poem with its new hero.

In some ways Cibber was a far more suitable hero than Theobald had been. He was better known. As poet laureate, as a celebrated actor and dramatist, as a gamester and a familiar companion of the sporting nobility—above all, as a kind of popular buffoon—he had a public far wider than that which interested itself merely in literature.[2] His fame, or notoriety, had been considerably increased by the publication in 1740 of his lively *Apology*. This book provided fresh material and several new reasons for satirizing the laureate, and Fielding[3] and others were not slow to take advantage of it. It is perhaps significant that in the anonymous *Tryal of Colley Cibber, Comedian, Etc. For Writing a book intitled An Apology for his Life . . .* (1740), Pope is indicted for "not exerting his Talents at this Juncture." Theobald, on the other hand, had proved something of a disappointment. As far as his work on Shakespeare was

---

1. *Gentleman's Magazine*, ii 1073. *The Universal Spectator*, Feb. 6, 1731, contains a *New Session of the Poets*, in which the contemporary poets are convened by the Goddess of Dullness, and the crown given to Cibber.

2. Cibber himself was alive to this fact. "He considers that my Face and Name are more known than those of many thousands of more consequence in the Kingdom: That therefore, right or wrong, a Lick at the *Laureat* will always be a sure Bait, *ad captandum vulgus* . . ." *Apology*, p. 31.

3. E.g. in *The Champion*, April 29, May 6, 1740, where the *Apology* is submitted to a caustic examination, and later (1742) in *Joseph Andrews*.

concerned he had vindicated his reputation, and Pope's ridicule tended to recoil on himself. Pope may well have been anxious to let the memory of Theobald alone; for since publishing his *Shakespeare Restored* he had gone on to edit the plays himself, and his edition was generally acknowledged to be superior to Pope's. Warburton, too, may have used his influence with Pope to bring about a change of hero. Theobald and he had once been fairly intimate friends, and though they had drifted apart Warburton may have felt some anxiety lest Theobald might one day let the world know what Mr Pope's new friend used to say about him in the old days. For Warburton, now the official commentator on Pope's works, it was a situation of some delicacy.

It has often been held that Cibber was quite unsuited to be the hero of a poem on dullness. Could he properly he called a dull man or a dull writer? Cibber very naturally had doubts on this point himself; and in at least some of his plays, in his *Apology*, and in his conversation he had shown himself to be, if not a wit, at least a thoroughly lively and amusing character. The proper answer to this objection is that in the word "dullness" Pope intended to include "every sort of rebellion against right reason and good taste."[1] In addition, he was an excellent example of that sort of natural, untaught writer against whom Pope, rightly or wrongly, was anxious to direct his satire. He was admittedly a different sort of dunce from Theobald, but his pertness was just as antipathetic to Pope as the other's pedantry. And as the egregious laureate of the Hanoverians, the consistent supporter of Walpole, and the satirist—if, indeed, that is not too grand a word—of the Jacobites, Cibber had laid further claims to Pope's contempt. This was the sort of coxcomb who made good in the reign of George II.[2]

The alterations required in the first three books to fit Cibber into the new scheme occasionally proved too much for even Pope's ingenuity: one or two passages, admirably pointed when Theobald was hero, became all but pointless when applied to his very different successor. Cibber himself observed that the account of Theo-

---

1. W. J. Courthope, EC iv 28.

2. By failing to make Cibber his hero in 1728, Pope missed a fine chance of anticipating history. To have called to the throne of Dullness the very man who in 1730 was to be given the laurel would have been a pretty irony. Cibber, too, would have made a better King of the 1728 dunces than Theobald.

bald's library in Book I was not applicable to himself: the books, as he remarked characteristically, "would never be looked into." On the other hand, some of Pope's alterations could scarcely be neater. When Theobald is raising a sacrifice of books to the goddess of Dullness, the last one that he places on the pile is his own translation of the *Ajax* of Sophocles in duodecimo:

And last, a little Ajax tips the spire. (A i 142.)

This will not do for Cibber, and so in 1743 the line becomes

A twisted Birth-day Ode completes the Spire. (B i 162.)

With the alterations in the text went some revision of the notes. Warburton had been invited by Pope[1] to be "in some measure, the editor of this new edition of the *Dunciad*," and had accepted the task. To the edition of 1743 he contributed the jocose "Ricardus Aristarchus Of the Hero of the Poem," an "Advertisement to the Reader" which had probably been drafted by Pope,[2] and additional notes in his heavy-handed style to all four books. After Pope's death Warburton continued to amplify the commentary, and in the edition of 1751 he used it more than once to castigate his own personal opponents.[3] As such notes are of interest to the student of Warburton rather than of Pope, they have not been reprinted in the present edition. Taken as a whole, Warburton's *Dunciad* notes shed darkness rather than light on the text of the poem. Too often his idea of annotating the *Dunciad* was to use the context for a display of mock pedantry which requires annotation in its turn if it is to be made intelligible to the modern reader.[4]

v

With the *Dunciad* of 1728 Pope had returned to original work; but, if no longer translating, he was yet burlesquing, or parodying, the Ancients. In this mock epic, as in *The Rape of the Lock*, he was

1. Nov. 27, 1742. EC ix 225.

2. See p. 251*n*.

3. Warburton's most notorious addition is a note to B iv 568 where he retaliated on Thomas Edwards, whose *Supplement to Mr Warburton's Edition of Shakespear. Being the Canons of Criticism* . . . (1748) had dealt some damaging blows at Warburton's reputation as an editor.

4. See, for example, his notes to B i 33, 37, 203.

careful to retain as many features of the true epic as possible; his model was, so to speak, the non-existent *Margites* of Homer.[1] In addition to the epic features enumerated by Pope in "Martinus Scriblerus Of the Poem," one may note in Book I the Proposition, Invocation, and Inscription; the Prayer to the Goddess and the Sacrifice (A i 135–212); the Intervention of the Goddess, and her Prophecy (213–16, 245–55); the Acclamation of the Hero (A 256–60, B 319–30); in Book II the Games, as in *Odyssey* XXIV and *Aeneid* V; in Book III the Visit to the Underworld, and the Vision of future glories, with Settle acting the part of Virgil's Sibyl. Pope's easy mockery of other and less important features of the classical epic will be found recorded in the notes; and Pope himself was careful to call attention to most of his verbal echoes of Homer, Virgil, Horace, and the other authors, both ancient and modern, with whom he had made free. While such notes may assist the uninformed reader, the *Dunciad* can make its full effect only upon one who is already sufficiently familiar with the classical poets to feel that small shock of delighted surprise which Pope intended by his irreverent shifting of the context. Appreciation of the *Dunciad* to-day necessarily suffers, not merely from the fading of its personalities, but from a change in English education.

If the *Dunciad* is indebted to the Ancients for its construction and some of its neatest effects, it also owes a good deal to the Moderns. In a note to A ii 132 Pope acknowledged Garth as his predecessor in this kind of satire; but he was also following Boileau and a whole generation of mock-heroic tradition.[2] Most important of all is his debt to Dryden's *Mac Flecknoe*, which gave Pope the idea of a succession to the throne of Dullness. In Dryden's poem Shadwell had succeeded Flecknoe; in Pope's, it is Theobald who succeeds Settle, but Flecknoe and Shadwell, now "gather'd to the Dull of antient days," remain impressive figures in the foggy background. In the literary ancestry of the *Dunciad* one should perhaps include that favourite genre, "The Sessions of the Poets," in which Apollo was represented as selecting a candidate for the vacant laureate-

---

1. See "Martinus Scriblerus, Of the Poem," p. 49.

2. For an account of Pope's predecessors in the mock-epic, see vol. ii, Introduction, pp. 107 ff. Pope was ready to take a hint from any writer—even, perhaps, from Blackmore, in whose poem, *The Kit-Cats*, 1708, the Grub Street poets seek the help of the god of Dullness.

ship.[1] Theobald himself had produced a prose version of this theme in his *Censor*, Jan. 24, 1717, when he made Apollo elect Quarles as laureate in preference to Dryden. "Ogilby," he writes, "brought in the Laurel and bound it round the Temples of *Quarles*; but, as soon as the sacred Leaves touch'd the Seat of Dullness, they faded and wither'd away . . ."

There was plenty of dullness in literature before the days of Dryden; but there can be little doubt that it was that wittiest of all Dryden's poems, *Mac Flecknoe*, that made it a fashionable literary topic. Wycherley was moved in his old age to write a poem on this theme, and the young Pope revised it carefully, methodized it, and augmented it with some verses of his own.[2] In the years before the appearance of the *Dunciad* one hears more and more about dullness. A writer who called himself "Will Sharpsight" may be found complaining in *The British Journal*, July 10, 1725, of the state of contemporary literature, and promising his readers "a Satyr upon Dullness" which would have as its chief aim "the Correction of petty Scribblers." The Scriblerus Club, with its professed intention of ridiculing "all the false tastes in learning," was only carrying out in a rather more specialized form the task that Addison and other wits had set themselves in their endeavours to correct the taste of the Town.[3] Such widely different writers as Oldham, Defoe, Swift, Blackmore, and the Duke of Buckingham had addressed themselves to the satirizing of dullness, obscenity, and other literary defects; the good work had been carried on by many of Pope's dunces themselves. Almost every writer in this age, even the dullest, seems to have been acutely conscious of dullness in the air; and criticism of his contemporaries—indignant, abusive, contemptuous, good-humoured according to the writer's disposition—was one of the favourite themes of the eighteenth-century man of letters. In the *Dunciad* it reached its most memorable expression.

1. In *Dunciad* A Theobald was represented as succeeding Settle as City Poet; in *Dunciad* B Cibber is proclaimed successor to Eusden as Poet Laureate. (A i 246 ff. B i 292 ff.).

2. EC vi 31. See vol. vi of this edition.

3. The *Dunciad* is, of course, one of the chief literary exhibits of the Scriblerus Club. How much it may have owed to the very informal meetings of the Club it is impossible to tell, but it is informed by the Scriblerus attitude to literature and scholarship.

2*

For the facetious commentary which Pope added in 1729 there were already some interesting precedents. The earlier editions of *A Tale of a Tub* had been lightly annotated; but to the fifth (1710) edition Swift added some notes signed "W. Wotton," as Pope was later in the *Dunciad* to attribute notes to Theobald and Bentley. Bentley's *Horace* (1711) was burlesqued in numerous pamphlets, and his notes parodied.[1] There was a mock-learned commentary to Dr Walter Pope's *Salisbury Ballad*, and William King's *Joan of Headington* in *Useful Miscellanies* (1712) has a burlesque of the learned preface. But nowhere before the *Dunciad* had the thing been done so elaborately, or to serve so many different purposes. In the *Dunciad* the Notes Variorum are frequently intended to discredit Theobald by ridiculing his scholarship and his various works; Pope has knocked him down in the poem, and now he pummels him in prose.[2] The same tactics were employed with the other dunces; and for some of those the notes had the additional advantage of giving the reader some much-needed information. More generally, the notes were intended to justify the personal satire of the poem, and to convince the public that the author was a good writer (of which the poem itself was a hilarious demonstration) and a good man, and that of the two he valued the second more highly than the first. The commentary, in fact, has considerable biographical value; it supplements the picture of the self-righteous poet that one meets so often in the Letters, and it makes clearer than ever the care that he took to preserve and to extend his literary reputation. To those two ends the various prefaces, notes, and appendices were all to contribute: Pope's enemies were to be humbled, but—equally important—Pope himself was to be aggrandized. At the same time, there is a good deal of fun in the commentary, and some excellent strokes of wit; the whole prose apparatus deserves more careful study than it usually gets. On the other hand, it is probably much more responsible

1. For an excellent account of the New Criticism and the hostility of the wits to Bentley, Theobald's master, see R. F. Jones, *Lewis Theobald*, 1919, pp. 31 ff., 256–7.

2. Pope occasionally drags into the notes passages from *Shakespeare Restored*. The most important of those have been noted as they occur, but there is a constant parody of Theobald's rather antiquated prose, more especially in the notes attributed to Scriblerus. Much reading of Elizabethan authors seems to have left its mark on Theobald's own style.

than the poem itself for the popular conception of the *Dunciad* as a bitter and merciless satire.

Even among the dunces there was a grudging acknowledgement of the fact that, however unjustified the satire might be, Pope's thrusts had frequently gone home. But John Dennis remained unimpressed, and in his own ponderous fashion he did succeed in bringing one serious charge against the poem. Not much notice need be taken of his ludicrous complaint that the action is full of improbabilities:

> But what Probability is there in *Pope*'s Rhapsody? What Probability in the Games which take up a third Part of the Piece? Is it not monstrous to imagine any Thing like that in the Master Street of a populous City; a Street eternally crowded with Carriages, Carts, Coaches, Chairs, and Men passing in the greatest Hurry about Private and Publick Affairs?[1]

By such criticism Dennis is only justifying his inclusion in the poem. But another of his complaints is more damaging: the *Dunciad*, he says, lacks action.[2] This objection has been repeated by friendlier critics than Dennis. "Surely it is not right," Warton remarks,[3] "that the hero should take no part in any thing that was transacted about him in the second book; and that in the third book he should be in a profound sleep." It might be replied that Pope is parodying epic action by having almost no action at all; but such a reply would scarcely meet the objection felt. Few readers of the *Dunciad* have any clear picture of what is going on, and for this Pope himself is largely to blame. The action is most intelligible in the second book, which is approximately on the same scale as those books in the *Iliad* and the *Aeneid* describing the heroic games which Pope is here travestying. Elsewhere there is very little happening at all, and such action as Pope supplies is out of all proportion to the long speeches given to Theobald, the Goddess, Settle, and Bentley. Considered simply as a mock epic, the *Dunciad* is less successful than *The Rape of the Lock*. The distinction between those two poems has been well put by a recent critic of Pope, who points out that while *The Rape of the Lock* is "an exquisitely diminished

---

1. *Remarks upon . . . the Dunciad*, 1729, p. 19.
2. *Ibid.*, pp. 17–18.
3. In his note to iv 20.

shadow cast by an entire epic poem," the *Dunciad* is "the ludicrous, grotesque, lifesize shadow cast by a piece of an epic poem."[1]
The mockery of the epic form is there; but in the *Dunciad* Pope's
primary concern is not to write mock epic, but to make use of that
form to satirize his enemies. The duncies come first, the *Dunciad*
second. Sometimes, indeed, the satire is so much detached from
the business of the poem that it looks as if Pope had simply slipped
in a few couplets that he had previously "hitched into rhyme."
The famous lines on Welsted ("Flow Welsted, flow! like thine
inspirer, Beer") occur in the course of the Vision in Book III:
one might reasonably expect a "Lo Welsted" rather than a "Flow
Welsted" at this point. Did the four lines on Welsted once form an
independent epigram? The couplet on Ralph, too, ("Silence, ye
Wolves . . .") reads like a detached epigram introduced abruptly
into Settle's descriptive harangue. But if the structure of the poem
is open to criticism, one is constantly astonished by its brilliant
detail, by its movement, and by the variety of tone which Pope
manages to impart to a poem almost wholly given up to denigra-
tion. Pope keeps up his ridicule and abuse for almost two thousand
lines: the effect *ought* to be monotonous; it is not.

The art which Pope lavished upon this poem has too often been
obscured by an unnecessary concern for his victims. Pope had
indeed embarked upon a comprehensive scheme of belittlement;
and the more duncies he could introduce, the better for his purpose,
since each dunce would catch the epidemic littleness from his
neighbour. To satirize one man is to run the risk of giving him
undue importance; to satirize the many is to make each individual
equally negligible. Yet his critics have frequently ignored the skill
with which he reduced his scribblers to Lilliputian dimensions, in
their indignation that he should have introduced some of them to
the *Dunciad* at all. Pope undoubtedly made some mistakes here;
and one or two of his duncies—Defoe and Bentley, for example—
have not been laughed into oblivion. But his success is to be
measured by the verdict of later generations upon such far from
stupid people as Theobald, Cibber, Welsted, Concanen, Mrs
Centlivre, and others. Pope's verdict has been accepted; he has succeeded in imposing his own values on almost all of his duncies. In
so far as they are remembered at all, it is as flies in the poet's amber.

1. Geoffrey Tillotson, *On the Poetry of Pope*, 1938, p. 55.

Much indignation, too, has been expended upon Pope's alleged malignity towards his dunces. Warton in particular keeps recurring to this conception of a wounded and angry poet retaliating bitterly upon his enemies. "What a state of anger and irritation must his mind (and such a mind!) have been in, during the many hours, nay years, he spent in writing the 1670 lines of the Dunciad!"[1] Jonathan Richardson handed on a story of how Pope read to him and his father one of the pamphlets that Cibber had written against him. "These things are my diversion," Pope told the two Richardsons, but they noticed that his face was writhing with anguish.[2] Undoubtedly Pope was too sensitive to the attacks made upon him; neither his physique nor his temperament was suited for the rough and tumble of public life in which he had become involved.[3] Cibber, a man of very different temperament, diagnosed Pope's irritability with real shrewdness:

> You seem in your *Dunciad*, to have been angry at the rain for wetting you, why then would you go into it? You could not but know, that an Author, when he publishes a Work, exposes himself to all weathers.[4]

Pope was indeed singularly vulnerable; and, as he told his friend Caryll, his pen was the only weapon he had. That weapon cannot always be drawn at a moment's notice: Pope's revenge was necessarily delayed, and, in consequence, deliberate, and his indignation with the offender was sometimes sustained over a long period, and must often have appeared even to his friends incommensurate with the offence.[5] Yet it would be absurd to see in the *Dunciad* nothing but the blind revenge of a very angry man. A very angry man could never have transfixed his opponents with

1. Warton, vol. iv, p. 213 (in his note to B iii 21).

2. T. Davies, *Life of Garrick*, 1780, ii 202.

3. Those who wish to dismiss the *Dunciad* as a product of Pope's spleen might, no doubt, find some evidence to confirm their views in the wretched state of the poet's health during the winter of 1727–8. "I have been in a worse condition of health than ever," he wrote to Swift, Feb. 1728 (EC vii 114).

4. *A Letter from Mr. Cibber to Mr. Pope*, 1742, p. 13.

5. Several complaints were made of the *cold-bloodedness* of Pope's satire. Cf. M. Concanen, *A Compleat Collection of all the Verses* . . . , p. x: "I said somewhere before that Mr P. had writ in his Anger: I beg his pardon, for he must be a very bad Man, if his Anger always continues till his Wit comes out."

such light-hearted precision, nor have written with such genial contempt of mediocre poets and pedantic scholars and disreputable booksellers. It has never been sufficiently recognized that in the *Dunciad* one of the greatest artists in English poetry found the perfect material for his art. Critical discussion of the poem began with the angry protests of the dunces, and has moved too exclusively along these lines ever since. It was not a mere paradox of Pope's that "the Poem was not made for these Authors, but these Authors for the Poem." Theobald, Smedley, Cibber, and the rest were admirable stuff for a satirist, and he revelled in their absurdities. Pope had, in fact, the artist's delight in his craft, the fencer's delight in the skilful use of his foil; and to such a master of ridicule, ridicule must have been extraordinarily pleasing. "What *Tully* says of War," he once observed,[1] "may be apply'd to Disputing, it should be always so manag'd as to remember that the only end of it is *Peace*; but generally true Disputants are like true Sportsmen, their whole delight is in the Pursuit; and a Disputant no more cares for the Truth, than the Sportsman for the Hare." Pope's callousness in the *Dunciad* is surely that of the sportsman; he concentrates on the pursuit, and thinks little of the victim. He rarely wrote anything in such high spirits as the *Dunciad* of 1728-9. James Ralph, for instance, sucked into the storm that followed the publication of the poem in its original form, attacked Pope in a clumsy satire called *Sawney*. Pope, casting about for a suitable reply, remembered Ralph's execrable *Night*, a poem in blank verse, and worked it into a delightful couplet:

> Silence, ye Wolves! while Ralph to Cynthia howls,
> And makes Night hideous—Answer him ye Owls!

There may be malice in these lines, but the author was scarcely writhing with anguish when he wrote them. It is in the commentary rather than the poem itself that the bitterness appears. His anxiety to prove in notes, prefaces, and appendices that he was not the sort of man that his enemies made him out to be is all part of "that unnecessary noise he used to make in boast of his morality," which so annoyed Aaron Hill.[2] As often as not Pope is think-

---

1. In his "Thoughts on Various Subjects," No. xix. *Miscellanies. The Second Volume*, 1727, p. 342.
2. S. Richardson, *Correspondence*, ed. A. L. Barbauld, 1804, i 106.

ing much less about the dunces than about himself—the picture of himself that he was painting for posterity in his poems, and, still more, in his carefully edited letters.

Even a superficial consideration of the minor characters in the *Dunciad* must show that they are not all people towards whom Pope felt a personal grudge. Sometimes he is taking up the cudgel on behalf of his friends, or merely following a satirical fashion. [1] There is, too, a nucleus of nobodies, introduced to act as a kind of solvent for those other persons with whom he is more particularly concerned. From Dryden and others he takes over such figures as Shadwell, Flecknoe, Settle, Blackmore, and Milbourne. Those men, whether dunces or not, had been baptised by Dryden, and were widely accepted as such by the age. [2] Again, such a comic butt as Tom Durfey is introduced, not because Pope felt spiteful towards him, but because almost every one was prepared to treat Durfey as a joke. The introduction of such men, and of Taylor, the water poet, Withers, Quarles, Ogilby, Tate, and others, was intended by Pope to put his scribblers in a historical setting of dullness. Every one was agreed about Ogilby and Tate; the assumption was that every one would see that Eusden and Welsted, Oldmixon and Cooke were of the same dull order, differing only in the scarcely relevant fact that they were still alive.

Again, even when he is dealing in the most unmerciful terms with his contemporaries, Pope is usually concerned with the offence as well as the offender. He lived in an age which still tended to regard everything that appeared in print as literature; and even when he is satirizing his scribblers he still pays them the compliment of treating their work as bad literature. [3] To-day a distinction between literature and reading matter has been forced upon us; it would seem to us almost irrelevant to complain about the literary quality of newspaper articles or pantomime librettos.

1. Particularly in Book IV. Many of Pope's victims in that book, e.g. the Virtuosi, the young Nobleman on the Grand Tour, the Antiquaries, had been previously satirized by Young, Bramston, Miller, and other writers.

2. Swift had added considerably to the list in *The Battle of the Books* and *A Tale of a Tub;* Ozell, looking for English equivalents of Boileau's butts, had accepted the judgments of Dryden and Swift, and introduced Ogilby, Bentley, Settle, Wesley, Quarles, Dunton, Blackmore, etc.

3. Cf. "Martinus Scriblerus Of the Poem," p. 49.

But Pope, no doubt because he lived at the beginning of a new era of popular publishing and weekly journalism, took a firm stand against the upstarts whom he saw invading the enclosed territory of literature. In the *Dunciad* of 1729 it is partly the *type* that he is attacking: the pedantic scholar like Hearne or Theobald; the weekly journalist like Roome and Concanen; the party hack like Oldmixon; the popular writer like Mrs Centlivre, Mrs Haywood, Ned Ward, or the author of *Robinson Crusoe*; the shameless publisher like Edmund Curll. In *The New Dunciad* he is generally more concerned with the class than with the individual. True, his satire is almost invariably tinged with some personal bitterness, but he genuinely despised all that the dunces stood for. Such writers *and such writing* seemed to Pope—as, indeed, to John Dennis—to threaten the standards of literature. The objections of both Pope and Dennis, whether they knew it or not, were partly those of the literary aristocrat, with the background of a classical education, who sees his privileges being encroached upon a by mob of facile and semi-literate authors. Pope's note on James Ralph (A iii 159) will show how the wind was blowing:

> He was wholly illiterate, and knew no Language not even *French*: Being advised to read the Rules of Dramatick Poetry before he began a Play, he smiled and reply'd, *Shakespear writ without Rules*.

Pope had good cause to be annoyed with the author of *Sawney* on purely personal grounds; but it is only fair to insist that he deplored such men as Ralph whether they had attacked him or not. The standards of literature must be kept up; the barbarians must be driven from the Capitol before it was too late. Men like Swift and Pope, conservative in their outlook, were honestly alarmed for the future of polite letters, and in 1728 there was some reason for alarm. For one *Cato* Pope saw a dozen *Nonjurors* and as many pantomimes and operas which appeared to be driving the regular drama from the stage. The "Rules" were being flouted; literature was falling into the hands of the uneducated or the half-educated.[1]

---

1. Dryden had felt all this about Settle. "Mr Settle having never studied any sort of learning but poetry, and that but slenderly, . . . must make very lame work on't; he himself declares, he neither reads, nor cares for conversation; so that he would persuade us he is a kind of fanatic in poetry, and has a light within him, and writes by an inspiration" (*Works*. ed. Scott-Saintsbury, xv 407).

What was happening in the theatre seemed, to some observers at least, to be happening in every branch of literature. "Art after Art goes out, and all is Night." Pope was exaggerating magnificently, and he must have known it; but the danger threatened, and it would be more than a mere threat if our Popes did not remain eternally vigilant.

It is frequently held that the bad writer should be left to the verdict of time; but that is a counsel of perfection. It should not be forgotten that when Nicholas Rowe died in 1718 such men as Oldmixon fancied their chances of becoming poet laureate,[1] and that Eusden actually was appointed; and when Eusden died in 1730 Theobald, if we are to believe what he wrote to Warburton,[2] very nearly got himself appointed in his place instead of the egregious Cibber. Pope's protest was partly one that lies behind most of the world's greatest satire; it was a protest against a wrong standard of values.[3] Time is the best judge, no doubt, but a little plain speaking from contemporaries may anticipate some of its verdicts, and prevent a total corruption of good taste. The words of Scriblerus are not to be taken as merely jocular:

> Do not gentle reader, rest too secure in thy contempt of the Instruments for such a revolution in learning, or despise such weak agents as have been described in our poem, but remember what the *Dutch* stories somewhere relate, that a great part of their Provinces was once overflow'd, by a small opening made in one of their dykes by a single *Water-Rat*.[4]

Pope's motives, therefore, were not so exclusively personal as has usually been suggested; and even when they were personal

---

1. See A ii 199n. There were rumours in 1715 that Dennis would succeed Tate.—*The Weekly Journal, With Fresh Advices Foreign and Domestick*, August 20, 1715.

2. J. Nichols, *Lit. Ill.*, ii 616–17.

3. In 1725 Leonard Welsted was addressed by one of his admiring contemporaries in some lines which Pope may or may not have seen, but which would certainly have struck him as ludicrously extravagant:

> While Britain makes thy matchless Works her Boast,
> And rival Bards strive, who shall grace thee most,
> Forgive, great Writer, these spontaneous Lays;
> The Tribute paid to Worth! the Song of Praise!

The London Journal, March 20, 1725.

4. A iii 337n.

they were not necessarily inspired by malice. The dunces complained loudly of what they called an unprovoked attack; and it is true that Pope was sometimes—though again not so often as has generally been assumed—the aggressor. But what the dunces could not see—how should they?—was that they annoyed by merely being themselves. "Gentlemen should consider that to some People Dulness is provoking; and that in such Case, to call Gentlemen dull is no Abuse, though it may be a Rudeness."[1] At the same time there was about Pope—and, for that matter, about Swift—an assumption of critical infallibility which was extremely annoying to their contemporaries, who frequently complained that Pope and Swift seemed to think that they and their friends had a monopoly of wit and good sense. Pope's satire, too, was sometimes the polished sneer of a man jealous of any rival; and he appeared to many of his contemporaries to be acting like Nero, "who, wisely resolving to be the only good Poet, and witty Man in his Time, set himself to destroy all that were conspicuous for those Characters."[2] In the *Dunciad*, too, Pope is sometimes too easily contemptuous of the author who writes for his bread, and too ready to assume that for that very reason he must write badly. It was easy for Smedley[3] to retort that Pope did not write for bread *now*; and the complaint of another author, "He reproaches his Enemies as poor and dull; and to prove them *poor*, he asserts they are *dull*; and to prove them *dull* he asserts they are *poor*,"[4] had a good deal of justification. Nor can it be denied that Pope's ridicule was sometimes directed against men who did not deserve it, and who were being ridiculed only because Pope was trying to laugh dangerous witnesses out of court. But there seems to be little danger of those facts being forgotten: the criticism of the nineteenth and twentieth centuries has been far too much concerned with the moral issues raised by Pope's satire, and too little interested in its purely aesthetic values.

---

1. *Essays, Letters, . . . Relating to the Late War of the Dunces*, p. 5.
2. *Characters of the Times*, 1728, pp. 21–2. Cf. also J. Smedley, *Gulliveriana*, p. ix.
3. Preface to *Gulliveriana*, p. xiii.
4. Letter signed "W.A.," *Mist's Journal*, June 8, 1728; reprinted in *Gulliveriana*, p. 312.

CHRONOLOGICAL TABLE

The standard biographies are G. Sherburn's *The Early Career of Alexander Pope*, 1934, and W. J. Courthope's life in vol. v of the Elwin-Courthope edition of Pope's works, 1871–89. Sherburn's account stops at 1727.

1688 (May 21) Alexander Pope born in London of elderly parents. Lewis Theobald born.

*c.*1700 Pope's family moved to Binfield, in Windsor Forest, [?] to comply with anti-Catholic regulations.
Death of Dryden.

*c.*1705 Pope started to make acquaintance with the literary society of London.

1709 (May) The *Pastorals* published in the sixth part of Tonson's *Miscellanies*.

1711 (May) *An Essay on Criticism* published; Pope's reference to Appius arouses the hostility of Dennis.

1712 (May) The *Messiah* published by Steele in *The Spectator*. Lintot's *Miscellany* published, containing the first version of *The Rape of the Lock*, and other poems by Pope. Pope was becoming acquainted with Swift, Gay, Parnell, and Arbuthnot, who together formed the Scriblerus Club.

1713 (March) *Windsor Forest*.
(April) Addison's *Cato* first acted, with a prologue by Pope. Pope was contributing to Steele's *Guardian*.
(October) Proposals issued for a translation of the *Iliad*.

1714 (March) The enlarged version of *The Rape of the Lock*.
(August) Death of Queen Anne.

1715 (February) *The Temple of Fame*.
(June 6) The *Iliad*, Books i–iv, published; followed two days later by Tickell's translation of *Iliad* i. Numerous attacks on Pope's *Iliad* in the newspapers and in several pamphlets. During this year [?], Pope wrote his character of Addison, and became acquainted with Lady Mary Wortley Montagu.

1716 (March) *Iliad*, vol. ii. Curll publishes *Court Poems*.
Pope takes his revenge in minor prose skits and by poison [Sherburn, ch. vi; N. Ault, *Pope's Prose*, pp. xciv ff.].
(April) Pope's family sold the house at Binfield, and settled at Chiswick, where their neighbour was Lord Burlington.

1717 (January) *Three Hours after Marriage* by Pope, Gay, and Arbuthnot, first acted. Cibber ridicules it at a performance of *The Rehearsal*. Further attacks on Pope in print.
(June) *Iliad*, vol. iii.
The collected volume of Pope's *Works*, containing *Verses to the Memory of an Unfortunate Lady* and *Eloisa to Abelard*.
(October) Pope's father died.

1718 (June) *Iliad*, vol. iv.
Death of Parnell. Pope and his mother moved to Twickenham late in the year.

1719 Death of Addison.

1720 (May) *Iliad*, vols. v and vi.

1721 (September) The *Epistle to Addison* prefixed to Tickell's edition of Addison's *Works*.
(December) The *Epistle to Oxford* prefixed to Pope's edition of Parnell's *Poems*.

1723 (January) Pope's edition of John Sheffield, Duke of Buckingham's *Works* published, and seized by the Government
on suspicion of Jacobitish passages.
(May) Pope called before the House of Lords as a witness at
Atterbury's trial.

1725 (March) Pope's edition of Shakespeare published in six
volumes. It is attacked in the weekly newspapers.
(April) *Odyssey*, vols. i–iii. Grub Street taunts at Pope as a
"poetical undertaker."
Bolingbroke returned from exile, and settled near Pope at
Dawley Farm, Uxbridge.

1726 (March) Theobald's *Shakespeare Restored: or, a Specimen of the
Many Errors . . . Committed . . . by Mr Pope*.
(June) *Odyssey*, vols. iv–v.
Pope visited by Swift. *Gulliver's Travels* published in Oc-
tober.

1727 (June) Pope-Swift *Miscellanies*, vols. i and ii.
Swift's second visit to Pope.

1728 (March) Pope-Swift *Miscellanies*, "last" volume. The *Peri
Bathous* arouses much angry comment.
(May) *The Dunciad*, in three books, with Theobald as hero.
Numerous letters in the newspapers, and pamphlets attack-
ing Pope.

1729 (April) *The Dunciad Variorum*.

1731 (December) *Epistle to Burlington* [Moral Essay iv].

1732 (October) Pope-Swift *Miscellanies*, "third" volume.
(December) Death of Gay.

1733 (January) *Epistle to Bathurst* [Moral Essay iii].
(February) The first *Imitation of Horace* [Sat. ii i].
(February-May) *An Essay on Man*, Epistles i–iii.
(June) Death of Pope's mother.

1734 (January) *Epistle to Cobham* [Moral Essay i].
      An Essay on Man, Epistle iv.
      (July) *Imitation of Horace* [Sat. II ii].
      (December) *Sober Advice from Horace.*

1735 (January) *Epistle to Dr Arbuthnot.*
      (February) *Of the Characters of Women* [Moral Essay ii].
      Death of Arbuthnot.
      (April) The *Works*, vol. ii.
      (May) Curll's edition of Pope's letters.
      Bolingbroke returned to France.

1737 (April) *Imitation of Horace* [Ep. II ii].
      (May) Pope's edition of his letters.
      Imitation of Horace [Ep. II i].
      An Essay on Man attacked by Crousaz, Professor of Mathe-
      matics and Philosophy at Lausanne.

1738 (January–March) *Imitations of Horace* [Eps. I vi and I i].
      (May–July) *Epilogue to the Satires.*
      Warburton commenced his replies to Crousaz.
      Pope visited by Bolingbroke.

1740 (April) Pope's first meeting with Warburton.
      An Apology for the Life of Mr. Colley Cibber, Comedian.

1742 (March) *The New Dunciad* [i.e. Book iv]. *A Letter from Mr.
      Cibber to Mr. Pope.*

1743 (October) *The Dunciad* in four books with Cibber enthroned
      in the place of Theobald.

1744 *Another Occasional Letter from Mr. Cibber to Mr. Pope.*
      (May 30) Death of Pope.

LIST OF THE PRINCIPAL POEMS
of Pope to be found in the other volumes

The translation of Homer is not included in this edition. The remaining poems will be found in volume vi.

ABBREVIATIONS

used in the footnotes and the biographical appendix

A. See Dunciad A.

Anonymous Key = A 4 pp. 12mo. Key to *The Dunciad*, without title-page or date.

Apology = An Apology for the Life of Mr. Colley Cibber, Comedian. 2nd ed., 1740.

Ayre = Memoirs of the Life and Writings of Alexander Pope. By William Ayre. 1745.

B. See Dunciad B.

Barker = Mr Cibber of Drury Lane. By R. H. Barker. 1939.

Bayle = A Dictionary Historical and Critical. By Pierre Bayle. 2nd ed., 1734–7.

Biog. App. = Biographical Appendix.

Bolingbroke, Works = The Works Of the Right Hon. Henry St John, Lord Viscount Bolingbroke. Ed. D. Mallet. 5 vols., 1754.

Boswell, Life = Boswell's Life of Johnson. Ed. G. B. Hill and L. F. Powell. 4 vols., 1934.

Bowles = The Works of Alexander Pope, Esq. Ed. W. L. Bowles. 10 vols., 1806.

Cibber, Lives = Lives of the Poets . . . By Mr Cibber and other Hands. 5 vols., 1753.

Dia. = Epilogue to the Satires.

Dilke = C. W. Dilke's MS. notes in his copy of the Poetical Works, ed. R. Carruthers (B.M. 12274 i 15).

DNB = Dictionary of National Biography.

Donne ii = The Second Satire of Dr John Donne.

Donne iv = The Fourth Satire of Dr John Donne.

Dunciad A = The Dunciad, Variorum [in three books], 1729.

Dunciad B = The Dunciad, In Four Books, 1743.

Dyce Copy of The New Dunciad = Annotated copy of The New Dunciad in Victoria and Albert Museum (Dyce 7747).

EC = The Works of Pope. Ed. W. Elwin and W. J. Courthope. 10 vols., 1871–89.

EC MS. = Copy of the Dunciad corrected by Jonathan Richardson from what he called "the first Broglio MS." [The corrections were transcribed by W. Elwin: EC iv 271 ff.]

EGMONT = Diary of the Earl of Egmont. Hist. MSS. Comm. 3 vols., 1920–3.

E. ON C. = Essay on Criticism.

EP. 1 i = The First Epistle of the First Book of Horace Imitated [to Bolingbroke].

EP. 1 vi = The Sixth Epistle of the First Book of Horace Imitated [to Murray].

EP. 11 i = The First Epistle of the Second Book of Horace, Imitated [to Augustus].

EP. 11 ii = The Second Epistle of the Second Book of Horace, Imitated.

EVANS = Warburton and the Warburtonians. By A. W. Evans. 1932.

GENT. MAG. = The Gentleman's Magazine.

GRIFFITH = Alexander Pope. A Bibliography. By R. H. Griffith. 1 vol. in two parts, 1922, 1927.

HANSON = Government and the Press, 1695–1763. By Laurence Hanson. 1936.

HERVEY MEMOIRS = Memoirs of the Reign of George II. By John, Lord Hervey. Ed. R. Sedgwick. 3 vols., 1931.

HOOKER = The Critical Works of John Dennis. Ed. Edward Niles Hooker. Vol. I, 1939.

JOHNSON, LIVES = Lives of the English Poets. By Samuel Johnson. Ed. G. Birkbeck Hill. 3 vols., 1905.

KEY = A Compleat Key to the Dunciad. By Edmund Curll. 1728. [References are to the third edition, unless otherwise stated.]

LETTER TO POPE = A Letter from Mr Cibber to Mr Pope. 1742.

MALONE = Malone's MS. notes for an edition of Pope's works. Bodleian MS. Malone 30.

MIST'S JOURNAL = The Weekly Journal; Or, Saturday's Post. 1716–28 (published by N. Mist).

MONK = Life of Richard Bentley. By J. H. Monk. 2 vols., 1833.

NICHOLS, LIT. ANEC. = Literary Anecdotes of the Eighteenth Century. By John Nichols. 9 vols., 1812–15.

NICHOLS, LIT. ILL. = Illustrations of the Literary History of the Eighteenth Century. By John Nichols. 8 vols., 1817–58.

OED = Oxford English Dictionary.

P = Note attributed to Pope in Warburton's edition of the Works, 1751.

POPE'S PROSE = The Prose Works of A. Pope. Ed. Norman Ault. Vol. i, 1936.

P.W. = Note attributed to Pope and Warburton jointly in Warburton's edition of the Works, 1751.

RALPH = A Critical History of the Administration of Sir Robert Walpole . . . [By James Ralph]. 1743.

READ'S JOURNAL = The Weekly Journal; Or, British Gazetteer. 1715+ (published by James Read).

R.E.S. = The Review of English Studies.

SAT. II i = The First Satire of the Second Book of Horace Imitated [to Fortescue].

SECOND LETTER = A Second Letter from Mr Cibber to Mr Pope. 1743.

SHERBURN = The Early Career of Alexander Pope. By George Sherburn. 1934.

SPENCE = Anecdotes . . . of Books and Men. By Joseph Spence. Ed. S. W. Singer. 1820.

SWIFT, CORRESPONDENCE = The Correspondence of Jonathan Swift, D.D. Ed. F. Elrington Ball. 6 vols., 1910–14.

WAKEFIELD = Observations on Pope. By G. Wakefield. 1796.

WALPOLE = Notes on the Poems of Pope, By Horatio, Earl of Orford, contributed by Sir W. A. Fraser. 1876.

W = Note attributed by Warburton to himself in his edition of the Works, 1751.

WARBURTON 1751 = Works of A. Pope. Ed. W. Warburton. 9 vols., 1751. First edition of 1751 quoted.

WARTON = Works of A. Pope. Ed. J. Warton. 9 vols., 1797. Edition of 1822 quoted.

THE
DUNCIAD
VARIORUM
WITH THE
PROLEGOMENA
OF
SCRIBLERUS

NOTE ON THE TEXT
of *Dunciad* A

The *Dunciad* advertised in the *Daily Post* of May 18, 1728 was a pamphlet of 52 pages, with a prefatory address, "The Publisher to the Reader," and nineteen brief footnotes. It has long been a matter of dispute among bibliographers whether the duodecimo or an almost identical octavo should be considered the first edition. The case for the duodecimo has been ably stated by Professor R. H. Griffith (*Modern Philology*, vol. xii, pp. 1 ff.; *Alexander Pope: A Bibliography*, vol. 1, pt. i, pp. 154 ff., vol. i, pt. ii, pp. 577 ff.; *The Colophon*, New Series, vol. iii, No. 4 (1938), pp. 569–86). In his catalogue of the Ashley Library, vol. iv, pp. 15 ff., Mr T. J. Wise argued in favour of the octavo, and he has had some supporters. The duodecimo-octavo dispute, however, is of more interest to the book collector than to the editor of Pope, for the textual differences are almost negligible, the only important divergence occurring in the opening line, where "Books and the man" of the duodecimo appears as "Book and the man" in the octavo. In the textual apparatus to the present edition the duodecimo (*1728a*) has been accepted as the first edition.

"The Second Edition" and "The Third Edition," both in duodecimo, followed in less than a month. The text was revised for both. The two variants of "The Third Edition" show so many differences from each other that it has been necessary in presenting the results of collation to separate them by giving them distinctive marks (*1728e, 1728f*: Griffith 203, 204). As Professor Griffith has shown (op. cit., vol. 1, pt. ii, p. 577), "the two variants of the Third Edition were each a complete re-printing as compared with the Second Edition or with each other." Yet another duodecimo edition (*1728c*: Griffith 200) which probably preceded the "Second Edition," since it incorporates none of the changes in the latter, is considered by Professor Griffith to be "most likely a pirated one, issued from the shop of Curll." Its most interesting textual feature is the substitution of "Gold chains" for "Glad chains" at i 86, a change which gave Pope the chance to write a mocking note in the name of Scriblerus. Professor Griffith regards Pope's note as "further evidence that the edition is a real pirated edition." It may be so; but, on the grounds that Pope was quite capable of instructing a printer to insert "Gold" for "Glad" merely to enable him to write the note he did, this edition has been collated with those others of 1728 which are certainly genuine. The Dublin edition of 1728 (Griffith 206) has not been included in the collation; it has, however, some textual interest on account of its guesses at the names of those dunces left blank by Pope.

In April 1729 appeared *The Dunciad Variorum* in quarto "Printed for A. Dod", with the Prolegomena of Scriblerus, notes variorum, and a number of appendices—the first edition of the *Dunciad* in this form. In some copies an additional leaf is found, without signature or pagination, headed "Addenda. M. Scriblerus Lectori." (Griffith 212. See p. 195*n.* of this edition.) An octavo "Printed for A. Dod" and another "Printed for Lawton Gilliver" followed a few days later. A variant of the Gilliver octavo (Griffith 215) has a two-page errata leaf, "M. Scriblerus Lectori", differing substantially from that of the quarto. (See p. 195*n.* of this edition.) Finally, still in 1729, came "The Second Edition, with some Additional Notes," of which Professor Griffith lists four variants. The Dublin editions of 1729 (Griffith 220, 221), and a London piracy "Printed for A. Dob," have been ignored for the purposes of collation.[1]

For the collected works in folio and quarto of 1735 Pope supplied Gilliver with a text that has several curious features. According to Professor Griffith (*Modern Philology*, vol. x (1912), p. 191), the folio was set up from a copy of the Gilliver "Second Edition" octavo of 1729. This statement he bases on the fact that the folio repeats the error, first found in the octavo, of omitting a line of French in a note to ii 165. This certainly seems to indicate that the notes at least were set up from a copy of the second octavo; but it is odd that the text of the poem should return on eight occasions to quarto (*1729a*) readings which were discarded in the octavo.[2] (Cf. ii 5, 159, 163, 168, 181, 341; iii 56, 282.) At iii 56, for instance, the quarto had printed "run forward"; this was corrected

1. For some elucidation of the Dod, Gilliver, and Dob octavos, see "The Dunciad of 1729," *The Modern Language Review*, vol. xxxi (1936), pp. 347 ff.

2. Cf. the editor's note to *Ep. to Arbuthnot* in vol. iv, pp. 92-3.

in the errata to "rush forward," and the correction was adopted by all the octavo editions of 1729. The folio and quarto of 1735, however, restore what was obviously a misprint of the quarto. All editions subsequent to *1735ab* return to "rush forward". It is difficult to escape the inference that for the folio text of the poem, as distinct from the notes, Pope sent Gilliver a copy of the quarto into which he had copied only some of the revisions made for the octavo editions of 1729. For the notes, which had been considerably expanded since the quarto was published, Gilliver would naturally give his printers a copy of "The Second Edition, with some Additional Notes". It should also be noted that the folio and quarto of 1735 contain numerous revisions of the text which were dropped in subsequent editions: later editions of *The Dunciad Variorum* up to 1742 accept the revisions made for the octavos of 1729. One piece, "By the Author A Declaration", first appeared in the folio.

To 1735 Professor Griffith assigns an undated octavo published by Gilliver (Griffith 392). Four new lines appear here for the first time at i 250, and there are other small revisions in both text and notes. Another Gilliver octavo, dated 1736, is a reissue of the sheets of the undated octavo, with a new title-page, and a revised note on the Rev. William Broome which compelled Pope to cancel the original leaf (o7) and substitute a new one.[1] The octavo issued as vol. iv of the works published by Gilliver and Clarke in 1736 was a reprint of Gilliver's octavo of 1735, but here again there was some revision.

In 1741 Henry Lintot included the *Dunciad* in the edition of Pope's works (vol. iii, pt. i) which he was publishing. The volume was reissued in 1742 with a new title-page. In a letter to Lintot, Jan. 31, 1741, Pope had assured him that he would "revise the edit. of ye Dunciad", but in fact his revision was of the slightest.

The present text of the poem is that of the quarto of 1729 (*1729a*). The typography of the quarto has been retained, but a number of misprints have been silently corrected (i 6, 8, 24, 38; ii 75, 317, 373; iii 56). To restore the typography of the 1728 duodecimo or octavo would have been, in a poem which had undergone so much revision and amplification in the course of twelve months, to

---

1. See *Dunciad A*, iii 327*n*.

produce a typographical pastiche. The punctuation of the quarto has been retained for the same reason, with three slight modifications of eighteenth-century usage. Pope or his printer occasionally omits to insert or to close inverted commas: these have been silently supplied. Again, Pope or his printer sometimes employs a mark of interrogation (e.g. "Heav'ns! what a pyle?" iii 69) where a mark of exclamation would now be used. On such occasions the exclamation mark has been substituted. Finally, apostrophes have been added where they are lacking.

In dealing with Pope's commentary a number of false references and misprints have been corrected. In Book II the printer numbered l. 163 as l. 165 and persisted in his error[1] to the end of the book; the numeration has been adjusted, and the corresponding adjustment made in the note references. Pope's very numerous misquotations have presented a special problem. To correct them all would have added seriously to an already congested page. Where the misquotation was clearly the printer's error it has been silently corrected; on other occasions it has been allowed to stand, but where there seemed to be any good reason for supplying the correct words (e.g. where Pope is deliberately falsifying the text, or softening some reflection upon himself) the actual words of the quotation are supplied in brackets. To save space, Pope's cross-references to the text of the poem have been frequently curtailed, and his distinction between "Imitations" and "Remarks," which involved his printers in difficulties which they never solved satisfactorily, has been ignored.

All editorial additions to Pope's commentary have been placed within diagonal brackets. If this does not add to the beauty of the page, it does at least enable the reader to tell at a glance whether he is about to read one of Pope's own notes or a further annotation of his editor's. All Pope's notes, or parts of notes, subsequent to those of the 1729 quarto have been dated. When a note was suppressed by Pope, the editions in which it did appear have been indicated.[2] Where no date is given, it can be assumed that the note first appeared in the quarto and continued unchanged

---

1. See Note, p. 6.

2. e.g. *1729a–d* following a note indicates that the note first appeared in the quarto of 1729, but was dropped from all editions after the octavo "Second Edition" of 1729.

through all editions up to 1742. It has proved impracticable within the compass of one volume to present a complete collation of the notes in the seventeen editions examined. Insignificant verbal changes have therefore been ignored, and the aim has been to record every textual revision in the notes that has any claim to importance.

The text of each of the prose pieces which precede and follow the poem is that of the quarto of 1729, collated with the quarto of 1743. The only exceptions are "Testimonies of Authors," which was so much amplified by Pope in subsequent editions that it has seemed best to give the final text of 1743, collated with the quarto of 1729, and "By the Author A Declaration," where the text is that of the folio of 1735, in which it first appeared. No useful purpose—or none, at least, commensurate with the labour involved—would have been served by giving a complete collation of the prose pieces. Pope's "Index of Things (including Authors)" has been retained, but there appeared to be no adequate reason for reprinting his serious "Index of Persons", "Index of the Authors of the Notes", and "Pieces contained in the Appendix", since the matter contained in those is given in the General Index to this volume.

Note. Professor Allen T. Hazen has pointed out to me that this statement is hardly fair to the printer. As I should have noted, leaf K_2 is a cancel, the printer having been faced with Pope's decision to omit the rather indecorous couplet that followed l. 152 in the editions of 1728. The printer duly adjusted the line numbering to accommodate this change, no doubt hoping that the difference would pass unnoticed.

KEY TO THE CRITICAL APPARATUS*

1728*a* = The Dunciad. An Heroic Poem. First (?) edition, duodecimo, Griffith 198.

1728*b* = Second (?) edition, octavo, Griffith 199.

1728*c* = Third (?) edition ("Gold chains"), duodecimo, Griffith 200.

1728*d* = "The Second Edition," duodecimo, Griffith 201.

1728*e* = "The Third Edition," duodecimo (Variant *a*), Griffith 203.

1728*f* = "The Third Edition," duodecimo (Variant *b*), Griffith 204.

1729*a* = The Dunciad, Variorum, First edition, quarto, Griffith 211.

1729*b* = Second edition, octavo (A. Dod), Griffith 213.

1729*c* = Third edition, octavo (Lawton Gilliver), Griffith 214.

1729*d* = "The Second Edition, with some Additional Notes", octavo, Griffith 224.

1735*a* = Works, vol. ii, folio, Griffith 370.

1735*b* = Works, vol. ii, quarto, Griffith 372.

1735*c* = The Dunciad. With Notes Variorum (n.d. 1735?), Griffith 392.

1736*a* = The Dunciad. An Heroic Poem (Gilliver), octavo, Griffith 405.

1736*b* = Works, vol. iv (Gilliver and Clarke), octavo, Griffith 431.

1741 = Works, vol. iii, part 2 (Lintot), octavo, Griffith 536.

1742 = Works, vol. iii, part 1 (Lintot), octavo, Griffith 545.

* See also p. 250.

ADVERTISEMENT

IT will be sufficient to say of this Edition, that the reader has here a much more correct and compleat copy of the DUNCIAD, than has hitherto appeared: I cannot answer but some mistakes may have slipt into it, but a vast number of others will be prevented, by the Names being now not only set at length, but justified by the authorities and reasons given. I make no doubt, the Author's own motive to use real rather than feign'd names, was his care to preserve the Innocent from any false Applications; whereas in the former editions which had no more than the Initial letters, he was made, by Keys printed here, to hurt the inoffensive; and (what was worse) to abuse his friends, by an impression at Dublin. 10

The Commentary which attends the Poem, was sent me from several hands, and consequently must be unequally written; yet will it have one advantage over most commentaries, that it is not made upon conjectures, or a remote distance of time: and the reader cannot but derive one pleasure from the very Obscurity of the persons it treats of, that it partakes of the 15 nature of a Secret, which most people love to be let into, tho' the Men or the Things be ever so inconsiderable or trivial.

Of the Persons it was judg'd proper to give some account: for since it is only in this monument that they must expect to survive, (and here survive they will, as long as the English tongue shall remain such as it 20 was in the reigns of Queen ANNE and King GEORGE) it seem'd but humanity to bestow a word or two upon each, just to tell what he was, what he writ, when he liv'd, or when he dy'd.

---

10. *at Dublin* ⟨This edition (Griffith, No. 206) reads "furious *Dryden*" for the "furious *D—n*" of the first edition (i 104*n*.); "*Hungerford*" for "*H—*" (i 244*n*.); "*Hughes*" for "*H—*" (ii 283*n*.); "*Savage*" for "*S—*" (ii 382*n*.).⟩

12. *several hands* ⟨See Introduction, p. xxivff.⟩

17. *trivial* ⟨Written ironically, no doubt; but the celebrity of the poem was largely due to the personalities introduced into the commentary. Theobald complained that "a Poetical War should confine itself to *Demerits* in the Science of Poetry"; for "to draw into the Quarrel Parts of *private character* . . . is intentionally to declare War against human Society."—*Mist's Journal*, June 22, 1728; *Gulliveriana*, p. 327.⟩

21. *GEORGE* ⟨The impermanence of the English language was, in fact, one of Pope's recurring anxieties. Cf. *E. on C.* 476–83, and G. Tillotson, *On the Poetry of Pope*, 1938, pp. 100 ff.⟩

23. *dy'd* ⟨"The notes I could wish to be very large, in what relates to the

If a word or two more are added upon the chief Offenders; 'tis only as a paper pinn'd upon the breast, to mark the Enormities for which they suffer'd; lest the Correction only should be remember'd, and the Crime forgotten.

In some Articles, it was thought sufficient barely to transcribe from Jacob, Curl, *and other writers of their own rank, who were much better acquainted with them than any of the Authors of this Comment can pretend to be. Most of them had drawn each other's Characters on certain occasions; but the few here inserted, are all that could be saved from the general destruction of such Works.* 5

10

Of the part of Scriblerus *I need say nothing: his Manner is well enough known, and approv'd by all but those who are too much concern'd to be judges.*

The Imitations *of the Ancients are added, to gratify those who either never read, or may have forgotten them; together with some of the Parodies,* 15 *and Allusions to the most excellent of the Moderns. If any man from the frequency of the former, may think the Poem too much a* Cento; *our Poet will but appear to have done the same thing in jest, which* Boileau *did in earnest; and upon which* Vida, Fracastorius, *and many of the most eminent Latin Poets professedly valued themselves.*

20

persons concerned; for I have long observed that twenty miles from London nobody understands hints, initial letters, or town facts and passages; and in a few years not even those who live in London. I would have the names of those scribblers printed indexically at the beginning or end of the poem, with an account of their works, for the reader to refer to."—Swift to Pope, July 16, 1728.⟩

4. *forgotten* ⟨Criminals sentenced to the pillory had frequently a paper pinned upon their breast (or, more usually, upon their back), setting forth the offences for which they were being punished.⟩

7. *Comment* ⟨For some identification of "the Authors of this Comment," see Introduction, pp. xxiv ff.⟩

16. *Moderns* ⟨"I would have all the parodies, as they are called, referred to the author they imitate."—Swift to Pope, July 16, 1728.⟩

20. ⟨It was originally Pope's intention to make use of a stanza from *The Faerie Queene* (i i 23: As gentle Shepheard in sweete euen-tide . . .) as a motto to his poem. Spence had seen it "written down in the first MS. copy of the Dunciad" (Spence, p. 296). It "hits the little impertinent poets", as Spence points out, but is in some of its details less applicable to the situation. When the poem was advertised by Mrs Dodd and others in the summer of 1728, the advertisements—perhaps the work of Edmund Curll—carried an adaptation

of Milton's lines in *Paradise Lost*, vi 856–8, 862, viz.:

> He, as an Herd
> Of Goats or tim'rous Flocks together throng'd,
> Drove them before him, Thunder struck pursu'd,
> Into the vast Profund.

See, for example, *The Whitehall Evening-Post*, June 6–8, 1728.⟩

L E T T E R

P U B L I S H E R,

Occasioned by the present   5

Edition of the D U N C I A D.

IT is with pleasure I hear that you have procured a correct
Edition of the DUNCIAD, which the many surreptitious
ones have rendered so necessary; and it is yet with more,
that I am informed it will be attended with a COMMENTARY: 10
a work so necessary, that I cannot think the Author himself
would have omitted it, had he approv'd of the first appearance
of this Poem.

Such Notes as have occurr'd to me I herewith send you; you
will oblige me by inserting them amongst those which are, or 15
will be, transmitted to you by others: since not only the Author's
friends, but even strangers, appear ingag'd by humanity, to
some care of an orphan of so much genius and spirit, which its
parent seems to have abandoned from the very beginning, and
suffered to step into the world naked, unguarded, and unat- 20
tended.

It was upon reading some of the abusive papers lately publish'd, that my great regard to a person whose friendship I shall
ever esteem as one of the chief honours of my life, and a much

---

The text is that of *1729a*, collated with *1743a*. Contractions such
as "I'm" or "tho' " are expanded in *1743a* to "I am" and "though":
such changes have not been separately noted here.
5 the present] the first correct   8 Edition] copy
9 necessary] requisite   17–18 to some care] to take some care
23–24 shall ever] *Om. 1743.*

---

13. *this Poem* ⟨See Introduction, p. xix ⟩

greater respect to Truth than to him or any man living, ingag'd me in Enquiries, of which the inclos'd Notes are the fruit.

I perceiv'd that most of these authors had been (doubtless very wisely) the first Aggressors: they had try'd till they were weary, what was to be got by railing at each other; no body was 5 either concern'd, or surpriz'd, if this or that Scribler was prov'd a Dunce: but every one was curious to read what could be said to prove Mr. POPE one, and was ready to pay something for such a discovery: A stratagem which wou'd they fairly own, might not only reconcile them to me, but screen them from the resent- 10 ment of their lawful superiors, whom they daily abuse, only (as I charitably hope) to get that by them, which they cannot get from them.

I found this was not all: ill success in that had transported them to personal abuse, either of himself, or (what I think he could 15 less forgive) of his friends. They had call'd men of virtue and honour Bad Men, long before he had either leisure or inclina- tion to call them Bad Writers: and some had been such old offenders, that he had quite forgotten their persons as well as their slanders, till they were pleas'd to revive them. 20

Now what had Mr. POPE done before to incense them? He had published those works which are in the hands of every body, in which not the least mention is made of any of them: And what has he done since? He has laugh'd and written the DUNCIAD. What has that said of them? a very serious truth 25 which the publick had said before, that they were dull: and what it had no sooner said, but they themselves were at great pains to procure or even purchase room in the prints, to testify under their hands to the truth of it.

I should still have been silent, if either I had seen any inclina- 30

---

9 might] it might   12–13 by . . . from] *by . . . from*

---

20 *revive them* ⟨See Pope's statement, Appendix II, p. 210. "Others of an elder date, having layn as waste paper many years, were upon the publication of the Dunciad brought out . . . "⟩

23. *any of them* ⟨This statement must be qualified. In *The Essay on Criticism* he had glanced at Dennis, Blackmore, and several others. In his satirical pamphlets on Curll, he had named a number of Curll's authors. See also N. Ault's Intro- duction to *Pope's Prose*, and Pope's note to an equally rash statement in Appen- dix I, p. 203*n*.⟩

tion in my friend to be serious with such accusers, or if they had only attack'd his writings: since whoever publishes, puts himself on his tryal by his country. But when his moral character was attack'd, and in a manner from which neither Truth nor Virtue can secure the most Innocent, in a manner which though it   5 annihilates the credit of the accusation with the just and impartial, yet aggravates very much the guilt of the accuser, (I mean by authors without Names:) Then I thought, since the danger is common to all, the concern ought to be so; and that it was an act of justice to detect the Authors, not only on this   10 account, but as many of them are the same, who for several years past, have made free with the greatest Names in Church and State, expos'd to the world the private misfortunes of Families, abus'd all even to Women, and whose prostituted papers (for one or other Party, in the unhappy Divisions of   15 their Country) have insulted the Fallen, the Friendless, the Exil'd, and the Dead.

Besides this, which I take to be a publick concern, I have already confess'd I had a private one. I am one of that number who have long lov'd and esteem'd Mr. POPE, and had often   20 declared it was not his Capacity or Writings (which we ever thought the least valuable part of his character) but the honest, open, and beneficent Man, that we most esteem'd and lov'd in him. Now if what these people say were believ'd, I must appear to all my friends either a fool or a knave, either impos'd   25 on my self, or imposing on them: So that I am as much interested in the confutation of these calumnies, as he is himself.

I am no Author, and consequently not to be suspected either

---

2 attack'd] meddled with   7 accuser] accusers   9 is] was

8. *without Names* ⟨The writer of this comment seems to forget that it is double-edged: the *Dunciad* had not been owned by its author.⟩

17. *the Dead* ⟨The authors referred to here are, no doubt, writers of scandalous memoirs like Mrs Haywood, and of political controversy like Oldmixon. Mrs Haywood was responsible for a scurrilous attack on Martha Blount (see Biog. App. HAYWOOD). Oxford and Bolingbroke, both "fallen," and Atterbury, "exiled," had been attacked persistently.⟩

27. *himself* ⟨In the Preface to his *Reflections upon an Essay upon Criticism*—a work which Pope read and marked—Dennis had written: "They who expose by a just Criticism the Absurdities of foolish fortunate Authors, attack all those

of jealousy or resentment against any of the men, of whom scarce one is known to me by sight; and as for their writings, I have sought them (on this one occasion) in vain, in the closets and libraries of all my acquaintance. I had still been in the dark, if a Gentleman had not procur'd me (I suppose from some of them-   5 selves, for they are generally much more dangerous friends than enemies) the passages I send you. I solemnly protest I have added nothing to the malice or absurdity of them, which it behoves me to declare, since the vouchers themselves will be so soon and so irrecoverably lost. You may in some measure prevent it, by 10 preserving at least their * Titles, and discovering (as far as you can depend on the truth of your information) the names of the conceal'd authors.

The first objection I have heard made to the Poem is, that the persons are too obscure for Satyre. The persons themselves, 15 rather than allow the objection, would forgive the Satyre; and if one could be tempted to afford it a serious answer, were not all assassinates, popular insurrections, the insolence of the rabble without doors and of domesticks within, most wrongfully chastized, if the Meanness of offenders indemnified them from 20 punishment? On the contrary, obscurity renders them more dangerous, as less thought of: Law can pronounce judgment only on open Facts, Morality alone can pass censure on Intentions of mischief; so that for secret calumny or the arrow flying in the dark, there is no publick punishment left, but what a good 25 writer inflicts.

The next objection is, that these sort of authors are Poor.

---

who commend and admire those Authors, and disturb perhaps by opening their Eyes, no fewer than a thousand Fops in the good Opinion which they have conceiv'd of themselves.">

4–5. *a Gentleman* ⟨If this statement is to be taken literally, the gentleman referred to is most probably Richard Savage, who was suspected of supplying Pope with "private intelligence and secret incidents" relating to the dunces.— Johnson, *Lives*, ɪɪ 362. See Introduction, pp. xxv f.⟩

*   Which we have done in a List in the *Appendix*, No. 2.

18. *assassinates* ⟨i.e. assassins.⟩

27. *Poor* ⟨This objection was frequently stated. Cf. a letter signed "W.A." in *Mist's Journal*, June 8, 1728: "It is, thro' the Whole, a merciless Satire on Poverty and Hunger, the Necessity and Distress of particular Men . . . *Supperless Bards, Books unpawn'd, unpaid Taylors*, etc. are the choice Flowers of our Poet."— *Gulliveriana*, p. 312.⟩

That might be pleaded as an excuse at the Old Baily for lesser crimes than defamation, for 'tis the case of almost all who are try'd there; but sure it can here be none, since no man will pretend that the robbing another of his reputation supplies the want of it in himself. I question not but such authors are poor, 5 and heartily wish the objection were removed by any honest livelihood. But Poverty here is the accident, not the subject: he who describes malice and villany to be pale and meagre, expresses not the least anger against paleness or leanness, but against malice and villany. The apothecary in ROMEO and JULIET is 10 poor, but is he therefore justified in vending poison? Not but poverty itself becomes a just subject of satyre, when it is the consequence of vice, prodigality, or neglect of one's lawful calling; for then it increases the publick burden, fills the streets and high-ways with Robbers, and the garrets with Clippers, 15 Coiners, and Weekly Journalists.

But admitting that two or three of these, offend less in their morals, than in their writings; must poverty make nonsense sacred? If so, the fame of bad authors would be much better taken care of, than that of all the good ones in the world; and 20 not one of a hundred had ever been call'd by his right name.

They mistake the whole matter: It is not charity to encourage them in the way they follow, but to get 'em out of it: For men are not bunglers because they are poor, but they are poor because they are bunglers. 25

Is it not pleasant enough to hear our authors crying out on the one hand, as if their persons and characters were too sacred for Satyre; and the publick objecting on the other, that they are too mean even for Ridicule? But whether bread or fame be

---

3 here] *Om. 1743.*   3 since no man} For who will
7 here is] is here   20 taken care of] consulted

13–14. *lawful calling* ⟨Cf. the passage from Dennis quoted at the end of this "Letter", and Savage's Preface to *An Author to be Let,* where it is argued that "tho' they are sad Writers, they might have been good Mechanicks." Young took the same line in *Two Epistles to Mr. Pope* . . . 1730, Ep. 1 51–4:
> His Hammer This, and That his Trowel quits,
> And wanting Sense for Tradesmen, serve for Wits.
> By thriving men subsists each other Trade,
> Of every *broken* Craft a *Writer's* made.⟩

3*

their end, it must be allow'd, our author by and in this poem, has mercifully given 'em a little of both.

There are two or three, who by their rank and fortune have no benefit from the former objections (supposing them good) and these I was sorry to see in such company. But if without any provocation, two or three gentlemen will fall upon one, in an affair wherein his interest and reputation are equally embark'd; they cannot certainly, after they had been content to print themselves his enemies, complain of being put into the number of them?

Others, I'm told, pretend to have been once his Friends; surely they are their enemies who say so, since nothing can be more odious than to treat a friend as they have done: but of this I can't persuade my self, when I consider the constant and eternal aversion of all bad writers to a good one.

Such as claim a merit from being his Admirers, I wou'd gladly ask, if it lays him under any personal obligation? at that rate he would be the most oblig'd humble servant in the world. I dare swear, for these in particular, he never desir'd them to be his Admirers, nor promis'd in return to be theirs; that had truly been a sign he was of their acquaintance; but wou'd not the malicious world have suspected such an approbation of some motive worse than ignorance, in the Author of the ESSAY on CRITICISM? Be it as it will, the reasons of their Admiration and of his Contempt are equally subsisting; for His Works and Theirs are the very same that they were.

One therefore of their accusations I believe may be just, "That he has a contempt for their writings." And there is

---

10 them?] them.   17 any] a   27 accusations] assertions
27 just] true

---

2. *both* ⟨Pope had given them fame by putting them in the *Dunciad*, and bread by enabling them to write their replies and sell them to the booksellers.⟩

3. *two or three* ⟨e.g. Thomas Burnet, George Duckett, Sir Richard Blackmore.⟩

11. *Friends* ⟨e.g. James Moore Smythe. Cf. *Ep. to Arbuthnot*, 346.⟩

18. *in the world* ⟨The writer may be answering here a charge brought against Pope by the author [Dennis?] of *A True Character* (p. 15), that Blackmore had complimented Pope on his Homer and so "had laid very great Obligations" on him.⟩

another which would probably be sooner allow'd by himself, than by any good judge beside, "That his own have found too much success with the publick." But as it cannot consist with his modesty to claim this as a justice, it lies not on him, but entirely on the publick, to defend its own judgment.   5

There remains what in my opinion might seem a better plea for these people, than any they have made use of. If Obscurity or Poverty were to exempt a man from satyr, much more should Folly or Dulness, which are still more involuntary, nay as much so as personal deformity. But even this will not help them: 10 Deformity becomes the object of ridicule when a man sets up for being handsome: and so must Dulness when he sets up for a Wit. They are not ridicul'd because Ridicule in itself is or ought to be a pleasure; but because it is just, to undeceive or vindicate the honest and unpretending part of mankind from imposition, 15 because particular interest ought to yield to general, and a great number who are not naturally Fools ought never to be made so in complaisance to a few who are. Accordingly we find that in all ages, all vain pretenders, were they ever so poor or ever so dull, have been constantly the topicks of the most 20 candid Satyrists, from the Codrus of JUVENAL to the Damon of BOILEAU.

Having mention'd BOILEAU, the greatest Poet and most judicious Critic of his age and country, admirable for his talents, and yet perhaps more admirable for his judgment in 25 the proper application of them; I cannot help remarking the resemblance betwixt Him and our Author in Qualities, Fame, and Fortune; in the distinctions shewn to them by their Superiors, in the general esteem of their Equals, and in their extended reputation amongst Foreigners; in the latter of which 30 ours has met with the better fortune, as he has had for his Translators persons of the most eminent rank and abilities in their respective Nations. * But the resemblance holds in nothing more, than in their being equally abus'd by the ignorant pretenders to Poetry of their times; of which not the least memory will 35

11 the] an   14 or] and   28 shewn to] shewn   31 fortune] fate

3. *the publick* ⟨This is the burden of Dennis's complaint against Pope.⟩
* Essay on Criticism in *French* Verse by General *Hamilton*. The same in

remain but in their own writings, and in the notes made upon
them. What BOILEAU has done in almost all his Poems, our
Author has only in this: I dare answer for him he will do it in
no more; and on his principle of attacking few but who had
slander'd him, he could not have done it at all had he been   5
confin'd from censuring obscure and worthless persons, for
scarce any other were his enemies. However, as the parity is so
remarkable, I hope it will continue to the last; and if ever he
shall give us an edition of this Poem himself, I may see some
of 'em treated as gently (on their repentance or better merit) as   10
Perault and Quinault were at last by BOILEAU.

In one point I must be allow'd to think the character of our
English Poet the more amiable. He has not been a follower of
fortune or success: He has liv'd with the Great without Flattery, been a friend to Men in power without Pensions, from   15
whom as he ask'd, so he receiv'd no favour but what was done
Him in his friends. As his Satyrs were the more just for being
delay'd, so were his Panegyricks; bestow'd only on such persons
as he had familiarly known, only for such virtues as he had

---

4 his] this

Verse also by Monsieur *Roboton*, Counsellor and Privy Secretary to King
George I.

Rape of the Lock, in *French, Paris*, 1728.

——— ——— In *Italian* Verse, by the Abbe *Conti*, a Noble *Venetian*; and
by the Marquess *Rangoni*, Envoy Extraordinary from *Modena* to King *George* II.

Others of his Works by *Salvini* of *Florence*, &c.

His Essays and Dissertations on *Homer*, in *French, Paris* 1728. ⟨General Hamilton's translation was not published, but an extract from it appeared in *Oeuvres
de Comte Antoine Hamilton*, 1812, p. 112. Robethon's *Essai sur la Critique* was
published in 1717. *La Boucle de Cheveux enlevée* was translated by the Abbé
Desfontaines, who was also responsible for *Remarques sur Homer etc.* In *1743a*
Pope attributed the first of these to the Princess of Conti. To this list Pope was
able to add in *1735a* the Abbé du Resnel's verse translation, *Essai sur la Critique*
(1730); and in *1743a* the prose *Essai sur L'Homme* of Silhouette (1736), and a
poetical version by du Resnel, and "others in French, Italian, and Latin."
See E. Audra, *Les Traductions Françaises de Pope, 1717–1825*.⟩

11. BOILEAU ⟨See *A Treatise of the Sublime . . . By Mr. Boileau*, 1712, pp. 96–7,
169–78. Mr John Butt has reminded me of Pope's partial amends to Thomas
Burnet (B iii 179*n.*), and his reference to Dennis in *Ep. to Arbuthnot*, 370–1,
where he claimed to be "Foe to his Pride, but Friend to his Distress."⟩

long observ'd in them, and only at such times as others cease
to praise if not begin to calumniate them, I mean when out of
Power or out of Fashion.† A Satyr therefore on writers so
notorious for the contrary, became no man so well as himself;
as none (it is plain) was so little in Their friendships, or so 5
much in that of those whom they had most abus'd, namely the
Greatest and Best of All Parties. Let me add a further reason,
that tho' ingag'd in their friendships, he never espous'd their
animosities; and can almost singly challenge this honour, not to
have written a line of any man, which thro' Guilt, thro' Shame, 10
or thro' Fear, thro' variety of Fortune, or change of Interests,
he was ever unwilling to own.

I shall conclude with remarking what a pleasure it must be
to every reader of humanity, to see all along, that our Author,
in his very laughter, is not indulging his own Ill nature, but 15
only punishing that of others. To his Poem those alone are
capable to do Justice, who to use the words of a great Writer,
know how hard it is (with regard both to his Subject and his
Manner) VETUSTIS DARE NOVITATEM, OBSOLETIS NITOREM,
OBSCURIS LUCEM, FASTIDITIS GRATIAM. I am, 20

Your most humble Servant,

WILLIAM CLELAND.

St. *James's*
  Dec. 22, 1728.

---

4 contrary] contrary practice   16 To] As to
17 to do] of doing it

---

† As Mr. *Wycherley*, at the time the Town declaim'd against his Book of
Poems: Mr. *Walsh*, after his death: Sir *William Trumbull*, when he had resign'd
the Office of Secretary of State; Lord *Bolingbroke* at his leaving *England* after
the Queen's death: Lord *Oxford* in his last decline of Life: Mr. Secretary *Craggs*
at the end of the South-Sea Year, and after his death: Others, only in *Epitaphs*.
⟨Cf. Pope to Fortescue (EC ix 109) on Sir Robert Walpole: "I have more
esteem for him, and will stay till he is out of power (according to my custom)
before I say what I think of him."⟩
  20. GRATIAM ⟨Pliny, *Natural History*, Preface § 15.⟩
  22. *CLELAND*] This Gentleman was of Scotland, and bred at the University
of Utrecht, with the Earl of Mar. He served in Spain under Earl Rivers. After
the Peace, he was made one of the Commissioners of the Customs in Scotland,

DENNIS, Rem. on Pr. *Arth.*

I Cannot but think it the most *reasonable* thing in the world, to distinguish Good writers, by discouraging the Bad. Nor is it an *ill-natur'd* thing, in relation even to the very *persons* upon whom the Reflections are made: It is true, it may deprive them,   5
a little the sooner, of a *short Profit* and a *transitory Reputation:* But then it may have a good effect, and oblige them (before it be too late) to decline that for which they are so very *unfit,* and to have recourse to *something* in which they may be more successful.

The *Persons* whom *Boileau* has attack'd in his writings, have 10
been for the most part *Authors,* and most of those Authors, *Poets:* And the censures he hath pass'd upon them have been *confirm'd by all Europe.* [Character of Mr. *P.* 1716.]

GILDON, Pref. to his *New Rehears.*

IT is the common cry of the *Poetasters* of the Town, and their 15
Fautors, that it is an *Ill-natur'd thing* to expose the *Pretenders* to Wit and Poetry. The Judges and Magistrates may with full as good reason be reproach'd with *Ill-nature,* for putting the Laws

and then of Taxes in England, in which having shewn himself for twenty years diligent, punctual, and incorruptible, though without any other assistance of Fortune, he was suddenly displaced by the Minister in the sixty eighth year of his age; and died two months after, in 1741. He was a person of Universal Learning, and an enlarged Conversation; no man had a warmer heart for his Friend, or a sincerer attachment to the Constitution of his Country. ⟨*1743a.* To this Warburton adds in *1751*:—"And yet, for all this, the Public will not allow him to be the Author of this Letter".—The public was sceptical from the first, and the opinion of the author of *Pope Alexander's Supremacy . . . examin'd* that Pope had "written a Letter to himself in the Name of one *William Cleland*" was widespread. Cf. *The Curliad,* p. 1. Swift was still wondering about Cleland when he wrote to Pope on Jan. 15, 1731: "As to his letter before the Dunciad I know not the secret, but should not suspect him for it." See Introduction, p. xxv, and Biog. App., CLELAND.⟩

1. *Rem. on Pr. Arth.* ⟨i.e. *Remarks on . . . Prince Arthur.* See *The Critical Works of John Dennis,* ed. E. N. Hooker, 1939, vol. i, p. 48.⟩

13. *Character of Mr. P. 1716* ⟨*A True Character of Mr. Pope,* p. 14. For the authorship of this pamphlet, see Testimonies of Authors, p. 25*n.*⟩

14. *New Rehears.* ⟨*A New Rehearsal, or Bays the Younger.* Pope has paraphrased the three opening sentences.⟩

in execution against a Thief or Impostor—The same will hold
in the Republick of Letters, if the Criticks and Judges will let
every *Ignorant Pretender* to Scribling, pass on the World.

THEOBALD, Lett. to *Mist*, Jun. 22, 1728.
ATTACKS may be levelled, either against *Failures in Genius,*   5
or against the *Pretensions* of *writing without one.*

CONCANEN, *Ded.* to the *Auth.* of the *Dunc.*
A *Satyre* upon *Dulness*, is a thing, that has been *used* and *allowed*
in *All Ages.*

Out of thine own Mouth will I judge thee, wicked Scribler!   10

7. *Auth. of the Dunc.* ⟨*A Compleat Collection of all the Verses* . . . 1728, p. xi.⟩

TESTIMONIES

OF

AUTHORS

Concerning our POET and his WORKS.

M. SCRIBLERUS Lectori S.

BEFORE we present thee with our exercitations on this
most delectable Poem (drawn from the many volumes
of our Adversaria on modern Authors) we shall here,
according to the laudable usage of editors, collect the various
judgments of the Learned concerning our Poet: Various indeed,   5
not only of different authors, but of the same author at different
seasons. Nor shall we gather only the Testimonies of such eminent Wits, as would of course descend to posterity, and consequently be read without our collection; but we shall likewise
with incredible labour seek out for divers others, which, but for   10
this our diligence, could never at the distance of a few months
appear to the eye of the most curious. Hereby thou may'st not
only receive the delectation of Variety, but also arrive at a
more certain judgment, by a grave and circumspect comparison
of the Witnesses with each other, or of each with himself. Hence   15
also thou wilt be enabled to draw reflections, not only of a
critical, but a moral nature, by being let into many particulars
of the Person as well as Genius, and of the Fortune as well as
Merit, of our Author: In which if I relate some things of little
concern peradventure to thee, and some of as little even to him;   20
I entreat thee to consider how minutely all true critics and
commentators are wont to insist upon such, and how material
they seem to themselves, if to none other. Forgive me, gentle

---

Pope added so persistently to the "Testimonies" that it has
seemed best to print the text in its final form of *1743a*. This has been
collated with *1729a*, in which the "Testimonies" first appeared.

1 this] the   2 Poem] Poem of the Dunciad
7 Testimonies] Testimonials
23 Forgive me,] Forgive me therefore

23

reader, if (following learned example) I ever and anon become tedious: allow me to take the same pains to find whether my author were good or bad, well or ill-natured, modest or arrogant; as another, whether his author was fair or brown, short or tall, or whether he wore a coat or a cassock.   5

We purposed to begin with his Life, Parentage, and Education: But as to these, even his cotemporaries do exceedingly differ. One saith[a], he was educated at home; another[b], that he was bred at St. Omer's by Jesuits; a third[c], not at St. Omer's, but at Oxford; a fourth[d], that he had no University education 10 at all. Those who allow him to be bred at home, differ as much concerning his Tutor: One saith[e], he was kept by his father on purpose; a second[f], that he was an itinerant priest; a third[g], that he was a parson; one[h] calleth him a secular clergyman of the Church of Rome; another[i], a monk. As little do they agree 15 about his Father, whom one[k] supposeth, like the Father of Hesiod, a tradesman or merchant; another[l], a husbandman; another[m], a hatter, &c. Nor has an author been wanting to give our Poet such a father as Apuleius hath to Plato, Jamblicus to

---

2 pains] pain   4 his author was] his were
9 bred] bred abroad   15 As . . . agree] As little agree they
17 another, a hatter &c.] Om. *1729a*.   18 has] hath

---

[a] Giles Jacob's Lives of Poets, vol. ii. in his Life. ⟨Vol. ii, p. 145.⟩

[b] Dennis's Reflect. on the Essay on Crit. ⟨p. 27. "He . . . must, I humbly conceive, derive his Religion from St. Omer's, as he seems to have done his Humanity and his Criticism." Dennis does not, of course, mean to be taken literally.⟩

[c] Dunciad dissected, p. 4.

[d] Guardian, N⁰ 40. ⟨An essay written by Pope himself. The reference is to par. 5. See Appendix V.⟩

[e] Jacob's Lives &c. vol. ii. ⟨p. 145.⟩

[f] Dunciad dissected, p. 4.

[g] Farmer P. and his son. ⟨In *The Dunciad Dissected*, p. 4.⟩

[h] Dunc. dissect. ⟨p. 4.⟩

[i] Characters of the times, p. 45.

[k] Female Dunc. p. ult. ⟨Pope is advised to consider "the former Distresses of his own Family. And that his Father was no Stranger to a *Statute* of *Bankrupt*."⟩

[l] Dunc. dissect. ⟨p. 3.⟩

[m] Roome, Paraphrase on the 4th of Genesis, printed 1729. ⟨For Roome, see Biog App.⟩

Pythagoras, and divers to Homer, namely a Dæmon: For thus
Mr. Gildon[n]: "Certain it is, that his original is not from Adam,
"but the Devil; and that he wanteth nothing but horns and tail
"to be the exact resemblance of his infernal Father." Finding,
therefore, such contrariety of opinions, and (whatever be ours 5
of this sort of generation) not being fond to enter into controversy, we shall defer writing the life of our Poet, 'till authors
can determine among themselves what Parents or Education
he had, or whether he had any Education or Parents at all.

Proceed we to what is more certain, his Works, tho' not less 10
uncertain the judgments concerning them; beginning with his
Essay on Criticism, of which hear first the most ancient of
Critics,

Mr. John Dennis.

"His precepts are false or trivial, or both; his thoughts are 15
"crude and abortive, his expressions absurd, his numbers harsh
"and unmusical, his rhymes trivial and common;—instead of
"majesty, we have something that is very mean; instead of
"gravity, something that is very boyish; and instead of per-
"spicuity and lucid order, we have but too often obscurity and 20
"confusion." And in another place: "What rare *numbers* are
"here! Would not one swear that this youngster had espoused
"some antiquated muse, who had sued out a divorce from some
"superannuated sinner, upon account of impotence, and who,
"being poxed by her former spouse, has got the gout in her 25
"decrepid age, which makes her *hobble so damnably*[o]." No less
peremptory is the censure of our hypercritical Historian

Mr. Oldmixon.

"I dare not say any thing of the Essay on Criticism in verse;

17 unmusical] unmusical, without cadence, or variety,
22 that] *Om. 1729a.*

[n] Character of Mr. P. and his Writings, in a Letter to a Friend, printed for
S. Popping, 1716. p. 10. Curl, in his Key to the Dunciad (first edit. said to be
printed for A. Dodd) in the 10th page, declared Gildon to be author of that
libel; though in the subsequent editions of his Key he left out this assertion,
and affirmed (in the Curliad, p. 4. and 8.) that it was writ by Dennis only.
⟨This note was amplified in *1729d* from a briefer statement in *1729a.*⟩
[o] Reflections critical and satyrical on a Rhapsody called An Essay on
Criticism. Printed for Bernard Lintot, octavo. ⟨p. 11.⟩

"but if any more curious reader has discovered in it something
"*new* which is not in Dryden's prefaces, dedications, and his
"essay on dramatic poetry, not to mention the French critics,
"I should be very glad to have the benefit of the discovery[p].

He is followed (as in fame, so in judgment) by the modest and   5
simple-minded

Mr. LEONARD WELSTED;

Who, out of great respect to our poet not naming him, doth
yet glance at his Essay, together with the Duke of Buckingham's, and the Criticisms of Dryden, and of Horace, which he   10
more openly taxeth[q]: "As to the numerous treatises, essays, arts,
"&c. both in verse and prose, that have been written by the
"moderns on this ground-work, they do but *hackney the same*
"*thoughts over again*, making them still more *trite*. Most of their
"pieces are nothing but a pert, insipid heap of *common place*.   15
"Horace has even in his Art of Poetry thrown out several things
"which plainly shew, he thought an Art of Poetry was of no use,
"even while he was writing one."

To all which great authorities, we can only oppose that of

Mr. ADDISON.   20

"[r]The Art of Criticism (saith he) which was published some
"months since, is a master-piece in its kind. The observations
"follow one another, like those in Horace's Art of Poetry, with-
"out that methodical regularity which would have been re-
"quisite in a prose-writer. They are some of them *uncommon*,   25
"but such as the reader must assent to, when he sees them
"explain'd with that ease and perspicuity in which they are
"delivered. As for those which are the *most known* and the most
"*receiv'd*, they are placed in so beautiful a light, and illustrated
"with such apt allusions, that they have in them all the graces   30
"of novelty; and make the reader, who was before acquainted
"with them, still more convinc'd of their truth and solidity.
"And here give me leave to mention what Monsieur Boileau has

---

[p] Essay on Criticism in prose, octavo, 1728. by the author of the Critical
History of England. ⟨p. 2. For Oldmixon, the author in question, see Biog. App.⟩

[q] Preface to his Poems, p. 18, 53. ⟨*Epistles, Odes*, etc. . . . 1724. Welsted is
called "simple-minded" because Pope and his friends classed him with Philips
among the consciously naïve writers. See A iii 163*n*.⟩

[r] Spectator, N⁰ 253.

"so well enlarged upon in the preface to his works: That wit
"and fine writing doth not consist so much in advancing things
"that are new, as in giving things that are known an agreeable
"turn. It is impossible for us who live in the latter ages of the
"world, to make observations in criticism, morality, or any art   5
"or science, which have not been touch'd upon by others; we
"have little else left us, but to represent the common sense of
"mankind in more strong, more beautiful, or more uncommon
"lights. If a reader examines Horace's Art of Poetry, he will
"find but few precepts in it, which he may not meet with in Ari-   10
"stotle, and which were not commonly known by all the poets of
"the Augustan age. His way of expressing, and applying them,
"not his invention of them, is what we are chiefly to admire.

"Longinus, in his Reflexions, has given us the same kind of
"sublime, which he observes in the several passages that oc-   15
"casioned them: I cannot but take notice that our English
"author has after the same manner exemplify'd several of the
"precepts in the very precepts themselves." He then produces
some instances of a particular beauty in the numbers, and concludes with saying, that "there are three poems in our tongue   20
"of the same nature, and each a master-piece in its kind; The
"Essay on Translated Verse; the Essay on the Art of Poetry;
"and the Essay on Criticism."

Of WINDSOR FOREST, positive is the judgment of the
affirmative   25

Mr. JOHN DENNIS,

"sThat it is a wretched rhapsody, impudently writ in emula-
"tion of the Cooper's Hill of Sir John Denham: The author of it
"is obscure, is ambiguous, is affected, is temerarious, is bar-
"barous."   30

But the author of the Dispensary

Dr. GARTH,

in the preface to his poem of Claremont, differs from this

19–20 the precepts] his Precepts   21 beauty] kind of beauty

23. ⟨By the Earl of Roscommon; by John Sheffield, Duke of Buckingham.⟩
s Letter to B. B. ⟨i.e. Barton Booth?⟩ at the end of the Remarks on Pope's
Homer, 1717 ⟨pp. 39, 44⟩.
32. Dr. Garth ⟨For Sir Samuel Garth (1661–1719), physician and poet, see
Biog. App., vol. iv.⟩

opinion: "Those who have seen these two excellent poems of
"Cooper's Hill, and Windsor Forest, the one written by Sir
"John Denham, the other by Mr. Pope, will shew a great deal
"of candour if they approve of this."

Of the Epistle of ELOISA, we are told by the obscure writer 5
of a poem called Sawney,[t] "That because Prior's Henry and
"Emma charm'd the finest tastes, our author writ his Eloise, *in*
"*opposition to it*; but forgot innocence and virtue: If you take
"away her tender thoughts, and her fierce desires, all the rest
"is of no value." In which, methinks, his judgment resembleth 10
that of a French taylor on a Villa and gardens by the Thames:
"All this is very fine, but take away the river, and it is good for
"nothing."

But very contrary hereunto was the opinion of

Mr. PRIOR   15

himself, saying in his *Alma*[v],

<blockquote>
O *Abelard!* ill fated youth,
Thy tale will justify this truth.
But well I weet thy cruel wrong
Adorns a nobler Poet's song: 20
Dan *Pope*, for thy misfortune griev'd,
With kind concern and skill has weav'd
A silken web; and ne'er shall fade
Its colours: gently has he laid
The mantle o'er thy sad distress,   25
And Venus shall the texture bless, *&c.*
</blockquote>

Come we now to his translation of the ILIAD, celebrated by
numerous pens, yet shall it suffice to mention the indefatigable.

Sir RICHARD BLACKMORE, Kt.

Who (tho' otherwise a severe censurer of our author) yet styleth 30
this a "laudable translation[w]." That ready writer

---

2 written by] by	5 writer] Author
10 resembleth] resembled	14 opinion] judgment

---

[t] Printed 1728, p. 12. ⟨This is a prose paraphrase of Ralph's prosaic blank
verse in *Sawney*, pp. 11–12. For Ralph, see Biog. App.⟩
[v] Alma, Cant. 2. ⟨287–96.⟩
[w] In his Essays, vol. i. printed for E. Curl. ⟨p. vi.⟩

Mr. OLDMIXON,

in his forementioned Essay, frequently commends the same. And the painful

Mr. LEWIS THEOBALD

thus extols it[x], "The spirit of Homer breathes all through this   5
"translation.—I am in doubt, whether I should most admire
"the justness to the original, or the force and beauty of the
"language, or the sounding variety of the numbers: But when I
"find all these meet, it puts me in mind of what the poet says of
"one of his heroes, That he alone rais'd and flung with ease a   10
"weighty stone, that two common men could not lift from the
"ground; just so, one single person has performed in this trans-
"lation, what I once despaired to have seen done by the force of
"several masterly hands." Indeed the same gentleman appears
to have chang'd his sentiment in his Essay on the Art of   15
sinking in reputation, (printed in Mist's Journal, March 30,
1728.) where he says thus: "In order to sink in reputation, let
"him take it into his head to descend into Homer (let the world
"wonder, as it will, how the devil he got there) and pretend to
"do him into English, so his version denote his neglect of the   20
"manner how." Strange Variation! We are told in

MIST'S JOURNAL, June 8.

"That this translation of the Iliad was not in all respects con-
"formable to the fine taste of his friend Mr. Addison; insomuch
"that he employed a *younger muse*, in an undertaking of this   25
"kind, which he supervised himself." Whether Mr. Addison
did find it conformable to his taste, or not, best appears from
his own testimony the year following its publication, in these
words:

Mr. ADDISON, FREEHOLDER, N° 40.   30

"When I consider myself as a British freeholder, I am in a
"particular manner pleased with the labours of those who have
"improved our language with the translations of old Greek and
"Latin authors.—We have already most of their Historians in

---

16 (printed . . . 1728)] *Om. 1729a.*
33 translations] translation

---

[x] Censor, vol. ii. n. 33. ⟨Jan. 5, 1717.⟩

"our own tongue, and what is more for the honour of our
"language, it has been taught to express with elegance the
"greatest of their Poets in each nation. The illiterate among our
"own countrymen may learn to judge from Dryden's Virgil of
"the most perfect Epic performance. And those parts of Homer   5
"which have been published already by Mr. Pope, give us
"reason to think that the Iliad will appear in English with as
"little disadvantage to that immortal poem."

As to the rest, there is a slight mistake, for this *younger muse*
was an *elder:* Nor was the gentleman (who is a friend of our   10
author) employ'd by Mr. Addison to translate it *after him*,
since he saith himself that he did it *before*[y]. Contrariwise that Mr.
Addison engaged our author in this work appeareth by declaration thereof in the preface to the Iliad, printed some time before
his death, and by his own letters of October 26, and November   15
2, 1713. where he declares it is his opinion, that no other person
was equal to it.

Next comes his Shakespear on the stage: "Let him (quoth
one, whom I take to be

Mr. THEOBALD, Mist's Journal, June 8, 1728.)   20

"publish such an author as he has least studied, and forget to
"discharge even the dull duty of an editor. In this project let him
"lend the bookseller his name (for a competent sum of money)
"to promote the credit of an exorbitant subscription." Gentle

---

3-4 our own] our   10 an *elder*] elder   14 time] years
16 it is] it   23 money] money tho'

---

[y] Vid. pref. to Mr. Tickel's translation of the first book of the Iliad, 4to.
⟨Tickell says that at one time he had intended to translate the whole of the
Iliad, "but had the pleasure of being diverted from that Design, by finding the
Work was fallen into a much abler Hand."—For the circumstances in which
Tickell's translation was undertaken and carried on, see Sherburn, pp. 127 ff.
His agreement with Tonson was signed on May 31, 1714: Pope's agreement
with Lintot is dated March 23, 1714, but he had been securing subscribers
since the previous October. Thomas Tickell (1686–1740), a minor poet of some
distinction, was Under-Secretary to Addison, and to his successor James Craggs.
He wrote a celebrated elegy on Addison's death, and edited his Works. For an
account of his literary career, see R. E. Tickell, *Thomas Tickell and the Eighteenth-
century Poets*, 1931.⟩

reader, be pleased to cast thine eye on the *Proposal* below quoted, and on what follows (some months after the former assertion) in the same Journalist of June 8. "The bookseller "proposed the book by subscription, and raised some thousands "of pounds for the same: I believe the gentleman did *not* share 5 "in the profits of this extravagant subscription."

"After the Iliad, he undertook (saith

MIST'S JOURNAL, June 8, 1728.)

"the sequel of that work, the Odyssey; and having secured the "success by a numerous subscription, he employed some *under-* 10 "*lings* to perform what, according to his proposals, should come "from his own hands." To which heavy charge we **can** in truth oppose nothing but the words of

Mr. POPE'S PROPOSAL for the ODYSSEY,
(printed by J. Watts, Jan. 10, 1724.) 15

"I take this occasion to declare that the subscription for Shake-"spear belongs wholly to Mr. Tonson: And that the benefit of "*this Proposal* is not solely for my own use, but for that of *two of* "*my friends,* who have *assisted me in this work.*" But these very gentlemen are extolled above our poet himself in another of 20 Mist's Journals, March 30, 1728. saying, "That he would not "advise Mr. Pope to try the experiment again of getting a great "part of a book done by assistants, lest those extraneous parts "should unhappily ascend to the sublime, and retard the de-"clension of the whole." Behold! these *Underlings* are become 25 good writers!

If any say, that before the said Proposals were printed, the subscription was begun without declaration of such assistance; verily those who set it on foot, or (as their term is) secured it, to wit, the right honourable the Lord Viscount HARCOURT, 30 were he living, would testify, and the right honourable the Lord BATHURST, now living, doth testify the same is a falshood.

---

1 pleased] pleased but	17 benefit] future Benefit
20 in] by	32 testify] testify that

---

32. *falshood* ⟨As to this, see Pope's letter to Broome, Nov. 1724 (EC viii 89), and Sherburn, pp. 250 ff. Up to December 1724 Pope seems to have been willing

Sorry I am, that persons professing to be learned, or of whatever rank of authors, should either falsely tax, or be falsely taxed. Yet let us, who are only reporters, be impartial in our citations, and proceed.

MIST'S JOURNAL, June 8, 1728.   5

"Mr. Addison raised this author from obscurity, obtained "him the acquaintance and friendship of the *whole body of our* "*nobility*, and transferred his powerful interests with those great "men to this rising bard, who frequently levied by that means "unusual contributions on the public." Which surely cannot be, 10 if, as the author of The Dunciad dissected reporteth; "Mr. "Wycherley had before introduced him into a familiar ac-"quaintance with the *greatest Peers* and *brightest Wits* then "living."

"No sooner (saith the same Journalist) was his body lifeless, 15 "but this author, reviving his resentment, libelled the memory "of his departed friend; and, what was still more heinous, made "the scandal public." Grievous the accusation! unknown the accuser! the person accused no witness in his own cause! the person, in whose regard accused, dead! But if there be living 20 any one nobleman whose friendship, yea any one gentleman whose subscription Mr. Addison procured to our author; let him stand forth, that truth may appear! *Amicus Plato, amicus Socrates, sed magis amica veritas.* In verity, the whole story of the libel is a lye; witness those persons of integrity, who several years 25 before Mr. Addison's decease, did see and approve of the said verses, in no wise a libel, but a friendly rebuke sent privately in

---

10 Which . . . living] *Om. 1729a.*
15 (saith the same Journalist)] *Om. 1729a.*
24 In verity] But in verity

---

to conceal the fact that in his translation of the *Odyssey* he had received considerable assistance from Broome and Fenton; and many of the subscribers (perhaps most of them) had been secured before that date.⟩

15. *the same Journalist* ⟨i.e. *Mist's Journal*, March 30, 1728. The contribution of June 8, 1728, is signed "W.A."; this is unsigned.⟩

23. *appear* ⟨Yet in his letter of Oct. 26, 1713, Addison had expressed his willingness to procure subscribers. "You cannot lay a greater obligation upon me than by employing me in such an office."—*The Letters of Joseph Addison*, ed. Walter Graham, 1941, p. 281. This letter, however, is not above suspicion.⟩

our author's own hand to Mr. Addison himself, and never made
public, 'till after their own Journals, and Curl had printed the
same. One name alone, which I am here authorised to declare,
will sufficiently evince this truth, that of the right honourable
the Earl of BURLINGTON.   5

Next is he taxed with a crime (in the opinion of some authors,
I doubt, more heinous than any in morality) to wit, Plagiarism,
from the inventive and quaint-conceited

JAMES MOORE SMITH Gent.

"ᶻUpon reading the third volume of Pope's Miscellanies, I   10
"found five lines which I thought excellent; and happening to
"praise them, a gentleman produced a modern comedy (the
"Rival Modes) published last year, where were the same
"verses to a tittle.

2–3 'till . . . same] till by *Curll* their own bookseller in his miscellanies, 12*mo.* 1727.   6 in the opinion of] with
14 tittle.] tittle, (speaking of women.)

> See how the world its pretty slaves rewards!
> A youth of frolicks, an old age of cards:
> Fair to no purpose; artful to no end;
> Young without lovers; old without a friend;
> A fop their passion, but their prize a sot;
> Alive, ridiculous; and dead, forgot.

---

1. *himself* ⟨See vol. vi, and Sherburn, pp. 146–8, where good reasons are
given for supposing that the "Atticus" lines were written in 1715, soon after
the appearance of Tickell's translation of the first book of the *Iliad*, and sent
to Addison in 1716. Pope stated (Spence, p. 149) that the lines had a salutary
effect on Addison. "He used me very civilly ever after . . ." See also N. Ault,
"Pope and Addison," *R.E.S.*, vol. xvii, 1941, pp. 428 ff., where the problem of
the Pope-Addison quarrel is reconsidered in detail. "Lord Oxford wrote in his
copy of the *Epistle to Arbuthnot*, 1734, now in the Bodleian, a note to line 209,
saying: 'The Assertion of some anonymous authors that Mr. P. writ this
Character after the Gentlemans death, was utterly untrue; it having been sent
him several years before, and then shown to Mr. Secretary Craggs, & yᵉ
present Earl of Burlington.' " N. Ault, loc. cit., p. 437.⟩

2–3. *the same* ⟨They were published in *The St. James's Journal*, Dec. 15, 1722,
and in Curll's *Cytheria*, 1723. See vol. vi.⟩

ᶻ Daily Journal, March 18, 1728. ⟨The letter is signed "Philo-Mauri".⟩

14. *tittle* ⟨They appeared in *Moral Es.* ii 243–8. For James Moore Smythe,
see A ii 46, and Biog. App., vol. iv.⟩

"These gentlemen are undoubtedly the first plagiaries, that
"pretend to make a reputation by stealing from a man's works
"in his own life-time, and out of a Public print." Let us join to
this what is written by the author of the Rival Modes, the said
Mr. James Moore Smith, in a letter to our author himself, who   5
had informed him, a month before that play was acted, Jan. 27,
172⅚, that "These verses, which he had before given him leave
"to insert in it, would be known for his, some copies being got
"abroad. He desires, nevertheless, that, since the lines had been
"read in his comedy to several, Mr. P. would not deprive it of   10
"them," &c. Surely if we add the testimonies of the Lord
BOLINGBROKE, of the Lady to whom the said verses were
originally addressed, of Hugh Bethel Esq. and others, who knew
them as our author's, long before the said gentleman composed
his play; it is hoped, the ingenuous that affect not error, will   15
rectify their opinion by the suffrage of so honourable personages.

And yet followeth another charge, insinuating no less than his
enmity both to Church and State, which could come from no
other informer than the said

Mr. JAMES MOORE SMITH.   20

"ªThe Memoirs of a Parish clerk was a very dull and unjust
"abuse of a person who wrote in defence of our Religion and
"Constitution, and who has been dead many years." This
seemeth also most untrue; it being known to divers that these
memoirs were written at the seat of the Lord Harcourt in   25
Oxfordshire, before that excellent person (bishop Burnet's)
death, and many years before the appearance of that history, of
which they are pretended to be an abuse. Most true it is, that
Mr. Moore had such a design, and was himself the man who
prest Dr. Arbuthnot and Mr. Pope to assist him therein; and   30
that he borrowed those Memoirs of our author, when that
History came forth, with intent to turn them to such abuse. But
being able to obtain from our author but one single hint, and

---

2 pretend] pretended   23 This] Verily this also
32 intent] intention

12. *Lady* ⟨Martha Blount.⟩
ª Daily Journal, April 3, 1728. ⟨This letter is signed "Philo-Ditto."⟩
22. *person* ⟨Bishop Burnet, who died in 1715.⟩

either changing his mind, or having more mind than ability, he contented himself to keep the said Memoirs, and read them as his own to all his acquaintance. A noble person there is, into whose company Mr. Pope once chanced to introduce him, who well remembereth the conversation of Mr. Moore to have turn- 5 ed upon the "Contempt he had for the work of that reverend "prelate, and how full he was of a design he declared himself to "have of exposing it." This noble person is the Earl of PETER-BOROUGH.

Here in truth should we crave pardon of all the foresaid right 10 honourable and worthy personages, for having mentioned them in the same page with such weekly riff-raff railers and rhymers; but that we had their ever-honoured commands for the same; and that they are introduced not as witnesses in the controversy, but as witnesses that cannot be controverted; not to dispute, but 15 to decide.

Certain it is, that dividing our writers into two classes, of such who were acquaintance, and of such who were strangers, to our author; the former are those who speak well, and the other those who speak evil of him. Of the first class, the most noble 20

JOHN Duke of BUCKINGHAM

sums up his character in these lines:

"[b]And yet so wond'rous, so sublime a thing,
"As the great Iliad, scarce could make me sing,
"Unless I justly could at once commend 25
"A *good companion,* and as *firm a friend;*
"One *moral,* or a mere *well-natur'd deed,*
"Can all desert in sciences exceed."

So also is he decyphered by the honourable
SIMON HARCOURT. 30
"[c]Say, wond'rous youth, what column wilt thou chuse,
"What laurel'd arch, for thy triumphant Muse?

---

7 himself] *himself*   22 character] personal character
24 could] should

---

[b]   Verses to Mr. P. on his translation of Homer. ⟨For John Sheffield, first Duke of Buckingham and Normanby (1648–1721), see Biog. App., vol. iv.⟩
[c]   Poem prefix'd to his works. ⟨The text of these lines in the *Works* (1717) varies slightly from that given here. The author was Pope's friend Simon, 2nd

> "Tho' each great ancient court thee to his shrine,
> "Tho' ev'ry laurel thro' the dome be thine,
> "Go to the *good* and *just*, an awful train!
> "*Thy soul's delight.*——

Recorded in like manner for his virtuous disposition, and gentle   5
bearing, by the ingenious

Mr. WALTER HART,

in this apostrophe:

> "[d]O! ever worthy, ever crown'd with praise!
> "Blest in thy *life* and blest in all thy *lays*.   10
> "Add, that the Sisters ev'ry thought refine,
> "And ev'n thy *life*, be *faultless* as thy line.
> "Yet envy still with fiercer rage pursues,
> "Obscures the *virtue*, and defames the Muse.
> "A soul like thine, in pain, in grief, resign'd,   15
> "Views with just scorn the malice of mankind."

The witty and moral satyrist

Dr. EDWARD YOUNG,

wishing some check to the corruption and evil manners of the
times, calleth out upon our poet to undertake a task so worthy 20
of his virtue:

> "[e]Why slumbers Pope, who leads the Muse's train,
> "Nor hears that *Virtue*, which he *loves*, complain?

Mr. MALLET,

In his epistle on Verbal Criticism: 25

> "Whose life, severely scan'd, transcends his lays;
> "For wit supreme is but his second praise."

---

16 just] vain   19 corruption] corruptions
20 calleth] calls
24 –p. 37, l. 11, Mr. MALLET . . . song] *Om. 1729a.*

---

son of Simon, 1st Viscount Harcourt, 1683–1720. See vol. vi for Pope's epitaph
on him.⟩
   [d]   In his Poems, printed for B. Lintot. ⟨They were published in 1727. For
the Rev. Walter Harte, see Biog. App.⟩
   [e]   Universal Passion, Satyr i. ⟨35–6.⟩
   24. *Mallet* ⟨For David Mallet, see Biog. App.⟩

Mr. HAMMOND,

That delicate and correct imitator of Tibullus, in his Love
Elegies, Elegy xiv.

"Now, fir'd by Pope and *Virtue*, leave the age,
  "In low pursuit of self-undoing wrong,   5
  "And trace the author thro' his moral page,
    "Whose blameless life still answers to his song."

Mr. THOMSON,

In his elegant and philosophical poem of the Seasons:
  "Altho' not sweeter his own Homer sings,   10
  "Yet is his *life* the more endearing song."

To the same tune also singeth that learned clerk of Suffolk
Mr. WILLIAM BROOME.

  "ᵗThus, nobly rising in fair *Virtue*'s cause,
  "From thy own *life* transcribe th' *unerring laws*."   15

And, to close all, hear the reverend Dean of St. Patrick's:
  "A Soul with ev'ry virtue fraught,
  "By Patriots, Priests, and Poets taught.
  "Whose filial Piety excells
  "Whatever Grecian story tells.   20
  "A genius for each bus'ness fit,
  "Whose meanest talent is his Wit," *&c.*

Let us now recreate thee by turning to the other side, and
shewing his Character drawn by those with whom he never

16–22 And, to close all, . . . Wit," *&c.*] *Om. 1729a, which reads:*
  And divers more, with which we will not tire the reader.
23 now] rather

---

1. *Hammond* ⟨For James Hammond, see Biog. App.⟩
11. *endearing song* ⟨*Winter*, ll. 554–5.⟩
  ᵗ In his Poems, and at the end of the Odyssey. ⟨"To Mr. Pope, On his
Works," 1726. The "learned clerk" was Rector of Oakley Magna, and Vicar
of Eye, Suffolk. See Biog. App.⟩
22. *Wit," &c.* ⟨"A Libel on D— *D*—. And a Certain Great Lord" (1730),
75 ff. *The Poems of Jonathan Swift*, ed. Harold Williams, 1937, vol. ii, p. 482.
Pope is quoting from memory, or from a different version sent to him by
Swift, or altering the text to please himself. In the printed version Swift has
"*Sages*" for "Patriots", and "all Stations" for "each bus'ness".⟩

conversed, and whose countenances he could not know, though turned against him: First again commencing with the high voiced and never enough quoted

Mr. JOHN DENNIS;

Who, in his Reflections on the Essay on Criticism, thus describ- 5
eth him: "A little affected hypocrite, who has nothing in his
"mouth but candour, truth, friendship, good-nature, human-
"ity, and magnanimity. He is so great a lover of falshood, that,
"whenever he has a mind to calumniate his cotemporaries, he
"brands them with some defect which is just *contrary to some good* 10
"*quality*, for which all their *friends and their acquaintance* commend
"them. He seems to have a particular pique to *People of Quality*,
"and authors of that rank.—He must derive his religion from
"St. Omer's."—But in the Character of Mr. P. and his
writings (printed by S. Popping, 1716.) he saith, "Though he 15
"is a professor of the worst religion, yet he *laughs at it*;" but that
"nevertheless, he is a *virulent Papist*; and yet a *Pillar* for the
"*Church of England.*"
Of both which opinions

Mr. LEWIS THEOBALD   20

seems also to be; declaring, in Mist's Journal of June 22, 1728.
"That, if he is not shrewdly abused, he made it his practice to
"cackle to both *parties* in their own sentiments." But, as to his
pique against *People of quality*, the same Journalist doth not
agree, but saith (May 8, 1728.) "He had, by some means or 25
"other, the *acquaintance* and *friendship* of the *whole body of our*
"*nobility.*"

However contradictory this may appear, Mr. Dennis and
Gildon, in the character last cited, make it all plain, by assuring
us, "That he is a creature that reconciles all contradictions; he 30
"is a beast, and a man; a Whig, and a Tory; a writer (at one and

---

4 Mr.] *Om. 1729a.*   10 brands] upbraids
20 LEWIS] *Om. 1729a.*   22 made] hath made

2-3. *high voiced* ⟨Perhaps in allusion to Dennis's pontifical pronouncements, or to that excitability mentioned several times in *The Narrative of Dr. Norris.*⟩
5. ⟨op. cit., pp. 22, 25, 27.⟩
14. *Character of Mr. P.* ⟨pp. 4, 5.⟩
25. *May 8, 1728* ⟨i.e. June 8, 1728.⟩

"the same time) of[g] Guardians and Examiners; an Assertor of
"liberty, and of the dispensing power of kings; a Jesuitical pro-
"fessor of truth; a base and a foul pretender to candour." So
that, upon the whole account, we must conclude him either to
have been a great hypocrite, or a very honest man; a terrible   5
imposer upon both parties, or very moderate to either.

Be it as to the judicious reader shall seem good. Sure it is, he is
little favoured of certain authors, whose wrath is perilous: For
one declares he ought to have a *price set on his head*, and to be
hunted down as a *wild beast*[h]. Another protests that he does not   10
know *what may happen*; advises him to *insure his person*; says he has
bitter enemies, and expresly declares it will be well if he *escapes with
his life*[i]. One desires he would *cut his own throat, or hang himself*[k].
But Pasquin seemed rather inclined it should be done by the
Government, representing him engaged in grievous designs   15
with a Lord of Parliament, then under prosecution[l]. Mr. Dennis
himself hath written to a *Minister*, that he is one of the most
dangerous persons in this kingdom[m]; and assureth the public, that
he is an *open* and *mortal enemy* to his *country*; a monster, that *will*,
one day, shew as *daring a soul* as a *mad Indian*, who runs a *muck*   20
to kill the first Christian he meets[n]. Another gives information
of *Treason* discovered in his poem[o]. Mr. Curl boldly supplies an
imperfect verse with *Kings* and *Princesses*[p]. And one Matthew

---

10–12 Another ... expresly declares] Another expresly, that
12 *escapes*] *escape*   14 But] *Om. 1729a.*
18–21 and assureth ... meets] *Om. 1729a.*   21 Another] A third
23 And one ... impudent,] and another yet bolder,

---

[g]   The Names of two weekly Papers.
3.   *candour* ⟨op. cit., p. 4.⟩
[h]   Theobald, Letter in Mist's Journal, June 22, 1728.
[i]   Smedley, Pref. to Gulliveriana, p. 14, 16.
[k]   Gulliveriana, p. 332.
[l]   Anno 1723. ⟨Feb. 20.⟩
[m]   Anno 1729.
[n]   Preface to Rem. on the Rape of the Lock, p. 12. and in the last page of
that treatise.
[o]   Page 6, 7. of the Preface, by Concanen, to a book intitled A Collection
of all the Letters, Essays, Verses, and Advertisements, occasioned by Pope and
Swift's Miscellanies. Printed for A. Moore, octavo, 1728.
[p]   Key to the Dunciad, 3d edit. p. 18.

Concanen, yet more impudent, publishes at length the Two most SACRED NAMES in this Nation, as members of the Dunciad[q]!

This is prodigious! yet it is almost as strange, that in the midst of these invectives his greatest Enemies have (I know not how) 5
born testimony to some merit in him.

Mr. THEOBALD,

in censuring his Shakespear, declares, "He has so great an
"*esteem* for Mr. Pope, and so high an *opinion* of his *genius* and
"*excellencies*; that, notwithstanding he professes a *veneration* 10
"*almost rising to Idolatry* for the writings of this inimitable poet,
"he would be very loth even to do *him* justice, at the expence of
"that *other gentleman*'s character[r]."

Mr. CHARLES GILDON,

after having violently attacked him in many pieces, at last came 15
to wish from his heart, "That Mr. Pope would be prevailed
"upon to give us Ovid's Epistles by his hand, for it is certain we
"see the original of Sappho to Phaon with much more life and
"likeness in his version, than in that of Sir Car. Scrope. And this
"(he adds) is the more to be wished, because in the English 20
"tongue we have scarce any thing truly and naturally written
"upon Love[s]." He also, in taxing Sir Richard Blackmore for his
heterodox opinions of Homer, challengeth him to answer what
Mr. Pope hath said in his preface to that poet.

Mr. OLDMIXON   25

calls him a great master of our tongue; declares "the purity and
"perfection of the English language to be found in his Homer;
"and, saying there are more good verses in Dryden's Virgil than
"in any other work, excepts this of our author only[t]."

---

4 it is . . . strange] is it no less strange
25 –p. 41, l. 5, Mr. OLDMIXON . . . that way." And] *Om. 1729a.*

---

[q] A List of Persons, &c. at the end of the forementioned Collection of all the Letters, Essays, &c.

[r] Introduction to his Shakespear restored, in quarto, p. 3.

[s] Commentary on the Duke of Buckingham's Essay, octavo, 1721, p. 97, 98.

[t] In his prose Essay on Criticism. ⟨p. 5.⟩

The Author of a Letter to Mr. CIBBER
says, "ᵛPope *was* so good a versifier [*once*] that his predecessor
"Mr. Dryden, and his cotemporary Mr. Prior excepted, the
"harmony of his numbers *is* equal to any body's. And, that he
"*had* all the merit that a man can have that way." And   5

Mr. THOMAS COOKE,

after much blemishing our author's Homer, crieth out,
    "But in his other works what beauties shine!
    "While sweetest Music dwells in ev'ry line.
    "These he admir'd, on these he stamp'd his praise,   10
    "And bade them live to brighten future daysᵂ."
So also one who takes the name of

H. STANHOPE,

the maker of certain verses to Duncan Campbellˣ, in that poem,
which is wholly a satyr on Mr. Pope, confesseth,   15
    " 'Tis true, if finest notes alone could show
    "(Tun'd justly high, or regularly low)
    "That we should fame to these mere vocals give;
    "Pope more than we can offer should receive:
    "For when some gliding river is his theme,   20
    "His lines run smoother than the smoothest stream," *&c.*

MIST'S JOURNAL, June 8, 1728.

Although he says, "The smooth numbers of the Dunciad are all
"that recommend it, nor has it any other merit;" yet that same

---

12 So also one] One ⟨*In 1729a this passage follows the citations
from Gildon.*⟩

ᵛ Printed by J. Roberts, 1742. p. 11. ⟨*A Letter to Mr. C—b—r, On his Letter to
Mr. P—*. The author was Lord Hervey.⟩

ᵂ Battle of Poets, folio, ⟨1725⟩ p. 15. ⟨For Cooke, see Biog. App.⟩

ˣ Printed under the title of the Progress of Dulness, duodecimo, 1728.
⟨Nothing is known of "H. Stanhope"; he may have been another "Joseph
Gay". A statement in *The Curliad*, p. 25, seems to indicate that he was in
reality William Bond (for whom see Biog. App.). In 1720 Curll issued "An
Epistle to his Royal Highness the Prince of Wales . . . By Mr. Stanhope", which,
owing to its criticism of the South Sea speculation, went through at least four
editions in a year. In the same year Curll published another political poem,
"The Governor," which was again by "Mr. Stanhope." The poem from which
Pope quotes is also dated 1720.⟩

paper hath these words: "The author is allowed to be a perfect
"master of an easy and elegant versification. *In all his works* we
"find the most *happy turns*, and *natural similes*, wonderfully short
"and thick sown."

The Essay on the Dunciad also owns, p. 25. it is very full of   5
beautiful images. But the panegyric, which crowns all that can be
said on this Poem, is bestowed by our Laureate,

Mr. COLLEY CIBBER,

who "grants it to be a better Poem of its kind than ever was
"writ;" but adds, "it was a victory over a parcel of poor   10
"wretches, whom it was almost cowardice to conquer.—A man
"might as well triumph for having killed so many silly flies that
"offended him. Could he have let them alone, by this time, poor
"souls! they had all been buried in oblivion[y]." Here we see our
excellent Laureate allows the justice of the satyr on every man in   15
it, but *himself*; as the great Mr. Dennis did before him.

The said

Mr. DENNIS and Mr. GILDON,

in the most furious of all their works (the forecited Character,
p. 5.) do in concert[z] confess, "That some men of *good under-*   20

8–16 But the panegyric, . . . before him.] *Om. 1729a.*
17 The said] *Om. 1729a.*   20 in concert] jointly

---

[y] Cibber's Letter to Mr. Pope, p. 9, 12.

[z] *In concert*] Hear how Mr. Dennis hath proved our mistake in this place;
"As to my writing in *concert* with Mr. Gildon, I declare upon the honour and
"word of a gentleman, that I never wrote so much as one line in *concert* with any
"one man whatsoever. And these two Letters from Mr. Gildon will plainly
shew that we are not writers in *concert* with each other.
    Sir,
—*The height of my Ambition is to please Men of the best Judgment; and finding that I
have entertained my Master agreeably, I have the extent of the Reward of my Labour.*
    Sir,
*I had not the opportunity of hearing of your excellent Pamphlet 'till this day. I am
infinitely satisfied and pleased with it, and hope you will meet with that encouragement
your admirable performance deserves, &c.*   CH. GILDON.
    "Now is it not plain, that any one who sends such compliments to another,
"has not been used to write in partnership with him to whom he sends them?"
Dennis, Rem. on the Dunc. p. 50. Mr. Dennis is therefore welcome to take this
piece to himself. ⟨Cf. "Errata," p. 197. In quoting from *A True Character,*

"*standing* value him for his rhymes." And (p. 17.) "That he has
"got, like Mr. Bays in the Rehearsal, (that is, like Mr. Dryden) a
"notable knack at rhyming, and writing smooth verse."

Of his Essay on Man, numerous were the praises bestowed by
his avowed enemies, in the imagination that the same was not 5
written by him, as it was printed anonymously.

Thus sang of it even

BEZALEEL MORRIS.

"Auspicious bard! while all admire thy strain,
"All but the selfish, ignorant, and vain; 10
"I, whom no bribe to servile flatt'ry drew,
"Must pay the tribute to thy merit due:
"Thy Muse, sublime, significant, and clear,
"Alike informs the Soul, and charms the Ear," &c.

And 15

Mr. LEONARD WELSTED

thus wrote[a] to the unknown author, on the first publication of
the said Essay: "I must own, after the reception which the vilest
"and most immoral ribaldry hath lately met with, I was sur-
"prised to see what I had long despaired, a performance deserv- 20
"ing the name of a poet. Such, Sir, is your work. It is, indeed,
"above all commendation, and ought to have been published in
"an age and country more worthy of it. If my testimony be of
"weight any where, you are sure to have it in the amplest
"manner," &c. &c. &c. 25

4–25 Of his Essay . . . &c. &c. &c.] Om. *1729a*.

Pope gives a completely false impression by leaving out half of a sentence.
After the word "rhymes" Dennis adds: "as they would be fond of an *Asseinego*,
that could sing his part in a Catch, or of a *Baboon* that could whistle *Walsingham*.">

14. *Ear*," &c. ⟨For Morris, see Biog. App. I am indebted to Mr Robert
W. Rogers of Harvard for tracing these lines for me: they are the opening
lines of a short poem prefixed to the anonymous pamphlet, *An Essay on the
Universe: A Poem*, 1733, (B.M. 11631 b 17), and are addressed "To the Author
of the *Essay on Man*." Since this pamphlet was advertised early in April 1733
(*The Bee*, i 497) Morris must have written his complimentary verses in ignorance
of the fact that he was complimenting Pope. *The Essay on Man* was published
anonymously towards the end of February 1733, and it was some time before
Pope's name was confidently connected with it.⟩

[a]   In a Letter under his hand, dated March 12, 1733.

Thus we see every one of his works hath been extolled by one or other of his most inveterate Enemies; and to the success of them all they do unanimously give testimony. But it is sufficient, *instar omnium*, to behold the great critic, Mr. Dennis, sorely lamenting it, even from the Essay on Criticism to this day of the 5 Dunciad! "A most notorious instance (quoth he) of the de- "pravity of genius and taste, the *approbation* this Essay meets "with[b]—I can safely affirm, that I never attacked any of these "writings, unless they had *success* infinitely beyond their merit. "—This, though an empty, has been a *popular* scribler. The 10 "epidemic madness of the times has given him *reputation*[c].—If, "after the cruel treatment so many extraordinary men (Spen- "cer, Lord Bacon, Ben. Johnson, Milton, Butler, Otway, and "others) have received from this country, for these last hundred "years, I should shift the scene, and shew all that penury 15 "changed at once to riot and profuseness; and more squand- "ered away upon *one object*, than would have satisfied the greater "part of those extraordinary men; the reader to whom this one "creature should be unknown, would fancy him a prodigy of "art and nature, would believe that all the great qualities of 20 "these persons were centered in him alone.—But if I should "venture to assure him, that the PEOPLE of ENGLAND had "made such a choice—the reader would either believe me a

---

1–3 Thus we see . . . testimony] To the *Success* of all his pieces, they do unanimously give testimony:
4 the] this last

---

[b]   Dennis, Pref. to his Reflect. on the Essay on Criticism.
[c]   Pref. to his Rem. on Homer. ⟨Dennis wrote (of his contemporaries in general): "I can safely affirm, that I never attack'd any of their Writings, unless I was provok'd to it, and unless they had Success abundantly beyond their Merit."⟩
18. *men* ⟨From *1729a–d* Pope added here the following note: "What this vast sum was Mr. DENNIS himself in another place informs us (pref. to his Remarks on the Rape of the Lock, p. 15) to wit, *a hundred a year*. Whereby we see how great he supposed the moderation of those extraordinary men; even greater than that of his friend Mr. *Giles Jacob*, who said of himself
    One hundred pounds a year, I think wou'd do
    For me, if single—Or if marry'd, two."
The lines are from "Human Happiness: a Poem," 1721, p. 22. Pope manages to introduce six errors into his quotation.⟩

"*malicious enemy*, and *slanderer*; or that the reign of the last "(Queen Anne's) *Ministry* was designed by fate to encourage "*Fools*[d]."

But it happens, that this our Poet never had any Place, Pension, or Gratuity, in any shape, from the said glorious Queen, or any of her Ministers. All he owed, in the whole course of his life, to any court, was a subscription, for his Homer, of 200 *l.* from King George I, and 100 *l.* from the prince and princess.

However, lest we imagine our Author's Success was constant and universal, they acquaint us of certain works in a less degree of repute, whereof, although owned by others, yet do they assure us he is the writer. Of this sort Mr. DENNIS[e] ascribes to him *two Farces*, whose names he does not tell, but assures us that *there is not one jest in them:* And an imitation of Horace, whose title he does not mention, but assures us *it is much more execrable than all his works*[f]. The DAILY JOURNAL, May 11, 1728. assures us, "He is below Tom. Durfey in the Drama, because (as that writer "thinks) the Marriage Hater matched, and the Boarding "School are better than the What-d'-ye-call-it;" which is not Mr. P.'s, but Mr. Gay's. Mr. GILDON assures us, in his New Rehearsal, p. 48. "That he was writing a *play* of the Lady Jane "Grey;" but it afterwards proved to be Mr. Row's. We are assured by another, "He wrote a pamphlet called Dr. Andrew "Tripe[g];" which proved to be one Dr. Wagstaff's. Mr. THEOBALD assures us, in Mist of the 27th of April, "That the treatise

5

10

15

20

4–8 But . . . princess.] *Om. 1729a.*   13 that] *Om. 1729a.*
21 p. 48] printed 1714, pag. 48,

---

[d]   Rem. on Homer, p. 8, 9.

[e]   Ibid. p. 8. ⟨The two farces are *What D'ye Call It*, 1715, and *Three Hours after Marriage*, 1717.⟩

[f]   Character of Mr. Pope, p. 7. ⟨This imitation has not been found. But see vol. iv, Introduction, p. xxvi.⟩

20. *Mr. Gay's* ⟨It was widely believed by Pope's contemporaries that he had a share in this farce. See Sherburn, pp. 124, 137–8. In a letter to Parnell, however, Gay refers to "my What-d'ye-call-it."—EC vii 455. Durfey's *The Marriage-Hater Match'd* was produced in 1692; his *Love for Money: or the Boarding School* in 1689–90; Rowe's *Lady Jane Gray* (ll. 21–22) in April 1715.⟩

[g]   Character of Mr. Pope, p. 6. ⟨The words of the text are: ". . . at the same time, that he openly extoll'd Sir *Richard Steele* in the highest manner, secretly publish'd the Infamous Libel of Dr. *Andrew Tripe* upon him." There

"of the *Profound* is very dull, and that Mr. Pope is the author of
"it." The writer of Gulliveriana is of another opinion; and says,
"the whole, or greatest part, of the merit of this treatise must and
"can only be ascribed to Gulliver[h]." [Here, gentle reader! cannot I but smile at the strange blindness and positiveness of men;   5
knowing the said treatise to appertain to none other but to me,
Martinus Scriblerus.]

We are assured, in Mist of June 8, "That his own *Plays* and
"*Farces* would better have adorned the Dunciad, than those of
"Mr. Theobald; for he had neither genius for Tragedy nor   10
"Comedy." Which whether true or not, is not easy to judge; in
as much as he hath attempted neither. Unless we will take it for
granted, with Mr. Cibber, that his being once very angry at
hearing a friend's Play abused, was an infallible proof the Play
was his own; the said Mr. Cibber thinking it impossible for a   15
man to be much concerned for any but himself: "Now let any
man judge (saith he) "by this concern, who was the true
"mother of the child[i]?"

But from all that hath been said, the discerning reader will
collect, that it little availed our author to have any Candour,   20
since when he declared he did not write for others, it was not
credited; as little to have any Modesty, since, when he declined
writing in any way himself, the presumption of others was imputed to him. If he singly enterprised one great work, he was
taxed of Boldness and Madness to a prodigy[k]: If he took assist-   25

---

8 We] Lastly we   12–18 Unless . . . child?] *Om. 1729a.*

---

seems to be no good ground for believing Dennis's charge. See Sherburn,
p. 154. The pamphlet referred to is *A Letter from the Facetious Doctor Andrew
Tripe, at Bath, to the Venerable Nestor Ironside,* 1714. It has also been attributed to
Swift; it is not included in *Miscellaneous Works of Dr. William Wagstaffe,* 1726.⟩
    1–2. *author of it* ⟨There is nothing in *Mist's Journal* of this date about the
Profound being "very dull."⟩
    [h]   Gulliv. p. 336.
    12. *attempted neither* ⟨After the performance of *Three Hours after Marriage*
Pope seems to have been willing that his share in it should be forgotten, if
possible. This farcical comedy was, no doubt, mainly the work of Gay, but in
the preface he acknowledged the assistance he had received from "two of my
friends," i.e. Pope and Arbuthnot.⟩
    [i]   Cibber's Letter to Mr. P. p. 19.
    [k]   Burnet's Homerides, p. 1. of his translation of the Iliad.

ants in another, it was complained of, and represented as a
great injury to the public[1]. The loftiest heroics, the lowest ballads, treatises against the state or church, satyrs on lords and
ladies, raillery on wits and authors, squabbles with booksellers, or even full and true accounts of monsters, poisons, and 5
murders; of any hereof was there nothing so good, nothing so
bad, which hath not at one or other season been to him ascribed.
If it bore no author's name, then lay he concealed; if it did, he
fathered it upon that author to be yet better concealed: If it
resembled any of his styles, then was it evident; if it did not, then 10
disguised he it on set purpose. Yea, even direct oppositions in
religion, principles, and politics, have equally been supposed in
him inherent. Surely a most rare and singular character! Of
which let the reader make what he can.

Doubtless most Commentators would hence take occasion to 15
turn all to their Author's advantage, and from the testimony of
his very Enemies would affirm, That his Capacity was boundless, as well as his Imagination; that he was a perfect master of
all Styles, and all Arguments; and that there was in those times
no other Writer, in any kind, of any degree of excellence, save 20
he himself. But as this is not our own sentiment, we shall determine on nothing; but leave thee, gentle reader, to steer thy
judgment equally between various opinions, and to chuse
whether thou wilt incline to the Testimonies of Authors avowed,
or of Authors concealed; of those who knew him, or of those 25
who knew him not.

---

3 satyrs] satyr   24–5 incline . . . concealed; of] believe

---

[1]   The London and Mist's Journals, on his undertaking of the Odyssey.
⟨e.g. *The London Journal*, July 17, 1725; *Mist's Journal*, March 30, June 8,
1728.⟩

MARTINUS SCRIBLERUS,

OF THE

P O E M.

THIS Poem, as it celebrateth the most grave and antient
of things, Chaos, Night and Dulness, so is it of the most
grave and antient kind. *Homer,* (saith *Aristotle*) was the
first who gave the *Form,* and (saith *Horace*) who adapted the
Measure, to heroic poesy. But even before this, may be rationally   5
presumed from what the antients have left written, was a piece
by *Homer* composed, of like nature and matter with this of our
Poet. For of Epic sort it appeareth to have been, yet of matter
surely not unpleasant, witness what is reported of it by the
learned Archbishop *Eustathius,* in Odyss. κ. And accordingly   10
Aristotle in his poetic, chap. 4. doth further set forth, that as the
Iliad and Odyssey gave example to Tragedy, so did this poem
to Comedy its first Idæa.

From these authors also it shou'd seem, that the Hero or chief
personage of it was no less *obscure,* and his *understanding* and   15
sentiments no less quaint and strange (if indeed not more so) than
any of the actors in our poem. MARGITES was the name of this
personage, whom Antiquity recordeth to have been *Dunce the
First*; and surely from what we hear of him, not unworthy to be
the root of so spreading a tree, and so numerous a posterity.   20
The poem therefore celebrating him, was properly and absolutely a *Dunciad*; which tho' now unhappily lost, yet is its
nature sufficiently known by the infallible tokens aforesaid.
And thus it doth appear, that the first Dunciad was the first
Epic poem, written by *Homer* himself, and anterior even to the   25
Iliad or Odyssey.

The text is that of *1729a,* collated with *1743a.* Changes in spelling
have not been noted. The spelling of *1729a* is rather more informal
than that of *1743a.*   17 in] of

---

10. *Odyssey K.* ⟨ὁ γὰρ Μαργίτης ἀνάλογον ἔχει, ὥσπερ ἡ Ἰλιὰς καὶ ἡ Ὀδύσσεια

48

Now forasmuch as our Poet had translated those two famous works of *Homer* which are yet left; he did conceive it in some sort of his duty to imitate that also which was lost: And was therefore induced to bestow on it the same Form which *Homer*'s is reported to have had, namely that of Epic poem, with 5 a title also framed after the antient *Greek* manner, to wit, that of *Dunciad*.

Wonderful it is, that so few of the moderns have been stimulated to attempt some Dunciad! Since in the opinion of the multitude, it might cost less pain and oil, than an imitation of 10 the greater Epic. But possible it is also that on due reflection, the maker might find it easier to paint a *Charlemagne*, a *Brute* or a *Godfry*, with just pomp and dignity heroic, than a *Margites*, a *Codrus*, a *Flecknoe*, or a *Tibbald*.

We shall next declare the occasion and the cause which 15 moved our Poet to this particular work. He lived in those days, when (after providence had permitted the Invention of Printing as a scourge for the Sins of the learned) Paper also became so cheap, and printers so numerous, that a deluge of authors cover'd the land: Whereby not only the peace of the honest 20 unwriting subject was daily molested, but unmerciful demands were made of his applause, yea of his money, by such as would neither earn the one, or deserve the other: At the same time, the Liberty of the Press was so unlimited, that it grew dangerous to refuse them either: For they would forthwith publish slanders 25 unpunish'd, the authors being anonymous; nay the immediate publishers thereof lay sculking under the wings of an Act of Parliament, assuredly intended for better purposes.

14 a *Flecknoe*, . . . *Tibbald*] or a Fleckno.   23 or] nor
24 Liberty . . . unlimited,] license of the Press was such,
26 nay . . . purposes] and skulking under the wings of Publishers,
    a set of men who never scrupled to vend either Calumny or
    Blasphemy, as long as the Town would call for it.

πρὸς τὰς τραγῳδίας, οὕτω καὶ οὗτος πρὸς τὰς κωμῳδίας.
For "Archbishop" *1729a* has "Arcbishop," which may be a Scriblerus spelling, but is more probably a misprint.〉
    27–28. *an Act of Parliament* 〈By "An act for laying several duties upon all sope and paper . . ", 10 Anne, C. 19, cxiii, it was laid down, "That during the [same] term of two and thirty years, no person whatsoever shall sell, or expose

[a]Now our author living in those times, did conceive it an endeavour well worthy an honest satyrist, to dissuade the dull and punish the malicious, *the only way that was left*. In that public-spirited view he laid the plan of this Poem, as the greatest service he was capable (without much hurt or being slain) to render his dear country. First, taking things from their original, he considereth the Causes creative of such authors, namely *Dulness* and *Poverty*; the one born with them, the other contracted, by neglect of their proper talent thro' self conceit of greater abilities. This truth he wrapp'd in an *Allegory*[b] (as the constitution of Epic poesy requires) and feigns, that one of these Goddesses had taken up her abode with the other, and that they jointly inspir'd all such writers and such works.[c] He proceedeth to shew the *qualities* they bestow on these authors, and the *effects* they produce: [d]Then the *materials* or *stock* with which they furnish them,[e] and (above all) that *self-opinion*[f] which causeth it to seem to themselves vastly greater than it is, and is the prime motive of their setting up in this sad and sorry merchandize. The great power of these Goddesses acting in alliance (whereof as the one is the mother of industry, so is the other of plodding) was to be exemplify'd in some *one, great* and *remarkable action.*[g] And none cou'd be more so than that which our poet hath chosen, the introduction of the lowest diversions of the rabble.

5

10

15

20

---

3 malicious] wicked

11 constitution] construction   requires] requireth

23 the introduction . . . *Latium*] *viz.* the restoration of the reign of Chaos and Night, by the ministry of Dulness their daughter, in the removal of her imperial seat from the City to the polite World; as the Action of the Æneid is the restoration of the empire of Troy, by the removal of the race from thence to Latium.

---

to sale, any [such] pamphlet, without the true respective name or names, and place or places of abode, of some known person or persons, by or for whom the same was really printed or published, written or printed thereupon . . ." The law was frequently ignored, either by the device of printing the name of a fictitious publisher on the title-page, or by printing the name of a genuine publisher (e.g. Anne Dodd) without obtaining his or her consent.⟩

[a] Vid. *Bossu, du poeme Epique*, ch. 8 ⟨*1729d*⟩.   [b] *Ibid.* ch. 7 ⟨*1729d*⟩.

[c] *Book* 1. *Verse* 32, &c. ⟨*1729d*⟩.   [d] *Verse* 45 to 52 ⟨*1729d*⟩.

[e] *Verse* 57 to 75 ⟨*1729d*⟩.   [f] *Verse* 80 ⟨*1729d*⟩.

[g] *Bossu*, ch. 7, 8 ⟨*1729d*⟩.

in *Smithfield* to be the entertainment of the court and town; or
in other words, the Action of the Dunciad is the[h] Removal of
the Imperial seat of Dulness from the City to the polite world; as
that of the Æneid is the Removal of the empire of *Troy* to
Latium. But as *Homer,* singing only the *Wrath* of *Achilles,* yet   5
includes in his poem the whole history of the *Trojan* war, in like
manner our author hath drawn into this single action the whole
history of Dulness and her children. To this end she is represented at the very[i] opening of the poem, taking a view of her
forces, which are distinguish'd into these three kinds, Party   10
writers, dull poets, and wild criticks.

A *Person* must be fix'd upon to support this action, who (to
agree with the said design) must be such an one as is capable of
being all three. This *phantom* in the poet's mind, must have a
name.[k] He seeks for one who hath been concerned in the   15
Journals, written bad *Plays* or *Poems,* and published low
Criticisms: He finds his name to be *Tibbald,* and he becomes of
course the Hero of the poem.

The *Fable* being thus according to best example one and
entire, as contain'd in the proposition; the *Machinary* is a con-   20
tinued chain of Allegories, setting forth the whole power, ministry, and empire of Dulness, extended thro' her subordinate
instruments, in all her various operations.

This is branched into *Episodes,* each of which hath its Moral
apart, tho' all conducive to the main end. The crowd assembled   25
in the second book demonstrates the design to be more extensive
than to bad poets only, and that we may expect other Episodes,
of the Patrons, Encouragers, or Paymasters of such authors, as
occasion shall bring them forth. And the third book, if well
consider'd, seemeth to embrace the whole world. Each of the   30
Games relateth to some or other vile class of writers. The first

---

8 To this end . . . criticks.] *Om. 1743.*
12 must] must next   who . . . three] *Om. 1743.*
15 He seeks . . . *Criticisms:*] *Om. 1743.*
17 He finds . . . *Tibbald,*] He finds it to be —;   19 best] the best

---

[h] *Verse* 1, 2 ⟨*1729d*⟩.
[i] *Verse* 95 to 104 ⟨*1729d*⟩.
[k] *Bossu,* ch. 8. Vide *Aristot. Poetic.* c.9 ⟨*1729d*⟩.

concerneth the Plagiary, to whom he giveth the name of *More*; the second the libellous Novellist, whom he styleth *Eliza*; the third the flattering Dedicator; the fourth the bawling Critick or noisy Poet; the fifth the dark and dirty Party-writer; and so of the rest, assigning to each some *proper name* or other, such as 5 he cou'd find.

As for the *Characters*, the publick hath already acknowledged how justly they are drawn: The manners are so depicted, and the sentiments so peculiar to those to whom applied, that surely to transfer them to any other, or wiser, personages, wou'd 10 be exceeding difficult. And certain it is, that every person concerned, being consulted apart, will readily own the resemblance of every portrait, his own excepted.

The Descriptions are singular; the Comparisons very quaint; the Narration various, yet of one colour. The purity and 15 chastity of Diction is so preserved, that in the places most suspicious not the *words* but only the *images* have been censured, and yet are those images no other than have been sanctified by antient and classical authority (tho' as was the manner of those good times, not so curiously wrapped up) yea and commented 20 upon by most grave doctors, and approved criticks.

As it beareth the name of Epic, it is thereby subjected to such severe indispensable rules as are laid on all Neotericks, a strict imitation of the antient; insomuch that any deviation accompanied with whatever poetic beauties, hath always been cen- 25 sured by the sound critick. How exact that Imitation hath been in this piece, appeareth not only by its general structure, but by particular allusions infinite, many whereof have escaped both the commentator and poet himself; yea divers by his exceeding diligence are so alter'd and interwoven with the rest, that several 30

---

12 will . . . own] hath . . . owned
13 excepted] *Add, 1743*: So Mr. Cibber calls them, "a parcel of
    poor wretches, so many *silly flies*[i]: but adds, our Author's Wit is
    remarkably more bare and barren, whenever it would fall foul
    on *Cibber*, than upon any other Person whatever."
  [i] Cibber's Letter to Mr. P. pag. 9, 12, 41.

---

  23. *Neotericks* ⟨i.e. Moderns.⟩

have already been, and more will be, by the ignorant abused, as altogether and originally his own.

In a word, the whole poem proveth itself to be the work of our Author when his faculties were in full vigour and perfection: at that exact time of life when years have ripened the judgment, 5 without diminishing the imagination; which by good criticks is held to be punctually at *forty*. For, at that season it was that *Virgil* finished his *Georgics*; and Sir *Richard Blackmore* at the like age composing his *Arthurs*, declared the same to be the very *Acme* and pitch of life for Epic poesy: tho' since he hath altered 10 it to *sixty*,* the year in which he published his *Alfred*. True it is, that the talents for Criticism, namely smartness, quick censure, vivacity of remark, certainty of asseveration, indeed all but acerbity, seem rather the gifts of Youth than of riper age: But it is far otherwise in *Poetry*; witness the works of Mr. *Rymer* and 15 Mr. *Dennis*, who beginning with criticism, became afterwards such Poets as no age hath parallel'd. With good reason therefore did our author chuse to write his *Essay* on that subject at twenty, and reserve for his maturer years, this great and wonderful work of the *Dunciad*. 20

---

5 of life] *Om. 1743.*

---

7. *forty* ⟨Pope was born on May 21, 1688: the *Dunciad* was published on May 18, 1728.⟩

*See his Essay on Heroic poetry. ⟨Pope has given the wrong reference here. In the second volume of his *Essays upon Several Subjects* (1717) Blackmore argues from the experience of Milton and Dryden that age does not necessarily weaken invention or fancy. "If a Person becomes an excellent Writer by Forty, it is certain he will continue so till Fifty . . . and the Parity of Reason will be extended to Sixty Years, and so forwards, if the Health of the Author does not decay . . ."—"An Essay upon Writing," op. cit., p. 283.⟩

DUNCIADOS PERIOCHA:

OR,

ARGUMENTS to the BOOKS.

BOOK the FIRST.

THE Proposition of the subject. The Invocation, and the Inscription. Then the Original of the great empire of *Dulness*, and cause of the continuance thereof. The beloved seat of the Goddess is described, with her chief attendants and officers, her functions, operations, and effects. Then 5 the poem hasts into the midst of things, presenting her on the evening of a Lord Mayor's day, revolving the long succession of her sons, and the glories past, and to come. She fixes her eye on *Tibbald* to be the instrument of that great event which is the subject of the poem. He is described pensive in his study, giving 10 up the cause, and apprehending the period of her empire from the old age of the present monarch *Settle*. Wherefore debating whether to betake himself to law or politicks, he raises an altar of proper books, and (making first his solemn prayer and declaration) purposes thereon to sacrifice all his unsuccessful writings. 15 As the pyle is kindled, the Goddess beholding the flame from her seat, flies in person and puts it out, by casting upon it the poem of *Thule*. She forthwith reveals her self to him, transports him to her Temple, unfolds all her arts, and initiates him into her mysteries; then announcing the death of *Settle* that night, 20 anoints, and proclaims him Successor.

Dunciados Periocha ⟨In *1735a* this title was dropped, and in *1735c* the arguments to the three books were placed at the head of each book.⟩

6. *things* ⟨Cf. Milton, *Par. Lost*, Argument to Bk. i. Curll pointed out, in *The Curliad*, p. 9, that the Arguments were a parody of those in *Paradise Lost*. They are not, however, so close a parody as he suggested.⟩

Book the Second.

THE King being proclaimed, the solemnity is graced with publick Games and sports of various kinds; (not instituted by the Hero, as by *Æneas* in *Virgil*, but for greater honour by the Goddess in person; in like manner as the games *Pythia, Isthmia, &c.* were anciently said to be by the Gods, 5 and as *Thetis* herself appearing according to *Homer* Odyss. 24. proposed the prizes in honour of her son *Achilles.* Hither flock the Poets and Criticks, attended (as is but just) with their Patrons and Book-sellers. The Goddess is first pleased for her disport to propose games to the latter, and setteth up the phantom of a 10 poet which the booksellers contend to overtake. The races described, with their divers accidents: Next, the game for a Poetess: Afterwards the exercises for the *Poets*, of Tickling, Vociferating, Diving: the first holds forth the arts and practices of Dedicators, the second of Disputants and fustian poets, the third 15 of profound, dark, and dirty authors. Lastly, for the *Criticks*, the Goddess proposes (with great propriety) an exercise not of their parts but their patience; in hearing the works of two voluminous authors, one in verse and the other in prose, deliberately read, without sleeping: The various effects of which, with the 20 several degrees and manners of their operation, are here most lively set forth: Till the whole number, not of criticks only, but of spectators, actors, and all present fall fast asleep, which naturally and necessarily ends the games.

Book the Third.

AFTER the other persons are disposed in their proper 25 places of rest, the Goddess transports the King to her Temple, and there lays him to slumber with his head on her lap; a position of marvellous virtue, which causes all the visions of wild enthusiasts, projectors, politicians, inamorato's, castle-builders, chymists and poets. He is immediately carry'd 30 on the wings of fancy to the *Elizian* shade, where on the banks of *Lethe* the souls of the dull are dip'd by *Bavius*, before their entrance into this world. There he is met by the ghost of

Settle, and by him made acquainted with the wonders of the   5
place, and with those which he is himself destin'd to perform.
He takes him to a *Mount of Vision*, from whence he shews him
the past triumphs of the empire of Dulness, then the present,
and lastly the future. How small a part of the world was ever
conquered by *Science*, how soon those conquests were stop'd, 10
and those very nations again reduced to her dominion. Then
distinguishing the Island of *Great Britain*, shews by what aids,
and by what persons, it shall be forthwith brought to her
empire. These he causes to pass in review before his eyes,
describing each by his proper figure, character, and qualifica- 15
tions. On a sudden the Scene shifts, and a vast number of
miracles and prodigies appear, utterly surprizing and unknown
to the King himself, till they are explained to be the wonders of
his own reign now commencing. On this subject *Settle* breaks
into a congratulation, yet not unmix'd with concern, that his 20
own times were but the types of these; He prophecies how first
the nation shall be overrun with farces, opera's, shows; and the
throne of Dulness advanced over both the Theatres: Then how
her sons shall preside in the seats of arts and sciences, till in conclusion all shall return to their original Chaos: A scene, of which 25
the present Action of the Dunciad is but a Type or Foretaste,
giving a Glimpse or *Pisgah-sight* of the promis'd Fulness of her
Glory; the Accomplishment whereof will, in all probability,
hereafter be the Theme of many other and greater Dunciads.

---

14. *future* ⟨Cf. Milton, *Par. Lost*, Argument to Bk. xi, where the Angel leads Adam
up to a high hill, "and sets before him in vision what shall happen till the Flood."⟩

THE
DUNCIAD,
IN
THREE BOOKS
WITH
NOTES VARIORUM

THE DUNCIAD*

Book the First

Books and the Man I sing, the first who brings
The Smithfield Muses to the Ear of Kings.

1 Books] Book *1728b*.   2 Ear] ears *1728a–f*.

---

* THE *Dunciad, Sic* M.S. It may be well disputed whether this be a right Reading. Ought it not rather to be spelled *Dunceiad*, as the Etymology evidently demands? *Dunce* with an *e*, therefore *Dunceiad* with an *e*. That accurate and punctual Man of Letters, the Restorer of *Shakespeare*, constantly observes the preservation of this very Letter *e*, in spelling the Name of his beloved Author, and not like his common careless Editors, with the omission of one, nay sometimes of two *ee*'s [as *Shak'spear*] which is utterly unpardonable. Nor is the neglect of a *Single Letter* so trivial as to some it may appear; the alteration whereof in a learned language is an *Atchievement that brings honour* to the Critick who advances it; and Dr. *B.* will be remembered to posterity for his performances of *this sort*, as long as the world shall have any Esteem for the Remains of *Menander* and *Philemon*. THEOBALD. ⟨This note is attributed to Theobald on account of the final sentence, which Pope has taken from *Shakespeare Restored*, p. 193. The epithet "punctual" which he applies to Theobald is intended, no doubt, to refer to the critic's interest in "commas and points." Rowe and Pope both used the spelling "Shakespear," and were followed in this by Hanmer and Warburton. See also B i *in*. "Dr. *B.*" is Bentley. Cf. B iv 217 f.⟩

I have a just value for the Letter E, and the same affection for the Name of this Poem, as the forecited Critic for that of his Author; yet cannot it induce me to agree with those who would add yet another *e* to it, and call it the *Dunceiade*; which being a French and foreign Termination, is no way proper to a word entirely English, and Vernacular. One *E* therefore in this case is right, and two *E*'s wrong; yet upon the whole I shall follow the Manuscript, and print it without any *E* at all; mov'd thereto by Authority, at all times with Criticks equal if not superior to Reason. In which method of proceeding, I can never enough praise my very good Friend, the exact Mr. *Tho. Hearne*; who, if any word occur which to him and all mankind is evidently wrong, yet keeps he it in the Text with due reverence, and only remarks in the Margin, *sic M.S.* In like manner we shall not amend this error in the Title itself, but only note it *obiter*, to evince to the learned that it was not our fault, nor any effect of our own Ignorance or Inattention. SCRIBLERUS. ⟨For Hearne see A iii 184*n*. and Biog. App.⟩

1. *Books and the Man I sing, etc.*] Wonderful is the stupidity of all the former Criticks and Commentators on this Poem! It breaks forth at the very first line.

The Author of the Critique prefix'd to *Sawney*, a Poem, *p.* 5. hath been so dull as to explain *The Man who brings*, &c. not of the Hero of the Piece, but of our Poet himself, as if he vaunted that *Kings* were to be his Readers (an Honour which tho' this Poem hath had, yet knoweth he how to receive it with more Modesty.) ⟨For James Ralph, author of *Sawney* (1728), see A iii 159 and Biog. App.⟩

We remit this Ignorant to the first lines of the *Æneid*; assuring him, that *Virgil* there speaketh not of himself, but of *Æneas*.

> *Arma virumq; cano, Trojæ qui primus ab oris,*
> *Italiam fato profugus, Lavinaq; venit*
> *Litora: multum ille & terris jactatus et alto, &c.*

I cite the whole three verses, that I may by the way offer a *Conjectural Emendation*, purely my own, upon each: First, *oris* should be read *aris*, it being as we see *Æn.* 2. 513, from the *altar* of *Jupiter Herçæus* that *Æneas* fled as soon as he saw *Priam* slain. In the second line I would read *flatu* for *fato*, since it is most clear it was by *Winds* that he arrived at the *Shore* of Italy; *Jactatus* in the third, is surely as improper apply'd to *terris*, as proper to *alto:* To say a man is *tost on land*, is much at one with saying he *walks at sea. Risum teneatis amici?* Correct it, as I doubt not it ought to be, *Vexatus.* SCRIBLERUS. ⟨The "Book" of *1728b* has been thought to refer to the book which particularly annoyed Pope: *Shakespeare Restored* (T. R. Lounsbury, *The First Editors of Shakespeare*, p. 290); but this reading does not occur in any later edition, and was almost certainly due to a printer's error.⟩

This Poem was writ in 1727 ⟨"in 1726"—*1735c–51*⟩. In the next year an imperfect Edition was published at Dublin, and re-printed at London in 12°. Another at Dublin, and re-printed at London in 8°, and three others in 12° the same year. But there was no perfect Edition before that of London in 4° 172⅞, which was attended with the following Notes.   We are willing to acquaint Posterity that this Poem (as it here stands) was presented to King George the Second and his Queen, by the hands of Sir R. Walpole, on the 12th of March 172⅞. ⟨*1735a–51*. As Professor Griffith points out (vol. i, pt. 1, p. 283), this is the earliest bibliography of the *Dunciad* of 1728. See also, however, Note on the Text of *Dunciad* A. He suggests (*The Colophon*, New Series, vol. iii, No. 4, p. 569) that this note was probably prepared by Jonathan Richardson from information supplied by Pope.⟩

2. *The* Smithfield-*Muses*] *Smithfield* is the place where Bartholomew Fair was kept, whose Shews, Machines, and Dramatical Entertainments, formerly agreeable only to the Taste of the Rabble, were, by the Hero of this Poem and others of equal Genius, brought to the Theatres of Covent-Garden, Lincolns-inn-Fields, and the Hay-Market, to be the reigning Pleasures of the Court and Town. This happened in the Year 1725, and continued to the Year 1728 ⟨many years—*1735a*⟩. See Book 3. Vers. 191, &c. ⟨Malone notes that in the Prologue to Gildon's *Measure for Measure* Oldmixon had used the phrase, "Smithfield-Bards."⟩

Say great Patricians! (since your selves inspire
These wond'rous works; so Jove and Fate require)
Say from what cause, in vain decry'd and curst,   5
Still Dunce the second reigns like Dunce the first?
   In eldest time, e'er mortals writ or read,
E'er Pallas issued from the Thund'rer's head,
Dulnes o'er all possess'd her antient right,
Daughter of Chaos and eternal Night: 10
Fate in their dotage this fair idiot gave,
Gross as her sire, and as her mother grave,
Laborious, heavy, busy, bold, and blind,
She rul'd, in native Anarchy, the mind.
   Still her old empire to confirm, she tries,   15

3. *Say great* Patricians (*since your selves inspire*
   These Wond'rous Works]—Ovid. *Met.* 1⟨2⟩.
            —*Dii cæptis* (*nam vos Mutastis & illas*).
5. *Say from what cause* ⟨An epic cliché. Cf. *Aen.* i 8 ff.⟩
6. Alluding to a verse of Mr. *Dryden*'s not in *Mac Flecno* (as it is said ignorantly
in the Key to the *Dunciad, pag.* 1.) but in his verses to Mr. *Congreve* ⟨l. 48⟩.
            And Tom *the Second reigns like* Tom *the First.*
⟨Pope is probably glancing at George II, who had succeeded his father less
than a year before the *Dunciad* was published. EC (vol. iv, p. 271) records an
earlier version of ll. 5–6:
            Say what the cause that still this taste remains,
            And when a Settle falls a Tibbald reigns.
After George I's death, in June 1727, Pope presumably hit upon the more
pointed couplet of the printed text. George II had disappointed the Opposition
by retaining Walpole, after an unsuccessful attempt to dismiss him, as his
chief minister. The "great Patricians" of l. 3 are the Whig aristocracy, who were
mainly responsible for bringing the Hanoverians to England in 1714.⟩
   10. *Daughter of* Chaos, *&c.*] The beauty of this whole Allegory being purely
of the Poetical kind, we think it not our proper business as a Scholiast, to
meddle with it; but leave it (as we shall in general all such) to the Reader:
remarking only, that *Chaos* (according to *Hesiod*, Θεογονία) was the Progenitor
of all the Gods. SCRIBL. ⟨Cf. also *Par. Lost*, ii 894–6:
            . . . where eldest Night
            And Chaos, ancestors of Nature, hold
            Eternal anarchy . . .
Dullness had already become a goddess in Swift's *Battle of the Books.*⟩
   12. *Gross as her sire* ⟨Dryden, *Aen.* vii 1044:
            Fam'd as his *Sire,* and as his Mother fair.—Wakefield.⟩

For born a Goddess, Dulness never dies.
 O thou! whatever Title please thine ear,
Dean, Drapier, Bickerstaff, or Gulliver!
Whether thou chuse Cervantes' serious air,
Or laugh and shake in Rab'lais' easy Chair,   20
Or praise the Court, or magnify Mankind,
Or thy griev'd Country's copper chains unbind;
From thy Bæotia tho' Her Pow'r retires,
Grieve not at ought our sister realm acquires:

17–26] *Om. 1728a–f.*

16. *For born a Goddess* ⟨Garth, *Dispensary*, i 116:
     With Godhead born, but curs'd, that cannot die!—Wakefield.⟩
  17. *Whatever Title* ⟨A god is frequently invoked in classical epic by different
names.⟩
  17–24. ⟨"It was my principal aim in the entire work to perpetuate the
friendship between us, and to show that the friends or the enemies of the one
were the friends or enemies of the other."—Pope to Swift, Oct. 9, 1729.—The
invocation to Swift was considerably revised before it appeared in print. For
an earlier version, see EC vii 104. Some Latin verses written by Charles Ford
in 1727 for Swift's birthday seem to anticipate the *Dunciad* invocation. See
Letters of Swift to Ford, ed. D. Nichol Smith, 1935, pp. 213–5.⟩
  18. *Bickerstaff* ⟨Isaac Bickerstaff, a pseudonym used by Swift in some of his
lighter satires, e.g. those on Partridge the Astrologer. The name was later
adopted by Steele for his *Tatler*.⟩
  20. *Rab'lais' easy Chair* ⟨"Dr. Swift was a great reader and admirer of Rabelais,
and used sometimes to scold me for not liking him enough" (Pope).—Spence,
p. 141.⟩
  21. *Or praise the Court, &c.*] *Ironicè*, alluding to *Gulliver's* Representations of
both—The next line relates to the Papers of the *Drapier* against the currency
of *Wood's* Copper Coin in Ireland, which upon the great discontent of the
people, his Majesty was graciously pleased to recal ⟨*1729b*⟩.
  23. *From thy* Bæotia] *Bæotia* of old lay under the Raillery of the neighbouring
Wits, as *Ireland* does now; tho' each of those nations produced one of the greatest
Wits, and greatest Generals, of their age. ⟨The wit produced by Bœotia was
Pindar, the general, Epaminondas. Ireland had produced two famous wits in
Swift and Congreve; her great general is presumably James Butler, Duke of
Ormonde—a hero to the Tories, at any rate. EC notes that Gay had previously
referred to Ireland as Bœotia in *A Welcome From Greece*, l. 103:
        Thou too, my *Swift*, dost breathe *Bæotian air*.⟩
  24. *Grieve not, my Swift! etc.*] *Ironicè iterum*. The Politicks of *England* and *Ireland*

Here pleas'd behold her mighty wings out-spread,   25
To hatch a new Saturnian age of Lead.
　　Where wave the tatter'd ensigns of Rag-Fair,
A yawning ruin hangs and nods in air;
Keen, hollow winds howl thro' the bleak recess,
Emblem of Music caus'd by Emptiness: 30
Here in one bed two shiv'ring sisters lye,

---

were at this time by some thought to be opposite, or interfering with each other: Dr. *Swift* of course was in the interest of the latter, our Author of the former ⟨*1729b*⟩.

26. *A new* Saturnian *Age of Lead*] The ancient Golden Age is by Poets stiled *Saturnian*; but in the Chymical language, *Saturn* is Lead.

27. Rag-fair] *Rag-fair* is a place near the *Tower* of *London*, where old cloaths and frippery are sold.

28.31. *&c. A yawning ruin &c.*] Hear upon this place the forecited Critick on the *Dunciad*. ⟨i.e. James Ralph, *Sawney*, p. viii. Pope afterwards altered those lines. Cf. *Dunciad* B i 33–4.⟩ "These lines (saith he) have no Construction, or are "Nonsense. The two shivering Sisters must be the sister Caves of Poverty and "Poetry, or the Bed and Cave of Poverty and Poetry must be the same, (*question-* "*less*) ⟨*if they lie in one bed—1729b–42*⟩ and the two Sisters the Lord knows who? O the Construction of Grammatical Heads! *Virgil* writeth thus: *Æn.* 1 ⟨166–8⟩—
> *Fronte sub adversa scopulis pendentibus antrum:*
> *Intus aquæ dulces, vivoq; sedilia saxo;*
> *Nympharum domus.*——

May we not say in like manner, "The Nymphs must be the Waters and the "Stones, or the Waters and the Stones must be the houses of the Nymphs? *Insulse!* The second line, *Intus aquæ, &c.* is in a parenthesis (as are the two lines of our Author, *Keen hollow Winds, &c.*) and it is the *Antrum*, and the *yawning Ruin*, in the line before that parenthesis, which are the *Domus*, and the *Cave*.

Let me again, I beseech thee Reader, present thee with another *Conjectural Emendation* on *Virgil's Scopulis pendentibus:* He is here describing a place, whither the weary Mariners of *Æneas* repaired to dress their Dinner.—*Fessi—frugesq; receptas Et torrere parant flammis:* What has *Scopulis pendentibus* here to do? Indeed the *aquæ dulces* and *sedilia* are something; *sweet Waters* to drink, and *Seats* to rest on. The other is surely an error of the Copyists. Restore it, without the least scruple, *Populis prandentibus.*

But for this and a thousand more, expect our Edition of *Virgil*; a Specimen whereof see in the Appendix ⟨IV⟩. SCRIBLERUS.

29. *Keen, hollow winds* ⟨*Windsor Forest*, 68:
　　　　The hollow winds thro' naked Temples roar.⟩
30. *Emblem of Music* ⟨The music, as Wakefield notes, is "bowel music."⟩

The cave of Poverty and Poetry.
This, the Great Mother dearer held than all
The clubs of Quidnunc's, or her own Guild-hall.
Here stood her Opium, here she nurs'd her Owls,   35
And destin'd here th' imperial seat of Fools.
Hence springs each weekly Muse, the living boast
Of Curl's chaste press, and Lintot's rubric post,
Hence hymning Tyburn's elegiac lay,

38 Curl's . . . Lintot's] *C—l's . . . L—t's 1728a–f.*

32. *The cave of Poverty* ⟨In 1714 Theobald had published *The Cave of Poverty, A Poem. Written in Imitation of Shakespeare.*⟩

33. *This the* Great Mother. *&c.*] *Æn.* 1⟨12, 15–18⟩.
>   *Urbs antiqua fuit—*
>   *Quam Juno fertur terris magis omnibus unam*
>   *Posthabita coluisse Samo; hic illius arma,*
>   *Hic currus fuit: hoc regnum Dea gentibus esse*
>   *(Siqua fata sinant) jam tum tenditq; fovetq;*

⟨Cf. Dryden's translation of ll. 17–18:
>   Here stood her Chariot, here, if heav'n were kind,
>   The Seat of awful Empire she design'd.⟩

33. *The* Great Mother] *Magna mater,* here applyed to *Dulness.* The *Quidnunc's* was a name given to the ancient Members of certain political Clubs, who were constantly enquiring, *Quid nunc?* what news? ⟨Cf. *The Quidnuncki's,* printed in Swift's and Pope's *Miscellanies,* 1727, and see R. J. Allen, *Clubs of Augustan London,* pp. 124 ff.⟩

34. *Guild-hall* ⟨The literary convention of laughing at the "cit" goes back to Elizabethan days or perhaps further, reaches its height in the Restoration period, and begins to die out about the middle of the eighteenth century.⟩

38. Curl*'s chaste press, and* Lintot*'s rubric post*] Two Booksellers, of whom see Book 2 ⟨49 ff.⟩. The former was fined by the Court of King's-Bench for publishing obscene books; ⟨*1729a–51*⟩ the latter usually adorn'd his shop with Titles in red letters. ⟨*1729b–51.* "Mr. CURLL, in the *Strand,* was fined by the Court of King's Bench 50 Marks, for publishing, 1. The Nun in her Smock, a Novel . . . Mr. LINTOT, in Fleet-street, is so fond of Red Letter Title-Pages to the Books he prints, that his Show-Boards and Posts before his Door are generally bedaubed with them."—Curll, *Key,* p. 7. Cf. *Ep. to Arbuthnot,* 215.⟩

39. *Hence hymning Tyburn—Hence, &c.*]
>   *—Genus unde Latinum*
>   *Albaniq; patres, atq; altæ moenia Romæ.*

Virg. ⟨*Aen.* i 6–7⟩.

39. *Hence hymning* Tyburn's *elegiac lay*] It is an ancient English custom for the

Hence the soft sing-song on Cecilia's day,   40
Sepulchral lyes our holy walls to grace,
And New-year Odes, and all the Grubstreet race.
  'Twas here in clouded majesty she shone;
Four guardian Virtues, round, support her Throne;
Fierce champion Fortitude, that knows no fears   45
Of hisses, blows, or want, or loss of ears:
Calm Temperance, whose blessings those partake
Who hunger, and who thirst, for scribling sake:

Malefactors to sing a Psalm at their Execution at *Tyburn*; and no less customary to print Elegies on their deaths, at the same time, or before.

VERSE 40 and 42, Allude to the annual Songs composed to Musick on St. *Cecilia*'s Feast, and those made by the Poet-Laureat for the time being to be sung at Court, on every New-Years-Day, the words of which are happily drown'd in the voices and Instruments. ⟨In *The Battle of the Poets* (1729) T. Cooke was to sneer at Pope's own *Ode on St. Cecilia's Day*.⟩

VERSE 41. Is a just Satyr on the Flatteries and Falsehoods admitted to be inscribed on the walls of Churches in Epitaphs. ⟨". . . the zeal of the first reformers was ill-placed in . . . suffering epitaphs (that is to say, flatteries and false history) to be the burden of church walls."—Pope to Allen, April 30, 1736.⟩

I must not here omit a Reflection, which will occur perpetually through this Poem, and cannot but greatly endear the Author to every attentive Observer of it: I mean that *Candour* and *Humanity* which every where appears in him, to those unhappy Objects of the Ridicule of all mankind, the bad Poets. He here imputes all scandalous rhimes, scurrilous weekly papers, lying news, base flatteries, wretched elegies, songs, and verses (even from those sung at Court, to ballads in the streets) not so much to Malice or Servility as to Dulness; and not so much to Dulness, as to Necessity; And thus at the very commencement of his Satyr, makes an Apology for all that are to be satyrized.

43. *In clouded Majesty she shone*] Milton, ⟨*Par. Lost*, iv 606–7⟩.
——*The Moon*
  Rising in clouded Majesty.——

44. *Four guardian Virtues* ⟨The four Cardinal Virtues were a recurring feature of the pageantry on a Lord Mayor's Day, and Pope may have associated them with the goddess for that reason. Cf. *London's Great Jubilee, Somers Tracts*, ed. Sir W. Scott, 1809–15, xi 584.⟩

45–6. *That knows no fears*] Horat. ⟨*Lib.* ii, *Sat.* vii 84⟩.
  Quem neq; pauperies, neq; mors, neq; vincula terrent.

48. *Who hunger, and who thirst*] "This is an infamous Burlesque on a Text in "Scripture, which shews the Author's delight in Prophaneness," (said *Curl* upon this place.) But 'tis very familiar with *Shakespeare* to allude to Passages of Scrip-

Prudence, whose glass presents th' approaching jayl:
Poetic Justice, with her lifted scale;   50
Where in nice balance, truth with gold she weighs,
And solid pudding against empty praise.
    Here she beholds the Chaos dark and deep,
Where nameless somethings in their causes sleep,
'Till genial Jacob, or a warm Third-day   55

ture. Out of a great number I'll select a few, in which he both alludes to, and
quotes the very Texts from holy Writ. In *All's well that ends well*, *I am no great
Nebucadnezzar*, *I have not much Skill in Grass*. Ibid. *They are for the flowry Way
that leads to the broad Gate, and the great Fire*. Mat. 7. 13. Much ado about nothing:
All, all, and moreover *God saw him when he was hid in the Garden*, Gen. 3. 8. (in a
very jocose Scene.) In Love's Labour lost, he talks of *Sampson*'s carrying the
Gates on his Back; in the Merry Wives of Windsor of *Goliah* and the Weaver's
Beam; and in Henry 4. *Falstaff*'s Soldiers are compared to *Lazarus* and the
Prodigal Son, &c. *The first part of this Note is Mr.* CURL'*s* ⟨*Key*, p. 8⟩: *The rest is
Mr.* THEOBALD'*s*. Shakespear Restor'd *Appendix, p.* 144. ⟨In later editions
Pope softened Curll's statement to "This is an allusion to a Text in Scripture
. . ." He paraphrases Theobald's words, and misquotes the passage from *All's
Well* which Theobald had quoted correctly. See also A i 168*n*.⟩

     49. *glass* ⟨The perspective glass through which Prudence was represented in
art as gazing.⟩

     50. *Poetic Justice* ⟨Cf. Pope's *Messiah*, 18:
                    Returning Justice lift aloft her scale.⟩

     53. *Here she beholds, &c.*] That is to say, unformed things, which are either
made into Poems or Plays, as the Booksellers or the Players bid most. These
lines allude to the following in *Garth's Dispensary, Cant.* 6 ⟨44–7⟩.
                    *Within the chambers of the Globe they spy
                    The beds where sleeping Vegetables lie,
                    'Till the glad summons of a genial ray
                    Unbinds the Glebe, and calls them out to day.*
⟨Cf. also *Par. Lost*, iii 11:
                    The rising world of waters dark and deep.
Garth, *Dispensary*, vi 113–14:
                    Here his forsaken Seat old *Chaos* keeps;
                    And undisturb'd by Form, in Silence sleeps.
Fo rthe source of Garth's lines, see Cowley's *Davideis*, i 75–80, and *Mac Flecknoe*,
72–8. Pope may also have had in mind Carew's line,
                    These Flowers as in their causes sleep.⟩

     55. *'Till genial Jacob* ⟨Jacob Tonson (1656?–1736), the leading publisher of his
generation. He specialized in plays and poetry.—The third day of a play's
run was regularly set apart for the author's benefit.—For the meaning of

Call forth each mass, a poem or a play.
How Hints, like spawn, scarce quick in embryo lie,
How new-born Nonsense first is taught to cry,
Maggots half-form'd, in rhyme exactly meet,
And learn to crawl upon poetic feet.   60
Here one poor Word a hundred clenches makes,
And ductile dulness new meanders takes;
There motley Images her fancy strike,
Figures ill-pair'd, and Similes unlike.
She sees a Mob of Metaphors advance,   65
Pleas'd with the Madness of the mazy dance:

56 Call] Calls *1728a–f.*

"warm" in this context, cf. James Miller's *Harlequin-Horace,* 1731: "You care
for nothing but a warm Third-Night": an extension of OED's sense 8, viz.
"well to do, rich, affluent." Pope, of course, is thinking also of a warmth
sufficient for incubation.⟩
    59–60. *Maggots* ⟨Cf. Parnell, "On Bishop Burnet's being set on Fire":
            Here crawls a Preface on its half-burn'd Maggots.
Maggot has two senses in this context: (a) grub, (b) "a whimsical or perverse
fancy" (OED). Pope may also have in mind Samuel Wesley's volume, *Maggots:
or Poems on several subjects,* 1685. Wesley (*W—y*) was introduced at i 126, in
some of the 1728 editions.⟩
    61. *Here one poor* Word *a hundred* clenches *makes*] It may not be amiss to give
an instance or two of these Operations of *Dulness* out of the Authors celebrated
in the Poem. A great Critick formerly held these Clenches ⟨puns⟩ in such
abhorrence, that he declared, "He that would Pun, would pick a Pocket."
Yet Mr. *Dennis's* Works afford us notable Examples in this kind. "*Alexander*
"Pope hath sent abroad into the world as many *Bulls* as his Namesake Pope
"*Alexander.*"—"Let us take the initial and final letters of his Surname, *viz.,*
"*A. P——E,* and they give you the Idea of an *Ape.——Pope* comes from the
"Latin word *Popa,* which signifies a little Wart; or from *Poppysma,* because he
"was continually *popping* out squibs of wit, or rather *Po-pysmata,* or *Po-pisms.*
DENNIS. *Daily-Journal* June 11. 1728. ⟨The letter is dated from Cambridge,
and signed "Philoscriblerus." Cf. also *Daily. Journal,* May 11, 1728.—The
"great Critick" referred to in Pope's note is Dennis himself. The anecdote
appears in Benjamin Victor's *Epistle to Sir Richard Steele,* 1722. After "DENNIS,"
1729b adds "on *Hom.* and," i.e. *Remarks on Homer,* pp. 91–2.—Pope probably
had in mind a line in *Mac Flecknoe,* 208:
            And torture one poor word Ten thousand ways.⟩
    62. *And ductile dulness*] A Parody on another in *Garth. Cant.* 1 ⟨26⟩.
            How ductile matter new meanders takes.

How Tragedy and Comedy embrace;
How Farce and Epic get a jumbled race;
How Time himself stands still at her command,
Realms shift their place, and Ocean turns to land.   70
Here gay Description Ægypt glads with showers;
Or gives to Zembla fruits, to Barca flowers;
Glitt'ring with ice here hoary hills are seen,
There painted vallies of eternal green,
On cold December fragrant chaplets blow,   75
And heavy harvests nod beneath the snow.
      All these and more, the cloud-compelling Queen
Beholds thro' fogs that magnify the scene:

74 There painted] Fast by, fair *1728a–c.*

68. *How* Farce *and* Epic, &c.] Allude to the Transgressions of the *Unities*, in the Plays of such Poets. For the Miracles wrought upon *Time* and *Place*, and the mixture of Tragedy, Comedy, Farce and Epic, *See* Pluto *and* Proserpine, Penelope, *&c. as yet extant.* ⟨"if yet extant"—*1735a–51.* Theobald wrote *A Dramatic Entertainment, Call'd Harlequin a Sorcerer: With the Loves of Pluto and Proserpine* in 1725 to take the place of his *Rape of Proserpine*, which had been unavoidably held up. *Penelope. An English Opera*, by John Mottley, assisted by Thomas Cooke, was acted at the Haymarket in May, 1728. For Pope's quarrel with Cooke, see ii 130*n.* and Biog. App.⟩

71. Ægypt *glads with Showers*] In the lower Ægypt Rain is of no use, the overflowing of the *Nyle* being sufficient to impregnate the soil.—These six verses represent the inconsistencies in the description of Poets, who heap together all glittering and gawdy Images, tho' incompatible in one season, or in one scene.—*See the* Guardian N° 40. *printed in the* Appendix ⟨V⟩, *Parag.* 6. *See also* Eusden's *whole Works (if to be found.)* ⟨*1729a–51.*⟩ It would not have been unpleasant, to have given Examples of all these Species of bad writing, from these Authors, but that it is already done in our Treatise of the *Bathos.* SCRIBL. ⟨*1729d.*⟩

72. *Zembla . . . Barca* ⟨For Zembla, cf. *The Temple of Fame*, 53 ff. Barca is the modern Barce, in Libya. Whatever improvements may have been made in this neighbourhood by the modern Italians, it was in Virgil's day "deserta siti regio."—*Aeneid*, iv 42.⟩

77. *The Cloud-compelling Queen*] From *Homer's* Epithet of *Jupiter,* νεφεληγερέτα Ζεύς.

78. *that magnify* ⟨Cf. i 218; and *E. on C.*, 392–3:

        As things seem large which we thro' mists descry,
        Dulness is ever apt to magnify.

The same idea is expressed again by Pope in a letter to Swift, Dec. 14, 1725.⟩

She, tinsel'd o'er in robes of varying hues,
With self-applause her wild creation views,   80
Sees momentary monsters rise and fall,
And with her own fool's colours gilds them all.
　'Twas on the day, when Thorold, rich and grave,
Like Cimon triumph'd, both on land and wave:
(Pomps without guilt, of bloodless swords and maces, 85
Glad chains, warm furs, broad banners, and broad faces)
Now Night descending, the proud scene was o'er,
But liv'd, in Settle's numbers, one day more.

82 gilds] gild *1735c*.　　83 Thorold] *Tho—d 1728a–f.*
86 Glad] Gold *1728c*.　　88 But] Yet *1728a–e.*

---

83. '*Twas on the Day when* Thorold] Sir *George Thorold* Lord Mayor of *London*, in the Year 1720. The Procession of a Lord Mayor is made partly by land, and partly by water. ⟨Thorold, Lord Mayor in 1719, died on Oct. 29, 1722.—*St. James's Journal*, Nov. 1, 1722. Cf. Introduction, p. xiv.⟩—*Cimon* the famous *Athenian* General obtained a Victory by sea, and another by land, on the same day, over the *Persians* and *Barbarians*. ⟨*1728a, 1729a–51*. The victory was at Salamis, B.C. 480.⟩

85. *Pomps* ⟨In the sense of πομπή, a procession.⟩

86. *Glad Chains*] The Ignorance of these Moderns! This was altered in one Edition to *Gold Chains*, shewing more regard to the metal of which the chains of Aldermen are made, than to the beauty of the Latinism and Grecism, nay of figurative speech itself.—*Lætas segetes*, glad, for making glad, *&c.* Scr.

88. *But liv'd in* Settle's *Numbers*] A beautiful manner of speaking, usual with the Poets in praise of Poetry, in which kind nothing is finer than those lines of Mr. *Addison* ⟨*A Letter from Italy*, 31–6⟩.

> *Sometimes misguided by the tuneful throng,*
> *I look for streams immortaliz'd in song,*
> *That lost in silence and oblivion lye,*
> *Dumb are their fountains, and their channels dry;*
> *Yet run for ever, by the Muses skill,*
> *And in the smooth description murmur still.*

Settle was alive at this time, and Poet to the City of *London*. His office was to compose yearly panegyricks upon the Lord Mayors, and Verses to be spoken in the Pageants: But that part of the shows being by the frugality of some Lord Mayors at length abolished, the employment of City Poet ceas'd; so that upon *Settle's* demise, there was no successor to that place. ⟨He died in 1724. His last important commission was in 1708, when the Goldsmiths' Company engaged him to prepare the pageants for the Lord Mayor's Show. The death of Prince George of Denmark two days before prevented their representation. The

Now May'rs and Shrieves all hush'd and satiate lay,
Yet eat in dreams the custard of the day;   90
While pensive Poets painful vigils keep,
Sleepless themselves to give their readers sleep.
Much to the mindful Queen the feast recalls,
What City-Swans once sung within the walls;
Much she revolves their arts, their ancient praise,   95
And sure succession down from Heywood's days.

89 all . . . lay,] in pleasing slumbers lay, *1728a–e.*
90 Yet] And *1728a–e.*   91 While] But *1728a–e.*
93 Much to her mind the solemn feast recalls, *1728a–f.*

substance of the two opening sentences of Pope's note appear in a note to
1728a, Bk i, l. 175.⟩ This important point of time our Poet has chosen, as the
Crisis of the Kingdom of *Dulness,* who thereupon decrees to remove her imperial
seat from the City, and over-spread the other parts of the Town: To which
great Enterprize all things being now ripe, she calls the Hero of this Poem.

Mr. *Settle* was once a writer in some vogue, particularly with his Party; for he
was the author or publisher of many noted Pamphlets in the time of King
Charles the second. He answered all *Dryden*'s political Poems; and being cry'd
up on one side, succeeded not a little in his Tragedy of the Empress of Morocco
(the first that was ever printed with Cuts.) "Upon this he grew insolent, the
"Wits writ against his Play, he replied, and the Town judged he had the
"better. In short *Settle* was then thought a formidable Rival to Mr. *Dryden*; and
"not only the Town, but the University of *Cambridge,* was divided which to
"prefer; and in both places the younger sort inclined to *Elkanah.* DENNIS. *Pref.
to Rem. on* Hom. ⟨Pope paraphrases Dennis freely.—Settle glanced at Dryden
in the dedication of *The Empress of Morocco* (1673), and again in a prologue to
The Heir of Morocco (1682). See Hugh Macdonald, *John Dryden. A Bibliography,*
1939, pp. 205 ff., 231. In 1674 he was attacked in *Notes and Observations on the
Empress of Morocco,* a pamphlet attributed to Dryden, Shadwell, and Crowne.
To this Settle replied in *Notes and Observations . . . Revised* (1674). He further
attacked Dryden in *Absalom Senior: Or Achitophel Transpros'd* (1682). (Hugh
Macdonald, op. cit., pp. 166, 209, 229 ff.)⟩

For the latter part of his History, see the third Book, verse ⟨281*n.*⟩.

92. *Sleepless themselves* ⟨Writing to Caryll, Jan. 18, 1718, about his translation of Homer, Pope says, "I charitably take pains for others' ease, and wake
to make you sleep!"⟩

96. *John Heywood*] Whose Enterludes were printed in the time of *Henry* the
eighth. ⟨*1728a–51.* In *Ep.* ii i 88 Pope was to refer to John Heywood as "eldest
Heywood." Here, however, he seems to be confusing him with the later
dramatist, Thomas Heywood (d. 1650?), who, like Settle after him, composed

> She saw with joy the line immortal run,
> Each sire imprest and glaring in his son;
> So watchful Bruin forms with plastic care
> Each growing lump, and brings it to a Bear.   100
> She saw old Pryn in restless Daniel shine,

101 old . . . Daniel] in *N—n* all his father *1728a–c.*

the Lord Mayor's pageants for many years.⟩
    sure succession ⟨Cf. Dryden's translation of Virgil's *Georgics*, iv 303:
        The immortal Line in sure Succession reigns.—Wakefield.
Cf. also Dryden's *Aeneid*, i 8, and *Donne* iv 161.⟩
    98. *Each sire imprest* ⟨Pope may be alluding here obliquely to the new coinage stamped on the accession of George II. Two hundred gold and eight hundred silver medals had been struck for the new King (A. Boyer, *Political State*, xxxiv 171); and the new silver and copper coinage must have been coming into circulation before Pope gave his poem its final revision.⟩
    101. *Old* Prynn *in restless* Daniel] *William Prynn* and *Daniel de Foe* were writers of Verses, as well as of Politicks; as appears by the Poem of the latter *De jure Divino*, and others, and by these lines in *Cowley's* Miscellanies of the former. ⟨*An Answer to a Copy of Verses Sent to me to Jersey*, 11–18. Pope has not quoted exactly.⟩

        —One lately did not fear
        (*Without the Muses leave*) *to plant Verse here.*
        But it produc'd such base, rough, crabbed hedge-
        Rhymes, as e'en set the hearers ears on edge:
        Written by William Prynn Esqui-re, *the*
        Year of our Lord, six hundred thirty three.
        Brave Jersey *Muse! and he's for his high stile*
        Call'd to this day the Homer *of the Isle.*

Both these Authors had a resemblance in their fates as well as writings, having been a-like sentenc'd to the Pillory. ⟨William Prynne (1600–69) was pilloried for writing *Histrio-mastix* (1633), and had his ears cut off. Defoe stood in the pillory in 1703 for writing *The Shortest Way with the Dissenters*. The title of Defoe's political poem is *Jure Divino*. See also Biog. App., Defoe. From *1729b* this note reads: "The first edition had it, *She saw in Norton all his father shine*; a great mistake! for *Daniel de Foe* had parts, but Norton de Foe was a wretched writer, and never attempted Poetry. Much more justly is *Daniel* himself made successor to *W. Pryn*, both of whom wrote Verses . . ." For Norton Defoe, see ii 383*n*.⟩
    Of *Eusden* and *Blackmore*, see ⟨iii 319*n*., ii 258*n*.⟩. And *Philips*, ⟨see iii 322*n*. Pope had already placed Ambrose Philips among the tortoises, which are "*slow and chill*, and, like Pastoral Writers, delight much in *Gardens*" (*Peri Bathous*, ch. vi). In *Ep. to Arbuthnot*, 182, Philips was said to strain "from hard-bound brains eight lines a-year," and in *Sandys' Ghost* Pope had alluded to his "costive head." See also Biog. App.⟩

5

And Eusden eke out Blackmore's endless line;
She saw slow Philips creep like Tate's poor page,
And all the Mighty Mad in Dennis rage.

102 Eusden] *E¹—n 1728a–f*.   Blackmore's] *Bl—'s 1728a–f*.
103 Philips . . . Tate's] *P—s . . . T—te's, 1728a–f*.
104 And furious *D—n* foam in *Wh—'s* rage *1728a–c*.
———— *D—s* ———— *W—'s* — *1728de*.
———— *D—s* ———— *W—y's* — *1728f*.

---

102. *And Eusden eke out* ⟨"Who sees not that *De F—* was the Poetical Son of *Withers*, . . . and *E—n* of *Bl—k—re?*"—*Peri Bathous*, ch. ix.⟩

103. *like Tate's poor page*] *Nahum Tate* ⟨1652–1715⟩ was Poet-Laureate, a cold writer, of no *invention*, but sometimes translated tolerably when befriended by Mr. *Dryden*. In his second part of *Absalom* and *Achitophel* are above two hundred admirable lines together of that great hand, which strongly shine through the insipidity of the rest. Something parallel may be observed of another Author here mention'd. ⟨*1729b–51*. Addison was thought to have helped Philips with his translation of Sappho which appeared in the *Spectator*.—EC iv 316. For Tate, see Biog. App., vol. iv.⟩

104. *And all the mighty Mad*] This is by no means to be understood literally, as if Mr. *D.* were really mad; Not that we are ignorant of the *Narrative* of Dr. *R. Norris*, but it deserveth no more regard than the *Pop upon P.* and the like idle Trash, written by *James Moor*, or other young and light Persons, who themselves better deserve to be blooded, scarified, or whipped, for such their ungracious merriment with their Elders. No—it is spoken of that *Excellent* and *Divine Madness*, so often mentioned by *Plato*, that poetical rage and enthusiasm, with which no doubt Mr. *D.* hath, in his time, been highly possessed; and of those *extraordinary hints* and *motions* whereof he himself so feelingly treats in the Preface to Pr. *Arth*. [See Notes on Book 2, verse 256.] SCRIBL. ⟨Part of this note ("Not that we are . . . Elders") appeared only in *1729a*, and was never again reprinted by Pope. From *1735–51* the words omitted were replaced by "according to the Narrative of Dr. Norris, in Swift and Pope's Miscellanies, Vol. 3." *The Narrative of Dr. Robert Norris* (1713), which Pope ironically condemns as "idle trash," was almost certainly his own. *A Popp upon Pope* (1728), which he here seems inclined to attribute to James Moore Smythe, he certainly believed at one time to be the work of Lady Mary Wortley Montagu. Cf. *Ep. to Arbuthnot*, l. 349n. and *Grub-Street Journal*, No. 20. He did not include *A Popp upon Pope* in the "List of Books" in Appendix ii.⟩

104. *And all the mighty Mad in* Dennis *rage*] This Verse in the surreptitious Editions stood thus, *And furious* D—*foam, &c.* which, in that printed in *Ireland*, was unaccountably filled up with the great name of *Dryden*. ⟨*1729a–d*. This (1728) Dublin edition was published by G. Faulkner and five other Dublin

booksellers. Many of the names left blank by Pope were supplied in the Dublin
edition by equally wild guesses. By "*D—n*" Pope intended John Dunton.
(EC iv 273). The *Wh—'s* of *1728a* was intended for "Whatley's." (For Stephen
Whatley, see Biog. App.) The EC MS. shows that he had also had Welsted in
mind. (EC iv 273). For "Whatley" the Irish edition read "Wharton," the
anonymous *Key*, "Whiston," and Curll's *Key*, "Mr. *Wesley* of *Westminster-
School*," i.e. Samuel Wesley the Younger, 1691–1739.⟩ *Mr. Theobald in the
Censor*, Vol. 2. Nº 33. ⟨Jan. 5, 1717⟩ also calls him by the Name of *Furius*.
"The modern *Furius* is to be look'd on as more the object of Pity, than of that
"which he daily provokes, laughter and contempt. Did we really know how
"much this *poor Man* (*I wish that reflection on* Poverty *had been spar'd*) suffers by
"being contradicted, or which is the same thing in effect, by hearing another
"praised; we should in compassion sometimes attend to him with a silent nod,
"and let him go away with the triumphs of his ill-nature. ⟨"I wish that reflection on Poverty had been spared" is Pope's gibe at those of his critics who
had complained almost in those words of his inhumanity in satirizing poverty.
Cf. *Mist's Journal*, March 30, June 8, 1728.⟩ "—*Poor* Furius (*again*) when any
"of his cotemporaries are spoken well of, quitting the ground of the present
"dispute, steps back a thousand years to call in the succour of the Ancients. His
"very *Panegyrick* is *spiteful*, and he uses it for the same reason as some Ladies do
"their commendations of a dead Beauty, who never would have had their good
"word, but that a living one happened to be mentioned in their company.
"His applause is not the tribute of his *Heart*, but the sacrifice of his *Revenge*," &c.
Indeed his pieces against our Poet are somewhat of an angry character, and as
they are now scarce extant, a taste of his stile may be satisfactory to the curious.
"A young squab, short Gentleman, whose outward form though it should be
"that of downright Monkey, would not differ so much from human shape, as
"his unthinking immaterial part does from human understanding.—He is as
"stupid and as venemous as a hunchbacked Toad.—A Book through which
"folly and ignorance, those bretheren so lame and impotent, do ridiculously
"look very big, and very dull, and strut, and hobble cheek by jowl, with their
"arms on kimbo, being led, and supported, and bully-backed by that blind
"Hector, Impudence. *Reflect. on the* Essay on Crit. *Page* 26. 29. 30. ⟨"As there is
no Creature in Nature so venomous, there is nothing so stupid and so impotent as a hunch-back'd Toad."—Dennis.⟩
    It would be unjust not to add his Reasons for this Fury, they are so strong
and so coercive. "I regard him (saith he) as an *Enemy*, not so much to me, as to
"my King, to my Country, to my Religion, and to that Liberty which has been
"the sole felicity of my life. A vagary of fortune, who is sometimes pleased to be
"frolicksome, and the epidemick *Madness of the times*, have given him *Reputation*,
"and Reputation (as *Hobbs* says) is *Power*, and *that has made him dangerous*.
"Therefore I look on it as my duty to *King George*, whose faithful subject I am,
"to my *Country*, of which I have appeared a constant lover; to the *Laws*, under
"whose protection I have so long lived; and to the *Liberty* of my *Country*, more
"dear than life to me, of which I have now for forty years been a constant

"asserter, &c. I look upon it as my duty, I say, to do—*you shall see what*—to pull
"the Lion's skin from this little Ass, which popular error has thrown round
"him; and to show, that this Author who has been lately so much in vogue, has
"neither sense in his thoughts, nor english in his expressions. DENNIS, *Rem. on*
Hom. *Pref. p.* 2. *and p.* 91. *&c.*) ⟨Quoted mainly from the Preface. The words
"*you shall see what*" are Pope's own.⟩

Besides these publick-spirited reasons, Mr. *D.* had a *private one*; which by his
manner of expressing it in page 92, appears to have been equally strong. He
was even in bodily fear of his Life, from the machinations of the said Mr. *P.*
"The story (says he) is too long to be told, but who would be acquainted with
"it, may hear it from Mr. *Curll* my Bookseller.—However, what my reason has
"suggested to me, that I have with a just *confidence* said, in defiance of his two
"clandestine weapons, his *Slander* and his *Poyson*". Which last words of his Book
plainly discover, Mr. *D*—his suspicion was that of being *poysoned*, in like manner
as Mr. *Curl* had been before him. Of which fact see *A full and true account of a*
horrid and barbarous revenge by Poyson on the body of Edmund Curl; printed in 1716,
the year antecedent to that wherein these Remarks of Mr. *Dennis* were published.
But what puts it beyond all question, is a passage in a very warm treatise in
which Mr. *D.* was also concerned, price two pence, called, *A true character of*
Mr. Pope *and his writings, printed for S. Popping*, 1716. in the tenth page whereof
he is said "to have insulted people on those calamities and diseases, which he
"himself gave them by administring *Poyson* to them"; and is called (*p.* 4.) *a*
lurking waylaying coward, and a stabber in the dark. Which (with many other things
most lively set forth in that piece) must have render'd him a terror, not to Mr.
Dennis only, but to all Christian People.

For the rest, Mr. *John Dennis* was the Son of a Sadler in *London*, born in 1657.
He paid court to Mr. *Dryden*; and having obtained some correspondence with
Mr. *Wycherly* and Mr. *Congreve*, he immediately obliged the publick with their
Letters ⟨*Letters Upon several Occasions*, 1696⟩. He made himself known to the
Government by many admirable Schemes and Projects; which the Ministry,
for reasons best known to themselves, constantly kept private. For his character
as a writer, it is given us as follows. "Mr. *Dennis* is *excellent* at pindarick writings,
"*perfectly regular* in all his performances, and a person of *sound Learning*. That
"he is master of a great deal of *Penetration* and *Judgment*, his criticisms (par-
"ticularly on Prince *Arthur*) do sufficiently demonstrate." From the same account it also appears, that he writ Plays "more to get *Reputation* than *Money*."
DENNIS *of himself.* See *Jacob's* Lives of Dram. Poets, page 68. 69. *compared with*
page 286. ⟨On p. 286 Jacob printed an additional note on Dennis, which
begins: "In the Account this Gentleman sent, he omitted . . . a Play wrote by
him." Pope, of course, is insinuating that the eulogy of Dennis which he has
quoted above was written by Dennis himself. It was, in fact, one of Jacob's
boasts that many of the accounts in his *Lives* had been supplied by the subjects
themselves. Jacob, however, in a letter to Dennis, dated April 24, 1729, charac-
terizes Pope's statement as "a malicious and scandalous Insinuation, without
the least Foundation of Truth; for I do solemnly declare . . . that you knew

> In each she marks her image full exprest,   105
> But chief, in Tibbald's monster-breeding breast;

nothing at all thereof, till the Book was printed, and publish'd by the Book-seller." Dennis published Jacob's vindication of his modesty in *Remarks upon . . . the Dunciad*, 1729, pp. 44–9. For some facts about those "admirable Schemes and Projects" which Dennis submitted to the Government, see Hooker, i 506.⟩

106. *But chief in* Tibbald] *Lewis Tibbald* (as pronounced) or *Theobald* (as written) was bred an Attorney, and Son to an Attorney (says Mr. *Jacob*) of *Sittenburn* in *Kent*. ⟨In his *Battle of the Poets*, T. Cooke (a friend of Theobald's) indicates how the name really was pronounced by writing: "Friend to all Worth, and Theobald his name," where the metre demands a tri-syllable.⟩ He was Author of many forgotten Plays, Poems, and other pieces, and of several anonymous Letters in praise of them in *Mist*'s Journal. ⟨There is no other authority for this charge. In view of Theobald's character it is highly unlikely that he puffed his own work.⟩ He was concerned in a Paper call'd the *Censor*, and a translation of *Ovid*, as we find from Mr. *Dennis*'s Remarks on *Pope*'s *Homer*, *p*. 9. 10. "There is a notorious Ideot, one hight *Whachum*, who "from an under-spur-leather to the Law, is become an under-strapper to the "Play-house, who has lately burlesqu'd the Metamorphoses of *Ovid* by a vile "Translation, &*c*. This Fellow is concerned in an impertinent Paper called the "*Censor*". But notwithstanding this severe character, another Critick says of him "That he has given us some Pieces which met with approbation; and that "*the Cave of Poverty* is an excellent Poem." *Giles Jacob*'s *Lives of the Poets*, vol. 2. p. 211. He had once a mind to translate the *Odyssey*, the first Book whereof was printed in 1717 by *B. Lintott*, and probably may yet be seen at his Shop. What is still in memory, is a piece now about a year old ⟨a piece printed in 4to—*1735*⟩, it had the arrogant Title of *Shakespear Restored:* Of this he was so proud himself, as to say in one of *Mist*'s *Journals*, *June* 8. "That to expose any Errors in it was impracticable." ⟨i.e. June 8, 1728. The letter (which is signed "W.A.," and is probably not by Theobald himself) says of Pope, ". . . it being impracticable to expose any Errors in that Work, he was extravagantly witty on some earlier Productions of his Antagonist."⟩ And in another, *April* 27. "That whatever "care for the future might be taken either by Mr. *P*. or any other assistants, "he would still give above 500 Emendations that *shall* escape them *all*." ⟨"And as my *Remarks* upon the whole Works of *Shakespeare* shall clearly attend upon the Publication of his Edition, I'll venture to promise without Arrogance, that I'll give above *five hundred* more fair *Emendations*, that shall escape *him* and all his Assistants."⟩ During the space of two years, while Mr. *Pope* was preparing his Edition of *Shakespear*, and published Advertisements, requesting all lovers of the Author to contribute to a more perfect one; this Restorer (who had then some correspondence with him, and was solliciting favours by Letters) did wholly conceal his design, 'till after its publication ⟨*1729a–42*⟩ (which he was since not asham'd to own, in a *Daily Journal* of *Nov*. 26, 1728.) And then an outcry was made in the Prints, that our Author had joined with

Sees Gods with Dæmons in strange league ingage,
And earth, and heav'n, and hell her battles wage.
She ey'd the Bard, where supperless he sate,
And pin'd, unconscious of his rising fate;   110

the Bookseller to raise an *extravagant subscription*; in which he had no share, of which he had no knowledge, and against which he had publickly advertised in his own Proposals for *Homer* ⟨*1729b–42*⟩. Probably that proceeding elevated him to the Dignity he holds in this Poem, which he seems to deserve no other way better than his brethren; unless we impute it to the share he had in the Journals, cited among the *Testimonies of Authors* prefixed to this work. ⟨In the advertisements which Tonson inserted in the newspapers of 1721-2, the assistance he asked for his editor was the loan of "old editions," i.e. quartos of the various plays. Theobald's position was given in a letter to the *Daily Journal*, Nov. 26, 1728: "I must own, I consider'd the Labour of Twelve Years Study upon this Author of too much Value, rashly to give either the Profit of it to a *Bookseller*, whom I had no Obligations to; or the Credit of it to an *Editor* so likely to be thankless." To the second (1728) edition of his *Shakespeare*, (vol. viii), Pope had appended a list of Theobald's emendations under the title of "Various Readings, Guesses etc.," and complained of his failure to communicate them voluntarily, "when we, by publick Advertisements, did request the assistance of all Lovers of this Author."—According to Theobald, the only favours he had solicited were that Pope should take a few tickets for a theatrical benefit: Pope had replied a month later, saying that he had been out of Town. Later, Theobald had asked him to promote his subscription for his *Aeschylus*: Pope had promised to do what he could, but he had not brought in a single subscriber, nor subscribed himself.—*Daily Journal*, April 17, 1729.⟩

106. Tibbald*'s monster-breeding breast, Sees Gods with Dæmons*, &c.] This alludes to the extravagancies of the Farces of that author ⟨*1728a–42*⟩; in which he alone could properly be represented as successor to *Settle*, who had written *Pope Joan, St. George for England*, and other pieces for *Bartlemew-Fair*. ⟨*1729b–42*. It was in the second of these farces that he acted the dragon "in a case of green leather of his own invention." J. Nichols, *Lit. Anec.*, i 44*n*. See also A iii 281*n*.⟩ See book 3. vers. 229, &c. ⟨*1728a–42*⟩.

109.—*Supper-less he sate*] It is amazing how the sense of this line hath been mistaken by all the former Commentators, who most idly suppose it to imply, that the Hero of the Poem wanted a supper. ⟨"Mr *Theobald* would give me no Thanks for assuring the World that he sits as seldom Supperless as the Author of this curious Line."—*A Compleat Collection of all the Verses* . . . (1728), p. xii. Yet in 1731 Theobald was complaining to Warburton: "I never was acquainted with such Wants since I knew the Use of Money."—R. F. Jones, *Lewis Theobald*, p. 280.⟩ In truth a great absurdity! Not that we are ignorant that the Hero of *Homer*'s *Odyssey* is frequently in that circumstance, and therefore it can

Studious he sate, with all his books around,
Sinking from thought to thought, a vast profound!
Plung'd for his sense, but found no bottom there;
Then writ, and flounder'd on, in mere despair.
He roll'd his eyes that witness'd huge dismay,   115
Where yet unpawn'd, much learned lumber lay,
Volumes, whose size the space exactly fill'd;
Or which fond authors were so good to gild;
Or where, by sculpture made for ever known,
The page admires new beauties, not its own.   120

no way derogate from the grandeur of Epic Poem to represent such Hero under
a Calamity, to which the greatest not only of Criticks and Poets, but of Kings
and Warriors, have been subject. But much more refin'd, I will venture to say,
is the meaning of our author: It was to give us obliquely a curious precept,
or what *Bossu* calls a *disguised sentence*, that "Temperance is the life of Study."
The language of Poesy brings all into Action; and to represent a Critic encom-
past with books, but without a supper, is a picture which lively expresseth
how much the true Critic prefers the diet of the mind to that of the body, one
of which he always castigates and often totally neglects, for the greater improvement of the other. SCRIBLERUS ⟨"I am so far of Opinion that our Common
Dreams proceed from Repletion and Indigestion, that, to prevent this fantastic
Disturbance of my slumbers, I have for some Years accustomed myself to go
supperless to Bed."—Theobald in *The Censor*, Jan. 17, 1717 (quoted by R. F.
Jones, *Lewis Theobald*, p. 130). It is unlikely that Pope's use of "supperless"
is more than a coincidence.⟩

  112. *Sinking from thought to thought* ⟨Earl of Rochester, *Satire against Mankind*,
l. 18:

      Stumbling from thought to thought, falls headlong down.
                                        —Wakefield.⟩

  115. *He roll'd his eyes that witness'd huge dismay*] Milt. ⟨*Par. Lost*, i 56–7⟩.—
Round he throws his eyes That witness'd huge affliction and dismay. The progress of a
bad Poet in his thoughts being (like the progress of the Devil in *Milton*) thro' a
Chaos, might probably suggest this imitation. ⟨See *Par. Lost*, ii 927 ff.⟩

  118. *fond authors.... gild* ⟨See *Dunciad* B, i 138n. By "fond" Pope may imply
(1) loving, tender, (2) infatuated, foolish. Both senses may be intended.⟩

  120. —*Admires new beauties not its own.* Virg. Geo. 2 ⟨82⟩.
                Miraturq; novas frondes, & non sua poma.
⟨In T. Newcomb's *Bibliotheca* (1712), mention is made of finely bound books
by Bentley, Blackmore, Ogilby, and Withers—

          Begging their readers to dispense
          With pretty cuts instead of sense.⟩
  VERSE id. *&c.*] This library is divided into two parts; the one (his polite

Here swells the shelf with Ogilby the great:
There, stamp'd with arms, Newcastle shines compleat,
Here all his suff'ring brotherhood retire,
And 'scape the martyrdom of jakes and fire;
A Gothic Vatican! of Greece and Rome   125
Well-purg'd, and worthy Withers, Quarles, and Blome.

126 Withers . . . Blome] *W—y, W—s,* and *Bl— 1728a–c.*
W—s, Q—s, and *Bl— 1728d.*

learning) consists of those books which seem'd to be the models of his poetry, and are preferr'd for one of these three reasons (usual with collectors of Libraries) that they fitted the shelves, or were gilded for shew, or adorned with pictures: The other class our author calls solid Learning; old bodies of Philosophy, old Commentators, old English Printers, or old English Translations; all very voluminous, and fit to erect Altars to Dulness.

121.—Ogilby *the great*] *John Ogilby* ⟨1600–76⟩ was one, who from a late initiation into literature, made such a progress as might well stile him the *Prodigy* of his time! sending into the world so many *large Volumes!* His translations of *Homer* and *Virgil, done to the life,* and with *such excellent Sculptures!* and (what added great grace to his works) he printed them all on *special good Paper,* and in a *very good Letter.* WINSTANLY, *Lives of Poets.* ⟨pp. 195–6. The title-pages of Ogilby's translations of the *Iliad* and the *Odyssey* announced that they were "Adorn'd with Sculpture."—According to Spence (p. 276), "Ogilby's translation of Homer was one of the first large poems that ever Mr. Pope read; and he still spoke of the pleasure it then gave him, with a sort of rapture, only in reflecting on it."⟩

122. *There, stamp'd with arms,* Newcastle *shines compleat*] The *Dutchess of Newcastle* was one who busied herself in the ravishing delights of Poetry; leaving to posterity in print three *ample Volumes* of her studious endeavours. WINSTANLY, *ibid.* ⟨pp. 188–9⟩. *Langbaine* reckons up eight Folio's of her Grace's; which were usually adorn'd with gilded Covers, and had her Coat of Arms upon them. ⟨*An Account of the English Dramatick Poets,* 1691, p. 394. Even Langbaine underestimates her productiveness. The DNB lists twelve separate works in folio.⟩

125. *Vatican* ⟨The word was frequently used for the Vatican Library. Cf. J. Norris (1694): "I . . . would not part with his Book for half a Vatican."—OED.⟩

126.—*Worthy* Withers, Quarles, *and* Blome] It was printed in the surreptitious Editions, *W—ly, W—s,* who were Persons eminent for good life; the one writ the Life of Christ in verse; the other some valuable pieces in the lyrick kind on pious subjects. The line is here restor'd according to its Original.

⟨*1729a–d, 1751.* In the EC MS. the reading given is "Withers $\left. {Quarles \atop Watts} \right\}$ and

> But high above, more solid Learning shone,
> The Classicks of an Age that heard of none;
> There Caxton slept, with Wynkin at his side,

Bloom." *W—y* is the Rev. Samuel Wesley, 1662–1735. Pope had probably no grievance against him, and introduced him only as a poetaster. He had already been satirized as such by Garth in the *Dispensary*, and by Swift in *The Battle of the Books*. Since Pope is thinking of works remarkable only for their illustrations, he may have had in mind Wesley's *History of the Old and New Testament attempted in Verse*, which was "adorned with Three Hundred and Thirty Sculptures." *The Life of our Blessed Lord*, a poem in ten books embellished with sixty copper-plates, was published in 1693. By 1730 Pope (who was friendly with Wesley's eldest son) was trying to interest Swift in Wesley's forthcoming work on Job (EC vii 184). Mr. Norman Ault has shown that Samuel Wesley the Younger resented Pope's sneering reference to his father, and probably complained to Pope directly, or through the Earl of Oxford. See vol. vi, pp. 294 f., "Upon a piece of News in Mist."—*W—s* is Isaac Watts (1674–1748), one of the most popular poets of his day. It was probably his popularity with humble readers that landed him in the *Dunciad*. According to one account, Watts's name was removed on his own "serious, though gentle, remonstrance" (J. Nichols, *Lit. Anec.*, v 218); according to another, at the request of Jonathan Richardson, the painter, a friend of both Watts and Pope (*Letters by Several Eminent Persons Deceased*, 1772, i 87).⟩

George Withers was a great pretender to poetical zeal against the vices of the times, and abused the greatest Personages in power, which brought upon him *frequent correction*. The *Marshalsea* and *Newgate* were no strangers to him. WINSTANLY ⟨pp. 165–6⟩. *Quarles* was as dull a writer, but an honester man. *Blome's* books are remarkable for their cuts. ⟨George Wither, or Withers (1588–1667), poet and pamphleteer. In writing contemptuously of Withers Pope was only following a tradition already well-established: he was not making an individual or peculiar judgment. Withers was frequently bracketed with Quarles as a type of feeble writer. Ayre (ii 192) refers to "the Children's Poet, Mr. Withers," and says of him and Quarles, "Their Writings were always recommended to all under twelve Years of Age, especially Female, by the three beforementioned great Wits" (i.e. Atterbury, Swift, and Pope).— Francis Quarles (1592–1644), the author of *Emblemes* (1635) and of much other religious verse. Quarles was popular with the lower orders, but generally despised by the cultured reader. The *Emblemes*, of course, owed much of their popularity to their quaint illustrations.—Richard Blome (d. 1705) was the publisher, and possibly the compiler, of numerous folios on heraldry, genealogy, geography, etc. These works were illustrated with "mapps and figures." Contempt for Blome was already a convention. See *Modern Philology*, xxx 371.⟩

129. *Caxton*] A Printer in the time of *Edw.* 4. *Rich.* 3. and *Henry* 7. *Wynkin de Word*, his successor in that of *Henry* 7 and 8. The former translated into prose

5*

One clasp'd in wood, and one in strong cow-hide.   130
There sav'd by spice, like mummies, many a year,
Old Bodies of Philosophy appear.
De Lyra here a dreadful front extends,
And there, the groaning shelves Philemon bends.
   Of these twelve volumes, twelve of amplest size,   135
Redeem'd from tapers and defrauded pyes,
Inspir'd he seizes: These an altar raise:

133 here] there *1728a–f, 1729b–42.*
134 there,] here, *1729b–42.*

Virgil's Æneis as a History; of which he speaks in his Proeme in a very singular manner, as of a book hardly known. *Vid. Append.* Tibbald quotes a rare passage from him in *Mist's Journal* of *March* 16, 1728. concerning a *straunge and mervayllouse beaste called Sagittarye,* which he would have *Shakespear* to mean rather than *Teucer,* the Archer celebrated by *Homer.* ⟨See Appendix iii, p. 213*n.* Pope seems to have been particularly annoyed at this exposure of Theobald's: he returns to his ridicule of Caxton and Wynkin in his notes to i 162, 166, 212. From *1735a* on, Pope omitted the Caxton Appendix, and printed instead an extended quotation in this note, viz. "Happened that to my hande . . . Vyrgyle made in metre."⟩

   131. *sav'd by spice* ⟨If this is the old joke about unwanted books being torn to pieces to wrap up spice (cf. *Ep.* ii i 418) it hardly seems to apply here.⟩

   133. *Nich. de Lyra,* or *Harpsfeld,* a very voluminous Commentator, whose works in five vast Folio's were printed in 1472. ⟨Pope has confused two men who lived two centuries apart. Nicholas de Lyra (d. 1340) was the author of the "five vast Folio's." His works were frequently reprinted in the fifteenth century. Nicholas Harpsfield, or Harpesfeld (1519?–75), theologian, wrote, among other works, *Historia Anglicana Ecclesiastica,* published in 1662.⟩

   134. *Philemon Holland,* Dr. in Physick. He translated *so many books,* that a man would think he had done *nothing else,* insomuch that he might be call'd *Translator General of his age.* The books alone of his turning into English, are sufficient to make a *Country Gentleman a compleat Library.* WINSTANLY ⟨pp. 146–7⟩. Cf. Gay's *Trivia,* ii 553:
      The bending shelves with ponderous scholiasts groan.⟩

   136. *Redeem'd from tapers* ⟨Garth, *Dispensary,* iv 133–4:
      Hither, retriev'd from *Cooks* and *Grocers,* come
      M—— Works entire, and endless Reams of *Bl——m.*
                    —Wakefield.
The thought is almost a commonplace at this period.—Theobald's pyre differs characteristically from that raised by the Baron in *The Rape of the Lock,* Canto ii. Both sacrifices are intended to parody those of classical epic.⟩

An hecatomb of pure, unsully'd lays
That altar crowns: A folio Common-place
Founds the whole pyle, of all his works the base;   140
Quarto's, Octavo's, shape the less'ning pyre,
And last, a little Ajax tips the spire.
     Then he. "Great Tamer of all human art!
First in my care, and nearest at my heart:
Dulness! whose good old cause I yet defend,   145
With whom my Muse began, with whom shall end!
O thou, of business the directing soul,
To human heads like byass to the bowl,
143 human] Wit and *1735ab*.

---

138. *hecatomb* ⟨Cf. G. Daniel, *Works* (ed. A. B. Grosart, 1878), i 85:
     Whole Hecatombes of Tribute Rhimes.
The epithet "unsully'd" is probably intended to refer to the sacrifices in
classical epic: the purity of the heifers offered on the altar is often stressed. But
Theobald's poems were also "unsully'd" in the sense that they had never been
thumbed by any reader. Cf. Cibber's sacrifice of his Works "unstain'd, untouch'd, and yet in maiden sheets" at B i 229.⟩
     142. *A little* Ajax] In *duodecimo*, translated from *Sophocles* by *Tibbald*. ⟨*1728a–42*.
—It is doubtful if this translation (1714) was by Theobald at all. He was under
contract to Lintot to translate four plays of Sophocles, but the *Ajax* was not one
of those. It is not attributed to him in any other contemporary account of his
work. Lintot advertised it (*Daily Courant*, March 15, 1714) as "Translated
from the Greek with Notes, by the best Hands," and again (*Post-Boy*, April
8–10, 1714) as "revis'd and corrected, with Notes: by N. Rowe Esq." Theobald
may have assisted only with the notes.⟩
     145. *good old cause* ⟨To the eighteenth-century reader this phrase connoted
the cause of the Puritans. It is unlikely, however, that Pope is here identifying
Dulness with Dissent. Theobald, at any rate, was not a Dissenter.⟩
     146. *With whom my Muse began, with whom shall end*] Virg. *Ecl.* 8 ⟨11⟩.
A te principium, tibi desinet ⟨*desinam*⟩—from *Theoc.* ⟨Id. xvii 1.⟩
     So *Horace* ⟨Ep. 1 i, i⟩,
Prima dicte mihi, summa dicende camœna.
     ⟨Mr Norman Ault has drawn my attention to Pope's *Iliàd* ix 132:
     With thee my cares began, in thee must end.
Cf. also A ii 51.⟩
     148. *like byas to the bowl* ⟨*Mac Flecknoe*, 189–90:
     This is that boasted Byas of thy mind,
     By which, one way, to dullness, 'tis inclined.

Which as more pond'rous makes their aim more true,
Obliquely wadling to the mark in view.   150
O ever gracious to perplex'd mankind!
Who spread a healing mist before the mind,
And, lest we err by Wit's wild, dancing light,
Secure us kindly in our native night.
Ah! still o'er Britain stretch that peaceful wand,   155
Which lulls th' Helvetian and Batavian land.
Where rebel to thy throne if Science rise,
She does but shew her coward face and dies:
There, thy good Scholiasts with unweary'd pains
. Make Horace flat, and humble Maro's strains;   160
Here studious I unlucky moderns save,
Nor sleeps one error in its father's grave,
Old puns restore, lost blunders nicely seek,

152 spread] spreads *1728c*.   154 night] *night 1728a–f*.
157 rebel . . . if] 'gainst thy throne if rebel *1728a–f*.

In touching up Wycherley's *Panegyric of Dulness* for publication, Pope had
already used the same simile:
> The Poize of Dulness to the heavy Skull,
> Is like the Leaden Byass to the Bowl,
> Which, as more pond'rous, makes its Aim more true,
> And guides it surer to the Mark in view.

—*The Posthumous Works of William Wycherley, Esq.*, 1728, vol. ii, p. 14. I am
indebted to Mr Norman Ault for drawing my attention to this second volume
of the *Posthumous Works*, 1729. See further "Lines Added to Wycherley's Poems"
in vol. vi.⟩

162–3. *Nor sleeps one error—Old puns restore, lost blunders, &c.*] As where he
laboured to prove *Shakespear* guilty of terrible *Anacronisms*, or low *Conundrums*,
which Time had cover'd; and conversant in such authors as *Caxton* and
Wynkin, rather than in *Homer* or *Chaucer*. ⟨Pope's misplaced efforts to remove
Shakespeare's anachronisms were exposed by Theobald in the Appendix to
Shakespeare Restored, pp. 134–5.⟩ Nay so far had he lost his reverence to this
incomparable author, as to say in print, *He deserved to be whipt*. ⟨"But indeed, if
ever the Poet deserved Whipping for low and indecent Ribaldry, it was for this
passage." (i.e. *Hamlet*, III ii 105).—*Shakespeare Restored*, p. 87.⟩ An insolence which
nothing sure can parallel! but that of *Dennis*, who can be proved to have
declared before Company, that *Shakespear was a Rascal. O tempora! O mores!*
SCRIBLERUS. ⟨This accusation had already been made in *The Narrative of
Dr. Robert Norris. See Pope's Prose*, i 166.⟩

And crucify poor Shakespear once a week.
For thee I dim these eyes, and stuff this head,   165
With all such reading as was never read;
For thee supplying, in the worst of days,
Notes to dull books, and prologues to dull plays;

164. *And crucify poor* Shakespear *once a week*]   For some time, once a week or fortnight, he printed in *Mist's Journal* a single remark or poor conjecture on some *word* or *pointing* of *Shakespear*, ⟨*1729a–42*⟩ either in his own name, or in letters to himself as from others without name. Upon these somebody made this Epigram,

> '*Tis generous* Tibald! *in thee and thy brothers,*
> *To help us thus to read the works of others:*
> *Never for this can just returns be shown;*
> *For who will help us e'er to read thy own?*

⟨*1729d–42*. Only two letters in Theobald's name on the subject of Shakespeare had appeared in *Mist's Journal* before the publication of the *Dunciad*.⟩

He since publish'd an Edition of Shakespeare with numerous alterations of the Text, upon bare *Conjectures*, either of his own, or of any others who sent them to him. To which Mr. *M.* ⟨Mallet⟩ alludes in those Verses of his very fine poem on that occasion ⟨*On Verbal Criticism*⟩.

> He with low Industry goes gleaning on,
> From good, from bad, from mean, neglecting none:
> His brother Bookworm so, on shelf or stall,
> Will feed alike on *Woolston* or on *Paul* . . .
> Such the grave Bird in Northern Seas is found
> (Whose name a Dutchman only knows to sound)
> Where'er the King of fish moves on before,
> This humble friend attends from shore to shore;
> With eye still earnest, and with bill declin'd,
> He picks up what his Patron drops behind;
> With such choice cates his palate to regale,
> And is the careful Tibbald of a Whale.

⟨*1735a–42*. In the Preface to his Shakespeare (1733) Theobald acknowledges the assistance he had received from various scholars, including "my most ingenious and ever-respected Friend, the Reverend Mr. William Warburton." See J. Nichols, *Lit. Ill.*, ii 730 ff.⟩

166. *With all such reading as was never read*]   Such as *Caxton* above-mentioned, the three destructions of *Troy* by *Wynkin*, and other like classicks.

168. *Notes to dull books, and prologues to dull plays*]   As to *Cook's Hesiod*, where sometimes a note, and sometimes even *half* a note, are carefully owned by him: And to *Moore's Comedy* of the *Rival Modes*, and other authors of the same rank: These were people who writ about the year 1726. ⟨James Moore Smythe's

For thee explain a thing till all men doubt it,
And write about it, Goddess, and about it;   170
So spins the silkworm small its slender store,
And labours, 'till it clouds itself all o'er.
Not that my quill to Critiques was confin'd,
My Verse gave ampler lessons to mankind;
So gravest precepts may successless prove,   175
But sad examples never fail to move.
As forc'd from wind-guns, lead itself can fly,
And pond'rous slugs cut swiftly thro' the sky;
As clocks to weight their nimble motion owe,
The wheels above urg'd by the load below;   180
Me, Emptiness and Dulness could inspire,
And were my Elasticity and Fire.

173 quill] pen *1728a–c*.   Critiques] criticks *1728a–c*.
175 gravest] written *1728a–c*; graver *1728de*.
182 Elasticity] Elasticity, *1728a–c*.

comedy, *The Rival Modes*, was first performed on Jan. 27, 1727, at Drury Lane.—
Thomas Cooke's translation of Hesiod was published in 1728. Theobald's
contribution consisted of two entire notes, and four parts of notes. These were
not, of course, "carefully owned" by Theobald; they had been quite properly
ascribed to him by Cooke. Cooke's acknowledgement, "The rest of the note
by Mr. Theobald," is parodied by Pope in his note to i 48.⟩
    169. *For thee explain a thing* ⟨Cf. *E. on C.*, 117:
                And those explain the meaning quite away.⟩
    175. *So gravest precepts* ⟨Cf. Wycherley's *To a Doctor of Physick* (revised by
Pope), *The Posthumous Works of . . . Wycherley*, vol. ii, p. 69:
                So when the noblest Precepts can't prevail
                To mend us, sad Examples never fail.
See also Pope's letter to Caryll, June 25, 1711.⟩
    177. *As forc'd from wind-guns*] The Thought of these four verses is found in a
poem of our author's of a very early date (namely writ at Fourteen Years old
and soon after printed, intitled, *To the Author of a Poem call'd* Successio,) where
they stand thus,
                The heaviest Muse the swiftest course has gone,
                As Clocks run fastest when most Lead is on.
                So forc'd from Engines Lead itself can fly,
                And pond'rous Slugs move nimbly thro' the Sky.
⟨*1735a–42*. The lines were used, with some minor alterations, to touch up
Wycherley's *Panegyrick of Dulness.*—*The Posthumous Works of . . . Wycherley*, ii 14.⟩

Had heav'n decreed such works a longer date,
Heav'n had decreed to spare the Grubstreet-state.
But see great Settle to the dust descend,   185
And all thy cause and empire at an end!
Cou'd Troy be sav'd by any single hand,
His gray-goose-weapon must have made her stand.
But what can I? my Flaccus cast aside,
Take up th' Attorney's (once my better) Guide?   190
Or rob the Roman geese of all their glories,

188 His] That *1735ab*.   190 Guide?] *guide? 1728a–c; Guide? 1728d–f.*
191 their] the *1742*.

See further "Lines Added to Wycherley's Poems" and "To the Author of . . .
Successio" in vol. vi.⟩
  183. *Had heav'n decreed such works a longer date,* &c.] Virg. Æn. 2 ⟨641–2⟩.
        Me si cælicolæ voluissent ducere vitam
        Has mihi servassent sedes.—
⟨In Dryden's translation:
        Had Heav'n decreed that I shou'd Life enjoy,
        Heav'n had decreed to save unhappy *Troy*.
Pitt's translation is even closer to Pope's parody:
        For me had Heav'n decreed a longer date,
        Heav'n had preserv'd for me the Dardan state.⟩
  187. *Could* Troy *be saved.—His gray-goose-weapon*] Virg. ibid. ⟨291–2⟩.
      —Si Pergama dextra
    Defendi possent, etiam hac defensa fuissent.
  189. *My* Flaccus] A familiar manner of speaking used by modern Criticks
of a favourite Author. Mr. *T.* might as justly speak thus of *Horace*, as a French
wit did of *Tully* seeing his works in a library, Ah! mon cher Ciceron! Je le connois
bien: c'est le même que Marc Tulle. ⟨Theobald was at one time under contract to
Lintot to translate the Satires and Epistles of Horace into English verse (J.
Nichols, *Lit. Ill.*, ii 707). It is possible that Pope had learnt of this fact from
Lintot himself, and intended an allusion to it here.⟩
  190. *Take up th'*Attorney's Guide] In allusion to his first profession of an
Attorney. ⟨The italics of the 1728 editions suggest that Pope may have had
some particular book in mind. There were a number of "Attorney's Guides" in
circulation, e.g. *The Practising Attorney: or Lawyer's Office*, but none, I believe,
actually called *The Attorney's Guide*.⟩
  191. *Or rob the* Roman *geese, &c.*] Relates to the well-known story of the
geese that saved the Capitol, of which *Virgil, Æn.* 8 ⟨655–6⟩. *Atq; hic auratis
volitans argenteus anser Porticibus, Gallos in limine adesse canebat.* ⟨In Dryden's translation: "The silver goose . . . by her cackle, sav'd the state."⟩ A passage

And save the state by cackling to the Tories?
Yes, to my Country I my pen consign,
Yes, from this moment, mighty Mist! am thine,
And rival, Curtius! of thy fame and zeal,   195
O'er head and ears plunge for the publick weal.
Adieu my children! better thus expire
Un-stall'd, unsold; thus glorious mount in fire
Fair without spot; than greas'd by grocer's hands,
Or shipp'd with Ward to ape and monkey lands,   200

200 Ward] *W—   1728a–e.   W—d 1728 f.*

I have always suspected. Who sees not the Antithesis of *auratis* and *argenteus*
to be unworthy the Virgilian Majesty? and what absurdity to say, a Goose
sings? canebat? Virgil gives a contrary character of the voice of this silly Bird, in
Ecl. 9 ⟨36⟩.—*argutos* interstrepere *anser olores.* Read it therefore *adesse strepebat.*
And why *auratis porticibus?* Does not the very verse preceding this inform us,
Romuleo recens horrebat regia culmo? Is this *Thatch* in one line, and *Gold* in another,
consistent? I scruple not (*repugnantibus omnibus manuscriptis*) to correct it, *auritis.*
Horace uses the same epithet in the same sense ⟨*Od.* I xii 11–12⟩,
                    —Auritas *fidibus canoris*
                    Ducere quercus.
And to say, that *Walls have Ears,* is common even to a proverb. SCRIBL.

194. *Mighty* Mist!] *Nathaniel Mist* was publisher of a famous Tory Paper
(see notes on l. ⟨lib.⟩ 3.) in which this Author was sometimes permitted to have a
part. ⟨Theobald denied that he had taken any part in the political side of the
paper: his contributions were confined to learning or entertainment.—*Mist's
Journal,* June 22, 1728. The only references to Mist or his journal in Book iii
occur in the notes to ll. 28, 272, 286. For Mist, see Biog. App.⟩

195. *Curtius* ⟨M. Curtius, the Roman youth who leapt, armed and mounted,
into the gulf which had opened in the Forum, *circa* 360 B.C.⟩

197. *Adieu my Children!*] This is a tender and passionate Apostrophe to his
own Works which he is going to sacrifice, agreeable to the nature of man in
great affliction, and reflecting like a parent, on the many miserable fates to
which they would otherwise be subject.
                    —*Felix Priameïa virgo!*
                    Jussa mori: quæ sortitus non pertulit ullos,
                    Nec victoris heri tetigit captiva cubile!
                    Nos patriâ incensâ, diversa per æquora vectæ, &c.
                              Virg. Æn. 3, ⟨321, 323–5⟩.

199. *greas'd by grocer's hands* ⟨The idea is a commonplace in the period.
Cf. Oldham, *A Satyr,* l. 101:
          But now are damn'd to wrapping Drugs, and Wares.⟩

200. Ward] *Edward Ward,* a very voluminous Poet in Hudibrastick Verse,

Or wafting ginger, round the streets to go,
And visit alehouse where ye first did grow."
With that, he lifted thrice the sparkling brand,
And thrice he dropt it from his quiv'ring hand:
Then lights the structure, with averted eyes;   205
The rowling smokes involve the sacrifice.
The opening clouds disclose each work by turns,
Now flames old Memnon, now Rodrigo burns,
In one quick flash see Proserpine expire,

201 go,] run, *1735ab*.   202 did grow.] begun. *1735ab*.

but best known by the *London Spy*, in Prose. He has of late Years kept a publick house in the City (but in a genteel way) and with his wit, humour, and good liquor (Ale) afforded his guests a pleasurable entertainment, especially those of the High-Church party. JACOB *Lives of Poets* ⟨i.e. *The Poetical Register*⟩ vol. 2. p. 225. Great numbers of his works are yearly sold into the Plantations ⟨*1729a–51*⟩. He wrote a wretched thing against our Author, call'd *Durgen*.— ⟨*1729d–51*. The word "Ale," inserted here parenthetically, is Pope's addition to Jacob.⟩ Ward in a Book call'd *Apollo's Maggot*, declar'd this account to be a great Falsity, protesting that his publick house was not in the City, but in Moor-fields. ⟨*1735a–51*. See *Apollo's Maggot*, pp. 30–1, 37–8. For Ward, see Biog. App. For "good liquor (Ale)" see pp. 198 and 467.⟩

202. *And visit Alehouse*] *Waller* on the Navy ⟨*To the King on his Navy*, 25–26⟩.
    Those towers of Oak o'er fertile plains may go,
    And visit Mountains where they once did grow.

203. *He lifted thrice the sparkling brand, And thrice he dropt it*] *Ovid of Althea* on the like occasion, burning her Offspring, Met. 8 ⟨462–3⟩.
    Tum conata quater flammis imponere torrem,
    Cæpta quater tenuit.—

205. *with averted eyes* ⟨Virgil, *Aen.* vi 223–4:
        et subiectam, more parentum
        Aversi, tenuere facem.—Wakefield.⟩

206. ⟨Cf. Dryden's *Aeneid*, viii 141:
        Thick Clouds of rowling Smoke involve the Sky.⟩

208. *Now flames old* Memnon, *&c.*] Virg. Æn. 2 ⟨310–12⟩.
        —*Jam Deiphobi dedit ampla ruinam*
        Vulcano superante, domus; jam proximus ardet
        Ucalegon.

208–9. *Memnon . . . Rodrigo . . . Proserpine*] *Memnon*, a Hero in the Persian Princess, very apt to take fire, as appears by these lines with which he begins the Play.
        By heav'n it fires my frozen blood with rage,
        And makes it scald my aged Trunk—

And last, his own cold Æschylus took fire.   210
Then gush'd the tears, as from the Trojan's eyes
When the last blaze sent Ilion to the skies.

⟨This tragedy of Theobald's, published in 1717, was "writ, and acted, [in 1711] before I was full Nineteen Years Old; and I expect that Age shall stand as a Plea for many Errors with the candid Reader."—Preface to *The Persian Princess*.⟩ *Rodrigo*, the chief personage of the Perfidious Brother, a play written between *T*. and a Watchmaker. ⟨This tragedy was published in 1715 as being "by Mr. Theobald." The following year Henry Meystayer, a watchmaker, published a different version of the play with a dedication to Theobald, in which he claimed that the play was substantially his. Theobald, while admitting that Meystayer brought him the story "wrought up into Something design'd to be call'd Tragedy," insisted that the play as it left his hands had been almost entirely re-written.—The hero is called Roderick, not Rodrigo.⟩ The *Rape* of *Proserpine*, one of the Farces of this Author, in which *Ceres* sets fire to a Corn-field, which endangered the burning of the Play-house. ⟨At the close of Scene V, the following stage-direction occurs: "Ceres here snatches flaming Branches from her Train, and sets the Corn etc. on Fire."—This pantomime was acted at Covent Garden in 1725.⟩

210. *His own cold Æschylus*] He had been (to use an expression of our Poet), *about Æschylus* for ten years, and had received Subscriptions for the same, but then went *about* other Books. The character of this tragic Poet is Fire and Boldness in a high degree; but our Author supposes it to be very much cooled by the translation; Upon sight of a specimen of it, was made this Epigram,

> Alas! poor *Æschylus!* unlucky Dog!
> Whom once a *Lobster* kill'd, and now a *Log*.

But this is a grievous error, for *Æschylus* was not slain by the fall of a Lobster on his head, but of a Tortoise, *teste* Val. Max. l. 9. cap. 12. SCRIBL. ⟨Theobald contracted with Lintot in 1713 to translate Aeschylus for ten guineas (J. Nichols, *Lit. Ill.*, ii 707). Later he issued proposals to publish the tragedies by subscription, but in his *Shakespeare Restored* (1726), and again in his edition of Shakespeare (1733) he was apologizing for their non-appearance. They never appeared; but according to Jacob (*Poetical Register*, i 259) Theobald had completed his translation. See R. F. Jones, *Lewis Theobald*, pp. 3–4, 201. According to *The Grub-Street Journal*, No. 40, Oct. 8, 1730, his proposals were dated Nov. 1723, "which asserted the Work to be then *ready for the Press*, and the *whole to be deliver'd the Easter following*." See also A iii 311n.⟩

212. *When the last blaze . . .*] See Virgil, *Aen.* 2, where I would advise the reader to peruse the story of *Troy*'s destruction, rather than in *Wynkin*. ⟨Cf. i 129n.⟩ But I caution him alike in both, to beware of a most grievous error, that of thinking it was brought about by I know not what *Trojan Horse*; there never having been any such thing. For first it was not *Trojan*, being made by the *Greeks*, and secondly it was not a Horse, but a Mare. This is clear from

Rowz'd by the light, old Dulness heav'd the head,
Then snatch'd a sheet of Thulè from her bed;
Sudden she flies, and whelms it o'er the pyre: 215
Down sink the flames, and with a hiss expire.
   Her ample presence fills up all the place;
A veil of fogs dilates her awful face;
Great in her charms! as when on Shrieves and May'rs
She looks, and breathes her self into their airs.   220
She bids him wait her to the sacred Dome;

---

many verses in *Virgil*,

            Uterum *armato milite complent*—
            Inclusos Utero *Danaos*—

Can a horse be said *Utero gerere?* Again,

            Uteroq; *recusso Insonuere cavæ*—
            Atq; utero *sonitum quater arma dedere.*

Nay is it not expressly said,

            Scandit fatalis machina muros
            Foeta *armis*—

How is it possible the word *fœta* can agree with a horse? and indeed can it be conceived, that the chaste and Virgin Goddess *Pallas* would employ her self in forming and fashioning the Male of that species? But this shall be proved to a Demonstration in our *Virgil Restored*. SCRIBLER. ⟨*1729b–51*⟩.

   214. *Thulè*] An unfinished Poem of that name, of which one sheet was printed fifteen Years ago; by *A. Ph.* a Northern Author. It is an usual method of putting out a fire, to cast wet sheets upon it. Some Criticks have been of opinion, that this sheet was of the nature of the *Asbestos*, which cannot be consumed by fire; but I rather think it only an allegorical allusion to the coldness and heaviness of the writing. ⟨*Thule*, by Ambrose Philips, was published in the *Freethinker*, No. IX (1718). Philips is called "a Northern Author" because Pope wishes to suggest that he is a cold writer. Cf. A i 103*n*. But the phrase makes a punning allusion to *Thule*, and perhaps to his well-known "winter-piece," *An Epistle to the Earl of Dorset*. For Philips, see Biog. App., vols. iv, v.⟩

   219. *Great in her charms! as when on Shrieves and May'rs*
     She looks, and breathes herself into their airs]
             Alma parens confessa Deam; qualisq; videri
             Cælicolis & quanta solet—Virg. Æn. 2.

⟨591–2. Cf. Dryden's translation:
          Great in her Charms, as when the Gods above
          She looks, and breaths her self into their Love.⟩
          —*Et lætos oculis afflarat honores.*—Id. Æn. 1 ⟨591⟩.

   221. —*The sacred* Dome] The *Cave of Poverty* above-mentioned; where he no sooner enters, but he Reconnoitres the place of his original; as *Plato* says the

Well-pleas'd he enter'd, and confess'd his Home:
So spirits ending their terrestrial race,
Ascend, and recognize their native place:
Raptur'd, he gazes round the dear retreat,   225
And in sweet numbers celebrates the seat.
    Here to her Chosen all her works she shows;
Prose swell'd to verse, Verse loitring into prose;
How random Thoughts now meaning chance to find,
Now leave all memory of sense behind: 230
How Prologues into Prefaces decay,
And these to Notes are fritter'd quite away.
How Index-learning turns no student pale,
Yet holds the Eel of science by the Tail.
How, with less reading than makes felons 'scape,   235

232 these] those *1728a–d.*

Spirits shall do, at their entrance into the celestial Regions. His Dialogue of the
Immortality of the Soul was translated by *T.* in the familiar modern stile of
Prithee Phædo, and *For God's sake Socrates:* printed for *B. Lintot,* 1713. ⟨Theobald
in his Preface excused the familiar style: "I dare not pretend to have done the
Original Justice in my Phrase, but . . . his Conceptions may strike the Mind as
powerfully, as if they were cloath'd in a more stately or florid Habit."⟩

226. *And in sweet numbers celebrates the seat*] He writ a Poem call'd the *Cave of
Poverty* ⟨*1728a*⟩, which concludes with a very extraordinary Wish, "That some
"great Genius, or man of distinguished merit may be *starved,* in order to cele-
"brate her power, and describe her Cave." It was printed in octavo, 1715.
⟨i.e. 1714. The words quoted are not, as might be supposed, Theobald's.
Pope is paraphrasing—and in doing so travesties—stanza cxx of Theobald's
poem.⟩

231. *Prefaces* ⟨"Prefaces have been daily growing upon us; and have, of late
years, arriv'd at such a monstrous size, that they sometimes equal . . . the
Book itself."—*Grub-Street Journal,* Jan. 29, 1736.⟩

233. *Index-learning* ⟨"The most accomplished way of using Books at present
is . . . to get a thorough Insight into the *Index,* by which the whole Book is
governed and turned, like *Fishes* by the *Tail.*"—Swift, *A Tale of a Tub,* Sect.
vii.⟩

235. *makes felons 'scape* ⟨"Benefit of clergy" was still available for criminals.
By an act of 5 Anne c. 6, it was allowed without the traditional reading test;
but as the century advanced the number of crimes for which the privilege
could be claimed became steadily smaller.—See *Johnson's England,* ed. A. S.
Turberville, 1933, i 314–15.⟩

Less human genius than God gives an ape,
Small thanks to France and none to Rome or Greece,
A past, vamp'd, future, old, reviv'd, new piece,
'Twixt Plautus, Fletcher, Congreve, and Corneille,
Can make a Cibber, Johnson, or Ozell.   240
    The Goddess then o'er his anointed head,
With mystic words, the sacred Opium shed;
And lo! her Bird (a monster of a fowl!

240 Cibber. . . Ozell.] *C—r, Jo—n,* or *O—ll. 1728a–f.*

---

240. *Can make a* Cibber] Mr. *Colly Cibber,* an Author and Actor; of a good share of wit, and *uncommon vivacity,* which are much improved by the *conversation* he enjoys, which is of the *best.* JACOB *Lives of* Dram. Poets. p. 8. Besides 2 Volumes of Plays in 4°, he has made up and translated several others. Mr. *Jacob* omitted to remark, that he is particularly admirable in Tragedy. ⟨For Cibber's plays, see *Dunciad* B, i 250, and for Cibber, see Biog. App.⟩

240. *—Johnson] Charles Johnson* ⟨1679–1748⟩, famous for writing a Play every season, and for being at *Button's* every day. He had probably thriven better in his Vocation had he been a small matter leaner. He may justly be called a Martyr to obesity, and to have fallen a victim to the rotundity of his parts. CHA. of the TIMES, printed by CURL, pag. 19. ⟨On Curl's pointing out that this pamphlet was in fact "Printed for *Read* in White-Fryars" (*The Curliad,* p. 31), Pope was compelled to omit his name.⟩ Some of his Plays are Love in a Forest (*Shakespear's* As you like it) Wife's Relief (*Shirley's* Gamester) The Victim (*Racine's* Iphigenia) The Sultaness (*Racine's* Bajazet, the prologue of which abused Dr. *Arbuthnot,* Mr. *Pope,* and Mr. *Gay.*) The *Cobler* of *Preston,* his own. ⟨Yet even this play is apparently based on *The Taming of the Shrew.*—The offending lines in *The Sultaness* (1717) were the following:

> Such Wags have been, who boldly durst adventure
> To Club a Farce by Tripartite-Indenture:
> But, let them share their Dividend of Praise,
> And their own Fools-Cap wear, instead of Bays.

Those lines were given added prominence when they were quoted on the title-page of Breval's *The Confederates.* For Johnson, see Biog. App.⟩

240. *Cibber, Johnson* ⟨The EC MS. has two variants here, viz. "Cibber, Bladen," and "Shadwell, Welsted." "Bladen" is almost certainly Col. Martin Bladen, author of *Solon.* But see *Dunciad* B, iv 560*n.*⟩

240. *—And* Ozell] Mr. *John Ozell,* if we credit Mr. *Jacob,* did go to School in "*Leicestershire,*" where *somebody* left him *something* ⟨"competent Means"— "Jacob⟩ to live on, when he shall retire from business. He was designed to be "sent to *Cambridge* in order for Priesthood; but he chose rather to be placed in "an *Office* of *accounts* in the City, being qualified for the same by his skill in

Something betwixt a H*** and Owl)
Perch'd on his crown. "All hail! and hail again,   245
My son! the promis'd land expects thy reign.
Know, Settle, cloy'd with custard and with praise,
Is gather'd to the Dull of antient days,
Safe, where no criticks damn, no duns molest,
Where Gildon, Banks, and high-born Howard rest.   250

244 H***] H***r *1729d.*   Heidegger *1735a–42.*
250 Gildon, Banks, . . . Howard] *G—n, B—, . . . H— 1728a–f*
(*H—d 1728f*): wretched *Withers, Banks,* and *Gildon, 1735c–42.*
Add *1735c–42*:
  And high-born *Howard,* more majestic sire,
  Impatient waits, till * * grace the quire.

"*Arithmetick,* and writing the necessary *hands.* He has oblig'd the world with "many translations ⟨"a great many valuable Translations"—Jacob⟩ of "French Plays." J ACOB *Lives of* Dram. Poets, p. 198. ⟨For further remarks on Ozell, see Pope's "Errata," added in *1729d,* p. 198 and Biog. App.⟩

 244. *A H—r*] A strange Bird from *Switzerland.* ⟨*1729a–d.* For John James Heidegger, a Swiss who became manager of the opera-house at Haymarket, see Biog. App.⟩ Here, in the *Dublin* edition, was absurdly inserted the name of an eminent Lawyer and Member of Parliament, who was a man of wit, and a friend of the author. ⟨*1729b–d.* The Dublin edition (1728) has *Hungerford,* i.e. John Hungerford (d. 1729), who unsuccessfully defended Christopher Layer, the Jacobite, in 1722. In a satirical *Collection of several Pictures by the best Hands* (n.d.) there is "A Droll Piece: By the late Mr. H—nger—f—d," which probably indicates that, like Heidegger, he had a peculiar appearance. From *1735–51* the note ran as follows: "A strange Bird from Switzerland, and not (as some have supposed) the name of an eminent Person, who was a man of Parts, and as was said of *Petronius, Arbiter Elegantiarum.*⟩

 250. *Where* Gildon, Banks, *and high-born* Howard *rest*] Charles Gildon ⟨1665–1724⟩, a writer of criticisms and libels of the last age: He published *Blount's* blasphemous books against the Divinity of Christ, the Oracles of reason, *&c.* ⟨1693⟩. He signalized himself as a Critic, having written some very bad plays; abused Mr. *P.* very scandalously in an anonymous Pamphlet of the Life of Mr. *Wycherly* printed by *Curl,* in another called the New Rehearsal printed in 1714, in a third entitled the compleat Art of English Poetry, in 2 Volumes, and others. ⟨In *Memoirs of the Life of William Wycherley, Esq.* (1718), Gildon called Pope "a little diminutive Creature, who had got a sort of Knack in smooth Versification" (p. 15), a "little *Aesopic* sort of an Animal in his own cropt Hair, and Dress agreeable to the Forest he came from" (p. 16). In *A New Rehearsal*

I see a King! who leads my chosen sons
To lands, that flow with clenches and with puns:
'Till each fam'd Theatre my empire own,
'Till Albion, as Hibernia, bless my throne!

251–4 I see a chief, who leads my chosen sons,
    All arm'd with points, antitheses and puns!
    I see a Monarch proud my race to own!
    A Nursing-mother, born to rock the throne!
    Schools, courts, and senates shall my laws obey,
    Till *Albion*, as *Hibernia*, bless my sway. *1735c–42*.

(1714) Pope was ridiculed as Sawney Dapper. See also Biog. App., Gildon.⟩

250. —*Banks*] Was author of the play of the Earl of Essex, Ann Boleyn, &c. He followed the law as a sollicitor, like *Tibbald*. ⟨In *1735ab* this sentence read: "He followed the law as a Sollicitor, and Poetry also, like Tibbald, with much the same success."—John Banks wrote seven plays between 1677 and 1696. He was not a polished writer, and his irregular blank verse must have proved very offensive to a correct age; but his plays have pathos and plenty of action. He appears in the *Dunciad* probably because his plays appealed to the undiscriminating. Pope asked his friend, Nicholas Rowe, to "rescue the Queen of Scots out of the hands of Banks."—Ayre, i 210.⟩

250. —*Hon.* Edward Howard, Author of the British Princes, and a great number of wonderful pieces, celebrated by the late Earls of *Dorset* and *Rochester*, Duke of *Buckingham*, Mr. *Waller*, &c. ⟨Howard, who was known as "foolish Ned," was the author of six plays. *The Brittish Princes. An Heroick Poem*, published in 1669, was much ridiculed by the wits.⟩

250. ⟨The EC MS. has "Where Dunton, Babor, Gildon, Howard rest." Babor is presumably J. Baber, author of *A Poem upon the Coronation* (1685) and another *To the King, upon the Queen's being delivered of a Son* (1688). He was ridiculed by his contemporaries for the latter poem.—To the additional couplet which first appeared in *1735c*, Pope added (*1735c–42*) the following note: "The reader may supply this verse with *H—y* or *V—y*, which he pleases, two noble Men who listed themselves with the Gentlemen of the Dunciad, but whether noble Writers may be judged by their works; a paper call'd *An Epistle to a Doctor of Divinity from Hampton-Court*, and another intitled *Dunces out of State*, both printed in 1733." —*H—y* is Lord Hervey; *V—y* is probably Richard Verney, Baron Willoughby de Broke, who scribbled a certain amount of verse. For Hervey, see vol. iv, pp. xix f., 363 f.⟩

254. ⟨To the reading of *1735c* ("A Nursing-mother," etc.) Pope added (*1735c–42*) the following note: "Some understand this of *Alma Mater*, (who is said in *lib. 3*. to *be dissolved in Port*) others of *Mother Osborne*."—For Mother Osborne, see *Dunciad* B, ii 312.⟩

I see! I see!—" Then rapt, she spoke no more.   255
"God save King Tibbald!" Grubstreet alleys roar.
So when Jove's block descended from on high,
(As sings thy great fore-father, Ogilby,)

255-6 She ceas'd: her owls responsive clap the wing,
    And *Grubstreet* garrets roar, God save the king. *1735c-42.*

---

258. *As sings thy great fore-father* Ogilby] See his *Æsop* Fab. where this excellent hemystic is to be found. ⟨*The Fables of Aesop, Paraphras'd in Verse . . . By
John Ogilby* (1651), p. 35.⟩ Our author shows here and elsewhere, a prodigious
Tenderness for a *bad writer.* We see he selects the only good passage perhaps in
all that ever *Ogilby* writ; which shows how candid and patient a reader he
must have been. What can be more kind and affectionate than these words in
the preface to his Poems, 4°. 1717. where he labours to call up all our humanity
and forgiveness toward them, ⟨toward these unlucky men.—*1729b-51*⟩ by the
most moderate representation of their case that has ever been given by any
Author? "Much may be said to extenuate the fault of bad Poets: What we call
"a *Genius* is hard to be distinguished, by a man himself, from a prevalent
"inclination: And if it be never so great, he can at first discover it no other way,
"than by that strong propensity, which renders him the more liable to be
"mistaken. He has no other method but to make the experiment by writing, and
"so appealing to the judgment of others: And if he happens to write ill (which
"is certainly no sin in itself) he is immediately made the Object of Ridicule!
"I wish we had the humanity to reflect, that even the worst Authors might
"endeavour to please us, and in that endeavour, deserve something at our
"hands. We have no cause to quarrel with them, but for their obstinacy in
"persisting, and even that may admit of alleviating circumstances: For their
"particular friends may be either ignorant, or unsincere; and the rest of the
"world too well-bred, to shock them with a truth, which generally their
'Booksellers are the first that inform them of'' ⟨*1729a-51*⟩.
    But how much all Indulgence is lost upon these people may appear from the
just Reflection made on their constant Conduct and constant Fate in the
following Epigram.

> Ye little wits, that gleam'd a-while,
>   When P–pe vouchsaf'd a ray,
> Alas! depriv'd of his kind smile,
>   How soon ye fade away!
> To compass Phoebus *Car* about
>   Thus empty Vapours rise;
> Each lends his Cloud, to put Him out
>   That rear'd him to the Skies.
> Alas! those Skies are not your Sphere;
>   There, He shall ever burn:

Loud thunder to its bottom shook the bog,
And the hoarse nation croak'd, God save King Log! 260

259 Loud] Hoarse *1728a–f.*   260 hoarse] loud *1728a–f.*

> *Weep, weep and fall! for Earth ye were,*
> *And must to Earth return.*   ⟨*1729d–51.*⟩

End of the First Book.

THE DUNCIAD.

Book the Second.

H IGH on a gorgeous seat, that far outshone
    Henley's gilt Tub, or Fleckno's Irish Throne,

1–12] *Om. 1728a–f.*

Two things there are, upon which the very Basis of all verbal Criticism is founded and supported: The first, that the Author could never fail to use the very best word, on every occasion: The second, that the Critick cannot chuse but know, which it is. This being granted, whenever any doth not fully content us, we take upon us to conclude, first that the author could never have us'd it, And secondly, that he must have used That very one which we conjecture in its stead.

We cannot therefore enough admire the learned *Scriblerus*, for his alteration of the Text in the two last verses of the preceding book, which in all the former editions stood thus

> *Hoarse Thunder to its bottom shook the bog,*
> *And the loud nation croak'd*, God save K. Log!

He has with great judgment transposed these two epithets, putting *hoarse* to the Nation, and *loud* to the Thunder: And this being evidently the true reading, he vouchsafed not so much as to mention the former; For which assertion of the just right of a Critick, he merits the acknowledgement of all sound Commentators.

1. *High on a gorgeous seat*] Parody of *Milton* ⟨*Par. Lost*, ii 1–5⟩,
> *High on a throne of royal state, that far*
> *Outshone the wealth of Ormus and of Ind,*
> *Or where the gorgeous East with richest hand*
> *Show'rs on her Kings barbaric pearl and gold,*
> *Satan exalted sate,*——

2. Henley's *gilt Tub*] The pulpit of a Dissenter is usually called a Tub; but that of Mr. Orator *Henley* was covered with velvet, and adorned with gold. He had also a fair altar, and over it this extraordinary inscription, *The Primitive Eucharist*. See the history of this person, book 3. verse 195.

2. *Or* Fleckno's *Irish Throne*] *Richard Flecknoe* ⟨d. 1678?⟩ was an Irish Priest, but had laid aside (as himself expressed it) the Mechanick part of Priesthood. He printed some Plays, Poems, Letters and Travels. I doubt not our Author took occasion to mention him in respect to the Poem of Mr. *Dryden*, to which this bears some resemblance; tho' of a character more different from it than that of the *Æneid* from the *Iliad*, or the *Lutrin* of Boileau from the *Defaite des Bouts*

Or that, where on her Curlls the Public pours
All-bounteous, fragrant grains, and golden show'rs;
Great Tibbald sate: The proud Parnassian sneer,   5
The conscious simper, and the jealous leer,
Mix on his look. All eyes direct their rays
On him, and crowds grow foolish as they gaze.
Not with more glee, by hands Pontific crown'd,
With scarlet hats, wide waving, circled round,   10
Rome in her Capitol saw Querno sit,
Thron'd on sev'n hills, the Antichrist of Wit.

5 sate:] nods: *1729b–d, 1735c–42.*

---

rimeès of *Sarazin.* ⟨For the "Irish Throne," cf. *Mac Flecknoe*, 106–7:
> The hoary Prince in Majesty appear'd,
> High on a Throne of his own Labours rear'd.⟩

3. *Or that, where on her* Curls *etc.*] *Edm. Curl* stood in the Pillory at *Charing-Cross*, in *March*, 1727–8. ⟨*1729a–51*. Cf. p. 199.⟩

N.B. Mr. *Curl* loudly complain'd of this Note as an Untruth, protesting "that he stood in the Pillory not in *March* but in *February*"; And of another on Verse 144. Saying, "he was not tost in a Blanket, but a *Rug*." Curliad in 12°. 1729. *pag.* 19 and 25. ⟨*1729d–51*. Curll stood in the pillory on Feb. 23, 1728, but was not pelted by the mob. He had been sentenced for publishing the *Memoirs* of John Ker of Kersland. Ker (who was now dead) had, in fact, received a royal warrant from Queen Anne for the publication, and Curll, in a printed paper which was handed out around the pillory, made this fact clear.—See *The Evening-Post*, Feb. 22/24, 1728.⟩

4. *grains* ⟨The refuse malt left after brewing. By "golden show'rs" Pope no doubt intends to suggest the yolk of rotten eggs.⟩

8. *crowds grow foolish* ⟨Addison, "To Sir Godfrey Kneller," 21–2:
> Whilst all his gracious aspect praise,
> And crowds grow loyal as they gaze.⟩

11. Querno] *Camillo Querno* was of *Apulia*, who hearing the great encouragement which *Leo* the tenth gave to Poets, travelled to *Rome* with a Harp in his hand, and sung to it twenty thousand verses of a Poem called *Alexias*. He was introduced as a Buffoon to *Leo*, and promoted to the honour of the Laurel; a jest, which the Court of *Rome* and the Pope himself entred into so far, as ⟨to cause him to ride on an Elephant to the Capitol, and—*1729b–51*⟩ to hold a solemn Festival on his Coronation, at which it is recorded the Poet himself was so transported, as to weep for joy. He was ever after a constant frequenter of the Pope's Table, drank abundantly, and poured forth verses without number. PAULUS JOVIUS, *Elog. Vir. doct. ch.* 72. Some idea of his Poetry is given ùs by *Fam. Strada* in his Prolusions. ⟨For further details about Camillo Querno, see "Of the Poet Laureate," p. 413f.⟩

To grace this honour'd day, the Queen proclaims
By herald hawkers, high, heroic Games.
She summons all her sons: An endless band   15
Pours forth, and leaves unpeopled half the land;
A motley mixture! in long wigs, in bags,
In silks, in crapes, in garters, and in rags;
From drawing rooms, from colleges, from garrets,
On horse, on foot, in hacks, and gilded chariots,   20
All who true dunces in her cause appear'd,
And all who knew those dunces to reward.

13–14 Now herald hawker's rusty voice proclaims
        Heroic prizes, and advent'rous Games;
    1728a–f. (In 1728 these lines follow l. 22.)
15 She . . . sons:] The sons of *Dulness* meet: *1728a–f.*
16 Pours] Pour *1741–42.*

13–14. ⟨Cf. Pope's *Odyssey*, xxiv 107–8:
            Thetis herself to all our peers proclaims
            Heroic prizes, and exequial games.—Wakefield.⟩

14. *hawkers* ⟨The word had a closer application to the situation in the eighteenth century than it now has. The "hawker" frequently cried newspapers and news in the streets. "I heard the Hawkers with great vehemence crying about a Paper."—*Spectator*, Aug. 22, 1711.⟩

15–16. *an endless band etc.* ⟨Virgil, *Aen.*, viii 7–8:
            undique cogunt
    auxilia et latos vastant cultoribus agros.—Wakefield.⟩

17. *bags* ⟨i.e. bag-wigs, in which the hair was enclosed in an ornamental bag. The bag-wig was most likely to be found on the head of the *young* dunce. Cf. *A Key to the Times* (1735), p. 21: "All the young Fellows [in Paris] . . . wear their Wigs in Bags . . ."⟩

18. *In silks, in crapes* ⟨Pope may intend no more here than a simple contrast between the wealthy dunces (in silk), and those of moderate means (in crape). But by "crape" he may be indicating the clerical dunce. ("*Crepe*, a thin stuff, loosely woven, of which the dress of the clergy is sometimes made."—Johnson's *Dictionary*, 1755. Cf. also *Moral Essays*, i 134.) The earliest example in OED of "silk" used to indicate a King's Counsel is in 1812.⟩

20. *chariots* ⟨Pronounced "charets." Swift records a pun of Prior's, who, on being set down by Lord Carteret in his chariot, thanked his lordship for his charity.—*Journal to Stella*, Jan. 4, 1711.⟩

22. Cf. Dryden's translation of *Aeneid*, vi 902–3:
            Those who, to worth their Bounty did extend;
            And those who knew that Bounty to commend.

    Amid that Area wide she took her stand,
  Where the tall May-pole once o'erlook'd the Strand;
  But now, so ANNE and Piety ordain,   25
  A Church collects the saints of Drury-lane.
    With Authors, Stationers obey'd the call,
  The field of glory is a field for all;
  Glory, and gain, th' industrious tribe provoke;
  And gentle Dulness ever loves a joke: 30
  A Poet's form she plac'd before their eyes,
  And bad the nimblest racer seize the prize;

23 Amid . . . she] In that wide space the Goddess *1728a–f.*
31 plac'd] sets *1728a–f.*   32 bad] bids *1728a–f.*

After l. 22 the EC MS. has:
      Ranked side by side the Patron and the Scrub,
      Each Quarles his Benlowes, and each Tibbald B—.
For Benlowes, see *Dunciad B,* iii 21*n.* For B— (i.e. George Bubb Dodington,
Baron Melcombe, a patron of Theobald's), see vol. iv, Biog. App. Theobald
had dedicated his *Double Falshood* to Dodington.⟩
    24. *May-pole* ⟨It stood on the site of the church referred to in l. 26, viz. St
Mary le Strand, one of the fifty new churches built in accordance with the
Act of 1711. The Maypole had been removed in 1718.⟩
    25–6. ⟨Dryden, *Mac Flecknoe,* 68–9:
        A watch Tower once, but now, so Fate ordains,
        Of all the Pile an empty name remains.
Drury Lane and the surrounding alleys had a bad reputation. Cf. Cibber's
reference to "the Passage-walking Nymphs of *Drury-Lane*" in his Prologue to
Mrs Centlivre's *The Man's Bewitch'd.* See also vol. iv, pp. 99*n.,* 139.⟩
    27. *Stationers* ⟨i.e. booksellers.⟩
    31. *A Poet's Form &c.*] This is what *Juno* does to deceive *Turnus, Æn.* 10
⟨636–40⟩.

      Tum dea nube cava, tenuem sine viribus umbram,
      In faciem Æneæ (visu mirabile monstrum)
      Dardaniis ornat telis, clypeumque jubasque
      Divini assimilat capitis——*Dat* inania verba,
      Dat sine mente sonum——

The Reader will observe how exactly some of these verses suit with their
allegorical application here to a Plagiary. There seems to me a great propriety
in this Episode, where such an one is imag'd by a phantom that deludes the
grasp of the expecting Bookseller. ⟨Pope had probably not forgotten the episode
in *The Battle of the Books,* where "the goddess *Dulness* took a cloud, formed into
the shape of Horace, . . . and placed it in a flying posture before him."⟩

No meagre, muse-rid mope, adust and thin,
In a dun night-gown of his own loose skin,
But such a bulk as no twelve bards could raise,   35
Twelve starveling bards of these degen'rate days.
All as a partridge plump, full-fed, and fair,
She form'd this image of well-bodied air,
With pert flat eyes she window'd well its head,
A brain of feathers, and a heart of lead,   40
And empty words she gave, and sounding strain,
But senseless, lifeless! Idol void and vain!

36 starveling] starving *1728a–f.*

33-42. ⟨"Dr. Young, who was well acquainted with More, told me that the portrait was not overcharged."—Warton. The picture given in those lines bears *some* resemblance to what is known of the appearance of James Moore Smythe. He was described in the *Grub-Street Journal*, June 25, 1730, as "a tall modest young Man, with yellowish Teeth, a sallow Complexion, and a flattish Eye; shaped somewhat like an *Italian* in the Shoulders, Hip, and back Parts ..." The "flattish eye" of this description corresponds to the "pert flat eyes" of l. 39. But from the MS. readings given in EC, iv 279, it appears as if Pope had intended originally to describe his own plump friend, John Gay. In this earlier version the phantom has "laughing eyes that twinkled in his head," he is "well-looked" and "well-fed," so that those who saw him "would swear, by G–d, it must be Gay." If this was Pope's original intention—i.e. to describe a phantom Gay, who was really Curll's author, "Joseph Gay"—nothing is left of it except the reference to Joseph Gay in l. 120. Pope is using "adust" in OED's sense 3: atrabilious, sallow.⟩

34. *In a dun night-gown* ⟨Malone notes the resemblance to Shakespeare, I *Henry IV*, III iii 3: "Why my skinne hangs about me like an olde Ladies loose Gowne." But a more immediate source is J. Oldham, *A Satyr*, 10:

    Like Morning-Gown about him hung his Skin.⟩

35. *But such a bulk etc.*] *Virg.* ⟨*Aen.* xii, 899–900⟩

    Vix illud lecti bis sex—
    Qualia nunc hominum producit corpora tellus.

⟨More generally, Pope appears to be imitating Homer's description of the stone lifted by Diomede.⟩

36. *Twelve starveling bards* ⟨"Then *Pindar* darted a Javelin, so large and weighty, that scarce a dozen *Cavaliers*, as *Cavaliers* are in our degenerate Days, could raise it from the Ground."—Swift, *The Battle of the Books*. The idea that human size and strength have degenerated from the heroic days is, of course an epic cliché ⟩

Never was dash'd out, at one lucky hit,
A Fool, so just a copy of a Wit;
So like, that criticks said and courtiers swore,   45
A wit it was, and call'd the phantom, More.

46 More.] *M—*. *1728a–f*.

---

43. *Never was dash'd out, &c.*] Our author here seems willing to give some account of the possibility of *Dulness* making a *Wit*, (which could be done no other way than by *chance.*) The fiction is the more reconcil'd to probability by the known story of *Apelles*, who being at a loss to express the foam of *Alexander*'s horse, dash'd his pencil in despair at the picture, and happen'd to do it by that fortunate stroke.

46. *And call'd the phantom*, More] Curl in his Key to the *Dunciad* ⟨p. 11⟩, affirm'd this to be *James Moore Smyth*, Esq; and it is probable (considering what is said of him in the Testimonies) that some might fancy our author obliged to represent this gentleman as a Plagiary, or to pass for one himself. His case indeed was like that of a man I have heard of, who as he was sitting in company, perceived his next neighbour had stolen his handkerchief. "Sir" (said the Thief, finding himself detected) "do not expose me, I did it for mere want: be so "good but to take it privately out of my pocket again, and say nothing." The honest man did so, but the other cry'd out, "See Gentlemen! what a Thief we "have among us! look, he is stealing my handkerchief" ⟨*1729a–51*⟩.

Some time before, he had borrowed of Dr. *Arbuthnot* a paper call'd an Historico-physical account of the *South-Sea*; and of Mr. *Pope* the Memoirs of a Parish Clark, which for two years he kept, and read to the Rev. Dr. *Young*, — *Billers*, Esq; and many others, as his own. ⟨Fettiplace Bellers, "an intimate Acquaintance of Mr. *Pope*'s, and much esteemed by him; . . . an exceeding good Judge of Poetry, and wrote several Things himself."—Ayre, i 283.⟩ Being apply'd to for them, he pretended they were lost; but there happening to be another copy of the latter, it came out in *Swift* and *Pope*'s Miscellanies. Upon this, it seems he was so far mistaken as to confess his proceeding by an endeavour to hide it: unguardedly printing (in the *Daily Journal* of *Apr.* 3. 1728.) "That the "contempt which he and others had for those pieces" (which only himself had shown, and handed about as his own) "occasion'd their being lost, and for "that cause only, not return'd." A fact, of which as none but he could be conscious, none but he could be the publisher of it. ⟨*1729a–d*. An unusually free paraphrase, even for Pope, of a letter signed "Philo-Ditto." The letter-writer states that the *Memoirs*, "when they were first handed about in Manuscript, gave so general an Offence, that so far from any Fear of their being robbed of them, it was generally expected that a certain Led Poet, maintain'd by the *Company* for that Purpose, would be order'd to own them." The *Historico-Physical Account* "was treated with no more Regard than was due to it, and thrown carelessly up and down till it was lost." But see "Testimonies of

All gaze with ardour: some, a Poet's name,

Authors," p. 34.⟩ The Plagiarisms of this person gave occasion to the following Epigram:

> M—re *always smiles whenever he recites;*
> *He smiles (you think) approving what he writes;*
> *And yet in this no Vanity is shown;*
> *A modest man may like what's not his own.*

⟨*1729d–51.* This epigram had been published, in a slightly different form, in *The Flying Post; or the Weekly Medley,* April 12, 1729, along with that on Roome (iii 146). Neither epigram appeared in the *Dunciad* until the "Second Edition" of (November) 1729. The modification which took place in both epigrams before they were printed in the *Dunciad* suggests that they were the work of Pope himself, although Pope was quite capable of touching up another man's epigram if he thought it could be improved. The last line is clearly indebted to a remark of Sir Samuel Tuke's, *viz.* "A modest Man may praise what's not his own."—*The Adventures of Five Hours,* 1663 (Prologue) ⟩.

This young Gentleman's whole misfortune was too inordinate a passion to be thought a Wit. Here is a very strong instance, attested by Mr. *Savage* son of the late Earl *Rivers;* who having shown some verses of his in manuscript to Mr. *Moore,* wherein Mr. *Pope* was call'd *first of the tuneful train* ⟨In *The Wanderer,* Canto I, 358, Pope is called "the Monarch of the tuneful train."⟩, *Mr. Moore* the next morning sent to Mr. *Savage* to desire him to give those verses another turn, to wit, "That *Pope* might now be the *first,* because *Moore* had left him "unrival'd in turning his style to Comedy." This was during the rehearsal of the *Rival Modes,* his first and only work; the Town condemn'd it in the action, but he printed it in 1726-7 with this modest Motto,

> *Hic cæstus, artemque repono.*

⟨The play ran for six nights at Drury Lane, from Jan. 27–Feb. 3, 1727. For the five lines in this comedy borrowed from Pope, see "Testimonies of Authors," p. 33.⟩ The smaller pieces which we have heard attributed to this author, are, An Epigram on the Bridge at *Blenheim,* by Dr. *Evans; Cosmelia,* by Mr. *Pit,* Mr. *Jones,* &c. ⟨Some verses *To Cosmelia,* ascribed to L. Jones, were published in *The London Magazine,* 1740, p. 398. Two epigrams on Cosmelia, No. ccxii and No. ccli, were published in *A Collection of Epigrams,* 1727.⟩ The Mock-marriage of a mad Divine, with a Cl— for a Parson, by Dr. *W.* ⟨i.e. Dr. Wagstaff?⟩. The Saw-pit, a Simile, by a *Friend.* ⟨The italics here possibly indicate that Dr Robert Freind (1667-1751) is intended.⟩ Certain Physical works on Sir *James Baker;* and some unown'd Letters, Advertisements and Epigrams against our author in the *Daily Journal.* ⟨See "A List of Books, Papers . . .," p. 209. For Sir James Baker, see below, ii 279*n.*⟩

Notwithstanding what is here collected of the Person imagin'd by *Curl* to be meant in this place, we cannot be of that opinion; since our Poet had certainly no need of vindicating half a dozen verses to himself which every reader had done for him; since the name itself is not spell'd *Moore* but *More;* and lastly,

Others, a sword-knot and lac'd suit inflame.
But lofty Lintot in the circle rose;
"This prize is mine; who tempt it, are my foes: 50
"With me began this genius, and shall end."
He spoke, and who with Lintot shall contend?
     Fear held them mute. Alone untaught to fear,

49 Lintot] *L—t 1728a–f.*   52 Lintot] *L—t 1728a–f.*
53 Alone] Alone, *1728a–f.*

---

since the learned *Scriblerus* has so well prov'd the contrary. ⟨From *1735a–42* this long note was printed in an abbreviated form.⟩

46. *The Phantom*, More] It appears from hence that this is not the name of a real person, but fictitious; *More* from μωρός, *stultus*, μωρία, *stultitia*, to represent the folly of a Plagiary. Thus *Erasmus: Admonuit me* Mori *cognomen tibi, quod tam ad* Moriæ *vocabulum accedit quam es ipse a re alienus.* Dedication of *Moriæ Encomion* to Sir *Tho. More*; the Farewell of which may be our Author's to his Plagiary. *Vale* More! & *Moriam tuam gnaviter defende. Adieu* More, *and be sure strongly to defend thy own folly.* SCRIBLERUS. ⟨Pope was always ready to improve upon a hint, even if it came from an enemy. In one of Concanen's weekly essays (*The London Journal*, Nov. 12, 1726) mention is made of a "phantom" Gay: "By the Number of their Writings, there ought to be at least Three Mr. POPE's; and for Mr. GAY, they have hatch'd a Kinsman and a Namesake . . . Thus the real Poet is unhappily toiling hard to raise a reputation, which the Phantom is pulling down as fast. I say *Phantom*; for tho' Mr. JOSEPH GAY be a very voluminous Author, yet no one living can ever bring any manner of Proof that there is or ever was any such Writer really in being." —For Joseph Gay, see l. 120.⟩

48. *sword-knot* ⟨A foppish adornment, such as a ribbon or tassel, to the sword. Moore Smythe was something of a beau.⟩

49. *But lofty* Lintot] We enter here upon the episode of the Booksellers: persons, whose names being more known and famous in the learned world than those of the authors in this Poem, do therefore need less explanation. The action of Mr. *Lintot* here imitates that of *Dares* in *Virgil* ⟨*Aen.*, v 381 ff.⟩, rising just in this manner to lay hold on a *Bull*. This eminent Bookseller printed the *Rival Modes* above-mentioned. ⟨He paid £105 for it—a high price. (J. Nichols, *Lit. Anec.*, viii 301.) Lintot was a large man, "a great sputtering fellow." (Spence, p. 355.) For Lintot's quarrel with Pope, see vol. iv, Biog. App.⟩

50. *This prize is mine* ⟨Cf. Pope's *Iliad*, xxiii 634–5:
         But this, my Prize, I never shall forego;
         This, who but touches, Warriors! is my Foe.—Wakefield.
The whole of the next passage (ll. 53–72) is a parody of the games in *Iliad*, xxiii, and of those in *Aeneid*, v.⟩

Stood dauntless Curl, "Behold that rival here!

54 Curl,] C—l. *1728a–f.*

54, &c.] Something like this is in *Homer, Il.* 10. *ver.* 220. of *Diomed.* Two different manners of the same author in his Similes, are also imitated in the two following; the first of the Bailiff, is short, unadorn'd, and (as the Critics well know) from *familiar life*; the second of the Water-fowl more extended, picturesque, and from *rural life.* The 55th verse is likewise a literal translation of one in *Homer.* ⟨This verse in Homer has not been identified.⟩

54. *Stood dauntless* Curl, *&c.*] We come now to a character of much respect, that of Mr. *Edmond Curl.* As a plain repetition of great actions is the best praise of them, we shall only say of this eminent man, that he carried the Trade many lengths beyond what it ever before had arrived at, and that he was the envy and admiration of all his profession. He possest himself of a command over all authors whatever; he caus'd them to write what he pleas'd; they could not call their very names their own. He was not only famous among these; he was taken notice of by the *State,* the *Church,* and the *Law,* and received particular marks of distinction from each. ⟨In 1716 Curll had published *An Account of the Tryal of the Earl of Winton,* for which he was reprimanded by the House of Lords, after having been kept in custody for about three weeks. In 1720 he was prosecuted for a libel on the Rev. William Clark. In 1722 he was before the House of Lords again for publishing the Duke of Buckingham's *Works.* In 1728 he was fined by the Court of King's Bench for publishing two obscene books, and sentenced to stand in the pillory for publishing the *Memoirs* of John Ker of Kersland. Cf. ii 3.⟩

It will be own'd that he is here introduc'd with all possible dignity: he speaks like the intrepid *Diomed*; he runs like the swift-footed *Achilles*; if he falls, 'tis like the beloved *Nisus*; and (what *Homer* makes to be the chief of all praises) he is *favour'd of the Gods:* He says but three words, and his prayer is heard; a Goddess conveys it to the seat of *Jupiter.* Tho' he loses the prize, he gains the victory; the great Mother her self comforts him, she inspires him with expedients, she honours him with an immortal present (such as *Achilles* receives from *Thetis* and *Æneas* from *Venus*) at once instructive and prophetical: After this, he is unrival'd and triumphant.

The tribute our author here pays him, is a grateful return for several un-merited obligations: Many weighty animadversions on the Publick affairs, and many excellent and diverting pieces on Private persons, has he given to his name. If ever he ow'd two verses to any other, he ow'd Mr. *Curl* some thousands. He was every day extending his fame, and inlarging his writings: witness innumerable instances! but it shall suffice only to mention the *Court-Poems,* which he meant to publish as the work of the true writer, a Lady of quality; but being first threaten'd, and afterwards punish'd, for it by Mr. *Pope,* he generously transferr'd it from *her* to *him,* and has now printed it twelve years ⟨ever since printed it—*1735a*⟩ in his name. The single time that ever he spoke to *C.* was on

"The race by vigor, not by vaunts is won;   55
"So take the hindmost Hell."—He said, and run.
Swift as a bard the bailiff leaves behind,
He left huge Lintot, and out-stript the wind.
As when a dab-chick waddles thro' the copse,
On feet and wings, and flies, and wades, and hops;   60
So lab'ring on, with shoulders, hands, and head,
Wide as a windmill all his figure spread,
With legs expanded Bernard urg'd the race,
And seem'd to emulate great Jacob's pace.
Full in the middle way there stood a lake,   65
Which Curl's Corinna chanc'd that morn to make,

58 Lintot] *L—t 1728a–f.*   60 feet] legs *1728a–f.*
63 With . . . Bernard] With steps unequal *L—t 1728a–f.*
66 Curl's] *C—l's 1728a–f.*

that affair, and to that happy incident he owes all the favours since received
from him. So true is the saying of Dr. *Sydenham*, that "any one shall be, at some
"time or other, the better or the worse, for having but *seen* or *spoken* to a good,
"or a bad man." ⟨Curll published *Court Poems* on March 23, 1716. In the
Advertisement the reader is given to understand that they may be the work
either of "a LADY of Quality" (i.e. Lady Mary Wortley Montagu), or of
"Mr. GAY," or of "the Judicious Translator of HOMER" (i.e. Pope). The
publication was unauthorized: Curll claimed that the poems had been "found
in a Pocket-Book taken up in Westminster-Hall." Of the three poems " 'The
Toilette' may be Gay's . . . ; but the other two are almost certainly Lady
Mary's" (Sherburn, p. 169). Pope's reply was the famous emetic administered
to Curll. The incident is narrated at length in his pamphlet, *A Full and True
Account of . . . Mr. Edmund Curll.* See N. Ault, *Pope's Prose*, I xcv f.⟩
    56. *So take the hindmost Hell*] *Horace de Art.* ⟨417⟩.
              Occupet extremum scabies; mihi turpe relinqui est.
    60. *On feet, and wings, &c.*] Milton ⟨*Par. Lost*, ii 947–50⟩,
                  ——*So eagerly the fiend*
        O'er bog, o'er steep, thro' strait, rough, dense, or rare,
        With head, hands, wings, or feet, pursues his way,
        And swims, or sinks, or wades, or creeps, or flies.
    64. *great Jacob's pace* ⟨Jacob Tonson (A i 55) had very ungainly legs.
Dryden in some satirical verses referred to his "two left legs." Cf. B ii 68. He
was further handicapped, according to Rowe, by what he called his "bunnians."
—"The Reconcilement between Jacob Tonson and Mr. Congreve," N. Rowe,
Works, 1751, ii 311.⟩
    66. *Curl's Corinna*] This name it seems was taken by one Mrs. *T——*

(Such was her wont, at early dawn to drop
Her evening cates before his neighbour's shop,)
Here fortun'd Curl to slide; loud shout the band,
And Bernard! Bernard! rings thro' all the Strand.   70
Obscene with filth the Miscreant lies bewray'd,

69 Curl] *C—l 1728a–f.*
70 Bernard! Bernard!] *L—t, L—t, 1728a–f.*   Lintot! Lintot!
1735ab.   71 Miscreant] varlet *1728a–e.*

⟨i.e. Thomas⟩, who procured some private Letters of Mr. *Pope*'s, while almost
a boy, to Mr. *Cromwell*, and sold them without the consent of either of those
gentlemen to *Curl*, who printed them in 12° 1727. He has discover'd her to be
the publisher in his *Key*, p. 11. But our Poet had no thought of reflecting on her
in this passage; on the contrary, he has been inform'd she is a decent woman
and in misfortunes. ⟨Curll's phrase (*The Curliad*, p. 31). This sentence was
omitted from *1735a–51*.⟩ We only take this opportunity of mentioning the
manner in which those Letters got abroad, which the author was asham'd of as
very trivial things, full not only of levities, but of wrong judgments of men and
books, and only excusable from the youth and inexperience of the writer. ⟨For
Mrs Elizabeth Thomas, see Biog. App. Curll justified his publication of the
letters on the grounds that "Mr. *Cromwell* made a free present of them to the
Gentlewoman . . . and when she had an Inclination to dispose of them otherwise, I see no reason she had to ask either Mr. *Cromwell*'s or Mr. *Pope*'s leave
for so doing."—*Key*, p. 22.⟩

68. *his neighbour's shop* ⟨Probably Curll's shop. He had moved about 1720 to
a shop "over against Catherine Street in the Strand." But it is not clear whether
"his" refers to Curll or Lintot. If Lintot's shop was the scene of Curll's fall, he
fell "at the *Cross-Keys*, between the Two Temple-Gates in Fleet Street."⟩

69. *Here fortun'd Curl to slide*] *Virg. Æn.* 5. ⟨329–30, 333⟩ of *Nisus.*

> *Labitur infelix, cæsis ut forte juvencis*
> *Fusus humum viridesq; super madefecerat herbas—*
> *Concidit, immundoque fimo, sacroque cruore.*

70. *And* Bernard, Bernard] *Virg.* Ecl. 6. ⟨44⟩

> *—Ut littus, Hyla, Hyla, omne sonaret.*

71. *Obscene with filth,* &c.] Tho' this incident may seem too low and base for
the dignity of an Epic Poem, the learned very well know it to be but a copy of
Homer and *Virgil*; the very words ὄνθος and *Fimus* are used by them, tho' our
Poet (in compliance to modern nicety) has remarkably enrich'd and colour'd
his language, as well as rais'd the versification, in these two Episodes. Mr.
Dryden in *Mac-Fleckno* has not scrupled to mention the *Morning Toast* at which
the fishes bite in the *Thames, Pissing Ally, Reliques of the Bum, Whipstich, Kiss my*
——, &c. but our author is more grave, and (as a fine writer says of *Virgil*
in his *Georgics*) *tosses about his* Dung *with an air of Majesty.* ⟨". . . he breaks the

Fal'n in the plash his wickedness had lay'd;
Then first (if Poets aught of truth declare)
The caitiff Vaticide conceiv'd a prayer.
   "Hear Jove! whose name my bards and I adore,   75
As much at least as any God's, or more;
And him and his if more devotion warms,
Down with the Bible, up with the Pope's Arms."
   A place there is, betwixt earth, air and seas,
Where from Ambrosia, Jove retires for ease.   80

76 God's,] Gods, *1728a–f.*

clods, and tosses the dung about, with an air of gracefulness."—Addison, *Essay on the Georgics.*⟩ If we consider that the Exercises of his *Authors* could with justice be no higher than *Tickling, Chatt'ring, Braying,* or *Diving,* it was no easy matter to invent such Games as were proportion'd to the meaner degree of *Booksellers.* In *Homer* and *Virgil, Ajax* and *Nisus,* the persons drawn in this plight are *Heroes;* whereas here they are such, with whom it had been great impropriety to have join'd any but vile ideas; besides the natural connection there is, between Libellers and common Nusances. Nevertheless I have often heard our author own, that this part of his Poem was (as it frequently happens) what cost him most trouble, and pleas'd him least: but that he hoped 'twas excusable, since levell'd at such as understand no delicate satire: Thus the politest men are sometimes obliged to *swear,* when they happen to have to do with Porters and Oyster-wenches. ⟨Cf. Pope's *Iliad,* xxiii 612–3 (of Ajax):
    Besmear'd with Filth, and blotted o'er with Clay,
    Obscene to sight, the ruefull Racer lay.
In his translation of *Aeneid* v 329–30 (of Nisus) Dryden had written:
    He fell, besmear'd with Filth and Holy Gore.⟩
  73. *if Poets &c.* ⟨Ovid, *Met.* xv 879:
    si quid habent veri vatum praesagia.—Wakefield.⟩
  74. *Vaticide* ⟨The poet was often called *vates.* Curll was a vaticide because he was a murderer of poets, either by paying them too little, or by producing inaccurate editions of their works. With Curll's prayer may be compared that of Cloanthus, *Aen.* v 234, or that of Ulysses, *Iliad,* xxiii 770.⟩
  78. *the* Bible, *the* Pope's Arms] The Bible, *Curl's* sign, the Cross-keys, *Lintot's.* ⟨*1728a–51.* Curll's sign had been "The Dial and Bible" for a number of years, but, as he pointed out (*Curliad,* pp. 23–4) it no longer was so. When the *Dunciad* was being written his usual imprint was "Printed for E. Curll in the Strand."⟩
  79. See *Lucian's Icaro-Menippus;* ⟨*1728a*⟩ where this Fiction is more extended ⟨*1729a–51*⟩.
  A place there is, betwixt earth, air and seas] Ovid Met. 12 ⟨39–40⟩.
    Orbe locus medio est, inter terrasq; fretumq;
    Cælestesq; plagas——

There in his seat two spacious Vents appear,
On this he sits, to that he leans his ear,
And hears the various Vows of fond mankind,
Some beg an eastern, some a western wind:
All vain petitions, mounting to the sky,   85
With reams abundant this abode supply;
Amus'd he reads, and then returns the bills
Sign'd with that Ichor which from Gods distills.
    In office here fair Cloacina stands,
And ministers to Jove with purest hands;   90
Forth from the heap she pick'd her Vot'ry's pray'r,
And plac'd it next him, a distinction rare!
Oft, as he fish'd her nether realms for wit,
The Goddess favour'd him, and favours yet.
Renew'd by ordure's sympathetic force,   95

83 And] There *1728a–f*.   84 beg] for *1735ab*.
85 All] Whose *1735ab*.   mounting . . . sky,] sent by winds on high,
1728a–f.

⟨For another source of this obscene fancy, see J. Ozell's translation of *La
Secchia Rapita* (1713), p. 51; G. Tillotson, *On the Poetry of Pope*, p. 157.⟩
  88. Alludes to *Homer, Iliad* 5.

      — ῥέε δ' ἄμβροτον αἷμα θέοιο,
  'Ιχὼρ, οἷος πέρ τε ῥέει μακάρεσσι θεοῖσιν.
  A stream of nectarous humour issuing flow'd,
  Sanguin, such as celestial Spirits may bleed.
               Milton ⟨*Par. Lost*, vi 332–3⟩.

⟨Cf. Hobbes's translation, *Iliad*, v 297–301:
             . . . out sprang the Blood Divine
  (Not such as men have in their Veins, but *Ichor*.
  For Gods that neither eat Bread nor drink Wine
  Have in their Veins another kind of Liquor . . .).
Pope told Spence that there were several passages in Hobbes's *Homer* which
might have been written on purpose to ridicule that poet. He instanced this
passage about the ichor.—Spence, p. 210.⟩
  89. *Cloacina*] The *Roman* Goddess of the Common-shores. ⟨She had ap-
peared in Gay's *Trivia*, ii 115.⟩
  93. *Oft as he fish'd*, &c.] See the Preface to *Swift* and *Pope*'s Miscellanies.
⟨"It has been humourously said, that some have fished the very Jakes, for
Papers left there by Men of Wit . . ." *Miscellanies in Prose and Verse*, 1727, i 12.⟩

As oil'd with magic juices for the course,
Vig'rous he rises; from th' effluvia strong
Imbibes new life, and scours and stinks along,
Re-passes Lintot, vindicates the race,
Nor heeds the brown dishonours of his face.   100
     And now the Victor stretch'd his eager hand
Where the tall Nothing stood, or seem'd to stand;
A shapeless shade! it melted from his sight,
Like forms in clouds, or visions of the night!
To seize his papers, Curl, was next thy care;   105
His papers light, fly diverse, tost in air:
Songs, sonnets, epigrams the winds uplift,
And whisk 'em back to Evans, Young, and Swift.

99 Lintot] *L—t 1728a–f.*
105–7 Baffled, yet present ev'n amidst despair,
        To seize his papers, *C—l*, was next thy care;
        His papers all, the sportive winds up-lift, *1728a–f.*
108 Evans . . . Swift.] to *G—*, to *Y—*, to *S—*.   *1728a–f.*
        Young] Younge *1736b–42.*

96. *As oil'd with magic juices*] Alluding to the opinion that there are Ointments us'd by Witches to enable them to fly in the air, *&c.*
   100. *the brown dishonours*] Virg. Æn. 5 ⟨357–8⟩.
                ——*faciem ostentabat, & udo*
                Turpia membra fimo——
⟨Wakefield draws attention to Parnell's version of the *Batrachomuomachia*, iii 86, where Psycarpax is smitten with a lump of mud which
                Dishonours his brown face, and blots his eyes.⟩
   103. *A shapeless shade*, &c.] Virg. Æn. 6 ⟨701–2⟩.
                ———*Effugit imago*
                Par levibus ventis, volucrique simillima somno.
   105. *To seize his papers* ⟨Cf. Pope's note to ii 66. Curll was continually publishing verses in which he had no legal property.⟩
   106. *His papers light, &c.*] Virg. ⟨Aen., vi 74–5⟩ of the Sybil's leaves,
                Carmina—turbata volent rapidis Ludibria Ventis.
The persons mentioned in the next line are some of those, whose Writings, Epigrams or Jests, he had own'd. ⟨Wakefield draws a parallel between this line and *Par. Lost*, x 282–7, but the resemblance seems remote enough to be accidental.⟩
   107. *sonnets* ⟨i.e. short poems.⟩
   108. *Evans* ⟨For Abel Evans (1679–1737)⟩ clergyman and minor poet,

Th' embroider'd Suit, at least, he deem'd his prey;
That suit, an unpaid Taylor snatch'd away!   110
No rag, no scrap, of all the beau, or wit,
That once so flutter'd, and that once so writ.
    Heav'n rings with laughter: Of the laughter vain,
Dulness, good Queen, repeats the jest again.
Three wicked imps of her own Grubstreet Choir   115
She deck'd like Congreve, Addison, and Prior;

see Biog. App. There is little of Young's published work that comes into the
category of "songs, sonnets, epigrams," but his letters show him to have been
a wit. The G— of 1728 is presumably Gay.⟩

    110. *An unpaid Taylor*] This line has been loudly complain'd of (in *Mist, June
8* ⟨1728⟩. *Dedic. to Sawney* ⟨by James Ralph⟩, and others) as a most inhuman
satire on the *Poverty* of *Poets*: but it is thought our author would be acquitted
by a Jury of *Taylors*. To me this instance seems unluckily chosen; if it be a satire
on any body, it must be on a bad PAYMASTER, since the person they have here
apply'd it to was a man of Fortune. ⟨Moore Smythe had run through his fortune
by 1727, and was unable to meet his creditors. Pope *is*, in fact, sneering at his
poverty. The printing of "PAYMASTER" in capitals is accounted for by the fact
that his grandfather, William Smythe, paymaster of the band of Gentlemen-
Pensioners, had obtained for him the reversion to this place on condition that
he assumed the additional name of Smythe. He must have succeeded his grandfather before Pope's note was written, for in J. Chamberlayne's *Present State of
Great Britain*, 1729, p. 188, the joint paymasters were said to be Arthur Moor and
James Moor.⟩ Not but Poets may well be jealous of so great a prerogative as
Non-payment: which Mr. *Dennis* so far asserts as boldly to pronounce, that "if
Homer himself was not in debt, it was because no body would trust him."
(*Pref. to Rem. on the Rape of the Lock, p.* 15.)

    116. *Like* Congreve, Addison, *and* Prior] These Authors being such whose
names will reach posterity, we shall not give any account of them, but proceed
to those of whom it is necessary. ⟨"Nay, these Fellows are arriv'd at that Height
of Impudence, as when an Author has publickly disown'd a spurious Piece,
they have disputed his own Name with him in printed Advertisements, which
has been practis'd to Mr. *Congreve* and Mr. *Prior*."—*Miscellanies in Prose and
Verse,* 1727, i 12. The Grub-Street hack in Savage's *Author to be Let*, p. 3, tells
how he was employed by Curll to write an obscene tale which "we agreed to
palm upon the World for a posthumous Piece of Mr. *Prior*." Curll did, in fact,
publish a spurious edition of Prior's poems in 1721. He seems also to have
passed off certain other poems as the work of Addison. See R. Straus, *The
Unspeakable Curll*, pp. 266, 267.⟩——*Besaleel Morris* was author of some Satyrs
on the Translators of *Homer* (Mr. *Tickel* and our author) with many other things
printed in News-papers.—*Bond* writ a Satyr against Mr. *P.*—Capt. *Breval* was

Mears, Warner, Wilkins run: Delusive thought!
Breval, Besaleel, Bond, the Varlets caught.
Curl stretches after Gay, but Gay is gone,
He grasps an empty Joseph for a John!   120
So Proteus, hunted in a nobler shape,
Became when seiz'd, a Puppy, or an Ape.

118 Breval . . . Varlets] **, **, and **, the wretches *1728a–e.*
   B—B—B, the Varlets *1728f.*   119 Curl] *C—l 1728a–f.*

---

author of *The Confederates*, an ingenious dramatic performance, to expose **Mr. P.**
Mr. *Gay*, Dr. *Arb*. and some Ladies of quality. CURL, *Key*, p. 11. ⟨Curll's actual
words were: "to expose that wretched Farce of *Gay's—Three Hours after
Marriage*." —For Bezaleel Morrice, William Bond, J. Durant Breval, see Biog.
App. Bond's satire has not been identified. From his note to l. 118 it looks as if
Pope himself did not know what it was called.⟩

117. *Mears, Warner, Wilkins*] Booksellers and Printers of much anonymous
stuff. ⟨See Biog. App., W. Mears, T. Warner, W. Wilkins.⟩

118. *Breval, Besaleel, Bond*] I foresee it will be objected from this line, that
we were in an error in our assertion on verse 46. of this Book, that *More* was a
fictitious name, since these persons are equally represented by the Poet as
phantoms. So at first sight it may seem; but be not deceived, Reader! these also
are not real persons. 'Tis true *Curl* declares *Breval* a Captain, author of a Libel
⟨a piece—*1729b*⟩ call'd *The Confederates*: But the same *Curl* first said ⟨on the
title-page⟩ it was written by *Joseph Gay*: Is his second assertion to be credited
any more than his first? He likewise affirms ⟨*Key*, p. 10⟩ *Bond* to be one who writ
a Satire on our Poet; but where is such a Satire to be found? where was such a
Writer ever heard of? As for *Besaleel*, it carries Forgery in the very name, nor is
it, as the others are, a surname. Thou may'st depend on it no such authors ever
lived: All phantoms! SCRIBLERUS.

120. *Joseph Gay*, a fictitious name put by *Curl* before several pamphlets
⟨*1728a*⟩, which made them pass with many for Mr. *Gay's*. ⟨"A pleasant
allusion to Ixion, embracing a cloud instead of Juno; or a parody on Homer,
Iliad, iii 376:
               And left an empty helmet in his hand."—Wakefield.
The verse gains additional meaning from a pun: a "Joseph" was a great-coat.—
"Joseph Gay" first appeared in 1716, when the name was used to conceal the
authorship of a poem, *The Hoop-Petticoat*, by Francis Chute (*Key*, p.12). Later,
J. D. Breval's *The Confederates* (1717) was said to be by Joseph Gay; and several
other compositions published in 1718–19 were attributed to this imaginary
author. He then seems to have been dropped, but he turns up again in 1733, to
be made responsible for *The Lure of Venus: Or, a Harlot's Progress*. The real Gay
had died in 1732, and Curll presumably hoped that the public would believe
this to be a posthumous work of his.⟩

6*

To him the Goddess. "Son! thy grief lay down,
And turn this whole illusion on the town.
As the sage dame, experienc'd in her trade,   125
By names of Toasts retails each batter'd jade,
(Whence hapless Monsieur much complains at Paris
Of wrongs from Duchesses and Lady Mary's)
Be thine, my stationer! this magic gift;
Cook shall be Prior, and Concanen, Swift;   130

130 Cook . . . Concanen,] *C— . . . C—n, 1728a–f.*

124. *And turn this whole illusion &c.*] It was a common practice of this Bookseller, to publish vile pieces of obscure hands under the names of eminent
authors. ⟨Pope had already exposed this practice in *A Full and True Account,*
where he makes Curll say: "I do sincerely pray Forgiveness for those indirect
Methods I have pursued in . . . putting Authors Names to Things they never
saw."—*Pope's Prose,* vol. i, p. 262.⟩

127–8. *hapless Monsieur . . . Lady Mary's* ⟨One of the purely private references
which Pope occasionally allowed himself, in order to gratify some pique: few
of his readers could have understood what was meant. The "hapless Monsieur"
here is the "wretched Monsieur" of *Sober Advice,* l. 53. For this man, M.
Rémond, and his financial and personal relations with Lady Mary Wortley
Montagu, see vol. iv, p. 79*n.* To any reader ignorant of the facts, there was
probably only one deduction to be drawn, in view of the "sage dame" and
"batter'd jade," as to the injury suffered by any one coming in contact with
Lady Mary. For the allusion in "Duchesses," see p. 467. Pope condescended
to throw some light on this passage in *1735ab,* but his note was withdrawn
again from later editions. The *1735ab* note reads: "This passage was thought
to allude to a famous Lady who cheated a French wit of 5000 pounds in the
South-Sea year. But the Author meant it in general of all bragging Travellers,
and of all Whores and Cheats under the name of Ladies."⟩

130. Cook *shall be* Prior] The man here specify'd was the son of a *Muggleto-*
nian, who kept a Publick-house at *Braintree* in *Essex.* He writ a thing call'd
The Battle of Poets ⟨1725: a revised edition appeared in 1729⟩, of which *Philips*
and *Welsted* were the heroes, and wherein our author was attack'd in his moral
character, in relation to his *Homer* and *Shakespear:* ⟨Cooke makes Dennis reproach Pope for merely seeking to make money out of "the deathless Grecian."
He is called a "mercenary Bard," and is said to have edited Shakespeare in this
same mercenary fashion. Pope's original poems, however, are praised by
Cooke.⟩ He writ moreover a Farce of *Penelope,* in the preface of which also he
was squinted at: ⟨*Penelope, A Dramatic Opera* (1728) was the joint work of Cooke
and John Mottley (1692–1750). The Preface contains a dull sneer at two lines
in Book xvii of Pope's translation of the *Odyssey.*⟩ and some malevolent things
in the *British, London* and *Daily Journals.* ⟨*1729a–51.* Some of those essays were

> So shall each hostile name become our own,

afterwards reprinted by Cooke in *The Letters of Atticus*, 1731.⟩ At the same time
the honest Gentleman wrote Letters to Mr. *P.* in the strongest terms protesting
his innocence. ⟨*1729d–51.* In a letter to Pope, dated Aug. 11, 1728, Cooke
denies that he is the author of "some scurrilous Pieces, which have been lately
printed in the Daily Papers," though admitting that he had formerly written
critically about him in a poem (presumably *The Battle of the Poets*). In a second
letter, Sept. 16, 1728, he promises to leave this poem out of his forthcoming
volume of Poems. Pope, however, was not reconciled to him, and Cooke
reprinted the poem, which now contained a much bitterer attack on Pope, in
his *Tales, Epistles, Odes, Fables* etc., 1729.—See Biog. App.⟩ His chief work was
a translation of *Hesiod*, to which *Theobald* writ notes, and half-notes, as hath
already been said. ⟨*1729a–51.* If Pope is making a specific charge in this line,
Cooke must have written something that Curll passed off as Prior's work.
Cooke was, in fact, one of Curll's authors. In 1726 Curll paid him £5 for
writing a Life of Marvell etc. (B.M. Add. MSS. 38,728 f. 52.) He may, as EC
suggests, be the hack writer in Savage's *Author to be Let* who was employed by
Curll to write "a merry tale" which was to be palmed upon the world as "a
posthumous Piece of Mr. Prior." Cf. A ii 116*n.*⟩

And Concanen, Swift] *Matthew Concanen,* an *Irishman,* an anonymous slanderer,
and publisher of other men's slanders, particularly on Dr. *Swift* to whom he had
obligations, and from whom he had received both in a collection of Poems for
his benefit and otherwise, no small assistance; To which *Smedley* (one of his
brethren in enmity to *Swift*) alludes in his *Metam.* of *Scriblerus,* p. 7. accusing
him of having "boasted of what he had not written, but others had revis'd
and done for him." ⟨Pope is here giving the substance of twenty lines of Smedley's poem.—To this charge Concanen replied in a letter to the *Daily Journal,*
Sept. 8, 1730: "I do in the most solemn Manner declare, that I never saw Dr.
Swift but *four* Times in my Life; that I never conversed with him but *twice,* at
one of which Times I dined with him, and that he then expressed some Intentions to serve me, which he declined at the next Visit I paid him . . . I do
assure you I never received any Gift, Kindness, or friendly Recommendation
from him whatever." Concanen does not explain, however, how he came to
publish several of Swift's poems in his volume of *Miscellaneous Poems, Original
and Translated, By Several Hands,* 1724. It is to this volume, no doubt, that Pope
refers.⟩ He was also author of several scurrilities in the *British* and *London Journals*
⟨and in a paper call'd the *Speculatist—1735a–51*⟩; and of a pamphlet call'd a
Supplement to the *Profund,* wherein he deals very unfairly with our Poet, not only
frequently blaming Mr. *Broome*'s verses as his, (for which he might indeed seem
in some degree accountable, having corrected what that gentleman did) but
those of the Duke of *Buckingham,* and others. To this rare piece, some-body
humorously caus'd him to take for his motto, *De profundis clamavi.* ⟨*1729a–51.*
Concanen afterwards collected his articles in the *British* and *London Journals,*
and published them with the title of *The Speculatist* (2nd ed. 1732)—not, he

And we too boast our Garth and Addison."

insisted, because he thought highly of them, but "to refute the Calumny of a rancorous and foul-mouth'd Railer who has asserted in print that the Author of them wrote *several Scurrilities* in those Papers." For references to Pope in *The Speculatist*, see pp. 40, 148, 187, 260.⟩

He was since a hired Scribler in the *Daily Courant*, where he pour'd forth much Billingsgate against the Lord Bolingbroke and others; after which this man was surprizingly promoted to administer Justice and Law in Jamaica. ⟨*1735a–51*. For Concanen, see Biog. App.⟩

132. *And we too boast our* Garth *and* Addison] Nothing is more remarkable than our author's love of praising good writers. He has celebrated Sir *Isaac Newton*, Mr. *Dryden*, Mr. *Congreve*, Mr. *Wycherley*, Dr. *Garth*, Mr. *Walsh*, Duke of *Buckingham*, Mr. *Addison*, Lord *Lansdown*; in a word, almost every man of his time that deserv'd it. It was very difficult to have that pleasure in a poem on This subject, yet he found means to insert their panegyrick, and here has made even Dulness out of her own mouth pronounce it. It must have been particularly agreeable to him to celebrate Dr. *Garth*; both as his constant friend thro' life, and as he was his predecessor in this kind of Satire. The *Dispensary* attack'd the whole Body of Apothecaries, a much more useful one undoubtedly than that of the bad Poets (if in truth this can be call'd a Body, of which no two members ever agreed). It also did what *Tibbald* says is unpardonable, drew in *parts of private character*, and introduced *persons independent of his Subject* ⟨*Mist's Journal*, June 22, 1728, in a letter signed W.A.⟩. Much more would *Boileau* have incurr'd his censure, who left all subjects whatever on all occasions, to fall upon the bad Poets; which it is to be fear'd wou'd have been more immediately His concern ⟨*1729a–51*⟩.

But certainly next to commending good Writers, the greatest service to learning is to expose the bad, who can only that one way be made of any use to it. This truth is very well set forth in these lines, addrest to our Author.

> The craven Rook, and pert Jackdaw,
>   (Tho' neither Birds of moral kind)
> Yet serve, if hang'd, or stuff'd with straw,
>   To show us, which way blows the wind.
> Thus dirty Knaves or chatt'ring Fools,
>   Strung up by dozens in thy Lay,
> Teach more by half than Dennis' rules
>   And point Instruction ev'ry way.
> With Egypt's art thy pen may strive
>   One potent drop let this but shed,
> And ev'ry Rogue that stunk alive
>   Becomes a precious Mummy dead.

⟨*1729d–51*. Griffith (1 i 205) says that this epigram appeared in *The Evening-Post*, June 26/28, 1729.⟩

> With that she gave him (piteous of his case,
> Yet smiling at his ruful length of face)

133 She gave him] the Goddess *1728a–f*.

---

133. ——*piteous of his case,*
    Yet smiling at his ruful length of face]
Virg. Æn. 5 ⟨358; 350–1⟩.
      ——*Risit pater optimus illi.*
      Me liceat casum miserari insontis amici——
      Sic fatus, tergum Gætuli immane leonis, &c.

134. *Ruful length of face*] "The decrepid person or figure of a man are no
"reflections upon his *Genius:* An honest mind will love and esteem a *man of*
"*worth,* tho' he be deform'd or poor. Yet the author of the Dunciad hath libell'd
"a person for his *ruful length of face!*" MIST'S JOURN. *June* 8 ⟨1728⟩. This
Genius and *man of worth* whom an honest mind should love, is Mr. *Curl.* True it is,
he stood in the Pillory; an accident which will lengthen the face of any mån
tho' it were ever so comely, therefore is no reflection on the natural beauty of
Mr. *Curl.* ⟨Curll was in person "very tall and thin, an ungainly, awkward,
white-faced man. His eyes were a light grey, large, projecting, gogle, and pur-
blind."—T. Amory, *The Life of John Buncle*, 1770, iv 137. "An ugly squinting
old fellow."—Mrs. L. Pilkington, *Memoirs*, 1749, ii 189.⟩ But as to reflections on
any man's Face, or Figure, Mr. *Dennis* saith excellently; "Natural deformity
"comes not by our fault, 'tis often occasioned by calamities and diseases, which
"a man can no more help, than a monster can his deformity. There is no one
"misfortune, and no one disease, but what all the rest of men are subject to.——
"But the deformity of this Author ⟨viz. Pope⟩ is visible, present, lasting, un-
"alterable, and peculiar to himself: it is the mark of God and Nature upon him,
"to give us warning that we should hold no society with him, as a creature not
"of our original, nor of our species: And they who have refused to take this
"warning which God and Nature have given them, and have in spite of it by a
"senseless presumption, ventur'd to be familiar with him, have severely suffer'd,
"&c. 'Tis certain his original is not from *Adam*, but from the Devil," &c.
DENNIS *and* GILDON: *Charact. of Mr.* P. 8°. 1716 ⟨p. 10⟩.

It is admirably observ'd by Mr. *Dennis* against Mr. *Law* ⟨*The Stage Defended,*
1726⟩, p. 33. "That the language of *Billingsgate* can never be the language of
Charity, nor consequently of Christianity." I should else be tempted to use the
language of a Critick: For what is more provoking to a Commentator, than to
behold his author thus pourtrayed? Yet I consider it really hurts not *Him;*
whereas maliciously to call some *others* dull, might do them prejudice with a
world too apt to believe it. Therefore tho' Mr. *D.* may call another a *little ass*
or a *young toad*, far be it from us to call him a *toothless lion*, or an *old serpent*. Indeed, had I written these notes (as was once my intent) in the learned language,
I might have given him the appellations of *Balatro, Calceatum caput*, or *Scurra in
triviis*, being phrases in good esteem, and frequent usage among the best learned:

But in our mother-tongue were I to tax any Gentleman of the Dunciad, surely it should be in words not to the vulgar intelligible, whereby christian charity, decency, and good accord among authors, might be preserved. SCRIBLERUS ⟨*1729a–51.* For "ass" and "toad" as applied by Dennis to Pope, see A i 104*n.*, and Appendix vi, p. 235.⟩

The good *Scriblerus* here, as on all occasions, eminently shows his Humanity. But it was far otherwise with the Gentlemen of the Dunciad, whose scurrilities were always Personal ⟨*1729d–51*⟩: They went so far as to libel an eminent Sculptor for making our author's *Busto* in marble, at the request of Mr. *Gibbs* the Architect: ⟨e.g. "To Mr. Reisbank, on his Carving A. POPE's *Busto*"— *Read's Weekly Journal,* March 29, 1729 (signed J.S., i.e. Jonathan Smedley (?)), and *Brice's Weekly Journal,* April 25, 1729⟩ which Rhimes had the undeserv'd honour to be answer'd in an *Impromptu* by the Earl of B——— ⟨probably Pope's friend, the Earl of Burlington, one of the three peers to whom he had assigned the copyright of the *Dunciad* of 1729⟩.

> *Well, Sir, suppose, the* Busto's *a damn'd head,*
> *Suppose, that* Pope's *an Elf;*
> *All he can say for't is, he neither made*
> *The* Busto *nor* Himself.

And by another Person of Quality,

> *Rysbrake, to make a* Pope *of Stone,*
> *Must labour hard and sore;*
> *But it would cost him labour none,*
> *To make a Stone of* Moor.

⟨*1729d–42.* John Michael Rysbrack (1693–1770) came to England in 1720 from Holland, and soon established himself as a favourite sculptor.—The "Moor" of the second epigram is James Moore Smythe.⟩ Their Scurrilities were of that nature as provoked every honest man but Mr. *Pope,* yet never to be lamented, since they occasion'd the following amiable Verses ⟨by D. Lewis (1683?–1760). See Boswell's *Life of Johnson,* ed. G. B. Hill, iv 307⟩.

> *While Malice,* Pope, *denies thy page*
> *It's own celestial Fire;*
> *While Critics, and while Bards in rage*
> *Admiring won't admire;*
>
> *While wayward Pens thy worth assail,*
> *And envious Tongues decry,*
> *These Times tho' many a Friend bewail,*
> *These Times bewail not I.*
>
> *But when the World's loud Praise is thine,*
> *And Spleen no more shall blame,*
> *When with thy* Homer *Thou shalt shine*
> *In one establish'd Fame,*

A shaggy Tap'stry, worthy to be spread   135
On Codrus' old, or Dunton's modern bed;
Instructive work! whose wry-mouth'd portraiture
Display'd the fates her confessors endure.
Earless on high, stood un-abash'd Defoe,

135 A . . . Tap'stry,] Gives him a cov'ring, *1728a–f.*
136 Dunton's] **'s *1728a–e.*   *D—on's 1728f.*
139 un-abash'd Defoe,] pillory'd *D— 1728a–f.*

> *When none shall rail, and ev'ry Lay*
> *Devote a Wreath to Thee;*
> *That Day (for come it will) that Day*
> *Shall I lament to see* ⟨*1729d–51*⟩.

135. *A shaggy Tap'stry*] A sorry kind of Tapestry frequent in old Inns, made of worsted or some coarser stuff: like that which is spoken of by Doctor *Donne* ⟨Satire iv, 225–6. Cf. also *E. on C.*, 587⟩—*Faces as frightful as theirs who whip Christ in old hangings.* The imagery woven in it alludes to the mantle of *Cloanthus* in *Æn.* 5. ⟨250–7. Pope's "mantle" is the "chlamydem auratam" of Virgil.⟩

136. *On* Codrus' *old, or* Dunton's *modern bed*] Of *Codrus* the Poet's bed see *Juvenal*, describing his *poverty* very copiously. *Sat.* 3. *v.* 203, &c.

> *Lectus erat Codro*, &c.

> Codrus *had but one bed, so short to boot,*
> *That his short* Wife's *short legs hung dangling out:*
> *His cupboard's head six earthen pitchers grac'd,*
> *Beneath them was his trusty tankard plac'd;*
> *And to support this noble Plate, there lay*
> *A bending Chiron, cast from honest clay.*
> *His few* Greek *books a rotten chest contain'd,*
> *Whose covers much of mouldiness complain'd,*
> *Where mice and rats devour'd poetic bread,*
> *And on Heroic Verse luxuriously were fed.*
> '*Tis true, poor* Codrus *nothing had to boast,*
> *And yet poor* Codrus *all that nothing lost.*
>
>   Dryd.

But Mr. C⟨oncanen⟩ in his dedication of the Letters, Advertisements. &c. to the Author of the *Dunciad*, assures us, that "*Juvenal* never satyrized the poverty of *Codrus*." ⟨*A Compleat Collection of all the Verses* . . . p. xi.⟩

John Dunton was a broken Bookseller and abusive scribler: he writ *Neck or Nothing* ⟨1713⟩, a violent satyr on some Ministers of State; *The danger* ⟨*Hazard*⟩ *of a death-bed repentance*, a libel on the late Duke of *Devonshire* and on the Rt. Rev. Bishop of *Peterborough.* &c. ⟨For Dunton, see Biog. App.⟩

138. *confessors* ⟨Accented by Pope, as by Shakespeare, on the first syllable.⟩
139. *Earless* ⟨Pope must have known that Defoe did not lose his ears.⟩

And Tutchin flagrant from the scourge, below: 140
There Ridpath, Roper, cudgell'd might ye view;
The very worsted still look'd black and blue:
Himself among the storied Chiefs he spies,

140 Tutchin] *T— 1728a–f.*   scourge,] lash, *1728a–f.*
141 Ridpath . . . cudgell'd] kick'd and cudgel'd *R— 1728a–f.*
143 among] amongst *1741–42.*

140. Tutchin] *John Tutchin*, author of some vile verses, and of a weekly
paper call'd the *Observator:* He was sentenc'd to be whipp'd thro' several towns
in the west of *England*, upon which he petition'd King *James* II. to be hànged.
When that Prince died in exile, he wrote an invective against his memory,
occasioned by some humane Elegies on his death. He liv'd to the time of Queen
Anne. ⟨Tutchin, a stubborn Whig, died in 1707, after being attacked in the
street by ruffians. He published in 1685 *Poems on several Occasions* (the "vile
verses"), and in 1701 the invective to which Pope alludes: *The British Muse:
or Tyranny exposed. A Satire; occasioned by all the fulsome and lying Poems and Elegies
that have been written on the Death of the late King James.*⟩
   141. Ridpath, Roper] Authors of the *Flying-Post* and *Post-Boy*, two scandalous papers on different sides, for which they equally and alternately were
cudgell'd, and deserv'd it. ⟨They died within one day of each other on Feb. 5
and Feb. 6, 1726 (*The London Journal*, Feb. 12, 1726). George Ridpath was
proprietor of the Whig *Flying Post*, Abel Roper of the Tory *Post-Boy*. Roper was
frequently threatened with a beating. (Cf. *Post-Boy*, April 28, 1713. Cf. also
Hereditary Right Exemplified . . . 1728, pp. 17–18). For Ridpath, Roper, see
Biog. App.⟩
   143. *Himself among the storied chiefs he spies*, &c.] Virg. Æn. 1 ⟨488; 459–60⟩.

> *Se quoq; principibus permixtum agnovit Achivis—*
> *Constitit & lacrymans: Quis jam locus, inquit, Achate!*
> *Quæ regio in terris nostri non plena laboris?*

⟨The whole business of the tapestry is imitated from *Aeneid*, Book i, where
Aeneas comes upon some tapestries in Dido's palace which portray the siege of
Troy and the various Trojan heroes, including himself.⟩
   143. *Himself . . . he spies*, &c.] The history of *Curl*'s being toss'd in a blanket,
and whipp'd by the scholars of *Westminster*, is ingeniously and pathetically
related in a poem entituled *Neck or Nothing*. ⟨By Samuel Wesley the Younger,
then head usher of Westminster School. In 1716 Curll had published, without
authority, a volume which he called *The Posthumous Works of Dr. South*, and had
included in it a funeral oration in Latin, spoken by John Barber, Captain of the
School, and son of the famous Alderman Barber, the printer. For this offence he
was tossed in a blanket by the Westminster boys, made to apologize to young
Barber, and finally kicked out of the School Yard amid "the Huzza's of the
Rabble."—Sherburn, pp. 171–2.⟩ Of his purging and vomiting, see *A full and*

As from the blanket high in air he flies,
"And oh! (he cry'd) what street, what lane, but knows
Our purgings, pumpings, blanketings and blows?   146
In ev'ry loom our labours shall be seen,
And the fresh vomit run for ever green!"
     See in the circle next, Eliza plac'd;

---

true account of a horrid revenge on the body of Edm. Curl, *&c.* ⟨in the 3d. vol. of Swift and Pope's Miscellanies.—*1735a–51*⟩.

148. *And the fresh vomit &c.*] A parody on these of a late noble author ⟨Lord Halifax, *Epistle to Lord Dorset*⟩,

> *His bleeding arm had furnish'd all their rooms,*
> *And run for ever purple in the looms.*

⟨Halifax actually wrote:

> *The wounded arm would furnish all their rooms,*
> *And bleed for ever scarlet in the looms.*

Pope had already allowed his imagination to dwell on this incident in *A Full and True Account* (*Pope's Prose*, i, p. 260) ". . . the Contents of his vomiting being as Green as Grass."⟩

149. *See in the circle next,* Eliza *plac'd*] In this game is expos'd in the most contemptuous manner, the profligate licenciousness of those shameless scriblers (for the most part of That sex, which ought least to be capable of such malice or impudence) who in libellous Memoirs and Novels, reveal the faults and misfortunes of both sexes, to the ruin or disturbance, of publick fame or private happiness. Our good Poet, (by the whole cast of his work being obliged not to take off the Irony) where he cou'd not show his Indignation, hath shewn his Contempt as much as possible: having here drawn as vile a picture, as could be represented in the colours of Epic poesy. SCRIBLERUS.

149. *Eliza Haywood*] This woman was authoress of those most scandalous books, call'd *The Court of Carimania* ⟨1727⟩, and *The new Utopia*. ⟨*Memoirs of a certain Island adjacent to the Kingdom of Utopia*, 1725. In this work Mrs. Haywood had made scandalous reflections on Pope's friend Martha Blount, and possibly on Pope himself.—Sherburn, p. 296.⟩ For the *two Babes of Love*, See CURL, *Key*, p. 12. ⟨"The two *Babes* of *Love* . . . the scandalous Chronicle records to be the Offspring of a *Poet* and a *Bookseller*."⟩ But whatever reflection he is pleas'd to throw upon this Lady, surely 'twas what from him she little deserv'd, who had celebrated his undertakings for *Reformation of Manners*, and declared her self "to be so perfectly acquainted with the *sweetness of his disposition*, and that "*tenderness with which he consider'd the errors of his fellow-creatures*; that tho' she "should find the *little inadvertencies* of her *own life* recorded in his papers, she was "certain it would be done in such a manner as she could not but approve," Mrs. HAYWOOD, Hist. of *Clar.⟨ina⟩* printed in the *Female Dunciad*, p. 18. ⟨These words are addressed to the editor of *The Female Dunciad*, who may, or may not,

Two babes of love close clinging to her waste;   150
Fair as before her works she stands confess'd,
In flow'rs and pearls by bounteous Kirkall dress'd.
The Goddess then: "Who best can send on high
"The salient spout, far-streaming to the sky;
"His be yon Juno of majestic size,   155
"With cow-like-udders, and with ox-like eyes.
"This China-Jordan, let the chief o'ercome
"Replenish, not ingloriously, at home."

152 In . . . pearls] In flow'r'd brocade *1728a–f.*
    Add *1728a -f:*
       Pearls on her neck, and roses in her hair,
       And her fore-buttocks to the navel bare.
154 far-streaming] fair-streaming *1728a–e.*

---

have been Curll. In "A List of Books, Papers . . ." (p. 210) Pope states that this
miscellany was "collected by the same Mr. *Curl.*" It was "Printed for T. Read
in *White-Fryers*"; but that does not necessarily absolve Curll from responsibility
for it.⟩
   150. *Two babes of love &c.*] Virg. Æn. 5 ⟨285⟩.
          Cressa genus, Pholoe, geminique sub ubere nati.
⟨It is just possible that Pope intended his reference to Virgil's "Pholoë of Cretan
stock" to go beyond the two babes. The Cretans were celebrated liars; they were
also notorious for unnatural love.⟩
   152. *Kirkall,* the Name of a Graver. This Lady's Works were printed in four
Volumes *duod.* with her picture thus dress'd up, before them. ⟨Elisha Kirkall
(1682?–1742). He introduced a new method of chiaroscuro engraving in 1722.⟩
   155.   ——*This* ⟨*Yon*⟩ Juno——
       With cow-like udders, and with ox-like eyes]
In allusion to *Homer's* Βοῶπις πότνια ῞Ηρη.
   157. *This* China *Jordan*, &c.] Virg. Æn. 5 ⟨314⟩.
         Tertius, Argolica hac galea contentus abito.
   This China *Jordan*] In the games of *Homer Il.* 23 ⟨262–5⟩, there are set together as prizes, a Lady and a Kettle ⟨τρίπους⟩; as in this place Mrs. *Haywood*
and a Jordan. But there the preference in value is given to the *Kettle*, at which
Mad. *Dacier* is justly displeas'd: Mrs. *H.* here is treated with distinction, and
acknowledg'd to be the more valuable of the two. ⟨"Je suis fort scandalisé de
voir que les Grecs estimoient deux d'avantage un trepied qu'une belle esclave
adroite et habile. Il me semble que cela est un peu grossier."—*L'Iliade D'Homere,
Traduite en François, Avec Des Remarques.* Madame Dacier, 1711, iii 585.⟩

> Chetwood and Curl accept the glorious strife,
> (Tho' one his son dissuades, and one his wife)   160
> This on his manly confidence relies,
> That on his vigor and superior size.
> First Chetwood lean'd against his letter'd post;
> It rose, and labour'd to a curve at most:
> So Jove's bright bow displays its watry round,   165
> (Sure sign, that no spectator shall be drown'd).
> A second effort brought but new disgrace,

159 Chetwood . . . Curl] *Ch—d . . . C—l 1728a–f.*   Chapman and
     Curl *1729d–36b.* Osborn and Curl *1741–42.*
163 Chetwood] *C—d 1728a–f.* Chapman, *1729d–36b.* Osborn,
     1741–42.

---

159. *Chetwood* the name of a Bookseller, whose Wife was said to have as great
an influence over her husband, as *Boileau*'s *Perruquiere.* See *Lutrin. Cant.* 2.—
Henry Curl, the worthy son of his father *Edmund.* ⟨For Chetwood, see Biog. App.
For Chapman, who was substituted in *1729d*, Pope added the following note:
"*Chapman*, a Bookseller who printed Mrs. *Haywood*'s *New Utopia* &c."—Worse
than that, however, he was one of the four booksellers concerned in the publication of Theobald's *Shakespeare Restored.* If Pope's note is correctly related to l.
159, Henry Curll, not his father, is the antagonist of Chetwood; but the note on
Henry Curll probably refers to "his son" of the line following. Henry Curll
(who died some time before 1742—R. Straus, *The Unspeakable Curll*, p. 190),
took over his father's business temporarily in 1726–7 when Edmund Curll was
in trouble with the authorities. For Samuel Chapman and Henry Curll, see
Biog. App.⟩
     161. *This on his manly confidence relies, That on his vigor*] Virg. Æn. 5 ⟨430–1⟩.

> *Ille* ⟨*pedum*⟩ *melior motu, fretusque juventa,*
> *Hic membris & mole valens——*

⟨Dryden translates:

> One on his Youth and pliant Limbs relies;
> One on his Sinews, and his Gyant size.⟩

     163. *letter'd post* ⟨See A i 38n.⟩
     165. *So Jove's bright bow—Sure sign*——] The words of *Homer* of the Rainbow,
in *Iliad* xi ⟨27–8⟩.

> ἅς τε Κρονίων
> Ἐν νέφεϊ στήριξε, τέρας μερόπων ἀνθρώπων.

Which Mad. *Dacier* thus renders, *Arcs merveilleux, que le fils de Saturn à fondez dans
les nües, pour etre dans tous les âges un signe à tous les mortels.*

For straining more, it flies in his own face;
Thus the small jett which hasty hands unlock,
Spirts in the gard'ner's eyes who turns the cock.   170
Not so from shameless Curl: Impetuous spread
The stream, and smoaking, flourish'd o'er his head.
So, (fam'd like thee for turbulence and horns,)
Eridanus his humble fountain scorns,
Thro' half the heav'ns he pours th' exalted urn;   175

168 The wild Mæander wash'd the Artist's face: *1729d–42.*
171 Curl] *C—l 1728a–f.*

---

173. *So (fam'd like thee for turbulence and horns) Eridanus] Virgil* mentions these
two qualifications of *Eridanus, Geor.* 4 ⟨371–3⟩.

> *Et gemina auratus taurino* cornua *vultu,*
> *Eridanus, quo non alius per pinguia culta*
> *In mare purpureum* violentior *effluit amnis.*

The Poets fabled of this River *Eridanus,* that it flow'd thro' the skies. *Denham,*
Cooper's Hill.

> *Heav'n her* Eridanus *no more shall boast,*
> *Whose Fame like thine in lesser currents lost,*
> *Thy nobler stream shall visit* Jove'*s abodes,*
> *To shine among the stars, and bathe the Gods;*

⟨Pope appears to be quoting, as usual, from memory, but he scarcely makes
sense of Denham's lines. Denham wrote (ll. 193–4):

> Whose Fame in thine, like lesser Currents lost,
> Thy Nobler streams shall visit *Jove's* aboads . . .

Pope is, of course, punning on "horns," the mark of the cuckold. I have found
no evidence to substantiate or disprove the charge against Curll's wife.⟩

175. *Thro' half the heavens he pours th' exalted urn]* In a manuscript Dunciad
(where are some marginal corrections of some gentlemen some time deceas'd)
I have found another reading of these lines, thus,

> *And lifts his urn thro' half the heav'ns to flow;*
> *His rapid waters in their passage glow.*

This I cannot but think the right: For first, tho' the difference between *burn* and
glow may seem not very material to others, to me I confess the latter has an elegance, a *Jenesçay quoy,* which is much easier to be conceiv'd than explain'd.
Secondly, every reader of our Poet must have observ'd how frequently he uses
this word *glow* in other parts of his works: To instance only in his *Homer.*

(1.) Iliad 9. v. 726.—*With one resentment glows.*
(2.) Iliad II. v. 626.—*There the battle glows.*
(3.) Ibid. 985.—*The closing flesh that instant ceas'd to glow.*
(4.) Il. 12. v. 55.—*Encompass'd* Hector *glows.*

His rapid waters in their passage burn.
   Swift as it mounts, all follow with their eyes;
Still happy Impudence obtains the prize.
Thou triumph'st, victor of the high-wrought day,
And the pleas'd dame soft-smiling leads away.   180

178 happy] happy, *1728a–f.*   180 leads] lead'st *1735ab.*

(5.) Ibid. 475.—*His beating breast with gen'rous ardour glows.*
(6.) Iliad 18. v. 591.—*Another part glow'd with refulgent arms.*
(7.) Ibid. v. 654.—*And curl'd on silver props in order glow.*

I am afraid of growing too luxuriant in examples, or I could stretch this catalogue to a great extent, but these are enough to prove his fondness for this
beautiful word, which therefore let all future Editions re-place here.

I am aware after all, that *burn* is the proper word to convey an idea of what
was said to be Mr. *Curl*'s condition at that time. But from that very reason I
infer the direct contrary. For surely every lover of our author will conclude he
had more humanity, than to insult a man on such a misfortune or calamity,
which could never befal him purely by his *own fault,* but from an unhappy
communication with another. *This Note is partly Mr.* THEOBALD, *partly*
SCRIBLERUS. ⟨It is "partly Mr. THEOBALD" because in his *Shakespeare Restored* (p. 11), after giving over three pages of parallels from Shakespeare to
illustrate one point, Theobald remarks, "I am afraid of growing too luxuriant
in Examples . . . Extent," as here.—There appears to be no clear evidence to support the unsavoury charge about Curll's "condition"; but he was "generally
held to be of an immoral character."—*New and General Biographical Dictionary*
(1798) iv 447. A writer in *Mist's Journal,* April 5, 1719, said that he was
"mark'd by Nature, for he has a bawdy Countenance, and a debauch'd Mien."⟩

179. *The high-wrought day*] Some affirm, this was originally—*the* well-p—st
day: but the Poet's decency would not suffer it. ⟨*1729d–51.* This is confirmed by
the EC MS., where the reading occurs. It is characteristic of Pope to retain his
beauties in the notes, even if he has removed them from the poem itself.⟩

Here the learned Scriblerus manifests great anger: he exclaims against all
such *Conjectural Emendations* in this manner. "Let it suffice, O Pallas! that every
noble ancient, Greek or Roman, hath suffer'd the impertinent correction of
every Dutch, German, and Switz Schoolmaster! Let our English at least escape,
whose intrinsic is scarce of Marble so solid, as not to be impair'd or soil'd by
such rude and dirty hands. Suffer them to call their Works their own, and after
death at least to find rest and sanctuary from Critics! When these men have
ceas'd to rail, let them not begin to do worse, to comment! let them not conjecture into nonsense, correct out of all correctness, and restore into obscurity
and confusion. Miserable fate! which can befall only the sprightliest Wits that
have written, and befall them only from such dull ones as could never write!
SCRIBLERUS ⟨*1735a–51*⟩.

Chetwood, thro' perfect modesty o'ercome,
Crown'd with the Jordan, walks contented home.
    But now for Authors nobler palms remain:
Room for my Lord! three Jockeys in his train;
Six huntsmen with a shout precede his chair;   185
He grins, and looks broad nonsense with a stare.
His honour'd meaning, Dulness thus exprest;
"He wins this Patron who can tickle best."
    He chinks his purse, and takes his seat of state:
With ready quills the dedicators wait;   190
Now at his head the dext'rous task commence,
And instant, fancy feels th' imputed sense;
Now gentle touches wanton o'er his face,
He struts Adonis, and affects grimace:
Rolli the feather to his ear conveys,   195
Then his nice taste directs our Operas:
Welsted his mouth with Classic flatt'ry opes,

---

181 Chetwood,] *Ch—d, 1728a–f.* Chapman, *1729d–36b.* Osborn,
    1741–42.
195 Rolli] *R— 1728a–f.*
197 Welsted] ** *1728a–e.* T— *1728f.* B—y *1735ab.* Bentley
    1735c–42.

---

    182. *Crown'd with the Jordan* ⟨"Among many other Pranks played in a
Drunken Debauch, Mr. *Chetwood* was sent Home with a Jordan . . . on his
Head.—Curll, *Key,* p. 13. If this is true, it may have suggested the whole episode
to Pope.⟩

    188. *tickle* ⟨Tickling with a feather seems to have been a well-understood
synonym for flattery. Cf. Swift, *A Letter of Advice to a Young Poet:* "I wou'd by no
means advise any young Man to make his first Essay in Panegyrick; . . . my
Counsel is, that you use the Point of your Pen, not the Feather. Let your first
Attempt be a *Coup d'Eclat* in the way of Libel, Lampoon, or Satyr."⟩

    195. *Paolo Antonio Rolli,* an *Italian* Poet, and writer of many Operas in that
language, which, partly by the help of his genius, prevail'd in *England* near ten
years ⟨*1729a–c:* "near twenty years"—*1729d–51*⟩. He taught Italian to some fine
Gentlemen who affected to direct the Opera's. ⟨*1735a–51.* For those "singing
Peers," see iv 45–49, 545–7. For Rolli, see Biog. App.⟩

    197. *Welsted*] See Note on verse 293 of this Book. ⟨To the reading "Bentley"
of *1735c* Pope appended a long note. See *Dunciad B,* ii 205.⟩

And the puff'd Orator bursts out in tropes.
But Oldmixon the Poet's healing balm

199 Oldmixon] *O— 1728a–f.*   Welsted most *1735a–42.*

198. tropes. ⟨Butler, *Hudibras*, 1 i 81–᷄2:
　　　　　For rhetoric he could not ope
　　　　　His mouth, but out there flew a trope.—WAKEFIELD.⟩
199. *But* Oldmixon, *&c.*] Mr. *John Oldmixon* (next to Mr. *Dennis* the most
ancient Critick of our Nation) not so happy as labᵣrious in Poetry, and therefore perhaps characteriz'd by the *Tatler*, N°. 62. by the name of *Omicron* the
unborn Poet. CURL, Key to the *D.* p. 13. An unjust censurer of Mr. *Addison*,
⟨in his Prose Essay on Criticism—*1729b–51. Op. cit.* pp. 7, 16.⟩ whom in his
imitation of *Bouhours* (call'd the *Arts of Logic and Rhetoric*) he misrepresents in
plain matter of fact. In p. 45. he cites the *Spectator* ⟨No. 169⟩ as abusing Dr.
Swift by name, where there is not the least hint of it: And in p. 304. is so injurious as to suggest, that Mr. *Addison* himself writ that *Tatler* N°. 43. which says
of his *own Simile*, that " 'tis as great as ever enter'd into the mind of man." This
person wrote numbers of books which are not come to our knowledge. "Drama-
"tick works, and a volume of Poetry, consisting of heroic Epistles, *&c.* some
"whereof are very well done," saith that great Judge Mr. JACOB. *Lives of Poets*,
Vol. 2. p. 303. ⟨Oldmixon wrote *The Grove, or Love's Paradise. An Opera*, 1700,
and *The Governour of Cyprus: a Tragedy*, 1703. He wrote a number of poems; the
volume mentioned by Jacob is apparently *Amores Britannici. Epistles Historical
and Gallant*, 1703.⟩
　　I remember a *Pastoral* of his on the *Battle of Blenheim*; a Critical History of
England; Essay on Criticism, in prose; The Arts of Logic and Rhetoric, in which
he frequently reflects on our Author. We find in the *Flying-Post* of *Apr. 13. 1728.*
some very flat verses of his against him and Dr. *Sw.* ⟨*1729a–42*⟩ and Mr. *Curl*
tells us in the *Curliad*, that he wrote the Ballad called The *Catholic Poet* against
the Version of *Homer*, before it appear'd to the public. ⟨*1729d–42.* Pope had
attributed this ballad to Mrs. *Centlivre*, and Curll had replied: ". . . the whole
by Mr. *Oldmixon*, not one word by Mrs. *Centlivre.*"—*Curliad*, p. 27. Pope accepted Oldmixon's authorship of the ballad, but never ceased to attribute it to
Mrs Centlivre as well. See ii 379*n*.⟩ He was all his life a hired writer for a Party,
and received his reward in a small place which he yet enjoys. ⟨*1729a–42.* He had
been Collector of Customs to the port of Bridgwater since 1716.⟩
　　But the Top of his Character was a Perverter of History, in that scandalous
one of the *Stuarts* in folio, and his Critical History of England, 2 vols. 8°. Being
imploy'd by Bishop Kennet in publishing the Historians in his Collection, he
falsified Daniel's Chronicle in numberless places. Yet this very man, in the
Preface to the first of these, advanc'd a *particular Fact* to charge three Eminent
Persons of falsifying the Lord Clarendon's History; which Fact has been disprov'd by the Bishop of Rochester, then the only survivor of them; and the
particular part produc'd since, after almost ninety Years, in that noble Author's

Strives to extract from his soft, giving palm;   200
Unlucky Oldmixon! thy lordly master
The more thou ticklest, gripes his fist the faster.
　　While thus each hand promotes the pleasing pain,
And quick sensations skip from vein to vein,

201 Oldmixon!] *O—! 1728a–f.* Welsted! *1735a–42.*　thy lordly]
thy unfeeling *1735a–42.*

own Hand. He was all his life a virulent Party-writer for hire, and received his
reward in a small place which he yet enjoys. ⟨*1735a–51.* In *1743* the last clause
was amended to: "which he enjoyed to his death." In *1730* Oldmixon pub-
lished "The History of England, During the Reigns of the Royal House of
Stuart . . . To all which is Prefix'd, Some Account of the *Liberties* taken with
Clarendon's History before it came to the Press, such *Liberties* as make it
Doubtful, What Part of it is Clarendon's, and what not." The three "eminent
Persons" whom Oldmixon accused of tampering with Clarendon's text were
Atterbury, George Smalridge (1663–1719), and Henry Aldrich (1647–1710).
The "particular fact" was adduced on the authority of George Duckett. Atter-
bury answered the charge in *The Late Bishop of Rochester's Vindication,* 1731.
Oldmixon was accused of falsifying Daniel's *Chronicle* in *Mr. Oldmixon's Reply . . .
Examin'd,* 1732. Pope repeated his charge against Oldmixon's veracity in
Donne iv 61, and *Ep. to Arbuthnot,* 146. For Oldmixon, see Biog. App., vols. iv, v.⟩
　　201. *thy lordly master* ⟨The noble patron may be a composite picture; but if
Pope intended to libel an individual peer it was most probably Thomas Pelham-
Holles, Duke of Newcastle, who was patron to all three dedicators named. As
Governor of the Academy of Music, founded in 1720, he was the patron of
Rolli, who dedicated to him his *L'Odio e L'Amore* in 1721. Welsted inscribed to
Newcastle his volume of *Epistles, Odes* etc. 1724 (with the "Dissertation" prefixed to it which annoyed Pope), and he had already complimented him on his
being created Duke in 1715. His flattering of the great had been adversely
commented upon by Bezaleel Morrice, who deplored his tendency "to seek
some courteous Noble's Grace | And greatly aim at Profit, or a Place" (*Epistle
to Mr. Welsted,* 1721, p. 8). Oldmixon had written to Jacob Tonson on Dec. 13,
1718, begging him to recommend him to Newcastle for the laureateship, vacant
through the death of Rowe (B.M. Add. MSS. 28, 275, f. 46)—a fact which was
quite probably known to Pope. It is perhaps significant that it is as a *poet* that
Oldmixon is mentioned here. Curll (*Key,* p. 13) asserted that three Dukes were
intended, viz. Newcastle, Grafton, and Bolton. A possible explanation of the
change in *1735a* from "unlucky Oldmixon" to "unlucky Welsted" is given by
Bowles, who prints a letter from Welsted to his patron Bubb Dodington, in
which he laments that he has offended him. For the Welsted-Dodington connection see EC iii 261*n.*⟩

A youth unknown to Phœbus, in despair,   205
Puts his last refuge all in Heav'n and Pray'r.
What force have pious vows! the Queen of Love
His Sister sends, her vot'ress, from above.
As taught by Venus, Paris learnt the art
To touch Achilles' only tender part;   210
Secure, thro' her, the noble prize to carry,
He marches off, his Grace's Secretary.
    "Now turn to diff'rent sports (the Goddess cries)
And learn, my sons, the wond'rous pow'r of Noise.
To move, to raise, to ravish ev'ry heart,   215
With Shakespear's nature, or with Johnson's art,
Let others aim: 'Tis yours to shake the soul
With thunder rumbling from the mustard-bowl,

206 and] in *1728a–c.*

---

205. *A youth unknown to* Phœbus, *&c.*] The satire of this Episode being levelled
at the base flatteries of authors to worthless wealth or greatness, concludeth here
with an excellent lesson to such men; That altho' their pens and praises were as
exquisite as they conceit of themselves, yet (even in their own mercenary views)
a creature unlettered, who serveth the passions, or pimpeth to the pleasures of
such vain, braggart, puft Nobility, shall with those patrons be much more inward, and of them much higher rewarded. SCRIBLERUS. ⟨Curll identified this
youth as "Webster" (*Key*, p. 13), i.e. Edward Webster, Chief Secretary to the
Duke of Bolton, Lord Lieutenant in Ireland. EC (iv 283–4, 331–2), while
suppressing some of the evidence, puts the ascription beyond all doubt. In the
EC MS. the youth is actually referred to as "sly W——r." See Biog. App.,
Webster.⟩

215. *To move, to raise, &c.—Let others aim—'Tis yours to shake, &c.*] Virgil,
Æn. 6 ⟨847–8, 851–2⟩.

> *Excudent alii spirantia mollius æra,*
> *Credo equidem, vivos ducent de marmore vultus, &c.*
> *Tu, regere imperio populos, Romane, memento,*
> *Hæ tibi erunt artes——*

218. *With Thunder &c.*] The old way of making Thunder and Mustard were
the same; but since it is more advantagiously perform'd by troughs of wood
with stops in them. Whether Mr. *Dennis* was the inventor of that improvement,
I know not; but it is certain, that being once at a Tragedy of a new Author with
a friend of his, he fell into a great passion at hearing some, and cry'd, "S'death!
"that is *my* Thunder." ⟨The Mustard Bowl is mentioned in *The Critical Specimen*,
1711 (*Pope's Prose*, i 16). Dennis's thunder first broke upon the world in his
tragedy, *Appius and Virginia*, 1709.—H. G. Paul, *John Dennis*, p. 45.⟩

With horns and trumpets now to madness swell,
Now sink in sorrows with a tolling Bell.   220
Such happy arts attention can command,
When fancy flags, and sense is at a stand.
Improve we these. Three cat-calls be the bribe
Of him, whose chatt'ring shames the Monkey tribe;
And his this Drum, whose hoarse heroic base   225
Drowns the loud clarion of the braying Ass."
        Now thousand tongues are heard in one loud din:
The Monkey-mimicks rush discordant in.
'Twas chatt'ring, grinning, mouthing, jabb'ring all,
And Noise, and Norton, Brangling, and Breval,   230
Dennis and Dissonance; and captious Art,
And Snip-snap short, and Interruption smart.

230 And Noise, and Norton,] And *R—*, and railing, *1728a–c.*
    Noise, Noncence, *N—n, 1728d–f.*   Breval,] *B—*, *1728a–f.*
231 Dennis] *D—s 1728a–f.*

220. *With a tolling Bell*] A mechanical help to the Pathetic, not unuseful to
the modern writers of Tragedy. ⟨*1729b–51.*—"I have known a bell introduced
into several tragedies with good effect; and have seen the whole assembly in a
very great alarm all the while it has been ringing."—Addison, *Spectator*, No. 44,
April 20, 1711.⟩
    223. *Three Catcalls*] Certain musical instruments used by one sort of Criticks
to confound the Poets of the Theatre ⟨*1729a–51*⟩. They are of great antiquity, if
we may credit *Florent. Christ.* on *Aristophanes* Ἱππεῖς, Act. i. *Parabasis Chori.*
⟨*1729b–d.* EC points out that Addison's Spectator, No. 361, is a humorous dissertation on cat-calls, whose origin is placed in remote antiquity. The cat-call
nuisance in the theatres was apparently increasing about 1728. A correspondent
in *The London Journal*, March 23, 1728, complained that "our English audience
have been for some time returning to their cattish nature; of which some particular sounds from the gallery have given us sufficient warning." (Quoted by
Charles Burney, *General History of Music*, iv 333, and ascribed to Arbuthnot.⟩
    228. ⟨In the EC MS.: "Welstead and Wickstead at each other grin."⟩
    230. *Norton.* [See verse 383.] *J. Durant Breval*, Author of a very extraordinary
Book of Travels, and some Poems. See before, V. 118. ⟨Breval published
Remarks on Several Parts of Europe in 1726. Further *Remarks* followed in 1738.
His poems include *The Art of Dress*, *MacDermot*, *Calpe, or Gibraltar*. There seems
to be nothing "very extraordinary" about his Book of Travels.⟩
    230. *And Noise* ⟨Cf. Bezaleel Morrice, *Three Satires*, 1719, p. 14:
                For noise and nonsense over all prevail.⟩

"Hold (cry'd the Queen) A Catcall each shall win,
Equal your merits! equal is your din!
But that this well-disputed game may end,   235
Sound forth, my Brayers, and the welkin rend."
     As when the long-ear'd milky mothers wait
At some sick miser's triple-bolted gate,
For their defrauded, absent foals they make
A moan so loud, that all the Guild awake,   240
Sore sighs Sir G * *, starting at the bray
From dreams of millions, and three groats to pay!
So swells each Windpipe; Ass intones to Ass,
Harmonic twang! of leather, horn, and brass.
Such, as from lab'ring lungs th' Enthusiast blows,   245
High sounds, attempred to the vocal nose.
But far o'er all, sonorous Blackmore's strain,

233 A Catcall each] ye all alike *1728a–f*.
236 forth,] *Omit comma 1728a–f*.
241 Sore] So *1728a–c*.   G **,] *G—t, 1728a–f*.   Gilbert, *1735c–42*.
246 sounds,] sound, *1735ab*.
247 Blackmore's] *Bl—'s 1728a–f*.

---

233. ——*A Catcall each shall win*, &c.] Virg. Ecl. 3 ⟨108–9⟩.
         Non inter nos est tantas componere lites,
         ⟨*Non nostrum inter vos tantas componere lites*⟩
         Et vitula tu dignus, & hic——
237. *milky mothers* ⟨Warton notes Pope's borrowing from *The Faerie Queene*, I VIII xi 7. For the tonic qualities of asses' milk, see *Ep. to Arbuthnot*, 306n.⟩
237–8. ⟨Gay, *Trivia*, ii 13:
         Before proud gates attending asses bray.⟩
237ff.] A *Simile* with a long tail, in the manner of *Homer*.
240. *Guild* ⟨Here "Guild" seems to mean nothing more precise than "company," or "fellowship"; i.e. the miser's neighbours in the City.⟩
241. *Sir G** ⟨Sir Gilbert Heathcote, who died Jan. 25, 1732–3, was reputed to be "worth 700,000 l. very honourably acquired." J. Nichols, *Lit. Ill.*, ii 22. His parsimonious habits were notorious. See *Ep.* II ii 240, and Biog. App., Vol. iv; and Swift to Alderman Barber: "She carries her liberality as much too high, as our friend Sir Gilbert did his avarice."—Swift, *Correspondence*, v 9.⟩
245. *Enthusiast* ⟨i.e. a man labouring under religious excitement, a fanatical preacher. In his *Discourse concerning the Mechanical Operation of the Spirit*, Swift had remarked on the Dissenter's habit of "conveying the sound thro' the nose."⟩

Walls, steeples, skies, bray back to him again:
In Tot'nam fields, the brethren with amaze
Prick all their ears up, and forget to graze;   250
Long Chanc'ry-lane retentive rolls the sound,
And courts to courts return it round and round:
Thames wafts it thence to Rufus' roaring hall,

248. —*bray back to him again*] A figure of speech taken from *Virgil*.
        Et vox assensu nemorum ingeminata remugit. Geor. 3 ⟨45⟩

        He hears his num'rous herds low o'er the plain,
        While neighb'ring hills low back to them again. Cowley.

⟨See Cowley's essay "Of Agriculture," where these lines form part of his translation (ll. 15–16) of Horace, *Od.* v ii.⟩

The poet here celebrated, Sir *R. B.* delighted much in the word *Bray*, which
he endeavour'd to ennoble by applying it to the sound of *Armour, War,* &c. In
imitation of him, and strengthen'd by his authority, our author has here admitted it into Heroic poetry. ⟨Wakefield points out that it had already been
admitted by Milton, *Par: Lost,* vi 209:
                Arms on armour clashing brayed
                Horrible discord.⟩

249. *Tot'nam fields* ⟨At this time open country. Cf. Gay, *To the Right Honourable William Pulteney,* 1717:
        Love flies the dusty town for shady woods.
        Then Tottenham fields with roving beauty swarm . . .
The EC MS. has "Tothill fields." These fields (in Westminster) were much
closer to the Strand than the "Tot'nam fields" of all the printed texts. The
reason for Pope's alteration is not clear: he may have preferred the more distant fields as a means of emphasizing the din.⟩

250. *Prick all their ears up, and forget to graze*] Virg. Ecl. 8 ⟨2⟩.
                Immemor herbarum quos est mirata juvenca.
The progress of the sound from place to place, and the scenary here of the
bordering regions, *Tot'nam fields, Chancery-lane,* the *Thames, Westminster-hall,* and
Hungerford-stairs, are imitated from *Virg. Æn.* 7 ⟨516 ff.⟩ on the sounding the
horn of *Alecto.*

        Audiit & Triviæ longe lacus, audiit amnis
        Sulphurea Nar albus aqua, fontesque Velini, &c.

251. *Long* Chanc'ry-lane] The place where the Courts of Chancery are kept:
The long detention of Clients in those Courts, and the difficulty of getting out
of them, is humorously allegoriz'd in these lines. ⟨Cf. "M. Scriblerus Lectori",
p. 196. The changes there made were adopted in subsequent editions.⟩

253. *Rufus' roaring hall* ⟨Westminster Hall. It was made noisy partly by the
lawyers who disputed there (cf. the "bawling Bar" of *Donne* iv 55); but even
more by the owners of stalls who took up a considerable amount of space in the

And Hungerford re-ecchoes, bawl for bawl.
All hail him victor in both gifts of Song,   255
Who sings so loudly, and who sings so long.

254 Hungerford]   *H — d 1728a–e.*

Hall. Cf. *Westminster Hall* (B.M., C 2 d 11, Vol. ii, p. 344):
        First from yᵉ Courts wᵗʰ clam'rous bawl
        The Criers their Attorneys call . . .
The accompanying print shows various stall-holders selling their wares.⟩

    254. *Hungerford* ⟨Hungerford Market. It was built in 1680 on the site of what is now Charing Cross Station. The reading *H——d* of *1728* seems to indicate that a surname was intended. Perhaps Pope left a blank so that those of his readers who cared to do so might assume that he was thinking of a celebrated lawyer, viz. John Hungerford. Cf. A i 244*n*. "Mr. Hungerford" is, in fact, the gloss of the anonymous Key.⟩

    256. *Who sings so loudly, and who sings so long*] A just character of Sir *Richard Blackmore*, Kt. who (as Mr. *Dryden* express'd it) *Writ to the rumbling of his Coach's wheels* ⟨Prologue to *The Pilgrim*, 1700⟩, and whose indefatigable Muse produced no less than six Epic poems: *Prince* and *King Arthur*, 20 Books; *Eliza*, 10; *Alfred*, 12; *The Redeemer*, 6: besides *Job* in folio, the whole *Book of Psalms, The Creation*, 7 Books, *Nature of Man*, 3 Books, and many more. 'Tis in this sense he is stiled afterwards, the *Everlasting Blackmore*. Notwithstanding all which, Mr. *Gildon* seems assured, that "this admirable author did not think himself upon "the *same foot* with *Homer*." *Comp. Art of Poetry*, Vol. i. p. 108. ⟨"As for Mr. *Lamode*'s putting the modern *Authors* on a Foot with *Homer*, I am very confident, that the *admirable* Author of *the Creation* has too much *Judgment*, and too much *Modesty*, to have any such Thought himself. Let it suffice, that the Author of the *Arthurs* has the glory of excelling Lucretius."⟩

    But how different is the judgment of the author of *Characters of the Times!* p. 25. who says, "Sir *Richard* is unfortunate in happening to mistake his proper "talents, and that he has not for many years been *so much as named*, or even "*thought of* among writers." Even Mr. *Dennis* differs greatly from his friend Mr. *Gildon*: "*Blackmore*'s Action (saith he) has neither unity, nor integrity, nor "morality, nor universality; and consequently he can have no *Fable*, and no "*Heroic Poem*: His Narration is neither probable, delightful, nor wonderful: His "Characters have none of the necessary qualifications.——The things contain'd "in his narration are neither in their own nature delightful, nor numerous "enough, nor rightly disposed, nor surprising, nor pathetic.——Nay he pro-"ceeds so far as to say Sir *Richard* has *no Genius*; first laying down that Genius is "caused by a *furious joy* and *pride of soul*, on the conception of an *extraordinary* "*Hint*. Many men (says he) have their *Hints*, without these motions of *fury* and "*pride of soul*, because they want fire enough to agitate their spirits; and these we "call cold writers: Others who have a great deal of fire, but have not excellent "organs, feel the foremention'd *motions*, without the *extraordinary hints*; And

This labour past, by Bridewell all descend,

"these we call fustian writers." But he declares, that "Sir *Richard* had neither the
"*Hints*, nor the *Motions*." *Remarks on Pr.* Arth. 8°. 1696. *Preface*.

This gentleman in his first works abused the character of Mr. *Dryden*, and in
his last of Mr. *Pope*, accusing him in very high and sober terms of prophaneness
and immorality (*Essay on polite writing*, Vol. 2. p. 270.) on a meer report from
Edm. Curl, that he was author of a Travestie on the first Psalm. ⟨*Key*, pp. 19–20.
In his *Essays upon Several Subjects*, ii 270, to which Pope refers, Blackmore expressed his abhorrence of this parody, but did not mention Pope by name.
"One of these Champions of Vice is the reputed Author of a detestable Paper . . .
in which the godless Author has burlesqu'd the *First Psalm* of *David* in so obscene and profane a manner, that perhaps no Age ever saw such an insolent
Affront offer'd to the establish'd Religion of their Country."—For details of
this burlesque, see Vol. vi.⟩ Mr. *Dennis* took up the same report, but with the
addition of what Sir *Richard* had neglected, an *Argument to prove it;* which being
very curious, we shall here transcribe. (*Remarks on* Homer. 8°. p. 27.) "It *was* he
"who burlesqu'd the Psalm of *David*. It is *apparent* to me that Psalm was bur-
"lesqu'd by a *Popish* rhymester. Let rhyming persons who have been brought up
"*Protestants* be otherwise what they will, let them be Rakes, let 'em be Scound-
"rels, let 'em be *Atheists*, yet education has made an invincible impression on
"them in behalf of the sacred writings. But a *Popish rhymester* has been brought
"up with a contempt for those sacred writings. Now show me another Popish
"rhymester but he."——This manner of argumentation is usual with Mr.
Dennis; he has employ'd the same against Sir *Richard* himself in a like charge of
Impiety and *Irreligion*. "All Mr. *Blackmore*'s celestial Machines, as they cannot be
"defended so much as by common receiv'd opinion, so are directly contrary to
"the doctrine of the Church of *England:* For the visible descent of an Angel
"must be a miracle. Now it is the doctrine of the Church of *England* that miracles
"had ceas'd a long time before Prince *Arthur* came into the world. Now if the
"doctrine of the Church of *England* be true, as we are oblig'd to believe, then are
"all the celestial machines in Prince *Arthur* unsufferable, as wanting not only
"human but divine probability. But if the machines are sufferable, that is if
"they have so much as divine probability, then it follows of necessity that the
"doctrine of the Church is false: So I leave it to every impartial Clergyman to
"consider, *&c*." *Preface to the Remarks on Prince* Arthur ⟨*1729a–51*⟩.

It has been suggested in the Character of Mr. *P.* that he had Obligations to
Sir *R. B*. He never had any, and never saw him but twice in his Life. ⟨*1729a-d*.
". . . he has attack'd no one so often, or with so much ridiculous, impotent Malice,
as Sir *Richard Blackmore*; . . . And what time has he chosen to do this? Why just
after that Gentleman had laid very great Obligations on him."—J. Dennis, *A
True Character* . . . , p. 15. In 1714 Pope had written to John Hughes (EC x 119):
"Pray make my most humble service acceptable to Sir Richard Blackmore"—
which suggests a more intimate acquaintance than Pope admits in his note. His
withdrawal of the two final sentences after *1729d* is significant.⟩

(As morning-pray'r and flagellation end.)
To where Fleet-ditch with disemboguing streams
Rolls the large tribute of dead dogs to Thames,   260
The King of Dykes! than whom, no sluice of mud
With deeper sable blots the silver flood.
"Here strip my children! here at once leap in!
"Here prove who best can dash thro' thick and thin,
"And who the most in love of dirt excel,   265

258. *As morning pray'r and flagellation end*] It is between eleven and twelve in the morning, after church service, that the criminals are whipp'd in *Bridewell* ⟨the House of Correction for women⟩.—This is to mark punctually the Time of the day: *Homer* does it by the circumstance of the Judges rising from court, or of the Labourer's dinner; our author by one very proper both to the *Persons* and the *Scene* of his Poem; which we may remember commenc'd in the evening of the Lord-mayor's day: The first book passed in that night; the next morning the games begin in the *Strand*, thence along *Fleetstreet* (places inhabited by Booksellers) then they proceed by *Bridewell* toward *Fleetditch*, and lastly thro' *Ludgate* to the City and the Temple of the Goddess.

259. *The* Diving] This I fancy (says a great Enemy to the Poem) is a Game which no body could ever think of but the Author: however it is work'd up admirably well, ⟨"and comes very near the Spirit of Mr. POPE"⟩, especially in those lines where he describes *Eusden* (he should say *Smedley*) rising up again. ESSAY on the DUNCIAD, p. 19.

259–60. ⟨Garth, *Dispensary*, iii 125–6:
     Nigh where *Fleet-Ditch* descends in sable Streams,
     To wash his sooty *Naiads* in the *Thames*.—Wakefield.
Pope had already written (*Odyss.*, iv 480)
     . . . the deep roar of disemboguing Nile.⟩

261. *The King of* Dykes, *&c.*] Virg. ⟨*Georg.* i 482, iv 372–3⟩.
     Eridanus, rex fluviorum——
     ——quo non alius, per pinguia culta,
     In mare purpureum violentior effluit amnis. ⟨Cf. A ii 173*n.*⟩

263 ff. ⟨Warton notes that the idea of the diving match is taken from the Earl of Dorset's verses *To Mr. Edward Howard On . . . The British Princes:*
     As skilful divers to the bottom fall
     Sooner than those who cannot swim at all;
     So in this way of writing without thinking,
     Thou hast a strange alacrity of sinking.⟩

264, 265, 266] The three chief qualifications of Party-writers; to stick at nothing, to delight in flinging dirt, and to slander in the dark by guess.

264. *thro' thick and thin* ⟨Dryden, *Absalom and Achitophel*, ii 414 (of Doeg):
     Spurd boldly on, and Dash'd thro' Thick and Thin.⟩

"Or dark dexterity of groping well.
"Who flings most filth, and wide pollutes around
"The stream, be his the Weekly Journals, bound.
"A pig of lead to him who dives the best.
"A peck of coals a-piece shall glad the rest."   270
     In naked majesty great Dennis stands,

267 filth,] mud, *1728a–f.*   268 Weekly] *** *1728a–f.*
271 great Dennis] great *D— 1728a–f.* Oldmixon *1735a–42.*

268. *The* Weekly Journals] Papers of news and scandal intermix'd, on different sides and parties and frequently shifting from one side to the other, call'd
the *London Journal, Mist's Journal, British Journal, Daily Journal,* &c. the writers
of which for some time were *Welsted* ⟨Oldmixon: *1735a–51*⟩, *Roome, Molloy*
⟨Arnall: *1735a–51*⟩, *Concanen,* and others; persons never seen by our author.
⟨EC MS. has two readings here: "The London Journals," "All Hoadley's
Journals," showing that Pope's first thought was to retaliate on Bishop Hoadly
for his "Britannicus" articles in *The London Journal* (1721) on Bishop Atterbury.
For Hoadly, see ii 338, 368, and Biog. App.; for Molloy, see Biog. App.—*The
London Journal,* a formidable critic of the government while John Trenchard
and Thomas Gordon were writing their celebrated "Cato's Letters" exposing
the South Sea directors, had become so popular that in 1722 the government
was forced to buy the paper outright and alter its policy. Gordon and Trenchard continued their attack in a new weekly, *The British Journal;* but that
paper too came under government control. From January 1728 William Arnall
was writing in it under the name of Roger Manly.—Hanson, pp. 106 ff.,
144–5. For the various other authors named, see Biog. App.⟩

270. *A peck of coals a-piece*] Our indulgent Poet, whenever he has spoken of
any dirty or low work, constantly puts us in mind of the Poverty of the offenders,
as the only extenuation of such practices. Let any one but remark, when a
Thief, a Pickpocket, a Highwayman or a Knight of the Post is spoken of, how
much our hatred to those characters is lessen'd, if they add, a *needy* Thief, a
poor Pickpocket, a *hungry* Highwayman, a *starving* Knight of the Post, *&c.*

271. *In naked majesty great* Dennis *stands*] The reader, who hath seen in the
course of these notes, what a constant attendance Mr. *Dennis* paid to our author,
might here expect a particular regard to be shewn him; and consequently may
be surprized at his sinking at once, in so few lines, never to rise again! But in
truth he looked upon him with some esteem, for having, more generously than
the rest, set his *name* to such works. He was not only a formidable Critick who
for many years had written against every thing that had success ⟨Pope is, no
doubt, recollecting the sentence from Dennis which he had quoted in his
"Testimonies of Authors," viz. "I never attack'd any of these writings unless
they had *Success,* infinitely beyond their merit."⟩, (the Antagonist of Sir
Richard Blackmore, Sir *Richard Steele,* Mr. *Addison,* and Mr. *Pope*) but a zealous

And, Milo-like, surveys his arms and hands,
Then sighing, thus. "And I am now threescore?
"Ah why, ye Gods! should two and two make four?"
He said, and climb'd a stranded Lighter's height,   275
Shot to the black abyss, and plung'd down-right.
The Senior's judgment all the crowd admire,
Who but to sink the deeper, rose the higher.
    Next Smedley div'd; slow circles dimpled o'er

279 Smedley] *E— 1728a–f.*

Politician (not only appearing in his works, where *Poetry* and the *State* are always equally concerned, but in many secret Hints and sage advices given to the Ministers of all reigns.) He is here likened to *Milo*, in allusion to that verse of *Ovid* ⟨*Met.* xv 228–30⟩.

> *—Fletque Milon senior, cum spectat inanes*
> *Herculeis similes, fluidos pendere lacertos;*

either with regard to his great Age, or because he was undone by trying to pull to pieces an Oak that was too strong for him.
⟨Cf. Dryden's translation, ll. 348 ff.:

> Now sapless on the verge of Death he stands,
> Contemplating his former Feet, and Hands;
> And *Milo*-like, his slacken'd Sinews sees . . .⟩
> ———*Remember* Milo's *End,*
> *Wedg'd in that timber which he strove to rend.*

        Lord *Rosc.* ⟨Lord Roscommon, *An Essay on Translated Verse*, 87–8⟩.

273. *—And am I now threescore?*] I shall here, to prove my impartiality, re-mark a great oversight in our author as to the age of Mr. *Dennis.* He must have been some years above threescore in the Mayoralty of Sir *George Thorold*, which was in 1720, and Mr. *Dennis* was born (as he himself inform'd us in Mr. *Jacob's* Lives before-mentioned) in 1657; since when he has happily liv'd eight ⟨ten: *1735a–42*⟩ years more, and is already senior to Mr. *Durfey*, who hitherto of all our Poets, enjoy'd the longest, bodily, Life. ⟨D'Urfey had died in 1723, aged seventy. The commas which Pope had carefully inserted to emphasize that D'Urfey's long life was *bodily* only, and did not extend to his poetic reputation, slipped out in later editions, and have never been restored since.⟩

275. *a stranded Lighter's height* ⟨Fleet Ditch was navigable at high-tide up to Holborn Bridge. "It had five feet of water at the lowest tide. The poet, as we see by the 'stranded lighter,' makes the diving match take place at low tide." —EC.⟩

279. Smedley] In the surreptitious editions this whole Episode was apply'd to an initial letter *E—*, by whom if they meant the Laureate, nothing was more absurd, no part agreeing with his character. ⟨Pope, of course, had merely

7

The quaking mud, that clos'd, and ope'd no more. 280
All look, all sigh, and call on Smedley lost;
Smedley in vain resounds thro' all the coast.
    Then * * try'd, but hardly snatch'd from sight,

281 Smedley] *E— 1728a–f.*   282 Smedley] *E— 1728a–f.*
283 Then ** try'd,] *H—* try'd the next, *1728a–f.*
283–4 Then ** [P** *1735ab*] essay'd: scarce vanish'd out of sight
    He buoys up instant, and returns to light; *1735a–42.*

changed his mind. In the EC MS. the reading is "Eusden."⟩ The Allegory
evidently demands a person dipp'd in scandal, and deeply immers'd in dirty
work: whereas Mr. *Eusden*'s writings rarely offended but by their length and
multitude, and accordingly are tax'd of nothing else in book 1. verse 102. But
the person here mention'd, an *Irishman*, was author and publisher of many
scurrilous pieces, a weekly *Whitehall Journal* in the year 1722, in the name of
Sir *James Baker*, and particularly whole Volumes of Billingsgate against Dr.
Swift and Mr. *Pope*, call'd *Gulliveriana* and *Alexand⟨e⟩riana*, printed in 8°. 1728.
⟨For Jonathan Smedley, see Biog. App. Sir James Baker was apparently an
actual knight, who for some reason became a butt of the wits, and whose name
was frequently taken in vain. (See *Mother Ross*, Defoe's *Works* (Bohn), iv 494 ff.)
A writer in *Mist's Journal* (June 30, 1722) charges the "Sir James Baker" of
The Whitehall Journal with writing *The St. James's Journal* as well.—*Gulliveriana*
and *Alexanderiana* make one volume of almost 400 pages.⟩

    281. ——*and call on* Smedley *lost*, &c.] Lord *Roscommon*'s translation of
Virgil's 6th Eclog. ⟨43–4⟩.

            Alcides *wept in vain for* Hylas *lost*,
            Hylas *in vain resounds thro' all the coast.*

    283. *Then * * try'd*] This is an instance of the Tenderness of our author. The
person here intended writ an angry preface against him, grounded on a Mistake, which he afterwards honourably acknowledg'd in another printed preface.
Since when, he fell under a second mistake, and abus'd both him and his Friend.
    He is a writer of Genius and Spirit, tho' in his youth he was guilty of some
pieces bordering upon bombast. Our Poet here gives him a Panegyric instead of
a Satire, being edify'd beyond measure, at this only instance he ever met with
in his life, of one who was much a Poet, confessing himself in an Error: And has
supprest his name, as thinking him capable of a second repentance. ⟨The
asterisks stand for "Aaron": the *H—* of *1728* stood for "Hill." See Biog. App.
for an account of Pope's relations with Aaron Hill. In 1731 Hill wrote to Pope
complaining of the references to him in the *Dunciad*. Pope replied at once that
the passage about him in the poem was an "oblique panegyric," but in a
subsequent letter he undertook to have the note omitted, and even to have it
stated ("if I have any influence on the editors") that Hill was not intended.

> Instant buoys up, and rises into light;
> He bears no token of the sabler streams,   285
> And mounts far off, among the swans of Thames.
>   True to the bottom, see Concanen creep,
> A cold, long-winded, native of the deep!
> If perseverance gain the Diver's prize,
> Not everlasting Blackmore this denies: 290

286 *Add 1728a–f:*
>   Far worse unhappy *D—r* succeeds,
>   He search'd for coral, but he gather'd weeds.
287 see Concanen] *** and *** *1728a–e. R—* and *Wh—y 1728f.*
288 A . . . native] Long-winded both, as natives *1728a–f.*
289 This only merit pleading for the prize, *1728a–f.*
290 Not] Nor *1728a–c.* Blackmore] *Bl— 1728a–f.*

He never went so far as that; but from *1735a* the note read: "A Gentleman of Genius and Spirit, who was secretly dipt in some papers of this kind, on whom our Poet bestows a Panegyric instead of a Satire, as deserving to be better imployed than in Party-quarrels and Personal Invectives." In the text of the poem, P * * of *1735ab*, if it is not a misprint (which is unlikely), was probably a further attempt to placate Hill. Asterisks were restored in *1736a*, possibly because P * * suggested Pope's friend, Christopher Pitt, whom he could scarcely have wished to satirize. For the "*H—* try'd" of *1728.* Curll and the anonymous *Key* both conjectured "Harte" (i.e. Walter Harte, whose tribute to Pope was cited in 1729 among the "Testimonies"); the Dublin edition of 1728 guessed "Hughes" (i.e. John Hughes, 1677–1720, or perhaps his brother Jabez, d. 1731).⟩

    286. ⟨"*D—r*" of the 1728 editions was the Rev. William Diaper, author of *Nereides: Or, Sea Eclogues,* to which Pope alludes in his couplet. He died in 1717, in his twenty-ninth year. It is difficult to see why Pope should introduce this inoffensive young poetaster, who had been dead for more than ten years when the *Dunciad* was published. The most likely explanation is that he was salvaging part of an epigram that he had written while Diaper was still alive. His omission from later editions was probably due to Swift, who had befriended him. See *Journal to Stella,* March 12, 21, Dec. 23, 1712.⟩

    287. *Concanen*] In the former editions there were only Asterisks in this place; this name was since inserted merely to fill up the verse, and give ease to the ear of the reader. ⟨The "*R—* and *Wh—y*" of *1728f* is explained by the EC MS., which reads "Roome and Whatley." For Roome, see iii 146 and Biog. App. For Stephen Whatley, see Biog. App.⟩

    290. *Not everlasting* Blackmore] Virg. Æn. 5 ⟨541⟩.

        Nec bonus Eurytion prælato invidit honori, &c.

No noise, no stir, no motion can'st thou make,
Th' unconscious flood sleeps o'er thee like a lake.
Not Welsted so: drawn endlong by his scull,

291–2 *Om.* *1728a–f.*
293 Not so bold Arnall, with a weight of scull, *1735a–42.*

292. *Th' unconscious flood* ⟨Cf. Parnell, *To Mr. Pope:*
On lazy lakes, unconscious of a flood,
Whose dull brown Naiads ever sleep in mud.⟩

293. *Welsted*] *Leonard Welsted*, author of the *Triumvirate*, or a Letter in verse from *Palæmon* to *Celia* at *Bath*, which was meant for a Satire on Mr. *P.* and some of his friends about the year 1718 ⟨i.e. 1717. It satirized Pope, Gay, and Arbuthnot for their farce, *Three Hours after Marriage*⟩. The strength of the metaphors in this passage is to express the great scurrility and fury of this writer, which may be seen, One day, in a Piece of his, call'd (as I think) *Labeo.* ⟨Afterwards incorporated in *One Epistle* (1730). See Pope's own statement in "A List of Books etc." This sentence was omitted in all editions from *1735a.*⟩ He writ other things which we cannot remember. *Smedley* in his *Metam.* of *Scrib.* mentions one, the *Hymn* of a *Gentleman* to the *Creator:* ⟨*1729a–51.* "A Hymn to the Creator: written by a Gentleman on occasion of the Death of his only daughter," 1726.⟩ and there was another in praise either of a *Cellar* or a *Garret.* ⟨*1729d–51.* "Oikographia," 1725, a pleasant poem, addressed to the Earl of Dorset, in which Welsted describes his house.⟩ *L. W.* characteris'd in the treatise περὶ βαθοῦς or the Art of sinking as a *Didapper*, and after as an *Eel*, is said to be this person, by DENNIS *Daily Journal* of *May* 11, 1728. He is mentioned again in book 3. ⟨*1729a–51.* See iii 163. The letter in the *Daily Journal* is unsigned; but it repeats some expressions already used by Dennis against Pope, and is in his furious manner.⟩ The foresaid dark anonymous Writers are characterized also under another animal, a *Mole*, by the author of the ensuing Simile, which was handed about, at the same time.

> *Dear* W—d, *mark, in dirty hole*
> *That painful animal, a Mole:*
> *Above ground never born to go,*
> *What mighty stir it keeps below!*
> *To make a Molehill, all this strife!*
> *It digs, pokes, undermines, for life;*
> *How proud, a little Dirt to spread!*
> *Conscious of nothing o'er its head:*
> *Till, lab'ring on for want of eyes,*
> *It blunders into Light—and dies.*

⟨*1729d–51.* Reprinted as No. xxviii of *Certain Epigrams* (1732) where it is inscribed "to Mr. Welsted, or Mr. Tibbald, no Matter which".—For William Arnall, substituted for Welsted in *1735a*, see B ii 315.⟩

Furious he sinks; precipitately dull.
Whirlpools and.storms his circling arm invest,   295
With all the Might of gravitation blest.
No crab more active in the dirty dance,
Downward to climb, and backward to advance;
He brings up half the bottom on his head,
And boldly claims the Journals and the Lead.   300
    Sudden, a burst of thunder shook the flood.
Lo Smedley rose, in majesty of mud!
Shaking the horrors of his ample brows,
And each ferocious feature grim with ooze.
Greater he looks, and more than mortal stares;   305
Then thus the wonders of the Deep declares.
    First he relates, how sinking to the chin,
Smit with his mien, the Mud-nymphs suck'd him in:
How young Lutetia, softer than the down,
Nigrina black, and Merdamante brown,   310
Vy'd for his love in jetty bow'rs below;

293–4 But nimbler *W—d* [*We—d 1728f*] reaches at the ground,
    Circles in mud, and darkness all around, *1728a–f.*
295–6 *Om. 1728a–f.*   298 and] or *1735ab.*   300 boldly] loudly
1735c–42.   302 Lo *E—* rose, tremendous all in mud! *1728a–f.*
303 ample] sable *1728a–f.*

302. ——*in Majesty of mud*] Milton ⟨*Par. Lost*, ii 266⟩,
               ——*in majesty of darkness round*
            Circled——⟨*Covers his throne*⟩.
    302. *Smedley rose* ⟨The reading of *1728a*, "tremendous all in mud," suggests
that Dennis, whose fondness for the word "tremendous" was well known, was
originally intended to win the diving match. This is confirmed by the EC MS.⟩
    305. *Greater he looks, and more than mortal stares*] Virg. ⟨*Aen*. vi 49–50⟩ of the
Sybil.
               ——*majorque videri*
            Nec mortale sonans——
⟨Dryden translates:
            Greater than Human Kind she seem'd to look:
            And with an Accent, more than Mortal, spoke.⟩
    309 f. ⟨"Lutetia" is the classical name for the modern Paris. The name
was thought to be derived from "its dirty situation." (*Grub-Street Journal*, April
17, 1735. Lutum=clay, mud.)—"Merdamante"=filth-loving.⟩

As Hylas fair was ravish'd long ago.
Then sung, how shown him by the nutbrown maids,
A branch of Styx here rises from the Shades,
That tinctur'd as it runs, with Lethe's streams,   315
And wafting vapours from the Land of Dreams,
(As under seas Alphæus' secret sluice
Bears Pisa's offerings to his Arethuse)
Pours into Thames: Each city-bowl is full
Of the mixt wave, and all who drink grow dull.   320
How to the banks where bards departed doze,

317 secret] sacred *1729a* (*corrected in* "*M. Scriblerus Lectori*").

312. *As Hylas fair*] Who was ravish'd by the water-nymphs and drawn into the river. The story is told at large by *Valerius Flaccus, Lib.* 3. Argon. See *Virg. Ecl.* 6 ⟨43–8⟩.

314, *&c. A branch of* Styx, *&c.*] Homer, *Il.* 2. Catal. ⟨751–5⟩.

> Ὁι τ' ἀμφ' ἱμερτὸν Τιταρησσὸν ἔργ' ἐνέμοντο,
> Ὅς ῥ' ἐς Πηνειὸν προῖει καλλίρροον ὕδωρ,
> Οὐδ' ὅ γε Πηνειῷ συμμίσγεται ἀργυροδίνῃ,
> Ἀλλά τέ μιν καθύπερθεν ἐπιρρέει ἠΰτ' ἔλαιον,
> Ὅρκου γὰρ δεινοῦ Στυγὸς ὕδατός ἐστιν ἀπορρώξ.

Of the land of Dreams in the same region, he makes mention, *Odyss.* 24 ⟨12⟩. See also *Lucian*'s true History. *Lethe* and the *Land* of *Dreams* allegorically represent the *Stupefaction* and *visionary Madness* of Poets equally dull and extravagant. Of *Alpheus* his waters gliding secretly under the sea of *Pisa*, to mix with those of *Arethuse* in *Sicily, vid. Moschus Idyl.* 8. *Virg. Ecl.* 10 ⟨4–5⟩,

> Sic tibi, cum fluctus subter labere Sicanos,
> Doris amara suam non intermisceat undam.

And again, *Æn.* 3 ⟨694–6⟩.

> —Alphæum, fama est, huc Elidis amnem
> Occultas egisse vias, subter mare, qui nunc
> Ore, Arethusa, tuo Siculis confunditur undis.

⟨But Pope here seems to be concealing, rather than revealing, the source of his imitation. Cf. Milton, *Arcades*, 30–1:

> Divine *Alpheus*, who, by secret sluse,
> Stole under Seas to meet his *Arethuse*.⟩

321. *How to the banks*, &c.] Virg. Ecl. 6 ⟨64, 66–70⟩.

> Tum canit errantem Permessi ad flumina Gallum,
> Utque viro Phœbi chorus assurexerit omnis;
> Ut Linus hæc illi divino carmine pastor,
> Floribus atque apio crines ornatus amaro,
> Dixerit, Hos tibi dant calamos, en accipe, Musæ,
> Ascræo quos ante seni—— &c.

They led him soft; how all the bards arose;
Taylor, sweet bird of Thames, majestic bows,
And Shadwell nods the poppy on his brows;
While Milbourn there, deputed by the rest,   325
Gave him the cassock, surcingle, and vest;
And "Take (he said) these robes which once were mine,
"Dulness is sacred in a sound Divine."
   He ceas'd, and show'd the robe; the crowd confess

---

323 bird] Swan *1735a–42*.   324 Shadwell] *Sh— 1728a–e.*
325 Milbourn] *M—n 1728a–c.*

---

323. Taylor, *sweet bird of* Thames] *John Taylor* the Water Poet, an honest
man, who owns he learn'd not so much as his *Accidence:* a rare example of
modesty in a Poet!

> *I must confess I do want eloquence,*
> *And never scarce did learn my Accidence,*
> *For having got from* Possum *to* Posset,
> *I there was gravell'd, could no farther get.*

He wrote fourscore books in the reign of *James* I. and *Charles* I. and afterwards
(like Mr. *Ward*) kept a Publick-house in *Long Acre*. He died in 1654. ⟨Pope's
information is derived from Winstanley's *Lives*, pp. 167–8. The lines from Taylor are, as is usual with Pope, incorrectly quoted.⟩

324. *And* Shadwell *nods the poppy*] *Shadwell* took Opium for many years, and
died of too large a dose of it, in the year 1692. ⟨He formed the habit owing to a
painful illness that had afflicted him for some years before his death. According
to Nicholas Brady, who preached his funeral sermon, "he never took his Dose
of *Opium*, but he solemnly recommended himself to God by Prayer."—A. S.
Borgman, *Thomas Shadwell*, 1928, p. 88. Cf. Dryden, *Mac Flecknoe*, 126–7 (of
Shadwell):

> His temples, last, with Poppies were o'erspread,
> That nodding seem'd to consecrate his head.

See Biog. App., Shadwell.⟩

325. Milbourn] *Luke Milbourn* ⟨1649–1720⟩ a Clergyman, the fairest of
Criticks; who when he wrote against Mr. *Dryden*'s *Virgil* ⟨*Notes on Dryden's
Virgil*, 1698⟩, did him justice, in printing at the same time his own translations
of him, which were intolerable. His manner of writing has a great resemblance
with that of the Gentlemen of the *Dunciad* against our author, as will be seen
in the Parallel of Mr. *Dryden* and him. *Append.* ⟨vi⟩.

326. *surcingle* ⟨a girdle or belt which confines the cassock: OED.⟩

328. *Dulness is sacred* ⟨Dryden, Prologue to *Troilus and Cressida*, l. 32:
    Dulness is decent in the Church and State.—EC.⟩

The rev'rend Flamen in his lengthen'd dress.   330
Slow moves the Goddess from the sable flood,
(Her Priest preceding) thro' the gates of Lud.
Her Criticks there she summons, and proclaims
A gentler exercise to close the games.
"Hear you! in whose grave heads, as equal scales,   335
I weigh what author's heaviness prevails,
Which most conduce to sooth the soul in slumbers,
My He*nley*'s periods, or my Blackmore's numbers?
Attend the trial we propose to make:
If there be man who o'er such works can wake,   340
Sleep's all-subduing charm who dares defy,
And boasts Ulysses' ear with Argus' eye;
To him we grant our amplest pow'rs to sit
Judge of all present, past, and future wit,
To cavil, censure, dictate, right or wrong,   345
Full, and eternal privilege of tongue."

331 moves . . . sable] mov'd . . . silver *1728a–c.*
338 He*nley*'s . . . Blackmore's] H—'s . . . *Bl*—'s *1728a–f.*
341 charm] pow'r *1728a–d.* charms *1729d, 1735c–42.*
342 boasts] boast *1728c.*   343 amplest] ample *1735ab.*

332. *Gates of* Lud] "King *Lud* repairing the City, call'd it after his own
"name, *Lud*'s Town; the strong gate which he built in the West part, he like-
"wise for his own honour named *Ludgate.* In the year 1260, this gate was beauti-
"fied with images of *Lud* and other Kings. Those images in the reign of *Edward*
"VI. had their heads smitten off, and were otherwise defaced by unadvised
"folks. Queen *Mary* did set new heads on their old bodies again. The 28th of
"Q. *Eliz.* the same gate was clean taken down, and newly and beautifully
"builded with images of *Lud* and others as afore." Stow's Survey of *London.*
⟨1720, vol. i, bk i, p. 20. The gate was removed in 1760.⟩
   338. *My Henley's periods* ⟨i.e. John ("Orator") Henley, for whom see iii 195*n.,*
and Biog. App. The half-italicized spelling remained in all editions from *1729a–
35b*; it is retained here because it may be intentional. In the EC MS. the reading
is "Hoadley's," and it cannot be doubted that Pope was thinking of Hoadly's
famous sermon alluded to at l. 368. (Cf. *Donne* iv 73: "And *Ho—y* for a Period
of a Mile.") Orator Henley had his faults, but he never sent any one to sleep,
and that is the qualification demanded by the context.⟩
   342] See *Hom. Odyss.* 12 ⟨192⟩. *Ovid, Met.* 1 ⟨625⟩.

Three Cambridge Sophs and three pert Templars came,
The same their talents, and their tastes the same,
Each prompt to query, answer, and debate,
And smit with love of Poesy and Prate.   350
The pond'rous books two gentle readers bring;
The heroes sit; the vulgar form a ring.
The clam'rous crowd is hush'd with mugs of Mum,
'Till all tun'd equal, send a gen'ral hum.
Then mount the clerks; and in one lazy tone,   355
Thro' the long, heavy, painful page, drawl on;
Soft, creeping, words on words, the sense compose,
At ev'ry line, they stretch, they yawn, they doze.
As to soft gales top-heavy pines bow low
Their heads, and lift them as they cease to blow,   360
Thus oft they rear, and oft the head decline,
As breathe, or pause, by fits, the airs divine:

357 Soft, creeping, . . . words,] *Omit commas 1728a–f, 1735ab.*

---

347. *Sophs* ⟨students in their second or third year.⟩
348. *The same their talents——Each prompt*, &c.] Virg. Ecl. 7 ⟨4–5⟩.

> *Ambo florentes ætatibus, Arcades ambo,*
> *Et cantare pares, & respondere parati.*

350.] *Smit with the love of sacred song*—Milton ⟨*Par. Lost*, iii 29⟩.
352. *The heroes sit;* &c.] Ovid, M⟨et.⟩ 13 ⟨1⟩.

> *Consedere duces, & vulgi stante corona.*

353. *Mum* ⟨A kind of beer originally brewed in Brunswick (OED). Pope gives it preference here, no doubt, because it allows him a quibble on "hush'd." Addison (*Spectator*, No. 9) had written of the Mum Club, a great "Enemy to Noise."⟩

356. *Thro' the long, heavy, painful page*, &c.] All these lines very well imitate the slow drowziness with which they proceed. It is impossible for any one who has a poetical ear to read them, without perceiving the heaviness that lags in the verse to imitate the action it describes. The Simile of the Pines is very just and well adapted to the subject. ESSAY on the DUNC. p. 21. ⟨The carrying over of the sense from "low" to "Their heads," with the marked pause that results at the end of the first foot, is a particularly bold liberty for Pope to take with the heroic couplet. "I have followed the significance of the numbers, and the adapting them to the sense, much more even than Dryden; and much oftener than any one minds it. Particularly in the translations of Homer, . . . and in the Dunciad, often, and indeed in all my poems."—Spence, p. 316.⟩

7*

And now to this side, now to that, they nod,
As verse, or prose, infuse the drowzy God.
Thrice Budgel aim'd to speak, but thrice supprest   365
By potent Arthur, knock'd his chin and breast.
Toland and Tindal, prompt at Priests to jeer,

365 Budgel] *B—l 1728a–f.*   366 Arthur] *Arthur 1728a–f.*
367 Toland and Tindal,] *C—s* and *T—d, 1728a–e. C—s* and
Toland, 1728f.

365. *Thrice* Budgel *aim'd to speak*] Famous for his speeches on many occasions
about the *South Sea* Scheme, &c. "He is a very ingenious gentleman, and hath
"written some excellent Epilogues to Plays, and *one small* piece on Love, which
"is very pretty." J ACOB Lives of Poets, vol. 2. p. 289. But this Gentleman has
since made himself much more eminent, and personally well-known to the
greatest statesmen of all parties ⟨as well as to all the Courts of Law—*1742–51*⟩,
in this nation. ⟨He spoke on Sept. 20 and Sept. 30, 1720, and printed his
speeches, which went through numerous editions. Budgell's oratorical gifts
are satirically referred to in *Donne* iv 51. He is said to have lost £20,000 in the
South Sea failure. Budgell's most famous epilogue was a humorous one which
he wrote for *The Distrest Mother* (1712) of Ambrose Philips. It was "received
with such uncommon applause, that it was called for by the audience during
the whole run of that tragedy, and continued to be spoken many years after,
at the representation of the same play." (*Biographia Britannica*, 2nd ed. Art.
B UDGELL.) For further elucidation of Pope's note, see Biog. App., Budgell.⟩

366. *Arthur* ⟨Blackmore's *Prince Arthur; an heroick poem*, appeared in 1695,
and was followed in 1697 by his *King Arthur. An Heroick Poem*. Both were
"pond'rous books" in folio. In the former, both in the preface and in the poem
itself, Blackmore had attacked Dryden.⟩

knock'd his chin ⟨Cf. Dryden's translation of the Ceyx-Alcyone episode, Ovid,
Met. xi 304–5:

> And rais'd his tardy Head, which sunk agen;
> And sinking on his Bosom knock'd his Chin.—EC.⟩

367. Toland *and* Tindal] Two persons not so happy as to be obscure, who
writ against the Religion of their Country. The surreptitious editions placed
here the name of a Gentleman, who, tho' no great friend to the Clergy is a
person of Morals and Ingenuity. ⟨This sentence was omitted in *1735ab* and
1742–51. The EC MS. makes it clear that "*C—s*" of *1728* was intended for
Anthony Collins, the deist (1676–1729). The name was printed in full in the
Dublin edition of 1728. He had been ridiculed by Swift in *Mr. C—ns's Discourse of Free-Thinking . . . For The Use of the Poor*, 1713.⟩ *Tindal* was Author of the
Rights of the Christian Church ⟨1706⟩: He also wrote an abusive pamphlet against
Earl *Stanhope* ⟨*S— 1729d–51*⟩, which was suppress'd while yet in manuscript by
an eminent Person then out of the Ministry, to whom he show'd it expecting

Yet silent bow'd to Christ's No kingdom here.
Who sate the nearest, by the words o'ercome
Slept first, the distant nodded to the hum.   370
Then down are roll'd the books; stretch'd o'er 'em lies
Each gèntle clerk, and mutt'ring seals his eyes.
As what a Dutchman plumps into the lakes,

368 Christ's No Kingdom] *Christ's no kingdom 1728a–f*.
373 As] At *1729a–c*.

his approbation. This Doctor afterwards publish'd the same piece, *mutatis mutandis*, against that very Person when he came into the Administration. ⟨The last six words were cancelled in *1729a* in "M. Scriblerus Lectori." (See p. 196.)—EC identifies the "abusive pamphlet" with *The Defection Consider'd* (1717). This pamphlet was aimed at Townshend, who had been dismissed from office in April 1717, and at Walpole, who had resigned in consequence, leaving Stanhope at the head of a new administration. If Pope's charge is correct, Tindal must have carried an anti-Stanhope pamphlet to either Townshend or Walpole, and then, after it had been rejected, rewritten it so as to put the case for Stanhope.—For Toland, see Biog. App.; for Tindall, see Biog. App. vol. iv.⟩

368. *Christ's No kingdom*, &c.] This is scandalously said by CURL, Key to *Dunc.* ⟨p. 15⟩ to allude to a Sermon of a reverend Bishop. But the context shows it to be meant of a famous publick Orator, not more remarkable for his long-winded periods, than his Disaffection to Ecclesiastical Hierarchy, and to the doctrine that Christ's Kingdom is of *this world*. ⟨From *1735a* onwards Pope omitted the last sentence of this note, and the word "scandalously" in the first sentence, thus giving a tacit approval to Curll's statement. Bishop Hoadly's famous discourse on "The Nature of the Kingdom or Church of Christ" was one of the least soporific sermons of its period. It occasioned the Bangorian controversy, and it had reached a fifteenth edition in the year of publication, 1717. Cf. T. Cooke, Preface to *The Battle of the Poets*, 1729: "He surely forgets, when he makes the Judges sleep over it, how long it keeped the whole Kingdom awake." In *1735ab* the note read as follows: "This is said by Curl, in his Key to the Dunciad, to allude to the Sermon of a reverend Bishop. If the Poet in this place, among mean and injurious Party-Writers, could have any thought of that Prelate; it must have been occasion'd by his having sometimes stoop'd to rank himself with them: or perhaps in particular for having in the London Journals borrow'd the name of Britannicus, to inflame the Accusations and aggravate the Sufferings of a Brother of his own Order in the Church, after he had satisfy'd the Rigour of the Law, and actually lay under those Pains and Penalties which continued his whole life: I mean the learned Bishop Atterbury."⟩

373 ff. ⟨These lines might be taken for a parody by Pope of his own lines in

One circle first, and then a second makes,
What Dulness dropt among her sons imprest   375
Like motion, from one circle to the rest;
So from the mid-most the nutation spreads
Round, and more round, o'er all the sea of heads.
At last Centlivre felt her voice to fail,
Old James himself unfinish'd left his tale,   380
Boyer the State, and Law the Stage gave o'er,

379 Centlivre] *C—re 1728a–e.*
380 Old James] And *** *1728a–f.* Motteux *1735a–42.*
381 Boyer . . . Stage] *T—s* and *T—* the church and state *1728a–f.*

The Temple of Fame, 436 ff.:

> As on the smooth Expanse of Chrystal Lakes,
> The sinking Stone at first a Circle makes . . .

As EC notes, however, the lines had been parodied twelve years earlier in *Aesop at the Bear-garden . . . By Mr.* Preston, 1715 (p. 30), where the obscene transmutation of Pope's simile had already been made. The passage is too unpleasant to quote, but there can be no doubt that Pope borrowed from it.⟩

378. *o'er all the sea of heads*] Blackm. Job.

> *A waving sea of heads was round me spread,*
> *And still fresh streams the gazing deluge fed.*

⟨This passage had already been picked out for ridicule in the *Peri Bathous*, ch. viii.⟩

379. *Centlivre*] Mrs. *Susanna Centlivre* ⟨1667?–1723. See Biog. App.⟩, wife to Mr. *Centlivre*, Yeoman of the Mouth to his Majesty. She writ many Plays, and a song (says Mr. *Jacob* ⟨*The Poetical Register*⟩, vol. I. p. 32.) before she was seven years old. She also writ a Ballad against Mr. *Pope's* Homer before he begun it. ⟨According to Curll (*Curliad*, p. 27) she had no hand in it. See ii 199*n*.⟩

380. *Old James* ⟨The annotators have ignored "old James" because he appears only in the editions of 1729. Perhaps he was the long-winded James Pitt, who was already writing as "Publicola" in *The London Journal* (P.R.O.—S.P.D. 36/11/85), and who was later characterized by Pope as "the eldest and gravest" of the newspaper writers. See *Dunciad* B, ii 312, and Biog. App.⟩

381. *Boyer the State, and Law the Stage gave o'er*] A. *Boyer*, a voluminous compiler of Annals, Political Collections, *&c.*——⟨Abel Boyer (1667–1729) wrote and compiled *The Political State of Great Britain* from 1711 till his death. Pope is perhaps referring to a statement of Boyer's in the number for Jan. 1729: ". . . I cannot entertain Hopes of being able to carry it on much longer, under the Disadvantage of a crazy Constitution, broken with Age, constant Labour, and a Complication of a Stubborn Gout and Rheumatism." He had also been forced by the hostility of certain booksellers to give up his monthly account

Nor Motteux talk'd, nor Naso whisper'd more;

382 Motteux . . . Naso] *** . . . S— *1728a–f.*   Motteux] Kelsey
1735a–42.

of Parliamentary Proceedings.—For Boyer, see Biog. App.⟩ *William Law,* A. M.
⟨1686–1761, author of *A Serious Call*⟩ wrote with great zeal against the Stage,
Mr. *Dennis* answer'd with as great. Their books were printed in 1726. Mr. *Law*
affirm'd that "the Playhouse is the Temple of the Devil, the peculiar pleasure
"of the Devil, where all they who go, yield to the Devil, where all the Laughter
"is a laughter among Devils, and that all who are there are hearing Musick in
"the very Porch of Hell." ⟨*The Absolute Unlawfulness of the Stage Entertainment . . .*
p. 15.⟩ To which Mr. *Dennis* replied, that "there is every jot as much difference
"between a true Play, and one made by a Poetaster, as between *Two religious*
"*books,* the *Bible* and the *Alcoran.*" Then he demonstrates that "all those who had
"written against the Stage were *Jacobites* and *Nonjurors,* and did it always at a
"time when something was to be done for the *Pretender.* Mr. *Collier* publish'd
"his *Short View* when *France* declar'd for the *Chevalier;* and his *Dissuasive* just
"at the *great Storm,* when the devastation which that Hurricane wrought had
"amazed and astonished the minds of men, and made them obnoxious to
"melancholy and desponding thoughts. Mr. *Law* took the opportunity to
"attack the Stage upon the great preparations he heard were making abroad,
"and which the *Jacobites* flatter'd themselves were design'd in their favour.
"And as for Mr. *Bedford's Serious Remonstrance,* tho' I know nothing of the time
"of publishing it, yet I dare to lay odds it was either upon the Duke *D'Aumont's*
"being at *Somerset-house,* or upon the *late Rebellion.*" DENNIS, Stage defended
against Mr. *Law,* pag. *ult.* ⟨i.e. *The Stage Defended, From Scripture, Reason,
Experience . . .* pp. 9, 32–4⟩.

    381. ⟨The "*T—s* and *T—*" of *1728a* is explained by the EC MS., which
reads:

          Travers and Trapp the church and state gave o'er.

For Trapp, see Biog. App. Travers was probably a coffee-house pundit. Cf.
"The Quidnunckis" (1724), *The Poems of Jonathan Swift,* ed. Harold Williams,
1937, iii 1120:

          How vain are mortal Man's Endeavours,
          Said, at St. *James's,* Master *Tra–ers!*⟩

    382. *Motteux . . . Naso* ⟨The loquacity of Motteux was again remarked upon
in *Donne* iv 50:

          Talkers, I've learn'd to bear; *Motteux* I knew.

For Motteux, see Biog. App., vol. iv. "Naso" may possibly be Spencer Compton, Earl of Wilmington, that "Roman in his nose alone" (*1740,* l. 65), but
there are many possible candidates. The *S—* of *1728* was taken by Curll (*Key*)
and by the author of the anonymous Key to be Shippen. William Shippen, the
Jacobite (1673–1743), was in the habit of speaking in the House in a low, rapid
voice which was rendered still more indistinct "by a habit he had contracted of

Norton, from Daniel and Ostrœa sprung,
Blest with his father's front, and mother's tongue,
Hung silent down his never-blushing head;   385
And all was hush'd, as Folly's self lay dead.
    Thus the soft gifts of Sleep conclude the day,
And stretch'd on bulks, as usual, Poets lay.
Why shou'd I sing what bards the nightly Muse
Did slumbring visit, and convey to stews?   390
Who prouder march'd, with magistrates in state,
To some fam'd round-house, ever open gate!

383-5 Ev'n *N—n*, gifted with his mother's tongue,
    Tho' born at *Wapping*, and from *Daniel* sprung,
    Ceas'd his loud bawling breath, and dropt the head;
    1728a-f.
385 Hung . . . his] Ev'n Arnall hung the *1735ab.*
391 Who] Or *1728a-f.*   392 round-house,] roundhouse' *1741-42.*

---

holding his glove before his mouth" (*Memoirs of Horace Walpole*, ed. Eliot
Warburton, 1851, i 305); but it is perhaps unlikely that Pope would wish to
introduce him into the *Dunciad*. The EC MS. has two readings: "Loughton,"
and "Selkirk." The latter is, no doubt, Charles Douglas, Earl of Selkirk (1663–
1739), who was to appear again in *Dia.* i 92; ii 61, 62, and who, if he is "The
Right Hon. E. of S." in the *Peri Bathous*, ch. vii, had already figured as one of
the Tortoises.—The "Kelsey" who first appeared in *1735a* has not been identified. The MS. gives "Kelsall," and this may be Henry Kelsall, who in 1729 was
one of the four Chief Clerks to the Treasury.⟩

    383. Norton] *Norton de Foe*, said to be the natural offspring of the famous
Daniel. Fortes creantur fortibus. One of the authors of the *Flying-Post*, in which
well-bred work Mr. *P.* had sometime the honour to be abus'd with his betters,
and of many hired scurrilities and daily papers to which he never set his name,
in a due fear of Laws and Cudgels. He is now writing the *Life of Colonel* Charteris.
⟨Several pamphlets dealing with the notorious career of Col. Francis Charteris
(1675–1732) were published about this time. The words "natural offspring"
were replaced by "offspring," and the last sentence was omitted from *1735a*
onwards. For Benjamin Norton Defoe, see Biog. App.

    "Ostrœa: that is, an oyster wench: hence, in the next verse, *his mother's
tongue*. He found this facetious name in Gay's *Trivia*, iii 185."—Wakefield.⟩

    386. *And all was hush'd,* &c.] Alludes to *Dryden*'s verse in the *Indian Emperor*
⟨III ii 1⟩,

        All things are hush'd, as Nature's self lay dead.

    392. *round-house* ⟨a lock-up.⟩

How Laurus lay inspir'd beside a sink,
And to mere mortals seem'd a Priest in drink?
While others timely, to the neighbouring Fleet   395
(Haunt of the Muses) made their safe retreat.

393 Laurus] *E— 1728a–f.*   395 While] All *1728a–f.*

393. *sink* ⟨a cess-pool, a conduit . . . for carrying away dirty water or sewage. (OED). Laurus was lying drunk in the street.⟩

393. *How* Laurus *lay* inspir'd, &c.] This line presents us with an excellent Moral, that we are never to pass judgment merely by *appearances*; a Lesson to all men who may happen to see a reverend person in the like situation, not to determine too rashly, since not only the Poets frequently describe a Bard inspir'd in this posture,

(*On* Cam's *fair bank where* Chaucer *lay inspir'd,*

and the like) but an eminent Casuist tells us, that if a Priest be seen in any indecent action, we ought to account it a deception of sight, or illusion of the Devil, who sometimes takes upon him the shape of Holy men on purpose to cause scandal. How little the prophane author of the *Characters of the Times* printed 8°. 1728. regarded this admonition, appears from these words pag. 26. (speaking of the reverend Mr. *Laurence Eusden*) "A most worthy successor of "*Tate* in the Laureatship, a man of insuperable modesty, since certainly it was "not his Ambition that led him to seek this illustrious post, but his affection to "the Perquisite of *Sack.*" A reflection as mean as it is scandalous! Scrib-lerus. ⟨Laurus is Eusden, the poet laureate. (See iii 315.) The final comment of Scriblerus (omitted from *1735a* onwards) is taken from Curll's *Key* (p. 16), where it is applied to l. 393. Pope's sneer gains added point from the fact that he believed Curll to be not only author of the *Key* (which here rebuts the charge of drunkenness brought against Eusden), but also part-author of *The Characters of the Times* where that same charge is made. Eusden's intemperate habits were well-known. "If he had any Beauty of Mind he darken'd it by Hard-drinking."—Ayre, i 260. And see *Ep. to Arbuthnot* 15, and Biog. App. to vol. iv.⟩

395. *Fleet*] A Prison for insolvent Debtors on the bank of the Ditch.

End of the Second Book.

THE DUNCIAD.

Book the Third.

B UT in her Temple's last recess inclos'd,
On Dulness lap th' Anointed head repos'd.
Him close she curtain'd round with vapors blue,
And soft besprinkled with Cimmerian dew.
Then raptures high the seat of sense o'erflow,   5
Which only heads, refin'd from reason, know.
Hence, from the straw where Bedlam's Prophet nods,
He hears loud Oracles, and talks with Gods.
Hence the Fool's paradise, the Statesman's scheme,
The air-built Castle, and the golden Dream,   10
The Maid's romantic wish, the Chymist's flame,
And Poet's vision of eternal fame.
    And now, on Fancy's easy wing convey'd,
The King descended to th' Elyzian shade.

5, 6, &c.] Hereby is intimated that the following Vision is no more than the
Chimera of the Dreamer's brain, and not a real or intended satire on the
Present Age, doubtless more learned, more inlighten'd, and more abounding
with great Genius's in Divinity, Politics, and whatever Arts and Sciences, than
all the preceding. For fear of any such mistake of our Poet's honest meaning, he
hath again at the end of this Vision, repeated this monition, saying that it all
past thro' the *Ivory gate*, which (according to the Ancients) denoteth Falsity.
SCRIBLERUS.

7. *Bedlam's Prophet* ⟨Pope may have had in mind one of the most striking
illustrations to Swift's *Tale of a Tub*, in which a lunatic is seen lying on the
straw of his cell.⟩

8.   *He hears loud Oracles, and talks with Gods.*
Virg. Æn. 7 ⟨90–1⟩.

            Et varias audit voces, fruiturque deorum
            Colloquio——

10–11. *the golden Dream . . . the Chymist's flame* ⟨Pope may be referring here to
Steele's unlucky ventures into alchemy. His search for *aurum potabile* at the
beginning of the century had been satirically recalled by Dennis in 1720 in
The Character and Conduct of Sir John Edgar, p. 18.⟩

There, in a dusky vale where Lethe rolls,   15
Old Bavius sits, to dip poetic souls,
And blunt the sense, and fit it for a scull
Of solid proof, impenetrably dull.

15. *There in a dusky vale*, &c.] Virg. Æn. 6 〈703 ff.〉.

——*Videt Æneas in valle reducta*
Seclusum nemus——
Lethæumque domos placidas qui prænatat amnem.
Hunc circum innumeræ gentes, &c.

16. *Old* Bavius *sits, &c.*] Alluding to the story of *Thetis* dipping *Achilles* to render him impenetrable.

At pater Anchises penitus convalle virenti
Inclusas animas, superumque ad lumen ituras,
Lustrabat——   Virg. Æn. 6.

〈679–81. Dryden, translating freely, had rendered Virgil's "inclusas animas" as "Spirits, which . . . new Bodies wait." Cf. l. 21 below.〉

16. *Old* Bavius *sits*] *Bavius* was an ancient Poet, celebrated by *Virgil* for the like cause as *Tibbald* by our author, tho' in less christian-like manner: For heathenishly it is declared by *Virgil* of *Bavius*, that he ought to be *hated* and *detested* for his evil works; *Qui Bavium non* odit——Whereas we have often had occasion to observe our Poet's great good nature and mercifulness, thro' the whole course of this Poem.

Mr. *Dennis* warmly contends that *Bavius* was no inconsiderable author; nay, that "he and *Mævius* had (even in *Augustus*'s days) a very formidable Party at "*Rome*, who thought them much superior to *Virgil* and *Horace:* For (saith he) "I cannot believe they would have fix'd that eternal brand upon them, if they "had not been coxcombs in more than ordinary credit." 〈Rem. on *Pr. Arthur*, part 2. c. 1.—*1729b–51.*〉 An argument which (if this Poem should last) will conduce to the honour of the Gentlemen of the *Dunciad*. In like manner he tells us of Mr. *Settle*, that "he was once a formidable Rival to Mr. *Dryden*, and "that in the University of *Cambridge* there were those who gave him the *prefer-* "*ence.*" 〈Pref. to *Remarks on Homer*. Cf. i 88*n.*〉 Mr. *Welsted* goes yet farther in his behalf. "Poor *Settle* was formerly the *Mighty Rival* of *Dryden:* nay, *for many years*, "bore his Reputation *above* him." [*Pref. to his Poems*, 8°. *p.* 51.] And Mr. *Mil-bourn* cry'd out, "How little was *Dryden* able, even when his blood run high, to "defend himself against Mr. *Settle!*" *Notes on Dryd. Virg. p.* 175. These are comfortable opinions! and no wonder some authors indulge them. SCRIBLERUS. 〈Curll (*Key*, p. 16) takes Bavius to be Shadwell. But when Pope mentions Shadwell at ii 324, and B iii 22, he does so by his own name. In a mock-epitaph, however, "In Obitum *Tho. Shadwell*, pinguis memoriae. 1693," Tom Brown had called him Bavius. At iii 315 Bavius is told to take the poppy from his brow. This certainly suggests that Bavius was Shadwell. Cf. ii 324*n.*〉

Instant when dipt, away they wing their flight,
Where Brown and Mears unbar the gates of Light,   20
Demand new bodies, and in Calf's array
Rush to the world, impatient for the day.
Millions and millions on these banks he views,
Thick as the stars of night, or morning dews,
As thick as bees o'er vernal blossoms fly,   25
As thick as eggs at Ward in Pillory.

24 or] and *1736b–42*.   26 Ward] *W—d 1728a–f*.

20. Brown *and* Mears] Booksellers, ⟨*1728a*⟩, Printers for *Tibbald*, Mrs. *Haywood*, or any body. ⟨See Biog. App., Brown, Mears.⟩—The Allegory of the souls of the Dull coming forth in the form of Books ⟨drest in calve's leather—*1735a–51*⟩, and being let abroad in vast numbers by Booksellers, is sufficiently intelligible.

20. *Unbar the gates of Light*] Milton ⟨*Par. Lost*, vi 4⟩.

22–3. ⟨*Temple of Fame*, ll. 481–2:
. . . impatient forth they flow,
And rush in Millions on the World below.⟩

23–5. *Millions and millions—Thick as the Stars*, &c.] Virg. ⟨*Aen.* vi 309 ff.⟩.
Quam multa in sylvis autumni frigore primo
Lapsa cadunt folia, aut ad terram gurgite ab alto
Quam multæ glomerantur aves, &c.

26. Ward *in Pillory*] *John Ward* of *Hackney*, Esq.; Member of Parliament, being convicted of Forgery, was first expelled the House, and then sentenc'd to the Pillory on the 17th of *Febr.* 1727. Mr. *Curl* ⟨having likewise stood there—*1735–51*⟩ looks upon the mention of such a Gentleman in a Satire, as a *great act of Barbarity. Key to the* Dunc. *3d Edit. p.* 16. And another Author ⟨Ned Ward⟩ thus reasons upon it. *Durgen*, 8°. pag. 11, 12. "How unworthy is it of *Christian* "*Charity* to animate the *rabble* to abuse a *worthy man* in such a situation? It was "in vain! he had no *Eggs* thrown at him; his *Merit* preserv'd him. What cou'd "move the Poet thus to mention a *brave Sufferer*, a *gallant Prisoner*, expos'd to the "view of all mankind! It was laying aside his *Senses*, it was committing a *Crime* "for which the *Law is deficient* not to punish him! nay a Crime which *Man can* "*scarce forgive*, nor *Time efface!* Nothing surely could have induced him but being "bribed to it by a great Lady," (to whom this brave, honest, worthy Gentleman was guilty of no offence but Forgery proved in open Court, &c.) ⟨*1729a–51.*⟩ But it is evident this verse cou'd not be meant of him; it being notorious that no *Eggs* were thrown at that Gentleman: Perhaps therefore it might be intended of Mr. *Edward Ward* the Poet. ⟨*1729d–51.* In adding this further note in *1729d* Pope omitted "It was in vain . . . preserv'd him." For Edward Ward, see i 200. He had been pilloried in 1705. In paraphrasing *Durgen* above, Pope has

Wond'ring he gaz'd: When lo! a Sage appears,
By his broad shoulders known, and length of ears,
Known by the band and suit which Settle wore,

given the substance of sixteen lines of Ward's verse. According to *Brice's Weekly Journal*, Feb. 24, 1727, the constables were so numerous when John Ward stood in the pillory "that whatever Dispositions there might be in any of the Spectators to pelt him, no body durst attempt it." The "great Lady" was Katherine, Duchess of Buckinghamshire. (See Pope's note to *Moral Essays*, iii 20.) From a letter of the Duchess to Pope (EC x 154) it appears that the poet had been exerting himself, through Lord Harcourt, to obtain justice for her. The charge that he was bribed to animate the rabble against Ward is repeated in *The Cudgel*, by Hercules Vinegar, Esq., 1742, p. 11. Curll (*Curliad*, p. 28) says that this was effected by "a small Copy of Verses which were handed about while Ward was in the pillory." For John Ward, see Biog. App., vol. iv.⟩

28. *And length of Ears*] This is a *sophisticated* reading. I think I may venture to affirm all the Copyists are mistaken here: I believe I may say the same of the Criticks; *Dennis, Oldmixon, Welsted*, have pass'd it in silence: I have always stumbled at it, and wonder'd how an error so manifest could escape such accurate persons. I dare assert it proceeded originally from the inadvertency of some Transcriber whose head run on the *Pillory* mention'd two lines before: It is therefore amazing that Mr. *Curl* himself should overlook it! ⟨Pope is punning on Curll's own acquaintance with the pillory. In eighteenth-century slang a man in the pillory was an "overseer."⟩ Yet that *Scholiast* takes not the least notice hereof. That the learned *Mist* ⟨June 8, 1728⟩ also read it thus, is plain, from his ranging this passage among those in which our Author was blamed for *personal Satire* on a *Man*'s *Face* (whereof doubtless he might take the *Ear* to be a part;) So likewise *Concanen, Ralph*, the *Flying-Post*, and all the Herd of Commentators.—*Tota armenta sequuntur.*

A very little Sagacity (which all these Gentlemen therefore wanted) will restore to us the true sense of the Poet, thus,

By his broad shoulders known, and length of years.

See how easy a change! of one single letter! That Mr. *Settle* was old is most certain, but he was (happily) a stranger to the Pillory. *This Note partly Mr.* THEOBALD, *partly* SCRIBLERUS. ⟨This note is ascribed to Theobald in part because it parodies two in *Shakespeare Restored*, pp. 19, 26. Cf. A 1 168n.—Settle was described by a writer in *The True Briton*, Feb. 19, 1724, as "a Man of tall Stature, red Face, short black Hair" (EC). Wakefield notes a distant parody here of Helen's description of Ajax, *Iliad* iii 226.⟩

29. *the band and suit* ⟨The collar or ruff ("band") worn by men in the seventeenth century had passed out of fashion long before Settle's death: that may be the point that Pope is making here. He may, however, be alluding to the dress worn by Settle as a poor brother of the Charterhouse, which he entered in 1718, "twice three years" before his death in 1724. Cf. O.E.D., "band", 4 b.⟩

(His only suit) for twice three years before: 30
All as the vest, appear'd the wearer's frame,
Old in new state, another yet the same.
Bland and familiar as in life, begun
Thus the great Father to the greater Son.
    "Oh born to see what none can see awake!   35
Behold the wonders of th' Oblivious Lake.
Thou, yet unborn, hast touch'd this sacred shore;
The hand of Bavius drench'd thee o'er and o'er.
But blind to former, as to future Fate,
What mortal knows his pre-existent state?   40
Who knows how long, thy transmigrating soul
Did from Bœotian to Bœotian roll?
How many Dutchmen she vouchsaf'd to thrid?
How many stages thro' old Monks she rid?
And all who since, in mild benighted days,   45
Mix'd the Owl's ivy with the Poet's bays?
As man's mæanders to the vital spring
Roll all their tydes, then back their circles bring;
Or whirligigs, twirl'd round by skilful swain,

42 Did] Might *1729b–42.*

---

32. *another yet the same* ⟨Cf. Horace, *Carmen Seculare*, 9–11:
               Alme Sol, curru nitido diem qui
               Promis et celas, aliusque et idem
               Nasceris . . .   —EC.⟩
35. ⟨Cf. Virgil, *Aen.* vi 390–1.—Wakefield.⟩
35 ff. ⟨Pope is here burlesquing the passage in *Aeneid* vi, where Aeneas
is guided by the Sibyl to the infernal regions, and is met by his father Anchises.
—Settle now speaks (ll. 35–222, 226–8, 247–356), and Theobald plays the
part of a spectator: he interrupts with only one question, at l. 246.⟩
42. *Did from* Bœotian, *&c.*] See the Remark on Book 1. V. 23.
46. *Mix'd the Owl's Ivy with the Poet's Bays*] Virg. Ec. 8 ⟨12–13⟩.
           ——*sine tempora circum*
        Inter victrices Hederam tibi serpere laurus.
47–8. ⟨These two lines formed part of an epic poem which Pope wrote when
a boy, and which he afterwards destroyed.—Spence, p. 25.⟩
49. *whirligigs* ⟨The OED offers three definitions of this ancient toy, and gives
a citation as far back as 1440. The toy of which Pope was thinking was probably

Suck the thread in, then yield it out again: 50
All nonsense thus, of old or modern date,
Shall in thee centre, from thee circulate.
For this, our Queen unfolds to vision true
Thy mental eye, for thou hast much to view:
Old scenes of glory, times long cast behind,   55
Shall first recall'd, rush forward to thy mind;
Then stretch thy sight o'er all her rising reign,
And let the past and future fire thy brain.
   "Ascend this hill, whose cloudy point commands
Her boundless Empire over seas and lands.   60
See round the Poles where keener spangles shine,
Where spices smoke beneath the burning Line,
(Earth's wide extreams) her sable flag display'd;
And all the nations cover'd in her shade!

56 rush] run *1729a* (*but corrected in "M. Scriblerus Lectori"*), *1735ab.*

---

one "consisting of a small spindle turned by means of string," rather than a
top or teetotum, or any eighteenth-century equivalent of diabolo or yo-yo.⟩

   53. *For this, our Queen &c.*] This has a resemblance to that passage in *Milton*
⟨*Par. Lost*, xi 411–13⟩, where the Angel,

> To nobler sights from Adam's eye remov'd
> The film; then purg'd with Euphrasie and Rue
> The visual nerve—For he had much to see.

There is a general allusion in what follows to that whole passage.

   59. *Ascend this hill* ⟨Cf. the words spoken by the Sibyl to Aeneas (*Aeneid*, vi
676) and by Michael to Adam (*Par. Lost*, xi 366–7) in similar circumstances.⟩

   61, 62. *See round the Poles*, &c.] Almost the whole Southern and Northern
Continent wrapt in Ignorance.

⟨Cf. Tickell's *A Poem on the Prospect of Peace*, 196 ff.

> Now o'er his Head the Polar Bear he spies,
> And freezing Spangles of the *Lapland* Skies;
> Now swells the Canvas to the sultry Line,
> With glittering Spoils where *Indian* Grottoes shine,
> Where Fumes of Incense glad the Southern Seas . . .
>> —Wakefield.

Pope quoted these lines with approval in a letter to John Caryll, Nov. 29, 1712.
The phrase "the burning line" occurs in the Rev. Thomas Newcomb's translation of Addison's Latin poem on the Peace of Ryswick, l. 82.⟩

"Far Eastward cast thine eye, from whence the Sun
And orient Science at a birth begun.   66
One man immortal all that pride confounds,
He, whose long Wall the wand'ring Tartar bounds.
Heav'ns! what a pyle! whole ages perish there:
And one bright blaze turns Learning into air.   70
    "Thence to the South extend thy gladden'd eyes;
There rival flames with equal glory rise,
From shelves to shelves see greedy Vulcan roll,
And lick up all their Physick of the Soul.
    "How little, mark! that portion of the ball,   75
Where, faint at best, the beams of Science fall.
Soon as they dawn, from Hyperborean skies,
Embody'd dark, what clouds of Vandals rise!
Lo where Mœotis sleeps, and hardly flows
The freezing Tanais thro' a waste of Snows,   80

65 thine] thy *1728a–f.*
67 man immortal] god-like Monarch *1735c–42.*
71 extend . . . eyes;] as far extend thy eyes; *1728a–f.*
75 mark!] see! *1728a–e.*
77 Soon . . . dawn,] Against her throne, *1728a–f.*
78 In dulness strong, th' avenging Vandals rise; *1728a–f.*
    dark] thick *1735ab.*

65.] Our Author favours the opinion that all Sciences came from the Eastern
nations.
    66. *Science* ⟨In its earlier sense of knowledge acquired by study.⟩
    69.] *Chi Ho-am-ti,* Emperor of *China,* the same who built the great wall be-
tween *China* and *Tartary,* destroyed all the books and learned men of that empire. ⟨*1728a–51.* His motive was pride: he wished all learning to date from his
reign. He made an exception of agricultural and medical works.⟩
    73, 74.] The *Caliph, Omar* I. having conquer'd *Ægypt,* caus'd his General to
burn the *Ptolomæan* library, on the gates of which was this inscription, *Medicina
Animæ, The Physick of the Soul.* ⟨*1728a–51.* Cf. Jonson, "An Execration upon Vulcan," 83–4 (on the burning of his library):
            These, had'st thou pleas'd either to dine or sup,
            Had made a meal for Vulcan to lick up.—J. Warton.⟩
    79–80. ⟨"I have been told that the couplet by which he declared his own
ear to be most gratified was this."—Johnson's *Lives,* iii 250.—The Mæotis and

The North by myriads pours her mighty sons,
Great nurse of Goths, of Alans, and of Huns.
See Alaric's stern port, the martial frame
Of Genseric! and Attila's dread name!
See, the bold Ostrogoths on Latium fall;   85
See, the fierce Visigoths on Spain and Gaul.
See, where the Morning gilds the palmy shore,
(The soil that arts and infant letters bore)
His conqu'ring tribes th' Arabian prophet draws,
And saving Ignorance enthrones by Laws.   90
See Christians, Jews, one heavy sabbath keep;
And all the Western World believe and sleep.

Tanais had been brought together by Seneca (*Hipp.* 715):

> Quis eluet me Tanais? aut quae barbaris
> Mæotis undis Pontico incumbens mari . . .

and again in *Herc. Furens*, 1323. In *Winter*, l. 888, James Thomson had written: "And Hecla flaming through a waste of snow." Though Pope hated cold weather, his imagination was stirred by "deserts of snow, seas of ice, and frozen skies" (EC vi 176). In a letter to Caryll, Dec. 21, 1712, he says that the severe weather has turned his studies "to those books which treat of the descriptions of the Arctic regions, Lapland, Nova Zembla, and Spitzberg." He then gives half a dozen examples of snow scenes from the poets.⟩

81–2. *The North by myriads, &c.* ⟨Cf. Milton, *Par. Lost*, i 351–4:

> A multitude, like which the populous North
> Pour'd never from her frozen loyns, to pass
> Rhene or the Danaw, when her barbarous Sons
> Came like a Deluge on the South . . .—EC.⟩

83. *Alaric* ⟨who led the Visigoths to the sack of Rome, A.D. 410.⟩

84. *Genseric* ⟨King of the Vandals.⟩

Attila ⟨"King of the *Huns*, surnamed the Scourge of God, lived in the Vth Century . . . The King of the *Huns* was of small Stature; but that did not hinder his striking a Terror into the most couragious, by his lofty Carriage and fierce Countenance." Bayle, Art. ATTILA.⟩

88. *The Soil that arts and infant letters bore*] *Phœnicia, Syria,* &c. where *Letters* are said to have been invented. In these Countries *Mahomet* began his Conquests.

91–2. *one heavy sabbath, &c.* ⟨Cf. Dryden, *To Sir Godfrey Kneller*, 57–8:

> Long time the Sister Arts, in Iron Sleep,
> A heavy Sabbath did supinely keep.—Wakefield.⟩

Pope had already observed (*E. on C.*, l. 692) that "the Monks finish'd what the Goths begun." In a letter to Caryll, June 25, 1711, he stated his difference of opinion from his friend Southcote about the monks: ". . . he thinks most sorts

"Lo Rome herself, proud mistress now no more
Of arts, but thund'ring against Heathen lore;
Her gray-hair'd Synods damning books unread,   95
And Bacon trembling for his brazen head:
Padua with sighs beholds her Livy burn;
And ev'n th' Antipodes Vigilius mourn.
See, the Cirque falls! th' unpillar'd Temple nods!
Streets pav'd with Heroes, Tyber choak'd with Gods!

97–102 Lo statues, temples, theatres o'erturned,
    Oh glorious ruin! and *** [*Apelles 1728f*] burn'd. *1728a–f.*

---

of learning *flourished* among them, and I am of opinion that only some sort of
learning was barely *kept alive* by them." Pope's independent views on such
matters offended many of his Catholic contemporaries.⟩

94. *Thund'ring against Heathen lore*] A strong instance of this pious rage is
plac'd to Pope *Gregory*'s account. *John of Salisbury* gives a very odd Encomium
to this Pope, at the same time that he mentions one of the strangest effects of
this excess of zeal in him. *Doctor sanctissimus ille Gregorius, qui melleo prædicationis
imbre totam rigavit & inebriavit ecclesiam, non modo* Mathesin *jussit ab aulâ; sed, ut
traditur a majoribus, incendio dedit* probatæ lectionis scripta, *Palatinus quæcunque
tenebat Apollo.* And in another place: *Fertur beatus Gregorius bibliothecam combussisse
gentilem; quo divinæ paginæ gratior esset locus, & major authoritas, & diligentia
studiosior. Desiderius* Archbishop of *Vienna* was sharply reproved by him for
teaching Grammar and Literature, and explaining the Poets; Because (says
this Pope) *in uno se ore cum Jovis laudibus, Christi laudes non capiunt: Et quam grave
nefandumque sit, Episcopis canere quod nec Laico religioso conveniat, ipse considera.* He is
said, among the rest, to have burn'd *Livy; Quia in superstitionibus & sacris Roman-
orum perpetuâ versatur.* The same Pope is accused by *Vossius* and others of having
caus'd the noble monuments of the old *Roman* magnificence to be destroyed,
lest those who came to *Rome* shou'd give more attention to Triumphal Arches,
&c. than to Holy Things. BAYLE, *Dict.* ⟨pp. 223–4⟩.

96. *And Bacon, &c.* ⟨Roger Bacon (1214?–94), the medieval philosopher who
was vulgarly supposed to have constructed a brazen head that could speak.
He is represented as trembling *because* he had made it, i.e. he was likely to incur
the displeasure of the Church.⟩

97. *Livy* ⟨See 94*n*. "It is said, that Livy was thus treated, because he insists
too much on the superstitious rites of the heathen."—Bayle, 224*n*.⟩

98. *Vigilius* ⟨Vigilius, or Virgilius, an eighth-century Bishop of Salzburg,
was publicly censured by the Archbishop of Mainz for professing his belief in
the existence of the Antipodes. Pope could have read a long account of the
incident in Bayle's *Dictionary*, from which he had quoted in his note to l. 94.⟩

99. *Cirque* ⟨probably the Coliseum at Rome.⟩

Till Peter's Keys some christen'd Jove adorn,   101
And Pan to Moses lends his Pagan horn;
See graceless Venus to a Virgin turn'd,
Or Phidias broken, and Apelles burn'd.

   "Behold yon' Isle, by Palmers, Pilgrims trod,   105
Men bearded, bald, cowl'd, uncowl'd, shod, unshod,
Peel'd, patch'd, and pyebald, linsey-woolsey brothers,
Grave mummers! sleeveless some, and shirtless others.
That once was Britain—Happy! had she seen
No fiercer sons, had Easter never been.   110

105 Behold yon'] See'st thou an *1728a–f.*

---

101. '*Till* Peter's *Keys*, &c.] After the Government of *Rome* devolved to the Popes, their zeal was for some time exerted in demolishing the Heathen Temples and Statues, so that the *Goths* scarce destroyed more Monuments of Antiquity out of Rage, than these out of Devotion. At length they spar'd some of the Temples by converting them to Churches, and some of the Statues, by modifying them into Images of Saints. In much later times, it was thought necessary to change the Statues of *Apollo* and *Pallas* on the tomb of *Sannazarius*, into *David* and *Judith*; the Lyre easily became a Harp, and the Gorgon's Head turn'd to that of *Holofernes*. ⟨Cf. *Epistle to Addison*, 11–14.⟩

102. *Moses* ⟨"The medieval belief was that Moses, after descending from Sinai, had horns on his head. The error began with St. Jerome in the Vulgate, the Hebrew word for 'ray' being also the word for 'horn,' and being translated adjectively 'cornutus'."—EC.⟩

107. *linsey-woolsey* ⟨Cf. Butler, *Hudibras*, 1 i 95–6:
        It was a party-colour'd dress
        Of patch'd and py-ball'd languages.
and 1 iii 1227–8:
        A Lawless Linsey Woolsy Brother,
        Half of one Order, half another.
Linsey-Woolsey: a textile material, woven from a mixture of wool and flax. Hence, adjectivally, "being neither one thing nor the other."—OED. For "Peel'd" three of OED's five senses give a possible meaning:—(1) reduced to destitution, (2) tonsured, (3) worn threadbare. Pope may have been conscious of all three.⟩

110. *Happy—had* Easter *never been*] Virg. Ecl. 6 ⟨45⟩.
        Et fortunatam, si nunquam armenta fuissent.

110. *Happy—had* Easter *never been*] Wars in *England* anciently, about the right time of celebrating *Easter*. ⟨*1728a.* "There is a passage in Bede highly commending the piety and learning of the Irish of that age, where, after abundance of praises, he overthrows them all, by lamenting that, alas! they kept Easter at a

In peace, great Goddess! ever be ador'd;
How keen the war, if Dulness draw the sword!
Thus visit not thy own! on this blest age
Oh spread thy Influence, but restrain thy Rage!
    "And see! my son, the hour is on its way,   115
That lifts our Goddess to imperial sway:
This fav'rite Isle, long sever'd from her reign,
Dove-like, she gathers to her wings again.
Now look thro' Fate! behold the scene she draws!
What aids, what armies, to assert her cause!   120
See all her progeny, illustrious sight!
Behold, and count them, as they rise to light.
As Berecynthia, while her offspring vye
In homage, to the mother of the sky,
Surveys around her in the blest abode   125
A hundred sons, and ev'ry son a God:
Not with less glory mighty Dulness crown'd,
Shall take thro' Grubstreet her triumphant round,

112 draw] whet *1728ef.*

---

wrong time of the year."—Swift to Pope, Sept. 29, 1725. The method of calculating Easter was discussed at the Council of Nicaea in A.D. 325; but differences
continued for some time afterwards.⟩
    117. *This fav'rite Isle* ⟨"An elegant allusion to the well-known passage in
Virgil's first Eclogue [l. 66]:
            et toto divisos orbe Britannos . . ."—Wakefield.⟩
    118. *Dove-like* ⟨Cf. Psalm xci 4.⟩
    119, 121. *Now look thro' Fate &c.]* Virg. Æn. 6 ⟨756 ff.⟩.
            Nunc age, Dardaniam prolem quæ deinde sequatur
            Gloria, qui maneant Itala de gente nepotes,
            Illustres animas, nostrumque in nomen ituras,
            Expediam——
    119. *draws* ⟨i.e. discloses, as when a stage-curtain is "drawn."⟩
    123. *As* Berecynthia, *&c.*]Virg. ib. ⟨784 ff.⟩
            Felix prole virum, qualis Berecynthia mater
            Invehitur curru Phrygias turrita per urbes,
            Læta deum partu, centum complexa nepotes,
            Omnes cælicolas, omnes supera alta tenentes.
    ⟨Cf. Dryden's translation of "invehitur curru Phrygias . . . per urbes": "she
makes the Phrygian round."⟩

And Her Parnassus glancing o'er at once,
Behold a hundred sons, and each a dunce.   130
  "Mark first the youth who takes the foremost place,
And thrusts his person full into your face.
With all thy Father's virtues blest, be born!
And a new Cibber shall the Stage adorn.
  "A second see, by meeker manners known,   135
And modest as the maid that sips alone:
From the strong fate of drams if thou get free,
Another Durfey, Ward! shall sing in thee.

129 Her] all *1728a–f.*
131 the youth] that youth *1729b–d, 1735c–42.*
134 Cibber] *C—r 1728a–f.*
135 See yet a younger, by his blushes known, *1728a–f.*
136 that] who *1728a–f.*
138 Ward!] *** *1728a–f.*

131. *Mark first the youth,* &c.] Virg. Æn. 6 ⟨760–1⟩.
        Ille vides, pura juvenis qui nititur hasta
        Proxima sorte tenet lucis loca.—
  133. *With all thy Father's virtues, &c.*] A manner of expression used by *Virgil*
⟨Ecl. viii 17⟩,
            Nascere! præque diem veniens, age Lucifer——
As also that of *Patriis virtutibus.* Ecl. 4 ⟨17⟩.
  134. *a new Cibber* ⟨Theophilus Cibber (1703–58), who was following his
father's profession, and had been appearing on the stage since 1721. See Biog.
App.⟩
  137. *From the strong fate of drams,* &c.] Virg. Æn. 6 ⟨882–3⟩.
            ——si qua fata aspera rumpas,
            Tu Marcellus eris!——
⟨The "strong fate of drams" has an obvious relevance to Ward's profession as a
tavern-keeper. (Cf. i 200*n.*) But in the editions of 1728 these words were applied
to an anonymous dunce who cannot have been Ward because he was introduced as being "yet a younger" man than young Cibber. The context requires
a young poet whose surname was a monosyllable. Cooke is perhaps the most
likely candidate, and Cooke (who, as Pope remarks, was the son of a man "who
kept a Publick-house at Braintree") could also be represented as getting free
from "the strong fate of drams," i.e. breaking away from his father's business.⟩
  138. Ward] *Vid.* Book 1. Ver. 200. ⟨For Ned Ward and Tom Durfey, see
also Biog. App.⟩

Thee shall each Ale-house, thee each Gill-house mourn,
And answ'ring Gin-shops sowrer sighs return!   140
   "Lo next two slip-shod Muses traipse along,
In lofty madness, meditating song,
With tresses staring from poetic dreams,
And never wash'd, but in Castalia's streams:
Haywood, Centlivre, Glories of their race!   145
Lo Horneck's fierce, and Roome's funereal face;

139 Thee . . . thee] For thee each Ale-house, and [thee *1735ab*]
   each *1728a–f, 1735ab*.
141 Lo] See *1728a–f*.
141–52 *In 1728a–f those lines follow l. 172*.
145 Haywood, Centlivre,] *H*—— and *T* ——, *1728a–f*.
146 Horneck's] *H—ck's 1728a–f*. Roome's funereal] *M*—'s rueful
   1728a–e. R—me's peculiar *1728f*. Roome's peculiar *1729d*.

---

  139. *Thee shall each Ale-house, &c.*] Æn. 7 ⟨759–60⟩.
           Te nemus Angitiae, vitrea te Fucinus unda,
           Te liquidi flevere lacus. ⟨*1729d*⟩.
Virgil again, *Ecl.* 10 ⟨13⟩.
           Illum etiam lauri, illum flevere myricæ, &c.
  Gill-house ⟨Johnson defines gill as "a malt liquor medicated with ground-
ivy."⟩
  141. ⟨The EC MS. reads:
           See Pix and slip-shod W— traipse along,
           With heads unpinned and meditating song.
—Mrs. Mary Pix wrote a number of tragedies and comedies without much
success. See Biog. App. "W—" stands, no doubt, for Wortley, i.e. Lady Mary
Wortley Montagu, for whom see ii 128*n*.⟩
  142. *meditating song* ⟨Gay, *Welcome from Greece*, 74:
           With *Winchilsea*, still meditating song.⟩
  143. *staring* ⟨standing up, bristling.⟩
  145. *Haywood, Centlivre*] See book 2. ⟨149, 379. For the "*H*— and *T*—" of
1728a Curll's *Key* and the anonymous Key give "Haywood and Trotter." Mrs
Catharine Trotter (1679–1749) had written several tragedies, and might fairly
lay claim to "lofty madness"; but she was a respectable woman, with a great
admiration for Pope, and is not known to have offended him personally. *T*—
is more probably Mrs Thomas (ii 66): she and Mrs Haywood make a better
pair, if the "lofty madness" is taken ironically.⟩
  146. *Lo Horneck's fierce and Roome's funereal face*] This stood in one edition
And M—'s *ruful face*. But the person who suppos'd himself meant applying to
our author in a modest manner, and with declarations of his innocence, he re-

> Lo sneering G * * de, half malice and half whim,
> A Fiend in glee, ridiculously grim.

147 G**de,] Goode, *1735a–42.*   147–8 *Om. 1728a–f.*

moved the occasion of his uneasiness ⟨*1729a–42*⟩. At the same time promising
to "do the like to any other who could give him the same assurance, of having
never writ scurrilously against him." ⟨*1729b–42*. The "*M—*" of all the 1728
editions except the last was identified by Curll (*Key*, p. 17) as "Mitchell—a
most wretched Rathonian Poetaster." The EC MS. proves that Curll guessed
right. For Joseph Mitchell (1684-1738, born at Ratho) see Biog. App.⟩

Horneck *and* Roome] These two are worthily coupled, being both virulent
Party-writers; and one wou'd think prophetically, since immediately after the
publishing of this Piece the former dying, the latter succeeded him in *Honour*
and *Employment*. ⟨Horneck's death was announced in *The Universal Spectator*,
Oct. 19, 1728, and on Oct. 26 the same paper announced that Edward Roome,
son of Stephen Roome, undertaker, had succeeded him as Solicitor to the
Treasury.⟩ The first was *Philip Horneck*, Author of a Billingsgate paper call'd
The High German Doctor, in the 2d Vol. of which Nº. 14. you may see the
regard he had for Mr. *P.*— ⟨In this number (Dec. 7-10, 1714) there is a dull,
obscure, and not very virulent attack on Pope's *Iliad*. For Horneck, see Biog.
App.⟩ *Edward Roome*, Son of an Undertaker for Funerals in *Fleet-street*, writ some
of the papers call'd *Pasquin*, and Mr. *Ducket* others, where by malicious Innuendos, it was endeavour'd to represent him guilty of malevolent practices
with a great man then under prosecution of Parliament. ⟨*1729a–51. Pasquin*,
No. xiii (Feb. 20, 1723) contains the suggestion that Pope was implicated in the
Jacobite plot for which, in August 1722, Atterbury had been committed to the
Tower on a charge of high treason. Cf. also *Pasquin*, No. xxxvi.⟩ He since
reflected on his, and Dr. Swift's Miscellanies, in his paper call'd the *Senator*.
⟨*1729b–42*. Op. cit., April 9, 1728.⟩ Of this Man was made the following
Epigram.

> *You ask why R— diverts you with his jokes,*
> *Yet, if he writes, is dull as other folks?*
> *You wonder at it—This Sir is the case,*
> *The Jest is lost, unless he prints his Face.*

⟨*1729d–51*. This epigram had been published, with considerable variations, in
The Flying Post: or The Weekly Medley, April 12, 1729. The alterations in the
Dunciad version probably indicate that Pope himself was the author. Cf. ii 46*n*.,
and see also *An Author to be Let*, p. 10. For Roome, see Biog. App.⟩

147. *G**de*] An ill-natur'd Critick who writ a Satire on our Author, yet
unprinted, call'd *The mock Æsop*. ⟨*1729a–51*.—call'd *The mock Aesop* or *Mac
Aesop*, to be father'd by James Moore. As it is yet unprinted, we have not set
his name at length.—*1729bc*.⟩ and many anonymous Libels in Newspapers for
Hire. ⟨*1735a–51*. For Barnham Goode, see Biog. App.⟩

Jacob, the Scourge of Grammar, mark with awe,
Nor less revere him, Blunderbuss of Law.   150
Lo Bond and Foxton, ev'ry nameless name,
All crowd, who foremost shall be damn'd to Fame?
Some strain in rhyme; the Muses, on their racks,
Scream, like the winding of ten thousand Jacks:
Some free from rhyme or reason, rule or check,   155

149 Jacob . . . Grammar,] *W—n*, the scourge of Scripture,
    1728a–e. Woolston, . . . of Gospel *1728f*.
150 Nor . . . him,] And mighty *J—b, 1728a–f*.
151 Bond and Foxton,] thousand thousand, *1728a–f*.
152 *Add 1728a–f*:
    How proud! how pale! how earnest all appear!
    How rhymes eternal gingle in their ear!
153–66 *Om. 1728a–f*.

149. Jacob] This *Gentleman* is Son of a *considerable Malster* of *Romsey* in *Southamptonshire*, and bred to the Law under a *very eminent Attorney:* who, between his *more laborious* Studies, has *diverted* himself with Poetry. He is a great admirer of Poets and their works, which has occasion'd him to try his genius that way—He has writ in prose the *Lives* of the *Poets, Essays*, and a great many Law-Books, *The Accomplish'd Conveyancer, Modern Justice*, &c. GILES JACOB of himself, *Lives* of Poets, Vol. 1. ⟨*1729a–51*. Pope's note is made up of excerpts from Jacob's *Poetical Register*, p. 318, and his *Historical Account*, pp. 299–300.⟩ He very grossly, and unprovok'd, abused in that book the Author's Friend Mr. *Gay*. ⟨*1729b–51*. Of *Three Hours after Marriage* Jacob wrote: "This Play has some extraordinary Scenes in it, which seem'd to trespass on Female Modesty" (*Poetical Register*, p. 115). In his account of Joseph Gay (*ibid*. p. 289), Jacob said that he was the author of an excellent farce, *The Confederates*, written "to expose the Obscenity and false Pretence to Wit" in *Three Hours after Marriage*. He then proceeded to quote the lines from the Prologue to Johnson's *Sultaness* alluded to by Pope at i 240*n*. For further remarks on Jacob, see Errata, p. 199. See also Biog. App.—*W—n* of *1728a* is Thomas Woolston (1670–1733), the freethinker. See iii 209 and Biog. App.⟩

150.] Virg. Æn. 6 ⟨842–3⟩.
————*duo fulmina belli*
Scipiadas, cladem Lybiæ!————

151. Bond *and* Foxton] Two inoffensive offenders against our poet; persons unknown, but by being mention'd by Mr. *Curl*. ⟨See Biog. App., Bond, Foxton.⟩

152. *damn'd to Fame* ⟨In a cancelled passage in *E. on C.*, to follow l. 123, Pope had written ". . . and Perault ne'er been damn'd to fame."⟩

Break Priscian's head, and Pegasus's neck;
Down, down they larum, with impetuous whirl,
The Pindars, and the Miltons, of a Curl.
　"Silence, ye Wolves! while Ralph to Cynthia howls,
And makes Night hideous—Answer him ye Owls!　160
　"Sense, speech, and measure, living tongues and dead,
Let all give way—and Durgen may be read.

162 Durgen] Morris *1735a–42*.

---

158. *Pindars . . . Miltons* ⟨Pope may not intend any particular allusion here;
but in 1720 Curll was advertising *The Olympic Odes of Pindar. In English Meetre*
(R. Straus, *The Unspeakable Curll*, p. 260); and Curll had frequently reprinted
the *Cider* of John Philips, a Miltonic imitation which, according to Warton,
Pope disliked intensely.⟩

159. *Ralph*] A name inserted after the first Editions, not known to our
Author till he writ a Swearing-piece call'd *Sawney*, very abusive of Dr. *Swift*,
Mr. *Gay*, and himself. These lines allude to a thing of his, intituled *Night* a *Poem*.
Shakespear, Hamlet ⟨I iv 53–4⟩.

> —*Visit thus the glimpses of the Moon,*
> *Making Night hideous*—

This low writer constantly attended his own works with Panegyricks in the
Journals, and once in particular prais'd himself highly above Mr. *Addison*, in
wretched remarks upon that Author's Account of English Poets, printed in a
London Journal, Sept. 1728. ⟨Pope may be right, but the remarks in question
were not ascribed to Ralph, nor acknowledged by him. In *The London Journal*
of Sept. 14 Addison's *Account of the Greatest English Poets* was contrasted un-
favourably with Ralph's *The Muses Address to the King: an Ode*, published in
August 1728. There were two long puffs for Ralph's *Night* in the *London Journal*
of May 11 and June 1, 1728, another in the *Evening Journal*, Feb. 7, 1728, and
another in *The British Journal*, June 24, 1727.⟩ He was wholly illiterate, and
knew no Language not even *French*: Being advised to read the Rules of Dramatick Poetry before he began a Play, he smiled and reply'd, *Shakespear writ
without Rules* ⟨*1729a–51*⟩. He ended at last in the common Sink of all such
writers, a Political News-paper, to which he was recommended by his Friend
Arnal, and receiv'd a small pittance for pay. ⟨*1735a–51*. Ralph was said by a
writer in *The Grub-Street Journal*, July 30, 1730, to have been editor of *The
Weekly Medley*, and to have killed it.—See Biog. App.⟩

162. *Durgen*] A ridiculous thing of *Ward*'s. ⟨Durgen is explained in Kersey's
Dictionary as "a little thick and short Person: a Dwarf." (Quoted in OED.)—
For Morris, substituted in 1735, see Biog. App.⟩

"Flow Welsted, flow! like thine inspirer, Beer,

163. *Flow*, Welsted, *flow!* &c.] Parody on *Denham, Cooper's Hill* ⟨188–91⟩.
> *O could I flow like thee, and make thy stream*
> *My great example, as it is my theme.*
> *Tho' deep, yet clear; tho' gentle, yet not dull;*
> *Strong, without rage; without o'erflowing, full.*

⟨These lines were so frequently parodied in the seventeenth and eighteenth
centuries that Swift in *Apollo's Edict* warned the poet not to attempt once more
"the Mimickry of *deep yet clear*." Welsted's verses had been rather similarly
characterized by Bezaleel Morrice, *An Epistle to Mr. Welsted*, 1721, p. 8:
> Thy harmless Verses, ever spruce and gay,
> In specious Gingle move one only Way.
> In easy Measures still they sliding go . . .

To Pope and his friends Welsted, like Philips, was too artless. Cf. *Peri Bathous*,
ch. ix, ". . . flow my Numbers with the quiet thoughtlessness of Mr. W—st—d?"
—There is little in Welsted's career to suggest that he was intemperate in his
habits, though Ayre (vol. i, p. 313) was willing to develop Pope's hint: "This
Gentleman, as many Gentlemen of his Class are, being apt to be bemus'd in
Beer . . ." Pope may have intended no more than a side-glance at one of Wel-
sted's best-known poems, Οἰκογραφία, in which he addressed the Duke of
Dorset on the emptiness of his cellar.⟩

Of this Author see the Remark on Book ii. v. 293. But (to be impartial) add
to it the following different character of him.

Mr. *Welsted* had, in his Youth, rais'd so great Expectations of his future
Genius, that there was a *kind of struggle* between the most eminent in the two
Universities, *which* shou'd have the Honour of his Education. To *compound* this,
he (*civilly*) became a Member of both, and after having pass'd some time at
the One, he removed to the Other. From thence he return'd to Town, where he
became the *darling Expectation* of *all the* polite Writers, whose encouragement he
acknowledg'd in his occasional Poems, in a manner that *will make no small part
of the Fame* of his Protectors. It also appears, from his *Works*, that he was happy
in the Patronage of the most illustrious Characters of the present Age—
Incourag'd by such a *Combination* in his favour, he—publish'd a book of Poems,
some in the *Ovidian*, some in the *Horatian* manner, in both which the most
exquisit Judges pronounce, he even *rival'd his masters*—His Love verses have
rescued that way of writing from Contempt—In his Translations, he has given
us the very soul and spirit of his author. His Ode—his Epistle—his Verses—his
Love-tale—all, are the most perfect things in all Poetry, etc. Welsted of *Himself.* Char. of the Times, 8⁰. 1728. pag. 23, 24. ⟨*1729d–51.* A slightly garbled
version of the account of Welsted in the work cited. Pope attributed the *Characters of the Times* to Curll and Welsted in "A List of Books," p. 208. Curll, however (*Curliad*, p. 31), said that "not one Word of it [was] wrote by the Persons to
whom it was assigned." It is unlikely that Welsted, a man of parts, was responsible for such a poor piece of hack-work, or that Curll had a hand in a

Tho' stale, not ripe; tho' thin, yet never clear;
So sweetly mawkish, and so smoothly dull;   165
Heady, not strong, and foaming tho' not full.
    "Ah Dennis! Gildon ah! what ill-starr'd rage
Divides a friendship, long confirm'd by age?
Blockheads with reason wicked wits abhor,
But fool with fool is barb'rous civil war.   170
Embrace, embrace my Sons! be foes no more!

167–172 *In 1728a–f these lines follow l. 180.*
167 Dennis! Gildon] *D—, G— 1728a–f.*
170 barb'rous] barb'rous, *1728a–f.*

work which he did not publish. For Welsted, see vol. iv, pp. 99, 123–4, and Biog. App.⟩

    167. *Ah Dennis*, &c.] The reader, who has seen thro' the course of these notes, what a constant attendance Mr. *Dennis* paid to our Author and all his works, may perhaps wonder he should be mention'd but twice, and so slightly touch'd, in this poem. But in truth he look'd upon him with some esteem, for having (more generously than all the rest) *set his Name* to such writings. He was also a very old man at this time. By his own account of himself in Mr. *Jacob's Lives*, he must have been above three score in the mayoralty of Sir *George Thorold* in 1720, and hath since happily lived ten years more. So that he is already senior to Mr. *Durfey*, who hitherto of all our Poets enjoy'd the longest Bodily life. ⟨*1735a–51.* Cf. ii 273*n.*⟩

    167. *what ill-starr'd rage* ⟨Nothing appears to be known of the quarrel between these two critics to which Pope alludes here. Farmer in his *Essay on the Learning of Shakespeare* suggests that their disagreement may have arisen over Shakespeare, Gildon believing that Shakespeare was a learned man, and Dennis taking the opposite view. Their names were frequently coupled, either for purposes of praise or blame. Aaron Hill in 1716 had dedicated *The Fatal Vision* to them because they could "distinguish excellencies, and detect absurdity."⟩

    169 f. ⟨This couplet, with certain minor variations, had already appeared in Pope's Prologue to *Three Hours after Marriage*, 1717. He is indebted to Dryden's Epilogue to *All for Love*, where, dealing with the same idea, Dryden writes:
        'Tis *Civil War* with their own Flesh and Blood.⟩

    171. *Embrace, embrace my Sons! be foes no more*] Virg. Æn. 6 ⟨832 ff.⟩.
        ——*Ne tanta animis assuescite bella,*
        Neu patriæ validas in viscera vertite vires:
        Tuq; prior, tu parce——sanguis meus!——
⟨Cf. Dryden's translation:
        Embrace again, my Sons; be Foes no more:
        Nor stain your Country with her Children's Gore.⟩

Nor glad vile Poets with true Criticks' gore.
"Behold yon Pair, in strict embraces join'd;
How like their manners, and how like their mind!
Fam'd for good-nature, B * * and for truth;   175

173–80 *In 1728a–f these lines follow l. 140.*
174 their . . . their] in . . . in *1735a–42.*
175 B**] Burnet *1729d–42.*

---

173. *Behold yon Pair, in strict embraces join'd*] Virg. Æn. 6 ⟨826–7⟩.
        Illæ autem paribus quas fulgere cernis in armis,
        Concordes animæ———
⟨Cf. Dryden's translation:
            The pair you see in equal Armour shine,
            (Now Friends below, in close Embraces join . . .)⟩.
And in the fifth ⟨i.e. *Aen.* v 295–6⟩,
        Euryalus, forma insignis viridique juventa,
        Nisus amore pio pueri.
    175–6. *Fam'd for good nature* B * *, *&c.*
        D * *, *for pious passion to the youth*]
The first of these was Son of the late Bishop of *S.* ⟨i.e. Gilbert Burnet, Bishop of
Salisbury⟩. Author of a weekly paper called *The Grumbler,* as the other was
concern'd in another call'd *Pasquin,* in which Mr. *Pope* was abused (particularly
with the late Duke of *Buckingham* and Bishop of *Rochester.*) ⟨For Francis Atterbury, Bishop of Rochester, see iii 146*n.* John Sheffield, Duke of Buckingham,
one of Pope's early patrons, died in 1721, and in 1723 Pope published an edition of his Works (Jan. 24). Three days later the unsold stock was seized on
account of Jacobite principles and expressions to be found in some of Buckingham's writings. Pope thus found himself, as the editor of a seditious work, in an
awkward situation, and hostile journalists made the most of it. He was attacked
in *Pasquin,* No. xii and No. xiii. See Sherburn, pp. 219–28.⟩ They also join'd in
a piece against his first undertaking to translate the *Iliad,* intituled *Homerides,*
by Sir *Iliad Dogrel,* printed by *Wilkins* 1715. And Mr. *D.* writ an Epilogue for
Powel's Puppet-show ⟨printed in *Homerides*—the second of the two pamphlets
bearing that title. This sentence was omitted from *1735a* onwards.⟩, reflecting on
the same work. Mr. *Curl* gives us this further account of Mr. *B.* "He did *himself*
"*write* a Letter to the E. of *Halifax, informing his Lordship* (as he tells him) *of what*
"*he knew much better before:* And he *publish'd in his own name* several political
"pamphlets, A certain information of a certain discourse, A second Tale of a
"Tub, *&c. All which* it is strongly affirmed *were written by* Colonel *Ducket.*"
CURL, Key, p. 17. ⟨This is not so. The joint authorship of the two men is
made clear from their correspondence. See *The Letters of Thomas Burnet to
George Duckett,* ed. D. Nichol Smith.—The pamphlet referred to by Curll is
The Necessity of Impeaching the Late Ministry. Burnet had written, rather oddly:

D * * for pious passion to the youth.

176 D**] Duckit *1729d–42.* pious passion] cordial friendship
    1728f.

"Give me Leave, my Lord, for once to inform your Lordship of Things which
you are much better acquainted with than my self . . ."⟩ But the author of the
Characters of the Times ⟨p. 14⟩ tells us, these political pieces were not approv'd
of by his *own Father*, the Reverend Bishop.

Of the other works of these Gentlemen, the world has heard no more, than it
wou'd of Mr. *Pope*'s, had their united laudable endeavours discourag'd him from
his undertakings. How few good works had ever appear'd (since men of true
merit are always the least presuming) had there been always such champions to
stifle them in their conception! And were it not better for the publick, that a
million of monsters came into the world ⟨which are sure to die as soon as born—
1729b–51⟩, than that the Serpents should have strangled one *Hercules* in his
cradle? ⟨*1729a–51.* In *1743a* this note was attributed to "C."—presumably
Colonel Cleland.⟩ The Union of these two Authors gave occasion to this
Epigram.

> Burnet *and* Duckit, *friends in spite,*
>   *Came hissing forth in Verse;*
> *Both were so forward, each wou'd write,*
>   *So dull, each hung an A——*
> *Thus* Amphisbœna (*I have read*)
>   *At either end assails;*
> *None knows which leads, or which is led,*
>   *For both Heads are but Tails.*—*1729d–42, 1751.*

⟨Most probably by Pope himself. The epigram appears to refer to their
collaboration in *Homerides*, which was a matter of great moment to Pope, but
perhaps to no one else. According to Griffith (p. 205), it appeared in *The Evening
Post*, June 26–8, 1729.—Pope no doubt intends the reference to Burnet's
good-nature and truth to be ironical; but the author of *The Characters of the
Times* says of him: "This is one of the most amiable Characters in Life: Mr.
Burnet is a frank, honest, good-natur'd Gentleman, of fine Wits, Parts, and
Knowledge." Perhaps Pope's reference to Burnet's good-nature was an ironical
comment on *The Grumbler.*—For Burnet and Duckett, see Biog. App.⟩

176. —— *for pious passion to the youth*] The verse is a literal translation of
Virgil, *Nisus amore pio pueri* ⟨*Aeneid*, v 296⟩——and here, as in the original,
apply'd to Friendship ⟨Cf. the reading of *1728f.*⟩: That between *Nisus* and
Euryalus is allow'd to make one of the most amiable Episodes in the world, and
surely was never interpreted in a perverse sense: But it will astonish the Reader
to hear, that on no other occasion than this line, a Dedication was written to
this Gentleman to induce him to think something farther. "Sir, you are known to
"have all that affection for the beautiful part of the creation which God and
"Nature design'd.—Sir, you have a very fine Lady—and, Sir, you have eight

Equal in wit, and equally polite,
Shall this a Pasquin, that a Grumbler write;
Like are their merits, like rewards they share,
That shines a Consul, this Commissioner.   180
    "But who is he, in closet close y-pent,
Of sober face, with learned dust besprent?
Right well mine eyes arede the myster wight,

181–6 *In 1728a–f these lines follow l. 190.*
182 Of . . . dust] With visage from his shelves with dust
    1728a–f.
183 the] that *1728a–f.*

"very fine Children,"—&c. [*Dedic.* to Dennis *Rem. on the Rape of the Lock.*]
The truth is, the poor Dedicator's brain was turn'd upon this article; he had
taken into his head that ever since some *Books* were written against the *Stage,*
and since the *Italian Opera* had prevail'd, the nation was infected with a vice
not fit to be nam'd. ⟨"I cannot here omit observing one Thing, That this
unnatural Sin has very much increased since *Collier's* Books were publish'd
against the Stage.—Dennis, *The Stage Defended,* p. 20.⟩ He went so far as to
print upon this subject, and concludes his argument with this remark, "that
"he cannot help thinking the Obscenity of Plays excusable at this juncture,
"since, when that execrable sin is spread so wide, it may be of use to the reduc-
"ing men's minds to the natural desire of women." DENNIS, *Stage defended*
against Mr. *Law,* p. 20. Our author has solemnly declared to me, he never
heard any creature but the Dedicator mention that Vice and this Gentleman
together. ⟨Pope may have been sincere in his protestations; but he never
suppressed the passage, nor the note calling attention to Dennis's interpretation
of it. Cf. N. Ault, *Pope's Prose,* p. lxxxvii.⟩

    180. *Consul . . . Commissioner* ⟨Burnet became British Consul at Lisbon in
1719. Duckett was one of the Commissioners for Managing the Excise on Beer
and Malt, at a salary of £1000 per annum.—*The True State of England,* 1729,
p. 124.⟩

    181. *But who is he,* &c.] Virg. Æn. 6 ⟨808 ff.⟩ questions and answers in this
manner, of *Numa,*

                Quis procul ille autem rami, insignis olivæ
                Sacra ferens?—nosco crines, incanaq; menta,&c.

    182. *with . . . dust besprent* ⟨Gay, *A Welcome from Greece,* 127–8:
                O *Wanley,* whence com'st thou with shorten'd hair,
                And visage from thy shelves with dust besprent?⟩

    183. AREDE] *Read* or *peruse;* tho' sometimes used for *counsel,* "READE
"THY READ, *take thy counsaile. Thomas Sternholde* in his translation of the first
"Psalm into *English* metre, hath *wisely* made use of this word,

On parchment scraps y-fed, and Wormius hight.

184 That wonnes in haulkes and hernes, and *H*— he hight.
1728a–f.

> *The man is blest that hath not bent*
> *To wicked* READ *his ear.*

"But in the last spurious editions of the Singing Psalms the word READ is
"changed into *men*. I say spurious editions, because not only here, but quite
"throughout the whole book of Psalms, are strange alterations, all for the
"worse! And yet the title-page stands as it us'd to do! and all (which is abomin-
"able in any book, much more in a sacred work) is ascribed to *Thomas Sternhold*,
"*John Hopkins, and others!* I am confident, were *Sternhold* and *Hopkins* now living,
"they would proceed against the innovators as cheats——A liberty which, to
"say no more of their intolerable alterations, ought by no means to be permitted
"or approved of, by such as are for *Uniformity*, and have any regard for the old
"*English Saxon* tongue. HERNE, *Gloss. on* Rob. *of* Gloc. *Art.* rede ⟨ii 698–700⟩.

I do herein agree with Mr. *H.* Little is it of avail to object that such words are
become *unintelligible*. Since they are *Truly English*, Men *ought* to understand
them; and such as are for *Uniformity* should think all alterations in a Language,
strange, abominable, and *unwarrantable*. Rightly therefore, I say again, hath our
Poet used ancient words, and poured them forth, as a precious ointment, upon
good old *Wormius* in this place. SCRIBLERUS. ⟨In this sarcastic note Pope is
indirectly stating the neo-classical demand for a diction polished and refined
from all uncouth or antiquated terms. His attitude to Hearne's antiquarian
researches was the normal one of the period. Curll wished that Hearne might
"reign unrivalled, *Legendary-grubber* to both Universities." (*An Apology for the
Writings of Walter Moyle,* 1727, p. 21.)—The phrase "haulkes and hernes" of *1728*
Pope found in Speght's *Chaucer*, where it appears in some verses addressed to the
editor. For Hearne, see Biog. App.⟩

Myster wight] Uncouth mortal.

184. *Wormius hight*] Let not this name, purely fictitious, be conceited to
mean the learned *Olaus Wormius*; much less (as it was unwarrantably foisted
into the surreptitious editions) our own Antiquary Mr. *Thomas Herne*, who had
no way aggrieved our Poet, but on the contrary published many curious tracts
which he hath to his great contentment perused.

Most rightly are ancient words here imployed in speaking of such who so
greatly delight in the same: We may say not only rightly, but *wisely*, yea *excellently*, inasmuch as for the like practise the like praise is given to *Hopkins*
and *Sternhold* by Mr. *Herne* himself. [*Glossar. to Rob. of Glocester*] *Artic.* BEHETT;
others say BEHIGHT, "*promised*, and so it is used *excellently well* by *Tho. Norton*
"in his translation into metre of the 116th Psalm, verse 14.

> *I to the Lord will pay my vows,*
> *That I to him* BEHIGHT.

"Where the modern innovators, not understanding the propriety of the word

To future ages may thy dulness last,   185
As thou preserv'st the dulness of the past!
    "There, dim in clouds, the poreing Scholiasts mark,
Wits, who like Owls see only in the dark,
A Lumberhouse of Books in ev'ry head,
For ever reading, never to be read.   190
    "But, where each Science lifts its modern Type,

187–8 Fast by, in darkness palpable inshrin'd
     W—s, B—r, M—n, [*M— 1728ef*] all the poring kind, *1728a–f.*
190 Are ever reading, and are never read. *1728a–f.*
191–4 Round him, each *Science* by its modern type
     Stands known; *Divinity* with box and pipe,
     And proud *Philosophy* with breeches tore,
     And *English Musick* with a dismal score:
     While happier *Hist'ry* with her comrade *Ale*,
     Sooths the sad series of her tedious tale. *1728a–f.*
     (*In 1728 these lines follow l. 200.*)

"(which is *Truly English,* from the *Saxon*) have most *unwarrantably* alter'd it thus,
                    I to the Lord will pay my vows,
                        With joy and great delight."
⟨*Robert of Gloucester's Chronicle,* ii 622⟩.

    VERSE ibid.—HIGHT] "In *Cumberland* they say to *hight,* for to *promise* or
"*vow;* but HIGHT usually signifies *was call'd:* and so it does in the North even to
"this day, notwithstanding what is done in *Cumberland.*" HERNE, *ibid.* ⟨ii 659.
Pope has mangled Hearne's note.⟩

    188. *Wits, who like Owls,* &c.] These few lines exactly describe the right
verbal Critick: He is to his Author as a Quack to his Patients, the more they
suffer and complain, the better he is pleas'd; like the famous Doctor of that sort,
who put up in his bills, *He delighted in matters of difficulty.* Some-body said well of
these men, that their heads were *Libraries out of order.* ⟨In a letter to Caryll,
Jan. 25, 1711, Pope had already remarked on this quack: ". . . you are like him
that put into his bills, 'Let no man be discouraged, for this doctor is one that
delighteth much in matters of difficulty.' "—The reading of *1728a* was elucidated
by Curll: "Watts, Baker, Milbourn"; and Baker was further said to be "the
Poẹt of *Enfield,*" who had published "some rueful Rhimes at his own Expence
both of Pocket and Understanding" (*Key,* p. 17). Curll refers to Henry Baker
(1698–1774). See Biog. App.⟩

    189. *A Lumberhouse of Books* ⟨Cf. *Essay of Criticism,* 613:
                With loads of learned lumber in his head.⟩

    191 ff. ⟨Of these verses as they stood in the editions of 1728 Ralph wrote
(Dedication to *Sawney*), "Can any Lines be more execrably dull?" It is signifi-

Hist'ry her Pot, Divinity his Pipe,
While proud Philosophy repines to show
Dishonest sight! his breeches rent below;
Imbrown'd with native Bronze, lo Henley stands,   195

195 Imbrown'd . . . Bronze,] Pass these to nobler sights: *1728a–f.*
Henley] *H— 1728a–e. He—y 1728f.*

---

cant that Pope revised them. He seems to be giving a contemptuous description
of Henley's neighbours in Butcher-Row. History is pictured as a female
gossiping over a pot of ale. The "English Musick" of the 1728 editions may be
a ballad-singer. But the lines remain obscure, and have never, perhaps, been
generally understood, even by Pope's editors, who have no comment to make.⟩

    195. ——*Lo! Henley stands,* &c.] *J. Henley,* the Orator; he preach'd on the
Sundays Theological matters, and on the Wednesdays upon all other sciences.
Each Auditor paid one shilling. He declaim'd some years unpunish'd against
the greatest persons, and occasionally did our author that honour. WELSTED,
in Oratory Transactions, Nº 1. publish'd by *Henley* himself, gives the following
account of him. "He was born at *Melton Mowbry* in *Leicestershire.* From his
"own Parish school he went to St. *John's* College in *Cambridge.* He began there
"to be uneasy; for it *shock'd* him to find he was *commanded to believe* against his
"judgment in points of Religion, Philosophy, *&c.* for his genius leading him
"freely to *dispute all propositions,* and *call all points to account,* he was impatient
"under those fetters of the free-born mind.——Being admitted to Priest's orders,
"he found the examination very short and superficial, and that it was *not*
"*necessary to conform to the Christian Religion* in order either to *Deaconship* or
"*Priesthood.*" ⟨Welstede adds: "but to subscribe (whether you have study'd
the Matter, or believe it, or no) to the System of the Church."⟩ He came to
Town, and after having for some years been a writer for Booksellers he had an
ambition to be so for Ministers of State. The only reason he did not rise in the
Church we are told "was the envy of others, and a disrelish entertain'd of him,
"because *he was not qualify'd to be a compleat Spaniel.*" ⟨Welstede: "This Popularity, with his enterprizing Spirit, and introducing regular Action into the Pulpit,
were the true Causes, why some obstructed his rising in Town, from Envy,
Jealousy, and a Disrelish of those who are not qualify'd to be compleat Spaniels."⟩
However he offer'd the service of his pen, in one morning, to two Great men of
opinions and interests directly opposite; by both of whom being rejected, he set
up a new Project, and stiled himself the *Restorer of ancient Eloquence.* He thought
"it as lawful to take a licence from the King and Parliament at one place, as
"another; at *Hick's* Hall, as at Doctors Commons; so set up his Oratory in
Newport-Market, Butcher-Row. There (says his friend) "he had the *assurance* to
"form a Plan which no mortal ever thought of; he had success against all
"opposition; challenged his adversaries to fair disputations, and *none would*
"*dispute with him;* writ, read and studied twelve hours a day; compos'd three

Tuning his voice, and balancing his hands.
How fluent nonsense trickles from his tongue!
How sweet the periods, neither said nor sung!
Still break the benches, Henley! with thy strain,
While K * *, B * *, W * *, preach in vain.   200

197 fluent] honey'd *1728a–f.*
199 Henley!] *H— 1728a–e. He—y 1728f.*
200 K**, B**, W**,] *K—, Br—, W— 1728a–f.*
    Kennet, Hare, and Gibson *1735a–42.*

"dissertations a week on all subjects; undertook to teach in *one year* what Schools
"and Universities teach in *five*; was not terrify'd by menaces, insults or satyrs,
"but still proceeded, matured his bold scheme, and put the *Church* and *all that,*
"in *danger.*"   WELSTED, *Narrative,* in *Orat. Transact.* N⁰. 1. ⟨Pope's usual
paraphrase. This *Narrative* by "Mr. Welstede"—not Welsted—was probably
written by Henley himself. The statement that he offered his pen to two great
men is not in the *Narrative*: it was denied by Henley (*Why How Now, Gossip
Pope?* 1743, p. 6), who said that he had never offered his services to Mr. P.
(i.e. Pulteney). He further denied (p. 7) that *he* had called himself the Restorer
of Ancient Eloquence, and claimed that he had never been prosecuted (p. 8).
This may be literally true; but he was certainly presented by the Grand Jury
(cf. *Read's Weekly Journal,* Jan. 18, 1729), and he was also arrested on Feb. 9,
1727 and forced to apply for bail. (P.R.O./S.P. 36/5/100.) See Biog. App.⟩

  After having stood some Prosecutions, he turned his Rhetorick to Buffoonry
upon all publick and private occurrences. All this passed in the same room;
where sometimes he broke Jests, and sometimes that Bread which he call'd
the *Primitive Eucharist.*——This wonderful person struck Medals, which he
dispersed as Tickets to his subscribers: The device, a Star rising to the Meridian,
with this Motto, AD SUMMA; and below, INVENIAM VIAM AUT FACIAM.

  196. *balancing his hands* ⟨This habit of Henley's—part of his theory of Oratory
—was glanced at in some verses in *The Grub-Street Journal,* No. 88: "H—l—y
the rostrum mounts, displays his hand . . ." He is said to have replied to Pope's
phrase by preaching on the text in the *Acts of the Apostles,* "And Paul stretched
forth his hands."—Ayre, i 277.—The "Bronze" of l. 195 is, of course, a *double
entendre.*⟩

  198. *neither said nor sung* ⟨Cf. *The Craftsman,* Dec. 26, 1726 (of Henley): "Such
was the Modulation of his Voice, that it inchanted our Ears, and seem'd more
like Musick than Speaking!"⟩

  199. *Still break the benches* ⟨Cf. Juvenal, *Sat.* vii 86:
            fregit subsellia versu.—Bowles.⟩

  200. *K**, B**, W** ⟨Curll (*Key,* 3rd ed., p. 17) says "Kennet, Bramston,
Warren," i.e. White Kennett (1660–1728), Bishop of Peterborough; Rev.
James Bramston (1694?–1744), a minor poet of some distinction; and possibly

Oh great Restorer of the good old Stage,
Preacher at once, and Zany of thy Age!
Oh worthy thou of Ægypt's wise abodes,
A decent Priest, where monkeys were the Gods!
But Fate with Butchers plac'd thy priestly Stall,   205
Meek modern faith to murder, hack, and mawl;
And bade thee live, to crown Britannia's praise,
In Toland's, Tindal's, and in Woolston's days.
    "Thou too, great Woolston! here exalt thy throne,
And prove, no Miracles can match thy own.   210
    "Yet oh my sons! a father's words attend:
(So may the fates preserve the ears you lend)
'Tis yours, a Bacon, or a Locke to blame,
A Newton's Genius, or a Seraph's flame:
But O! with one, immortal One dispense,   215

201–28 *Om. Add 1728a–f:*
        But oh! what scenes, what miracles behind?
        Now stretch thy view, and open all thy mind.
209–10 *Om. 1735a–42.*   212 you] ye *1735ab.*
214 Seraph's] Milton's *1735a–42.*

Dr. Robert Warren, whose sermons in three volumes were published in 1723. It would be rash to assume that Pope intends to praise any of them. The line may be read as an encomium of fine preaching thrown away on unappreciative congregations, or a criticism of the ineffectiveness of their sermons. Pope was not likely to compliment Kennet (cf. *Ep.* II ii 220*n.*); but there seems to have been no reason why he should be rude to Bramston, whose *Art of Politicks* he thought "pretty" (EC vi 326). Curll may be mistaken in thinking that "W—" is "Warren": there are other names that would fit the metre, e.g. Wesley, Whiston, Richard Welton the nonjuror. The change to "Hare" and "Gibson" in 1735 does not lessen the possibility that Pope intended the line to be satirical. See *Dunciad B,* iii 204*n.*⟩

    208. Of *Toland* and *Tindal,* see book 2 ⟨l. 367⟩. *Tho. Woolston,* an impious madman, who wrote in a most insolent style against the Miracles of the Gospel; in the years 1726, 27, *&c.* ⟨See Biog. App.⟩

    213. *blame* ⟨perhaps in OED's Sense 3: "to bring into disrepute, to discredit." Pope could have found this use of the word in the Authorised Version of the Bible.⟩

    214. *Seraph's* ⟨The substitution of "Milton's" in 1735 was no doubt intended to reflect on Bentley's notorious edition of *Paradise Lost,* 1732.⟩

8*

The source of Newton's Light, of Bacon's Sense!
Content, each Emanation of his fires
That beams on earth, each Virtue he inspires,
Each Art he prompts, each Charm he can create,
What-e'er he gives, are giv'n for You to hate.   220
Persist, by all divine in Man un-aw'd,
But learn, ye Dunces! not to scorn your GOD."
    Thus he, for then a ray of Reason stole
Half thro' the solid darkness of his soul;
But soon the Cloud return'd—and thus the Sire: 225
"See now, what Dulness and her sons admire;
See! what the charms, that smite the simple heart
Not touch'd by Nature, and not reach'd by Art."
    He look'd, and saw a sable Sorc'rer rise,
Swift to whose hand a winged volume flies: 230

229 Sorc'rer rise,] seer arise, *1728a–f.*

216. *Newton's Light* ⟨i.e. his enlightenment. But Pope probably intended a secondary reference to Newton's famous researches on Optics. Cf. his epigram on Newton in vol. vi.⟩

222. *But learn, ye Dunces! not to scorn your God*] *Virg. Æn.* 6. ⟨620⟩ puts this precept into the mouth of a wicked man ⟨Phlegyas⟩, as here of a stupid one,
         Discite justitiam moniti, & non temnere divos!
⟨Settle's advice is ironical. It is safe enough to despise a Milton or a Locke; it is *not* safe (as Woolston found) to indulge in blasphemy.⟩

229. ——*a sable Sorc'rer*] Dr. *Faustus*, the subject of a set of Farces which lasted in vogue two or three seasons, in which both Play-houses strove to outdo each other in the years 1726, 27. ⟨Dr Faustus seems to have become the vogue in 1723. In that year Thurmond's *Harlequin Doctor Faustus* was performed at Drury Lane, and *The Necromancer: or, Harlequin's Doctor Faustus* at Lincoln's Inn Fields.⟩ All the extravagancies in the sixteen lines following were introduced on the Stage, and frequented by persons of the first quality in *England* to the twentieth and thirtieth time. ⟨In Theobald's *Rape of Proserpine*, Sc. iv, Ceres "appears in the Air in her Chariot drawn by Dragons." Later, "an earthquake is felt, and part of the Building falls . . . Mount Ætna emits Flames. Beneath, a Giant is seen to rise . . ." In Scene v there follows "a Dance of Daemons." The earth then opens, and Pluto's chariot rises. Cyane "offering to speak, is turn'd into a Brook" on the stage, etc.⟩

230. *a winged volume* ⟨This was one of John Rich's tricks. In a satire on his *Doctor Faustus* (*The British Stage; or, the exploits of Harlequin*), Harlequin cries: "You, Mr. Book on yonder Shelf, repair to your Master at the Word of Com-

All sudden, Gorgons hiss, and Dragons glare,
And ten-horn'd fiends and Giants rush to war.
Hell rises, Heav'n descends, and dance on Earth,
Gods, imps, and monsters, music, rage, and mirth,
A fire, a jig, a battle, and a ball,   235
Till one wide Conflagration swallows all.
　　Thence a new world, to Nature's laws unknown,
Breaks out refulgent, with a heav'n its own:
Another Cynthia her new journey runs,
And other planets circle other suns: 240
The forests dance, the rivers upward rise,
Whales sport in woods, and dolphins in the skies,
And last, to give the whole creation grace,
Lo! one vast Egg produces human race.

232 rush to] threaten *1728a–f.*   233 and] to *1728a–f.*
234 imps, and monsters,] monsters, furies, *1728a–f.*
237 Thence] Then *1728a–f.*
238 Breaks out refulgent,] Refulgent rises, *1728a–f.*

mand." According to the stage direction, "The Book is toss'd to him by a Hand behind the Shelf.">

233. *Hell rises, &c.*] This monstrous absurdity was actually represented in *Tibbald's Rape of Proserpine*. ⟨In Scene vi the "Heavens open, and disclose Jupiter." Immediately afterwards the Earth opens "and Pluto and Proserpine rise as from Hell." The scene closes with a Grand Ballet.⟩

240. *And other planets*] Virg. Æn. 6 ⟨641⟩.
　　　　　　　——*solemque suum, sua sydera norunt.*

241. *The forests dance* ⟨Pope meant these words to be taken literally; but cf. his *Messiah*, 26:
　　　　　See nodding forests on the mountains dance.⟩

242. *Whales sport in woods, &c.*] Hor. ⟨*De Arte Poetica*, 30⟩
　　　　　Delphinum sylvis appingit, fluctibus aprum.

244. *Lo! one vast Egg*] In another of these Farces *Harlequin* is hatch'd upon the Stage, out of a large Egg. ⟨This took place in *The Rape of Proserpine*, and it was one of Rich's most admired performances. "From the first chipping of the egg, his receiving motion, his feeling the ground, his standing upright, to his quick Harlequin trip round the empty shell . . . every limb had its tongue, and every action a voice."—John Jackson, *History of the Scottish Stage*, 1793, p. 368. Christopher Pitt in "The Art of Preaching" refers to Rich as "just hatch'd, and breaking from his egg."⟩

    Joy fills his soul, joy innocent of thought: 245
"What pow'r," he cries, "what pow'r these wonders
      wrought?"
    "Son! what thou seek'st is in thee. Look, and find
Each monster meets his likeness in thy mind.
Yet would'st thou more? In yonder cloud, behold!
Whose sarcenet skirts are edg'd with flamy gold,   250
A matchless youth: His nod these worlds controuls,
Wings the red lightning, and the thunder rolls.
Angel of Dulness, sent to scatter round
Her magic charms o'er all unclassic ground:

245–6 Silent the monarch gaz'd; yet ask'd in thought
    What God or Dæmon all these wonders wrought? *1728a–f.*
247–8 *Om. 1728a–f.*
249 Yet . . . more?] To whom the Sire: *1728a–f.*
251–2 A godlike youth: See *Jove*'s own bolt he flings
    Rolls the loud thunder, and the light'ning wings! *1728a–f.*
254 o'er] on *1728a–f.*

---

   247. *Son! what thou seek'st is in thee*]
              Quod petis in te est——
              Ne te quæsiveris extra. Pers. ⟨*Sat.* i 7⟩.
   250. *Whose sarcenet skirts, &c.* ⟨In *The Arts of Logic and Rhetorick*, p. 371,
Oldmixon quotes a line:
          Like Clouds, whose fleecy Skirts are gilt with Gold
which appears to derive from Milton, *Par. Lost*, v 187,
         Till the Sun paint your fleecy Skirts with Gold.⟩.
   251. *A matchless youth* ⟨John Rich was by no means a youth in 1728. He was
born *circa* 1682.⟩
   252. *Wings the red lightning, &c.*] Like *Salmoneus* in *Æn.* 6 ⟨586, 590–1⟩.
         Dum flammas Jovis, & sonitus imitatur Olympi,
        ——*Nimbos, & non imitabile fulmen,*
        Ære & cornipedum cursu simularat æquorum.
   252. *the thunder rolls* ⟨The inventory of clothes, scenes, and properties in
Covent Garden Theatre in 1744 (B.M. Add. MSS. 12,201) includes "86
thunder balls, 6 baskets to dᵒ . . . 4 candlesticks for the thunder . . . the thunder
ball and line." EC suggests that in his comic account of theatrical machinery
Pope may be recollecting a similar *jeu d'esprit* in *The Spectator* No. 592, Sept.
10, 1714.⟩
   254. ——*o'er all unclassic ground*] alludes to Mr. *Addison*'s verse in the praises

Yon stars, yon suns, he rears at pleasure higher,   255
Illumes their light, and sets their flames on fire.
Immortal Rich! how calm he sits at ease
Mid snows of paper, and fierce hail of pease;
And proud his mistress' orders to perform,
Rides in the whirlwind, and directs the storm.   260
    "But lo! to dark encounter in mid air
New wizards rise: here Booth, and Cibber there:
Booth in his cloudy tabernacle shrin'd,
On grinning dragons Cibber mounts the wind:
Dire is the conflict, dismal is the din,   265
Here shouts all Drury, there all Lincoln's-Inn;
Contending Theatres our empire raise,

257 Rich!] *R—ch! 1728a–f.*
262 Booth, and Cibber] *B—th, and C—r 1728a–f.*
263 Booth] *B—th 1728a–f.*   264 Cibber] *C—r 1728a–f.*

of *Italy* ⟨i.e. *A Letter from Italy*, 11–12⟩,
> *Poetic fields incompass me around,*
> *And still I seem to tread on Classic ground.*

As verse ⟨259 and⟩ 260 is a Parody on a noble one of the same Author in the *Campaign* ⟨291–2⟩; and verse 255, 256. on two sublime verses of Dr. *Y.* ⟨*An Epistle to the Right Hon. George Lord Lansdowne*, by Edward Young, 467–8:
> Who the Sun's height can raise at pleasure higher,
> His lamp illumine, set his flames on fire.⟩

257. *Immortal* Rich] Mr. *John Rich*, Master of the Theatre in *Lincolns-Inn-Fields*, was the first that excell'd this way. ⟨See Biog. App.⟩

262. *Booth* and *Cibber*, two of the managers of the Theatre in *Drury-Lane.* ⟨"Two noted Actors, managers of the Theatre in Drury-Lane, who however in these performances, imitated Mr. Rich, *non passibus aequis."—1735ab.* For Booth, see Biog. App., vol. iv.⟩

263. *in his cloudy tabernacle* ⟨Milton, *Par. Lost*, vii 248:
> Shee in a cloudie Tabernacle
> Sojourn'd the while.⟩

265. *Dire is the conflict* ⟨Milton, *Par. Lost*, vi 211–13:
> . . . dire was the noise
> Of conflict; over head the dismal hiss
> Of fiery Darts . . .⟩

267. *Contending Theatres* ⟨In his *Apology*, ch. xv, Cibber refers to "that succession of monstrous medlies that have so long infested the stage, and which arose upon one another alternately, at both houses, outvying, in expence, like

Alike their labours, and alike their praise.
"And are these wonders, Son, to thee unknown?
Unknown to thee? These wonders are thy own.   270
For works like these let deathless Journals tell,
'None but Thy self can be thy parallel.'

271–2 Om. 1728a–f.

contending bribes on both sides at an election, to secure a majority of the multitude." He asserts that he was forced to provide pantomimes at Drury Lane, or else lose his audiences to Rich at Covent Garden.⟩

272. *None but thy self can be thy parallel*] A marvellous line of *Theobald*; unless the Play call'd the *Double Falshood* be, (as he would have it believed) *Shakespear*'s: But whether this line be his or not, he proves *Shakespear* to have written as bad, (which methinks in an author for whom he has a Veneration almost *rising to idolatry*, might have been concealed) as for example,

> Try what *Repentance* can: What can it not?
> But what can it, when one cannot *repent?*
> ——For *Cogitation*
> Resides not in the Man who does not *think, &c.*
> Mɪsᴛ's Jᴏᴜʀɴ.

It is granted they are all of a piece, and no man doubts but herein he is able to imitate *Shakespeare*. ⟨The "marvellous line" of Theobald's occurs in *Double Falshood*, iii i 18—"None but Itself can be its Parallel." This play, produced in 1727, was put forward by Theobald as a work of Shakespeare's, which it certainly was not, though it may have been written by one of his contemporaries and revised by Theobald. In a letter to Aaron Hill, June 9, 1738, Pope says that he never supposed the play to be by Theobald, but took it to be of the Shakespearean age.—In *Shakespeare Restored* (p. iii) Theobald had written: "I confess a Veneration, almost rising to Idolatry, for the work of this inimitable Poet."—The two passages (*Hamlet* iii iii 65–6; *Winter's Tale* i ii 258–9) were quoted by Theobald in *Mist's Journal*, April 27, 1728. From *1735a–42* the last sentence of this note was omitted, and the following added: "But the last of these is ño man's nonsense but Tibbald's, as he might have found had he read what follows,

> Who does not think
> My Wife is slippery.—*Cymbeline.*"

In his article in *Mist's Journal* Theobald had quoted the passage from *Winter's Tale* to excuse the "None but Itself can be its Parallel" of *Double Falshood*. The punctuation of the first Folio—

> (for Cogitation
> Resides not in that man, that do's not thinke)

—appeared to justify him. He must, however, have taken Pope's criticism to heart, for in his edition of Shakespeare's plays he accepted the reading of the second Folio, which adds *it* after *thinke*.⟩

272. The former Annotator seeming to be of opinion that the *Double Fals-hood* is not *Shakespear*'s; it is but justice to give Mr. *Theobald*'s Arguments to the contrary ⟨in "The Preface of the Editor" to *Double Falshood*⟩: First that the MS. was above sixty years old; secondly, that once Mr. *Betterton* had it, or he hath heard so; thirdly, that some-body told him the author gave it to a bastard-daughter of his: But fourthly and above all, "that he has a *great mind* every thing "that is good in our tongue *should be* Shakespeare's." ⟨". . . my Partiality for *Shakespeare* makes me wish, that Every Thing which is good, or pleasing, in our Tongue, had been owing to his Pen."⟩ I allow these reasons to be truly critical; but what I am infinitely concern'd at is, that so many Errors have escaped the learned Editor: a few whereof we shall here amend, out of a much greater number, as an instance of our regard to this *dear Relick*. ⟨Theobald's own phrase in his dedication of the play to Bubb Dodington.⟩

ACT 1. SCENE 1.

I have his letters of a modern date,
Wherein by *Julio, good Camillo*'s son
(Who as he says, [ ] shall follow hard upon,
And whom I with the growing hour [ ] expect)
He doth sollicit the return of gold,
To purchase certain horse that *like him well*.

This place is corrupted: the epithet *good* is a meer insignificant expletive, but the alteration of that single word restores a clear light to the whole context, thus,

I have his letters of a modern date,
Wherein, by *July*, (by *Camillo*'s son,
Who, as he *saith*, shall follow hard upon,
And whom I with the growing hours expect)
He doth sollicit the return of gold.

Here you have not only the *Person* specify'd, by whose hands the return was to be made, but the most necessary part, the *Time*, by which it was required. *Camillo*'s son was to follow hard upon—What? Why upon *July*.—*Horse* that *like him well*, is very absurd: Read it, without contradiction,

——Horse, that *he likes well*.

ACT 1. at the end.

——I must stoop to gain her,
Throw all my gay *Comparisons* aside,
And turn my proud additions out of service:

saith *Henriquez* of a maiden of low condition, objecting his high quality: What have his *Comparisons* here to do? Correct it boldly,

Throw all my gay *Caparisons* aside,
And turn my proud additions out of service.

ACT 2. SCENE 1.

All the verse of this Scene is confounded with prose.

——O that a man
Could reason down this *Feaver* of the blood,

> Or sooth with *words* the tumult in his heart!
> Then *Julio*, I might be *indeed* thy friend.

Read——this *fervor* of the blood,

> Then *Julio* I might be in *deed* thy friend.

marking the just opposition of deeds and words.

ACT 4. SCENE 1.

> How his eyes *shake* fire!—said by *Violante*,

observing how the lustful shepherd looks at her. It must be, as the sense plainly demands,

> ——How his eyes *take* fire!
> And measure every piece of youth about me!

Ibid. That, tho' I *wore disguises* for some *ends.*

She had but one disguise, and wore it but for one end. Restore it, with the alteration but of two letters,

> That, tho' I *were disguised* for some *end.*

ACT 4. SCENE 2.

> —To oaths no more give credit,
> To tears, to vows; false *both!*—

False Grammar I'm sure. *Both* can relate but to *two* things: And see! how easy a change sets it right!

> To tears, to vows, false *troth*—

I could shew you that very word troth, in *Shakespear* a hundred times.

> *Ib.* For there is nothing left thee now to look for,
> That can bring *comfort,* but a *quiet grave.*

This I fear is of a piece with *None but itself can be its parallel:* for the grave *puts an end* to all sorrow, it can then need no *comfort.* Yet let us vindicate *Shakespear* where we can: I make no doubt he wrote thus,

> For there is nothing left thee now to look for,
> *Nothing* that can bring *quiet,* but the grave.

Which reduplication of the word gives a much stronger emphasis to *Violante*'s concern. This figure is call'd *Anadyplosis.* I could shew you a hundred just such in him, if I had nothing else to do. SCRIBLERUS.

⟨The reference to *Anadyplosis* is a satirical thrust at Theobald's pedantry: he had mentioned this figure in *Shakespeare Restored,* p. 13. The whole note is a parody of Theobald's editorial method and idiom. In *Shakespeare Restored* he is fond of such phrases as "Restore it without the least Scruple," "an idle Expletive," "the minute Alteration of a *single* Letter or *two,*" "Correct with the greatest Certainty." In a letter printed in *Mist's Journal,* March 16, 1728, he writes: "And so in a great number of passages more, that I could produce were there any occasion."—In spite of Pope's ridicule of *Double Falshood,* it had reached a second edition by March 1728, and was being advertised as by "Mr. Theobald, the Author of *Shakespear Restored*" (*Whitehall Evening Post,* March 12/14, 1728)—an added reason, perhaps, for Pope's exposure of its faults.⟩

These, Fate reserv'd to grace thy reign divine,
Foreseen by me, but ah! with-held from mine.
In Lud's old walls, tho' long I rul'd renown'd,   275
Far, as loud Bow's stupendous bells resound;
Tho' my own Aldermen conferr'd my bays,
To me committing their eternal praise,
Their full-fed Heroes, their pacific May'rs,
Their annual trophies, and their monthly wars.   280
Tho' long my Party built on me their hopes,
For writing pamphlets, and for burning Popes;
(Diff'rent our parties, but with equal grace
The Goddess smiles on Whig and Tory race,

282 burning] roasting *1729b–d, 1735c–42*.
284 The] Our *1728a–f*.

274. *Foreseen by me* ⟨Settle's pageants for the Lord Mayor's shows had in a sense anticipated Theobald's pantomimes.⟩

279. *pacific May'rs* ⟨Cf. the "bloodless swords and maces" of i 85.⟩

280. Annual trophies, on the *Lord Mayor's Day*; and monthly wars, in the *Artillery Ground*. ⟨The old City Trainbands afforded a traditional theme for satire. Their military exercises had been delightfully ridiculed by Steele in *The Tatler*, No. 41, July 14, 1709.⟩

281. *Tho' long my Party*] *Settle*, like most Party-writers, was very uncertain in his political principles. He was employ'd to hold the pen in the *Character* of a *Popish successor* ⟨1681⟩, but afterwards printed his *Narrative* ⟨1683⟩ on the contrary side. He had managed the Ceremony of a famous Pope-burning on *Nov.* 17, 1680: then became a Trooper of King *James*'s army at *Hounslow-heath*: After the Revolution he kept a Booth at *Bartlemew-fair*, where in his Droll call'd St. *George for England*, he acted in his old age in a Dragon of green leather of his own invention. He was at last taken into the Charterhouse, and there dyed, aged about 60 years. ⟨Settle was probably one of the first authors that Pope read. He told Atterbury that when he was a boy "he read over the controversy of James the Second's time; that his father had them all, and that they were the only books he had in the country."—Spence, p. 364*n.*; EC ix 11. Edward Young referred again to Settle's activities as a dragon in *Two Epistles to Mr. Pope*, 1730, i 263 ff. The substance of this note had appeared in *1728a*, at iii 233.⟩

283–84.   ——*With equal grace*
                 Our Goddess smiles on Whig and Tory race]
Virg. Æn. 10 ⟨108, 112⟩,
                 Tros Rutulusve fuat, nullo discrimine habebo.
                 ——*Rex Jupiter omnibus idem.*

'Tis the same rope at sev'ral ends they twist,   285
To Dulness, Ridpath is as dear as Mist.)
Yet lo! in me what authors have to brag on!
Reduc'd at last to hiss in my own dragon.
Avert it, heav'n! that thou or Cibber e'er
Should wag two serpent tails in Smithfield fair.   290
Like the vile straw that's blown about the streets
The needy Poet sticks to all he meets,
Coach'd, carted, trod upon, now loose, now fast,
In the Dog's tail his progress ends at last.
Happier thy fortunes! like a rolling stone,   295
Thy giddy dulness still shall lumber on,
Safe in its heaviness, can never stray,
And licks up every blockhead in the way.
Thy dragons Magistrates and Peers shall taste,
And from each show rise duller than the last: 300

289 Cibber] *C—r 1728a–f*.
294 In . . . ends] And carry'd off in some Dog's tail *1735a–42*.
296 shall] may *1735ab*.
297 Too safe in inborn heaviness to stray, *1735ab*.
298 licks] lick *1735ab*.
299 Magistrates and Peers] ** and ** *1728a–e*.

---

286. *To Dulness,* Ridpath *is as dear as* Mist] *George Ridpath*, author for several years of the *Flying-Post*, a Whig-paper; *Nathaniel Mist*, publisher of the Weekly Journal, a Tory-paper. ⟨For Ridpath, see ii 141*n*. and Biog. App. For Mist, see i 194*n*. and Biog. App.⟩

299. *Magistrates and Peers*] It stood in the first edition with blanks, *Thy dragons ** and ***. *Concanen* was sure, "they must needs mean no-body but the "*King* and *Queen*, and said he would insist it was so, till the Poet clear'd himself "by filling up the blanks otherwise agreeably to the context, and consistent "with his *allegiance*. [Pref. to a Collection of Verses, Essays, Letters, &c. against Mr. *P.* printed for *A. Moore*, pag. 6.]

⟨Concanen wanted to fill in the blanks with "George" and "Caroline". Curll (*Key*, p. 18) suggested "Kings and Princesses." In Nov. 1728 the Prince of Wales and the Princesses did, in fact, see a performance of Theobald's pantomime, *Perseus and Andromeda*, at Drury Lane. (*Weekly Medley*, Nov. 23, 1728.) The EC MS. shows that Pope had the royal family in mind: it reads "Peers and Potentates."⟩

Till rais'd from Booths to Theatre, to Court,
Her seat imperial, Dulness shall transport.
Already, Opera prepares the way,
The sure fore-runner of her gentle sway.
To aid her cause, if heav'n thou can'st not bend,   305
Hell thou shalt move; for Faustus is thy friend:
Pluto with Cato thou for her shalt join,
And link the Mourning-Bride to Proserpine.
Grubstreet! thy fall should men and Gods conspire,
Thy stage shall stand, ensure it but from Fire.   310
Another Æschylus appears! prepare

302 imperial,] *Omit comma 1728a–f.*

---

303. *Opera* ⟨See *Dunciad B*, iv 45–70.⟩

305. —*If heav'n thou canst not bend, &c.*]
Virg. Æn. 7 ⟨312⟩.

Flectere si nequeo superos, Acheronta movebo.

307. —*Faustus is thy friend*, Pluto *with* Cato, *&c.*] Names of miserable Farces of *Tibbald* and others, which it was their custom to get acted at the end of the best Tragedies, to spoil the digestion of the audience. ⟨Congreve's *The Mourning Bride*, 1697; Addison's *Cato*, 1713. See iii 229n. There seems to have been no piece called *Pluto*: Pope is probably thinking of *Harlequin a Sorcerer, with the Loves of Pluto and Proserpine*, which was performed at the Lincoln's Inn Fields theatre in Jan. 1725.

By the beginning of the eighteenth century it had become customary to supplement the performance of a tragedy with entertainments of singing and dancing. Soon the farcical after-piece became popular. To make room for such light entertainment plays were frequently acted in a shortened version.⟩

310. ——*ensure it but from fire*] In *Tibbald*'s Farce of *Proserpine* a Corn-field was set on fire; whereupon the other Playhouse had a Barn burnt down for the recreation of the spectators. They also rival'd each other in showing the Burnings of Hell-fire, in Dr. *Faustus*. ⟨Cf. i 208n. On Oct. 26, 1727—just about the time that those words were written—a riot had occurred at the opening performance of Cibber's *Henry VIII* at Drury Lane, owing to a cry of "Fire!" raised among the audience. Several people were injured, and one woman crushed to death. See R. H. Barker, *Mr. Cibber of Drury Lane*, 1939, p. 140. Pope may have had the circumstance in mind.⟩

311. *Another Æschylus appears!* &c.] It is reported of *Æschylus*, that when his Tragedy of the *Furies* was acted, the audience were so terrify'd that the children fell into fits, and the big-bellied women miscarried ⟨*1728a*⟩. *Tibbald* is translating this author: he printed a specimen of him many years ago, of which I only remember that the first Note contains some comparison between *Prometheus* and

For new Abortions, all ye pregnant Fair!
In flames, like Semeles, be brought to bed,
While opening Hell spouts wild-fire at your head.
    "Now Bavius, take the poppy from thy brow,   315
And place it here! here all ye Heroes bow!
This, this is He, foretold by ancient rhymes,
Th' Augustus born to bring Saturnian times:
Beneath his reign, shall Eusden wear the bays,

319 Eusden] *E—n 1728a-f.*

Christ crucify'd. ⟨Two passages from the *Prometheus* of Aeschylus were printed in Theobald's *Censor*, March 9, 1717, and another in *The Grove*, a poetical miscellany of 1721. Dennis had seen a specimen of the Aeschylus which "would make Pope blush for his Homer" (*Remarks upon the Dunciad*, p. 56). Theobald spoilt Pope's joke by failing to publish his Aeschylus. Cf. i 210*n.*

The introduction of Æschylus here is rather abrupt. It is possible that ll. 311-12 formed a complete epigram that Pope had written when Theobald published his specimen of Æschylus "many years ago," and that he had now worked it into the texture of the *Dunciad.*⟩

313. ——*Like Semeles*——] See *Ovid, Met.* 3. ⟨Warton suggests that there may be an allusion here to Congreve's opera *Semele*, III vii, but that seems improbable. Pope was unlikely to sneer at Congreve, and by 1728 *Semele*, never a popular work, must have been almost forgotten. It is not clear whether "Semeles" is in the possessive case or nominative plural.⟩

317. *This, this is he, &c.*] Virg. Æn. 6 ⟨791-4⟩.

> Hic vir, hic est! tibi quem promitti sæpius audis,
> Augustus Cæsar, divum genus; aurea condet
> Sæcula qui rursus Latio, regnata per arva
> Saturno quondam——

Saturnian here relates to the age of *Lead*, mention'd book 1. ver. 26. ⟨Wakefield draws attention to ll. 5-7 of Dryden's translation of Virgil's fourth Eclogue, to which Pope is clearly indebted:

> The last great Age, foretold by sacred Rhymes,
> Renews its finish'd Course, *Saturnian* times
> Rowl round again . . .⟩

319. Eusden *wear the bays*] *Laurence Eusden*, Poet-Laureate: Mr. *Jacob* gives a catalogue of some few only of his works, which were very numerous. Mr. *Cook* in his *Battle of Poets* ⟨1725, p. 13⟩ saith of him,

> Eusden, *a laurel'd Bard, by fortune rais'd,*
> *By very few was read, by fewer prais'd.*

Mr. *Oldmixon* in his Arts of Logic and Rhetoric, p. 413, 414. affirms, "That

Cibber preside Lord-Chancellor of Plays,   320

320 Cibber] *C—r 1728a–f.*

"of all the Galimatia's he ever met with, none comes up to some verses of this
"Poet, which have as much of the Ridiculum and the Fustian in 'em as can well
"be jumbled together, and are of that sort of nonsense which so perfectly con-
"founds all Ideas, that there is no distinct one left in the mind. Further he says
"of him, that he hath prophesy'd his own poetry shall be sweeter than *Catullus,*
"*Ovid,* and *Tibullus,* but we have little hope of the accomplishment of it from
"what he hath lately publish'd." Upon which Mr. *Oldmixon* has not spar'd a
reflection, "That the putting the Laurel on the head of one who writ such verses,
"will give futurity a very lively idea of the Judgment and Justice of those who
"bestow'd it." *Ibid. p.* 417. But the well-known learning of that Noble Person
who was then Lord Chamberlain, might have screen'd him from this un-
mannerly reflection. ⟨Eusden's appointment (Dec. 24, 1718) was due to the
Duke of Newcastle, then Lord Chamberlain, whom he had courted with a very
flattering poem on the occasion of the Duke's marriage in 1717 to Lady Hen-
rietta Godolphin. Pope no doubt intends the phrase "the well-known learning"
to be ironical. Oldmixon's wrath is partly to be explained by the fact that he
regarded himself as being in the running for the laureateship. For Eusden, see
Biog. App., vol iv.⟩   Mr. *Eusden* was made *Laureate* for the same reason that
Mr. *Tibbald* was made *Hero* of This Poem, because there was *no better to be had.*
Nor ought Mr. *Oldmixon* to complain, so long after, that the Laurel would better
have become his own brows, or any other's: It were decent to acquiesce in the
opinion of the Duke of *Buckingham* upon this matter.

> —*In rush'd* Eusden, *and cry'd, Who shall have it,*
> *But I the true Laureate to whom the King gave it?*
> Apollo *begg'd pardon, and granted his claim,*
> *But vow'd, that till then he ne'er heard of his name.*
>   Session of Poets ⟨*1729a–42*⟩.

I have before observ'd something like Prophesy in our Author. Eusden,
whom he here couples with Cibber, no sooner died but his place of Laureate was
supply'd by Cibber, in the year 1730, on which was made the ensuing Epigram.

> In merry old England it once was a rule,
> The King had his Poet, and also his Fool:
> But now we're so frugal, I'd have you to know it,
> That C**r can serve both for Fool and for Poet.

⟨*1735a–42.* Cf. B i 104*n.*⟩

320. *Lord-Chancellor of Plays* ⟨As one of the three patentees of Drury Lane,
Cibber was in a position to accept or refuse new plays submitted for performance. Complaints about his handling of dramatists were frequent. He is said to
have rejected the *Mariamne* of Pope's friend, Fenton, in an insolent manner.—
Johnson, *Lives,* ii 260. He also turned down *The Beggar's Opera.*⟩

> B * * sole Judge of Architecture sit,
>   And Namby Pamby be prefer'd for Wit!

321 B**] *B—n 1728ef.* Benson *1735a–42.*
322 Namby Pamby] *A—e P—s 1728a–f.* Ambrose Philips *1735c–42.*

---

321. B** *sole judge of Architecture*] W——m B—ns—n (late Surveyor of the Buildings to his Majesty King *George* I.) gave in a report ⟨Jan. 21, 1719⟩ to the *Lords*, that Their House and the Painted Chamber adjoining were in immediate danger of falling. Whereupon the Lords met in a Committee to appoint some other place to sit in, while the House should be taken down. But it being proposed to cause some other Builders first to inspect it, they found it in very good condition. The Lords, upon this, were going upon an address to the King against *B—ns—n*, for such a misrepresentation; but the Earl of *Sunderland*, then Secretary, gave them an assurance that his Majesty would remove him, which was done accordingly. In favour of this man, the famous Sir *Christopher Wren*, who had been Architect to the Crown for above fifty years, who laid the first stone of St. *Paul*'s, and lived to finish it, had been displac'd from his employment at the age of near ninety years. ⟨Pope's account of Benson's dismissal differs considerably from that given in the *Journals of the House of Lords*, vol. xxi, p. 143b. There it appears that the Lord Chamberlain acquainted the House on April 16, 1719 that the King "had given order for the suspending the said William Benson from the Execution of his Office; and would give fuller Orders for his effectual prosecution." For Benson, see *Dunciad B*, iv 110, and Biog. App.⟩

322. *And* Namby Pamby] An author ⟨i.e. Ambrose Philips⟩ whose eminence in the Infantine stile obtain'd him this name. He was (saith Mr. JACOB) "one "of the Wits at *Button*'s, and a Justice of the Peace." ⟨*The Poetical Register*, vol. i, p. 203, vol. ii, p. 139.⟩ But since he hath met with higher preferment, in *Ireland*: and a much greater character we have of him in Mr. GILDON's Compleat Art of Poetry, vol. 1. p. 157. "Indeed he confesses, he dares not set him *quite* "*on the same foot* with *Virgil*, lest it should *seem* Flattery: but he is much mistaken "if posterity does not afford him a *greater esteem* then he *at present enjoys*." This is said of his Pastorals, of which see in the Appendix the *Guardian*, at large. He endeavour'd to create some mis-understanding between our author and Mr. *Addison*, whom also soon after he abused as much. His constant cry was, that Mr. *P.* was an Enemy to the government; and in particular he was the avowed author of a report very industriously spread, that he had a hand in a Party-paper call'd the *Examiner:* A falshood well known to those yet living, who had the direction and publication of it.

> Qui *meprise* Cotin, n'estime point son Roy,
>   Et n'a, (*selon* Cotin,) ni Dieu, ni Foy, ni Loy.

⟨Boileau, Satire ix 306–7.—For Philips, see i 103, Appendix v, and Biog. App.—Writing to Swift, Oct. 15, 1725, Pope indicates that l. 322—and possibly the *Dunciad* in an earlier form—was already in existence. See Introduction, p. ix.⟩

> While naked mourns the Dormitory wall,
> And Jones' and Boyle's united labours fall,
> While Wren with sorrow to the grave descends,   325
> Gay dies un-pension'd with a hundred Friends,

323 While . . . the] I see th' unfinish'd *1728a–f*.
324 I see the *Savoy* totter to her fall! *1728a–f*.   325–32 *Om. 1728a–f*.

323. *Dormitory wall*] The Dormitory in *Westminster* was a building intended for the lodging of the King's Scholars; toward which a sum was left by Dr. *Edw. Hannes*, the rest was raised by contributions procured from several eminent persons by the interest of *Francis* late Bishop of *Rochester*, and Dean of *Westminster*. He requested the Earl of *Burlington* to be the Architect, who carry'd on the work till the Bill against that learned Prelate was brought in, which ended in his banishment. The shell being finished according to his Lordship's design, the succeeding Dean and Chapter employ'd a common builder to do the inside, which is perform'd *accordingly*.

⟨Sir Edward Hannes (d. 1710) was physician to the Duke of Gloucester, and later to his mother, Queen Anne. He left £1,000 to Westminster School for the erection of the new dormitory mentioned by Pope.—For Francis Atterbury, Bishop of Rochester (1662–1732) see Biog. App., vol iv. For Richard Boyle, third Earl of Burlington (1695–1753) see vol. iii.⟩

324. Jones' *and* Boyle's *united labours*] At the time when this Poem was written, the Banquetting-house of *Whitehall*, the Church and Piazza of *Covent-garden*, and the Palace and Chappel of *Somerset-house*, the works of the famous *Inigo Jones*, had been for many years so neglected, as to be in danger of ruin. The Portico of *Covent-garden* Church had been just then ⟨1727⟩ restored and beautify'd at the expence of *Richard* ⟨Boyle⟩ Earl of *Burlington*; who, at the same time, by his publication of the designs of that great Master and *Palladio*, as well as by many noble buildings of his own, revived the true Taste of Architecture in this Kingdom. ⟨Cf. vol. iv, p. 63*n*. In 1727 William Kent (1684–1748) published, with the assistance of Burlington, *Designs of Inigo Jones*. This work included one design by Palladio, and a few by Burlington. In 1730 Burlington brought out an edition of Palladio's *Fabbriche Antiche*.—The reading of *1728a-f* refers to the dilapidated condition of Savoy House in the Strand, which Strype reported in 1720 to be "at this present a very ruinous building."—J. Stow, *A Survey of London*, ed. J. Strype, iv 107.⟩

326. Gay *dies un-pension'd*, &c.] See Mr. *Gay*'s Fable of the *Hare* and *Many Friends*. ⟨According to Swift (*Correspondence*, vol. iv, p. 375), when Queen Caroline came to the throne she told Lady Suffolk (then Mrs Howard) that she would "take up the hare," but all that Gay was offered was the post of Gentleman Usher to one of the Princesses, a sinecure worth £200 per annum. This, on the advice of his friends, he declined. Pope is using the word "unpension'd" to comment on Gay's failure to find a suitable appointment, but also, no doubt, as a term of praise; i.e. Gay was not a "pensioner" of Walpole's. Cf. *Sat.* II i 116.⟩

Hibernian Politicks, O Swift, thy doom,

327 doom,] fate, *1736a–42*.

This gentleman was early in the friendship of our author, which has continued many years. He wrote several works of humour with great success, the *Shepherd's Week*, *Trivia*, the *What d'ye call it*, &c. (printed together in 4°. by *J. Tonson*) *Fables*; and lastly, the celebrated *Beggar's Opera*; a piece of Satire which hit all tastes and degrees of men, from those of the highest Quality to the very Rabble: That verse of *Horace* ⟨Sat. II i 69⟩

Primores populi arripuit, populumque tributim,

could never be so justly applied as to this. The vast success of it was unprecedented, and almost incredible: What is related of the wonderful effects of the ancient Music or Tragedy hardly came up to it: *Sophocles* and *Euripides* were less follow'd and famous. It was acted in *London* sixty-three days, uninterrupted; and renew'd the next season with equal applauses. ⟨Pope is more enthusiastic than accurate here. The play was first performed on Jan. 29, 1728. It was repeated on Jan. 31, and then ran without a break till Tuesday, March 5. Thereafter it was performed at frequent intervals until June 19.—A. Nicoll, *History of Early Eighteenth Century Drama*, 1925, p. 331.⟩ It spread into all the great towns of *England*, was play'd in many places to the 30th, and 40th time, at *Bath* and *Bristol* 50, &c. It made its progress into *Wales*, *Scotland*, and *Ireland*, where it was performed 24 days together ⟨*1729b–51*⟩. It was lastly acted in *Minorca* ⟨*1729b–51*⟩. The fame of it was not confin'd to the author only; the Ladies carry'd about with 'em the favourite songs of it in Fans; and houses were furnish'd with it in Screens. The person who acted *Polly*, till then obscure, became all at once the favourite of the town; her *Pictures* were ingraved and sold in great numbers; her *Life* written; books of *Letters* and *Verses* to her publish'd; and pamphlets made even of her *Sayings* and *Jests*. ⟨e.g. *Polly Peachum's Jests*, 1728; *The Life of Lavinia Beswick, alias Fenton* . . . 1728; *Letters in Prose and Verse to the Celebrated Polly Peachum*, 1728. Lavinia Fenton (1708–60), the actress who played the part of Polly, became the mistress, and, in 1751, the wife, of Charles Paulet, third Duke of Bolton.⟩

Furthermore, it drove out of *England* ⟨for that season—*1735c–51*⟩ the *Italian Opera*, which had carry'd all before it for ten years: That Idol of the Nobility and the people, which the great Critick Mr. *Dennis* by the labours and outcries of a whole life could not overthrow, was demolish'd in one winter by a single stroke of this gentleman's pen. This remarkable period happen'd in the year 1728. Yet so great was his modesty, that he constantly prefixed to all the editions of it this Motto, *Nos hæc novimus esse nihil.* ⟨*1729a–51*.—The Opera House was closed in the autumn of 1728, the Royal Academy of Music having withdrawn its support. Handel, however, engaged a new set of Italian singers the following autumn, and they were performing in London early in December.—Dennis had written frequently against the Italian opera, but his chief attack was made in his *Essay on the Operas after the Italian Manner*, 1706.⟩

327. Hibernian *politicks*] The Politicks of *England* and *Ireland* at this time

And Pope's, translating three whole years with Broome.
  "Proceed great days! till Learning fly the shore,
Till Birch shall blush with noble blood no more,   330
Till Thames see Eton's sons for ever play,
Till Westminster's whole year be holiday;
Till Isis' Elders reel, their Pupils' sport;
And Alma Mater lye dissolv'd in Port!
  "Signs following signs lead on the Mighty Year; 335

328 translating . . . Broome.] whole years to comment and
    translate. *1736a–42*.
333 The sons of *Isis* reel! the towns-mens sport; *1728a–f.*
334 lye] all *1728a–f.*
335 Signs . . . on] Then, when these signs declare *1728a–f.*

were thought by some to be opposite or interfering with each other. Dr. *Swift* of course was in the interests of the latter. ⟨The "Drapier Letters" were publish-ed in 1724. Cf. i 24*n*.⟩

  328. *And* Pope'*s, translating*] He concludes his Irony with a stroke upon him-self: For whoever imagines this a sarcasm on the other ingenious person is greatly mistaken. The opinion our author had of him was sufficiently shown, by his joining him in the undertaking of the *Odyssey:* in which Mr. *Broome* having ingaged without any previous agreement, discharged his part so much to Mr. *Pope*'s satisfaction, that he gratified him with the full sum of *Five hundred pounds*, and a present of all those books for which his own interest could procure him Subscribers, to the value of *One hundred more*. The author only seems to lament, that he was imploy'd in Translation at all. ⟨In *1735c* the concluding words read: "so long imploy'd in translation."—Pope's note is disingenuous; he did, in fact, intend the reference to Broome as a sarcasm, for the two men had quar-relled. (See Biog. App., Broome.) In 1735 Broome and Pope were reconciled, with the result that Pope struck out the reference to Broome in *1736a*, and sub-stituted the following note: "The Author here seems to lament ⟨plainly laments—*1736b–51*⟩ that he was so long imployed in translating and com-menting. He began the Iliad in 1713 and finish'd it in 1719. The Edition of Shakespear, which he undertook merely because he thought no body else would, took up nearly two years more in the drudgery of comparing Impres-sions, rectifying the Scenary, &c. and the translation of half the Odyssey employ'd him from that time to 1725."—Pope told Broome, Jan. 12, 1736, that he had been compelled "to cancel an impression of a thousand leaves" to make this alteration. See the Pope-Broome correspondence EC viii pp. 178, 180. 181.⟩

  329. *Proceed great days*] Virg. Ecl. 4 ⟨12⟩,
      ——*Incipient magni procedere menses*

See! the dull stars roll round and re-appear.
She comes! the Cloud-compelling Pow'r, behold!
With Night Primæval, and with Chaos old.
Lo! the great Anarch's ancient reign restor'd,
Light dies before her uncreating word: 340
As one by one, at dread Medæa's strain,
The sick'ning Stars fade off th' æthereal plain;
As Argus' eyes, by Hermes' wand opprest,
Clos'd one by one to everlasting rest;

336 See!] When *1728a–f.* stars] star *1736b–42.*
337–54 Let there be darkness! (the dread pow'r shall say)
        All shall be darkness, as it ne'er were Day; *1728a–f.*
342 th' æthereal] the a'thereal *1729a.*

337, &c. *She comes! the Cloud-compelling pow'r, behold!* &c.] Here the Muse, like *Jove*'s Eagle, after a sudden stoop at ignoble game, soareth again to the skies. As Prophecy hath ever been one of the chief provinces of Poesy, our poet here foretells from what we feel, what we are to fear; and in the style of other Prophets, hath used the future tense for the preterit: since what he says shall be, is already to be seen, in the writings of some even of our most adored authors, in Divinity, Philosophy, Physics, Metaphysics, *&c.* (who are too good indeed to be named in such company.) Do not gentle reader, rest too secure in thy contempt of the Instruments for such a revolution in learning, or despise such weak agents as have been described in our poem, but remember what the *Dutch* stories somewhere relate, that a great part of their Provinces was once overflow'd, by a small opening made in one of their dykes by a single *Water-Rat* ⟨and lately much indanger'd by certain Worms breeding in their Piles.— *1735ab.*⟩.

However, that such is not seriously the judgment of our Poet, but that he conceiveth better hopes from the diligence of our Schools, from the regularity of our Universities, the discernment of our Great men, the encouragement of our Patrons, and the genius of our Writers in all kinds, (notwithstanding some few exceptions in each) may plainly be seen from his conclusion; where by causing all this Vision to pass thro' the *Ivory Gate*, he expressly in the language of poesy declares all such imaginations to be wild, ungrounded, and fictitious.

                                                            SCRIBLERUS.

341. *Medæa's strain* ⟨See Seneca's *Medea*, Act. iv.⟩
343. *As* Argus' *eyes &c.*] Ovid Met. 1 ⟨686–7; 713–14⟩.
        Et quamvis sopor est oculorum parte receptus,

        Parte tamen vigilat—Vidit Cyllenius omnes
        Succubuisse oculos, &c. ibid.

Thus at her felt approach, and secret might,   345
Art after Art goes out, and all is Night.
See sculking Truth in her old cavern lye,
Secur'd by mountains of heap'd casuistry:
Philosophy, that touch'd the Heavens before,
Shrinks to her hidden cause, and is no more: 350
See Physic beg the Stagyrite's defence!
See Metaphysic call for aid on Sence!
See Mystery to Mathematicks fly!
In vain! they gaze, turn giddy, rave, and die.
Thy hand great Dulness! lets the curtain fall,   355
And universal Darkness covers all."
    "Enough! enough!" the raptur'd Monarch cries;

355 To their first Chaos Wit's vain works shall fall, *1728a–f.*
356 Darkness covers] Dulness cover *1728a–f.* Darkness buries
    1729b–42.
357–8 No more the Monarch could such raptures bear;
    He wak'd, and all the Vision mix'd with air. *1728a–f.*

347. *Truth in her old cavern lye*] Alludes to the saying of *Democritus*, that Truth lay at the bottom of a deep well.

349–50. *Philosophy . . . is no more* ⟨To the edition of 1751 Warburton added a note stating that this couplet "was intended as a censure of the Newtonian philosophy. For the poet had been misled by the prejudices of foreigners, as if that philosophy had recurred to the *occult qualities of Aristotle.* This was the idea he received of it from a man educated much abroad, who had read every thing, but every thing superficially. Had his excellent friend Dr. A. been consulted in this matter, it is certain that so unjust a reflection had never discredited so noble a satire. When I hinted to him how he had been imposed upon, he changed the lines with great pleasure into a compliment (as they now stand) on that divine genius, and a satire on the folly by which he himself had been misled."—For the alteration in the text, see B iv 643–4. The "excellent friend" is clearly Arbuthnot; the "man educated much abroad" is almost certainly Bolingbroke. The compliment to Newton is obscure. Cf. also B 643*n.*⟩

351. *See Physic &c.* ⟨Physic=natural science. For Warburton's elucidation, see B iv 645, 646*n.*⟩

353. *Mystery* ⟨In its theological sense: "a religious truth known only from divine revelation; usually . . . a doctrine of the faith involving difficulties which human reason is incapable of solving."—OED. See also B iv 647*n.*⟩

356. ⟨Cf. Pope's *Iliad,* iv 199, vi 199, xii 80.⟩

And thro' the Ivory Gate the Vision flies.

358. *And thro' the Ivory Gate the Vision flies*] Virg. Æn. 6 ⟨893–6⟩

> *Sunt geminæ somni portæ; quarum altera fertur*
> *Cornea, qua veris facilis datur exitus umbris;*
> *Altera, candenti perfecta nitens elephanto,*
> *Sed falsa ad cælum mittunt insomnia manes.*

F I N I S.

M. SCRIBLERUS Lectori.

THE *Errata* of this Edition[1] we thought (gentle reader) to have trusted to thy candor and benignity, to correct with thy pen, as accidental Faults escaped the press: But seeing that certain Censors do give to such the name of *Corruptions of the Text* and *false Readings*, charge them on the Editor, and judge that correcting the same is to be called *Restoring*, and an *Atchievement that brings Honour to the Critic*; we have in like manner taken it upon ourselves.

Book i. Verse 8. *E'er Pallas issu'd from the Thund'rers head. E'er* is the contraction of *ever*, but that is by no means the sense in this place: Correct it, without the least scruple, *E're*, the contraction of *or-ere*, an old *English* word for *before*. What Ignorance of our mother tongue!

Verse 6. *Still Dunce [ ] second reigns like Dunce the first.* Read infallibly, still Dunce *the* second—Want of knowledge in the very Measure!

Verse 23, 24.——*tho' her power* retires,
    Grieve not at ought our sister realms acquire.
Read,—*our sister* realm acquires. Want of Ear even in Rhime!

Verse 38. ——Lintot*'s rubric's post.* Read, *rubric post.* I am aware, there is such a Substantive as *Rubric, The Rubric*; but here (I can assure the Editor) it is an Adjective.

Verse 189. Remarks. *C'est le mem quem* Mare ⟨Marc⟩ Tulle. Correct it boldly, *le meme que* Mare ⟨Marc⟩ Tulle. Ignorance in the *French!*

---

[1] ⟨The edition of *1729a*. This piece has been reprinted here since it shows how even in correcting the errors of the press Pope still pursued his aim of satirizing Theobald and the other verbal critics who set commas and points "exactly right." In some copies of *1729a* a quite different "M. Scriblerus Lectori" follows p. 84. (See Griffith, vol. 1, pt. 1, p. 167. The British Museum copy, 642 k 2(1) has this extra leaf.) In *1729b* there is again an "M. Scriblerus Lectori" differing from that printed here, and continuing the satirical banter at the expense of textual critics.

In the opening paragraph of this piece Pope is glancing at Theobald's *Shakespeare Restored*, and to some extent parodying his style of writing in that work. Cf. A i 1n.⟩

Book ii. verse 79. Imitations.—Terrasque *fretamque*. Read *fretumque*, Neut. Unskilfulness in *Latin!*

Ibid. verse 88.—ῥέε δ' Ἀμβροτον, correct the Accents thus, ῥέε δ' Ἄμβροτον—πέργε, Corr. πέρ τε. Want of understanding in *Greek!*

Book i. verse 258. Rem. Tenderness for *a bad writer*, read *the bad writers*. Plur. False *English:* No Relative!

Verse 197. Rem. *Incensa* [. ,] make it a plain Comma; [,] a strange sort of Punctuation this, [. ,] invented sure by the Editor!

Verse 208. Imit. *Uc, alegon.* Monstrous Division! away with that Comma!

Book ii. verse 369. Leave out these words—*When he came into the Administration*; For these Gentlemen never write against any man *in power*. This betrays great want of knowledge in Authors!

After so shameful ignorance in *Greek, Latin, French, English,* Quantity, Accent, Rhyme, Grammar, we cannot wonder at such Errors as the following. Book i. verse 101. *Rem.* for 254, read 258. and for 300, read 281.——Book ii. verse 75, for *Here* r. *Hear*, Verse 118. Rem. col. 2. for *Libel*, read *silly book*, it deserves not the name of a Libel. Verse 251, for *Courts* of *Chancery* r. *Offices*, for *those Courts*, r. *that Court*, and for *them* r. *it.* Verse 317. for *sacred* r. *secret.* Book iii. verse 46. Imit. for *hedæram* r. *hederam.* Verse 56. for *run forward* r. *rush forward.* We must also observe the careless manner of spelling sometimes *Satyr*, sometimes *Satire*, in the Notes, probably from the different Orthography of the various Annotators; however no excuse for the Editor, who ought constantly to have spelled it *Satire.*

In our Prolegomena likewise, pag. 12. line 6. where it is said, certain Verses were *never made publick till by Curl their own Bookseller;* Correct and strengthen the passage thus, *never made publick till in* their own Journals, *and by Curl* their own Bookseller, *&c.* But this, gentle reader, be so candid as to believe the Error only of the Printer.

Vale & fruere.

ERRATA.[1]

M. Scriblerus Lectori.

WE should think (gentle Reader) that we but ill perform'd our Part, if we corrected not as well *our own Errours* now, as formerly those of the *Printer*.[2] Since what moved us to this Work, was solely the Love of *Truth*, not in the least any Vainglory, or Desire to contend with *Great Authors*. And farther, our Mistakes we conceive will the rather be pardoned, as scarce possible to be avoided in writing of such Persons and Works as do ever shun the Light. However, that we may not any way soften or extenuate the same, we give them thee in the very Words of our Antagonists: not defending, but retracting them from our heart, and craving excuse of the Parties offended: For surely in this Work, it hath been above all things our desire, *to provoke no Man.*

Errour I. *Testimonies*, page 35 ⟨42⟩. Mr. Gildon *and* Dennis *in their* Character of Mr. P— *&c.*] Hear how Mr. *Dennis* hath prov'd our Mistake in this place. "As to my writing *in concert* with Mr. "*Gildon*, I declare upon the word and honour of a *Gentleman*, that I "never wrote so much as one Line[3] *in concert with any one Man what-* "*soever*; and these two Letters from Mr. *Gildon* will plainly show, "that we are not Writers *in concert* with each other.

Sir,—The height of my Ambition is to please Men of the best Judgment; and finding that I have entertain'd my Master agreeably, I have the Extent of the Reward of my Labour, &c.

Sir, I had not the opportunity of hearing[4] your excellent Pamphlet 'till this Day: I am infinitely satisfied and pleas'd with it, and hope you will meet with that Encouragement which your admirable Performance deserves, &c.

CH: GILDON.

---

1. ⟨This "Errata" appears in *1729d* only. In subsequent editions the matter contained in it was incorporated among the notes.⟩

2. ⟨In the "M. Scriblerus Lectori" of *1729a* and *1729bc*.⟩

3. ⟨Dennis added here: "that was afterwards printed." A work advertised in the *Daily Post*, Feb. 5, 1720: *A new Project for the Regulation of the Stage*, is attributed to "Mr. D—nis and Mr. G—don." I have not seen a copy, but the half-concealed names of Dennis and Gildon in the advertisement seem to indicate that it may have been a skit, and not the work of those two critics.⟩

4. ⟨In his later years Gildon became blind: the pamphlet had apparently been read to him.⟩

197

"Now is it not plain, that any one who sends such Compliments
"to another, has not been us'd to write in *Partnership* with him to
"whom he sends them?" [Dennis'*s Remarks on the* Dunciad, *pag.* 50.]
Mr. *Dennis* is therefore welcome to take this Piece to himself.

ERROUR II. Book 1. Note on Verse 200. Edward Ward *has of
late kept a publick House in the City.*] The said *Edward Ward* declares
this to be a great Falsity; protesting, that "He selleth *Port*; neither
"is his publick House in the *City*, but in *Moor-Fields*." [Ward *in the
Notes on* Apollo'*s* Maggot, 8vo.]

ERROUR III. Book 1. Verse 240. Ozell.] Mr. *Jacob*'s Character
of Mr. *Ozell*, seems vastly short of his Merits; and he ought to have
further Justice done him, having since fully confuted all Sarcasms
on his Learning and Genius, by an Advertisement of *Sept.* 20, 1729.
in a Paper call'd the *Weekly Medley*, &c. "As to my *Learning*, this
"envious Wretch knew, and every body knows, that the *whole
"Bench of Bishops*, not long ago, were pleas'd to give me a *Purse of
"Guineas*, for discovering the erroneous Translations of the Com-
"mon-Prayer in *Portuguese, Spanish, French, Italian*, &c.[1] As for my
"*Genius*, let Mr. *Cleland* shew better Verses in all *Pope*'s Works than
"*Ozell*'s Version of *Boileau*'s *Lutrin*, which the late Lord *Halifax*
"was so pleas'd with, that he complimented him with Leave to
"dedicate it to him, *&c. &c.* Let him show better and truer Poetry
"in the *Rape of the Locke*, than in *Ozell*'s *Rape of the Bucket*, (*la
"Secchia rapita*) which, because an ingenious Author[2] happen'd to
"mention in the same breath with *Pope*'s, viz. *Let* Ozell *sing the
"Bucket*, Pope *the Lock*, the little Gentleman had like to run mad.—
"And Mr. *Toland* and Mr. *Gildon* publickly declar'd, *Ozell*'s
"Translation of *Homer* to be, as it was *prior*, so likewise *superior* to
"*Pope*'s.—Surely, surely, every Man is free to deserve well of his
"Country!

JOHN OZELL."

We cannot but subscribe to such Reverend Testimonies, as
those of the *Bench of Bishops*, Mr. *Toland*, and Mr. *Gildon*.[3]

---

1. ⟨Ozell had published in 1722 *Common Prayer not Common Sense*, in which he
exposed errors in the translation of the English liturgy into various languages.⟩
2. ⟨Giles Jacob, in his *Rape of the Smock*, i ff.⟩
3. ⟨Pope's "reverend" is, of course, sarcastic when applied to Toland,

ERROUR IV. Book 2. Note on Verse 3. Edm. Curll *stood in the Pillory at* Charing-Cross, *in* March 172⅞.] "This, saith *Edm. Curll,* "is a false Assertion,—"I had indeed the Corporal punishment of "what the Gentlemen of the Long Robe are pleas'd jocosely to call, "*mounting the Rostrum,* for one Hour: But that *Scene of Action* was not "in the Month of *March,* but in *February*." [*Curliad* 12°. *pag.* 19.]

ERROUR V. Book 2. Note on Verse 143. *The History of* Curl's *being tost in a Blanket.*] "Here, quoth *Curl, ibid.* pag. 25. *Scriblerus!* "Thou leesest in what thou assertest, concerning a Blanket: It was "not a *Blanket,* but a *Rug.*"

ERROUR VI. Book 3. Note on Verse 147. Goode *writ a Satyr on our Author, call'd the* Mock Æsop.] "*Bar. Goode* maketh Oath, with "most solemn Protestation, that herein he is greatly wronged; and "wisheth the most heavy Curses to fall on himself and his Family, "if ever he wrote any such thing.
                    Jurat. coram nos,
                    J. Dennis, D. Mallet, R. Savage."
We find this to be true; for the Satyr he writ, was call'd not Mock Esop, *but* Mack Esop.

ERROUR VII. Book 3. Ver. 149.
          Jacob, *the Scourge of Grammar, mark with awe;*
          Nor less revere him Blunderbuss of Law.]
There may seem some Error in these Verses, Mr. *Jacob* having proved our Author to have a Respect for him, by this undeniable Argument. "He had once a *Regard* for my *Judgment*; otherwise he "would never have subscribed Two Guineas to me, for one small "Book in *Octavo*." [Jacob's *Letter* to Dennis, *in his Remarks on the* Dunciad, pag. 49.] Therefore I should think the Appellation of *Blunderbuss* to Mr. *Jacob,* like that of *Thunderbolt* to *Scipio,* was meant in his Honour.[1]

"prompt at Priests to jeer" (A ii 367), and to Gildon, who had "published *Blount's* blasphemous books against the Divinity of Christ" (A i 250n.⟩

1. ⟨The "one small Book in *Octavo*" was Giles Jacob's *Poetical Register,* in which an account of Pope was included. The proofs of this were sent to Pope by Jacob, and this fact was afterwards perverted by Curll and others into a statement that he had written the life himself. See R. Straus, *The Unspeakable Curll,* pp. 156–7.⟩

Mr. *Dennis* argues the same way. "My Writings having made "great Impression on the Minds of all sensible Men, Mr. *P— re-* "*pented*, and to *give proof of his Repentance*, subscribed to my Two "Volumes of select Works—and afterwards to my Two Volumes "of Letters." [*Ibid.* pag. 40.] We should hence believe, the Name of Mr. *Dennis* hath also crept into this Poem by some Mistake. From hence, gentle Reader! thou may'st beware, when thou givest to such Authors, not to flatter thy self that thy Motives are Good Nature, or Charity.[1] But whereas Mr. *Dennis* adds, that a Letter which our Author writ to him, was also *in acknowledgment of that Repentance*, in this surely he erreth; for the said Letter was but a civil Answer to one of his own, whereby it should seem that he himself was first touch'd with Repentance, and with some Guineas.

SIR,   April 29, 1721.

*A*S *you have subscrib'd for two of my Books, I have order'd them to be left for you at Mr.* Congreve's *Lodgings: As most of those Letters were writ during the Time that I was so unhappy as to be in a State of War with you, I was forced to maim and mangle at least ten of them, that no Footsteps might remain of that Quarrel. I particularly left out about half the Letter which was writ upon publishing the Paper call'd the* Guardian.

I am,
SIR,
Your most obedient,
Humble Servant,
JOHN DENNIS.

---

1. ⟨The rest of this note was omitted from *1735a* onwards.⟩

APPENDIX.

I.

PREFACE *prefix'd to the five imperfect Editions of the* DUNCIAD, *printed at* Dublin *and* London, *in Octavo &* Duod.

(*a*) The PUBLISHER to the READER.

I T will be found a true observation, tho' somewhat surprizing, that when any scandal is vented against a man of
the highest distinction and character, either in the State or
in Literature, the publick in general afford it a most quiet reception; and the larger part accept it as favourably as if it were   5

The text is that of *1729a*, collated with the first edition, *1728a*,
and with *1743a*. Unimportant verbal changes in Pope's notes
have not been entered. Additions made by Pope to the notes of
1729a are supplied from *1743a*, but the edition in which they were
first published is noted on each occasion.

PREFACE . . . *Duod.*] Qm. *1728*. PREFACE Prefixed to the five first
imperfect Editions of the DUNCIAD, in three books, printed at
DUBLIN and LONDON, in octavo and duodecimo, *1727.—1743.*

Duod. ⟨Cf. A 1 in., and Griffith, vol. i, pt. i, p. 283.⟩

(*a*) *The Publisher*] Who he was is uncertain; but *Edward Ward* tells us in his
Preface to *Durgen* ⟨p. iii⟩, that "most Judges are of opinion this Preface is not
of *English* Extraction but *Hibernian*, &c." He means Dr. *Swift*, who whether
Publisher or not, may be said in a sort to be Author of the Poem: For when He,
together with Mr. *Pope*, (for reasons specify'd in their Preface to the Miscellanies) determin'd to own the most trifling pieces in which they had any hand,
and to destroy all that remain'd in their power, the first sketch of this poem was
snatch'd from the fire by Dr. *Swift*, who persuaded his friend to proceed in it,
and to him it was therefore Inscribed. ⟨*1729a.*⟩ But the occasion of printing it
was as follows. There was publish'd in those Miscellanies, a Treatise of the
Bathos, or *Art of Sinking in Poetry*, in which was a Chapter, where the Species
of bad Writers were rang'd in Classes, and initial Letters of Names prefix'd,
for the most part at random. But such was the number of Poets eminent in
that Art, that some one or other took every Letter to himself. All fell into so

some kindness done to themselves: Whereas if a known scoundrel or blockhead chance but to be touch'd upon, a whole
legion is up in arms, and it becomes the common cause of all
Scriblers, Booksellers, and Printers whatsoever.

Not to search too deeply into the *Reason* hereof, I will only   5
observe as a *Fact*, that every week for these two Months past,
the town has been persecuted with (*b*) Pamphlets, Advertisements, Letters, and weekly Essays, not only against the Wit and
Writings, but against the Character and Person of Mr. *Pope*.
And that of all those men who have received pleasure from his   10
Writings (which by modest computation may be about a (*c*)

---

2 chance but to be] *chance to be but 1728*; but chance to be *1743*.
11 Writings] works *1743*.

---

violent a fury, that for half a year or more the common News-Papers (in most
of which they had some Property, as being hired Writers) were filled with the
most abusive Falsehoods and Scurrilities they could possibly devise: A Liberty
in no way to be wonder'd at in those People, and in those Papers, that, for
many years during the uncontrolled License of the Press, had aspersed almost
all the great Characters of the Age, and this with Impunity, their own Persons
and Names being utterly secret and obscure. This gave Mr. Pope the Thought,
that he had now some Opportunity of doing good, by detecting and dragging
into light these common Enemies of Mankind; since to invalidate this universal
Slander, it sufficed to shew what contemptible Men were the Authors of it.
He was not without hopes, that by manifesting the Dullness of those who had
only Malice to recommend them, either the Booksellers would not find their
Account in employing them, or the Men themselves, when discovered, want
Courage to proceed in so unlawful an occupation. This it was that gave birth
to the Dunciad, and he thought it an happiness, that by the late Flood of
Slander on himself, he had acquired such a peculiar right over their Names as
was necessary to his Design. ⟨*1735a*. The statement added in *1735a* had
appeared as part of the Dedication (pp. v–vi) to *A Collection of Pieces in Verse and
Prose . . . on Occasion of the Dunciad*, 1732. This dedication, though signed by
Richard Savage, was apparently written by Pope.—Johnson, *Lives of the Poets*,
iii 147.⟩

(*b*) *Pamphlets, Advertisements*, &c.] See the List of these anonymous papers
with their dates and Authors thereunto annexed. N° 2. ⟨*1729a*. The attacks
followed upon the publication, on March 8, of the *Peri Bathous* in *Miscellanies.
The Last Volume*.⟩

(*c*) *About a hundred thousand*] It is surprizing with what stupidity this Preface,
which is almost a continued Irony, was taken by these Authors. This passage
among others they understood to be serious. ⟨*1729a*. In *1743a* this last sentence

hundred thousand in these Kingdoms of *England* and *Ireland*, not to mention *Jersey*, *Guernsey*, the *Orcades*, those in the *New world*, and *Foreigners* who have translated him into their languages) of all this number, not a man hath stood up to say one word in his defence.   5

The only exception is the (*d*) Author of the following Poem, who doubtless had either a better insight into the grounds of this clamour, or a better opinion of Mr. *Pope*'s integrity, join'd with a greater personal love for him, than any other of his numerous friends and admirers.   10

Further, that he was in his peculiar intimacy, appears from the knowledge he manifests of the most *private* Authors of all the *anonymous* pieces against him, and from his having in this Poem attacked (*e*) no man living, who had not before printed or published some scandal against this particular Gentlemen.   15

How I became possest of it, is of no concern to the Reader; but it would have been a wrong to him, had I detain'd this publication: since those *Names* which are its chief ornaments, die off daily so fast, as must render it too soon unintelligible. If it pro-

---

14–15 or published some scandal] *and published 1728.*
15 particular] *Om. 1743.*
16 became] came *1743.*   of no concern] no concern *1743.*
17 this] the *1743.*

---

became: "All such passages as these were understood by Curl, Cook, Cibber, and others, to be serious."⟩ Hear the Laureate (Letter to Mr. Pope, p. 9). "Though I grant the Dunciad a better Poem of its kind than ever was writ; yet, when I read it with those *vain-glorious* encumbrances of Notes and Remarks upon it, &c.—it is amazing, that you, who have writ with such masterly spirit upon the ruling Passion, should be so blind a slave to your own, as not to see how far a *low avarice of Praise*, &c. (taking it for granted that the notes of Scriblerus and others, were the author's own.) ⟨*1743a.*⟩

(*d*) *The Author of the following Poem*, &c.] A very plain Irony, speaking of Mr. *Pope* himself ⟨*1729a*⟩.

13. *against him* ⟨No such knowledge can be presumed from the *Dunciad* of 1728. This remark of the prefacer has much more application to the *Dunciad Variorum* of the following year. Cf. Introduction, p. xx.⟩

(*e*) The Publisher in these words went a little too far: but it is certain whatever Names the Reader finds that are unknown to him, are of such: and the exception is only of two or three, whose dulness or scurrility ⟨whose dulness,

voke the Author to give us a more perfect edition, I have my end.

Who he is, I cannot say, and (which is great pity) there is certainly (*f*) nothing in his style and manner of writing, which can distinguish, or discover him. For if it bears any resemblance 5 to that of Mr. *P.* 'tis not improbable but it might be done on purpose, with a view to have it pass for his. But by the frequency of his allusions to *Virgil*, and a *labor'd* (not to say *affected*) *shortness* in imitation of him, I should think him more an admirer of the *Roman* Poet than of the *Grecian*, and in that not of the same taste 10 with his Friend.

I have been well inform'd, that this work was the labour of full (*g*) *six* years of his life, and that he retired himself entirely

---

6 P.] Pope *1743*.
13 retired himself entirely] wholly retired himself *1743*.

---

impudent scurrility, or self-conceit—*1743a*⟩ all mankind agree to have justly entitled them to a place in the Dunciad. ⟨*1729a*. So far, the prefacer's aim appears to have been to suggest that the poem was written as a reply to attacks (mostly recent) on Pope. But a few lines lower down he says ironically that it was the labour of six years. The note to 1 i in *1735a* states that the poem was written in 1727, and in *1736a*, that it was written in 1726. If Pope noticed such discrepancies he probably thought them immaterial.⟩

(*f*) *There is certainly nothing in his Style,* &c.] This Irony had small effect in concealing the Author. The Dunciad, imperfect as it was, had not been publish'd two days, but the whole Town gave it to Mr. *Pope* ⟨*1729a*⟩.

(*g*) *The Labour of full* six *years,* &c.] This also was honestly and seriously believ'd, by divers of the Gentlemen of the Dunciad. *J. Ralph,* Pref. to *Sawney* ⟨pp. iii–iv⟩, "We are told it was the labour of *six years,* with the utmost *assiduity* "and *application:* It is no great compliment to the Author's sense ⟨"or Good-nature"—Ralph⟩, to have employed so *large a part* of his *Life,* &c." ⟨"in a Piece of unjustifiable *Satyr,* which was calculated only to gratify a malicious Temper"—Ralph.⟩ So also *Ward,* Pref. to *Durg.* ⟨i.e. *Durgen,* pp. ii, v.⟩ "The "Dunciad, as the Publisher very *wisely* confesses, cost the Author *six years* "*retirement from all the pleasures of life,* to but half finish his abusive undertaking— "tho' it is somewhat difficult to conceive, from either its Bulk or Beauty, that it "cou'd be so long in hatching, *&c.* But the *length of time* and *closeness of application* "were mentioned to prepossess the reader with a good opinion of it."

Nevertheless the Prefacer to Mr. *Curl's Key* (a great Critick) was of a different sentiment, and thought it might be written in *six days.* ⟨"He must be a very great DUNCE, who, from a Plan so extensive, could not have raised a much nobler Structure in Six Days."—Curll, *Key,* p. iv.⟩

It is to be hoped they will as well understand, and write as gravely upon what

from all the avocations and pleasures of the world, to attend
diligently to its correction and perfection; and six years more he
intended to bestow upon it, as it should seem by this verse of
Statius, which was cited at the head of his manuscript.

> *Oh mihi bissenos multum vigilata per annos,*   5
> (*h*) *Duncia!*

Hence also we learn the true *Title* of the Poem; which with
the same certainty as we call that of *Homer* the *Iliad*, of *Virgil* the
Æneid, of *Camoens* the *Lusiad*, of *Voltaire* the *Henriad* (*i*), we may
pronounce could have been, and can be no other, than   10

The DUNCIAD.

It is styled *Heroic*, as being *doubly* so; not only with respect to
its nature, which according to the best Rules of the Ancients and
strictest ideas of the Moderns, is critically such; but also with
regard to the Heroical disposition and high courage of the   15
Writer, who dar'd to stir up such a formidable, irritable, and
implacable race of mortals.

The time and date of the Action is evidently in the last reign,
when the office of City Poet expir'd upon the death of *Elkanah
Settle*, and he has fix'd it to the Mayoralty of Sir *Geo. Thorold*. 20
But there may arise some obscurity in Chronology from the
Names in the Poem, by the inevitable removal of some Authors,
and insertion of others, in their Niches. For whoever will con-
sider the Unity of the whole design, will be sensible, that the
Poem was not made for these Authors, but these Authors for the Poem: 25

---

9 of *Voltaire* the *Henriad*] *Om. 1743.*
18–20 The time . . . *Thorold.*] *Om. 1743.*
20 *Thorold*] Tho—ld. *1728.*   21 But there] There *1743.*

Scriblerus hath said of this Poem. ⟨*1729a.* "They just as well understood what
Scriblerus said of the Poem."—*1743a.*⟩

(*h*) The same learned Prefacer took this word to be really in *Statius.* "By a
quibble on the word *Duncia*, the Dunciad is formed," ⟨Curll, *Key*⟩ *pag.* 3.
Mr. *Ward* also follows him in the same opinion. ⟨*1729a. Durgen*, p. ii. The first
line is from the *Thebaid*, xi 810.⟩

(*i*) *The Henriad*] The French Poem of Monsieur *Voltaire*, entitled *La Henriade*,
had been publish'd at *London* the year before. ⟨*1729a. Om. 1743a.*⟩

20. *Thorold* ⟨Cf. A i 88*n.*, 83*n.*⟩

And I should judge they were clapp'd in as they rose, fresh and
fresh, and chang'd from day to day, in like manner as when the
old boughs wither, we thrust new ones into a chimney.

I would not have the reader too much troubled or anxious, if
he cannot decypher them; since when he shall have found them   5
out, he will probably know no more of the Persons than before.

Yet we judg'd it better to preserve them as they are, than to
change them for *fictitious names*, by which the Satyr would only
be multiplied, and applied to many instead of one. Had the
Hero, for instance, been called *Codrus*, how many would have   10
affirm'd him to be Mr. *W——* Mr. *D——* Sir *R——B——*, *&c.*
but now, all that unjust scandal is saved, by calling him
Theobald, which by good luck happens to be the name of a real
person.

I am indeed aware, that this name may to some appear too   15
mean, for the Hero of an Epic Poem: But it is hoped, they will
alter that opinion, when they find, that an Author no less
eminent than *la Bruyere* has thought him worthy a place in his
Characters.

Voudriez vous, THEOBALDE, *que je crusse que vous êtes baisse?* 20
*que vous n'êtes plus Poete, ni bel esprit? que vous êtes presentement aussi
mauvais Juge de tout genre d'Ouvrage, que mechant Auteur? Votre air
libre & presumptueux me rassure, & me persuade tout le contraire, &c.*
Characteres, Vol. I. *de la Societe & de la Conversation, pag.* 176.
Edit. Amst. 1720.   25

---

1 And I] I *1743*.
11 Mr. *W—* Mr. *D—*] Mr. T. Mr. E. *1743*.
13 *Theobald*] by a name *1743*.   the name] that *1743*.
15–25 I am . . . 1720.] *Om. 1743*.   16 Poem:] Poem? *1728*.

---

9. *of one* ⟨For a different justification of personal satire, see Pope's letter of
Aug. 2, 1734, to Arbuthnot, answering a request that he should "study more to
reform than chastise." Pope told Arbuthnot, *inter alia*, that "it is only by hunting
one or two from the herd that any examples can be made."⟩

II.

A List of Books, Papers, and Verses, in which our Author was abused, printed before the Publication of the Dunciad: *With the true Names of the Authors.*

REFLECTIONS Critical and Satyrical on a late Rhapsody called an Essay on Criticism. By Mr. *Dennis.* Printed for *B. Lintot.* Price 6*d.*

A New Rehearsal, or Bays the Younger, Containing an Examen of Mr. *Rowe*'s Plays, and a word or two upon Mr. *Pope*'s Rape of the Locke. Anon. [*Charles Gildon.*] Printed for *J. Roberts,* 1714. Price 1*s.*

Homerides, or a Letter to Mr. *Pope,* occasion'd by his intended Translation of Homer. By Sir *Iliad Doggrel.* [*T. Burnet* and *G. Ducket* Esquires] Printed for *W. Wilkins,* 1715. Price 6*d.*[1]

Æsop at the Bear-garden. A Vision in imitation of the Temple of Fame. By Mr. *Preston.* Sold by *John Morphew,* 1715. Price 6*d.*[2]

The Catholic Poet, or Protestant Barnaby's sorrowful Lamentation, a Ballad about Homer's Iliad [by Mrs. *Centlivre* and others] 1715. Price 1*d.*[3]

An Epilogue to a Puppet-show at Bath, concerning the said Iliad, by *George Ducket* Esq; Printed by *E. Curl.*[4]

A compleat Key to the What-d'ye-call-it, Anon. [Mr. *Th—*] Printed for *J. Roberts,* 1715.[5]

---

1. ⟨This is the earlier of the two pamphlets bearing this title. It was to be called "The Hump Conference", but Addison persuaded Burnet to strike out all references to Pope's person.—*The Letters of Thomas Burnet to George Duckett,* ed. D. Nichol Smith, pp. 85, 91. The title of the second *Homerides* pamphlet is *Homerides: Or Homer's First Book Moderniz'd,* 1716.⟩

2. ⟨"Mr. Preston" was probably one of the wits at Button's. The real Mr. Preston was the "bear-marshal" at Hockley in the Hole. See Sherburn, p. 136.⟩

3. ⟨". . . the Person on whom it is charged is falsely accused. The Ballad, here referred to, being wrote by Mr. *Oldmixon.*"—*The Curliad,* p. 27.⟩

4. ⟨This first appeared in May 1715 in the second of the two pamphlets called *Homerides.* The sting of Duckett's satire lies in his reference to Pope's diminutive body: he was about four feet six inches in height.⟩

5. ⟨"Anon. by Griffin a Player, supervis'd by Mr. Th—." *1735a.* "Mr.

9*

A true character of Mr. *Pope* and his Writings, in a Letter to a Friend, Anon. [Messieurs *Gildon* and *Dennis*.] Printed for *S. Popping*, 1716. Price 3*d*.[1]

The Confederates, a Farce. By *Joseph Gay* [*J. D. Breval*.] Printed for *R. Burleigh*, 1717. Price 1*s*.

Remarks upon Mr. *Pope*'s Translation of Homer, with two Letters concerning the Windsor Forrest and the Temple of Fame. By Mr. *Dennis*. Printed for *E. Curl*, 1717. Price 1*s*. 6*d*.

Satires on the Translators of Homer, Mr. *P*. and Mr. *T*. Anon. [*Bez. Morris*] 1717. Price 6*d*.

The Triumvirate, or a Letter from Palæmon to Celia at Bath. Anon. [*Leonard Welsted*.] Price 1*s*. 1718. Folio.

The Battle of Poets, a Heroic Poem. [By *Tho. Cooke*] Printed for *J. Roberts*. Folio. 1725.[2]

Memoirs of Lilliput, Anon. [Mrs. *Eliz. Haywood*.] 8°. Printed 1727.

An Essay on Criticism, in Prose, by the Author of the Critical History of England [*J. Oldmixon*] 8° 1728.

Gulliveriana, and Alexandriana. With an ample Preface and Critique on *Swift* and *Pope*'s Miscellanies [By *Jonathan Smedley*.] Printed for *J. Roberts* 8° 1728. Advertised before the publication of the Dunciad in the Daily Journal, *April* 13. 1728.

Characters of the Times, or an Account of the Writings, Characters, &c. of several Gentlemen libell'd by *S*— and *P*— in a late Miscellany, 8° 1728. [*C—l* and *W—d*.][3]

Remarks on Mr. *Pope*'s Rape of the Lock, in Letters to a Friend. [By Mr. *Dennis*.] Written in 1714, tho' not printed till 1728. 8°.

Th—" is Theobald. "Why Theobald, who in 1717 was friendly to Pope, should be joined to Griffin as author, unless through malice *ex post facto*, is hard to say."—Sherburn, p. 138.⟩

1. ⟨From *1735a* this pamphlet was attributed to Dennis alone. It has all the marks of his abusive style. Cf. "Testimonies of Authors", p. 25*n*., and "Errata," p. 197.⟩

2. ⟨Pope was very mildly dealt with in this (1725) version of the poem. In the revised version of 1729, after he had been placed in the *Dunciad*, Cooke attacked Pope much more sharply.⟩

3. ⟨i.e. Curll and Welsted. The names were omitted from *1735a*. See A i 240 and iii 163*n*. In his account of this pamphlet (*Curliad*, p. 11), Curll states that he refused it "upon the many Errors I perceived in it, only on a cursory View of the Manuscript".⟩

Verses, Letters, Essays, or Advertisements in the publick Prints.

British Journal, *Nov.* 25, 1727. A Letter on *Swift* and *Pope*'s Miscellanies. [Writ by *Concanen.*]

Daily Journal, *March* 18, 1728. A Letter by *Philomauri.* [*James Moore Smyth.*] [1]

Id. *March* 29. A Letter about *Thersites* and accusing the Author of Disaffection to the Government. [*James Moore Smyth.*]

Mist's Weekly Journal, *March* 30. An Essay on the Arts of a Poets sinking in reputation, Or a supplement to the Art of sinking in Poetry [supposed by Mr. *Theobald.*]

Daily Journal, *April* 3. A Letter under the name of *Philo-ditto* [by *James Moore Smyth.*]

Flying-Post, *April* 4. A Letter against *Gulliver* and Mr. *P.* [Mr. *Oldmixon.*]

Daily Journal, *April* 5. An Auction of Goods at *Twickenham,* [by *J. Moore Smyth.*]

Flying-Post. *April* 6. A Fragment of a Treatise upon *Swift* and *Pope,* [by Mr. *Oldmixon.*]

The Senator, *April* 9. On the same, [by *Edward Roome.*]

Daily Journal, *April* 8. Advertisement [by *James Moore Smyth.*]

Daily Journal, *April* 9. Letter and Verses against Dr. *Swift,* [by ** Esq;] [2]

Flying-Post, *April* 13. Verses against the same, and against Mr. *P—*'s *Homer,* [by *J. Oldmixon.*]

Daily Journal, *April* 16. Verses on Mr. *P.* [by **Esq;.]

Id. *April* 23. Letter about a Translation of the character of *Thersites* in *Homer,* [*J—D—,* &c.] [3]

Mist's Weekly Journal, *April* 27. A Letter of *Lewis Theobald.*

Daily Journal, *May* 11. A Letter against Mr. *P.* at large, Anon. [*John Dennis.*]

All these were afterwards reprinted in a Pamphlet entitled,

1. ⟨EC suggests (vol. iii, p. 112) that Pope was "in all probability" the writer of this letter.⟩

2. ⟨From *1735a* onwards this entry, and the next but one, were omitted. The author of these two attacks was Aaron Hill, and Hill had now made his peace with Pope. See Biog. App., Hill.⟩

3. ⟨In *1729b* this piece was attributed to "*Tho. Cook, D—,* etc": in *1735a* to "Tho. Cook, &c." The fact that Pope should print "J— D—" instead of "John Dennis" probably indicates that he was uncertain about Dennis's share in it.⟩

A collection of all the Verses, Essays, Letters and Advertisements occasion'd by *Pope* and *Swift*'s Miscellanies. Prefaced by *Concanen*, Anonymous. 8°. Printed for *A. Moore*, 1728. Price 1*s*. Others of an elder date, having layn as waste paper many years, were upon the publication of the Dunciad brought out, and their Authors betrayed by the mercenary Booksellers (in hope of some possibility of vending a few) by advertising them in this manner—*The Confederates*, a Farce, By Capt. *Breval*, (for which he is *put into the Dunciad*.) An *Epilogue to Powel's Puppetshow*, by Col. *Ducket*, (for which he is *put into the Dunciad*.) Essays, *&c*. by Sir *Rich. Blackmore*. *N.B.* It is for a passage in pag. — of this book that Sir *Richard* was *put into the Dunciad*.)[1] And so of others.

After the DUNCIAD, 1728.

AN Essay on the Dunciad, 8°. Printed for *J. Roberts*. [In this book, *pag*. 9. it was formally declared "That the complaint "of the aforesaid Pieces, Libels, and Advertisements, was "forged and untrue, that all mouths had been silent except in "Mr. *Pope*'s praise, and nothing against him publish'd, but, by "Mr. THEOBALD." *Price* 6*d*.

Sawney, in blank Verse, occasion'd by the Dunciad, with a Critique on that Poem. [By *J. Ralph*, a person never mention'd in it at first, but inserted after this.] Printed for *J. Roberts*. 8°. Price 1*s*.

A compleat Key to the Dunciad, by *E. Curl*. 12°. Price 6*d*.

A second and third Edition of the same, with Additions. 12°.

The Popiad, by *E. Curl*, extracted from *J. Dennis*, Sir *R. Blackmore*, &c. 12°. Price 6*d*.

The Curliad, by the same E. Curl ⟨*1735a*⟩.

The Female Dunciad, collected by the same Mr. *Curl*. 12°. Price 6*d*. With the Metamorphosis of *P*— into a stinging Nettle, [by Mr. *Foxton*.] 12°.

The Metamorphosis of *Scriblerus* into *Snarlerus*, [by *J. Smedley*.] Printed for *A. Moore*. Folio. Price 6*d*.

The Dunciad dissected, or Farmer *P*. and his Son, by *Curl*. 12° ⟨*1729a–d*. By Curl, and one Mrs. Thomas. *1735a*⟩.

---

1. ⟨See Blackmore's *Essays upon Several Subjects*, vol. ii, p. 270, and A ii 258*n*.⟩

An Essay on the Taste and Writings of the present times, said to be writ by a Gentleman of C. C. C. *Oxon*. Printed for *J. Roberts*, 8°.[1]

The Arts of Logic and Rhetorick, partly taken from *Bouhours*, with new Reflections, *&c*. [by *John Oldmixon*.] 8°.

Remarks on the Dunciad, by Mr. Dennis, Dedicated to Mr. Theobald. 8° ⟨*1735a*⟩.

A Supplement to the Profund, Anon. [By *Matthew Concanen*.] 8°.

Mist's Weekly Journal, *June* 8. A long Letter sign'd *W. A.* [*Dennis, Theobald*, and others.][2]

Daily Journal, *June* 11. A Letter sign'd *Philoscriblerus*, on the name of *Pope*.—Letter to Mr. *Theobald* in Verse, sign'd *B. M.* against Mr. *P.*—Many other little Epigrams about this time in the same papers, [by *James Moore* and others.][3]

Mist's Journal, *June* 22. A Letter by *Lewis Theobald*.

Flying-Post, *August* 8. Letter on *Pope* and *Swift*.

Daily Journal, *August* 8. Letter charging the Author of the Dunciad with Treason.

Durgen, A plain Satyr on a pompous Satyrist. [By *Edw. Ward*, with a little of *James Moore*.][4]

Apollo's Maggot in his Cups, by E. Ward ⟨*1735a*⟩.

Labeo, [A Paper of Verses written by *Leonard Welsted*.] ⟨*1729a–d*⟩, which after came into *One Epistle*, and was publish'd by James

---

1. ⟨Pope tried hard to discover who wrote this pamphlet, and even went so far as to ask his friend Fortescue to ask Walpole, to whom it was dedicated, for the name of the author. See EC ix 124.⟩

2. ⟨*A—ld, D—s, Th.* and others.—*1729b*. In *1729d* the words in brackets were omitted, and the following added: "[These initial Letters were subscribed to cast the slander of writing this on Mr. *A—ll*, the present Author of the *British Journal* ⟨i.e. William Arnall⟩, who has justify'd himself from this and all other offence to Mr. *P.*]." Arnall having given Pope offence, those words were omitted from *1735a* onwards. From *1729d* the note concludes with a further statement: "It was writ by some or other of the Club of *Th—, D—s, M—re, C—n, C—ke*, who for some time, held constant Weekly meetings for these kind of performances." From *1735a* the names were spelled in full, viz. Theobald, Dennis, Moore, Concanen, Cooke.⟩

3. ⟨From *1735a* Pope added in brackets after "B.M." the name in full, viz. Bezaleel Morris.⟩

4. ⟨"Mr. *James Moor* had not the least Finger in the Poem call'd the *Durgen* . . ." E. Ward, *Apollo's Maggot in his Cups*, p. 35.⟩

Moore. 4to. 1730. Another part of it came out in Welsted's own name in 1731, under the just Title of *Dulness and Scandal*, fol. ⟨*1735a.*⟩[1]

Gulliveriana Secunda, Being a collection of many of the Libels in the News papers, like the former Volume under the same title, by *Smedley*. Advertised in the Craftsman *November* 9, 1728. with this remarkable promise, that "*any thing* which *any body* shou'd "send as Mr. *Pope*'s or Dr. *Swift*'s, shou'd be inserted and published "as Theirs."

Pope Alexander's Supremacy and Infallibility examin'd &c. 4to. By Geo. Ducket and John Dennis ⟨*1735a*⟩.[2]

Dean Jonathan's Paraphrase on the 4th Chapter of Genesis. Writ by E. Room, fol. 1729 ⟨*1735a*⟩.

Verses on the Imitator of *Horace* by a Lady [or between a Lady, a Lord, and a Court Squire] Printed for *J. Roberts*, fol. 1733 ⟨*1736a*⟩.[3]

An Epistle from a Nobleman to a Dr. of Divinity, from *Hampton Court* [Lord *H—y*] Printed for *J. Roberts* also, fol. 1733 ⟨*1736a*⟩.[4]

A Letter from Mr. Cibber to Mr. Pope. Printed for W. Lewis in Covent Garden, octavo ⟨*1743a*⟩.[5]

---

1. ⟨*One Epistle* was attributed to "the son of an Alehouse keeper [i.e. T. Cooke?], the son of a Footman, and the Son of a —." *Grub-Street Journal*, May 14, 1730. On May 21 the same journal suggested that a lady had "some hand in this piece".⟩

2. ⟨"The book is writ by Burnet, and a person who has great obligations to me, and the cut is done by Ducket."—Pope to Lord Oxford, May 16, 1729. But he was not sure of this, for he immediately added: "I would fain come at the proof of this."⟩

3. ⟨By Lady Mary Wortley Montagu, assisted by Lord Hervey. See vol. iv, pp. xvii–xix.⟩

4. ⟨For this lampoon of Lord Hervey's, see vol. iv, pp. xix–xx.⟩

5. ⟨Cibber's letter is dated July 7, 1742.—This list of books and pamphlets is very far from being complete. Even Pope probably failed to keep an account of all the attacks upon him that appeared in the *London Journal, London Evening-Post, Whitehall Evening Post, Daily Journal, Read's Weekly Journal, Mist's Weekly Journal, Flying-Post*, etc.; but one or two attacks are missing from his list that one might have expected to see there, e.g., *A Popp unpon Pope*, 1728. After 1729 he had clearly decided to make no further additions to his list unless for special reasons, e.g. to justify his references from *1735c* onwards to Lord Hervey (A i 251).⟩

III.

A Copy of CAXTON's *Preface to his Translation of* VIRGIL.[1]

AFTER dyuerse Werkes, made translated and achieued, hauyng noo werke in hande I sittyng in my studye where as laye many dyuerse paunflettes and bookys. happened that to my hande cam a lytlyl booke in frenshe. whiche late was translated oute of latyn by some noble clerke of fraunce whiche booke is named *Eneydos* (made in latyn by that noble poete & grete clerke *Vyrgyle*) whiche booke I sawe over and redde therein. How after the generall destruccyon of the grete *Troye*, *Eneas* departed berynge his olde fader *anchises* upon his sholdres, his lytyl son *yolas* on his hande. his wyfe wyth moche other people followynge, and how he shipped and departed wyth alle thystorye of his aduentures that he had *er he cam to the atchieuement of his conquest of ytalye* as all a longe shall be shewed in this present boke. In whiche booke I had grete playsyr. by cause of the fayr and honest termes & wordes in frenshe Whyche I neuer sawe to fore lyke. ne none so playsaunt ne so wel ordred. whiche booke as me semed sholde be moche requysyte to noble men to see as wel for the eloquence as the historyes. How wel that many hondred yerys passed was the sayd booke of *Eneydos* wyth other workes made and lerned dayly in scolis specyally in *ytalye* and other places, whiche historye the sayd *Vyrgyle* made in metre, And whan I had aduysed me in this sayd booke. *I delybered and concluded* to translate it in to englyshe. And forthwyth toke a

---

1. ⟨This Appendix appeared in the editions of 1729 only. (Cf. A i 129*n*.) The extract from Caxton was copied for Pope by Lord Oxford's amanuensis in the summer of 1728. (EC viii 236.) In *Mist's Journal*, March 16, 1728, Theobald had cited Caxton to clear up a passage in *Troilus and Cressida*, v v 14: "The dreadfull Sagittary Appauls our numbers." Pope had assumed that the Sagittary was Teucer; but Theobald (with the help of Caxton) was able to show that it was "a mervayllouse beste"; in fact, a Centaur. The mistake probably rankled, and Pope took refuge once again in ridicule; but the joke at Caxton's expense amounts to no more than laughing at a man because his clothes are old-fashioned. Gay had played the same joke in the antiquated "Proeme to the Courteous Reader" in his *Shepherd's Week*, 1714.⟩

penne and ynke and wrote a leef or tweyne, whyche I ouersawe
agayn to corecte it, And whan I sawe the fayr & straunge termes
therein, I doubted that it sholde not please some gentylmen whiche
late blamed me sayeng that in my translacyons I had ouer curyous
termes whiche coude not be vnderstande of comyn peple, and
desired me to vse olde and homely termes in my translacyons. and
fayn wolde I satysfye euery man, and so to doo toke an olde boke
and redde therein, and certaynly the englyshe was so rude and
brood that I coude not wele vnderstande it. And also my lorde
Abbot of *Westmynster* ded do shewe to me late certayn euydences
wryton in olde englyshe for to reduce it in to our englyshe now
vsid, And certaynly it was wryton in suche wyse that it was more
lyke to dutche than englyshe I coude not reduce ne brynge it to be
vnderstonden, And certaynly our langage now vsed varyeth
ferre from that whiche was vsed and spoken whan I was borne,
For we englyshe men, ben borne vnder the domynacyon of the
mone. whiche is neuer stedfaste, but euer wauerynge, wexynge one
season, and waneth & dyscreaseth another season, And that
comyn englyshe that is spoken in one shyre varyeth from another.
In so moche that in my dayes happened that certayn marchants
were in a ship in Tamyse for to haue sayled ouer the see into
Zelande, and for lacke of wynde thei taryed atte forlond. and wente
to lande for to refreshe them And one of theym named *Sheffelde* a
mercer cam in to an hows and axed for mete. and specyally he
axyd after eggys. And the goode wyf answerde. that she coude
speke no frenshe. And the merchant was angry. for he also coude
speke no frenshe. but wolde haue hadde egges, and she vnderstode
hym not, And thenne at laste another sayd that he wolde haue
eyren, then the good wyf sayd that she vnderstod hym wel, Loo
what sholde a man in thyse dayes now wryte. egges or eyren,
certaynly it is harde to playse every man, by cause of dyuersite
& change of langage. For in these dayes euery man that is in ony
reputacyon in his contre. wyll vtter his comynycacyon and maters
in suche maners & termes, that fewe men shall vnderstonde
theym, And som honest and grete clerkes haue ben wyth me and
desired me to wryte the moste curyous termes that I coude fynde,
And thus bytwene playn rude, & curyous I stande abashed. but in
my Judgemente, the comyn termes that be dayli vsed ben lyghter
to be vnderstonde than the olde and ancyent englyshe, And for as

moche as this present booke is not *for a rude vplondyshe man* to laboure
therein, ne rede it, but onely for a clerke & a noble gentylman that
feleth and vnderstondeth in faytes of armes in loue & in noble
chyualrye, Therefore in a meane betwene bothe I haue reduced &
translated this sayd booke in to our englyshe not ouer rude ne
curyous but in suche termes as shall be vnderstanden by goddys
grace accordynge to my copye. And yf ony man wyll enter mete
in redyng of hit and fyndeth suche termes that he can not vnderstande late hym goo rede and lerne *Vyrgyll*, or the pystles of *Ouyde*,
and ther he shall see and vnderstonde lyghtly all, Yf he haue a
good redar & enformer, For this booke is not for euery rude and
vnconnynge man to see, but to clerkys & very gentylmen that
understande gentylnes and scyence. Thenne I praye alle theym
that shall rede in this lytyl treatys to holde me for excused for the
translatynge of hit. For I knowleche my selfe ignorant of connynge
to enpryse on me so hie and noble a werke, But I praye Mayster
John Skelton late created poete laureate in the vnyuersite of *Oxen-
forde* to ouersee and correcte this sayd booke. And t'addresse and
expowne where as shall be founde faulte to theym that shall
requyre it. For hym I knowe for suffycyent to expowne and
englyshe euery dyffyculte that is therein, For he hath late translated the epystlys of *Tulle*, and the boke of *Dyodorus Syculus*. and
diuerse others werkes oute of latyn in to englyshe not in rude and
olde langage. but in *polysshed and ornate termes* craftely, as he that
hath redde *Vyrgyle, Ouyde, Tullye*, and all the other noble poetes
and oratours, to me unknown: And also he hath redde the ix
muses and vnderstande theyr musicalle scyences. and to whom of
theym eche scyence is appropred. I suppose he hath dronken of
Elycons well. Then I praye hym & suche other to correcte adde or
mynysshe where as he or they shall fynde faulte, For I haue but
folowed my copye in frenche as nygh as me is possyble, And yf ony
worde be sayd therein well, I am glad. and yf otherwyse I submytte
my sayd boke to theyr correctyon, Whiche boke I presente vnto
the hye born my *tocomynge* naturall & souerayn lord *Arthur* by the
grace of God Prynce of *Walys*, Duke of *Cornewayll*. & Erle of *Chester*
first bygoten Son and heyer vnto our most dradde naturall &
souerayn lorde & most crysten kynge, *Henry* the vij. by the grace
of God kynge of *Englonde* and of *Fraunce* & lord of *Irelonde*, byseech-
ing his noble grace to receyue it in thanke of me his moste humble

subget & seruant, And I shall praye vnto almyghty God for his prosperous encreasyng in vertue, wysedom, and humanyte that he may be egal wyth the most renômed of alle his noble progenytours. And so to lyue in this present lyf, that after this transitorye lyfe he and we alle may come to everlastynge lyf in heuen, *Amen:*

At the end of the Book.

Here fynyssheth the boke of *Eneydos*, compyled by *Vyrgyle*, whiche hathe be translated out of *latyne* in to *frenshe*, and out of *frenshe* reduced in to *Englysshe* by me *Wyllm. Caxton*, the xxij daye of *Juyn*. the yere of our lorde. M. iiij C lxxxx. The fythe yere of the Regne of kyng *Henry* the seuenth.

IV.

VIRGILIUS RESTAURATUS:[1]
SEU
MARTINI SCRIBLERI
Summi Critici
CASTIGATIONUM in ÆNEIDEM
S P E C I M E N :

ÆNEIDEM totam, Amice Lector, innumerabilibus pœne mendis scaturientem, ad pristinum sensum revocabimus. In singulis ferè versibus spuriæ occurrunt lectiones, in omnibus quos unquam vidi codicibus aut vulgatis aut ineditis, ad opprobrium usque Criticorum, in hunc diem existentes. Interea adverte oculos, & his paucis fruere. At si quæ sint in hisce castigationibus de quibus non satis liquet, syllabarum quantitates, προλεγόμενα nostra Libro ipsi præfigenda, ut consulas, moneo.

I. SPECIMEN LIBRI PRIMI, VERS. I. (*a*)

A R MA Virumque cano, Trojæ qui primus ab *oris*
  Italiam, *fato* profugus, Lavinaque venit
  Litora: multum ille & terris *jactatus* & alto,
Vi superum————

---

1. ⟨This Appendix appeared in the editions of 1729 only. It was presumably dropped from the *Dunciad* because it was included in *Miscellanies. The Third Volume.* 1732. The title is intended to ridicule Theobald's *Shakespeare Restored.* For Arbuthnot's connection with this piece, see Introduction, pp. xvf. A number of misprints in *1729a* have been silently corrected from the "Addenda. M. Scriblerus Lectori" which appears in some copies of that edition, in an unnumbered leaf following p. 84.—See Griffith, vol. i, pt. i, p. 167.⟩

 (*a*) Arma Virumque cano, Trojæ qui primus ab *Aris*
   Italiam, *flatu* profugus, *Latinaque* venit
   Litora: multum ille & terris *vexatus*, & alto,
   Vi superum————
  Ab *aris*, nempe Hercæi Jovis, vide lib. 2. vers. 512, 550.—*Flatu*, ventorum

II. VERS. 52. (b)
—Et quisquis *Numen* Junonis adoret?

III. VERS. 86. (c)
—Venti velut *agmine facto*
Qua data porta ruunt—

IV. VERS. 117. (d)
Fidumque vehebat *Orontem.*

V. VERS. 119. (e)
Excutitur, pronusque *magister*
Volvitur in caput———

VI. VERS. 122. (f)
Apparent rari nantes in gurgite vasto
Arma virùm———

VII. VERS. 151. (g)
Atque rotis *summas* leviter perlabitur *undas.*

Æoli, ut sequitur—*Latina* certè littora cum Æneas aderat, *Lavina* non nisi postea ab ipso nominata, Lib. 12. vers. 193—*Jactatus, terris* non convenit.

(b) ———Et quisquis *Nomen* Junonis adoret?
Longè melius, quam ut antea, *Numen.*
Et Procul dubio sic Virgilius.

(c) —Venti velut *aggere fracto*
Qua data porta ruunt——
Sic corrige, meo periculo.

(d) *Fortemque* vehebat *Orontem:*
Non *fidum*, quia Epitheton *Achatæ* notissimum,
Oronti nunquam datur.

(e) —Excutitur: pronusque magis tèr
Volvitur in caput——
Aio Virgilium aliter non scripsisse, quod planè confirmatur ex sequentibus—
Ast illum ter *fluctus ibidem Torquet*——

(f) *Armi hominum*: Ridicule anteà *Arma virum* quæ ex ferro conflata, quomodo possunt *natare?*

(g) Atque rotis *spumas* leviter perlabitur *udas. Summas*, & *leviter perlabi*, pleonasmus est: Mirificè altera lectio Neptuni agilitatem & celeritatem exprimit; simili modo Noster de Camilla, Æn. 11.—*intactæ segetis per summa volaret*, &c. hyperbolicè.

VIII. Vers. 154. (*h*)

Jamque *faces* & saxa volant, *furor arma ministrat.*

IX. Vers. 170. (*i*)

Fronte sub adversa *scopulis pendentibus* antrum,
Intus aquæ dulces, vivoque sedilia saxo.

X. Vers. 188. (*k*)

————Tres littore *cervos*
Prospicit errantes: hos *tota armenta* sequuntur
A tergo————

XI. Vers. 748.

Arcturum pluviasque Hyades, *geminosque Triones;*
Error gravissimus. Corrige,—*septemque Triones.*

XII. Vers. 631. (*l*)

Quare agite O juvenes, *tectis* succedite nostris.

(*h*) Jam *fæces* & saxa volant, *fugiuntque Ministri:* Uti solent, instanti periculo.
—*Fæces, facibus* longe præstant, quid enim nisi fæces jactarent vulgus sordidum?

(*i*) Fronte sub adversa *populis prandentibus* antrum.
Sic malim, longe potiùs quam *scopulis pendentibus:* Nugæ! Nonne vides versu
sequenti *dulces aquas* ad potandum & sedilia ad discubendum dari? In quorum
usum? prandentium.

(*k*) ————Tres litore *corvos*
Aspicit errantes: hos *agmina tota* sequuntur
A tergo—*Cervi,* lectio vulgata, absurditas notissima: hæc animalia in Africa
non inveniri, quis nescit? At motus & ambulandi ritus Corvorum, quis non
agnovit hoc loco? Litore, locus ubi errant Corvi, uti Noster alibi,
Et sola secum sicca spaciatur arena.
Omen præclarissimum, immo et *agminibus* Militum frequentèr observatum, ut
patet ex Historicis.

(*l*) Quare agite O Juvenes, *tectis* succedite nostris.
Lectis potius dicebat Dido, polita magis oratione, & quæ unica voce et Torum
& Mensam exprimebat: Hanc lectionem probe confirmat appellatio O
Juvenes! Duplicem hunc sensum alibi etiam Maro lepidè innuit,
Æn. 4. vers. 19. Huic uni forsan potui succumbere *culpæ:*
Anna! fatebor enim—
Corrige, *Huic uni* [*Viro* scil.] potui succumbere; Culpas
Anna? fatebor enim, *&c.* Vox *succumbere* quam eleganter ambigua!

LIBER SECUNDUS. Vers. 1. (*a*)

*C*ONTICUERE omnes, intentique ora tenebant,
Inde toro *Pater* Æneas sic orsus ab alto:

Vers. 3. (*b*)

Infandum Regina jubes renovare dolorem.

Vers. 4. (*c*)

Trojanas ut *opes*, & lamentabile regnum.

Vers. 5. (*d*)

Eruerint Danai, Quæque ipse *miserrima vidi*
Et quorum pars magna fui.

Vers. 7. (*e*)

—Quis talia *fando*
Temperet *a* lacrymis?

LIB. II. Vers. 1. *&c.*

(*a*) *Concubuere* omnes, intentèque ora tenebant;
Inde toro *satur* Æneas sic orsus ab alto.

Concubuere, quia toro Æneam vidimus accumbentem: quin & altera ratio, scil. *Conticuere* & *ora tenebant*, tautologicè dictum. In Manuscripto perquam rarissimo in Patris Musæo, legitur *ore gemebant*; sed magis ingeniosè quam verè. *Satur* Æneas, quippe qui jam-jam a prandio surrexit: *Pater* nihil ad rem attinet.

(*b*) *Infantum* regina jubes renovare dolorem. Sic haud dubito veterrimis codicibus scriptum fuisse: hoc satis constat ex perantiqua illa Brittannorum Cantilena vocata *Chevy-Chace*, cujus autor hunc locum sibi ascivit in hæc verba,
The Child may rue that is unborn.

(*c*) Trojanas ut *Oves* & lamentabile regnum *Diruerint*—Mallem *oves* potius quam *opes*, quoniam in antiquissimis illis temporibus oves & armenta divitiæ regum fuere. Vel fortasse *Oves Paridis* innuit, quas super Idam nuperrime pascebat, & jam in vindictam pro Helenæ raptu, a Menelao, Ajace aliisque ducibus, meritò occisas.

(*d*) —Quœque ipse *miserrimus audi*,
Et quorum pars magna fui——

Omnia tam *audita* quam *visa* recta distinctione enarrare hic Æneas profitetur: Multa quorum nox ea fatalis sola conscia fuit, Vir probus & pius tanquam *visa* referre non potuit.

(*e*) ——Quis talia *flendo*,
Temperet *in* lachrymis?——Major enim doloris indicatio, absque modo lachrymare, quam solummodo *a* lachrymis non temperare?

VERS. 9. (*f*)
Et jam nox *humida* cœlo
Præcipitat, suadentque *cadentia* sydera somnos.
Sed si tantus amor *casus* cognoscere *nostros*, (*g*)
Et *breviter* Trojæ *supremum* audire laborem,
Quanquam animus meminisse horret, *luctuque refugit*, (*h*)
Incipiam.

VERS. 13. (*i*)
Fracti bello, fatisque repulsi,
Ductores Danaûm, tot jam labentibus annis,
Instar montis *Equum*, divina Palladis arte,
Ædificant——*&c.*

(*f*) Et jam nox *lumina* cœlo
Præcipitat, suadentque *latentia* sydera somnos.
Lectio, *humida*, vespertinum rorem solum innuere videtur: magis mi arridet
Lumina, quæ *latentia* postquam *præcipitantur*, Auroræ adventum annunciant.

(*g*) Sed si tantus amor *curas* cognoscere *noctis*,
Et *brevì ter* Trojæ, *superumque* audire *labores.*

Curæ Noctis (scilicet Noctis Excidii Trojani) magis compendiosè (vel ut dixit
ipse *breviter*) totam Belli catastrophen denotat, quam diffusa illa & indeterminata
lectio, *casus nostros. Ter* audire gratum esse Didoni, patet ex libro quarto, ubi
dicitur, *Iliacosque iterum demens audire labores Exposcit: Ter* enim pro *sæpe* usurpatur.
Trojæ, superumque labores, rectè, quia non tantum homines sed & Dii sese his
laboribus immiscuerunt. Vide Æn. 2. vers. 610, *&c.*

(*h*) Quamquam animus meminisse horret, *luctusque resurgit. Resurgit* multò
proprius dolorem renascentem notat, quam ut hactenus, *refugit.*

(*i*) *Tracti* bello, fatisque repulsi.
Tracti & *Repulsi*, Antithesis perpulcra!
Fracti frigidè & vulgaritèr.

Equum jam *Trojanum*, (ut vulgus loquitur) adeamus; quem si *Equam Græcam*
vocabis Lector, minimè pecces: Solæ enim femellæ utero gestant. Uterumque
armato milite complent—Uteroque *recusso Insonuere cavæ*——*Atque* utero *sonitum
quater arma dedere.*—*Inclusos utero Danaos* &c. Vox *fœta* non convenit maribus,—
Scandit fatalis machina muros, Foeta armis——Palladem Virginem, Equo mari
fabricando invigilare decuisse quis putat? Incredibile prorsus! Quamobrem
existimo veram *Equæ* lectionem passim restituendam, nisi ubi forte metri
caussa, *Equum* potius quam *Equam, Genus* pro *Sexu*, dixit Maro. Vale! dum
hæc paucula corriges, majus opus moveo.

V.

A Continuation of the GUARDIAN: On the Subject of PASTORALS.[1]

Compulerantque greges Corydon & Thyrsis in unum.
Ex illo Corydon, Corydon est tempore nobis ⟨Virg. Ecl. vii⟩.

Monday, April 27, 1713 ⟨No. 40⟩.

1.   I Designed to have troubled the Reader with no farther
         Discourses of *Pastorals*, but being informed that I am
         taxed of Partiality in not mentioning an Author whose
Eclogues are published in the same Volume with Mr. *Philips*'s;
I shall employ this Paper in Observations upon him, written in   5
the *free Spirit of Criticism*, and without apprehension of offending
that Gentleman, whose character it is that he takes the greatest
care of his Works before they are published, and has the least
concern for them afterwards.

   2. I have laid it down as the first rule of Pastoral, that its Idea   10
should be taken from the manners of the *Golden Age*, and the
Moral form'd upon the representation of *Innocence*; 'tis therefore plain that any Deviations from that design degrade a Poem

The text is that of *1729a*, collated with *The Guardian*, April 27,
1713. In reprinting his essay as an Appendix to the *Dunciad*,
Pope italicized many words and phrases which had an ironical
significance. Those departures from the original text have not
been separately noted.

   1. ⟨Omitted from *1735a–42*; it was restored to the *Dunciad* in *1743a*.
In the spring of 1713 a number of essays on pastoral poetry appeared in *The
Guardian* (Nos. 22, 23, 28, 30, 32). They are usually attributed to Steele, but
J. E. Butt has offered evidence to show that they may be the work of Thomas
Tickell.—*Bodleian Quarterly Record*, v 299 ff. In those essays Ambrose Philips was
highly praised, Pope not even mentioned. Pope thereupon wrote a further
essay, ironically praising the pastorals of Philips and condemning his own for
the want of that simplicity which was so obvious in those of Philips. This was
sent to Steele, who published it on April 27, without suspecting the irony.—
See Sherburn, pp. 118–21.⟩

from being true Pastoral. In this view it will appear that *Virgil* can only have *two* of his Eclogues allowed to be such: His first and ninth must be rejected, because they describe the ravages of Armies, and oppressions of the Innocent; *Corydon*'s criminal Passion for *Alexis* throws out the second; the calumny and rail- 5 ing in the third are not proper to that state of Concord; the eighth represents unlawful ways of procuring Love by Inchant- ments, and introduces a Shepherd whom an inviting Precipice tempts to Self-Murder. As to the fourth, sixth, and tenth, they are given up by (*a*) *Heinsius, Salmasius, Rapin,* and the Criticks in 10 general. They likewise observe that but *eleven* of all the *Idyllia* of *Theocritus* are to be admitted as Pastorals; and even out of that number the greater part will be excluded for *one* or *other* of the *Reasons abovementioned.* So that when I remark'd in a former paper, that *Virgil*'s Eclogues taken all together are rather *select* 15 *Poems* than *Pastorals*; I might have said the same thing with no less truth of *Theocritus.* The reason of this I take to be yet un- observed by the Criticks, *viz. They never meant them all for Pastorals.*

Now it is plain *Philips* hath done this, and *in that Particular* excelled both *Theocritus* and *Virgil.* 20

3. As *Simplicity* is the distinguishing Characteristick of Pas- toral, *Virgil* hath been thought guilty of too courtly a Stile; his Language is *perfectly pure,* and he often forgets he is among Peas- ants. I have frequently wonder'd, that since he was so conver- sant in the writings of *Ennius,* he had not imitated the *Rusticity* of 25 the *Doric,* as well by the help of the *old obsolete Roman* Language, as *Philips* hath by the *antiquated English:* For example, might he not have said *Quoi* instead of *Cui; quoijum* for *cujum; volt* for *vult,* &c. as well as our Modern hath *Welladay* for *Alas, whilome* for *of old, make mock* for *deride,* and *witless Younglings* for *simple Lambs,* 30 &c. by which means he had attained as much of the Air of *Theocritus,* as *Philips* hath of *Spencer?*

4. Mr. *Pope* hath fallen into the *same error with Virgil.* His Clowns do not converse in *all the Simplicity* proper to the Coun- try: His names are borrow'd from *Theocritus* and *Virgil,* which 35 are improper to the Scene of his Pastorals. He introduces *Daph-*

---

19 Now . . . this] Which it is plain *Philips* hath done, *1713*

(*a*) *See* Rapin *de* Carm. Past. *pars* 3.

nis, Alexis and *Thyrsis* on *British* Plains, as *Virgil* had done before
him on the *Mantuan:* Whereas *Philips*, who hath the strictest
regard to Propriety, makes choice of names *peculiar to the Country*,
and more agreeable to a Reader of *Delicacy*; such as *Hobbinol*,
Lobbin, Cuddy, and *Colin Clout.*

   5. So easie as Pastoral Writing may seem, (in the *Simplicity*   5
we have described it) yet it requires great *Reading*, both of the
Ancients and *Moderns*, to be a master of it. *Philips* hath given us
manifest proofs of his *Knowledge of Books:* It must be confessed
his competitor hath imitated some *single thoughts* of the Ancients
well enough, (if we consider he had not the happiness of an   10
University Education) but he hath dispersed them, *here* and
there, without that order and method which Mr. *Philips* observes,
whose *whole* third Pastoral is an instance how well he hath
studied the fifth of *Virgil*, and how judiciously *reduced Virgil's*
thoughts to the standard of Pastoral; as his contention of *Colin*   15
Clout and the *Nightingale* shows with what *exactness* he hath imitated *every line* in *Strada.*

   6. When I remarked it as a principal fault, to introduce *Fruits*
and *Flowers* of a *Foreign growth*, in descriptions where the Scene
lies in our *own Country*, I did not design that observation should   20
extend also to *Animals*, or the *sensitive Life*; for *Philips* hath with
great judgment described *Wolves* in *England* in his first Pastoral.
Nor would I have a Poet slavishly confine himself (as Mr. *Pope*
hath done) to one particular *season* of the Year, one certain
time of the *day*, and one *unbroken Scene* in each Eclogue. 'Tis plain   25
Spencer neglected this Pedantry, who in his Pastoral of *November*
mentions the mournful song of the *Nightingale*:
       Sad Philomel *her song in Tears doth steep.*
   And Mr. *Philips*, by a poetical Creation, hath raised up finer
beds of Flowers than the most industrious Gardiner; his Roses,   30
Endives, Lillies, Kingcups and Daffadils blow *all in the same*
season.

   7. But the better to discover the merits of our two contemporary Pastoral Writers, I shall endeavour to draw a Parallel of
them, by setting several of their particular thoughts in the same   35

17 *every line* in] *Om. 1713.*   20 our *own*] our *1713.*
31 Endives . . . Kingcups] *Om. 1713.*   *all*] *Om. 1713.*

light, whereby it will be obvious how much *Philips* hath the advantage. With what Simplicity he introduces two Shepherds singing alternately!

Hobb.   *Come,* Rosalind, *O come, for without thee*
          What Pleasure can the Country have for me: 5
          Come, Rosalind, *O come; my brinded Kine,*
          My snowy Sheep, my Farm, and all, is thine.

Lanq.   *Come* Rosalind, *O come; here shady Bowers*
          Here are cool Fountains, and here springing Flow'rs.
          Come, Rosalind; *Here ever let us stay,*   10
          And sweetly wast, our live-long time away.

Our other Pastoral Writer, in expressing the same thought, deviates into *downright Poetry.*

Streph. *In Spring the Fields, in Autumn Hills I love,*
          At Morn the Plains, at Noon the shady Grove,   15
          But Delia *always; forc'd from* Delia*'s sight,*
          Nor Plains at Morn, nor Groves at Noon delight.

Daph.   Sylvia*'s like Autumn ripe, yet mild as* May,
          More bright than Noon, yet fresh as early Day;
          Ev'n Spring displeases, when she shines not here,   20
          But blest with her, 'tis Spring throughout the Year.

In the first of these Authors, two Shepherds thus *innocently* describe the Behaviour of their Mistresses.

Hobb.   *As* Marian *bath'd, by chance I passed by,*
          She blush'd, and at me cast a side-long Eye: 25
          Then swift beneath the crystal Wave she try'd
          Her beauteous Form, but all in vain, to hide.

Lanq.   *As I to cool me bath'd one sultry day,*
          Fond Lydia *lurking in the Sedges lay.*
          The wanton laugh'd, and seem'd in haste to fly;   30
          Yet often stopp'd, and often turn'd her Eye.

The other Modern (who it must be confessed hath a *knack of versifying*) hath it as follows.

Streph. *Me gentle* Delia *beckons from the Plain,*
         Then, hid in Shades, eludes her eager Swain;
         But feigns a Laugh, to see me search around,
         And by that Laugh the willing Fair is found.

Daph.   *The sprightly* Sylvia *trips along the Green,*   5
         She runs, but hopes she does not run unseen;
         While a kind glance at her Pursuer flyes,
         How much at variance are her Feet and Eyes!

There is nothing the Writers of this kind of Poetry are fonder of,
than descriptions of Pastoral Presents. *Philips* says thus of a 10
Sheep-hook.

         Of season'd Elm; where studs of Brass appear,
         To speak the Giver's name, the month and year.
         The hook of polish'd Steel, the handle turn'd,
         And richly by the Graver's skill adorn'd.   15

The other of a Bowl embossed with Figures.

         ————*where wanton Ivy twines,*
         And swelling Clusters bend the curling Vines;
         Four Figures rising from the work appear,
         The various Seasons of the rolling year;   20
         And What is that which binds the radiant Sky,
         Where twelve bright Signs in beauteous order lie?

The simplicity of the Swain in this place, who forgets the name
of the *Zodiack*, is no ill imitation of *Virgil*; but how much more
plainly and unaffectedly would *Philips* have dressed this 25
Thought in his *Doric?*

         And what that hight, which girds the Welkin sheen,
         Where twelve gay Signs in meet array are seen?

   If the Reader would indulge his curiosity any farther in the
comparison of Particulars, he may read the first Pastoral of 30
Philips with the second of his Contemporary, and the fourth and
sixth of the former with the fourth and first of the latter; where
several parallel places will occur to every one.

   Having now shown some parts, in which these two Writers
may be compared, it is a justice I owe to Mr. *Philips*, to discover 35

those in which *no man can compare with him*. First, That *beautiful Rusticity*, of which I shall only produce two Instances, out of a hundred not yet quoted.

> *O woful day! O day of Woe, quoth he,*
> *And woful I, who live the day to see!*   5

The simplicity of Diction, the melancholy flowing of the Numbers, the solemnity of the Sound, and the easie turn of the Words, in this *Dirge*, (to make use of our Author's Expression) are extreamly elegant.

In another of his Pastorals, a Shepherd utters a *Dirge* not 10
much inferior to the former, in the following lines.

> *Ah me the while! ah me! the luckless day,*
> *Ah luckless Lad! the rather might I say;*
> *Ah silly I! more silly than my Sheep,*
> *Which on the flowry Plains I once did keep.*   15

How he still charms the ear with these *artful Repetitions* of the Epithets; and how *significant* is the last verse! I defy the most common Reader to repeat them, without feeling some *motions of compassion*.

In the next place I shall rank his *Proverbs*, in which I formerly 20
observed he excells: For example,

> *A* rolling Stone *is ever bare of* Moss;
> *And to their cost*, green years old proverbs *cross*.
> —*He that* late lyes down, *as* late will rise,
> *And Sluggard-like, till noon-day snoaring lyes.*   25
> *Against* Ill-Luck *all cunning* Fore-sight *fails*;
> *Whether we sleep or wake, it nought avails.*
> —*Nor fear, from* upright *Sentence*, wrong.

Lastly, his *elegant Dialect*, which alone might prove him the eldest born of *Spencer*, and our only true *Arcadian*. I should think 30
it proper for the several writers of Pastoral, to confine themselves to their several *Counties*. *Spencer* seems to have been of this opinion: for he hath laid the scene of one of his Pastorals in *Wales*, where with all the Simplicity natural to that part of our

---

6 The simplicity] That simplicity *1713*.

Island, one Shepherd bids the other *good morrow* in an unusual
and elegant manner.

> Diggon Davy, *I bid hur God-day:*
> *Or* Diggon *hur is, or I mis-say.*

Diggon answers,   5

> *Hur was hur, while it was day-light;*
> *But now hur is a most wretched wight,* &c.

But the most beautiful example of this kind that I ever met
with, is in a very valuable Piece, which I chanced to find among
some old Manuscripts, entituled, *A Pastoral Ballad:* which I 10
think, for its nature and simplicity, may (notwithstanding the
modesty of the Title) be allowed a perfect Pastoral: It is composed in the *Somersetshire* Dialect, and the names such as are
proper to the Country People. It may be observed, as a further
beauty of this Pastoral, the words *Nymph, Dryad, Naiad, Fawn,* 15
Cupid, or *Satyr,* are not once mentioned through the whole. I
shall make no Apology for inserting some few lines of this excellent Piece. *Cicily* breaks thus into the subject, as she is going a
Milking:

Cicily.   Rager *go vetch tha* (*b*) *Kee, or else tha Zun*   20
          Will quite be go, be vore c'have half a don.

Roger.   *Thou shouldst not ax ma tweece, but I've a be*
          To dreave our Bull to bull tha Parson's Kee.

It is to be observed, that this whole Dialogue is formed upon
the *Passion of Jealousie*; and his mentioning the Parson's Kine 25
naturally revives the Jealousie of the Shepherdess *Cicily,* which
she expresses as follows:

Cicily.   *Ah* Rager, Rager, *chez was zore avraid*
          When in yond Vield you kiss'd tha Parson's Maid:
          Is this tha Love that once to me you zed,   30
          When from tha Wake thou brought'st me Gingerbread?

(*b*) That is the *Kine* or *Cows.*

Roger.   Cicily *thou charg'st me valse,—I'll zwear to thee,*
            Tha Parson's Maid is still a Maid for me.

In which Answer of his are express'd at once that *Spirit of Religion*, and that *Innocence of the Golden Age*, so necessary to be observed by all Writers of Pastoral.   5

    At the conclusion of this piece, the Author reconciles the Lovers, and ends the Eclogue the most *simply* in the world.

        So Rager *parted vor to vetch tha Kee,*
        And vor her Bucket in went Cicily.

I am loath to show my fondness for Antiquity so far as to prefer 10
this ancient *British* Author to our present *English* Writers of Pastoral; but I cannot avoid making this obvious Remark, that *Philips* hath hit into the *same Road* with this old *West Country* Bard of ours.

    After all that hath been said, I hope none can think it any 15
Injustice to Mr. *Pope*, that I forbore to mention him as a Pastoral Writer; since upon the whole, he is of the same class with *Moschus* and *Bion*, whom we have excluded that rank; and of whose Eclogues, as well as some of *Virgil*'s, it may be said, that (according to the description we have given of this sort of 20
Poetry) they are by no means *Pastorals*, but *something better*.

---

13 *Philips* hath] Both *Spencer* and *Philips* have *1713*.

VI.

A PARALLEL

OF THE

CHARACTERS

OF

Mr. DRYDEN and Mr. POPE,

As drawn by certain of their Cotemporaries.

Mr. DRYDEN.
His POLITICKS, RELIGION, MORALS.

M R. *Dryden* is a mere Renegado from *Monarchy, Poetry,* and *good Sense.* (*a*) A true *Republican* Son of a *monarchical* Church. (*b*) A Republican *Atheist.* (*c*) *Dryden* was from the beginning an ἀλλοπρόσαλλος, and I doubt not will continue so to the last. (*d*)   5

In the Poem call'd *Absalom and Achitophel* are notoriously traduced, The KING, the QUEEN, the LORDS and GENTLE-MEN, not only their Honourable Persons exposed, but the WHOLE NATION and its REPRESENTATIVES notoriously libell'd; It is *Scandalum Magnatum,* yea of MAJESTY itself. (*e*)   10

He looks upon *God's Gospel* as a *foolish Fable,* like the *Pope,* to whom he is a pitiful Purveyor. (*f*) His very *Christianity* may be questioned. (*g*) He ought to expect more Severity than other

---

The text is that of *1729a,* collated with *1743a.* This piece first appeared in *1729a.*

Cotemporaries] Contemporaries *1743.*
2 of a] of *1743.*

(*a*) *Milbourn on Dryden's Virgil,* 8° 1698. *p.* 6.
(*b*) *pag.* 38.   (*c*) *pag.* 192.   (*d*) *pag.* 8.
(*e*) *Whip and Key,* 4°, *printed for R. Janeway* 1682. *Preface.*
(*f*) *ibid.*   (*g*) *Milbourn, p.* 9.

VI.

A PARALLEL

OF THE

CHARACTERS

OF

Mr. DRYDEN and Mr. POPE,

Mr. POPE.

His POLITICKS, RELIGION, MORALS.

M R. *Pope* is an open and mortal *Enemy* to his *Country*, and the *Commonwealth* of *Learning*. (*a*) Some call him a Popish *Whig*, which is directly inconsistent. (*b*) *Pope* as a Papist must be a *Tory* and *High-flyer*. (*c*) He is *both* a *Whig* and a *Tory*. (*d*) He hath made it his custom to cackle to   5
more than one Party in their own Sentiments. (*e*)

In his *Miscellanies*, the Persons abused are, The KING, the QUEEN, His late MAJESTY, both Houses of PARLIAMENT, the *Privy-Council*, the Bench of *Bishops*, the Establish'd CHURCH, the present MINISTRY, &c. To make sense of some passages,   10
they must be constru'd into ROYAL SCANDAL. (*f*)

He is a *Popish* Rhymester, bred up with a *Contempt* of the *Sacred Writings*. (*g*) His *Religion* allows him to *destroy Hereticks*, not only with his pen, but with fire and sword; and such were

---

4 a *Tory.*] tory *1743.*

(*a*) *Dennis*, Remarks on the Rape of the Lock, pref. p. 12.

(*b*) Dunciad dissected ⟨p. 7⟩.   (*c*) Preface to *Gulliveriana*.

(*d*) *Denn.* and *Gild.* Character of Mr. *P.* ⟨p. 4⟩.

(*e*) *Theobald*, Letter in *Mist's* Journal, *June* 22, 1728. ⟨Theobald was answering Pope's charge in *Dunciad A* i 192 that he had "cackled" to the Tories. His letters to *Mist's Journal* had always, he claimed, been on "learning or entertainment". Pope, on the other hand, "or he is shrewdly abus'd, has made it his Custom to *cackle* to more than *one* Party in their own Sentiments."⟩

(*f*) List, at the end of a Collection of Verses, Letters, Advertisements, 8°. Printed for *A. Moore*, 1728. and the Preface to it, pag. 6.

(*g*) *Dennis's* Remarks on *Homer*, p. 27.

10

men, as he is *most unmerciful* in his own *Reflections* on others. (*h*)
With as good right as his *Holiness*, he sets up for *Poetical Infallibility*. (*i*)

Mr. DRYDEN only a Versifyer.

His whole Libel is all *bad matter*, beautify'd (which is *all* that   5
can be said of it) with *good metre*. (*k*) Mr. *Dryden*'s Genius did not
appear in any thing more than his *Versification*, and whether he
is to be ennobled for *that only*, is a question. (*l*)

Mr. DRYDEN's VIRGIL.

Tonson calls it *Dryden*'s *Virgil*, to show that this is not that *Vir-*   10
gil so admired in the Augustæan age, but a *Virgil* of another
stamp, a *silly, impertinent, nonsensical* Writer. (*m*) None but a
Bavius, a *Mævius*, or a *Bathyllus* carp'd at *Virgil*, and none but
such unthinking Vermin *admire* his Translator. (*n*) It is true,
soft and easy lines might become *Ovid*'s Epistles or Art of Love—   15
But *Virgil* who is all great and majestic, *&c.* requires strength of
lines, weight of words, and closeness of expressions, not an
ambling Muse running on a Carpet-ground, and shod as lightly
as a *Newmarket* racer.—He has numberless faults in his *English*,
in *Sense*, in his *Author's meaning*, and in propriety of *Expression*. (*o*)   20

Mr. DRYDEN understood no *Greek* or *Latin*.

Mr. *Dryden* was *once*, I have heard, at *Westminster School*: Dr.
Busby wou'd have *whipt him* for so childish a Paraphrase. (*p*)
The meanest Pedant in *England* wou'd *whip a Lubber* of twelve for
construing so absurdly. (*q*) The Translator is *mad, every line* betrays   25
his Stupidity. (*r*) The faults are innumerable, and convince me
that Mr. *Dryden* did not, or would not *understand his Author*. (*s*)
This shows how fit Mr. *D.* may be to *translate Homer!* A mistake
in a single letter might fall on the *Printer* well enough, but Εἴχωρ
for Ἴχωρ must be the error of the *Author:* Nor had he art enough   30
to correct it at the Press. (*t*) Mr. *Dryden* writes for the *Court
Ladies*—He writes for the *Ladies*, and not for use. (*u*)

---

19 in his *English*, in *Sense*] *Om.* 1743.

(*h*) ibid. *p.* 175.   (*i*) *pag.* 39.   (*k*) *Whip and Key, pref.*
(*l*) *Oldmixon, Essay on Criticism*, p. 84.   (*m*) *Milbourn*, pag. 4.   (*n*) Pag. 35.
(*o*) Pag. 22, and 192.   (*p*) *Milbourn*, pag. 72.   (*q*) Pag. 203.
(*r*) Pag. 78.   (*s*) Pag. 206.   (*t*) Pag. 19.   (*u*) Pag. 124, 190.

all those *unhappy Wits* whom he sacrificed to his *accursed Popish Principles*. (*h*) It deserved Vengeance to suggest, that Mr. *Pope* had less *Infallibility* than his *Namesake at Rome*. (*i*)

Mr. POPE only a Versifyer.

The *smooth numbers* of the Dunciad are *all* that recommend it, 5
nor has it *any other merit*. (*k*) It must be own'd that he hath got a
notable *Knack* of rhymeing, and writing *smooth verse*. (*l*)

Mr. POPE's HOMER.

The *Homer* which *Lintot* prints, does not talk like *Homer*, but
like *Pope*; and he who translated him one wou'd swear had a 10
Hill in *Tipperary* for his *Parnassus*, and a puddle in some Bog for
his *Hippocrene*. (*m*) He has no *Admirers* among those that can
distinguish, discern, and judge. (*n*)

He hath a knack at *smooth verse*, but without either *Genius* or
good *Sense*, or any tolerable knowledge of *English*. The qualities 15
which distinguish *Homer* are the beauties of his *Diction* and the
harmony of his Versification——But this little Author who is so
much in vogue, has neither *Sense* in his *Thoughts*, nor *English* in
his *Expressions*. (*o*)

Mr. POPE understood no *Greek*. 20

He hath undertaken to translate *Homer* from the *Greek*, of
which he knows not *one word*, into *English*, of which he understands ⟨almost⟩ *as little*. (*p*) I wonder how this Gentleman
wou'd look should it be discover'd, that he has not translated
ten verses together in any book of *Homer* with justice to the Poet, 25
and yet he dares reproach his fellow-writers with *not understanding Greek*. (*q*) He has stuck so little to his Original, as to have his
knowledge in Greek called in question. (*r*) I should be glad to know
which it is of all *Homer*'s Excellencies, which has so delighted the
Ladies, and the Gentlemen who judge like *Ladies*. (*s*) 30

But he has a notable talent at *Burlesque*; his genius slides so

---

(*h*) Preface to *Gulliveriana*, p. 11.　　(*i*) Dedication to the Collection of
Verses, Letters, pag. 9.　　(*k*) *Mist's Journal, of June* 8, 1728.

(*l*) *Character of Mr.* P. and *Dennis on Homer* ⟨p. 16.⟩　　(*m*) *Dennis's* Remarks
on *Pope's Homer*, pag. 12.　　(*n*) *Ibid*.　　(*o*) Character of Mr. *P.* pag. 17.
and Remarks on *Homer*, p. 91.　　(*p*) *Dennis's* Remarks on *Homer*, p. 12.

(*q*) Daily Journal of *April* 23, 1728.　　(*r*) Supplement to the Profund. Pref.
⟨p. v⟩.　　(*s*) *Oldmixon*, Essay on Criticism, p. 66

The Translator puts in a little *Burlesque* now and then into
Virgil, for a Ragout to his *cheated Subscribers*. (*w*)

Mr. DRYDEN trick'd his Subscribers.

I wonder that any man who cou'd not but be conscious of his
own *unfitness* for it, shou'd go to amuse the learned world with   5
such an *Undertaking!* A man ought to value his *Reputation* more
than *Money*; and not to hope that those who can read for themselves, will be *Imposed upon*, merely by a *partially and unseasonably-
celebrated Name.* (*x*) *Poetis quidlibet audendi* shall be Mr. *Dryden*'s
Motto, tho' it should extend to *Picking of Pockets.* (*y*)   10

Names bestow'd on Mr. DRYDEN.

An APE.] A crafty *Ape* drest up in a gaudy Gown—Whips
put into an *Ape*'s paw, to play pranks with—None but *Apish* and
Papish Brats will heed him. *Whip and Key, Pref.*

An ASS.] A Camel will take upon him no more burden than   15
is sufficient for his strength, but there is *another Beast* that
crouches under all: Mr. *Dryden*, &c. *Milb.* p. 105.

A FROG.] Poet *Squab* indued with Poet *Maro*'s Spirit! an
ugly, *croaking* kind of *Vermine*, which would swell to the bulk of
an *Oxe.* Pag. 11.   20

A COWARD.] A *Clinias* or a *Damætas*, or a man of Mr.
Dryden's *own Courage.* Pag. 176.

A KNAVE.] Mr. *Dryden* has heard of *Paul, the Knave of Jesus
Christ:* And if I mistake not, I've read somewhere of *John
Dryden Servant to his Majesty.* Pag. 57.   25

A FOOL.] Had he not been such a self-conceited *Fool—Whip
and Key, pref.* Some great Poets are positive *Blockheads. Milbourn*,
p. 34.

A THING.] So little a *Thing* as Mr. *Dryden. Ibid.* pag. 35.

17 Mr. *Dryden*, &c.] *Om. 1743.*

(*w*) Pag. 67.   (*x*) *Milbourn*, p. 192.   (*y*) *Ibid.* p. 125.

naturally into it, that he hath burlesqu'd *Homer* without designing it. (*t*)

Mr. POPE trick'd his Subscribers.

'Tis indeed somewhat *bold*, and almost *prodigious*, for *a single man* to undertake such a work! But 'tis too late to dissuade by 5 demonstrating the *madness* of your Project: The Subscribers' expectations have been rais'd, in proportion to what their *Pockets have been drain'd of.* (*u*) *Pope* has been concern'd in Jobbs, and hired out his *Name* to Booksellers. (*x*)

Names bestow'd on Mr. POPE.   10

An APE.] Let us take the initial letter of his christian name, and the initial and final letters of his surname, *viz.* A. P. E. and they give you the same Idea of an *Ape*, as his face, *&c. Dennis, Daily Journal, May* 11, 1728.

An ASS.] It is my duty to pull off the Lion's skin from this little 15 *Ass. Dennis's* Rem. on *Homer*, pref.

A FROG.] A *squab* short Gentleman—a little creature that like the *Frog* in the Fable, swells and is angry that it is not allow'd *to be as big as an Oxe. Dennis's Remarks on the Rape of the Lock, pref. p.* 9.   20

A COWARD.] A lurking, way-laying *Coward. Char. of Mr. P. pag. 3.*

A KNAVE.] He is one whom God and nature have mark'd for *want* of common *honesty. Ibid.*

A FOOL.] Great *Fools* will be christen'd by the names of great 25 Poets, and *Pope* will be called *Homer. Dennis's* Rem. on *Homer, p. 37.*

A THING.] A little, abject, *Thing. Ibid. p. 8.*

---

6 your] the *1743.*

(*t*) *Dennis's* Remarks, p. 28.   (*u*) *Burnet, Homerides. p.* 1, &c.

(*x*) *British Journal, Nov.* 25, 1727.

27. ⟨"If the Translation of Ancient Poets is carry'd on but a little farther at the Rate that it has been in that of HOMER and OVID; why then we may expect, that in a very short Time, the Names of the Ancient Poets will sink as vilely low, as those of their Heroes, or those of their Goddesses. And as Dogs are called by the Names of their Heroes, HECTOR, and CAESAR, and POMPEY ... so great Fools will be christen'd anew by the Names of their great Poets, HOMER, and HORACE, and OVID; and then Pope and the *Censor* will not be the Translators of HOMER and OVID, but HOMER and OVID Themselves."⟩

VII.

A

L I S T

OF

All our AUTHOR's Genuine Works.[1]

THE Works of Mr. ALEXANDER POPE, in quarto and   5
folio. Printed for *Jacob Tonson* and *Bernard Lintot*, in the
year 1717. This Edition contains whatsoever is his,
except these few following, which have been written since that
time.

INSCRIPTION to Dr. *Parnel*'s Poems; To the Right Honour- 10
able ROBERT Earl of OXFORD and Earl MORTIMER.

VERSES on Mr. ADDISON's Treatise of *Medals*, first printed
after his death in Mr. *Tickel*'s Edition of his Works.

EPITAPHS: On the Honourable *Simon Harcourt:* on the
Honourable *Robert Digby:* on Mrs. *Corbett*; and another intend- 15
ed for Mr. *Rowe.*

The WHOLE ILIAD of HOMER, with the PREFACE, and the
NOTES, (except the *Extracts from Eustathius* in the four last
volumes, made by Mr. *Broome*; and the *Essay* on the *Life* and
Writings of *Homer*, which tho' collected by our Author, was put 20
together by Dr. *Parnell*.)

TWELVE BOOKS of the ODYSSEY, with some parts of other
Books; and the *Dissertation* by way of *Postscript* at the end.

The *Preface* to Mr. *Tonson*'s Edition of SHAKESPEAR.

MISCELLANIES by Dr. *Swift* and our Author, *&c.* Printed 25
for *B. Motte.*

And some *Spectators* and *Guardians.*

---

1. ⟨In the editions of 1729 only. See Vol. vi, and *Pope's Prose*, where this list
is considerably extended.⟩

By the AUTHOR

A DECLARATION.

𝖂𝖍𝖊𝖗𝖊𝖆𝖘 certain Haberdashers of Points and Particles, being instigated by the spirit of Pride, and assuming to themselves the name of Critics and Restorers, have taken upon them to adulterate the common and current sense of our Glorious Ancestors, Poets of this Realm, by clipping, coining, defacing the images, mixing their own 5 base allay, or otherwise falsifying the same; which they publish, utter, and vend as genuine: The said haberdashers having no right thereto, as neither heirs, executors, administrators, assigns, or in any sort related to such Poets, to all or any of them: Now We, having carefully revised this our Dunciad,[a] 10

The text is that of *1735a*, in which this piece first appeared, collated with *1743a*.

---

[a] Read thus confidently, instead of "beginning with the word *Books*, and "ending with the word *flies*," as formerly it stood; Read also "containing the entire "sum of *one thousand, seven hundred, and fifty four* verses," instead of "*one thousand and* "*twelve* lines;" such being the initial and final words, and such the true and entire contents, of this Poem.

Thou art to know, reader! that the first Edition thereof, like that of Milton, was never seen by the Author (though living and not blind;) The Editor himself confest as much in his Preface: And no two poems were ever published in so arbitrary a manner. The Editor of this, had as boldly suppressed whole Passages, yea the entire last book; as the Editor of Paradise lost, added and augmented. Milton himself gave but *ten* books, his editor *twelve*; this Author gave *four* books, his Editor only *three*. But we have happily done justice to both; and presume we shall live, in this our last labour, as long as in any of our others. Bentley. ⟨*1743a*.

beginning with the word Books, and ending with the words buries
all, containing the entire sum of one thousand and twelve Lines,
do declare every word, figure, point, and comma of this impres=
sion to be authentic: And do therefore strictly enjoin and forbid
any person or persons whatsoever, to erase, reverse, put be-   5
tween hooks, or by any other means directly or indirectly change
or mangle any of them. And we do hereby earnestly exhort all
our brethren to follow this our example, which we heartily wish
our Great Predecessors had heretofore set, as a remedy and
prevention of all such abuses. Provided always, that nothing in   10
this Declaration shall be construed to limit the lawful and undoubted right of every subject of this Realm, to judge, censure,
or condemn, in the whole or in part, any Poem or Poet whatsoever.

> Given under our hand at London, this third day of 15
> January, in the year of our Lord One thou-
> sand, seven hundred, thirty and two.

Declarat' cor' me,
JOHN BARBER, Mayor.

---

1   word] words   Books] The Mighty Mother
2   one thousand and twelve Lines] one thousand seven hundred
and fifty four verses   3 do declare] declare

The first edition of Milton's poem was, as the note indicates, in ten books: *Paradise
Lost. A Poem Written in Ten Books by John Milton* . . . 1667. The second edition
(1674) was in twelve books: *Paradise Lost. A Poem in Twelve Books* . . . *Revised
and Augmented by the same Author.*⟩

6. *hooks* ⟨Bentley's word for the brackets by which he indicated the passages
in *Paradise Lost* that he considered spurious. Cf. B iv 194*n*.⟩

John Barber, Mayor ⟨See Biog. App.—Writing to Swift, Jan. 13, 1732/3,
Arbuthnot informed him that Pope had "affixed to the new edition of his Dun-
ciad, a royal declaration against the haberdashers of points and particles . . ."
The date of Arbuthnot's letter confirms the date of the "Declaration."⟩

INDEX[1]

Of THINGS (including AUTHORS) to be found in the
NOTES, &c. The first Number denotes the BOOK, the
second the VERSE. Test. Testimonies. Ap. Appendix.

A.

ADDISON (Mr.) written against
with vehemence, by *J. Dennis.*
Book ii. verse 271. Railed at by
A. Philips. iii. 322.

Abused by *J. Oldmixon,* in his Prose-
Essay on Criticism, *&c.* ii. 199.

—by *J. Ralph,* in a London Journal,
iii. 159.

—Celebrated by our Author—Upon
his Discourse of Medals—In his
Prologue to *Cato*—and in this Poem.
ii. 132.

False Facts concerning him and our
Author related by anonymous Persons in *Mist*'s Journals, *&c. Test.
pag.* 9, 10, 11 ⟨29 ff.⟩.

Disprov'd by the Testimonies of

—The Earl of *Burlington,* 12 ⟨33⟩.

—Mr. *Tickel,* 10 ⟨30⟩.

—Mr. *Addison* himself, *Ibid.* and 9 ⟨29⟩.

Anger, one of the Characteristics of
Mr. *Dennis*'s Critical Writings, i.
104.

—*Affirmation,* another: *Test.* p. 5 ⟨27⟩.

[To which are added by Mr. *Theobald, Ill-nature, Spite, Revenge,* i. 104.]

Altar of *Tibbald*'s Works, how built,
and how founded? i. 135, *&c.*

Æschylus, How long he was *about* him,
i. 210.

In what respect like him, iii. 311.

Asses, at a Citizen's gate in a morning,
ii. 237.

Appearances, that we are never to judge
by them, especially of Poets and
Divines, ii. 394.

Alehouse, The Birth-place of many
Poems, i. 202.

—And of some Poets, ii. 130.

—One kept by *Taylor* the Water-poet,
ii. 323.

—and by *Edward Ward,* i. 200.

B.

*B*AVIUS, Book iii. verse 16. Mr.
Dennis his great opinion of him,
ibid.

Bawdry, in Plays, not disapprov'd of
by Mr. *Dennis,* iii. 176.

---

1. ⟨The text is that of *1729a,* in which this index first appeared. Errors or omissions in references to the text of the poem and to its various appendices have been
silently corrected or supplied. Where Pope's references are to the pages of *1729a,*
the corresponding page references to the present edition have been added in
brackets.

An index to a poem of this kind was by no means an innovation: Blackmore provided one for his *Prince Arthur* and *King Arthur,* and Gay had one for
his *Trivia.* For the *jocular* index there were several precedents, e.g. *Dr. Bentley's
Dissertations on the Epistles of Phalaris . . . Examin'd,* 2nd ed. 1698.⟩

F I N I S.

THE

D U N C I A D,

IN

FOUR BOOKS.

Printed according to the complete Copy
found in the Year 1742.

WITH THE

P ROLEGOMENA of S CRIBLERUS,

AND

N OTES V ARIORUM.

To which are added,

S EVERAL N OTES now first publish'd, the H YPERCRITICS
of A RISTARCHUS, and his *Dissertation* on the H ERO of
the P OEM.

Tandem *Phœbus* adest, morsusque inferre parantem
Congelat, et patulos, ut erant, indurat hiatus.   O VID.

NOTE ON THE TEXT
of *Dunciad* B

The New Dunciad: As it was Found in the Year 1741 was published by T. Cooper in March 1742; it was a quarto of 48 pages.[1] A second quarto (Griffith 549) contains a number of slight revisions in the text of both poem and notes, and two additional lines. Late in April Cooper published what he described on the title-page as "The Second Edition", but what was, in fact, a reissue of the sheets of the second quarto, with a new title-page (Griffith 556). An octavo which probably preceded it is suspected by Professor Griffith of being a piracy, although it carries Cooper's name on the title-page. It must certainly be suspect, for Cooper was advertising in the *London Evening-Post*, April 22–4, 1742, that there was no genuine edition of the poem except in quarto, "nor will there be one in any other Form till it is joined with the rest of the Author's Works in the Duodecimo Volume." This octavo, which was set up from a copy of the first quarto and incorporates none of the revisions of the second quarto described above, has been collated here with the other Cooper editions; but though it has been given the benefit of the doubt it has almost certainly no textual authority. Two 1742 octavo piracies "Printed for J. H. Hubbard" (Professor Griffith suspects that Edmund Curll was behind them), and two Dublin editions of the same date, have not been collated. The "Duodecimo Volume" mentioned in Cooper's advertisement was the small octavo Works (vol. iii, pt. ii) published in July, containing "The Dunciad, Book IV And The Memoirs of Scriblerus." The text had been revised slightly; it was revised again for a further edition of this volume later in the same year.

During 1743 Pope was at work on the new version of the *Dunciad* in which Theobald was to be dethroned in favour of Colley Cibber; it was published in quarto by M. Cooper towards the end of October as *The Dunciad, In Four Books*. This is generally regarded as the first edition of the Cibber *Dunciad*, but there is a

---

1. A Large Paper quarto is catalogued in the Ashley Library (Griffith 547).

248

puzzling complication. At some date in 1743 Dodsley and Cooper issued a third edition of the small octavo Works, vol. iii, pt. ii. Here *The New Dunciad* has been expanded from the 618 lines of *1742a* to 648 lines: the 1743 quarto has 650. The volume is made up of remainder sheets of the previous (i.e. second) edition of the Works, vol. iii, pt. ii, but many new leaves have been inserted to allow for extensive revision of both poem and notes. The new readings frequently differ from those in the quarto, and differ in such a way as to suggest that the octavo was "a trial version, ante-dating in time of composition the text of the quarto" (Griffith, op. cit., vol. i, pt. ii, p. 464). It would have been odd indeed if Dodsley and Cooper had prejudiced the sale of their seven-and-sixpenny quarto by publishing this botched-up octavo before it; but Professor Griffith is probably right in suggesting that it may have been *printed* at about the time the 1743 quarto was at press. The first three books of the Cibber *Dunciad* were republished together in 1743 by Dodsley and Cooper in the Works as vol. iii, pt. i, and were obviously intended to be sold along with the third edition of vol. iii, pt. ii. just mentioned.

In 1750 J. and P. Knapton published the complete *Dunciad* in octavo (dated 1749). The text of the first three books was made up for the most part of the unsold sheets of the 1743 octavo; the fourth book was set up from a copy of the 1743 quarto, with four additional lines replacing the asterisks at ll. 115–18. Those lines however, appear in some copies of the quarto containing a cancelled leaf issued in 1744. (See *Dunciad B*, iv 115*n.*; Griffith, op. cit., vol. i, pt. ii, p. 477.)

With only a few slight changes Warburton's 1751 text of the poem follows the quarto. With the commentary, however, Warburton took notorious liberties, adding to those of his earlier notes which Pope had seen and approved others which Pope did not live to read, and which he would almost certainly have disapproved. In the present edition, where Warburton's 1751 notes throw any new light on the poem they have been included among the other editorial matter; where he is merely indulging personal animosities or displaying his learning, they have been ignored. In his edition of 1751 Warburton indicated the authorship of many of the notes by the initial letters "P.W." and "W." Those letters have been retained in the present edition. In the first three books all notes

by Pope and Warburton additional to those which had appeared
in *Dunciad A* were first published in the quarto of 1743, and no indication of their date has been necessary. In Book IV, on the other
hand, all but a few of the notes first appeared in *The New Dunciad* of
1742. To avoid a tedious repetition of *1742a* after almost every note
in Book IV, it has seemed best in that book to leave *1742a* notes undated, and to date all the rest.

The present text accepts the final revision of the 1743 quarto.
Typography and punctuation are those of the quarto, but a few
misprints have been silently corrected. Notes and other prose
pieces which were repeated substantially unchanged from *The
Dunciad Variorum* have not been reprinted, but a cross reference has
been given on every occasion to enable the reader to turn to the
passage in question in the earlier version of the poem. To reprint
the commentary and appendices in their entirety would undoubtedly have been more convenient for the reader, but would
have necessitated two volumes instead of one. The editorial treatment of the text of the poem and of the commentary follows that
adopted for *The Dunciad Variorum*. (See pp. 4ff.)

KEY TO THE CRITICAL APPARATUS

1742*a* = The New Dunciad. First edition, quarto, Griffith 546.
1742*b* = Second (?) edition, octavo, Griffith 551.
1742*c* = Third (?) edition, quarto, Griffith 549.
1742*d* = "The Second Edition", quarto, Griffith 556.
1742*e* = Works, vol. iii, part 2, octavo, Griffith 566.
1742*f* = Works, vol. iii, part 2, octavo, Griffith 567.
1743*a* = The Dunciad, In Four Books, quarto, Griffith 578.
1743*a*² = The Dunciad, In Four Books, quarto [as above, but
              with the cancelled leaf, X3].
1743*b* = Works, vol. iii, part 2 [MDCCXLII], octavo, Griffith 579.
1743*c* = Works, vol. iii, part 1, octavo, Griffith 585.
1749 = The Dunciad, Complete, In Four Books [1750],
              octavo, Griffith 638.
1751 = Works, ed. Warburton, vol. v, Griffith 647.

ADVERTISEMENT

TO THE

READER.[1]

I Have long had a design of giving some sort of Notes on the Works of this Poet. Before I had the happiness of his acquaintance, I had written a Commentary on his Essay on Man, and have since finished another on the Essay on Criticism. There was one already on the Dunciad, which had met with general approbation: but I still thought some additions were wanting (of a more serious kind) to the humorous Notes of Scriblerus, and even to those written by Mr. Cleland, Dr. Arbuthnot, and others. I had lately the pleasure to pass some months with the Author in the Country,[2] where I prevailed upon him to do what I had long desired, and favour me with his explanation of several passages in his Works. It happen'd, that just at that juncture was published a ridiculous book[3] against him, full of Personal Reflections which furnished him with a lucky opportunity of improving This Poem, by giving it the only thing it wanted, a more considerable Hero. He was always sensible of its defect in that particular, and owned he had let it pass with the Hero it had, purely for want of a better; not entertaining the least expectation that such an one was reserved for this Post, as has since obtained the Laurel: But since that had happened, he could no longer deny this justice either to him or the Dunciad.

And yet I will venture to say, there was another motive which had still more weight with our Author: This person was one, who from every Folly (not to say Vice) of which another would be ashamed, has constantly derived a Vanity; and therefore was the man in the world who would least be hurt by it.

W. W.[4]

---

1. ⟨The text is that of *1743a*, in which this piece first appeared, collated with *1751*. The *1751* text shows no variations.⟩

2. ⟨Warburton probably refers here to the visit he paid to the house of Ralph Allen at Prior Park early in 1742.⟩

3. ⟨*A Letter from Mr. Cibber to Mr. Pope*, 1742. See Introduction, p. xxxiii.⟩

4. ⟨Though Warburton initialled this Advertisement, he had probably not much more to do with writing it than Cleland had to do with the "Letter to the Publisher" of 1729. "I have scratched out a sort of *avis au lecteur*, . . . which if you disapprove not, you will make your own."—Pope to Warburton, Nov. 27, 1742.⟩

By AUTHORITY.[1]

𝕭𝔂 virtue of the Authority in Us vested by the Act for subjecting
Poets to the power of a Licenser, we have revised this Piece;
where finding the style and appellation of Kɪɴɢ to have been
given to a certain Pretender, Pseudo-Poet, or Phantom, of the
name of Tɪʙʙᴀʟᴅ; and apprehending the same may be deemed in
some sort a Reflection on Majesty, or at least an insult on that
Legal Authority which has bestowed on another person the Crown
of Poesy: We have ordered the said Pretender, Pseudo-Poet, or
Phantom, utterly to vanish, and evaporate out of this work:[2] And
do declare the said Throne of Poesy from henceforth to be abdicated
and vacant, unless duly and lawfully supplied by the Lᴀᴜʀᴇᴀᴛᴇ
himself. And it is hereby enacted, that no other person do presume
to fill the same.

OC. Ch.[3]

---

1. ⟨The text is that of *1743a* in which this piece first appeared.⟩

2. ⟨Theobald still appears, however, at i 133, 286, and in several of the
notes.⟩

3. ⟨None of Pope's editors has taken any notice of this cryptic signature. The
"Ch." presumably stands for "Chamberlain," since it was the Lord Chamberlain
who had the power loosely referred to in Pope's mock-proclamation—if he is
thinking of the Licensing Act of 1737, which, however, concerned *dramatic* poets.
The Lord Chamberlain in 1743 was Charles, second Duke of Grafton, whose
father was a natural son of Charles II. Charles II had a monogram made of two
capital C's interlocked, the first C being reversed; and as his grandson was also
a Charles the signature may be intended to recall the royal monogram.

Pope's problem in this satirical piece was to produce a reasonably realistic
parody that would not get him into trouble. The poet—and his artist—appear to
have taken a rather impudent chance with the Duke of Grafton and his royal
master. Apart from the absence of GR on the royal arms, and a suspiciously human expression on the lion's face, there seems to be little in the coat of arms to
suggest that it was not being used "by authority."⟩

MARTINUS SCRIBLERUS

HIS

Prolegomena and Illustrations

TO THE

D U N C I A D:

WITH THE

Hyper-critics of ARISTARCHUS

★

DENNIS, Remarks on Pr. ARTHUR.
⟨See pp. 20–21.⟩

A LETTER TO THE PUBLISHER,
Occasioned by the first correct
EDITION of the DUNCIAD.
⟨See pp. 11–19.⟩

TESTIMONIES OF AUTHORS
Concerning our POET and his WORKS.
⟨See pp. 23–47.⟩

MARTINUS SCRIBLERUS
of the POEM.
⟨See pp. 48–53.⟩

RICARDUS ARISTARCHUS

OF THE

HERO of the POEM

O F the Nature of *Dunciad* in general, whence derived, and on what authority founded, as well as of the art and conduct of this our poem in particular, the learn-ed and laborious Scriblerus hath, according to his manner, and with tolerable share of judgment, dissertated. But when he 5 cometh to speak of the *Person* of the *Hero* fitted for such poem, in truth he miserably halts and hallucinates. For, misled by one Monsieur Bossu, a Gallic critic, he prateth of I cannot tell what *Phantom of a Hero*, only raised up to support the Fable. A putid conceit! As if Homer and Virgil, like modern Undertakers, who 10 first build their house and then seek out for a tenant, had con-trived the story of a War and a Wandering, before they once thought either of Achilles or Æneas. We shall therefore set our good brother and the world also right in this particular, by giving our word, that in the *greater Epic*, the prime intention of 15 the Muse is to exalt Heroic Virtue, in order to propagate the love of it among the children of men; and consequently that the Poet's first thought must needs be turned upon a real subject meet for laud and celebration; not one whom he is to make, but

---

9 putid] putrid *1743a*.   15 giving our word] assuring them
17 children] *children*

Poem. ⟨The text is that of *1743a*, in which this piece first appeared, collated with *1751*. Ricardus Aristarchus is, of course, Richard Bentley. Warburton's *1751* additions to this piece of his have been included in the text, but enclosed in square brackets. For Warburton's authorship of this piece, cf. EC ix 226.⟩

8. Bossu ⟨*Traité du poëme épique*, I I 5.⟩

9. putid ⟨The "putid" of *1751* is almost certainly the right reading, and has accordingly been adopted in the text. The word was used by Bentley, whose style is being burlesqued here. Cf. *Dissertation upon the Epistles of Phalaris* (*Works*, ed. A. Dyce, ii 169): "What a scene of putid and senseless formality . . ."⟩

one whom he may find, truly illustrious. This is the *primum mobile* of his poetic world, whence every thing is to receive life and motion. For this subject being found, he is immediately ordained, or rather acknowledged, an *Hero*, and put upon such action as befitteth the dignity of his character.   5

But the Muse ceases not here her Eagle-flight. Sometimes, satiated with the contemplation of these *Suns* of glory, she turneth downward on her wing, and darts like lightning on the *Goose* and *Serpent* kind. For we may apply to the Muse in her various moods, what an ancient master of Wisdom affirmeth of 10 the Gods in general: *Si Dii non irascuntur impiis et injustis, nec pios utique justosque diligunt. In rebus enim diversis, aut in utramque partem moveri necesse est, aut in neutram. Itaque qui bonos diligit, & malos odit; & qui malos non odit, nec bonos diligit. Quia & diligere bonos ex odio malorum venit; & malos odisse ex bonorum caritate descendit.* 15 Which in the vernacular idiom may be thus interpreted: "If the "Gods be not provoked at evil men, neither are they delighted "with the good and just. For contrary objects must either excite "contrary affections, or no affections at all. So that he who "loveth good men, must at the same time hate the bad; and he 20 "who hateth not bad men, cannot love the good; because to love "good men proceedeth from an aversion to evil, and to hate evil "men from a tenderness to the good." From this delicacy of the Muse arose the *little Epic*, (more lively and choleric than her elder sister, whose bulk and complexion incline her to the flegmatic) 25 and for this some notorious Vehicle of vice and folly was sought out, to make thereof an example. An early instance of which (nor could it escape the accurate Scriblerus) the Father of Epic poem himself affordeth us. From him the practice descended to the Greek Dramatic poets, his offspring; who in the com- 30 position of their *Tetralogy*, or set of four pieces, were wont to make the last a *Satyric Tragedy*. Happily one of these ancient *Dunciads* (as we may well term it) is come down to us amongst

---

6 Sometimes] For sometimes
8 like lightning] with Jove's lightning
16 the vernacular] our vernacular   33 to us] unto us

---

15. *descendit* ⟨Lactantius, *De Ira Dei*, v 10. For this reference I am indebted to Mr. E. H. Blakeney.⟩

the Tragedies of Euripides. And what doth the reader think
may be the subject? Why truly, and it is worth his observation,
the unequal Contention of an *old, dull, debauched, buffoon Cyclops*,
with the heaven-directed *Favourite of* Minerva; who after having
quietly born all the monster's obscene and impious ribaldry,   5
endeth the farce in punishing him with the mark of an indelible
brand in his *forehead.* May we not then be excused, if for the
future we consider the Epics of Homer, Virgil, and Milton,
together with this our poem, as a complete *Tetralogy*, in which
the last worthily holdeth the place or station of the *satyric* piece? 10

Proceed we therefore in our subject. It hath been long, and
alas for pity! still remaineth a question, whether the Hero of
the *greater Epic* should be an *honest man?* or, as the French critics
express it, *un honnête homme*[a]; but it never admitted of any
doubt that the Hero of the *little Epic* should *not* be so. Hence, 15
to the advantage of our Dunciad, we may observe how much
juster the *Moral* of that Poem must needs be, where so important a question is previously decided.

But then it is not every Knave, nor (let me add) Fool, that is
a fit subject for a Dunciad. There must still exist some Ana- 20
logy, if not Resemblance of Qualities, between the Heroes
of the two Poems; and this in order to admit what Neoteric
critics call the *Parody*, one of the liveliest graces of the little
Epic. Thus it being agreed that the constituent qualities of the
greater Epic Hero, are *Wisdom, Bravery*, and *Love*, from whence 25
springeth *heroic Virtue*; it followeth that those of the lesser Epic
Hero, should be *Vanity, Impudence*, and *Debauchery*, from which
happy assemblage resulteth *heroic Dulness*, the never-dying
subject of this our Poem.

This being confessed, come we now to particulars. It is the 30
character of true *Wisdom*, to seek its chief support and confidence within itself; and to place that support in the resources

---

1 think] suppose
2 subject] subject thereof   Why truly,] Why in truth,
    worth his] worthy
15 *not* be so.] be just the contrary.   19 Fool] every Fool

---

[a] Si un Heros Poëtique doit être un honnête homme. Bossu, du Poême
Epique, lib. v. ch. 5.

which proceed from a conscious rectitude of Will.—And are
the advantages of *Vanity*, when arising to the heroic standard,
at all short of this self-complacence? Nay, are they not, in the
opinion of the enamoured owner, far beyond it? "Let the
world (will such an one say) "impute to me what Folly or   5
"weakness they please; but till *Wisdom* can give me something
"that will make me more heartily happy, I am content to be
"GAZED AT[b]." This we see is *Vanity* according to the *heroic*
gage or measure; not that low and ignoble species which
pretendeth to *Virtues* we *have not*, but the laudable ambition of   10
being *gazed at* for glorying in those *Vices* which all the world
know *we have*. "The world may ask (says he) why I make my
"follies publick? Why not? I have passed my time very
"pleasantly with them[c]." In short, there is no sort of Vanity
such a Hero would scruple, but that which might go near   15
to degrade him from his high station in this our Dunciad;
namely, "Whether it would not be *Vanity* in him, to take
"shame to himself for *not being* a *wise man*[d]?"

Bravery, the second attribute of the true Hero, is Courage
manifesting itself in every limb; while, in its correspondent   20
virtue in the mock Hero, that Courage is all collected into the
Face. And as Power when drawn together, must needs be more
strong than when dispersed, we generally find this kind of
courage in so high and heroic a degree, that it insults not only
Men, but Gods. Mezentius is without doubt the bravest   25
character in all the Æneis; but how? His bravery, we know,
was an high courage of blasphemy. And can we say less of this
brave man's, who having told us that he placed "his *Summum*
"*bonum* in those follies, which he was not content barely to
"possess but would likewise glory in," adds, "*If I am mis-*   30
"*guided*, 'TIS NATURE'S FAULT, *and I follow* HER[e]." Nor
can we be mistaken in making this happy quality a species of

---

11 all the world know] every body knows
20 while, in its] while its
21 that Courage] is that same Courage
22–23 be more strong] have more force and spirit

---

[b] Dedication to the Life of C.C.   [c] Life, p. 2. octavo Ed.
[d] Life, ibid.   [e] Life, p. 23 octavo.

Courage, when we consider those illustrious marks of it, which
made his *Face* "more known (as he justly boasteth) than
"most in the kingdom," and his *Language* to consist of what
we must allow to be the most *daring* Figure of Speech, that
which is taken from the *Name of God*.   5

Gentle Love, the next ingredient in the true Hero's composition, is a mere bird of passage, or (as Shakespear calls it) *summer-
teeming Lust*, and evaporates in the heat of *Youth*; doubtless by
that refinement it suffers in passing through those *certain
strainers* which our Poet somewhere speaketh of. But when it is 10
let alone to work upon the *Lees*, it acquireth strength by *Old
age*; and becometh a standing ornament to the little Epic. It
is true indeed, there is one objection to its fitness for such an
use: For not only the Ignorant may think it *common*, but it is
admitted to be so, even by Him who best knoweth its nature. 15
"Don't you think (saith he) to say only *a man has his Whore*,
"ought to go for little or nothing? Because *defendit numerus*, take
"the first ten thousand men you meet, and I believe you would
"be no loser if you betted ten to one, that every single sinner
"of them, one with another, had been guilty of the same 20
"frailty[f]." But here he seemeth not to have done himself justice: The man is sure enough a Hero, who has his Lady at
fourscore. How doth his Modesty herein lessen the merit of a
whole well-spent Life: not taking to himself the commendation

---

12 standing] lasting   15 nature] value   16 saith] argueth
21–22 done himself justice] done justice to himself

---

5. *God* ⟨For Cibber's blasphemous language, cf. B i 115*n*.⟩

8. *Lust* ⟨*Macbeth*, IV iii 86. The reading of the first Folio is "Summer-
seeming". "Summer-teeming" is Warburton's emendation: lust, he says,
"lasts no longer than the *heat* of life," and "goes off in the *winter* of age".⟩

9–10. *certain strainers* ⟨"Lust, thro' some certain strainers well refin'd."—
Essay on Man, ii 189.⟩

17. ought . . . nothing ⟨Cibber's words are: ". . . is the flattest Piece of Satyr
that ever fell from the formidable Pen of Mr. *Pope*." He is answering Pope's reference to him in *Ep. to Arbuthnot* 97:

And has not *Colly* still his Lord, and Whore?

[f] Letter to Mr. P. p. 46.

23. fourscore ⟨"If the private Anecdotes of *Drury-lane* Theatre can carry any
Authority, the Laureat was, within these four Years, in great Danger of being
lost to the Poetick World by the Malady of an unfortunate Amour with a

(which *Horace* accounted the greatest in a theatrical character)
of continuing to the very *dregs*, the same he was from the
beginning,

———— *Servetur ad* IMUM
Qualis ab incepto processerat ————   5

But let us farther remark, that the calling her *his* whore,
implieth she was *his own*, and not his *neighbour*'s. Truly a com-
mendable Continence! and such as Scipio himself must have
applauded. For how much Self-denial was necessary not to
covet his Neighbour's whore? and what disorders must the   10
coveting her have occasioned, in that Society, where (according to this Political Calculator) *nine* in *ten* of all ages have their
concubines?

We have now, as briefly as we could devise, gone through
the three constituent Qualities of either Hero. But it is not in   15
any, or all of these, that Heroism properly or essentially
resideth. It is a lucky result rather from the collision of these
lively Qualities against one another. Thus, as from Wisdom,
Bravery, and Love, ariseth *Magnanimity*, the object of *Admiration*, which is the aim of the greater Epic; so from Vanity, Im-   20
pudence, and Debauchery, springeth *Buffoonry*, the source of
Ridicule, that "laughing ornament," as he well termeth it[g], of
the little Epic.

He is not ashamed (God forbid he ever should be ashamed!)
of this Character; who deemeth, that not *Reason* but *Risibility*   25
distinguisheth the human species from the brutal. "As Nature
(saith this profound Philosopher) distinguished our species
"from the mute creation by our Risibility, her design MUST
"have been by *that faculty* as evidently to raise our HAPPINESS
"as by OUR *os sublime* (OUR ERECTED FACES) to lift the   30
"dignity of our FORM above them[h]." All this considered, how
complete a Hero must he be, as well as how *happy* a Man,

---

6 But] But here, in justice both to the Poet and the Hero,
9 necessary] exerted   16 or all] or in all

---

young Actress."—*The Universal Spectator*, Aug. 21, 1742. In 1743 Cibber was
seventy-two years old.⟩
    5. *processerat* ⟨Horace, *Ars Poetica*, 126.⟩   [g] Letter to Mr. P. p. 31.
    [h] *Life*, p. 23, 24.

whose Risibility lieth not barely in his *muscles* as in the
common sort, but (as himself informeth us) in his very *spirits?*
And whose *Os sublime* is not simply an *erect face*, but a Brazen
head, as should seem by his comparing it with one of Iron,
said to belong to the late king of Sweden[i]!   5
    But whatever personal qualities a Hero may have, the
examples of Achilles and Æneas shew us, that all those are of
small avail, without the constant *assistance of the* GODS: for the
subversion and erection of Empires have never been judged
the work of Man. How greatly soever then we may esteem of   10
his high talents, we can hardly conceive his personal prowess
alone sufficient to restore the decayed empire of Dulness. So
weighty an atchievement must require the particular favour
and protection of the GREAT: who being the natural patrons
and supporters of *Letters*, as the ancient Gods were of *Troy*,   15
must first be drawn off and engaged in another Interest,
before the total subversion of them can be accomplished. To
surmount, therefore, this last and greatest difficulty, we have
in this excellent man a professed Favourite and Intimado of the
Great. And look of what force ancient Piety was to draw the   20
Gods into the party of Æneas, that, and much stronger is
modern Incense, to engage the Great in the party of Dulness.
    Thus have we essayed to pourtray or shadow out this noble
Imp of Fame. But now the impatient reader will be apt to say,
if so many and various graces go to the making up a Hero,   25
what mortal shall suffice to bear this character? Ill hath he
read, who sees not in every trace of this picture, that *individual*, ALL-ACCOMPLISHED PERSON, in whom these rare
virtues and lucky circumstances have agreed to meet and con-
centre with the strongest lustre and fullest harmony.   30
    The good Scriblerus indeed, nay the World itself might be
imposed on in the late spurious editions, by I can't tell what

---

4 comparing it with] preferring it to
9 judged] adjudged   26 this] his   27 sees] seeth

---

[i] Letter, p. 8. ⟨"These old Soldiers, fired with Resentment, returned home,
crying as they went: Down with this Head of Iron! Since he's resolved to perish,
let him perish!"—*The History of Charles XII . . . By M. De Voltaire*, 1732, Bk. vi,
p. 86.⟩

Sham-hero, or *Phantom:* But it was not so easy to impose on HIM whom this egregious error most of all concerned. For no sooner had the fourth book laid open the high and swelling scene, but he recognized his own heroic Acts: And when he came to the words,   5
>   *Soft on her lap her Laureat son reclines,*
(though *Laureat* imply no more than *one crowned with laurel*, as befitteth any Associate or Consort in Empire) he ROAR'D (like a Lion) and VINDICATED HIS RIGHT OF FAME: Indeed not without cause, he being there represented as *fast* 10 *asleep*; so unbeseeming the eye of Empire, which, like that of Providence, should never slumber. "Hah! (saith he) fast "asleep it seems! that's a little too strong. Pert and dull at least "you might have allowed me, but as seldom asleep as any "fool[k]." However, the injured Hero may comfort him- 15 self with this reflexion, that tho' it be *sleep*, yet it is not the *sleep of death*, but of *immortality*. Here he will[l] *live* at least, tho' not *awake*; and in no worse condition than many an enchanted Warrior before him. The famous *Durandarte*, for instance, was, like him, cast into a long slumber by *Merlin* 20 the *British Bard* and Necromancer: and his example, for submitting to it with so good a grace, might be of use to our Hero. For this disastrous knight being sorely pressed or driven to make his answer by several *persons of quality*, only replied with a sigh, *Patience, and shuffle the cards*[m].   25

But now, as nothing in this world, no not the most sacred or perfect things either of Religion or Government, can escape the teeth or tongue of Envy, methinks I already hear these carpers objecting to the clear title of our Hero.

"It would never (say they) have been esteemed sufficient 30 "to make an Hero for the Iliad or Æneis, that Achilles was

---

8 he ROAR'D . . . FAME:] he loudly resented this indignity to
    violated Majesty.
11 unbeseeming] misbeseeming   12 slumber] doze nor slumber
22 so good a] a good   23 this] that   28 teeth or tongue] sting
29 clear . . . Hero.] clearness of our Hero's title.

---

[k] Letter, p. 53.   [l] Letter, p. 1.
[m] Don Quixote, Part ii. Book ii. ch. 22.

"brave enough to overturn one Empire, or Æneas pious
"enough to raise another, had they not been Goddess-born,
"and Princes bred. What then did this Author mean, by
"erecting a Player instead of one of his Patrons, (a person
"never a hero even on the stage[n]",) to this dignity of Col-   5
"legue in the empire of Dulness, and Atchiever of a work
"that neither old Omar, Attila, nor John of Leiden could
"entirely compass?"

To all this we have, as we conceive, a sufficient answer
from the Roman historian, *Fabrum esse suæ quemque fortunæ:*   10
Every man is the Smith *of his own fortune.* The politic Florentine
Nicholas Machiavel goeth still farther, and affirms that a
man needs but to *believe himself a Hero* to be one of the best.
"Let him (saith he) but fancy himself capable of the highest
"things, and he will of course be able to atchieve them."   15
Laying this down as a principle, it will certainly and incon-
testably follow, that, if ever Hero *was* such a character,
OURS *is:* For if ever man *thought* himself such, OURS *doth.* Hear
how he constantly paragons himself, at one time to A L E X -
ANDER the Great and CHARLES the XII. of S W E D E N , for   20
the excess and delicacy of his Ambition[o]; to H E N R Y the IV.
of F R A N C E, for honest Policy[p]; to the first B R U T U S, for love of
Liberty[q]; and to Sir R O B E R T W A L P O L E, for good Govern-
ment while in power[r]: At another time, to the godlike
S O C R A T E S, for his diversions and amusements[s]; to H O R A C E,   25
M O N T A I G N E, and Sir W I L L I A M T E M P L E, for an elegant
Vanity that makes them for ever read and admired[t]; to TWO

---

8 compass] bring to pass   11 *Every*] *That every*
12–13 affirms . . . needs] affirmeth . . . needeth
16–18 Laying . . . *doth.*] From this principle it follows, that no-
    thing can exceed our Hero's prowess; as nothing ever equalled
    the greatness of his conceptions.   27 makes] maketh

---

[n] See Life, p. 148.
10. historian ⟨Sallust, *Ad Caesarem Senem De Re Publica Oratio.*⟩
    [o] Life, p. 149.   [p] P. 424.   [q] P. 366.
    [r] P. 457. ⟨Cibber does not name Walpole, but notes the tendency in
England to create "a Clamour against every different Ministry for the time
being".⟩   [s] P. 18.   [t] P. 425.

Lord CHANCELLORS, for Law, from whom, when confeder-
ate against him at the bar, he carried away the prize of Eloquence[v]; and, to say all in a word, to the right reverend the
Lord BISHOP of LONDON himself, in the art of writing
pastoral letters[w].   5

Nor did his *Actions* fall short of the sublimity of his Conceptions. In his early youth he *met the Revolution* at Nottingham[x]
face to face, at a time when his betters contented themselves
with *following* her. [It was here he got acquainted with *Old
Battle-array*, of whom he hath made so honourable mention 10
in one of his immortal Odes.] But he shone in Courts as well as
Camps: He was *called up* when *the nation fell in labour* of this
Revolution[y]: and was a gossip at her christening, with the
Bishop and the ladies[z].

As to his *Birth*, it is true he pretendeth no relation either to 15
Heathen God or Goddess; but, what is as good, he was
descended from a *Maker* of both[a]. And that he did not pass
himself on the world for a Hero, as well by birth as education,
was his own fault: For, his lineage he bringeth into his life as
an Anecdote, and is sensible he had it in his power *to be* 20
thought no body's son at all[b]: And what is that but coming into
the world a Hero?

[But be it, (the punctilious Laws of Epic Poesy so requiring)
that a Hero of more than mortal birth must needs be had,
even for this we have a remedy. We can easily derive our 25

6–7 Conceptions] Conceit
7–8 at Nottingham . . . face] face to face in Nottingham
9–11 It was here . . . Odes]*Om. 1743a.*
23ff. But be it . . . *Chaos?*] *Om. 1743a.*

---

[v] P. 436, 437.   [w] P. 52. ⟨No bishop is named by Cibber.⟩   [x] P. 47.
10. *Battle-array* ⟨"*Old Battle-array*" is a gibe at Cibber's New-Year ode for
1733 (*Gent. Mag.* iii 40). He had allowed himself to write:

> As freedom the jewel of life is,
> 'Twas bought by old battle-array.

The lines were parodied by Isaac Hawkins Browne in *A Pipe of Tobacco*.⟩
[y] P. 57.   [z] P. 58, 59.
[a] A Statuary. ⟨i.e. Caius Gabriel Cibber, 1630–1700. He executed a
Pallas and an Apollo for the first Duke of Devonshire.⟩
[b] Life, p. 6.

11

Hero's Pedigree from a Goddess of no small power and authority amongst men; and legitimate and install him after the right classical and authentic fashion: For, like as the ancient Sages found a Son of Mars in a mighty warrior; a Son of Neptune in a skilful Seaman; a Son of Phœbus in a har- 5 monious Poet; so have we here, if need be, a Son of FORTUNE in an artful *Gamester*. And who fitter than the Offspring of *Chance*, to assist in restoring the Empire of *Night* and *Chaos*?]

There is in truth another objection of greater weight, 10 namely, "That this Hero still existeth, and hath not yet "finished his earthly course. For if Solon said well, that no "man could be called happy till his death, surely much less "can any one, till then, be pronounced a Hero: this species "of men being far more subject than others to the caprices of 15 "Fortune and Humour." But to this also we have an answer, that will be deemed (we hope) decisive. It cometh from *himself*, who, to cut this dispute short, hath solemnly pro- tested that *he will never change or amend*.

With regard to his *Vanity*, he declareth that nothing shall 20 ever part them. "Nature (saith he) hath amply supplied me "in Vanity; a pleasure which neither the pertness of Wit, nor "the gravity of Wisdom, will ever persuade me to part with[c]." Our poet had charitably endeavoured to administer a cure to it: But he telleth us plainly, "My superiors perhaps may be 25 "mended by him; but for my part I own myself incorrigible. "I look upon my Follies as the best part of my Fortune[d]." And with good reason: We see to what they have brought him!

Secondly, as to *Buffoonry*, "Is it (saith he) a time of day for 30 "me to leave off these fooleries, and set up a new character? "I can no more put off my Follies than my Skin; I have often "tried, but they stick too close to me; nor am I sure my "friends are displeased with them, for in this light I afford "them frequent matter of mirth, *&c. &c.*[e]." Having then so 35

17 will . . . decisive.] will (we hope) be deemed decisive.
18 dispute] matter

[c] P. 424.   [d] P. 19.

publickly declared himself *incorrigible*, he is become *dead in law*, (I mean the *law Epopœian*) and descendeth to the Poet as his property: who may take him, and deal with him, as if he had been dead as long as an old Egyptian hero; that is to say, *embowel* and *embalm him for posterity*.   5

Nothing therefore (we conceive) remains to hinder his own Prophecy of himself from taking immediate effect. A rare felicity! and what few prophets have had the satisfaction to see, alive! Nor can we conclude better than with that extraordinary one of his, which is conceived in these Oraculous words, 10 MY DULNESS WILL FIND SOMEBODY TO DO IT RIGHT[f].

> [*Tandem Phœbus adest, morsusque inferre parantem*
> *Congelat, et patulos, ut erant, INDURAT hiatus.*][g]

---

2 descendeth to] devolveth upon
6 remains] remaineth
12–13 *Tandem . . . hiatus*] *Om. 1743a.*

---

[e] P. 17.   [f] Ibid. p. 243. octavo edit.
[g] [*Ovid*, of the serpent biting at Orpheus's head.—*1751.*]

ARGUMENT

BOOK the FIRST

THE Proposition, the Invocation, and the Inscription. Then the Original of the great Empire of Dulness, *and cause of the continuance thereof. The College of the* Goddess *in the City, with her private Academy for Poets in particular; the Governors of it, and the four Cardinal Virtues. Then the Poem* hastes into the midst 5 of things, *presenting her, on the evening of a Lord Mayor's day, revolving the long succession of her Sons, and the glories past and to come. She fixes her eye on* Bays *to be the Instrument of that great Event which is the Subject of the Poem. He is described pensive among his Books, giving up the Cause, and apprehending the* 10 *Period of her Empire: After debating whether to betake himself to the Church, or to Gaming, or to Party-writing, he raises an Altar of proper books, and (making first his solemn prayer and declaration) purposes thereon to sacrifice all his unsuccessful writings. As the pile is kindled, the Goddess beholding the flame from her seat,* 15 *flies and puts it out by casting upon it the poem of* Thulé. *She forthwith reveals herself to him, transports him to her Temple, unfolds her Arts, and initiates him into her Mysteries; then announcing the death of* Eusden *the Poet Laureate, anoints him, carries him to Court, and proclaims him Successor.* 20

THE DUNCIAD

BOOK the FIRST

THE Mighty Mother, and her Son who brings
The Smithfield Muses to the ear of Kings,

The DUNCIAD, sic MS. It may well be disputed whether this be a right
reading: Ought it not rather to be spelled *Dunceiad*, as the Etymology evidently
demands? *Dunce* with an *e*, therefore *Dunceiad* with an *e*. That accurate and
punctual Man of Letters, the Restorer of *Shakespeare*, constantly observes the
preservation of this very Letter *e*, in spelling the Name of his beloved Author,
and not like his common careless Editors, with the omission of one, nay sometimes of two *ee's*, [as *Shakspear*] which is utterly unpardonable. "Nor is the
"neglect of a *Single Letter* so trivial as to some it may appear; the alteration
"whereof in a learned language is an Atchievement that brings honour to the
"Critic who advances it; and Dr. Bentley will be remembered to posterity for
"his performances of this sort, as long as the world shall have any esteem for
"the remains of Menander and Philemon." THEOBALD. ⟨Cf. A i 1 *n.*⟩

This is surely a slip in the learned author of the foregoing note; there having
been since produced by an accurate Antiquary, an *Autograph* of *Shakspeare* himself, whereby it appears that he spelled his own name without the first *e*. ⟨The
reference must almost certainly be to Shakespeare's will, on each sheet of which
(three in all) he signs without the first *e*. The will was discovered by Joseph
Greene (1712–90), master of the Stratford Grammar School from 1735, but
the date of his discovery is not known. (See E. K. Chambers, *William Shakespeare*,
ii 169, 239.) In sending a copy of the will to James West in 1747, Greene makes it
clear that he had discovered it some time before, since he had lost the first copy
which he made. See J. O. Halliwell-Phillipps, *Life of William Shakespeare*, 1848,
p. 274.⟩ And upon this authority it was, that those most Critical Curators of
his Monument in Westminster Abby erased the former wrong reading, and
restored the true spelling on a new piece of old Ægyptian Granite. Nor for this
only do they deserve our thanks, but for exhibiting on the same Monument the
first Specimen of an *Edition* of an author in *Marble*; where (as may be seen on
comparing the Tomb with the Book) in the space of five lines, two Words and
a whole Verse are changed, and it is to be hoped will there stand, and outlast
whatever hath been hitherto done in Paper; as for the future, our Learned
Sister University (the other Eye of England) is taking care to perpetuate a
Total new Shakespear, at the Clarendon press. BENTL.

It is to be noted, that this great Critic also has omitted one circumstance;
which is, that the Inscription with the Name of Shakspeare was intended to be
placed on the Marble Scroll to which he points with his hand; instead of which

it is now placed behind his back, and that Specimen of an Edition is put on the Scroll, which indeed Shakspeare hath great reason to point at. ANON.

⟨The inscription on the marble scroll of the Shakespeare monument reads as follows:

> The Cloud capt Tow'rs,
> The Gorgeous Palaces
> The Solemn Temples,
> The Great Globe itself,
> Yea all which it Inherit,
>   Shall Dissolve;
> And like the baseless Fabrick of a Vision
> Leave not a wreck behind.

The Folio reads "this vision" and "rack". In the Folio, too, the seventh line of the inscription comes before "The cloud-capp'd towers", and is replaced by "And, like this insubstantial pageant faded". In the Preface to his *Shakespeare* (2nd ed., 1740) Theobald had pointed out that "Mr. *Pope*, or his Graver" had perpetuated an error in the Latin inscription under Shakespeare's monument at Stratford. The badinage about the mistakes in the passage from *The Tempest* may be an answer to Theobald's criticism. See also *Gent. Mag.* xi 276.—The "Total new Shakespear" is Hanmer's edition, which was published at the Clarendon Press, Oxford, soon after this note was written, in 1743-4. Different accounts of Hanmer's quarrel with Warburton, which arose in 1739 over Hanmer's projected edition of Shakespeare, were given by the two men, each claiming to be the injured party. See Evans, pp. 147–55, and *Dunciad* iv 105*n.*, 113*n.*⟩

Though I have as just a value for the letter *E* . . . SCRIBLERUS ⟨A i i⟩.

This Poem was written in the year 1726 . . . SCHOL. VET. ⟨A i i⟩.

It was expresly confessed in the Preface to the first edition, that this Poem was not published by the Author himself. ⟨Cf. Bentley's excuse for his extensive emendation of the text of *Paradise Lost*, that the poem had not been "published by the Author himself", owing to his blindness.⟩ It was printed originally in a foreign Country. And what foreign Country? Why, one notorious for blunders; where finding blanks only instead of proper names, these blunderers filled them up at their pleasure. ⟨Cf. A i 104*n.*⟩

The very *Hero* of the Poem hath been mistaken to this hour; so that we are obliged to open our Notes with a discovery who he really was. We learn from the former Editor, that this Piece was presented by the Hands of Sir Robert Walpole to King George II. ⟨Cf. A i 1*n.*⟩ Now the author directly tells us, his Hero is the Man

> ————*who brings*
> *The Smithfield Muses to the ear of Kings.*

And it is notorious who was the person on whom this Prince conferred the honour of the *Laurel.*

It appears as plainly from the *Apostrophe* to the *Great* in the third verse, that

I sing. Say you, her instruments the Great!
Call'd to this work by Dulness, Jove, and Fate;
You by whose care, in vain decry'd and curst,   5
Still Dunce the second reigns like Dunce the first;
Say how the Goddess bade Britannia sleep,
And pour'd her Spirit o'er the land and deep.
   In eldest time, e'er mortals writ or read,
E'er Pallas issu'd from the Thund'rer's head,   10
Dulness o'er all possess'd her ancient right,
Daughter of Chaos and eternal Night:
Fate in their dotage this fair Ideot gave,

Tibbald could not be the person, who was never an Author in fashion, or caressed by the Great; whereas this single characteristic is sufficient to point out the true Hero; who, above all other Poets of his time, was the *Peculiar Delight* and *Chosen Companion* of the Nobility of England; and wrote, as he himself tells us, certain of his Works at the *earnest Desire* of *Persons of Quality.* ⟨See *Letter to Pope*, p. 1.⟩

Lastly, The sixth verse affords full proof; this Poet being the only one who was universally known to have had a *Son* ⟨Theophilus Cibber. See Biog. App.⟩ so exactly like him, in his poetical, theatrical, political, and moral Capacities, that it could justly be said of him

           Still Dunce the second reign'd like Dunce the first.   BENTL.

1. *The Mighty Mother, and her Son, &c.*] The Reader ought here to be cautioned, that the *Mother*, and not the *Son*, is the principal Agent of this Poem: The latter of them is only chosen as her Collegue (as was anciently the custom in Rome before some great Expedition) the main action of the Poem being by no means the Coronation of the Laureate, which is performed in the very first book, but the Restoration of the Empire of Dulness in Britain, which is not accomplished 'till the last. W. ⟨Apparently an attempt by Warburton to answer a frequent criticism of the *Dunciad*, viz. that the hero *did* nothing.⟩

Ibid.—*her Son who brings, &c.*] Wonderful is the stupidity . . . SCRIBLERUS ⟨A i i⟩.

2. *The Smithfield Muses*] Smithfield is the place . . . Court and Town ⟨A i 2⟩. This happened in the Reigns of King George I, and II. See Book 3.

4. *By Dulness, Jove, and Fate:*] i.e. By their *Judgments*, their *Interests*, and their *Inclinations.* W.

5. *You by whose care* ⟨The change from the reading of 1729, viz. "Say from what cause," probably indicates that Pope, now actively supporting the Opposition, intended a more obvious thrust at the great Whig families who had played the chief part in 1714 in bringing over the Hanoverians.⟩

12. *Daughter of Chaos, &c.* ⟨A i 10⟩.

Gross as her sire, and as her mother grave,
Laborious, heavy, busy, bold, and blind,   15
She rul'd, in native Anarchy, the mind.
　　Still her old Empire to restore she tries,
For, born a Goddess, Dulness never dies.
　　O Thou! whatever title please thine ear,
Dean, Drapier, Bickerstaff, or Gulliver!   20
Whether thou chuse Cervantes' serious air,
Or laugh and shake in Rab'lais' easy chair,

---

15. *Laborious, heavy, busy, bold, &c.*] I wonder the learned Scriblerus has omitted to advertise the Reader, at the opening of this Poem, that Dulness here is not to be taken contractedly for mere Stupidity, but in the enlarged sense of the word, for all Slowness of Apprehension, Shortness of Sight, or imperfect Sense of things. It includes (as we see by the Poet's own words) Labour, Industry, and some degree of Activity and Boldness: a ruling principle not inert, but turning topsy-turvy the Understanding, and inducing an Anarchy or confused State of Mind. This remark ought to be carried along with the reader throughout the work; and without this caution he will be apt to mistake the Importance of many of the Characters, as well as of the Design of the Poet. Hence it is that some have complained he chuses too mean a subject, and imagined he employs himself, like Domitian, in killing flies; whereas those who have the true key will find he sports with nobler quarry, and embraces a larger compass; or (as one saith, on a like occasion)

　　Will see his Work, like Jacob's ladder, rise,
　　Its foot in dirt, its head amid the skies.   BENTL.

⟨For the source of this quotation, see p. 466.⟩

16. *She rul'd, in native Anarchy, the mind*] *The native Anarchy of the mind* is that state which precedes the time of Reason's assuming the rule of the Passions. But in that state, the uncontrolled violence of the Passions would soon bring things to confusion, were it not for the intervention of Dulness in this absence of Reason; who, though she cannot regulate them like Reason, yet blunts and deadens their Vigour, and, indeed, produces some of the good effects of it: Hence it is that Dulness has often the appearance of Reason. This is the only good she ever did; and the Poet takes particular care to tell it in the very introduction of his Poem. It is to be observed indeed, that this is spoken of the universal rule of Dulness in ancient days, but we may form an idea of it from her partial Government in later times. W. ⟨Warburton is, no doubt, playing on the word "partial". The period of Whig ascendency was to Pope and his friends one of partial dullness, only saved from being completely dull by the Opposition; it was also to them a period of partiality in government.⟩

17. *Still her old Empire to restore*] This Restoration makes the Completion of the Poem. *Vide* Book 4.

Or praise the Court, or magnify Mankind,
Or thy griev'd Country's copper chains unbind;
From thy Bœotia tho' her Pow'r retires,   25
Mourn not, my S w i f t, at ought our Realm acquires,
Here pleas'd behold her mighty wings out-spread
To hatch a new Saturnian age of Lead.

    Close to those walls where Folly holds her throne,
And laughs to think Monroe would take her down,   30
Where o'er the gates, by his fam'd father's hand
Great Cibber's brazen, brainless brothers stand;
One Cell there is, conceal'd from vulgär eye,

23. *Or praise the Court, &c.* ⟨A i 21⟩.

28. *To hatch a new Saturnian age of Lead*] The ancient . . . Lead ⟨A i 26⟩. She is said here only to be spreading her wings to hatch this age; which is not produced completely till the fourth book.

30. *Monroe* ⟨James Monro, M.D., 1680–1752, physician to Bethlehem Hospital for the insane—the place "where Folly holds her throne" (l. 29). For Monro, see *Ep.* ii ii 70, and Biog. App. vol. iv.⟩

31. *By his fam'd father's hand*] Mr. Caius-Gabriel Cibber, father of the Poet Laureate. The two Statues of the Lunatics over the gates of Bedlam-hospital were done by him, and (as the son justly says of them) are no ill monuments of his fame as an Artist. ⟨The statues, however, as Colley Cibber pointed out, are of stone, not of bronze. (Cf. B ii 3.) Rather than sacrifice the admirable epithet "brazen", Pope wrote a facetious note acknowledging the inaccuracy. See B ii 3*n*. These two recumbent statues of "Raving Madness" and "Melancholy Madness" were executed by Caius Gabriel Cibber about the year 1680. They are now in the possession of the Corporation of London at the Guildhall.⟩

33. *One Cell there is*] The cell of poor Poetry is here very properly represented as a little *unendowed Hall* in the neighbourhood of the Magnific *College* of Bedlam; and as the surest Seminary to supply those learned walls with Professors. For there cannot be a plainer indication of madness than in men's persisting to starve themselves and offend the public by scribling,
      Escape in Monsters, and amaze the town.
when they might have benefited themselves and others in profitable and honest employments. The *Qualities* and *Productions* of the students of this private Academy are afterwards described in this first book; as are also their *Actions* throughout the second; by which it appears, how near allied Dulness is to Madness. This naturally prepares us for the subject of the third book, where we find them in union, and acting in conjunction to produce the Catastrophe of the fourth; a mad poetical Sibyl leading our Hero through the Regions of Vision, to animate him in the present undertaking, by a view of the past

11*

The Cave of Poverty and Poetry.
Keen, hollow winds howl thro' the bleak recess,   35
Emblem of Music caus'd by Emptiness.
Hence Bards, like Proteus long in vain ty'd down,

triumphs of Barbarism over Science. W. ⟨The Cell of Poverty and Poetry, situated in *Dunciad A* in the neighbourhood of Rag Fair, was shifted in *1743a* to the neighbourhood of Bedlam. Warburton's reference to "a little unendowed Hall" is obscure; but, in view of the mention of "Professors" immediately afterwards, the Hall may perhaps be identified with Sion College, close to Bedlam. Dr. Joseph Trapp, Professor of Poetry at Oxford from 1708–18, was, at the time Warburton's note was written, President of Sion College; and on April 26, 1743 he had published a *Concio ad Clerum Londinensem*. For Trapp, see Biog. App. He was a frequent subject of ridicule by the wits.⟩

34. *Poverty and Poetry*] I cannot here omit a remark that will greatly endear our Author to every one, who shall attentively observe that Humanity and Candor, which every where appears in him towards those unhappy objects of the ridicule of all mankind, the bad Poets. He here imputes . . . to be satyrized ⟨A i 41⟩.

37. *Hence Bards, like Proteus*]

> *Sunt quibus in plures jus est transire figuras:*
> *Ut tibi, complexi terram maris incola, Proteu;*
> *Nunc violentus aper, nunc quem tetigisse timerent,*
> *Anguis eras, modo te faciebant cornua Taurum,*
> *Sæpe Lapis poteras.*   Ovid. Met. viii ⟨730 ff.⟩.

Neither Palæphatus, Phurnutus, nor Heraclides give us any steddy light into the mythology of this mysterious fable. If I be not deceived in a part of learning which has so long exercised my pen, by *Proteus* must certainly be meant a hacknied Town scribler; and by his Transformations, the various disguises such a one assumes, to elude the pursuit of his irreconcilable enemy, the Bailiff. Proteus is represented as one bred of the mud and slime of Ægypt, the original soil of Arts and Letters: And what is a Town-scribler, but a creature made up of the excrements of luxurious Science? By the change then into a *Boar* is meant his character of a *furious and dirty Party-writer*; the *Snake* signifies a *Libeller*; and the *Horns of the Bull*, the *Dilemmas* of a *Polemical Answerer*. These are the three great parts he acts under; and when he has completed his circle, he sinks back again, as the last change into a *Stone* denotes, into his natural state of immoveable Stupidity. If I may expect thanks of the learned world for this discovery, I would by no means deprive that excellent Critic of his share, who discovered before me, that in the character of Proteus was designed *Sophistam, Magum, Politicum, præsertim rebus omnibus sese accommodantem.* Which in English is, *A Political writer, a Libeller, and a Disputer, writing indifferently for or against every party in the State, every sect in Religion, and every character in private life.* See my *Fables of Ovid explained.* ABBE BANIER. W. ⟨Banier's name is set by Warburton to this

Escape in Monsters, and amaze the town.
Hence Miscellanies spring, the weekly boast
Of Curl's chaste press, and Lintot's rubric post: 40
Hence hymning Tyburn's elegiac lines,
Hence Journals, Medleys, Merc'ries, Magazines:
Sepulchral Lyes, our holy walls to grace,

---

note because he was the author of *La Mythologie et les fables expliquées par l'histoire*, 3 vols. 1738–40. The English translation had just appeared, 1739–40.—In an undated letter to Warburton (B.M. Egerton MS. 1946 f. 62), Pope writes: "I like the note on Proteus much." Warburton himself was so pleased with this note that he added to it considerably in *1751*.⟩

39. *Miscellanies* ⟨By "Miscellanies" Pope may intend no more than those volumes of occasional verse, the "Poems on Several Occasions" so frequently published in this period. He refers to Crashaw (EC vi 116) as one of the "poetical writers of miscellanies." In view of the sarcastic reference to Curll's "chaste press",—which, however, also occurs in *Dunciad A*—he may be glancing at compilations like the obscene *Merryland Miscellany* which Curll published early in 1742. Several other *Merryland* books had appeared in the preceding months.—Ll. 39–41 recall a much earlier opinion of Pope's in a letter to H. Cromwell, Nov. 1, 1708, that "those names very rarely last . . . many days, which are planted either in Jacob Tonson's or the Ordinary of Newgate's Miscellanies".⟩

40. *Curl's chaste press, &c.* ⟨A i 38⟩.

41, 42. *Hence hymning Tyburn's* ⟨A i 39⟩.

41. *Hence hymning Tyburn's elegiac lines*] It is an ancient English custom . . . before ⟨A i 39⟩.

42. *Magazines*] Miscellanies in prose and verse, in which at some times
         ——*new-born nonsense first is taught to cry*;
at others, dead-born Dulness appears in a thousand shapes. These were thrown out weekly and monthly by every miserable scribler; or picked up piece-meal and stolen from any body, under the title of Papers, Essays, Queries, Verses, Epigrams, Riddles, &c. equally the disgrace of human Wit, Morality, and Decency. P.W. ⟨Several "Weekly Journals" were appearing when this line was written, and a "Daily Journal". The word "medley" was frequently used to denote a literary miscellany, and sometimes a miscellany of cartoons brought together on a single sheet. *The Flying-Post: Or, The Weekly Medley* ran from 1728–30. "Mercury", popular in the seventeenth century as a title for news-papers, had fallen out of favour, but was still in ordinary use as a synonym for "newspaper". A weekly *London Mercury* ran from 1721–2. *The Gentleman's Magazine* had been appearing regularly since 1731, *The London Magazine* since 1732, *The Scots Magazine* since 1739⟩.

43. *Sepulchral Lyes* ⟨A i 41⟩.

And New-year Odes, and all the Grub-street race.
    In clouded Majesty here Dulness shone;   45
Four guardian Virtues, round, support her throne:
Fierce champion Fortitude, that knows no fears
Of hisses, blows, or want, or loss of ears:
Calm Temperance, whose blessings those partake
Who hunger, and who thirst for scribling sake: 50
Prudence, whose glass presents th' approaching jayl:
Poetic Justice, with her lifted scale,
Where, in nice balance, truth with gold she weighs,
And solid pudding against empty praise.
    Here she beholds the Chaos dark and deep,   55
Where nameless Somethings in their causes sleep,
'Till genial Jacob, or a warm Third day,
Call forth each mass, a Poem, or a Play:
How hints, like spawn, scarce quick in embryo lie,
How new-born nonsense first is taught to cry,   60
Maggots half-form'd in rhyme exactly meet,
And learn to crawl upon poetic feet.
Here one poor word an hundred clenches makes,
And ductile dulness new meanders takes;

---

44. *New-year Odes*] Made by the Poet Laureate for the time being, to be
sung at Court on every New-year's day, the words of which are happily drowned
in the voices and instruments. ⟨Cf. A i 40.⟩ The *New-year Odes* of the Hero of
this work were of a cast distinguished from all that preceded him, and made a
conspicuous part of his character as a writer, which doubtless induced our
Author to mention them here so particularly.

45. *In clouded Majesty* ⟨A i 43⟩.

45. *In clouded Majesty here Dulness shone*] See this Cloud removed, or rolled
back, or gathered up to her head, book iv. ver. 17, 18. It is worth while to
compare this description of the Majesty of Dulness in a state of peace and tran-
quillity, with that more busy scene where she mounts the throne in triumph,
and is not so much supported by her own Virtues, as by the princely consciousness of having destroyed all other. SCRIBL. W.

47. ——*that knows no fears, &c.* ⟨A i 45–6⟩.

50. *Who hunger, and who thirst, &c.* ⟨A i 48⟩.

55. *Here she beholds, &c.* ⟨A i 53⟩.

63. *Here one poor word, &c.* ⟨A i 61⟩.

64. *And ductile Dulness, &c.* ⟨A i 62⟩.

There motley Images her fancy strike,   65
Figures ill pair'd, and Similies unlike.
She sees a Mob of Metaphors advance,
Pleas'd with the madness of the mazy dance:
How Tragedy and Comedy embrace;
How Farce and Epic get a jumbled race;   70
How Time himself stands still at her command,
Realms shift their place, and Ocean turns to land.
Here gay Description Ægypt glads with show'rs,
Or gives to Zembla fruits, to Barca flow'rs;
Glitt'ring with ice here hoary hills are seen,   75
There painted vallies of eternal green,
In cold December fragrant chaplets blow,
And heavy harvests nod beneath the snow.
    All these, and more, the cloud-compelling Queen
Beholds thro' fogs, that magnify the scene.   80
She, tinsel'd o'er in robes of varying hues,
With self-applause her wild creation views;
Sees momentary monsters rise and fall,
And with her own fools-colours gilds them all.
    'Twas on the day, when * * rich and grave,   85
Like Cimon, triumph'd both on land and wave:
(Pomps without guilt, of bloodless swords and maces,
Glad chains, warm furs, broad banners, and broad faces)

77 In] On *1743c, 1749.*

70, *&c. How Farce and Epic, &c.* ⟨A i 68⟩.

73. *Ægypt glads with show'rs* ⟨A i 71⟩.

79. *The cloud-compelling Queen* ⟨A i 77⟩.

85, 86. *'Twas on the Day, when ** rich and grave, Like Cimon, triumph'd*] Viz. a Lord Mayor's Day; his name the author had left in blanks, but most certainly could never be that which the Editor foisted in formerly, and which no way agrees with the chronology of the poem. BENTL. ⟨The dropping of Thorold's name was one of the numerous small changes made necessary by the change of hero and the passage of years. Bentley's idiom is caught: in his edition of *Paradise Lost* (p. 22), he had drawn attention to some words which he held to have been "foisted in by the Man he trusted his Copy with".⟩

The Procession . . .Barbarians ⟨A i 83⟩.

88. *Glad chains* ⟨A i 86⟩.

Now Night descending, the proud scene was o'er,
But liv'd, in Settle's numbers, one day more.   90
Now May'rs and Shrieves all hush'd and satiate lay,
Yet eat, in dreams, the custard of the day;
While pensive Poets painful vigils keep,
Sleepless themselves, to give their readers sleep.
Much to the mindful Queen the feast recalls   95
What City Swans once sung within the walls;
Much she revolves their arts, their ancient praise,
And sure succession down from Heywood's days.
She saw, with joy, the line immortal run,
Each sire imprest and glaring in his son: 100
So watchful Bruin forms, with plastic care,
Each growing lump, and brings it to a Bear.
She saw old Pryn in restless Daniel shine,
And Eusden eke out Blackmore's endless line;

---

90. *But liv'd, in Settle's numbers* ⟨A i 88⟩.

Ibid. *But liv'd, in Settle's numbers, one day more*] Settle was poet to the City of London. His office . . . that place ⟨A i 88⟩.

98. *Heywood* ⟨A i 96⟩.

103. *Old Pryn, &c.* ⟨A i 101⟩.

104. *And Eusden eke out, &c.*] Laurence Eusden . . . reflection ⟨A iii 319⟩. Nor ought Mr. Oldmixon to complain, so long after, that the Laurel would have better become his own brows, or any other's: It were more decent to acquiesce in the opinion of the Duke of *Buckingham* upon this matter:

> ——*In rush'd Eusden, and cry'd, Who shall have it,*
> *But I, the true Laureate, to whom the King gave it?*
> *Apollo beg'd pardon, and granted his claim,*
> *But vow'd that 'till then he ne'er heard of his name.*

Session of Poets.

The same plea might also serve for his successor, Mr. Cibber; and is further strengthened in the following Epigram, made on that occasion:

> *In merry old England it once was a rule,*
> *The King had his Poet, and also his Fool:*
> *But now we're so frugal, I'd have you to know it,*
> *That Cibber can serve both for Fool and for Poet.*

⟨This epigram was attributed by Cibber to Pope himself.—*Letter to Pope*, p. 39.⟩
Of Blackmore, see Book 2. Of Philips, Book 1. ver. 258. and Book 3. *prope fin.*
Nahum Tate . . . mentioned ⟨A i 103⟩.

She saw slow Philips creep like Tate's poor page,   105
And all the mighty Mad in Dennis rage.
    In each she marks her Image full exprest,
But chief in B A Y s's monster-breeding breast;
Bays, form'd by nature Stage and Town to bless,
And act, and be, a Coxcomb with success.   110
Dulness with transport eyes the lively Dunce,
Remembring she herself was Pertness once.
Now (shame to Fortune!) an ill Run at Play

---

106. *And all the mighty Mad* ⟨A i 104⟩.

106. *And all the mighty Mad in Dennis rage*] Mr. Theobald, in the Censor . . . p. 286 ⟨A i 104⟩.

108. *BAYS'S monster-breeding breast* ⟨EC suggests (iv 317) that Pope may have intended a reference to the character Bayes in *The Rehearsal*, which Cibber was playing when he made a ludicrous reference to the Mummy and Crocodile in *Three Hours after Marriage*. It is hardly likely, however, that Pope would rake up this, to him, offensive episode. "Monster-breeding," which might seem to refer to the crocodile, was in fact applied to Theobald in the earlier editions.⟩

109. *Bays, form'd by Nature, &c.*] It is hoped the poet here hath done full justice to his Hero's Character, which it were a great mistake to imagine was wholly sunk in stupidity; he is allowed to have supported it with a wonderful mixture of Vivacity. This character is heightened according to his own desire, in a Letter he wrote to our author."Pert and dull at least you might have "allowed me. What! am I only to be dull, and dull still, and again, and for ever?" He then solemnly appealed to his own conscience, that "he could not "think himself so, nor believe that our poet did; but that he spoke worse of "him than he could possibly think; and concluded it must be merely to shew "his *Wit*, or for some *Profit* or *Lucre* to himself." Life of C. C. chap. vii. and Letter to Mr. P. pag. 15. 40. 53.

110. *And act . . . a Coxcomb* ⟨"In some Parts he does mighty well; in the *Buffoon*, the *Coxcomb*, the *Pert*, the *Impudent*, the *Bamster*."—*The Craftsman*, June 7, 1729. Similar tributes to his successful presentation of Sir Courtly Nice and Lord Foppington were paid to Cibber by Aaron Hill in *The Prompter*, Nov. 19, 1734. The coxcomb was Cibber's best theatrical part.⟩

112. *Pertness* ⟨Cibber's prologues had been cited by Pope as examples of "pertness" in the *Peri Bathous*, ch. xii. Warburton has a note on this line in *1751* which does little to clarify Pope's meaning. Dullness was presumably pert in her younger days; she is now "grave" and "laborious." Cf. A i 14, 15.⟩

113. *shame to Fortune!*] Because she usually shews favour to persons of this Character, who have a three-fold pretence to it. ⟨For Cibber's gambling habits,

Blank'd his bold visage, and a thin Third day:
Swearing and supperless the Hero sate,   115
Blasphem'd his Gods, the Dice, and damn'd his Fate.
Then gnaw'd his pen, then dash'd it on the ground,
Sinking from thought to thought, a vast profound!
Plung'd for his sense, but found no bottom there,
Yet wrote and flounder'd on, in mere despair.   120
Round him much Embryo, much Abortion lay,
Much future Ode, and abdicated Play;
Nonsense precipitate, like running Lead,
That slip'd thro' Cracks and Zig-zags of the Head;
All that on Folly Frenzy could beget,   125
Fruits of dull Heat, and Sooterkins of Wit.
Next, o'er his Books his eyes began to roll,

---

see *The Laureat* (1740), p. 123, and Barker, p. 13. He was a member of White's, a club much frequented by the nobility, where play ran high.⟩

114. *Blank'd* ⟨Either in OED's sense 1, to whiten, make pale; or in sense 2, to put out of countenance.⟩

Third day ⟨Cf. A i 55*n*.⟩

115. *supperless the Hero sate*] It is amazing . . .SCRIBL. ⟨A i 109⟩.

But since the discovery of the true Hero of the poem, may we not add that nothing was so natural, after so great a loss of Money at Dice, or of Reputation by his Play, as that the Poet should have no great stomach to eat a supper? Besides, how well has the Poet consulted his Heroic Character, in adding that he *swore* all the time! BENTL. ⟨The point of this last sentence appears to be that the heroes of the ancient epics frequently swear that they will perform certain actions. Cibber's profanity was notorious. Gentlemen delighted to hear him "invent new oaths at play."—*The Laureat* (1740), p. 106. Cf. B i 204.⟩

122. *abdicated* ⟨Possibly in OED's sense 1: to disown. Cibber, however, was not in the habit of disowning his plays. Pope appears to be thinking of half-written plays which Cibber had given up in disgust or despair. The word may have occurred to him while thinking of Cibber's *King John*. Cf. B i 252.⟩

123. *precipitate* ⟨Perhaps in its adjectival sense only of "violently hurried." But in seventeenth-century Chemistry, the word was "applied specially to certain preparations of mercury obtained by precipitation" (OED). Pope may have had this other idea in mind too, though the word scarcely fits the context, a precipitate being normally in the form of powder.⟩

126. *Sooterkins of Wit* ⟨Dryden, *MacFlecknoe*, l. 196:
        But sure thou'rt but a *Kilderkin* of wit.

"Sooterkin: A joke upon the Dutch women, supposing that by their constant

In pleasing memory of all he stole,
How here he sipp'd, how there he plunder'd snug
And suck'd all o'er, like an industrious Bug.   130
Here lay poor Fletcher's half-eat scenes, and here
The Frippery of crucify'd Moliere;
There hapless Shakespear, yet of Tibbald sore,
Wish'd he had blotted for himself before.

use of stoves, which they place under their petticoats, they breed a kind of small animal in their bodies, called a sooterkin, of the size of a mouse, which when mature slips out."—Grose, *A Classical Dictionary of the Vulgar Tongue.*⟩

131. *poor Fletcher's half-eat scenes*] A great number of them taken out to patch up his Plays. ⟨e.g. *Caesar in Egypt* is indebted to *The False One; The Rival Fools*, to *Wit at Several Weapons; Love Makes a Man*, to *The Custom of the Country* and *The Elder Brother.*⟩

132. *The Frippery*] "When I fitted up an old play, it was as a good housewife "will mend old linnen, when she has not better employment." Life, p. 217. octavo. ⟨For Molière, see Pope's note to B i 253.⟩

133. *hapless Shakespear, &c.*] It is not to be doubted but Bays was a subscriber to Tibbald's Shakespear. ⟨Cibber *was* a subscriber.⟩ He was frequently liberal this way; and, as he tells us, "subscribed to Mr. Pope's Homer, out of pure "Generosity and Civility; but when Mr. Pope did so to his Nonjuror, he con- "cluded it could be nothing but a joke." Letter to Mr. P. p. 24. ⟨Pope's purchase of four tickets for the author's night of *The Nonjuror* was, in Cibber's opinion, a "bountiful banter"; i.e. Pope was contemptuously repaying Cibber for his subscription to the *Homer*. "I had, not long before, been a Subscriber to your *Homer*: And now, to make up our Poetical Accounts, as you call'd it, you sent me a Note, with four Guineas inclosed, for four Tickets, for the Author's Day of *such a Play as The Non-Juror.*—Cibber, op. ci t. pp. 24–5.⟩ This Tibbald, or Theobald, published an edition of Shakespear, of which he was so proud himself as to say, in one of Mist's Journals, June 8, "That to "expose any Errors in it was impracticable." And in another, April 27, "That "whatever care might for the future be taken by any other Editor, he would still "give above five hundred Emendations, that *shall* escape them all." ⟨For what Theobald really said, see A i 106n. The statement in *Mist's Journal*, June 8, 1728, (possibly not by Theobald at all) referred to his *Shakespeare Restored*, and not to his edition of Shakespeare, which did not appear till 1734.⟩

134. *Wish'd he had blotted*] It was a ridiculous praise which the Players gave to Shakespear, "that he never blotted a line." ⟨"And what he thought, he vttered with that easinesse, that wee haue scarse receiued from him a blot in his papers."—"To the great Variety of Readers", John Heminge and Henrie Condell in the first Folio of Shakespeare's *Works*. See also Ben Jonson, *Discoveries* (*Workes*, 1641, p. 97).⟩ Ben Johnson honestly wished he had blotted a

The rest on Out-side merit but presume,   135
Or serve (like other Fools) to fill a room;
Such with their shelves as due proportion hold,
Or their fond Parents drest in red and gold;
Or where the pictures for the page attone,
And Quarles is sav'd by Beauties not his own.   140
Here swells the shelf with Ogilby the great;
There, stamp'd with arms, Newcastle shines complete:
Here all his suff'ring brotherhood retire,
And 'scape the martyrdom of jakes and fire:
A Gothic Library! of Greece and Rome   145
Well purg'd, and worthy Settle, Banks, and Broome.

thousand; and Shakespear would certainly have wished the same, if he had lived to see those alterations in his works, which, not the Actors only (and especially the daring Hero of this poem) have made on the *Stage*, but the presumptuous Critics of our days in their *Editions*. ⟨For alterations of Shakespeare's plays made by Cibber and his contemporaries, see G. C. D. Odell, *Shakespeare from Betterton to Irving*, 2 vols. 1921.—The "presumptuous Critics" are presumably Theobald and, in anticipation of his forthcoming edition, Sir Thomas Hanmer.⟩

135. *The rest on Out-side merit, &c.*] This Library is divided into three parts; the first consists of those authors from whom he stole, and whose works he mangled; the second, of such as fitted the shelves, or were gilded for shew, or adorned with pictures; the third class our author calls solid learning, old bodies of Divinity, old Commentaries, old English Printers, or old English Translations; all very voluminous, and fit to erect altars to Dulness. ⟨Cf. A i 120.⟩

138. *red and gold* ⟨Those volumes "drest in red and gold" were presumably presentation copies from Cibber's writing friends. Morocco gilt—generally, but not invariably red morocco—was the usual binding for author's presentation copies. Many such copies have survived, including a considerable number of elaborate specimens bound for Settle's patrons.⟩

140. *Quarles is saved* ⟨The quaint illustrations to Francis Quarles's *Emblemes*. (1635) were executed by William Marshall. Cf. A i 126*n*.⟩

141. *Ogilby the great* ⟨A i 121⟩.

142. *Newcastle shines complete* ⟨A i 122⟩.

146. *Worthy Settle, Banks, and Broome*] The Poet has mentioned these three authors in particular, as they are parallel to our Hero in his three capacities: 1. Settle was his Brother Laureate; only indeed upon half-pay, for the City instead of the Court; but equally famous for unintelligible flights in his poems on public occasions, such as Shows, Birth-days, &c. 2. Banks was his Rival in *Tragedy* (tho' more successful in one of his Tragedies, the *Earl of Essex*, which is

> But, high above, more solid Learning shone,
> The Classics of an Age that heard of none;
> There Caxton slept, with Wynkyn at his side,
> One clasp'd in wood, and one in strong cow-hide; 150
> There, sav'd by spice, like Mummies, many a year,
> Dry Bodies of Divinity appear:
> De Lyra there a dreadful front extends,
> And here the groaning shelves Philemon bends.
> Of these twelve volumes, twelve of amplest size, 155

yet alive: *Anna Boleyn*, the *Queen of Scots*, and *Cyrus the Great*, are dead and gone. These he drest in a sort of *Beggars Velvet*, or a happy mixture of the *thick Fustian* and *thin Prosaic*; exactly imitated in *Perolla and Isidora*, *Cæsar in Ægypt*, and the *Heroic Daughter*. 3. Broome was a serving-man of Ben. Johnson, who once picked up a *Comedy* from his Betters, or from some cast scenes of his Master, not entirely contemptible. ⟨For Settle and Banks, see A i 88*n.*, iii 281*n.*, and i 250*n.* *The Earl of Essex* was revived at least once every year from 1733–8, and twice in 1740. *Anna Bullen* was revived in 1733 at Goodman's Fields. The three plays in which Banks is "exactly imitated" are by Cibber.—Richard Brome (d. 1652?) was author or part-author of more than twenty plays. One of these, *A Joviall Crew*, was altered for the stage by Sir W. Yonge and by Concanen and Roome, two of Pope's dunces. As the name is generally spelled "Brome" (which gives a perfect eye-rhyme to "Rome"), the spelling "Broome" seems to be deliberate, and was no doubt intended to reflect on Pope's collaborator in the translation of the *Odyssey*, the Rev. William Broome. After being removed from the *Dunciad* at his own request (cf. A iii 328*n.*), Broome appears to have been brought in again by this back-door.⟩

147. *More solid Learning*] Some have objected, that books of this sort suit not so well the library of our Bays, which they imagine consisted of Novels, Plays, and obscene books; but they are to consider, that he furnished his shelves only for ornament, and read these books no more than the *Dry bodies of Divinity*, which, no doubt, were purchased by his Father when he designed him for the Gown. See the note on v. 200. ⟨Cf. Introduction, p. xxxvii.⟩

149. *Caxton*] A Printer . . . hardly known ⟨A i 129⟩. "Happened that to my "hande . . . Vyrgyle made in metre" ⟨A i 129⟩.

152. *Dry Bodies of Divinity* ⟨The change from the earlier reading, "Old Bodies of Philosophy", may have been made to enable Pope to ridicule the Rev. Thomas Stackhouse, who had written against Pope's friend Atterbury in his *Memoirs of the Life . . . of Dr. Francis Atterbury* (1723). In 1729 Stackhouse had published his *Complete Body of Divinity*, which Pope may be glancing at here, and more recently his *New History of the Holy Bible*, another vast work.⟩

153. *De Lyra* ⟨A i 133⟩.
154. *Philemon* ⟨A i 134⟩.

Redeem'd from tapers and defrauded pies,
Inspir'd he seizes: These an altar raise:
An hecatomb of pure, unsully'd lays
That altar crowns: A folio Common-place
Founds the whole pile, of all his works the base: 160
Quartos, octavos, shape the less'ning pyre;
A twisted Birth-day Ode completes the spire.
    Then he: "Great Tamer of all human art!
First in my care, and ever at my heart;
Dulness! whose good old cause I yet defend,   165
With whom my Muse began, with whom shall end;
E'er since Sir Fopling's Periwig was Praise,
To the last honours of the Butt and Bays:
O thou! of Bus'ness the directing soul!
To this our head like byass to the bowl,   170
Which, as more pond'rous, made its aim more true,
Obliquely wadling to the mark in view:

162. *A twisted Birth-day Ode* ⟨The change from Theobald's "little Ajax" was forced on the poet; but he has met it with an admirable substitute. The words suggest a fools-cap for George II, the recipient of Cibber's birthday odes.⟩

166. *With whom my Muse began, &c.* ⟨A i 146⟩.

167. *Sir Fopling's Periwig*] The first visible cause of the passion of the Town for our Hero, was a fair flaxen full-bottom'd Periwig, which, he tells us, he wore in his first play of the *Fool in fashion* ⟨*Love's Last Shift, or The Fool in Fashion*, produced in 1696⟩. It attracted, in a particular manner, the Friendship of Col. Brett, who wanted to purchase it. "Whatever contempt (says he) Philosophers "may have for a fine Periwig, my friend, who was not to despise the world but "to live in it, knew very well that so material an article of dress upon the head "of a man of sense, if it became him, could never fail of drawing to him a "more partial Regard and Benevolence, than could possibly be hoped for in an "ill-made one. This perhaps, may soften the grave censure which so youthful "a purchase might otherwise have laid upon him. In a word, he made his "attack upon this Periwig, as your young fellows generally do upon a lady of "pleasure, first by a few familiar praises of her person, and then a civil enquiry "into the price of it; and we finished our bargain that night over a bottle." See Life, octavo p. 303. This remarkable Periwig usually made its entrance upon the stage in a sedan, brought in by two chairmen, with infinite approbation of the audience.

168. *the Butt and Bays* ⟨i.e. the laureate's butt of sack and his laurel crown.⟩

O! ever gracious to perplex'd mankind,
Still spread a healing mist before the mind;
And lest we err by Wit's wild dancing light,   175
Secure us kindly in our native night.
Or, if to Wit a coxcomb make pretence,
Guard the sure barrier between that and Sense;
Or quite unravel all the reas'ning thread,
And hang some curious cobweb in its stead!   180
As, forc'd from wind-guns, lead itself can fly,
And pond'rous slugs cut swiftly thro the sky;
As clocks to weight their nimble motion owe,
The wheels above urg'd by the load below:
Me Emptiness, and Dulness could inspire,   185
And were my Elasticity, and Fire.
Some Dæmon stole my pen (forgive th' offence)
And once betray'd me into common sense:
Else all my Prose and Verse were much the same;
This, prose on stilts; that, poetry fall'n lame.   190
Did on the stage my Fops appear confin'd?
My Life gave ampler lessons to mankind.
Did the dead Letter unsuccessful prove?
The brisk Example never fail'd to move.
Yet sure had Heav'n decreed to save the State,   195
Heav'n had decreed these works a longer date.
Could Troy be sav'd by any single hand,
This grey-goose weapon must have made her stand.

194 brisk] sad *1743c 1749.*
196 these] those *1743c, 1749.*

178, 179. *Guard the sure barrier—Or quite unravel, &c.*] For *Wit* or *Reasoning* are never greatly hurtful to Dulness, but when the first is founded in *Truth,* and the other in *Usefulness.* W.

188. *And once betray'd me* ⟨in *The Careless Husband.* Cf. *Ep.* II i 92.⟩

194. *brisk* ⟨Pope seems to have appropriated this word from Cibber himself, who describes himself as "a brisk blockhead" in his youth.—*Apology,* p. 244.⟩

195. *Had Heav'n decreed, &c.* ⟨A i 183⟩.

197, 198. *Could Troy be sav'd—This grey-goose weapon* ⟨A i 187⟩.

What can I now? my Fletcher cast aside,
Take up the Bible, once my better guide?   200
Or tread the path by vent'rous Heroes trod,
This Box my Thunder, this right hand my God?
Or chair'd at White's amidst the Doctors sit,
Teach Oaths to Gamesters, and to Nobles Wit?
Or bidst thou rather Party to embrace?   205

201–2 *Om. 1743c, 1749.*
204 Nobles Wit?] Nobles —— Wit? *1743c, 1749.*

199. *my Fletcher*] A familiar manner of speaking, used by modern Critics, of a favourite author. Bays might as justly speak thus of Fletcher, as a French Wit did of Tully, seeing his works in a library, "Ah! mon cher Ciceron! "je le connois bien; c'est le même que Marc Tulle." But he had a better title to call Fletcher *his own*, having made so free with him. ⟨Cf. A i 189.⟩

200. *Take up the Bible*] When, according to his Father's intention, he had been a *Clergyman*, or (as he thinks himself) a *Bishop* of the Church of England. Hear his own words: "At the time that the fate of King James, the Prince of "Orange and Myself ⟨Cibber: "that of so minute a Being as myself"⟩, were on "the anvil, Providence thought fit to postpone mine, 'till theirs were deter- "mined: But had my father carried me a month sooner to the University, who "knows but that purer fountain might have washed my Imperfections into a "capacity of writing, instead of Plays and annual *Odes*, Sermons and *Pastoral* "*Letters?*" Apology for his Life, chap. iii. ⟨p. 52. Cf. A i 190.⟩

202. *This Box my Thunder, this Right hand my God*]
          Dextra mihi Deus, *& telum* quod missile libro.
Virgil ⟨*Aen.* x 773⟩ of the Gods of Mezentius.
⟨Box=dice-box.⟩

203. *at* White's *amidst the* Doctors] "These Doctors had a modest and fair "Appearance, and, like true Masters of Arts, were habited in *black* and *white*; "they were justly styled *subtiles* and *graves*, but not always *irrefragabiles*, being "sometimes examined, laid open, and split." SCRIBL. W.
This learned Critic is to be understood allegorically: The *Doctors* in this place mean no more than *false Dice*, a Cant phrase used amongst Gamesters. So the meaning of these four sonorous Lines is only this, "Shall I play fair, or foul?" ⟨The *subtiles* and *graves* of Warburton's pedantic joke are used for the purpose of punning on the two senses of "Doctors" intended here, viz. Doctors of a University and false dice. Taken with the former, the words have their Latin sense of "ingenious" and "venerable"; taken with the latter, they mean "tricky" and "heavy" (i.e. "loaded"). A weighted die was exposed by splitting it. "Irrefragabiles" refers to the title assumed by certain Doctors of the early Christian Church, and affords Warburton another laboured pun.—For White's, see B i 113*n*.⟩

(A friend to Party thou, and all her race;
'Tis the same rope at different ends they twist;
To Dulness Ridpath is as dear as Mist.)
Shall I, like Curtius, desp'rate in my zeal,
O'er head and ears plunge for the Commonweal?   210
Or rob Rome's ancient geese of all their glories,
And cackling save the Monarchy of Tories?
Hold—to the Minister I more incline;
To serve his cause, O Queen! is serving thine.
And see! thy very Gazetteers give o'er,   215
Ev'n Ralph repents, and Henly writes no more.

213 the] some *1743c, 1749*.   215 And see!] Now, see *1743c, 1749*.
216 repents,] is lost, *1743c, 1749*.

208. *Ridpath—Mist*] George Ridpath, author of a Whig paper, called the
Flying post; Nathanael Mist, of a famous Tory Journal.
211. *Or rob Rome's ancient geese* ⟨A i 191⟩.
212. *And cackling save the Monarchy of Tories?*] Not out of any preference or
affection to the Tories. For what Hobbes so ingenuously confesses of himself,
is true of all Party-writers whatsoever: "That he defends the supreme powers,
"as the *Geese* by their *cackling* defended the Romans, who held the Capitol; for
"they favoured them no more than the Gauls their Enemies, but were as ready
"to have defended the Gauls if they had been *possessed of the Capitol.*" Epist.
Dedic. to the Leviathan. W.
213. *the Minister* ⟨i.e. Walpole.⟩
214. *O Queen!* ⟨i.e. Dullness. But Pope was probably thinking too of Queen
Caroline, whose understanding with Walpole was complete. To serve Walpole
was to serve Queen Caroline.⟩
215. *Gazetteers*] A band of ministerial writers, hired at the price mentioned
in the note on book ii. ver. 316, who on the very day their Patron quitted his
post, laid down their paper, and declared they would never more meddle in
Politics. ⟨The *Daily Gazetteer*, however, continued to appear for many years after
the fall of Walpole (Jan. 28, 1742), though in a less markedly political form.
On Feb. 22, 1742, it announced that "as the Gazetteer-Legion never had any
other Existence than in the Imagination of some of our Brother-News-Writers,
so they had certainly a Right to disband the Troops they had rais'd, whenever
they saw fit . . . and as to the Conduct of the *Gazetteer* for the future, . . . we
shall continue to use our utmost Diligence and best Endeavour to please *all
Parties* and to *offend none*".⟩
216. *Ev'n Ralph repents, &c.* ⟨Ralph, once a writer for *The Daily Gazetteer*,
had "repented" by becoming an anti-ministerial writer in *The Champion*, which

What then remains? Ourself. Still, still remain
Cibberian forehead, and Cibberian brain.
This brazen Brightness, to the 'Squire so dear;
This polish'd Hardness, that reflects the Peer;   220
This arch Absurd, that wit and fool delights;
This Mess, toss'd up of Hockley-hole and White's;
Where Dukes and Butchers join to wreathe my crown,
At once the Bear and Fiddle of the town.
  "O born in sin, and forth in folly brought!   225
Works damn'd, or to be damn'd! (your father's fault)
Go, purify'd by flames ascend the sky,
My better and more christian progeny!

227 flames] flame, *1743c, 1749.*

had been appearing since the autumn of 1739.—The Bodleian file for Henley's
Hyp Doctor, a ministerial paper, ends with the number for Jan. 20, 1741. For
Ralph, and Henley, see Biog. App.⟩

 217. *What then remains? Ourself* ⟨"A happy parody on the famous M O Y of
Corneille in his *Medea* . . . But the original is in Seneca's Tragedy of *Medea.—*
'Medea superest.' " [v 164]—Warton.⟩

 218. *Cibberian forehead*] So indeed all the MSS. read; but I make no scruple
to pronounce them all wrong, the Laureate being elsewhere celebrated by our
Poet for his great *Modesty—modest Cibber—*Read, therefore, at my peril, *Cer-*
berian forehead. This is perfectly classical, and, what is more, *Homerical*; the *Dog*
was the ancient, as the *Bitch* is the modern, symbol of Impudence: (Κυνὸς
ὄμματ᾽ ἔχων, says Achilles to Agamemnon) which, when in a superlative
degree, may well be denominated from *Cerberus,* the *Dog with three heads.*—But
as to the latter part of this verse, *Cibberian brain,* that is certainly the genuine
reading. B E N T L. W.

 222. *Hockley-hole* ⟨i.e. Hockley-in-the-Hole, a place near Clerkenwell-Green,
famous for the baiting of bulls and bears, dog-fights, trials of skill, etc.⟩

 224. *Bear and Fiddle* ⟨Cibber is at once the person baited and the jester. Cf.
OED, "fiddle", sense 2 b. In illustrating this meaning of "fiddle" OED quotes a
sentence from Cibber's *Apology,* Ch. i, which Pope may have had in mind: "His
easy humour, whenever he is called to it [company], can still make himself the
fiddle of it." "Bear" and "Fiddle" are associated through bear-baiting, at which
playing on the fiddle seems to have been a preliminary. Cf. *Hudibras,* Pt. i,
Canto 2.⟩

 225. *O born in sin, &c.* ⟨A i 197⟩.

 228. *My better and more christian progeny*] "It may be observable, that my muse
"and my spouse were equally prolific; that the one was seldom the mother of a

Unstain'd, untouch'd, and yet in maiden sheets;
While all your smutty sisters walk the streets.   230
Ye shall not beg, like gratis-given Bland,
Sent with a Pass, and vagrant thro' the land;
Not sail, with Ward, to Ape-and-monkey climes,
Where vile Mundungus trucks for viler rhymes;
Not sulphur-tipt, emblaze an Ale-house fire;   235
Not wrap up Oranges, to pelt your sire!
O! pass more innocent, in infant state,
To the mild Limbo of our Father Tate:
Or peaceably forgot, at once be blest
In Shadwell's bosom with eternal Rest!   240

229 untouch'd,] unstitch'd, *1743c, 1749.*
231 Bland,] B—d, *1743c, 1749.*

"Child, but in the same year the other made me the father of a Play. I think we
"had a dozen of each sort between us; of both which kinds some *died* in their
"*Infancy*," *&c.* Life of C. C. p. 217. 8vo edit. ⟨Among Cibber's less Christian
progeny was the notorious Theophilus Cibber, and Mrs Charlotte Charke. The
latter's irregular life may be alluded to in the phrase "walk the streets", l. 230.
The surface meaning is, of course, that *other* copies of Cibber's works were
hawked about the streets: those that were now to be burnt were fresh from the
press, still "in sheets".⟩

    229. *Unstain'd, untouch'd, &c.* ⟨A i 197⟩.

    231. *gratis-given Bland—Sent with a Pass*] It was a practice so to give the Daily
Gazetteer and ministerial pamphlets (in which this B. was a writer) and to send
them *Post-free* to all the Towns in the kingdom. ⟨For Bland, see Biog. App.—
Between 1735 and 1737 John Walthoe was paid on an average about £900
each quarter for *Daily Gazetteers* sent to the Post Office. See *Calendar of Treasury
Books and Papers, 1735–8*, ed. W. A. Shaw, and cf. B ii 314*n*.⟩

    233. *Ward* ⟨A i 200⟩.

    234. *vile Mundungus* ⟨i.e. tobacco of poor quality. Cf. J. Oldham, *A Satyr*,
ll. 107, 109:

         And truck for pots of Ale next Stourbridge-Fair . . .
         To vile Mundungus made a Martyr flame.—Wakefield.⟩

    236. *Oranges* ⟨Oranges were regularly sold in the theatres, and were occasion-
ally used for pelting the actors when they or the play failed to give satisfaction.⟩

    238, 240. *Tate—Shadwell*] Two of his predecessors in the Laurel. ⟨See
A i 103, and A ii 324. In l. 240 there is what Wakefield calls "an indecorous
allusion" to *Luke* xvi 22.⟩

Soon to that mass of Nonsense to return,
Where things destroy'd are swept to things unborn."
   With that, a Tear (portentous sign of Grace!)
Stole from the Master of the sev'nfold Face:
And thrice he lifted high the Birth-day brand,   245
And thrice he dropt it from his quiv'ring hand;
Then lights the structure, with averted eyes:
The rowling smokes involve the sacrifice.
The op'ning clouds disclose each work by turns,
Now flames the Cid, and now Perolla burns;   250

241. *And thrice he lifted, &c.* ⟨A i 203⟩.

241–2. ⟨Cf. Rochester's translation of Seneca's "Post mortem nihil est" (*Works*, ed. John Hayward, 1926, pp. 48–9):

> And to that Mass of Matter shall be swept
> Where things destroy'd, with things unborn are kept.⟩

243. *With that, a Tear (portentous sign of Grace!) &c.*] It is to be observed that our Poet hath made his Hero, in imitation of Virgil's, obnoxious to the tender Passions. He was indeed so given to weeping, that he tells us, when Goodman the player swore, if he did not *make a good actor, he'd be damn'd*; "the surprise of "being commended by one who had been himself so eminent on the stage, and "in so *positive a manner*, was more than he could support. In a word (says he) "it almost took away my breath and (laugh if you please) fairly drew tears "from my eyes." P. 149. of his Life, octavo. W.

244. *the sev'nfold Face* ⟨Wakefield notes the parody of Ovid, *Met.* xiii 2: "clypei dominus septemplicis"—which Dryden translates: "the Master of the sev'nfold Shield." The phrase describes Cibber's impenetrable assurance, but also suggests the mobile face of the born actor.⟩

250. *Now flames the Cid, &c.* ⟨A i 208⟩.

250. *Now flames the Cid, &c.*] In the first notes on the Dunciad ⟨A i 240⟩ it was said, that this Author was particularly excellent at Tragedy. "This (says "he) is as unjust as to say I could not dance on a Rope" ⟨*Letter to Pope*, p. 35⟩. But certain it is that he had attempted to dance on this Rope, and fell most shamefully, having produced no less than four Tragedies (the names of which the Poet preserves in these few lines) the three first of them were fairly printed, acted, and damned; the fourth suppressed, in fear of the like treatment. ⟨Cibber's *Perolla and Izadora* was first performed in 1705, his *Ximena: or The Heroick Daughter* (based on *Le Cid* of Corneille), in 1712, and his *Caesar in Egypt* in 1724. His *Papal Tyranny* was not performed till 1745, but it had been rehearsed for performance about ten years earlier at Drury Lane, and then withdrawn by Cibber before production owing to hostile criticism.—"Colley after having laid out immense Pains, upon altering Shakespear's Play of *King John*,

Great Cæsar roars, and hisses in the fires;
King John in silence modestly expires:
No merit now the dear Nonjuror claims,
Moliere's old stubble in a moment flames.
Tears gush'd again, as from pale Priam's eyes   255
When the last blaze sent Ilion to the skies.
    Rowz'd by the light, old Dulness heav'd the head;
Then snatch'd a sheet of Thulè from her bed,
Sudden she flies, and whelms it o'er the pyre;
Down sink the flames, and with a hiss expire.   260
    Her ample presence fills up all the place;
A veil of fogs dilates her awful face:
Great in her charms! as when on Shrieves and May'rs
She looks, and breathes herself into their airs.
She bids him wait her to her sacred Dome: 265
Well pleas'd he enter'd, and confess'd his home.

---

modestly withdrew it when it had been several Times rehears'd, lest per-adventure it should meet the sad Fate of the others."—*Sawney and Colley* (1742), p. 9*n*. It was in this way that the play expired "in silence": the facts were well known to the Town when Pope wrote.⟩

253. *the dear Nonjuror—Moliere's old stubble*] A Comedy threshed out of Moliere's Tartuffe, and so much the Translator's favourite, that he assures us all our author's dislike to it could only arise from *disaffection to the Government*;
          Qui méprise Cotin, n'estime point son Roi,
          Et n'a, selon Cotin, ni Dieu, ni foi, ni loi.   Boil. ⟨Satire ix⟩.
He assures us, that "when he had the honour to kiss his Majesty's hand upon "presenting his dedication of it, he was graciously pleased, out of his Royal "bounty, to order him two hundred pounds for it. And this he doubts not "*grieved* Mr. P." ⟨*Letter to Pope*, p. 24.—George I paid a visit to the theatre to see Cibber's play "and seem'd to be mightily pleas'd."—*Some Cursory Remarks on the Play call'd the Non-Juror*, 1718, p. 29. In the Public Record Office (S.P. 35/11/33) there is a letter of Cibber's to the Earl of Sunderland, dated March 10, 1718, reminding him that some proposal had been made to reward him for the *Nonjuror*, but that nothing so far had come of it. The *Nonjuror* is a Whig and Protestant play, containing much crude satire of Catholics and Nonjurors as the real or supposed enemies of George I and his Whig government.⟩

256. *When the last blaze, &c.* ⟨A i 212⟩.
258. *Thulè* ⟨A i 214⟩.
263. *Great in her charms! &c.* ⟨A i 219⟩.
265. *sacred Dome*] Where he no sooner enters . . . regions ⟨A i 221⟩.

So Spirits ending their terrestrial race,
Ascend, and recognize their Native Place.
This the Great Mother dearer held than all
The clubs of Quidnuncs, or her own Guild-hall: 270
Here stood her Opium, here she nurs'd her Owls,
And here she plann'd th' Imperial seat of Fools.

Here to her Chosen all her works she shews;
Prose swell'd to verse, verse loit'ring into prose:
How random thoughts now meaning chance to find, 275
Now leave all memory of sense behind:
How Prologues into Prefaces decay,
And these to Notes are fritter'd quite away:
How Index-learning turns no student pale,
Yet holds the eel of science by the tail: 280
How, with less reading than makes felons scape,
Less human genius than God gives an ape,
Small thanks to France, and none to Rome or Greece,
A past, vamp'd, future, old, reviv'd, new piece,
'Twixt Plautus, Fletcher, Shakespear, and Corneille, 285
Can make a Cibber, Tibbald, or Ozell.

The Goddess then, o'er his anointed head,
With mystic words, the sacred Opium shed.
And lo! her bird, (a monster of a fowl,
Something betwixt a Heideggre and owl,) 290

---

269. *This the Great Mother, &c.* ⟨A i 33⟩.

269. *Great Mother* ⟨A i 33⟩.

286. *Tibbald*] Lewis Tibbald (as pronounced) or Theobald (as written) was bred an Attorney, and son to an Attorney (says Mr. Jacob) of Sittenburn in Kent. He was Author of some forgotten Plays, Translations, and other pieces. He was concerned in a paper called the Censor, and a Translation of Ovid. "There is a notorious Idiot, one hight Whachum, who, from an under-spur-"leather to the Law, is become an under-strapper to the Play-house, who hath "lately burlesqued the Metamorphoses of Ovid by a vile Translation, &c. This "fellow is concerned in an impertinent paper called the Censor." DENNIS Rem. on Pope's Hom. p. 9, 10. ⟨Cf. A i 106.⟩

Ibid. *Ozell* ⟨A i 240, and Errata, p. 198.⟩

290. *A Heideggre* ⟨A i 244⟩.

Perch'd on his crown. "All hail! and hail again,
My son! the promis'd land expects thy reign.
Know, Eusden thirsts no more for sack or praise;
He sleeps among the dull of ancient days;
Safe, where no Critics damn, no duns molest,   295
Where wretched Withers, Ward, and Gildon rest,
And high-born Howard, more majestic sire,
With Fool of Quality compleats the quire.
Thou Cibber! thou, his Laurel shalt support,
Folly, my son, has still a Friend at Court.   300
Lift up your gates, ye Princes, see him come!
Sound, sound ye Viols, be the Cat-call dumb!
Bring, bring the madding Bay, the drunken Vine;
The creeping, dirty, courtly Ivy join.
And thou! his Aid de camp, lead on my sons,   305

298 Impatient waits 'till H—y grace the quire. *1743c, 1749.*
299–300 Yet, yet a while, at Court my H—y stay!
    See Cibber enters! haste, and turn the Key. *1743c, 1749.*
304 courtly] Courtly *1743c, 1749.*   305 on] out *1743c, 1749.*

---

293. *Eusden* ⟨He died in 1730. Cf. A ii 393.⟩
296. *Withers* ⟨A i 126⟩.
Ibid. *Gildon* ⟨A i 250⟩.
296. *Ward, and Gildon* ⟨Ward had died in 1731; Gildon, in 1724.⟩
297. *Howard* ⟨A i 250⟩.
298. *Fool of Quality* ⟨i.e. Lord Hervey. The death of Hervey, August 5, 1743, enabled Pope to make this last-minute change in the text. From *1735c–42* the line had run: "Impatient waits, till ** grace the quire." The next twelve lines are among the most obscure that Pope ever wrote, owing to the difficulty of understanding to whom the "his" of 299, 305, 308, and 309 and the "him" of 301 refer. The meaning appears to be: "You, Cibber, shall support his (i.e. Eusden's) laurel . . . Lift up your gates, ye Princes, see him (i.e. Cibber) come . . . And thou (i.e. Lord Hervey), his *Aide de camp*, lead on my sons . . . Let Bawdry etc. support his (i.e. Cibber's) front . . . And under his (i.e. Cibber's) wing Grub-Street shall skulk behind the King."—For Lord Hervey, see vol. iv, Introduction and Biog. App.⟩
304. *The creeping . . . Ivy* ⟨"Not only as it anciently belonged to Poets in general; but as it is emblematical of the three virtues of a court poet in particular; it is creeping, dirty, and dangling."—See below, "Of the Poet Laureate," p. 415. Warburton's reference in his edition of 1751 to the "Hederae sequaces" of Persius (Sat. I, Prol. 6) seems hardly necessary.⟩

Light-arm'd with Points, Antitheses, and Puns.
Let Bawdry, Bilingsgate, my daughters dear,
Support his front, and Oaths bring up the rear:
And under his, and under Archer's wing,
Gaming and Grub-street skulk behind the King.   310
   "O! when shall rise a Monarch all our own,

307 my daughters] two sisters *1743c, 1749.*
309 Archer's] Ar—r's *1743c, 1749.*

306. *Points, Antitheses* ⟨Lord Hervey's fondness for antithesis was well-known. Cf. *Ep. to Arbuthnot,* 325.⟩

308. *front* ⟨There is almost certainly a *double entendre* here, "front" being contrasted with "rear," but also carrying the further, and now nearly obsolete, sense of "impudence."⟩

309, 310. *Under Archer's wing,—Gaming, &c.*] When the Statute against Gaming was drawn up, it was represented, that the King, by ancient custom, plays at Hazard one night in the year ⟨i.e. Twelfth Night⟩; and therefore a clause was inserted, with an exception as to that particular. Under this pretence, the Groom-porter had a Room appropriated to Gaming all the summer the Court was at Kensington, which his Majesty accidentally being acquainted of, with a just indignation prohibited. It is reported, the same practice is yet continued wherever the Court resides, and the Hazard Table there open to all the professed Gamesters in town.

> Greatest *and* justest SOV'REIGN! *know you this?*
> *Alas! no more, than* Thames' *calm* head *can know*
> *Whose meads his* arms *drown, or whose corn o'erflow.*
>   Donne to Queen Eliz.

⟨Pope, quoting from Satire v 28–30, manages to introduce four errors into these three lines.—Thomas Archer, who died May 23, 1743, several months before these lines were published, was Groom-Porter to Anne, George I, and George II. The Groom-Porter "has the Inspection of the King's Lodgings, and takes care that they are provided with Tables, Chairs, Firing, etc. As also to provide Cards, Dice, etc. when there is Playing at Court; and to decide Disputes which arise in Gaming."—*The True State of England,* 1729, p. 43. The office is now extinct. Archer died worth more than £100,000.—*Gent. Mag.* xiii 275. See Biog. App.⟩

311. *O when shall rise a Monarch, &c.*] Boileau, Lutrin, Chant. 2 ⟨51–6⟩.

> *Helas! qu'est devenu ce tems, cet heureux tems,*
> *Où les Rois s'honoroient du nom de Faineans:*
> *S'endormoient sur le trone, & me servant sans honte,*
> *Laissoient leur sceptre au mains ou d'un mair, ou d'un comte:*
> *Aucun soin n'approchoit de leur paisible cour,*
> *On reposoit la nuit, on dormoit tout le jour, &c.*

And I, a Nursing-mother, rock the throne,
'Twixt Prince and People close the Curtain draw,
Shade him from Light, and cover him from Law;
Fatten the Courtier, starve the learned band,   315
And suckle Armies, and dry-nurse the land:
'Till Senates nod to Lullabies divine,
And all be sleep, as at an Ode of thine."

She ceas'd. Then swells the Chapel-royal throat:
"God save king Cibber!" mounts in ev'ry note.   320
Familiar White's, "God save king Colley!" cries;
"God save king Colley!" Drury-lane replies:
To Needham's quick the voice triumphal rode,
But pious Needham dropt the name of God;

311-18. *O! when shall rise, &c.* ⟨In these lines Pope comes very near to a direct criticism of George II's reign. The charge of "suckling armies" reverts to a complaint frequently made by the Opposition. In 1735 Parliament had approved a treaty with Denmark by which 6000 Danish horse and foot were taken into pay. In 1743, not long before these lines were published, George II's Hanoverian troops had been taken into British pay.⟩

319. *Chapel-royal*] The Voices and Instruments used in the service of the Chapel-royal being also employed in the performance of the Birth-day and New-year Odes.

321. *God save king Colley!* ⟨It was customary at White's to greet Cibber with cries of "O King Coll! Come in, King Coll! Welcome, welcome, King Colley" (T. Davies, *Life of Garrick*, ii 360). Whether this custom was known to Pope, or whether it actually arose from these lines in the *Dunciad*, is not clear. For the "echo" effect of ll. 320-1, cf. B ii 263 ff. and *The Rape of the Lock*, iv 96*n.* in vol. ii, p. 188.⟩

324. *Needham*] A Matron of great fame, and very religious in her way; whose constant prayer it was, that she might "get enough by her profession to "leave it off in time, and make her peace with God." But her fate was not so happy; for being convicted, and set in the pillory, she was (to the lasting shame of all her great Friends and Votaries) so ill used by the populace, that it put an end to her days. ⟨Mother Needham was convicted on April 29, 1731, for keeping a disorderly house: she was fined one shilling, and sentenced to stand twice in the pillory. She stood only once, for she was handled so roughly by the mob that she died on May 3.—*Daily Post*, May 4, 1731. Her foul language was evi-

Back to the Devil the last echoes roll,   325
And "Coll!" each Butcher roars at Hockley-hole.
    So when Jove's block descended from on high
(As sings thy great forefather Ogilby)
Loud thunder to its bottom shook the bog,
And the hoarse nation croak'd, "God save King Log!"

---

dently notorious. Cf. James Bramston's *The Art of Politicks*, 1729:

> Try not with Jests obscene to force a Smile,
> Nor lard your Speech with Mother Needham's Stile.

She is the handsome old procuress in Hogarth's *The Harlot's Progress*, Plate I.⟩
    325. *Back to the Devil*] The Devil Tavern in Fleet-street, where these Odes are usually rehearsed before they are performed at Court ⟨*1743a–51*⟩. Upon which a Wit of those times made this epigram:

> When Laureates make Odes, do you ask of what sort?
> Do you ask if they're good, or are evil?
> You may judge—from the Devil they come to the Court,
> And go from the Court to the Devil.

⟨*1743b–51*. See further vol. vi, where this epigram is tentatively ascribed to Pope.⟩
    326. *And Coll! &c.* ⟨Cf. *MacFlecknoe*, 47–8:

> Echoes from Pissing-Ally, *Sh*— call,
> And *Sh*— they resound from *A*— *Hall*.

For Hockley-hole, see B i 222*n*.⟩
    328. *—Ogilby)—God save king Log!*] ⟨A i 258. The note underwent some slight revision.⟩

The End of the First Book

THE DUNCIAD

Book the Second

ARGUMENT

The King being proclaimed, the solemnity is graced with public Games *and sports of various kinds; not instituted by the Hero, as by Æneas in Virgil, but for greater honour by the* Goddess *in person (in like manner as the games Pythia, Isthmia, &c. were anciently said to be ordained by the Gods, and as Thetis herself appearing, according to Homer, Odyss. 24. proposed the prizes in honour of her son Achilles.) Hither flock the Poets and Critics, attended, as is but just, with their Patrons and Booksellers. The Goddess is first pleased, for her disport, to propose games to the* Booksellers, *and setteth up the Phantom of a Poet, which they contend to overtake. The Races described, with their divers accidents. Next, the game for a* Poetess. *Then follow the Exercises for the* Poets, *of tickling, vociferating, diving: The first holds forth the arts and practices of* Dedicators, *the second of* Disputants *and fustian Poets, the third of profound, dark, and dirty Party-writers. Lastly, for the* Critics, *the Goddess proposes (with great propriety) an Exercise, not of their parts, but their patience, in hearing the works of two voluminous Authors, one in* verse, *and the other in* prose, *deliberately read, without sleeping: The various effects of which, with the several degrees and manners of their operation, are here set forth; 'till the whole number, not of Critics only, but of spectators, actors, and all present, fall fast asleep; which naturally and necessarily ends the games.*

THE DUNCIAD

Book the Second

High on a gorgeous seat, that far out-shone
Henley's gilt tub, or Fleckno's Irish throne,
Or that where on her Curls the Public pours,
All-bounteous, fragrant Grains and Golden show'rs,
Great Cibber sate: The proud Parnassian sneer,   5
The conscious simper, and the jealous leer,
Mix on his look: All eyes direct their rays
On him, and crowds turn Coxcombs as they gaze.
His Peers shine round him with reflected grace,
New edge their dulness, and new bronze their face.   10
So from the Sun's broad beam, in shallow urns
Heav'ns twinkling Sparks draw light, and point their
        horns.

10 edge] point *1743c, 1749.*   12 twinkling] Starry *1743c, 1749.*

Two things there are . . . all sound Commentators ⟨A ii⟩.

1. *High on a gorgeous seat* ⟨A ii 1⟩.

2. *Henley's gilt tub* ⟨A ii 2⟩.

Ibid. *or Fleckno's Irish throne*] Richard Fleckno . . . Sarazin ⟨A ii 2⟩.

It may be just worth mentioning, that the Eminence from whence the ancient Sophists entertained their auditors, was called by the pompous name of a Throne;—ἐπὶ θρόνου τινος ὑψηλοῦ μάλα σοφιστικῶς καὶ σοβαρῶς. Themistius, Orat. i.

3. *Or that where on her Curls, &c.*] Edmund Curl . . . p. 19, 25 ⟨A ii 3⟩. Much in the same manner Mr. Cibber remonstrated that his Brothers at Bedlam, mentioned Book i. were not *Brazen*, but *Blocks*; yet our author let it pass unaltered, as a trifle, that no way lessened the Relationship. ⟨*Second Letter*, p. 4. Pope had been warned by William Bowyer that he would probably have trouble over the epithet "brazen." On Nov. 13 [1742?] he replied: "Just now I receive yrs abt ye *Brazen* Image. I wd have it stand as it is, & no matter if ye Criticks dispute abt it."—B.M. Egerton MS. 1946 f. 63.⟩

9. *Peers* ⟨Cibber's "peers" are his brother dunces of the pen, but also those among the English nobility who delighted in his society at White's and elsewhere. Cf. B i 220.⟩

11–12. *Heav'n's twinkling Sparks, &c.* ⟨*Paradise Lost*, vii 364–6:
        Hither, as to their fountain, other stars

296

> Not with more glee, by hands Pontific crown'd,
> With scarlet hats wide-waving circled round,
> Rome in her Capitol saw Querno sit,   15
> Thron'd on sev'n hills, the Antichrist of wit.
>   And now the Queen, to glad her sons, proclaims
> By herald Hawkers, high heroic Games.
> They summon all her Race: An endless band
> Pours forth, and leaves unpeopled half the land.   20
> A motley mixture! in long wigs, in bags,
> In silks, in crapes, in Garters, and in rags,
> From drawing rooms, from colleges, from garrets,
> On horse, on foot, in hacks, and gilded chariots:
> All who true Dunces in her cause appear'd,   25
> And all who knew those Dunces to reward.
>   Amid that area wide they took their stand,
> Where the tall may-pole once o'er-look'd the Strand;
> But now (so ANNE and Piety ordain)
> A Church collects the saints of Drury-lane.   30
>   With Authors, Stationers obey'd the call,
> (The field of glory is a field for all.)
> Glory, and gain, th'industrious tribe provoke;
> And gentle Dulness ever loves a joke.
> A Poet's form she plac'd before their eyes,   35
> And bade the nimblest racer seize the prize;
> No meagre, muse-rid mope, adust and thin,
> In a dun night-gown of his own loose skin;

13–16 *In 1743c, 1749, these lines follow l. 26.*
17 And . . . sons,] To grace her dauntless Son, she now
1743c, 1749.

> Repairing, in their golden urns draw light,
> And hence the morning planet gilds her horns.
>   —Wakefield.⟩

15. *Querno*] Camillo Querno . . . Prolusions. ⟨A ii 11. After the words "weep for joy" *1743a* has a note, "See Life of C. C. chap. vi. p. 149"—a reference to Cibber's delight at Goodman's prophecy. See B iii 232*n*.⟩
35. *A Poet's form, &c.* ⟨A ii 31⟩.

But such a bulk as no twelve bards could raise,
Twelve starv'ling bards of these degen'rate days.   40
All as a partridge plump, full-fed, and fair,
She form'd this image of well-body'd air;
With pert flat eyes she window'd well its head;
A brain of feathers, and a heart of lead;
And empty words she gave, and sounding strain,   45
But senseless, lifeless! idol void and vain!
Never was dash'd out, at one lucky hit,
A fool, so just a copy of a wit;
So like, that critics said, and courtiers swore,
A Wit it was, and call'd the phantom More.   50
　　All gaze with ardour: Some a poet's name,
Others a sword-knot and lac'd suit inflame.
But lofty Lintot in the circle rose:
"This prize is mine; who tempt it are my foes;
With me began this genius, and shall end."   55
He spoke: and who with Lintot shall contend?
　　Fear held them mute. Alone, untaught to fear,
Stood dauntless Curl; "Behold that rival here!
"The race by vigour, not by vaunts is won;
"So take the hindmost, Hell."—He said, and run.   60
Swift as a bard the bailiff leaves behind,
He left huge Lintot, and out-strip'd the wind.
As when a dab-chick waddles thro' the copse

---

39. *But such a bulk, &c.* ⟨A ii 35⟩.
44. *A brain . . . lead*] i.e.
　　　　　　　　　A trifling head, *and a* contracted heart,
as the poet, book 4 ⟨504⟩ describes the *accomplished* Sons of Dulness; of whom this
is only an *Image*, or Scarecrow, and so stuffed out with these corresponding
materials. SCRIBL. W.
47. *Never was dash'd out, &c.* ⟨A ii 43⟩.
50. *and call'd the phantom More*] CURL, in his Key . . . handkerchief!" ⟨A ii 46⟩.
The plagiarisms . . . *repono* ⟨A ii 46⟩.
50. *the phantom More* ⟨A ii 46⟩.　　　53. *But lofty Lintot* ⟨A ii 49⟩.
58. *Stood dauntless Curl* ⟨A ii 54⟩.　　　60. *So take the hindmost, Hell* ⟨A ii 56⟩.
61, *&c.* ⟨A ii 54⟩.

On feet and wings, and flies, and wades, and hops;
So lab'ring on, with shoulders, hands, and head,   65
Wide as a wind-mill all his figures spread,
With arms expanded Bernard rows his state,
And left-legg'd Jacob seems to emulate.
Full in the middle way there stood a lake,
Which Curl's Corinna chanc'd that morn to make: 70
(Such was her wont, at early dawn to drop
Her evening cates before his neighbour's shop,)
Here fortun'd Curl to slide; loud shout the band,
And Bernard! Bernard! rings thro' all the Strand.
Obscene with filth the miscreant lies bewray'd,   75
Fal'n in the plash his wickedness had laid:
Then first (if Poets aught of truth declare)
The caitiff Vaticide conceiv'd a pray'r.
   Hear Jove! whose name my bards and I adore,
As much at least as any God's, or more;   80
And him and his, if more devotion warms,
Down with the Bible, up with the Pope's Arms.
   A place there is, betwixt earth, air, and seas,
Where, from Ambrosia, Jove retires for ease.
There in his seat two spacious vents appear,   85

64, 65. *On feet and wings, &c.* ⟨A ii 60⟩.
67, 68. *With arms expanded, Bernard rows his state,*
       And left-legg'd Jacob seems to emulate]
Milton, of the motion of the Swan ⟨*Par. Lost*, vii 440⟩,

         ————*rows*

       His state with oary feet.
And Dryden, of another's,—*With two left legs*—⟨Cf. A ii 64*n*.⟩
   68. *left-legg'd Jacob* ⟨In some lines on Tonson Dryden had remarked on his "two left Legs." Pope was here returning to a reading which he had discarded in 1728.—See EC iv 280.⟩
   70. *Curl's Corinna* ⟨A ii 66⟩.
   73. *Here fortun'd Curl to slide* ⟨A ii 69⟩.
   74. *And Bernard! Bernard!* ⟨A ii 70⟩.
   75. *Obscene with filth, &c.* ⟨A ii 71⟩.
   82. *the Bible . . . the Pope's Arms* ⟨A ii 78⟩.
   83. ⟨A ii 79⟩.   Ibid. *A place there is, &c.* ⟨A ii 79⟩.

On this he sits, to that he leans his ear,
And hears the various vows of fond mankind;
Some beg an eastern, some a western wind:
All vain petitions, mounting to the sky,
With reams abundant this abode supply;   90
Amus'd he reads, and then returns the bills
Sign'd with that Ichor which from Gods distils.
    In office here fair Cloacina stands,
And ministers to Jove with purest hands.
Forth from the heap she pick'd her Vot'ry's pray'r,   95
And plac'd it next him, a distinction rare!
Oft had the Goddess heard her servant's call,
From her black grottos near the Temple-wall,
List'ning delighted to the jest unclean
Of link-boys vile, and watermen obscene;   100
Where as he fish'd her nether realms for Wit,
She oft had favour'd him, and favours yet.
Renew'd by ordure's sympathetic force,
As oil'd with magic juices for the course,
Vig'rous he rises; from th' effluvia strong   105
Imbibes new life, and scours and stinks along;
Re-passes Lintot, vindicates the race,
Nor heeds the brown dishonours of his face.
    And now the victor stretch'd his eager hand
Where the tall Nothing stood, or seem'd to stand;   110
A shapeless shade, it melted from his sight,
Like forms in clouds, or visions of the night.

---

92. ⟨A ii 88⟩.
93. *Cloacina* ⟨A ii 89⟩.
98. *black grottos* ⟨Coal wharves on the Thames, or in Fleet Ditch⟩.
99–100. ⟨This admirable couplet belonged to an earlier stage in the composition of the poem. It appears in the EC MS. with a slight variation in the first line. See EC iv 280.⟩
101. *Where as he fish'd, &c.* ⟨A ii 93⟩.
104. *As oil'd with magic juices* ⟨A ii 96⟩.
108. *the brown dishonours* ⟨A ii 100⟩.
111. *A shapeless shade, &c.* ⟨A ii 103⟩.

To seize his papers, Curl, was next thy care;
His papers light, fly diverse, tost in air;
Songs, sonnets, epigrams the winds uplift,   115
And whisk 'em back to Evans, Young, and Swift.
Th'embroider'd suit at least he deem'd his prey;
That suit an unpay'd taylor snatch'd away.
No rag, no scrap, of all the beau, or wit,
That once so flutter'd, and that once so writ.   120
      Heav'n rings with laughter: Of the laughter vain,
Dulness, good Queen, repeats the jest again.
Three wicked imps, of her own Grubstreet choir,
She deck'd like Congreve, Addison, and Prior;
Mears, Warner, Wilkins run: delusive thought!   125
Breval, Bond, Besaleel, the varlets caught.
Curl stretches after Gay, but Gay is gone,
He grasps an empty Joseph for a John:
So Proteus, hunted in a nobler shape,
Became, when seiz'd, a puppy, or an ape.   130
      To him the Goddess: "Son! thy grief lay down,
And turn this whole illusion on the town:
As the sage dame, experienc'd in her trade,
By names of Toasts retails each batter'd jade;
(Whence hapless Monsieur much complains at Paris 135
Of wrongs from Duchesses and Lady Maries;)
Be thine, my stationer! this magic gift;
Cook shall be Prior, and Concanen, Swift:

---

114. *His papers light, &c.* ⟨A ii 106⟩.
116. *Evans, Young, and Swift*] Some of those persons whose writings, epigrams, or jests he had owned. See Note on ver. 50.
118. *an unpay'd taylor* ⟨A ii 111⟩.
124. *like Congreve, Addison, and Prior* ⟨A ii 116⟩.
125. *Mears, Warner, Wilkins* ⟨A ii 117⟩.
126. *Breval, Bond, Besaleel* ⟨A ii 118⟩.
128. *Gay* ⟨A ii 120⟩.
132. *And turn this whole illusion, &c.* ⟨A ii 124⟩.
138. *Cook shall be Prior* ⟨As in A ii 130, with some small revisions⟩.
138. *and Concanen, Swift* ⟨A ii 287⟩.

So shall each hostile name become our own,
And we too boast our Garth and Addison."   140
      With that she gave him (piteous of his case,
Yet smiling at his rueful length of face)
A shaggy Tap'stry, worthy to be spread
On Codrus' old, or Dunton's modern bed;
Instructive work! whose wry-mouth'd portraiture   145
Display'd the fates her confessors endure.
Earless on high, stood unabash'd De Foe,
And Tutchin flagrant from the scourge below.
There Ridpath, Roper, cudgell'd might ye view,
The very worsted still look'd black and blue.   150
Himself among the story'd chiefs he spies,
As from the blanket high in air he flies,

---

140. *And we too boast our Garth and Addison*] Nothing . . . Mr. Addison; ⟨A ii 132⟩ in a word, almost every man of his time that deserved it; even Cibber himself (presuming him to be author of the Careless Husband.) It was very difficult . . . *dead.* ⟨A ii 132. Cibber's authorship of *The Careless Husband*, on which doubt is cast in this note, was questioned by many of his contemporaries. The author of *Sawney and Colley*, 1742 (p. 8) asserted that "the great A—ll wrote ev'ry Line." Cibber himself may have been responsible for this notion, for, in dedicating his play to the Duke of Argyll, he says modestly: "I owe most of it to the many stolen observations I have made from Your Grace's manner of conversing."⟩

141, 142. ——*piteous of his case, &c.* ⟨A ii 133⟩.

142. *rueful length of face* ⟨A ii 134⟩.

The good Scriblerus here, as on all occasions, eminently shews his humanity. But it was far otherwise with the gentlemen of the Dunciad, whose scurrilities were always personal, and of that nature which provoked every honest man but Mr. Pope; yet never to be lamented . . . *to see* ⟨A ii 134⟩.

143. *A shaggy Tap'stry* ⟨A ii 135⟩.

144. *On Codrus' old, or Dunton's modern bed* ⟨A ii 136⟩.

148. *Tutchin* ⟨A ii 140⟩.

149. *Ridpath, Roper*] Authors of the Flying-post and Post-boy, two scandalous papers on different sides, for which they equally and alternately deserved to be cudgelled, and were so ⟨Cf. A ii 141⟩.

151. *Himself . . . he spies* ⟨A ii 143⟩.

151. *Himself . . . he spies*] The history of Curl's being tossed in a blanket, and whipped by the scholars of Westminster, is well known. Of his purging . . . in Swift and Pope's Miscell. ⟨A ii 143⟩.

"And oh! (he cry'd) what street, what lane but knows,
Our purgings, pumpings, blankettings, and blows?
In ev'ry loom our labours shall be seen,   155
And the fresh vomit run for ever green!"
    See in the circle next, Eliza plac'd,
Two babes of love close clinging to her waist;
Fair as before her works she stands confess'd,
In flow'rs and pearls by bounteous Kirkall dress'd.   160
The Goddess then: "Who best can send on high
"The salient spout, far-streaming to the sky;
"His be yon Juno of majestic size,
"With cow-like udders, and with ox-like eyes.
"This China Jordan let the chief o'ercome   165
"Replenish, not ingloriously, at home."
Osborne and Curl accept the glorious strife,

---

156. *And the fresh vomit, &c.* ⟨A ii 148⟩.
157. *See in the circle next* ⟨A ii 149⟩.
Ibid. *Eliza Haywood* ⟨A ii 149⟩.
158. *Two babes of love. &c.* ⟨A ii 150⟩.
160. *Kirkall* (A ii 152).
163. *yon Juno, &c.* ⟨A ii 155⟩.
165. *This China Jordan* ⟨A ii 157⟩.
167. *Osborne*] A Bookseller in Grays-Inn, very well qualified by his impudence
to act this part; and therefore placed here instead of a less deserving Predecessor.
This man published advertisements for a year together, pretending to sell Mr.
Pope's Subscription books of Homer's Iliad at half the price: Of which books
he had none, but cut to the size of them (which was Quarto) the common
books in folio, without Copper-plates, on a worse paper, and never above half
the value. ⟨"Thomas Osborne, Bookseller in Gray's-Inn, Having purchased
the few remaining Copies of Mr. Pope's Homer's Iliad's, 6 vol. and Odysseys
5 vol. in . . . Folio, the Subscription Price of which was, for the large Paper
1*l*. 1*s*. and for the small Paper 12*s*. in Sheets each Vol. now offers them to the
Publick at the following reasonable Rates, viz. The large Paper at 8*s*. per Vol.
and small Paper at 6*s*. per Vol. in Sheets . . ."—*The Daily Gazetteer*, May 29,
1739.⟩
Upon this Advertisement the Gazetteer harangued thus, July 6, 1739.
"How melancholy must it be to a Writer to be so unhappy as to see his works
"hawked for sale in a manner so fatal to his fame! How, with Honour to your
"self, and Justice to your Subscribers, can this be done? What an Ingratitude
"to be charged on the *Only honest Poet* that lived in 1738! and than whom

(Tho' this his Son dissuades, and that his Wife.)
One on his manly confidence relies,
One on his vigour and superior size.   170
First Osborne lean'd against his letter'd post;
It rose, and labour'd to a curve at most.
So Jove's bright bow displays its wat'ry round,
(Sure sign, that no spectator shall be drown'd)
A second effort brought but new disgrace,   175
The wild Meander wash'd the Artist's face:
Thus the small jett, which hasty hands unlock,
Spirts in the gard'ner's eyes who turns the cock.
Not so from shameless Curl; impetuous spread
The stream, and smoking flourish'd o'er his head.   180
So (fam'd like thee for turbulence and horns)
Eridanus his humble fountain scorns;
Thro' half the heav'ns he pours th'exalted urn;
His rapid waters in their passage burn.
     Swift as it mounts, all follow with their eyes: 185
Still happy Impudence obtains the prize.
Thou triumph'st, Victor of the high-wrought day,
And the pleas'd dame, soft-smiling, lead'st away.
Osborne, thro' perfect modesty o'ercome,
Crown'd with the Jordan, walks contented home.   190
     But now for Authors nobler palms remain;

"*Virtue* has not had a *shriller Trumpeter* for many ages! That you were once
"*generally admired and esteemed* can be denied by none; but that you and your
"works are now despised, is verified by *this fact:*" which being utterly false, did
not indeed much humble the Author, but drew this just chastisement on the
Bookseller. ⟨*1741.* "He told me when he was doing that which raised Pope's
resentment, that he should be put in the *Dunciad.*"—Johnson, *Lives,* iii 187.
For Osborne, see Biog. App.⟩
     169, 170. *One on his manly confidence, &c.* ⟨A ii 161⟩.
     173, 174. *So Jove's bright bow, &c.* ⟨A ii 165⟩.
     176. *wild Meander* ⟨Cf. Addison, *A Letter from Italy,* 46 (of the River Boyne):
                    And unobserved in wild mæanders played.⟩
     181, 182. *So (fam'd like thee, &c.* ⟨A ii 173⟩.
     183. *Thro' half the heav'ns, &c.*⟨A ii 175⟩.
     187. *the high-wrought day* ⟨A ii 179⟩.

Room for my Lord! three jockeys in his train;
Six huntsmen with a shout precede his chair:
He grins, and looks broad nonsense with a stare.
His Honour's meaning Dulness thus exprest,   195
"He wins this Patron, who can tickle best."
    He chinks his purse, and takes his seat of state:
With ready quills the Dedicators wait;
Now at his head the dextrous task commence,
And, instant, fancy feels th' imputed sense;   200
Now gentle touches wanton o'er his face,
He struts Adonis, and affects grimace:
Rolli the feather to his ear conveys,
Then his nice taste directs our Operas:
Bentley his mouth with classic flatt'ry opes,   205

---

203. *Paolo Antonio Rolli* ⟨A ii 195⟩.

205. *Bentley his mouth, &c.*] Not spoken of the famous Dr. Richard Bentley, but of one Thom. Bentley, a small critic, who aped his uncle in a *little Horace*. The great one was intended to be dedicated to the Lord Hallifax, but (on a change of the Ministry) was given to the Earl of Oxford; for which reason the little one was dedicated to his son the Lord Harley. A taste of this *Classic Elocution* may be seen in his following Panegyric on the Peace of Utrecht. *Cupimus Patrem tuum, fulgentissimum illud Orbis Anglicani jubar*, adorare. *O ingens* Reipublicæ *nostræ columen! O fortunatam tanto* Heroe *Britanniam! Illi tali tantoque viro* DEUM *per* Omnia *adfuisse, manumque ejus & mentem direxisse*, CERTISSIMUM EST. Hujus *enim* Unius *ferme opera*, æquissimis & perhonorificis conditionibus, diuturno, heu nimium! bello, finem impositum videmus. O Diem æterna memoria dignissimam! qua terrores Patriæ omnes excidit*, Pacem*que diu exoptatam toti fere Europæ restituit, ille Populi Anglicani Amor, Harleius.*

Thus critically (that is verbally) translated:

"Thy Father, that most refulgent star of the Anglican Orb, we much desire
"to *adore!* Oh mighty Column of our *Republic!* Oh Britain, fortunate in such an
"*Hero!* That to such and so great a Man GOD was ever present, in *every thing*,
"and all along directed both his hand and his heart, is a *Most Absolute Certainty!*
"For it is in a manner by the operation of this *Man alone*, that we behold a *War*
"(alas! how much too long an one!) brought at length to an end, *on the most*
"*just and most honourable Conditions*. Oh Day eternally to be memorated! wherein
"All the Terrors of his Country were ended, and a PEACE (long wish'd for by
"*almost all Europe*) was restored by HARLEY, the Love and Delight of the
"People of England."

But that this Gentleman can write in a different style, may be seen in a letter

And the puff'd orator bursts out in tropes.
But Welsted most the Poet's healing balm
Strives to extract from his soft, giving palm;
Unlucky Welsted! thy unfeeling master,
The more thou ticklest, gripes his fist the faster.   210
    While thus each hand promotes the pleasing pain,
And quick sensations skip from vein to vein;
A youth unknown to Phœbus, in despair,
Puts his last refuge all in heav'n and pray'r.
What force have pious vows! The Queen of Love   215
His sister sends, her vot'ress, from above.
As taught by Venus, Paris learnt the art
To touch Achilles' only tender part;
Secure, thro' her, the noble prize to carry,
He marches off, his Grace's Secretary.   220
    "Now turn to diff'rent sports (the Goddess cries)
And learn, my sons, the wond'rous pow'r of Noise.
To move, to raise, to ravish ev'ry heart,

---

he printed to Mr. Pope ⟨in a *Letter to Mr.* Pope *occasion'd by Sober Advice from Horace—1735c–42*⟩, wherein several Noble Lords are treated in a most extraordinary language, particularly the Lord Bolingbroke abused for that very PEACE which he here makes the *single work* of the Earl of Oxford, directed by *God Almighty.* ⟨*1735c*. The change to "B—y" was made in *1735a*, and to "Bentley" in *1735c*; but Bentley was in Pope's mind at a much earlier stage. (See EC iv 283.) His original intention was probably to satirize Dr. Richard Bentley in this passage, and the note added to the "Bentley" reading of *1735c* referring the reader to Thomas Bentley, the nephew, must be attributed to the latter's *A Letter to Mr. Pope, Occasion'd by Sober Advice from Horace*, 1735, in which Pope is severely handled. For Thomas Bentley, see Biog. App. If the passage was originally written with Dr. Bentley in mind, the "classic flatt'ry" may have been the Latin speech delivered by Bentley at Cambridge, July 6, 1725. This speech, printed by Bentley in his *Terence*, 1726, celebrated, among other things, the beneficence of George I to the University.—The phrase, "Thus critically (that is verbally) translated", with which Pope introduces his rendering of the Latin panegyric, is another thrust at the verbal criticism by which Bentley had become famous, and in which Theobald had had considerable success.⟩

207. *Welsted* ⟨As A ii 293, with a few slight omissions⟩.

213. *A youth unknown to Phœbus, &c.* ⟨A ii 205⟩.

223, 225. *To move, to raise, &c.* ⟨A ii 215⟩.

With Shakespear's nature, or with Johnson's art,
Let others aim: 'Tis yours to shake the soul   225
With Thunder rumbling from the mustard bowl,
With horns and trumpets now to madness swell,
Now sink in sorrows with a tolling bell;
Such happy arts attention can command,
When fancy flags, and sense is at a stand.   230
Improve we these. Three Cat-calls be the bribe
Of him, whose chatt'ring shames the Monkey tribe:
And his this Drum, whose hoarse heroic base
Drowns the loud clarion of the braying Ass."
    Now thousand tongues are heard in one loud din: 235
The Monkey-mimics rush discordant in;
'Twas chatt'ring, grinning, mouthing, jabb'ring all,
And Noise and Norton, Brangling and Breval,
Dennis and Dissonance, and captious Art,
And Snip-snap short, and Interruption smart,   240
And Demonstration thin, and Theses thick,
And Major, Minor, and Conclusion quick.
"Hold (cry'd the Queen) a Cat-call each shall win;
Equal your merits! equal is your din!
But that this well-disputed game may end,   245
Sound forth my Brayers, and the welkin rend."
    As when the long-ear'd milky mothers wait
At some sick miser's triple-bolted gate,
For their defrauded, absent foals they make
A moan so loud, that all the guild awake;   250
Sore sighs Sir Gilbert, starting at the bray,
From dreams of millions, and three groats to pay.
So swells each wind-pipe; Ass intones to Ass,
Harmonic twang! of leather, horn, and brass;

---

226. *With Thunder, &c.* ⟨A ii 218⟩.   228. *—with a tolling bell* ⟨A ii 220⟩.
231. *Three Cat-calls* ⟨A ii 223⟩.
238. *Norton*] See ver. 417.—*J. Durant Breval,* Author of a very extraordinary
Book of Travels, and some Poems. See before, Note on ver. 126 ⟨A ii 230⟩.
243. *a Cat-call, &c.* ⟨A ii 233⟩.   247. *As when the, &c.* ⟨A ii 239⟩.

Such as from lab'ring lungs th' Enthusiast blows,   255
High Sound, attemp'red to the vocal nose;
Or such as bellow from the deep Divine;
There Webster! peal'd thy voice, and Whitfield! thine.
But far o'er all, sonorous Blackmore's strain;
Walls, steeples, skies, bray back to him again.   260
In Tot'nam fields, the brethren, with amaze,
Prick all their ears up, and forget to graze;
Long Chanc'ry-lane retentive rolls the sound,
And courts to courts return it round and round;
Thames wafts it thence to Rufus' roaring hall,   265
And Hungerford re-echoes bawl for bawl.
All hail him victor in both gifts of song,
Who sings so loudly, and who sings so long.
    This labour past, by Bridewell all descend,
(As morning pray'r, and flagellation end)   270
To where Fleet-ditch with disemboguing streams

256 Sound,] Notes, *1743c, 1749.*

258. *Webster—and Whitfield*] The one the writer of a News-paper called the
Weekly Miscellany, the other a Field-preacher. This thought the only means
of advancing Christianity was by the New-birth of religious madness; That,
by the old death of fire and faggot: And therefore they agreed in this, though in
no other earthly thing, to abuse all the sober Clergy. From the small success
of these two extraordinary persons, we may learn how little hurtful *Bigotry* and
Enthusiasm are, while the Civil Magistrate prudently forbears to lend his power
to the one, in order to the employing it against the other. W. ⟨For Dr. William
Webster and George Whitefield, see Biog. App. The two were probably introduced to please Warburton. They are brought together in the same line as a
sort of Roper and Ridpath of the religious world, Webster's *Weekly Miscellany*
being one of the bitterest of anti-Methodist journals.—Whitefield had a voice
"of great compass and audible at immense distances" (DNB). Webster's voice
"pealed" in his *Weekly Miscellany*, and in other miscellaneous writings.⟩
    260. *bray back to him again* ⟨A ii 248⟩.
    262. *Prick all their ears up, &c.* ⟨A ii 250⟩.
    263. *Long Chanc'ry-lane* ⟨A ii 251⟩.
    268. *Who sings so loudly, &c.* ⟨A ii 256⟩.
    270. *As morning pray'r, &c.* ⟨A ii 258⟩.
    271. *Fleet-ditch* ⟨Since this line first appeared, the Fleetditch had been brick-
ed over (in 1737) from Holborn Bridge to Fleet Street. The remaining portion
from Fleet Street to the River remained uncovered till 1765.⟩

Rolls the large tribute of dead dogs to Thames,
The King of dykes! than whom no sluice of mud
With deeper sable blots the silver flood.
"Here strip, my children! here at once leap in,   275
"Here prove who best can dash thro' thick and thin,
"And who the most in love of dirt excel,
"Or dark dexterity of groping well.
"Who flings most filth, and wide pollutes around
"The stream, be his the Weekly Journals bound,   280
"A pig of lead to him who dives the best;
"A peck of coals a-piece shall glad the rest."
In naked majesty Oldmixon stands,
And Milo-like surveys his arms and hands;
Then sighing, thus, "And am I now three-score?   285
"Ah why, ye Gods! should two and two make four?"
He said, and clim'd a stranded lighter's height,
Shot to the black abyss, and plung'd down-right.
The Senior's judgment all the crowd admire,
Who but to sink the deeper, rose the higher.   290
　　Next Smedley div'd; slow circles dimpled o'er

273. *The King of dykes! &c.* ⟨A ii 261⟩.
276, 277, 278. ⟨A ii 264⟩.
280. *the Weekly Journals* ⟨A ii 268⟩.
282. "*A peck of coals a-piece*" ⟨A ii 270⟩.
283. *Oldmixon*] Mr. JOHN OLDMIXON ... vol. ii. p. 303 ⟨A ii 199, with a few omissions⟩.
In his Essay on Criticism ... death ⟨A ii 199⟩.
He is here likened to Milo ... Lord Rosc. ⟨A ii 271⟩.
286. "*Ah why, ye Gods! should two and two make four?*"] Very reasonably doth this ancient Critic complain: Without doubt it was a fault in the Constitution of things. For the *World*, as a great writer saith, *being given to man for a subject of disputation*, he might think himself mock'd with a penurious gift, were any thing made certain. Hence those superior masters of wisdom, the *Sceptics* and *Academics*, reasonably conclude that *two and two do not make four*. SCRIBL. W.
But we need not go so far, to remark what the Poet principally intended, the absurdity of complaining of *old age*, which must necessarily happen, as long as we are indulged in our desires of adding one year to another.
291. *Smedley*] The person here mentioned ... in octavo, 1728 ⟨A ii 279⟩.

The quaking mud, that clos'd, and op'd no more.
All look, all sigh, and call on Smedley lost;
Smedley in vain resounds thro' all the coast.
　　Then * essay'd; scarce vanish'd out of sight,　　　295
He buoys up instant, and returns to light:
He bears no token of the sabler streams,
And mounts far off among the Swans of Thames.
　　True to the bottom, see Concanen creep,
A cold, long-winded, native of the deep:　　　　　300
If perseverance gain the Diver's prize,
Not everlasting Blackmore this denies:
No noise, no stir, no motion can'st thou make,
Th' unconscious stream sleeps o'er thee like a lake.
　　Next plung'd a feeble, but a desp'rate pack,　　　305
With each a sickly brother at his back:
Sons of a Day! just buoyant on the flood,
Then number'd with the puppies in the mud.
Ask ye their names? I could as soon disclose
The names of these blind puppies as of those.　　　310
Fast by, like Niobe (her children gone)

309 could as soon] sooner could *1743c, 1749.*
310 as] than *1743c, 1749.*

293. *and call on Smedley lost; &c.* ⟨A ii 281⟩.

295. *Then * essay'd* ⟨See A ii 283*n.*⟩.

299. *Concanen*] MATTHEW CONCANEN, an Irishman, bred to the law. Smedley (one of his brethren in enmity to Swift) in his Metamorphosis of Scriblerus, p. 7. accuses him of "having boasted . . . Jamaica ⟨A ii 130⟩.

302. *Not everlasting Blackmore* ⟨A ii 290⟩.

306, 307. *With each a sickly brother, &c.*] These were daily Papers, a number of which, to lessen the expence, were printed one on the back of another. ⟨Pope seems to be referring to such papers as *The Daily Courant*, which printed a country edition for sending down to the country reader on post-days three times a week. The news for two days was thus printed on a "Double Courant", most of the advertisements, which normally filled the back page, being omitted.⟩

309. *Ask ye their names?* ⟨Cf. Dryden's translation of Juvenal, *Sat.* x 348: "Ask me their Names, I sooner cou'd relate . . ."
　　　　　　　　　　　　　　　　　　　　　　—Wakefield.⟩

311. *like Niobe*] See the story in Ovid, Met. vii. where the miserable Petre-faction of this old Lady is pathetically described.

Sits Mother Osborne, stupify'd to stone!
And Monumental Brass this record bears,
"These are,—ah no! these were, the Gazetteers!"

312. *Osborne*] A name assumed by the eldest and gravest of these writers, who at last being ashamed of his Pupils, gave his paper over, and in his age remained silent. ⟨See Biog. App., James Pitt.—"Mr. *P—t*, formerly a country School-Master, conducted the *London Journal* under the Name of *Fr. Osborne*; which the Country Writers, from the Heaviness of the Style, converted into *Mother Osborne*."—Ralph, pp. 517–18. Pitt continued to write under the same pseudonym in *The Daily Gazetteer*.⟩

313. *And Monumental Brass, &c.* ⟨Writing to Swift, May 17, 1739, Pope gives an earlier version of this line, viz.:

      And rueful Paxton tells the world with tears.

Paxton was Solicitor to the Treasury. See Biog. App., vol. iv.⟩

314. *Gazetteers*] We ought not to suppress that a modern Critic here taxeth the Poet with an Anachronism, affirming these Gazetteers not to have lived within the time of his poem, and challenging us to produce any such paper of that date. But we may with equal assurance assert, these Gazetteers not to have lived since, and challenge all the learned world to produce one such paper at this day. Surely therefore, where the point is so obscure, our author ought not to be censured too rashly. Scribl.

Notwithstanding this affected ignorance of the good Scriblerus, the *Daily Gazetteer* was a title given very properly to certain papers, each of which lasted but a day. Into this, as a common sink, was received all the trash, which had been before dispersed in several Journals, and circulated at the public expence of the nation. ⟨"In the Year 1735, it was thought fit to unite all the Strength of the Party, in order to animate one Paper, to which Mr. *Osborne* was to give solid Reason, Mr. *Walsingham* Wit, and the occasional Gentlemen Humour or Secret History, as the Exigencies of the Patron might require."—Ralph, p. 518. And see B i 231*n*.⟩ The authors were the same obscure men; though sometimes relieved by occasional essays from Statesmen, Courtiers, Bishops, Deans, and Doctors ⟨e.g. Dr. Henry Bland, Dean of Durham; Francis Hare, Bishop of Chichester; Horace Walpole, Sir Robert's brother; Benjamin Hoadly, Bishop of Winchester, etc.⟩. The meaner sort were rewarded with Money; others with Places or Benefices, from an hundred to a thousand a year. It appears from the *Report* of the *Secret Committee* for enquiring into the Conduct of R. Earl of O. ⟨*A Further Report from the Committee of Secresy, appointed to enquire into the Conduct of Robert Earl of Orford* . . . 1742, Appendix xiii⟩ "That no less "than *fifty-thousand, seventy-seven pounds, eighteen shillings*, were paid to Authors "and Printers of News-papers, such as Free-Britons, Daily-Courants, Corn-"Cutter's Journals, Gazetteers, and other political papers, between Feb. 10, "1731. and Feb. 10, 1741." Which shews the Benevolence of One Minister to have expended, for the current dulness of ten years in Britain, double the sum

Not so bold Arnall; with a weight of skull,   315
Furious he dives, precipitately dull.
Whirlpools and storms his circling arm invest,
With all the might of gravitation blest.
No crab more active in the dirty dance,
Downward to climb, and backward to advance.   320
He brings up half the bottom on his head,
And loudly claims the Journals and the Lead.
The plunging Prelate, and his pond'rous Grace,

which gained Louis XIV. so much honour, in annual Pensions to Learned men all over Europe. In which, and in a much longer time, not a Pension at Court, nor Preferment in the Church or Universities, of any Consideration, was bestowed on any man distinguished for his Learning separately from Party-merit, or Pamphlet-writing.

It is worth a reflection, that of all the Panegyrics bestowed by these writers on this great Minister, not one is at this day extant or remembred; nor even so much credit done to his Personal character by all they have written, as by one short occasional compliment of our Author.

> Seen him I have; but in his happier hour
> Of social pleasure, ill exchang'd for Pow'r!
> Seen him, uncumber'd by the Venal Tribe,
> Smile without Art, and win without a Bribe.

⟨Epilogue to the Satires, i 29-32.⟩

315. Arnall] WILLIAM ARNALL, bred an Attorney, was a perfect Genius in this sort of work. He began under twenty with furious Party-papers; then succeeded Concanen in the British Journal. At the first publication of the Dunciad, he prevailed on the Author not to give him his due place in it, by a letter professing his detestation of such practices as his Predecessor's. But since, by the most unexampled insolence, and personal abuse of several great men, the Poet's particular friends, he most amply deserved a niche in the Temple of Infamy: Witness a paper, called the Free Briton, a Dedication intituled To the Genuine Blunderer, 1732, and many others. ⟨In The Free Briton, No. 138, July 20, Lord Bolingbroke was attacked by Arnall in a "Dedication addressed to the Genuine Blunderer." This was in reply to the publication of a collection of papers from Fog's Journal which had been dedicated to "the greatest blunderer in Christendom," i.e. Walpole. See Gent. Mag., vol. ii, pp. 856, 863.⟩ He writ for hire, and valued himself upon it; ⟨1735a⟩ not indeed without cause, it appearing by the aforesaid REPORT, that he received "for Free Britons, and "other writings, in the space of four years, no less than ten thousand nine hundred "and ninety-seven pounds, six shillings, and eight pence, out of the Treasury." ⟨1743.⟩

323. The plunging Prelate, &c. ⟨"It having been invidiously insinuated that by this Title was meant a truly great Prelate, as respectable for his defence of

With holy envy gave one Layman place.
When lo! a burst of thunder shook the flood.   325
Slow rose a form, in majesty of Mud;
Shaking the horrors of his sable brows,
And each ferocious feature grim with ooze.
Greater he looks, and more than mortal stares:
Then thus the wonders of the deep declares.   330
    First he relates, how sinking to the chin,
Smit with his mien, the Mud-nymphs suck'd him in:
How young Lutetia, softer than the down,

the present balance of power in the *civil* constitution, as for his opposition to
no power at all, in the *religious*; I owe so much to the memory of my deceased
friend as to declare, that when, a little before his death, I informed him of this
insinuation, he called it vile and malicious, as any candid Man, he said, might
understand, by his having paid a willing compliment to this very Prelate in
another part of the Poem."—Warburton, *1751*. Warburton is here trying to
shield Thomas Sherlock, Bishop of London, with whom he was on terms of
friendship. Pope's disclaimer, however, can have convinced few readers of the
Dunciad, and can hardly have deceived Warburton himself. According to
Warton, Sir Robert Walpole used to relate an anecdote of Sherlock, who was
his contemporary at Eton, "that when some of the Scholars, going to bathe in
the Thames, stood shivering on the Bank, Sherlock plunged in immediately
over his head and ears". That this anecdote was well known is suggested by an
epigram in *The Craftsman*, April 3, 1731:
> ... By the River whilst trembling stood each *Eton* Dunce,
> G—d d— ye (cry'd *Sh*—) e'en plunge in at once;
> At *School* and in *S—te* the same he appears;
> The *Man*, like the *Boy*, souses o'er Head and Ears.
If the "plunging Prelate" is not Sherlock, who is he? It should be noted that
Pope apparently offered Warburton no alternative name. Sherlock was a
consistent supporter of Walpole in the House of Lords. Recently—in Feb. 1741
—he had spoken in his favour on the crucial motion introduced by Lord
Carteret that Walpole be removed from the person and councils of the King
for ever.—By "his pond'rous Grace," Pope most probably intended John
Potter (1674?–1747), Archbishop of Canterbury. He was an enemy of Warburton's, and is said to have tried to enlist the London clergy to write against
his *Divine Legation* (R. Hurd, *Letters of a late Eminent Prelate*, 1808, p. 85). He
left several learned works in folio, which might account for the epithet "ponderous." His portrait in the Examination Schools at Oxford shows him to
have been a man of heavy appearance. It is just possible that Potter's predecessor, William Wake, is intended; he had written against Atterbury.⟩
    329. *Greater he looks, &c.* ⟨A ii 305⟩.

Nigrina black, and Merdamante brown,
Vy'd for his love in jetty bow'rs below,　　　　335
As Hylas fair was ravish'd long ago.
Then sung, how shown him by the Nut-brown maids
A branch of Styx here rises from the Shades,
That tinctur'd as it runs with Lethe's streams,
And wafting Vapours from the Land of dreams,　　　340
(As under seas Alphæus' secret sluice
Bears Pisa's off'rings to his Arethuse)
Pours into Thames: and hence the mingled wave
Intoxicates the pert, and lulls the grave:
Here brisker vapours o'er the Temple creep,　　　345
There, all from Paul's to Aldgate drink and sleep.

　　Thence to the banks where rev'rend Bards repose,
They led him soft; each rev'rend Bard arose;
And Milbourn chief, deputed by the rest,
· Gave him the cassock, surcingle, and vest.　　　350
"Receive (he said) these robes which once were mine,
"Dulness is sacred in a sound divine."
　　He ceas'd, and spread the robe; the crowd confess
The rev'rend Flamen in his lengthen'd dress.
Around him wide a sable Army stand,　　　355

347 rev'rend Bards repose] Bards departed doze *1743c, 1749.*

---

336. *As Hylas fair* ⟨A ii 312⟩.　　　338. *A branch of Styx, &c.* ⟨A ii 314⟩.
347. *Thence to the banks, &c.* ⟨A ii 321⟩.　　　349. *Milbourn* ⟨A ii 325⟩.

　　355. *Around him wide, &c.*] It is to be hoped that the satyr in these lines will be understood in the confined sense in which the Author meant it, of such only of the Clergy, who, tho' solemnly engaged in the service of Religion, dedicate themselves for venal and corrupt ends to that of Ministers or Factions; and tho' educated under an entire ignorance of the world, aspire to interfere in the government of it, and, consequently, to disturb and disorder it; in which they fall short only of their Predecessors, when invested with a larger share of power and authority, which they employed indifferently (as is hinted at in the lines above) either in supporting arbitrary power, or in exciting rebellion; in canonizing the vices of Tyrants, or in blackening the virtues of Patriots; in corrupting religion by superstition, or betraying it by libertinism, as either was thought best to serve the ends of Policy, or flatter the follies of the Great. W. ⟨In spite

A low-born, cell-bred, selfish, servile band,
Prompt or to guard or stab, to saint or damn,
Heav'n's Swiss, who fight for any God, or Man.
    Thro' Lud's fam'd gates, along the well-known Fleet
Rolls the black troop, and overshades the street,   360
'Till show'rs of Sermons, Characters, Essays,
In circling fleeces whiten all the ways:
So clouds replenish'd from some bog below,
Mount in dark volumes, and descend in snow.
Here stopt the Goddess; and in pomp proclaims   365
A gentler exercise to close the games.
    "Ye Critics! in whose heads, as equal scales,
"I weigh what author's heaviness prevails;
"Which most conduce to sooth the soul in slumbers,
"My H—ley's periods, or my Blackmore's numbers; 370
"Attend the trial we propose to make:
"If there be man, who o'er such works can wake,
"Sleep's all-subduing charms who dares defy,
"And boasts Ulysses' ear with Argus' eye;
"To him we grant our amplest pow'rs to sit   375
"Judge of all present, past, and future wit;
"To cavil, censure, dictate, right or wrong,
"Full and eternal privilege of tongue."
    Three College Sophs, and three pert Templars came,
The same their talents, and their tastes the same;   380

---

of Warburton's explanation, this passage gave offence to some of the clergy.
Cf. Pope to Warburton, Jan. 12, 1744.⟩

356. *cell-bred* ⟨i.e. bred in ignorance of the world⟩.

357. *to saint* ⟨to canonize, endow with saintly attributes⟩.

358. *Swiss* ⟨The Swiss mercenary soldiers were famous. "Swiss" is frequently
used in this period as a term of contempt for a hireling supporter, and Dryden
had already so used it of the clergy (*The Hind and the Panther*, iii 177: "Those
Swisses fight on any side for pay."). Pope seems to be thinking more particularly
here of the clerical journalists, such as Hoadly, Bland, Henley.⟩

359. *Lud's fam'd gates* ⟨A ii 332⟩.

364. *volumes* ⟨Pope probably means to play on the word.⟩

374. ⟨A ii 342⟩.

380, 381. *The same their talents, &c.* ⟨A ii 348⟩.

Each prompt to query, answer, and debate,
And smit with love of Poesy and Prate.
The pond'rous books two gentle readers bring;
The heroes sit, the vulgar form a ring.
The clam'rous crowd is hush'd with mugs of Mum,   385
'Till all tun'd equal, send a gen'ral hum.
Then mount the Clerks, and in one lazy tone
Thro' the long, heavy, painful page drawl on;
Soft creeping, words on words, the sense compose,
At ev'ry line they stretch, they yawn, they doze.   390
As to soft gales top-heavy pines bow low
Their heads, and lift them as they cease to blow:
Thus oft they rear, and oft the head decline,
As breathe, or pause, by fits, the airs divine.
And now to this side, now to that they nod,   395
As verse, or prose, infuse the drowzy God.
Thrice Budgel aim'd to speak, but thrice supprest
By potent Arthur, knock'd his chin and breast.
Toland and Tindal, prompt at priests to jeer,
Yet silent bow'd to Christ's No kingdom here.   400
Who sate the nearest, by the words o'ercome,
Slept first; the distant nodded to the hum.
Then down are roll'd the books; stretch'd o'er 'em lies
Each gentle clerk, and mutt'ring seals his eyes.
As what a Dutchman plumps into the lakes,   405

382. *And smit with love, &c.* ⟨A ii 350⟩.

384. *The heroes sit, &c.* ⟨A ii 352⟩.

388. *Thro' the long, heavy, painful page, &c.* ⟨A ii 356⟩.

397. *Thrice Budgel aim'd to speak* ⟨A ii 365⟩.

399. *Toland and Tindal*] Two persons, not so happy as to be obscure, who writ against the Religion of their Country. ⟨Cf. A ii 367.⟩

400. *Christ's No kingdom, &c.*] This is said by Curl, Key to Dunc. to allude to a sermon of a reverend Bishop. ⟨Cf. A ii 368.⟩

405. *As what a Dutchman, &c.*] It is a common and foolish mistake, that a ludicrous parody of a grave and celebrated passage is a ridicule of that passage. The reader therefore, if he will, may call this a parody of the author's own Similitude in the Essay on Man, Ep. iv. ⟨364 ff.⟩
          As the small pebble, &c.

One circle first, and then a second makes;
What Dulness dropt among her sons imprest
Like motion from one circle to the rest;
So from the mid-most the nutation spreads
Round and more round, o'er all the sea of heads.   410
At last Centlivre felt her voice to fail,
Motteux himself unfinish'd left his tale,
Boyer the State, and Law the Stage gave o'er,
Morgan and Mandevil could prate no more;
Norton, from Daniel and Ostrœa sprung,   415

---

but will any body therefore suspect the one to be a ridicule of the other? A ridicule indeed there is in every parody; but when the image is transferred from one subject to another, and the subject is not a *poem burlesqued* (which Scriblerus hopes the reader will distinguish from a *burlesque poem*) there the ridicule falls not on the thing *imitated*, but *imitating*. Thus, for instance, when

> Old Edward's armour beams on Cibber's breast ⟨Ep. ii i 319⟩,

it is, without doubt, an object ridiculous enough. But I think it falls neither on old king Edward, nor his armour, but on his *armour-bearer* only. Let this be said to explain our Author's Parodies (a figure that has always a good effect in a mock epic poem) either from profane or sacred writers. W. ⟨Warburton's note ignores the fact that the so-called parody of the simile in the *Essay on Man* had appeared in the *Dunciad* of 1728, long before the *Essay* was written.⟩

410. *O'er all the sea of heads* ⟨A ii 378⟩.

411. *Centlivre* ⟨A ii 379⟩.

413. *Boyer the State, and Law the Stage gave o'er* ⟨A ii 381⟩.

414. *Morgan*] A writer against Religion, distinguished no otherwise from the rabble of his tribe than by the pompousness of his Title; for having stolen his Morality from Tindal, and his Philosophy from Spinoza, he calls himself, by the courtesy of England, a *Moral Philosopher*. W. ⟨For Thomas Morgan, deist, author of *The Moral Philosopher*, see Biog. App.⟩

Ibid. *Mandevil*] This writer, who prided himself as much in the reputation of an *Immoral Philosopher*, was author of a famous book called the Fable of the Bees; which may seem written to prove, that Moral Virtue is the invention of knaves, and Christian Virtue the imposition of fools; and that Vice is necessary, and alone sufficient to render Society flourishing and happy. W. ⟨Bernard Mandeville (1670?—1733) published the first part of *The Fable of the Bees* in 1714, and a second part in 1729. Warburton does not attempt in this note to do justice to Mandeville's argument, viz. that "private vices are public benefits." It is significant that in his edition of 1751 the words "which may seem written to prove" become simply "written to prove".⟩

415. *Norton*] Norton De Foe . . . his name ⟨A ii 383⟩.

Bless'd with his father's front, and mother's tongue,
Hung silent down his never-blushing head;
And all was hush'd, as Folly's self lay dead.
    Thus the soft gifts of Sleep conclude the day,
And stretch'd on bulks, as usual, Poets lay.   420
Why should I sing what bards the nightly Muse
Did slumb'ring visit, and convey to stews;
Who prouder march'd, with magistrates in state,
To some fam'd round-house, ever open gate!
How Henley lay inspir'd beside a sink,   425
And to mere mortals seem'd a Priest in drink:
While others, timely, to the neighb'ring Fleet
(Haunt of the Muses) made their safe retreat.

418. *And all was hush'd, &c.* ⟨A ii 386⟩.
426. *And to mere mortals, &c.*] This line presents . . . to cause scandal."
SCRIBL. ⟨A ii 393⟩.
427. *Fleet* ⟨A ii· 395⟩.

The End of the SECOND BOOK

ARGUMENT

BOOK the THIRD

*After the other persons are disposed in their proper places of rest, the God-
dess transports the King to her Temple, and there lays him to slumber
with his head on her lap; a position of marvellous virtue, which causes
all the Visions of wild enthusiasts, projectors, politicians, inamoratos,
castle-builders, chemists, and poets. He is immediately carried on the* 5
wings of Fancy, and led by a mad Poetical Sibyl, to the Elysian shade;
where, on the banks of Lethe, *the souls of the dull are dipped by*
Bavius, *before their entrance into this world. There he is met by the
ghost of* Settle, *and by him made acquainted with the wonders of the
place, and with those which he himself is destined to perform. He takes* 10
him to a Mount of Vision, *from whence he shews him the past
triumphs of the Empire of Dulness, then the present, and lastly the
future: how small a part of the world was ever conquered by Science,
how soon those conquests were stopped, and those very nations again
reduced to her dominion. Then distinguishing the Island of* Great- 15
Britain, *shews by what aids, by what persons, and by what degrees it
shall be brought to her Empire. Some of the persons he causes to pass in
review before his eyes, describing each by his proper figure, character,
and qualifications. On a sudden the Scene shifts, and a vast number of
miracles and prodigies appear, utterly surprising and unknown to the* 20
*King himself, 'till they are explained to be the wonders of his own
reign now commencing. On this Subject* Settle *breaks into a congratulation, yet not unmixed with concern, that his own times were but
the types of these. He prophesies how first the nation shall be over-run
with* Farces, Operas, *and* Shows; *how the throne of Dulness shall be* 25
advanced over the Theatres, *and set up even at* Court: *then how her
Sons shall preside in the seats of* Arts *and* Sciences: *giving a glimpse,
or Pisgah-sight of the future Fulness of her Glory, the accomplishment
whereof is the subject of the fourth and last book.*

THE DUNCIAD

Book the Third

B‌UT in her Temple's last recess inclos'd,
On Dulness' lap th' Anointed head repos'd.
Him close she curtains round with Vapours blue,
And soft besprinkles with Cimmerian dew.
Then raptures high the seat of Sense o'erflow,   5
Which only heads refin'd from Reason know.
Hence, from the straw where Bedlam's Prophet nods,
He hears loud Oracles, and talks with Gods:
Hence the Fool's Paradise, the Statesman's Scheme,
The air-built Castle, and the golden Dream,   10
The Maid's romantic wish, the Chemist's flame,
And Poet's vision of eternal Fame.

    And now, on Fancy's easy wing convey'd,
The King descending, views th' Elysian Shade.
A slip-shod Sibyl led his steps along,   15

3 curtains] curtain'd *1743c, 1749.*
4 besprinkles] besprinkled *1743c, 1749.*

5, 6, &c. ⟨A iii 5, 6⟩.
How much the good Scriblerus was mistaken, may be seen from the Fourth
book, which, it is plain from hence, he had never seen. BENT.
7, 8. *Hence, from the straw, &c.* ⟨A iii 8⟩.
15. *A slip-shod Sibyl*] This allegory is extremely just, no conformation of the
mind so much subjecting it to real *Madness,* as that which produces real *Dulness.*
Hence we find the religious (as well as the poetical) Enthusiasts of all ages were
ever, in their natural state, most heavy and lumpish; but on the least application of *heat,* they run like lead, which of all metals falls quickest into fusion.
Whereas *fire* in a Genius is truly Promethean, it hurts not its constituent parts,
but only fits it (as it does well-tempered steel) for the necessary impressions of
art. But the common people have been taught (I do not know on what foundation) to regard Lunacy as a mark of *Wit,* just as the Turks and our modern
Methodists do of *Holiness.* But if the cause of Madness assigned by a great
Philosopher be true, it will unavoidably fall upon the dunces. He supposes it

In lofty madness meditating song;
Her tresses staring from Poetic dreams,
And never wash'd, but in Castalia's streams.
Taylor, their better Charon, lends an oar,
(Once swan of Thames, tho' now he sings no more.)   20
Benlowes, propitious still to blockheads, bows;
And Shadwell nods the Poppy on his brows.
Here, in a dusky vale where Lethe rolls,
Old Bavius sits, to dip poetic souls,
And blunt the sense, and fit it for a skull   25
Of solid proof, impenetrably dull:
Instant, when dipt, away they wing their flight,
Where Brown and Mears unbar the gates of Light,
Demand new bodies, and in Calf's array,
Rush to the world, impatient for the day.   30

⟨Locke, *An Essay concerning Humane Understanding*, Bk. ii, ch. xi, s. 13⟩ to be the *dwelling over long on one object or idea:* Now as this attention is occasioned either by Grief or Study, it will be fixed by Dulness; which hath not quickness enough to comprehend what it seeks, nor force and vigour enough to divert the imagination from the object it laments. W.

19. *Taylor* ⟨A ii 323⟩.

21. *Benlowes*] A country gentleman, famous for his own bad Poetry, and for patronizing bad Poets, as may be seen from many Dedications of Quarles and others to him. Some of these anagram'd his name, *Benlowes* into *Benevolus:* to verify which, he spent his whole estate upon them. ⟨Edward Benlowes (1602–76), author of *Theophila, or Love's Sacrifice* and other works. Anthony Wood records that he squandered his estate on "poets, flatterers (which he loved), in buying of curiosities (which some called baubles), on musicians, buffoons, etc." Quarles acknowledged his patronage in the Epistle to his *Emblemes* (1635). Pope may have taken a special interest in Benlowes because his niece had married Walter Blount of Mapledurham. For new light on Benlowes, see articles by C. Niemeyer and by H. Jenkins, *R.E.S.*, vol. xii, 1936, pp. 31 ff., 273 ff.⟩

22. *Shadwell* ⟨A ii 324⟩.

23. *Here in a dusky vale, &c.* ⟨A iii 15⟩.

24. *Old Bavius sits* ⟨A iii 16⟩.

24. *Old Bavius sits*] Bavius . . . the gentlemen of the Dunciad ⟨A iii 16⟩.

28. *unbar the gates of Light* ⟨A iii 20⟩.

28. *Brown and Mears*] Booksellers, Printers for any body.—The allegory . . . intelligible ⟨A iii 20⟩.

Millions and millions on these banks he views,
Thick as the stars of night, or morning dews,
As thick as bees o'er vernal blossoms fly,
As thick as eggs at Ward in Pillory.

Wond'ring he gaz'd: When lo! a Sage appears,   35
By his broad shoulders known, and length of ears,
Known by the band and suit which Settle wore
(His only suit) for twice three years before:
All as the vest, appear'd the wearer's frame,
Old in new state, another yet the same.   40
Bland and familiar as in life, begun
Thus the great Father to the greater Son.

"Oh born to see what none can see awake!
Behold the wonders of th' oblivious Lake.
Thou, yet unborn, hast touch'd this sacred shore;   45
The hand of Bavius drench'd thee o'er and o'er.
But blind to former as to future fate,
What mortal knows his pre-existent state?
Who knows how long thy transmigrating soul
Might from Bœotian to Bœotian roll?   50

31, 32. *Millions and millions—Thick as the stars, &c.* ⟨A iii 23⟩.

34. *Ward in Pillory* ⟨A iii 26⟩.

36. *and length of ears* ⟨A iii 28⟩.

37. *Settle*] Elkanah Settle was once a Writer in vogue, as well as Cibber, both for Dramatic Poetry and Politics. Mr. Dennis tells us that "he was a "formidable rival to Mr. Dryden, and that in the University of Cambridge "there were those who gave him the *preference*." Mr. Welsted goes yet farther in his behalf: "Poor Settle was formerly the *Mighty rival* of Dryden; nay, for "*many years*, bore his reputation *above* him." Pref. to his Poems, 8vo. p. 31. And Mr. Milbourn cried out, "How little was Dryden able, even when his "blood run high, to defend himself against Mr. Settle!" Notes on Dryd. Virg. p. 175. These are comfortable opinions! and no wonder some authors indulge them.

He was author or publisher . . . *Rem. on* Hom. ⟨A i 88⟩.

50. *Might from Bœotian, &c.*] Bœotia lay under the ridicule of the Wits formerly, as Ireland does now; tho' it produced one of the greatest Poets and one of the greatest Generals of Greece:

Bœotum crasso jurares aere natum.   Horat.

⟨*Ep.* ii i 244. For Pope's alteration of this note, cf. A i 23.⟩

How many Dutchmen she vouchsaf'd to thrid?
How many stages thro' old Monks she rid?
And all who since, in mild benighted days,
Mix'd the Owl's ivy with the Poet's bays?
As man's Mæanders to the vital spring   55
Roll all their tides, then back their circles bring;
Or whirligigs, twirl'd round by skilful swain,
Suck the thread in, then yield it out again:
All nonsense thus, of old or modern date,
Shall in thee centre, from thee circulate.   60
For this, our Queen unfolds to vision true
Thy mental eye, for thou hast much to view:
Old scenes of glory, times long cast behind
Shall, first recall'd, rush forward to thy mind:
Then stretch thy sight o'er all her rising reign,   65
And let the past and future fire thy brain.

     "Ascend this hill, whose cloudy point commands
Her boundless empire over seas and lands.
See, round the Poles where keener spangles shine,
Where spices smoke beneath the burning Line,   70
(Earth's wide extremes) her sable flag display'd,
And all the nations cover'd in her shade!
     "Far eastward cast thine eye, from whence the Sun
And orient Science their bright course begun:

61 this,] *Om. comma, 1743a.*   74 their bright] first their *1743c, 1749.*

---

54. *Mix'd the Owl's ivy* ⟨A iii 46⟩.

61, 62. *For this, our Queen, &c.* ⟨A iii 53⟩.

67. *Ascend this hill, &c.*] The scenes of this vision are remarkable for the order of their appearance. First, from ver. 67 to 73. those places of the globe are shewn where Science *never* rose; then from ver. 73 to 83, those where she was destroyed by *Tyranny*; from ver. 85 to 95, by inundations of *Barbarians*; from ver. 96 to 106, by *Superstition.* Then Rome, the Mistress of Arts, described in her degeneracy; and lastly Britain, the scene of the action of the poem; which furnishes the occasion of drawing out the Progeny of Dulness in review. W.

69. *See, round the Poles, &c.* ⟨A iii 61, 62⟩.

73. ⟨A iii 65⟩.

74. *their bright course* ⟨In a note to his 1751 edition Warburton accounts for

One god-like Monarch all that pride confounds,   75
He, whose long wall the wand'ring Tartar bounds;
Heav'ns! what a pile! whole ages perish there,
And one bright blaze turns Learning into air.
    "Thence to the south extend thy gladden'd eyes;
There rival flames with equal glory rise,   80
From shelves to shelves see greedy Vulcan roll,
And lick up all their Physic of the Soul.
    "How little, mark! that portion of the ball,
Where, faint at best, the beams of Science fall:
Soon as they dawn, from Hyperborean skies   85
Embody'd dark, what clouds of Vandals rise!
Lo! where Mæotis sleeps, and hardly flows
The freezing Tanais thro' a waste of snows,
The North by myriads pours her mighty sons,
Great nurse of Goths, of Alans, and of Huns!   90
See Alaric's stern port! the martial frame
Of Genseric! and Attila's dread name!
See the bold Ostrogoths on Latium fall;
See the fierce Visigoths on Spain and Gaul!
See, where the morning gilds the palmy shore   95
(The soil that arts and infant letters bore)
His conqu'ring tribes th' Arabian prophet draws,
And saving Ignorance enthrones by Laws.
See Christians, Jews, one heavy sabbath keep,
And all the western world believe and sleep.   100
    "Lo! Rome herself, proud mistress now no more
Of arts, but thund'ring against heathen lore;

---

the change from the earlier reading, "at a birth". "As this was thought to contradict that Line of the Introduction,

In eldest times e'er Mortals writ or read,

which supposes the sun and science did not set out together, it was alter'd to *their bright course begun.* But this slip, as usual, escaped the gentlemen of the Dunciad."⟩

75. ⟨A iii 69⟩.   81, 82. ⟨A iii 73, 74⟩.   96. ⟨A iii 88⟩.
102. *thund'ring against heathen lore* ⟨A iii 94⟩.

Her grey-hair'd Synods damning books unread,
And Bacon trembling for his brazen head.
Padua, with sighs, beholds her Livy burn,   105
And ev'n th' Antipodes Vigilius mourn.
See, the Cirque falls, th' unpillar'd Temple nods,
Streets pav'd with Heroes, Tyber choak'd with Gods:
'Till Peter's keys some christ'ned Jove adorn,
And Pan to Moses lends his pagan horn;   110
See graceless Venus to a Virgin turn'd,
Or Phidias broken, and Apelles burn'd.
      "Behold yon' Isle, by Palmers, Pilgrims trod,
Men bearded, bald, cowl'd, uncowl'd, shod, unshod,
Peel'd, patch'd, and pyebald, linsey-wolsey brothers, 115
Grave Mummers! sleeveless some, and shirtless others.
That once was Britain—Happy! had she seen
No fiercer sons, had Easter never been.
In peace, great Goddess, ever be ador'd;
How keen the war, if Dulness draw the sword!   120
Thus visit not thy own! on this blest age
Oh spread thy Influence, but restrain thy Rage.
      "And see, my son! the hour is on its way,
That lifts our Goddess to imperial sway;
This fav'rite Isle, long sever'd from her reign,   125
Dove-like, she gathers to her wings again.
Now look thro' Fate! behold the scene she draws!
What aids, what armies to assert her cause!
See all her progeny, illustrious sight!

---

109. *'Till Peter's keys, &c.* ⟨A iii 101⟩.

117, 118. *Happy!—had Easter never been!* ⟨A iii 110⟩.

126. *Dove-like, she gathers*] This is fulfilled in the fourth book.

127, 129. *Now look thro' Fate! &c.* ⟨A iii 119⟩.

128. *What aids, what armies, &c.*] i.e. Of Poets, Antiquaries, Critics, Divines, Free-thinkers. But as this Revolution is only here set on foot by the first of these Classes, the Poets, they only are here particularly celebrated, and they only properly fall under the Care and Review of this Collegue of Dulness, the Laureate. The others, who finish the great work, are reserved for the fourth book, when the Goddess herself appears in full Glory. W.

Behold, and count them, as they rise to light.   130
As Berecynthia, while her offspring vye
In homage to the Mother of the sky,
Surveys around her, in the blest abode,
An hundred sons, and ev'ry son a God:
Not with less glory mighty Dulness crown'd,   135
Shall take thro' Grub-street her triumphant round;
And her Parnassus glancing o'er at once,
Behold an hundred sons, and each a Dunce.
    "Mark first that Youth who takes the foremost place,
And thrusts his person full into your face.   140
With all thy Father's virtues blest, be born!
And a new Cibber shall the stage adorn.
    "A second see, by meeker manners known,
And modest as the maid that sips alone;
From the strong fate of drams if thou get free,   145
Another Durfey, Ward! shall sing in thee.
Thee shall each ale-house, thee each gill-house mourn,

---

131. *As Berecynthia, &c.* ⟨A iii 123⟩.
139. *Mark first that Youth, &c.* ⟨A iii 131⟩.
141. *With all thy Father's virtues, &c.*] A manner of expression . . . Ecl. iv.
⟨A iii 133⟩.
It was very natural to shew to the Hero, before all others, his own Son, who
had already begun to emulate him in his theatrical, poetical, and even political
capacities. By the attitude in which he here presents himself, the reader may be
cautioned against ascribing wholly to the Father the merit of the epithet
Cibberian, which is equally to be understood with an eye to the Son. ⟨In remarking on T. Cibber's "political capacities," Pope may have in mind "A
Letter from T—ph—s C—r, at —, to Mr. POPE, at Twickenham," which
appeared in *The Universal Spectator*, Oct. 16, 1742. Here Cibber remarks, or is
made to remark: "I could not, by defending Sir *R— W— totis viribus*, offend
the little Bard; unless—he was an Enemy to the *Government*."⟩
141–2. *With all thy Father's virtues blest, &c.* ⟨Since they first appeared in 1728
these lines had taken on a more unpleasant significance for old Cibber. Theophilus had in 1738 become notorious through an unsuccessful attempt to
enrich himself by the adultery of his wife, Susanna Maria Cibber, which he
himself had encouraged.—See Barker, pp. 184 ff.⟩
145. *From the strong fate of drams* ⟨A iii 137⟩.
147. *Thee shall each ale-house, &c.* ⟨A iii 139⟩.

And answ'ring gin-shops sowrer sighs return.
   "Jacob, the scourge of Grammar, mark with awe,
Nor less revere him, blunderbuss of Law.   150
Lo P‑‑p‑‑le's brow, tremendous to the town,
Horneck's fierce eye, and Roome's funereal Frown.
Lo sneering Goode, half malice and half whim,
A Fiend in glee, ridiculously grim.
Each Cygnet sweet of Bath and Tunbridge race,   155
Whose tuneful whistling makes the waters pass:

151 P‑‑p‑‑le's] P—le's *1743c, 1749*.

---

149. *Jacob* ⟨A iii 149⟩.

149, 150. There may seem some error . . . Charity. ⟨As in "Errata," p. 199.⟩

150. ⟨A iii 150⟩.

152. *Horneck and Roome*] These two were virulent Party-writers, worthily coupled together, and one would think prophetically, since, after the publishing of this piece, the former dying, the latter succeeded him in *Honour* and *Employment*. The first was Philip Horneck, Author of a Billingsgate paper call'd The High German Doctor. Edward Roome was son of an Undertaker for Funerals in Fleetstreet, and writ some of the papers call'd Pasquin, where by malicious Innuendos he endeavoured to represent our Author guilty of malevolent practices with a great man then under prosecution of Parliament. P—le was the author of some vile Plays and Pamphlets. He published abuses on our author in a Paper called the Prompter. ⟨Cf. A iii 146. For William Popple and *The Prompter*, see Biog. App.⟩

153. *Goode* ⟨A iii 147⟩.

155–6. *Each Cygnet sweet, &c.* ⟨E. Young, *The Universal Passion*, Sat. i 279–80:

> At Bath, in summer, chants the reigning lass,
> And sweetly whistles as the waters pass.

                         —Warton.⟩

156. *Whose tuneful whistling makes the waters pass*] There were several successions of these sort of minor poets, at Tunbridge, Bath, &c. singing the praise of the Annuals flourishing for that season; whose names indeed would be nameless, and therefore the Poet slurs them over with others in general. ⟨*Tunbrigalia. Or The Tunbridge Miscellany, For the Years 1737, 1738, 1739* was published in 1740. On pp. 17–19 the profane "Parody on the 4th Chapter of Genesis," a lampoon on Pope which he attributed to Roome, was reprinted. There was a *Bath Miscellany, For the Year 1740*, in the preface to which the publisher stated that it was his aim "to convince *Pope* and *Swift* that there are more poets in England than themselves."⟩

Each Songster, Riddler, ev'ry nameless name,
All crowd, who foremost shall be damn'd to Fame.
Some strain in rhyme; the Muses, on their racks,
Scream like the winding of ten thousand jacks: 160
Some free from rhyme or reason, rule or check,
Break Priscian's head, and Pegasus's neck;
Down, down they larum, with impetuous whirl,
The Pindars, and the Miltons of a Curl.

  "Silence, ye Wolves! while Ralph to Cynthia howls, 165
And makes Night hideous—Answer him, ye Owls!

  "Sense, speech, and measure, living tongues and dead,
Let all give way—and Morris may be read.

  "Flow Welsted, flow! like thine inspirer, Beer,
Tho' stale, not ripe; tho' thin, yet never clear;   170
So sweetly mawkish, and so smoothly dull;
Heady, not strong; o'erflowing, tho' not full.

  "Ah Dennis! Gildon ah! what ill-starr'd rage
Divides a friendship long confirm'd by age?

157 Each . . . Riddler,] Ænigma Bard, and *1743c, 1749*.

---

  157. *Riddler* ⟨Poetical riddles, of the kind found in Anglo-Saxon poetry, were an occasional feature of the Miscellanies.⟩

  165. *Ralph*] James Ralph . . . Sept. 1728 ⟨A iii 159⟩. He ended at last . . . a small pittance for pay ⟨A iii 159⟩.

  168. *Morris*] *Besaleel*, see Book 2 ⟨126⟩.

  169. *Flow Welsted, flow! &c.* ⟨A iii 163⟩.

  169. *Flow* Welsted, *&c.*] Of this Author . . . *pag*. 23, 24 ⟨A iii 163⟩. It should not be forgot to his honour, that he received at one time the sum of 500 pounds for secret service, among the other excellent authors hired to write anonymously for the Ministry. See Report of the Secret Committee, &c. in 1742. ⟨"But this gentleman some years afterwards declared to Mr. Walthoe, an alderman of St. Albans, 'that he received it for Sir Richard Steele, and paid it to him'; a declaration which is now abundantly confirmed by the unsuspicious testimony of Steele himself."—*The Works of Leonard Welsted*, ed. John Nichols, 1787, p. xxii *n*. See also *The Correspondence of Richard Steele*, ed. Rae Blanchard, 1941, pp. 310–11.⟩

  173. *Ah Dennis, &c.*] The reader . . . at this time ⟨A iii 167⟩. By his own account of himself in Mr. *Jacob's Lives*, he must have been above threescore, and happily lived many years after. So that he was senior to Mr. *Durfey*, who hitherto of all our Poets enjoy'd the longest Bodily life. ⟨Cf. A ii 273*n*.⟩

Blockheads with reason wicked wits abhor,   175
But fool with fool is barb'rous civil war.
Embrace, embrace my sons! be foes no more!
Nor glad vile Poets with true Critic's gore.
  "Behold yon Pair, in strict embraces join'd;
How like in manners, and how like in mind!   180
Equal in wit, and equally polite,
Shall this a Pasquin, that a Grumbler write;
Like are their merits, like rewards they share,
That shines a consul, this Commissioner."
  "But who is he, in closet close y-pent,   185
Of sober face, with learned dust besprent?"
"Right well mine eyes arede the myster wight,
On parchment scraps y-fed, and Wormius hight.
To future ages may thy dulness last,
As thou preserv'st the dulness of the past!   190
  "There, dim in clouds, the poring Scholiasts mark,
Wits, who like owls, see only in the dark,
A Lumberhouse of books in ev'ry head,
For ever reading, never to be read!
  "But, where each Science lifts its modern type,   195

177. *Embrace, embrace my sons!* ⟨A iii 171⟩.
179. *Behold yon Pair, &c.* ⟨A iii 173⟩.
179. *Behold yon Pair, &c.*] One of these . . . 1715 ⟨A iii 175⟩.
Of the other works of these Gentlemen the world has heard no more, than
it would of Mr. *Pope*'s, had their united laudable endeavours discourag'd him
from pursuing his studies . . . Cradle? C. ⟨A iii 175⟩.
After many Editions of this poem, the Author thought fit to omit the names
of these two persons, whose injury to him was of so old a date. In the verses he
omitted, it was said that one of them had a *pious passion* for the other. It was a
literal translation of *Virgil*, *Nisus amore pio pueri*—and there, as in the original,
applied to Friendship: That between *Nisus* . . . Gentleman together ⟨A iii 176⟩.
184. *That shines a* Consul, *this* Commissioner] Such places were given at this
time to such sort of Writers.
185. *But who is he, &c.* ⟨A iii 181⟩.   187. *arede* ⟨A iii 183⟩.
Ibid. *myster wight* ⟨A iii 183⟩.   188. Wormius *hight* ⟨A iii 184⟩.
188. *hight* ⟨A iii 184⟩.
192. *Wits, who, like owls, &c.* ⟨A iii 188⟩.

Hist'ry her Pot, Divinity his Pipe,
While proud Philosophy repines to show,
Dishonest sight! his breeches rent below;
Imbrown'd with native bronze, lo! Henley stands,
Tuning his voice, and balancing his hands.   200
How fluent nonsense trickles from his tongue!
How sweet the periods, neither said, nor sung!
Still break the benches, Henley! with thy strain,
While Sherlock, Hare, and Gibson preach in vain.
Oh great Restorer of the good old Stage,   205
Preacher at once, and Zany of thy age!
Oh worthy thou of Ægypt's wise abodes,
A decent priest, where monkeys were the gods!
But fate with butchers plac'd thy priestly stall,
Meek modern faith to murder, hack, and mawl;   210
And bade thee live, to crown Britannia's praise,
In Toland's, Tindal's, and in Woolston's days.
    "Yet oh, my sons! a father's words attend:

196 his Pipe] her Pipe *1743a–51*. [Cf. A iii 192.]
204 Sherlock] Kennet *1743c, 1749*.

196. *his Pipe* ⟨The change in *1743a* to "her Pipe" is almost certainly a printer's error.⟩

199. *lo! Henley stands, &c.*] J. Henley the Orator . . . FACIAM ⟨A iii 195⟩. This man had an hundred pounds a year given him for the secret service of a weekly paper of unintelligible nonsense, called the Hyp-Doctor. ⟨It appeared weekly from Dec. 15, 1730 to January(?) 1741.⟩

204. *Sherlock, Hare, Gibson*] Bishops of Salisbury, Chichester, and London. ⟨To this Warburton added in *1751*, "whose Sermons and Pastoral Letters did honour to their country as well as stations." It is by no means certain, however, that Pope intended his line to be a panegyric. Cf. A iii 200*n*. For Sherlock, see B ii 323*n*., and Biog. App. For Francis Hare, Bishop of Chichester, and Edmund Gibson, Bishop of London, see Biog. App., vol. iv.⟩

212. ⟨A iii 208⟩.

213. *Yet oh, my sons! &c.*] The caution against Blasphemy here given by a departed Son of Dulness to his yet existing brethren, is, as the Poet rightly intimates, not out of tenderness to the ears of others, but their own. And so we see that when that danger is removed, on the open establishment of the Goddess in the fourth book, she encourages her sons, and they beg assistance

(So may the fates preserve the ears you lend)
'Tis yours, a Bacon or a Locke to blame,　　　　　215
A Newton's genius, or a Milton's flame:
But oh! with One, immortal one dispense,
The source of Newton's Light, of Bacon's Sense!
Content, each Emanation of his fires
That beams on earth, each Virtue he inspires,　　　220
Each Art he prompts, each Charm he can create,
Whate'er he gives, are giv'n for you to hate.
Persist, by all divine in Man unaw'd,
But, 'Learn, ye D U N C E S ! not to scorn your G o D.' "
　　　Thus he, for then a ray of Reason stole　　　225
Half thro' the solid darkness of his soul;
But soon the cloud return'd—and thus the Sire:
"See now, what Dulness and her sons admire!
See what the charms, that smite the simple heart
Not touch'd by Nature, and not reach'd by Art."　　230
　　　His never-blushing head he turn'd aside,
(Not half so pleas'd when Goodman prophesy'd)
And look'd, and saw a sable Sorc'rer rise,
Swift to whose hand a winged volume flies:
All sudden, Gorgons hiss, and Dragons glare,　　　235

to pollute the Source of Light itself, with the same virulence they had before
done the purest emanations from it. W.

224. *But, "Learn, ye Dunces! not to scorn your God"* ⟨A iii 222⟩.

Ibid. *"not to scorn your God"*] See this subject pursued in Book 4.

226. *the solid darkness* ⟨Cowley, *Davideis,* i 85–6:
　　　　　　　　. . . the Sun's lovely face,
　　　　　Strikes through the Solid darkness of the place.⟩

　232. (*Not half so pleas'd when Goodman prophesy'd*)] Mr. Cibber tells us, in his
Life, p. 149. that Goodman being at the rehearsal of a play, in which he had a
part, clapped him on the shoulder, and cried, "If he does not make a good
"actor, I'll be d—d—" "And (says Mr. Cibber) I make it a question, whether
"Alexander himself, or Charles the twelfth of Sweden, when at the head of their
"first victorious armies, could feel a greater transport in their bosoms than I
"did in mine."

　233. *a sable Sorc'rer* ⟨A iii 229. For "the years 1726, 27," *1743* has "some
years."⟩

And ten-horn'd fiends and Giants rush to war.
Hell rises, Heav'n descends, and dance on Earth:
Gods, imps, and monsters, music, rage, and mirth,
A fire, a jigg, a battle, and a ball,
'Till one wide conflagration swallows all.   240
    Thence a new world to Nature's laws unknown,
Breaks out refulgent, with a heav'n its own:
Another Cynthia her new journey runs,
And other planets circle other suns.
The forests dance, the rivers upward rise,   245
Whales sport in woods, and dolphins in the skies;
And last, to give the whole creation grace,
Lo! one vast Egg produces human race.
    Joy fills his soul, joy innocent of thought;
"What pow'r, he cries, what pow'r these wonders   250
      wrought?"
"Son; what thou seek'st is in thee! Look, and find
Each Monster meets his likeness in thy mind.
Yet would'st thou more? In yonder cloud behold,
Whose sarsenet skirts are edg'd with flamy gold,
A matchless Youth! his nod these worlds controuls,   255
Wings the red lightning, and the thunder rolls.
Angel of Dulness, sent to scatter round
Her magic charms o'er all unclassic ground:
Yon stars, yon suns, he rears at pleasure higher,
Illumes their light, and sets their flames on fire.   260
Immortal Rich! how calm he sits at ease
'Mid snows of paper, and fierce hail of pease;

---

237. *Hell rises, &c.* ⟨A iii 233⟩.
244. *And other planets* ⟨A iii 240⟩.
246. *Whales sport in woods, &c.* ⟨A iii 242⟩.
248. *Lo! one vast Egg* ⟨A iii 244⟩.
251. *Son; what thou seek'st, &c.* ⟨A iii 247⟩.
256. *Wings the red light'ning, &c.* ⟨A iii 252⟩.
258. *—o'er all unclassic ground* ⟨A iii 254⟩.
261. *Immortal Rich!* ⟨A iii 257⟩.

And proud his Mistress' orders to perform,
Rides in the whirlwind, and directs the storm.
    "But lo! to dark encounter in mid air   265
New wizards rise; I see my Cibber there!
Booth in his cloudy tabernacle shrin'd,
On grinning dragons thou shalt mount the wind.
Dire is the conflict, dismal is the din,
Here shouts all Drury, there all Lincoln's-inn;   270
Contending Theatres our empire raise,
Alike their labours, and alike their praise.
    "And are these wonders, Son, to thee unknown?
Unknown to thee? These wonders are thy own.
These Fate reserv'd to grace thy reign divine,   275
Foreseen by me, but ah! with-held from mine.
In Lud's old walls tho' long I rul'd, renown'd
Far as loud Bow's stupendous bells resound;
Tho' my own Aldermen confer'd the bays,
To me committing their eternal praise,   280

---

266. *I see my Cibber there!*] The history of the foregoing absurdities is verified
by himself, in these words (Life, chap. xv.) "Then sprung forth that succession
"of monstrous medleys that have so long infested the stage, which arose upon
"one another alternately at both houses, out-vying each other in expence."
He then proceeds to excuse his own part in them, as follows: "If I am asked
"why I assented? I have no better excuse for my error than to confess I did it
"against my conscience, and had not virtue enough to starve. ⟨Cibber adds:
"by opposing a Multitude, that would have been too hard for me."⟩ Had
"Henry IV. of France a better for changing his Religion? I was still in my
"heart, as much as he could be, on the side of Truth and Sense; but with this
"difference, that I had their leave to quit them when they could not support
"me.—But let the question go which way it will, Harry IVth has *always been*
"*allowed a great man*" ⟨pp. 423–4⟩. This must be confest a full answer, only the
question still seems to be, 1. How the doing a thing against one's conscience is
an excuse for it? and, 2dly, It will be hard to prove how he got the leave of
Truth and Sense to quit their service, unless he can produce a Certificate that
he ever was in it.

266, 267. *Booth* and *Cibber* were joint managers of the Theatre in Drury-lane.

268. *On grinning dragons, &c.*] In his Letter to Mr. P. ⟨p. 37⟩ Mr. C. solemnly
declares this not to be *literally true*. We hope therefore the reader will understand it *allegorically* only.

Their full-fed Heroes, their pacific May'rs,
Their annual trophies, and their monthly wars:
Tho' long my Party built on me their hopes,
For writing Pamphlets, and for roasting Popes;
Yet lo! in me what authors have to brag on!   285
Reduc'd at last to hiss in my own dragon.
Avert it Heav'n! that thou, my Cibber, e'er
Should'st wag a serpent-tail in Smithfield fair!
Like the vile straw that's blown about the streets,
The needy Poet sticks to all he meets,   290
Coach'd, carted, trod upon, now loose, now fast,
And carry'd off in some Dog's tail at last.
Happier thy fortunes! like a rolling stone,
Thy giddy dulness still shall lumber on,
Safe in its heaviness, shall never stray,   295
But lick up ev'ry blockhead in the way.
Thee shall the Patriot, thee the Courtier taste,
And ev'ry year be duller than the last.
'Till rais'd from booths, to Theatre, to Court,
Her seat imperial Dulness shall transport.   300
Already Opera prepares the way,
The sure fore-runner of her gentle sway:
Let her thy heart, next Drabs and Dice, engage,
The third mad passion of thy doting age.
Teach thou the warb'ling Polypheme to roar,   305

295 shall] can *1743c, 1749*.   296 But lick] And licks *1743c, 1749*.

282. ⟨A iii 280⟩.   283. *Tho' long my Party* ⟨A iii 281⟩.

297. *Thee shall the Patriot, &c.* ⟨A iii 299⟩.

302. *the sure fore-runner* ⟨The wits had been complaining of the effect of Opera on public taste since the beginning of the century. In the epilogue to *Tamerlane* (1702), Rowe had written anxiously of the effect upon tragedy of "Harmony with Beauty join'd"; and in the prologue to *The Royal Convert* (1707) he had told his audience that their taste was rapidly degenerating:

> Now Fidling, and the Charms of Sing-Song, win ye;
> Harmonious *Peg*, and warbling *Valentini*.⟩

305. *Polypheme*] He translated the Italian Opera of Polifemo; but unfortunately lost the whole jest of the story. The Cyclops asks Ulysses his *name*, who tells him his name is *Noman:* After his eye is put out, he roars and calls the Brother

And scream thyself as none e'er scream'd before!
To aid our cause, if Heav'n thou can'st not bend,
Hell thou shalt move; for Faustus is our friend:
Pluto with Cato thou for this shalt join,
And link the Mourning Bride to Proserpine.   310
Grubstreet! thy fall should men and Gods conspire,
Thy stage shall stand, ensure it but from Fire.
Another Æschylus appears! prepare
For new abortions, all ye pregnant fair!
In flames, like Semele's, be brought to bed,   315
While op'ning Hell spouts wild-fire at your head.
  "Now Bavius take the poppy from thy brow,
And place it here! here all ye Heroes bow!
This, this is he, foretold by ancient rhymes:
Th' Augustus born to bring Saturnian times.   320
Signs following signs lead on the mighty year!
See! the dull stars roll round and re-appear.
See, see, our own true Phœbus wears the bays!
Our Midas sits Lord Chancellor of Plays!

Cyclops to his aid: They enquire *who has hurt him?* he answers *Noman*; where-upon they all go away again. Our ingenious Translator made Ulysses answer, *I take no name*, whereby all that follow'd became unintelligible. Hence it appears that Mr. Cibber (who values himself on subscribing to the English Translation of Homer's Iliad) had not that merit with respect to the Odyssey, or he might have been better instructed in the Greek *Pun-nology*. ⟨For further details of Cibber's blunder, see Barker, p. 176. *Polifemo*, a melodrama by Rolli, was published in 1735 in Italian and English.—For the allusion to the *Iliad* in Pope's note, see *Letter to Pope*, pp. 24–5.⟩

306. *And scream thyself* ⟨Cibber's voice was a frequent subject of jest.—". . . his voice was rather shrill than loud or articulate, and crack'd extremely, when he endeavour'd to raise it."—*The Laureat*, 1740, p. 103. Cf. also *The Prompter*, No. 3, Nov. 19, 1734, where his voice is compared with that of a suffering pig.⟩

308, 309. *Faustus, Pluto, &c.*] Names of miserable Farces which . . . audience ⟨A iii 307⟩.

312. *ensure it but from Fire* ⟨A iii 310⟩.

313. *Another Æschylus appears!*] It is reported . . . miscarried ⟨A iii 311⟩.

315. *like Semele's* ⟨A iii 313⟩.   319, 320. *This, this is he, &c.* ⟨A iii 317⟩.

323. *Phœbus* ⟨See iv 61*n.*, 93*n.*⟩

324. *Midas* ⟨i.e. Cibber is as bad a judge of poetry as Midas, who, called

13*

On Poets' Tombs see Benson's titles writ!   325
Lo! Ambrose Philips is prefer'd for Wit!
See under Ripley rise a new White-hall,
While Jones' and Boyle's united labours fall:
While Wren with sorrow to the grave descends,
Gay dies unpension'd with a hundred friends,   330
Hibernian Politics, O Swift! thy fate;
And Pope's, ten years to comment and translate.
    "Proceed, great days! 'till Learning fly the shore,
'Till Birch shall blush with noble blood no more,
'Till Thames see Eaton's sons for ever play,   335
'Till Westminster's whole year be holiday,
'Till Isis' Elders reel, their pupils' sport,
And Alma mater lie dissolv'd in Port!"
    "Enough! enough!" the raptur'd Monarch cries;
And thro' the Iv'ry Gate the Vision flies.   340

upon to judge between Apollo and Pan, awarded the prize to Pan. There may
be a secondary suggestion that Cibber was coining money for himself from the
theatre.⟩

325. *Benson's titles writ* ⟨A iii 321.—Benson's connection with "Poets'
Tombs" is explained in the note to iv 110. See also Biog. App.⟩

326. *Ambrose Philips*] He was (saith Mr. JACOB) ... *enjoys"* ⟨A iii 322⟩. He
endeavour'd ... of it ⟨A iii 322⟩.

327. *Ripley* ⟨For Thomas Ripley, architect (d. 1758), see Biog. App., vol. iv.—
By "a new White-hall" Pope probably means the Admiralty building which
was going up in 1724–6.⟩

328. *Jones' and Boyle's united labours* ⟨A iii 324⟩.

330. *Gay dies unpension'd, &c.* ⟨A iii 326⟩.

331. *Hibernian Politics*] See book i. ver. 26.

332. *And Pope's ... to comment and translate* ⟨A iii 328n. For the change from
the text of 1729, see also Biog. App., Broome.⟩

333. *Proceed, great days! &c.*] It may perhaps seem incredible, that so great a
Revolution in Learning as is here prophesied, should be brought about by such
weak Instruments as have been [hitherto] described in our poem: But do not thou,
gentle reader, rest too secure in thy contempt of these Instruments. Remember
what the Dutch stories ... SCRIBL. ⟨A iii 337⟩.

340. *And thro' the Iv'ry Gate, &c.* ⟨A iii 358⟩.

The End of the THIRD BOOK

THE DUNCIAD

A R G U M E N T[1]

The Poet being, in this Book, to declare the Completion *of the* Prophecies *mention'd at the end of the former, makes a new* Invocation;
*as the greater Poets are wont, when some high and worthy matter is to
be sung. He shews the Goddess coming in her Majesty, to destroy*
Order *and* Science, *and to substitute the* Kingdom of the Dull   5
upon earth. How she leads captive the Sciences, *and silenceth the*
Muses; *and* what *they be who succeed in their stead. All her Children,
by a wonderful attraction, are drawn about her; and bear along with
them divers others, who promote her Empire by connivance, weak re-
sistance, or discouragement of Arts; such as Half-wits, tasteless Ad-*   10
*mirers, vain Pretenders, the Flatterers of Dunces, or the Patrons of
them. All these crowd round her; one of them offering to approach her,
is driven back by a Rival, but she commends and encourages both. The
first who speak in form are the* Genius's *of the* Schools, *who assure
her of their care to advance her Cause, by confining Youth to* Words,   15
*and keeping them out of the way of real Knowledge. Their Address,
and her gracious Answer; with her Charge to them and the Universities.
The* Universities *appear by their proper Deputies, and assure her
that the same method is observ'd in the progress of* Education; *The
speech of* Aristarchus *on this subject. They are driven off by a band of*   20
young Gentlemen return'd from Travel *with their* Tutors; *one of
whom delivers to the Goddess, in a polite oration, an account of the
whole Conduct and Fruits of their* Travels: *presenting to her at the
same time a young Nobleman perfectly accomplished. She receives him
graciously, and indues him with the happy quality of* Want of Shame.   25
She sees loitering about her a number of Indolent Persons *abandon-
ing all business and duty, and dying with laziness: To these approaches*

9 *them*] them also *1742a.*   27 *these*] whom *1742a.*

---

1. Collated with *1742a.*

337

the Antiquary Annius, *intreating her to make them* Virtuosos, *and assign them over to him: But* Mummius, *another Antiquary, complaining of his fraudulent proceeding, she finds a method to reconcile their difference. Then enter a Troop of people fantastically adorn'd, offering her strange and exotic presents: Amongst them, one stands forth and demands justice on another, who had deprived him of one of*   5 *the greatest Curiosities in nature: but he justifies himself so well, that the Goddess gives them both her approbation. She recommends to them to find proper employment for the* Indolents *before-mentioned, in the study of* Butterflies, Shells, Birds-nests, Moss, *&c. but with particular caution, not to proceed beyond* Trifles, *to any useful or* 10 *extensive views of Nature, or of the Author of Nature. Against the last of these apprehensions, she is secured by a hearty Address from the* Minute Philosophers *and* Freethinkers, *one of whom speaks in the name of the rest. The Youth thus instructed and principled, are delivered to her in a body, by the hands of* Silenus; *and then admitted* 15 *to taste the Cup of the* Magus *her High Priest, which causes a total oblivion of all Obligations, divine, civil, moral, or rational. To these her Adepts she sends* Priests, Attendants, *and* Comforters, *of various kinds; confers on them* Orders *and* Degrees; *and then dismissing them with a speech, confirming to each his* Privileges *and tell-* 20 *ing what she expects from each, concludes with a* Yawn *of extraordinary virtue: The Progress and Effects whereof on all Orders of men, and the Consummation of all, in the Restoration of* Night *and* Chaos, *conclude the Poem.*

---

19 *confers*] then confers *1742a*.

19–24 *and then dismissing . . . Poem.*] and finally dismissing them with a speech, confirms to each his *Privileges*, warns *One* in particular not to exceed them, and concludes with a *Yawn* of extraordinary virtue, the effects of which are not unfelt at this day. *1742a*.

THE DUNCIAD

Book the Fourth

Yet, yet a moment, one dim Ray of Light
Indulge, dread Chaos, and eternal Night!
Of darkness visible so much be lent,
As half to shew, half veil the deep Intent.
Ye Pow'rs! whose Mysteries restor'd I sing,   5
To whom Time bears me on his rapid wing,

The Dunciad, Book IV.] This Book may properly be distinguished from
the former, by the Name of the Greater Dunciad, not so indeed in Size,
but in Subject; and so far contrary to the distinction anciently made of the
Greater and *Lesser Iliad*. But much are they mistaken who imagine this Work
in any wise inferior to the former, or of any other hand than of our Poet; of
which I am much more certain than that the *Iliad* itself was the Work of
Solomon, or the *Batrachomuomachia* of *Homer*, as *Barnes* hath affirmed. Bent. P.W.
⟨Joshua Barnes, 1654–1712, editor of Homer. In *1742* this note was given to
Scriblerus, and the following sentence added: "Nor is it imperfect or incorrect,
save in some few places, which we shall remark."⟩

1, &c.] This is an Invocation of much Piety. The Poet willing to approve
himself a genuine Son, beginneth by shewing (what is ever agreeable to *Dulness*)
his high respect for *Antiquity* and a *Great Family*, how dull, or dark soever:
Next declareth his love for *Mystery* and *Obscurity*; and lastly his Impatience to
be *re-united* to her. Scribl. P.W. ⟨The allusion in "a Great Family" seems to
be to the custom among poets of dedicating their works to noble patrons.⟩

2. *dread Chaos, and eternal Night!*] Invoked, as the Restoration of their Empire
is the Action of the Poem. P.W.

3. *Of darkness visible* ⟨Cf. *Paradise Lost*, i 63.⟩

4. *half to shew, half veil*] This is a great propriety, for a dull Poet can never
express himself otherwise than by *halves*, or imperfectly. Scribl. P.W.

I understand it very differently; the Author in this work had indeed a *deep
Intent*; there were in it *Mysteries* or ἀπόρρητα which he durst not fully reveal, and
doubtless in divers verses (according to *Milton*)

—— *more is meant than meets the ear* ⟨*Il Penseroso*, l. 120⟩.

Bent. P.W.

6. *To whom Time bears me*] Fair and softly, good Poet! (cries the gentle
Scriblerus on this place.) For sure in spite of his unusual modesty, he shall not
travel so fast toward Oblivion, as divers others of more Confidence have done:
For when I revolve in my mind the Catalogue of those who have the most

> Suspend a while your Force inertly strong,
> Then take at once the Poet and the Song.
>   Now flam'd the Dog-star's unpropitious ray,
> Smote ev'ry Brain, and wither'd ev'ry Bay;   10
> Sick was the Sun, the Owl forsook his bow'r,
> The moon-struck Prophet felt the madding hour:
> Then rose the Seed of Chaos, and of Night,
> To blot out Order, and extinguish Light,

9 Now flam'd] 'Twas when *1742a–f, 1743b.*

---

boldly promised to themselves Immortality, *viz. Pindar, Luis Gongora, Ronsard, Oldham,* Lyrics; *Lycophron, Statius,* ⟨*Camoens,—1742*⟩ *Chapman, Blackmore,* Heroics; I find the one half to be already dead, and the other in utter darkness. But it becometh not us, who have taken upon us the office of Commentator, to suffer our Poet thus prodigally to cast away his Life; contrariwise, the more hidden and abstruse is his work, and the more remote its beauties from common Understanding, the more is it our duty to draw forth and exalt the same, in the face of Men and Angels. Herein shall we imitate the laudable Spirit of those, who have (for this very reason) delighted to comment on the Fragments of *dark* and *uncouth* Authors, preferred *Ennius* to *Virgil,* and chosen to turn the dark Lanthorn of *Lycophron,* rather than to trim the everlasting Lamp of *Homer* ⟨chosen to give light to *Lycophron,* rather than to hold a candle to *Homer.— 1742.*⟩. SCRIBL. P.W.

⟨The pointed reference to Lycophron is presumably a thrust at Archbishop Potter, whose edition of Lycophron appeared in 1697. But the note has a more general application to scholars like Bentley, whose annotations extended to such obscure works as Nicander's medical epic, *Theriaca.* Cf. iv 226*n.*⟩

7. *Force inertly strong*] Alluding to the *Vis inertiæ of Matter,* which, tho' it really be no Power, is yet the Foundation of all the Qualities and Attributes of that sluggish Substance. P.W.

9. *the Dog-star's . . . ray* ⟨Cf. *Ep. to Arbuthnot,* 3*n.*⟩

11, 12. *Sick was the Sun, &c.*] The Poet introduceth this, (as all great events are supposed by sage Historians to be preceded) by an *Eclipse of the Sun;* but with a peculiar propriety, as the Sun is the *Emblem* of that intellectual light which dies before the face of Dulness. Very apposite likewise is it to make this *Eclipse,* which is occasioned by the *Moon's predominancy,* the very time when *Dulness* and *Madness* are in *Conjunction;* whose relation and influence on each other the poet hath shewn in many places, Book 1. ver. 22. Book 3. ver. 5, *& seq.* W. ⟨*1743.*⟩

14. *To blot out Order, and extinguish Light*] The two great Ends of her Mission; the one in quality of Daughter of *Chaos,* the other as Daughter of *Night. Order* here is to be understood extensively, both as Civil and Moral, the distinctions

> Of dull and venal a new World to mold,   15
> And bring Saturnian days of Lead and Gold.
>   She mounts the Throne: her head a Cloud conceal'd,
> In broad Effulgence all below reveal'd,
> ('Tis thus aspiring Dulness ever shines)
> Soft on her lap her Laureat son reclines.   20

between high and low in Society, and true and false in Individuals: *Light*, as Intellectual only, Wit, Science, Arts. P.W.

15. *Of dull and venal*] The Allegory continued; *dull* referring to the extinction of Light or Science, *venal* to the destruction of Order, or the Truth of Things. P.W.

Ibid. *a new World*] In allusion to the Epicurean opinion, that from the Dissolution of the natural World into Night and Chaos, a new one should arise; this the Poet alluding to, in the Production of a new moral World, makes it partake of its original Principles. P.W.

16. Lead *and* Gold] *i.e.* dull and venal. P.W.

18. *all below reveal'd*] Vet. Adag. 𝕿𝖍𝖊 𝖍𝖎𝖌𝖍𝖊𝖗 𝖞𝖔𝖚 𝖈𝖑𝖎𝖒𝖇, 𝖙𝖍𝖊 𝖒𝖔𝖗𝖊 𝖞𝖔𝖚 𝖘𝖍𝖊𝖜 𝖞𝖔𝖚𝖗 𝕬——. Verified in no instance more than in Dulness aspiring. Emblematized also by an Ape climbing and exposing his posteriors. ⟨It was the opinion of the Ancients, that the Divinities manifested themselves to Men by their Back-parts, Virg. *Aen.* I. [402]

            — & avertens, *rosea cervice refulsit.*

But this passage may admit of a more modern Exposition, by the Adage, . . . *1742, 1751.*⟩ Scribl. P.W.

20. *her Laureat son reclines*] With great judgment it is imagined by the Poet, that such a Collegue as Dulness had elected, should sleep on the Throne, and have very little share in the Action of the Poem. Accordingly he hath done little or nothing from the day of his Anointing; having past through the second book without taking part in any thing that was transacted about him, and thro' the third in profound Sleep. Nor ought this, well considered, to seem strange in our days, when so many *King-consorts* have done the like. Scribl. ⟨P.W.—*1742*. The sneer at King-consorts was probably intended for George II, who was content in political matters, whether he knew it or not, to follow his Queen. As a contemporary lampoon put it: "We know 'tis Queen Caroline, not you that reign."⟩

This verse our excellent Laureate took so to heart, that he appealed to all mankind, "if he was not as *seldom asleep as any fool?*" ⟨*Letter to Pope*, p. 53⟩. But it is hoped the Poet hath not injured him, but rather verified his Prophecy (p. 243. of his own Life, 8vo. ch. ix.) where he says "*the Reader will be as much* "*pleased to find me a* Dunce *in my* Old age, *as he was to prove me a* brisk blockhead "*in my* Youth." Wherever there was any room for Briskness, or Alacrity of any sort, *even in sinking*, he hath had it allowed him; but here, where there is nothing for him to do but to take his natural rest, he must permit his Historian to be

Beneath her foot-stool, *Science* groans in Chains,
And *Wit* dreads Exile, Penalties and Pains.
There foam'd rebellious *Logic*, gagg'd and bound,
There, stript, fair *Rhet'ric* languish'd on the ground;
His blunted Arms by *Sophistry* are born,   25
And shameless *Billingsgate* her Robes adorn.
Morality, by her false Guardians drawn,

---

silent. It is from their *actions* only that Princes have their character, and Poets from their *works:* And if in *those* he be *as much asleep as any fool*, the Poet must leave him and them to *sleep to all eternity*. BENT. ⟨P. *1743.*⟩

Ibid. *her Laureat*] "When I find my Name in the satyrical works of this Poet, ⟨"of our most celebrated living Author"—Cibber⟩ I never look upon it as "any malice meant to me, ⟨Cibber adds: "for he knows I never provok'd it"⟩ "but PROFIT to himself. For he considers that *my Face* is more *known* than "most in the nation; ⟨Cibber has: "than those of many thousands of more "consequence in the Kingdom."⟩ and therefore *a Lick at the Laureate* will be a "sure bait *ad captandum vulgus*, to catch little readers." Life of Colley Cibber, chap. ii ⟨pp. 31–2⟩.

Now if it be certain, that the works of our Poet have owed their success to this ingenious expedient, we hence derive an unanswerable Argument, that this Fourth DUNCIAD, as well as the former three, hath had the Author's last hand, and was by him intended for the Press: Or else to what purpose hath he crowned it, as we see, by this finishing stroke, the profitable *Lick* at the *Laureate?* BENT. ⟨P.W. *1742.*⟩

21, 22. *Beneath her footstool, &c.*] We are next presented with the pictures of those whom the Goddess leads in Captivity. *Science* is only depressed and confined so as to be rendered useless; but *Wit* or *Genius*, as a more dangerous and active enemy, punished, or driven away: *Dulness* being often reconciled in some degree with Learning, but never upon any terms with Wit. And accordingly it will be seen that she admits something *like* each Science, as Casuistry, Sophistry, &c. P.W.

22. *Wit dreads Exile, &c.* ⟨Cf. James Miller's *Are these Things so?* 1740:

. . . if his rebel Wit
Can to such Pains and Penalties submit.

Pope may have had in mind the fate of Gay's *Polly*, or the more recent misfortunes of Paul Whitehead, who absconded when summoned before the House of Lords for his *Manners* in 1739. Atterbury and Bolingbroke, both friends of Pope, had spent several years in exile; a bill of Pains and Penalties was enacted against the former for his complicity in the Jacobite plot of 1722.⟩

27. *by her false Guardians drawn*] *Morality* is the Daughter of *Astræa*. This alludes to the Mythology of the ancient Poets; who tell us that in the *Gold* and *Silver* ages, or in the *State of Nature*, the Gods cohabited with Men here on Earth;

> *Chicane* in Furs, and *Casuistry* in Lawn,
> Gasps, as they straiten at each end the cord,
> And dies, when Dulness gives her Page the word.   30
> Mad *Mathesis* alone was unconfin'd,
> Too mad for mere material chains to bind,
> Now to pure Space lifts her extatic stare,
> Now running round the Circle, finds it square.
> But held in ten-fold bonds the *Muses* lie,   35
> Watch'd both by Envy's and by Flatt'ry's eye:

but when by reason of human degeneracy men were forced to have recourse to a *Magistrate*, and that the Ages of *Brass* and *Iron* came on, (that is, when Laws were wrote on brazen tablets and inforced by the Sword of Justice) the Celestials soon retired from Earth, and Astræa last of all; and then it was she left this her Orphan Daughter in the hands of the *Guardians* aforesaid. SCRIBL. ⟨W. *1743*.⟩

28. *in Furs . . . in Lawn* ⟨i.e. in the Law . . . in the Church. The "Furs" are the ermine robes of the judges. "Lawn" is the fine linen used for the sleeves of a bishop. (Cf. *Moral Es.* i 136: "A Saint in Crape is twice a Saint in Lawn.")⟩

30. *gives her* Page *the word*] There was a Judge of this name, always ready to hang any man, of which he was suffered to give a hundred miserable examples during a long life, even to his dotage. ⟨*1742e*.⟩ Tho' the candid *Scriblerus* imagined ⟨see *1742a*⟩ *Page* here to mean no more than a *Page* or *Mute*, and to allude to the custom of strangling State Criminals in *Turkey* by Mutes or Pages. A practice more decent than that of *our Page*, who before he hanged any person, loaded him with reproachful language. SCRIBL. ⟨P.W. For Sir Francis Page, the notorious "hanging judge," see Biog. App. The second half of this note appeared, with some slight differences, in *1742*.⟩

31. *Mad* Mathesis] Alluding to the strange Conclusions some Mathematicians have deduced from their principles concerning the *real Quantity of Matter*, the *Reality of Space, &c.* ⟨P.W. Among the works of Martinus Scriblerus was "an investigation of the quantity of real matter in the universe"; and he had also "enriched mathematics with many precise and geometrical quadratures of the circle."—"Memoirs of Martinus Scriblerus": *The Life and Works of John Arbuthnot*, ed. G. A. Aitken, p. 356. In spite of their admiration for Newton, Pope and his brother wits were fond of ridiculing Mathematics and mathematicians. Arbuthnot was perhaps the only member of the Scriblerus Club who had any real knowledge of the subject.⟩

33. *pure Space*] i.e. pure and defæcated from Matter ⟨*1742*⟩.—*extatic Stare*, the action of men who look about with full assurance of seeing what does not exist, such as those who expect to find *Space* a real being. ⟨W. *1743*.⟩

34. *finds it square*] Regards the wild and fruitless attempts of *squaring the Circle*. P.W.

36. *Watch'd both by* Envy's *and by* Flatt'ry's *eye*] One of the misfortunes

There to her heart sad Tragedy addrest
The dagger wont to pierce the Tyrant's breast;
But sober History restrain'd her rage,

37 There] Oft *1742ab*.
39–42 Oft her gay Sister's life and spirit fled;
But History and Satire held their head: *1742ab*.

---

falling on Authors, from the *Act* for subjecting *Plays* to the power of a *Licenser*, being the false representations to which they were expos'd, from such as either gratify'd their Envy to Merit, or made their Court to Greatness, by perverting general Reflections against Vice into Libels on particular Persons. ⟨P.W. This trouble existed before the Licensing Act. Cf. *Remarks on the Tragedy of Eurydice*, which was said to be "writ in favour of the Pretender," and *Remarks on an Historical Play, Called, The Fall of Mortimer*, 1731, which was claimed as "a libel against the present Administration." B.M. 641 e 28 (3-4).⟩

39. *But Sober* History] History attends on Tragedy, Satyr on Comedy, as their substitutes in the discharge of their distinct functions: the one in high life, recording the crimes and punishments of the great; the other in low, exposing the vices or follies of the common people ⟨*1742a*, with a few verbal changes⟩. But it may be asked, How came *History* and *Satyr* to be admitted with impunity to minister comfort to the Muses, even in the presence of the Goddess, and in the midst of all her triumphs? A question, says *Scriblerus*, which we thus resolve: *History* was brought up in her infancy by Dulness herself; but being afterwards espoused into a noble house, she forgot (as is usual) the humility of her birth, and the cares of her early friends. This occasioned a long estrangement between her and Dulness. At length, in process of time, they met together in a Monk's Cell, were reconciled, and became better friends than ever. After this they had a second quarrel, but it held not long, and are now again on reasonable terms, and so are like to continue. This accounts for the connivance shewn to History on this occasion. But the boldness of *Satyr* springs from a very different cause; for the reader ought to know, that she alone of all the sisters is unconquerable, never to be silenced, when truly inspired and animated (as should seem) from above, for this very purpose, to oppose the kingdom of Dulness to her last breath. ⟨W. *1742c*. History was "espoused into a noble house" when Clarendon wrote his *History of the Rebellion*. By its subsequent relapse into dullness "in a Monk's Cell" Warburton may intend an allusion to Bossuet, or possibly—by a stretching of terms—to Burnet's *History of his own Times*. Cf. *Donne* iv 61n. In his *Critical and Philosophical Enquiry into . . . Miracles*, 1727, Warburton had insisted that Raleigh and Clarendon were "the only two our Nation has yet produced of a *true historic Genius*" (p. 60); and he had condemned the Abbé Vertot for having "invented an entirely new Species of historic Writing, that meddles only with the Revolutions of a Country." It is possible that in excepting History Pope is thinking of one of the few methods by which the Opposition was able to criticize Walpole's administration, viz. by citing

And promis'd Vengeance on a barb'rous age.   40
There sunk Thalia, nerveless, cold, and dead,
Had not her Sister Satyr held her head:
Nor cou'd'st thou, C H E S T E R F I E L D! a tear refuse,
Thou wept'st, and with thee wept each gentle Muse.
    When lo! a Harlot form soft sliding by,   45
With mincing step, small voice, and languid eye;
Foreign her air, her robe's discordant pride

41 cold] faint *1742cd.*

---

events from English or Roman history which afforded an obvious parallel to
what was happening in contemporary England.⟩

    43. *Nor cou'd'st thou, &c.*] This Noble Person in the year 1737, when the Act
aforesaid was brought into the House of Lords, opposed it in an excellent speech
(says Mr. *Cibber*) "with a lively spirit, and uncommon eloquence." ⟨*Apology*,
p. 233. Cibber applies these words, however, to the speeches of the Opposition,
and not specifically to that of Lord Chesterfield.⟩ This speech had the honour
to be answered by the said Mr. *Cibber*, with a lively spirit also, and in a manner
very uncommon, in the 8th Chapter of his *Life and Manners*. And here, gentle
Reader, would I gladly insert the other speech, whereby thou mightest judge
between them: but I must defer it on account of some differences not yet
adjusted between the noble Author and myself, concerning the *True Reading*
of certain passages. Scribl. ⟨P.W. Chesterfield's speech was reported in
Fog's Journal at considerable length. In *The Gentleman's Magazine* for May 1737
(vol. vii, pp. 409–11) the speech was published again with many additions to
the version given in *Fog's*. A letter which was prefixed to this fuller version of
the speech claimed that it "added many entire passages actually delivered
by that Noble Lord, and restored others." It may be to this difference in re-
porting that the Scriblerus note refers.—For Chesterfield, see Biog. App., vol. iv.⟩

    45. *When lo! a Harlot form*] Every Reader will see, that from this verse to the
68th is a detach'd piece. We suppose it rightly inserted here, from what is said
of her casting a scornful look on the *prostrate Muses*: but if any one can show us
a properer place we shall be obliged to him ⟨*1742. Om. 1743a–51*⟩. The Attitude given to this Phantom represents the nature and genius of the *Italian* Opera;
its affected airs, its effeminate sounds, and the practice of patching up these
Operas with favourite Songs, incoherently put together. These things were
supported by the subscriptions of the Nobility ⟨*1742*⟩. This circumstance that
Opera should prepare for the opening of the grand Sessions, was prophesied of
in Book 3. ver. 304.

        Already Opera prepares the way,
        The sure fore-runner of her gentle sway.
                            ⟨P.W. *1743.*⟩

In patch-work flutt'ring, and her head aside·
By singing Peers up-held on either hand,
She tripp'd and laugh'd, too pretty much to stand;   50
Cast on the prostrate Nine a scornful look,
Then thus in quaint Recitativo spoke.
     "O *Cara! Cara!* silence all that train:
Joy to great Chaos! let Division reign:

54. *let Division reign*] Alluding to the false taste of playing tricks in Music with numberless divisions, to the neglect of that harmony which conforms to the Sense, and applies to the Passions. Mr. *Handel* had introduced a great number of Hands, and more variety of Instruments into the Orchestra, and employed even Drums and Cannon to make a fuller Chorus; which prov'd so much too manly for the fine Gentlemen of his age, that he was obliged to remove his Music into *Ireland*. After which they were reduced, for want of Composers, to practise the patch-work above mentioned. ⟨P.W. Senesino was particularly celebrated for his "divisions," i.e. breaking up each of a succession of long notes into a number of short ones, and so dwelling on a single syllable of the word he was singing.—The reasons given here for Handel's having to "remove his Music into Ireland" leave much out of account. Handel's misfortunes were due to a variety of causes, among which his quarrels with singers and others must be reckoned. He became bankrupt in 1737, and suffered a period of eclipse in London. His oratorio, the *Messiah*, was performed in Dublin in 1742 with great success, but was received some time later in London without much enthusiasm. It was not until some years after Pope's death that Handel recovered his popularity with the London public.—On Handel's employment of "Drums and Cannon" Mr John Butt has communicated the following note: "There is no mention of Handel's use of cannon in any of his scores (not even the Fireworks Music, in spite of one biographer to the contrary) nor in Burney nor Hawkins; but Horatio Townsend (*An Account of the Visit of Handel to Dublin*, 1852, p. 103) remembered hearing 'many years ago, from a very respectable authority in matters of musical history, the tradition that Handel once, during the performance of one of his choruses, exclaimed, with enthusiasm, "Oh! that I had cannon!" ' Tympani in the orchestra were not a novelty, since Lully and Purcell had been using them in the 1670's. But Handel was specially fond of them. Percy Scholes (*Companion to Music*, Art. 'Tympani') refers to the tradition that after the battle of Dettingen (1743) Handel used a pair of kettledrums captured in the field."⟩

54. *Joy to great Chaos* ⟨"*Joy to great Cæsar*—The beginning of a famous old Song."—Warburton, *1751*. The song was one of Tom D'Urfey's. In the reign of Charles II it "gave the Whigs such a blow as they were not able to recover that whole reign."—*The Guardian*, No. 67, May 28, 1713.⟩

> Chromatic tortures soon shall drive them hence,   55
> Break all their nerves, and fritter all their sense:
> One Trill shall harmonize joy, grief, and rage,
> Wake the dull Church, and lull the ranting Stage;
> To the same notes thy sons shall hum, or snore,
> And all thy yawning daughters cry, *encore*.   60
> Another Phœbus, thy own Phœbus, reigns,
> Joys in my jiggs, and dances in my chains.
> But soon, ah soon Rebellion will commence,

55 Chromatic] My Racks and *1742a–e*.

---

55. *Chromatic tortures*] That species of the ancient music called the *Chromatic* was a variation and embellishment, in odd irregularities, of the *Diatonic* kind. They say it was invented about the time of *Alexander*, and that the *Spartans* forbad the use of it, as languid and effeminate. W. ⟨*1743*. According to Dr Burney (*General History of Music*, iv 364), Handel, whom Pope praises a few lines further on, was the first to introduce those tortures. Pope, in fact, had little understanding, or appreciation, of music. Cf. Burney, op. cit., iv 65.⟩

58. *Wake the dull Church . . . Stage* ⟨"i.e. Dissipate the *devotion* of the one by light and wanton airs; and subdue the *Pathos* of the other by recitative and sing-song."—W. *1751*.⟩

60. *encore* ⟨The crying of *"encore"* at the Opera was apparently a new thing when Addison wrote his *Spectator*, No. 314, Feb. 29, 1712. Perhaps Pope is sneering at the female lovers of opera for their un-English affectations.⟩

61. *thy own* Phœbus *reigns*]

> *Tuus jam regnat Apollo.*   Virg. ⟨Ecl. iv 10.⟩

Not the ancient *Phœbus*, the God of Harmony, but a modern *Phœbus* of *French* extraction, married to the Princess *Galimathia*, one of the handmaids of Dulness, and an assistant to Opera. Of whom see *Bouhours*, and other Critics of that nation. Scribl. P.W. ⟨"The *French* express this kind of Nonsense by the Term *Phebus*; in which Figure, if we may so call it, there must be an Appearance of Light glimmering over the Obscurity, a Semblance of Meaning without any real Sense; whereas in *Galimatias*, the Obscurity is compleat. The *Phebus* is so term'd, from that Appearance of Light, which is very often so little, that the Thought is so obscure as not to be understood . . . The *Opera* is of a Nature not to be supported without this Figure; every thing is Shew, and there is no more need of Sense than there is of Philosophy."—D. Bouhours, *The Arts of Logick and Rhetorick*, trs. J. Oldmixon, 1728, pp. 365, 372. Pope may have taken a hint from Fielding's *Historical Register* (1736), where in Act III, Sc. i, a bastard Apollo appears on the stage, who has "the entire direction of all our play-houses and poetical performances whatever."⟩

If Music meanly borrows aid from Sense:
Strong in new Arms, lo! Giant Handel stands,   65
Like bold Briareus, with a hundred hands;
To stir, to rouze, to shake the Soul he comes,
And Jove's own Thunders follow Mars's Drums.
Arrest him, Empress; or you sleep no more"—
She heard, and drove him to th' Hibernian shore.   70
      And now had Fame's posterior Trumpet blown,
And all the Nations summon'd to the Throne.
The young, the old, who feel her inward sway,
One instinct seizes, and transports away.
None need a guide, by sure Attraction led,   75
And strong impulsive gravity of Head:

---

64. *Music meanly borrows aid, &c.* ⟨Pope appears to be referring to Handel's
oratorios. This form of musical composition had recently been introduced from
Italy. Pope himself had written the book for Handel's first oratorio, *Esther*, 1720.
See vol. vi. Cf. Tickell's lines *To Mr. Addison, on his Opera of Rosamond:*

> From words so sweet new grace the notes receive,
> And Music borrows help she us'd to give.⟩

66. *Like bold Briareus* ⟨Cf. iv 54n.⟩

71. *Fame's posterior Trumpet*] *Posterior*, viz. her *second* or *more certain* Report:
unless we imagine this word *posterior* to relate to the position of one of her
Trumpets, according to *Hudibras:*

> She blows not both with the same Wind,
> But one before and one behind;
> And therefore modern Authors name
> One good, and t'other evil Fame.   P.W.

⟨An inaccurate quotation from *Hudibras*, Pt. II, Canto i, 71-2, 75-6.⟩

75. *None need a guide, &c.*] The sons of Dulness want no instructors in study,
nor guides in life: they are their own masters in all Sciences, and their own
Heralds and Introducers into all places. P.W. ⟨*1743.* In *1742* this note read:
"The sons of Dulness are αὐτοδίδακτος, and can introduce themselves into
all places, they want no instructors in study, nor guides in life."⟩

76. *gravity of Head* ⟨Cf. B ii 315-18.⟩

76 to 101.] It ought to be observed that here are three classes in this assembly.
The first of men absolutely and avowedly dull, who naturally adhere to the
Goddess, and are imaged in the simile of the Bees about their Queen. The
second involuntarily drawn to her, tho' not caring to own her influence; from
ver. 81 to 90. The third of such, as, tho' not members of her state, yet advance
her service by flattering Dulness, cultivating mistaken talents, patronizing

None want a place, for all their Centre found,
Hung to the Goddess, and coher'd around.
Not closer, orb in orb, conglob'd are seen
The buzzing Bees about their dusky Queen.   80
    The gath'ring number, as it moves along,
Involves a vast involuntary throng,
Who gently drawn, and struggling less and less,
Roll in her Vortex, and her pow'r confess.
Not those alone who passive own her laws,   85
But who, weak rebels, more advance her cause.
Whate'er of dunce in College or in Town
Sneers at another, in toupee or gown;
Whate'er of mungril no one class admits,
A wit with dunces, and a dunce with wits.   90
    Nor absent they, no members of her state,
Who pay her homage in her sons, the Great;

---

vile scriblers, discouraging living merit, or setting up for wits, and Men of taste in arts they understand not; from ver. 91 to 101 ⟨*1742*⟩. In this new world of Dulness each of these three classes hath its appointed station, as best suits its nature, and concurs to the harmony of the System. The *first* drawn only by the strong and simple impulse of Attraction, are represented as falling directly down into her; as conglobed into her substance, and resting in her centre.

> —— *All their centre found,*
> *Hung to the Goddess, and coher'd around.*

'The *second*, tho' within the sphere of her attraction, yet having at the same time a different motion, they are carried, by the composition of these two, in planetary revolutions round her centre, some nearer to it, some further off:

> *Who gently drawn, and struggling less and less,*
> *Roll in her Vortex, and her pow'r confess.*

The *third* are properly *excentrical*, and no constant members of her state or system: sometimes at an immense distance from her influence, and sometimes again almost on the surface of her *broad effulgence*. Their use in their Perihelion, or nearest approach to Dulness, is the same in the moral World, as that of *Comets* in the natural, namely to refresh and recreate the Dryness and decays of the system; in the manner marked out from ver. 91 to 98. P.W. ⟨*1743*⟩.

88. *toupee* ⟨"A curl or artificial lock of hair on the top of the head, esp. as a crowning feature of the periwig; a periwig in which the front hair was combed up, over a pad, into such a top-knot" (OED). The dunces in toupee are the men of fashion, as opposed to the scholars.⟩

Who false to Phœbus, bow the knee to Baal;
Or impious, preach his Word without a call.
Patrons, who sneak from living worth to dead,   95
With-hold the pension, and set up the head;
Or vest dull Flatt'ry in the sacred Gown;
Or give from fool to fool the Laurel crown.

93. *false to* Phœbus] Spoken of the ancient and true *Phœbus*, not the *French Phœbus*, who hath no chosen Priests or Poets, but equally inspires any man that pleaseth to sing or preach. SCRIBL. ⟨Cf. iv 61*n*.⟩

96. *With-hold the pension, &c.* ⟨The circumstance of the poet neglected while still alive and then commemorated in sculpture after his death was a poetical vein very fruitfully worked by the wits of the period. Besides Pope's own lines on Halifax-Dodington in the *Ep. to Arbuthnot*, 235–48, and Samuel Wesley's epigram, "While *Butler*, needy Wretch! was yet alive," Swift's caustic lines on Queen Caroline's collection of "heads" at Richmond may have been in Pope's mind:

> Lewis the living Learned fed,
> And rais'd the scientific Head:
> Our frugal Queen to save her Meat,
> Exalts the Heads that cannot eat.

See *The Poems of Jonathan Swift*, ed. Harold Williams, ii 662–3. Cf. also iv 110*n*.⟩

97. *Or vest dull Flatt'ry* ⟨The line has a general application to all patrons of ecclesiastical livings who bestow them on some successful flatterer; but Pope's editors have sought, no doubt with justification, for a more specific allusion. EC suggests the thirty-year-old story of Bishop Kennett (see *Ep.* ii ii 220*n*.); but a more likely candidate is Dr. Alured Clarke, 1696–1742. Pope himself told Spence—

> "Let Clarke make half his life the poor's support,
> But let him give the other half to court

was a couplet in the manuscript for the fourth book of the Dunciad: but I believe I shall omit it; though, if rightly understood, it has more of commendation than satire in it."—Spence, p. 211. Cf. *Ep. to the Satires*, ii 164*n*.⟩

98. *Or give from fool to fool, &c.* ⟨"In an anonymous Ode written by Pope for Cibber, is this conclusion,

> So shall the Crown and Laurel too
> Descend from fool to fool."—Walpole.

See N. Ault, *New Light on Pope*, pp. 315–22, and *The Poetical Works of John Gay*, ed. G. C. Faber, 1926, p. 653. Pope is here satirizing by implication the Duke of Newcastle, who chose Eusden as laureate in 1718, and the Duke of Grafton, who chose Cibber in 1730.⟩

And (last and worst) with all the cant of wit,
Without the soul, the Muse's Hypocrit.   100
    There march'd the bard and blockhead, side by side,
Who rhym'd for hire, and patroniz'd for pride.
Narcissus, prais'd with all a Parson's pow'r,
Look'd a white lilly sunk beneath a show'r.
There mov'd Montalto with superior air;   105
His stretch'd-out arm display'd a Volume fair;

99, 100. *And (last and worst) &c.*] In this division are reckoned up 1. The Idolizers of Dulness in the Great—2. Ill Judges,—3. Ill Writers,—4. Ill Patrons. But the *last and worst*, as he justly calls him, is the *Muse*'s *Hypocrite*, who is as it were the Epitome of them all. He who thinks the only end of poetry is to amuse, and the only business of the poet to be witty; and consequently who cultivates only such trifling talents in himself, and encourages only such in others. W. ⟨*1743.* Pope would almost certainly have included Lord Hervey among the "Muse's Hypocrits."⟩

103–4. *Narcissus* ⟨Lord Hervey, to whom Dr Conyers Middleton dedicated his *Life of Cicero* in 1741 (Walpole). Hervey was an epileptic, and had a noticeably white face. (Pope writes of the "pale Narcissus" flower in his verses in imitation of Cowley.) Middleton's dedication extends to fourteen pages. . . . "The public will naturally expect that in chusing a Patron for *the Life of* Cicero, I should address myself to some person of illustrious rank, distinguished by his parts and eloquence, and bearing a principal share in the great affairs of the Nation . . ." Middleton goes on to praise Hervey's hospitality, his love of learning and literature, his "singular temperance in diet," his "sprightly compositions of various kinds."—Pope was one of the subscribers to the *Life*, Warburton another. Mr. G. Tillotson has suggested to me that Pope may have been indebted for his simile of the white lily to Dryden's translation of *Aeneid*, ix 583–4:

               Like a white Poppy sinking on the Plain,
               Whose heavy Head is overcharg'd with Rain.⟩

105. *Montalto* ⟨The "decent Knight" of l. 113, i.e. Sir Thomas Hanmer. The name was obviously intended to suggest Hanmer's pompous manner. He was "a portly old gentleman, of a very stately carriage, accustomed to walk solemnly to church twice on every Sunday, followed by all his servants, and moving from his iron gates to the porch of the church between two ranks of his tenants and adherents, who stood, hat in hand, bowing reverently low, while the great man acknowledged their salutations by a few words and a dignified condescension."—Sir C. Bunbury, *Life of Sir Thomas Hanmer*, p. 95. If this local ritual was known to Pope, he may be referring to it at ll. 107–8.⟩

106. *a Volume* ⟨i.e. his edition of Shakespeare. See l. 113.⟩

Courtiers and Patriots in two ranks divide,
Thro' both he pass'd, and bow'd from side to side:
But as in graceful act, with awful eye
Compos'd he stood, bold Benson thrust him by: 110
On two unequal crutches propt he came,
Milton's on this, on that one Johnston's name.
The decent Knight retir'd with sober rage,
Withdrew his hand, and clos'd the pompous page.
[But (happy for him as the times went then)   115

110 Benson] B—s—n *1742a–e*.
114 "What! no respect, he cry'd, for Shakespear's page?" *1743a²*,
    1749.   115–18 *1743a²*, *1749–51*. Om. *1742a–43b*.

107. *Courtiers and Patriots* ⟨The "Courtiers" are the Court party, the supporters of the administration. By the "Patriots" Pope probably intends the
whole "Country-Party," i.e. the Opposition of Whigs led by Pulteney, and of
Tories led by Bolingbroke (till his death in 1740) by Sir William Wyndham.⟩
108. *bow'd from side to side* ⟨"As being of no *one* party."—Warburton, *1751*.—
Hanmer belonged to the "Whimsicals," or Hanoverian Tories.⟩
110. *bold* Benson] This man endeavoured to raise himself to Fame by erecting
monuments, striking coins, setting up heads, and procuring translations, of
Milton; and afterwards by a great passion for *Arthur Johnston*, a *Scotch* physician's
Version of the Psalms, of which he printed many fine Editions. See more of him,
Book 3. ver. 325. P.W. ⟨For William Benson, see Biog. App. His admiration
for Milton resulted in his setting up a monument to him in the Abbey (1737),
having a medal of him engraved, and commissioning William Dobson to turn
Paradise Lost into Latin for a fee of £1,000. He had a bust of Johnston executed
by Rysbrach.—Arthur Johnston, M.D. (1587–1641), a Scots physician and
writer of Latin verse. His *Psalmorum Davidis Paraphrasis Poetica* was published
at Aberdeen in 1637. Benson's editions appeared in 1740, 1741, 1743. EC
suggests that he is "bold" Benson because he dedicated to the King.⟩
113. *The decent* Knight] An eminent person, who was about to publish a very
pompous Edition of a great Author, *at his own expence* ⟨very much at his own
expence indeed.—*1742*⟩. P.W. ⟨Hanmer's edition of Shakespeare appeared in
1743–4. The italics may be intended to suggest that the publication was at the
expense of his reputation as well as of his pocket. According to Warburton he
was "at the expence of his purse in procuring cuts for his edition."—*The
Castrated Letter of Sir Thomas Hanmer*, 1763, p. 28. For the reasons for Hanmer's
inclusion in the *Dunciad*, see Biog. App., Hanmer.⟩
115–18. ⟨"These four lines were printed in a separate leaf by Mr. Pope in
the last edition, which he himself gave, of the Dunciad, with directions to the
printer, to put this leaf into its place as soon as Sir T. H's Shakespear should be

Appear'd Apollo's May'r and Aldermen,
On whom three hundred gold-capt youths await,
To lug the pond'rous volume off in state.]
    When Dulness, smiling—"Thus revive the Wits!
But murder first, and mince them all to bits;   120
As erst Medea (cruel, so to save!)
A new Edition of old Æson gave,
Let standard-Authors, thus, like trophies born,

published. B."—*1751*. The "B" to whom this note is attributed may be the printer, William Bowyer. The copy of the quarto of 1743 in the British Museum (641 l. 17) contains the substituted leaf.—A passage in one of Pope's letters to Warburton, dated Jan. 18 (1743), throws light on these four lines. Writing of Hanmer's *Shakespeare* Pope says: "The heads of some houses have subscribed 100, and 50, at three guineas the book, which they refund by putting them off to the gentlemen commoners, and this way the press is paid."〉

116. *Apollo's May'r and Aldermen* 〈In the context this appears to be the Vice-Chancellor of Oxford University, and the Heads of the various colleges. The Clarendon Press was about to publish Hanmer's *Shakespeare*; but Pope had a quarrel with Oxford of a more serious kind. In the summer of 1741 both Pope and Warburton had been unofficially approached to discover whether they would be willing to accept a Doctor's degree from the University of Oxford. Both men were willing, but unhappily for Warburton his enemies in Oxford succeeded in having the proposal, so far as it related to him, outvoted. Pope thereupon told Warburton: "I will be doctored with you, or not at all," and refused to accept the degree offered to him. In a note to a letter from Pope to himself, dated Sept. 20, 1741, Warburton states that Pope's "resentment of this low trick gave birth to the celebrated lines, of Apollo's Mayor and Aldermen." Cf. iv 577–8, and see Evans, pp. 85–6.〉

117. *gold-capt* 〈The Gentleman-Commoner at Oxford wore a gold tassel on his cap.〉

119. "*Thus revive, &c.*] The Goddess applauds the practice of tacking the obscure names of Persons not eminent in any branch of learning, to those of the most distinguished Writers; either by printing *Editions* of their works with impertinent alterations of their Text, as in the former instances, or by setting up *Monuments* disgraced with their own vile names and inscriptions, as in the latter. P.W.

122. *old Æson*] Of whom Ovid (very applicable to these restored authors)

> Æson *miratur,*
> Dissimilemque animum *subiit*——〈Met. vii.〉
>   P.W.

123. *standard-Authors* 〈Pope is, of course, playing on the word "standard."〉

Appear more glorious as more hack'd and torn,
And you, my Critics! in the chequer'd shade,   125
Admire new light thro' holes yourselves have made.
     "Leave not a foot of verse, a foot of stone,
A Page, a Grave, that they can call their own;
But spread, my sons, your glory thin or thick,
On passive paper, or on solid brick.   130
So by each Bard an Alderman shall sit,
A heavy Lord shall hang at ev'ry Wit,
And while on Fame's triumphal Car they ride,
Some Slave of mine be pinion'd to their side."
     Now crowds on crowds around the Goddess press,   135
Each eager to present the first Address.
Dunce scorning Dunce beholds the next advance,

133 triumphal] triumphant *1742a–d.*

---

126. *Admire new light, &c.* ⟨Cf. Waller:
          The Soul's dark cottage, batter'd and decay'd,
          Lets in new light through chinks that time has made.
The "chequer'd shade" is a reminiscence of Milton's *L'Allegro*, l. 96.⟩

128. *A Page, a Grave*] For what less than a Grave can be granted to a dead author? or what less than a Page can be allow'd a living one? P.W.

Ibid. *A Page*] *Pagina*, not *Pedissequus*. A Page of a Book, not a Servant, Follower, or Attendant; no Poet having had a *Page* since the death of Mr. Thomas Durfey. SCRIBL. P.W. ⟨Steele refers jocularly to Durfey's page in *The Lover*, No. 40, May 27, 1714: "That gentleman has so long appeared in the cities of London and Westminster, attended only by one servant, and him all along *under age*, that the generality have too familiar a conception of him."⟩

131. *So by each Bard and Alderman, &c.*] Vide the *Tombs of the Poets*, Editio Westmonasteriensis. P.W. ⟨"Alluding to the monument erected for Butler by Alderman Barber."—Warburton, *1751.* At the end of the Latin inscription on the monument appear the words:
          Hoc tandem, posito Marmore, curavit
          Johannes Barber, Civis Londinensis, 1721.
For Barber, see Biog. App.⟩

134. *Some Slave of mine* ⟨In allusion to the custom in ancient Rome of placing a chained slave beside a victorious general as he rode through the city.⟩

137, 138, *Dunce scorning dunce, &c.*] This is not to be ascribed so much to the different manners of a Court and College, as to the different effects which a pretence to Learning, and a pretence to Wit, have on Blockheads. For as Judgment consists in finding out the *differences* in things, and Wit in finding out

But Fop shews Fop superior complaisance.
When lo! a Spectre rose, whose index-hand
Held forth the Virtue of the dreadful wand;   140
His beaver'd brow a birchen garland wears,
Dropping with Infant's blood, and Mother's tears.
O'er ev'ry vein a shudd'ring horror runs;
Eton and Winton shake thro' all their Sons.
All Flesh is humbled, Westminster's bold race   145
Shrink, and confess the Genius of the place:
The pale Boy-Senator yet tingling stands,

141 wears,] bears, *1742a–f, 1743b*.
143–4 *Om. 1742a–f, 1743b*.
145 Westminster's . . . race] Youth's bold courage cools, *1742a–f, 1743b*.
146 Each shudd'ring owns the Genius of the Schools; *1742a–f, 1743b*.

---

their *likenesses,* so the Dunce is all discord and dissension, and constantly busied in *reproving, examining, confuting, &c.* while the Fop flourishes in peace, with Songs and Hymns of Praise, *Addresses, Characters, Epithalamiums, &c.* W. ⟨*1743*⟩.

   139. *a Spectre* ⟨The ghost of Dr Busby, the famous headmaster of Westminster School.⟩

   140. *the dreadful wand*] A Cane usually born by Schoolmasters, which drives the poor Souls about like the wand of Mercury. SCRIBL. P.W.

   141. *His beaver'd brow* ⟨Perhaps the fur cap worn by Doctors, or merely the hat that Busby habitually wore. (In the portrait of Busby reproduced in Nichols, *Lit. Ill.*, vol. iv, he is wearing an enormous hat which shades his brow.) Or Pope may be alluding to the well-known story of how Busby kept his hat on his head while showing Charles II round Westminster School, lest the boys should think that there was any one greater than himself.⟩

   142. *Dropping with Infant's blood &c.* ⟨Warburton (*1751*) notes the imitation of *Paradise Lost,* i 392–3:

        First Moloch, horrid King besmear'd with blood
        Of human sacrifice, and parents tears.⟩

   144. *Eton and Winton shake &c.* ⟨EC notes Pope's rendering of *Iliad* xvi 672:

        Troy at the loss through all her legions shook.⟩

   145. *bold* ⟨Perhaps with particular reference to the exploit mentioned in *Dunciad* A ii 143*n*.⟩

And holds his breeches close with both his hands.
   Then thus. "Since Man from beast by Words is known,
Words are Man's province, Words we teach alone.   150
When Reason doubtful, like the Samian letter,
Points him two ways, the narrower is the better.
Plac'd at the door of Learning, youth to guide,
We never suffer it to stand too wide.
To ask, to guess, to know, as they commence,   155

---

148. *And holds his breeches*] An effect of Fear somewhat like this, is described in the 7th Æneid ⟨515, 518⟩,

> *Contremuit nemus——*
> *Et trepidæ matres pressere ad pectora natos.*

nothing being so natural in any apprehension, as to lay close hold on whatever is suppos'd to be most in danger. But let it not be imagined the author would insinuate these youthful Senators (tho' so lately come from school) to be under the undue influence of any *Master*. SCRIBL. P.W. ⟨The italics indicate that some particular individual is intended. Most probably the note implies that the young senators, i.e. members of the upper (and lower?) House, come under the influence of Walpole, and vote as he wishes. The allusion can scarcely be to Bentley, the Master of Trinity, though he appears in person at l. 203.⟩

149 etc. ⟨The next two hundred lines (149–336) deal with different aspects of contemporary education. "What was first designed for an Epistle on Education, as part of my essay-scheme, is now inserted in the fourth book of the Dunciad" (Pope to Spence, p. 289). Warton writes a long and indignant note in defence of eighteenth-century education, and suggests that Pope perhaps "adopted this false opinion from that idle book on education, which Locke disgraced himself by writing"; but much of Pope's criticism of the classical education of the day is shrewd enough.⟩

151. *like the Samian letter*] The letter Y, used by Pythagoras ⟨a native of Samos⟩ as an emblem of the different roads of Virtue and Vice.

> *Et tibi quae Samios diduxit litera ramos.*
> Persius ⟨Sat. iii 56⟩. P.W.

153. *Plac'd at the door, &c.*] This circumstance of the *Genius Loci* (with that of the Index-hand before) seems to be an allusion to the *Table of Cebes*, where the Genius of human Nature points out the road to be pursued by those entering into life. 'Ο δὲ γέρων ὁ ἄνω ἑστηκὼς ἔχων χάρτην τινα ἐν τῇ χειρὶ, καὶ τῇ ἑτέρᾳ ὥσπερ δεικνύων τι οὗτος Δαίμων καλεῖται. *&c.* P.W. ⟨To Cebes, a disciple of Socrates, is attributed the Πίναξ or *Tabula*, a collection of philosophical reflections on life.⟩

154. *to stand too wide* ⟨"A pleasant allusion to the description of the door of Wisdom in the *Table of Cebes*, θύραν τινα μικράν."—Warburton, *1751*.⟩

As Fancy opens the quick springs of Sense,
We ply the Memory, we load the brain,
Bind rebel Wit, and double chain on chain,
Confine the thought, to exercise the breath;
And keep them in the pale of Words till death.   160
Whate'er the talents, or howe'er design'd,
We hang one jingling padlock on the mind:
A Poet the first day, he dips his quill;
And what the last? a very Poet still.
Pity! the charm works only in our wall,   165
Lost, lost too soon in yonder House or Hall.
There truant W Y N D H A M ev'ry Muse gave o'er,
There T A L B O T sunk, and was a Wit no more!
How sweet an Ovid, M U R R A Y was our boast!
How many Martials were in P U L T' N E Y lost!   170
Else sure some Bard, to our eternal praise,

---

159. *to exercise the breath*] By obliging them to get the classic poets by heart, which furnishes them with endless matter for Conversation, and Verbal amusement for their whole lives. P.W.

162. *We hang one jingling padlock, &c.*] For youth being used like Pack-horses and beaten on under a heavy load of Words, lest they should tire, their instructors contrive to make the Words jingle in rhyme or metre. W. ⟨*1743*⟩.

165. *our wall* ⟨Busby is speaking. He refers to the "Dormitory wall" mentioned in A iii 323*n*.⟩

166. *in yonder* House *or* Hall] Westminster-hall and the House of Commons ⟨*1743*⟩.

167. WYNDHAM ⟨For Sir William Wyndham, see Biog. App., vol. iv.⟩

168. TALBOT ⟨For Charles Talbot, Baron Talbot, see Biog. App., vol. iv. "He was extolled by his contemporaries as a prodigy of wit and a paragon of virtue."—DNB.⟩

169. *How sweet an Ovid*, MURRAY ⟨For William Murray, Earl of Mansfield, see Biog. App., vol. iv. He won a prize at Oxford for a Latin poem on the death of George I. A MS. poem of Murray's, *Aedes Blenhamianae*, is listed in H.M.C., Sixth Report, App. p. 680. He was a Westminster scholar (cf. Busby's "*our* boast").⟩

170. PULT'NEY ⟨Both William Pulteney and his cousin Daniel (d. 1731) published Latin verses; but Pope, who is certainly referring to the former, calls him a Martial probably in allusion to his lampoons in *The Craftsman*. See Biog. App., vol. iv, William Pulteney.⟩

In twice ten thousand rhyming nights and days,
Had reach'd the Work, the All that mortal can;
And South beheld that Master-piece of Man."
    "Oh (cry'd the Goddess) for some pedant Reign!   175
Some gentle J A M E S , to bless the land again;

174. *that Master-piece of Man*] viz. an *Epigram*. The famous Dr. *South* declared a perfect Epigram to be as difficult a performance as an Epic Poem. And the Critics say, "an Epic Poem is the greatest work human nature is capable of." P.W. ⟨This last statement had already been made by Pope in the *Peri Bathous*, ch. xv, "A Receipt to make an Epic Poem." EC traces South's statement about epigram to his *Sermons* (ed. 1710) ii 128.⟩

175. *Oh (cry'd the Goddess) &c.*] The matter under debate is how to confine men to Words for life. The instructors of youth shew how well they do their parts; but complain that when men come into the world they are apt to forget their Learning, and turn themselves to useful Knowledge. This was an evil that wanted to be redressed. And this the Goddess assures them will need a more extensive Tyranny than that of Grammar schools. She therefore points out to them the remedy, in her wishes for *arbitrary Power*; whose interest it being to keep men from the study of *things*, will encourage the propagation of *words* and *sounds*; and to make all sure, she wishes for another *Pedant Monarch*. The sooner to obtain so great a blessing, she is willing even for once to violate the fundamental principle of her politics, in having her sons taught at least *one thing*; but that sufficient, the *Doctrine of Divine Right*.

Nothing can be juster than the observation here insinuated, that no branch of Learning thrives well under Arbitrary government but *Verbal*. The reasons are evident. It is unsafe under such Governments to cultivate the study of things of importance. Besides, when men have lost their public virtue, they naturally delight in trifles, if their private morals secure them from being vicious. Hence so great a Cloud of Scholiasts and Grammarians so soon overspread the Learning of Greece and Rome, when once those famous Communities had lost their Liberties. Another reason is the *encouragement* which arbitrary governments give to the study of *words*, in order to busy and amuse active genius's, who might otherwise prove troublesome and inquisitive. So when Cardinal Richelieu had destroyed the poor remains of his Country's liberties, and made the supreme Court of Parliament merely *ministerial*, he instituted the *French Academy*. What was said upon that occasion, by a brave Magistrate, when the letters-patent of its erection came to be verified in the Parliament of Paris, deserves to be remembered: He told the assembly, that *this adventure put him in mind after what manner an Emperor of Rome once treated his Senate; who when he had deprived them of the cognizance of Public matters, sent a message to them in form for their opinion about the best Sauce for a Turbot.* W. ⟨*1743*⟩.

176. *Some gentle* J A M E S, *&c.*] Wilson tells us that this King, *James* the first, took upon himself to teach the Latin tongue to Car, Earl of Somerset; and that

To stick the Doctor's Chair into the Throne,
Give law to Words, or war with Words alone,
Senates and Courts with Greek and Latin rule,
And turn the Council to a Grammar School!   180
For sure, if Dulness sees a grateful Day,

Gondomar the Spanish Ambassador wou'd speak false Latin to him, on purpose to give him the pleasure of correcting it, whereby he wrought himself into
his good graces. ⟨Arthur Wilson, *History of Great Britain, Being the Life and Reign
of King James The First, 1653.*—"The reign of Pedantry with us is generally
reckoned that of King James I."—*Grub-Street Journal,* Feb. 26, 1736.⟩

This great Prince was the first who assumed the title of *Sacred Majesty,* which
his loyal Clergy transfer'd from *God* to *Him.* "The principles of Passive Obedi-
"ence and Non-resistance (says the Author ⟨Bolingbroke⟩ of the Dissertation
"on Parties, Letter 8.) which before his time had skulk'd perhaps in some old
"Homily, were talk'd, written, and preach'd into vogue in that inglorious
"reign. P.W. ⟨"Under James the First, which was absolutely the worst reign
we ever had, except perhaps that of James the Second."—Pope to Spence,
p. 155.⟩

181, 182. *if Dulness sees, &c.*] And grateful it is in Dulness to make this confession. I will not say she alludes to that celebrated verse of Claudian ⟨*De
Consulatu Stilichonis,* iii 113⟩,

> ——*nunquam* Libertas *gratior extat*
> *Quam sub* Rege pio——

But this I will say, that the words *Liberty* and *Monarchy* have been frequently
confounded and mistaken one for the other by the gravest authors. I should
therefore conjecture, that the genuine reading of the forecited verse was thus,

> ——*nunquam* Libertas *gratior exstat*
> *Quam sub* Lege *pia*——

and that *Rege* was the reading only of Dulness herself: And therefore she might
allude to it. SCRIBL.

I judge quite otherwise of this passage: The genuine reading is *Libertas,* and
Rege: So Claudian gave it. But the error lies in the first verse: It should be
Exit, not *Exstat,* and then the meaning will be, that Liberty was never *lost,* or
went away with so good a grace, as under a good King: it being without doubt
a tenfold shame to lose it under a bad one.

This farther leads me to animadvert upon a most grievous piece of nonsense
to be found in all the Editions of the Author of the Dunciad himself. A most
capital one it is, and owing to the confusion above mentioned by Scriblerus, of
the two words *Liberty* and *Monarchy.* Essay on Crit. ⟨90–1⟩.

> *Nature, like* Monarchy, *is but restrain'd*
> *By the same Laws herself at first ordain'd.*

Who sees not, it should be, *Nature like* Liberty? Correct it therefore *repugnantibus*

'Tis in the shade of Arbitrary Sway.
O! if my sons may learn one earthly thing,
Teach but that one, sufficient for a King;
That which my Priests, and mine alone, maintain,   185
Which as it dies, or lives, we fall, or reign:
May you, may Cam, and Isis preach it long!
'The R I G H T D I V I N E of Kings to govern wrong.' "
     Prompt at the call, around the Goddess roll
Broad hats, and hoods, and caps, a sable shoal: 190
Thick and more thick the black blockade extends,
A hundred head of Aristotle's friends.

---

omnibus (even tho' the Author himself should oppugn) in all the impressions which have been, or shall be, made of his works. BENTL. P.W. ⟨Pope, or Warburton, has misquoted, or Pope has belatedly improved, the second line of the couplet, viz. "By the same laws which first herself ordain'd."⟩

187. *Cam, and Isis* ⟨The two Universities were still preaching the doctrine of passive obedience. Oxford in particular remained very cool to the Hanoverians, and correspondingly sympathetic to the Jacobites and to Nonjurors.⟩

188. *The* RIGHT DIVINE *of Kings* ⟨If there was one doctrine that the Whigs might have been expected to maintain, it was opposition to the Divine Right of Kings. But cf. *The Champion*, May 22, 1740: "We have lived to see the Day, when Whigs, or those who call themselves so, have had the Front to acknowledge openly, that the Parliament ought to be dependent on the Crown."—The line is, no doubt, directed against George II, who, though far from being an absolute monarch, gave his ministers many awkward moments.⟩

190. *shoal* ⟨i.e. school. The word is applied to fish, frogs, seals, etc.⟩

191. *blockade* ⟨Perhaps suggested to Pope by the similarity in sound to "blockhead."⟩

192. *A hundred head of Aristotle's friends*] The Philosophy of *Aristotle* had suffered a long disgrace in this learned University: being first expelled by the *Cartesian*, which, in its turn, gave place to the *Newtonian*. But it had all this while some faithful followers in secret, who never bowed the knee to *Baal*, nor acknowledged any strange God in Philosophy. These, on this new appearance of the Goddess, come out like Confessors, and make an open profession of the ancient faith in the *ipse dixit* of their Master. Thus far SCRIBLERUS.

But the learned Mr. *Colley Cibber* takes the matter quite otherwise; and that this *various fortune of Aristotle* relates not to his *natural*, but his *moral* Philosophy. For speaking of that University in his time, he says, *they seemed to have as implicit a Reverence for Shakespear and Johnson, as formerly for the* ETHICS *of Aristotle*. See his Life, p. 385. One would think this learned professor had mistaken *Ethics* for *Physics*; unless he might imagine the Morals too were grown into disuse,

Nor wert thou, Isis! wanting to the day,
  [Tho' Christ-church long kept prudishly away.]
Each staunch Polemic, stubborn as a rock,   195
Each fierce Logician, still expelling Locke,
Came whip and spur, and dash'd thro' thin and thick
On German Crouzaz, and Dutch Burgersdyck.

---

from the relaxation they admitted of during the time he mentions, *viz.* while
He and the Players were ⟨in 1713⟩ at Oxford. W. ⟨*1743.*⟩

  Ibid. *A hundred head, &c.*] It appears by this the Goddess has been careful of
keeping up a Succession, according to the rule,

> *Semper enim refice: ac ne post amissa requiras,*
> *Anteveni*; *& sobolem* armento *sortire* quotannis.

⟨Virgil, *Georg.* iii 70–1⟩. It is remarkable with what dignity the Poet here
describes the *friends* of this ancient Philosopher. Horace does not observe the
same decorum with regard to those of another sect, when he says *Cum ridere
voles Epicuri de* grege *Porcum* ⟨*Ep.* i iv 16⟩. But the word *Drove, Armentum,* here
understood, is a word of honour, as the most noble *Festus* the *Grammarian* assures us, *Armentum id genus pecoris appellatur, quod est idoneum opus* armorum. And
alluding to the temper of this *warlike breed,* our poet very appositely calls them
a hundred head. SCRIBL. W. ⟨*1743.* Warburton's ironical note is intended
to emphasize, rather than conceal, the fact that by using the word "head" Pope
is thinking of his academic dunces as cattle.⟩

  194. [*Tho' Christ-church*] This line is doubtless spurious, and foisted in by the
impertinence of the Editor; and accordingly we have put it between Hooks.
For I affirm this College came as early as any other, by its *proper Deputies*; nor
did any College pay homage to Dulness in its *whole body.* BENTL. P.W. ⟨In the
Preface to his edition of *Paradise Lost* Bentley explained that those passages in
the poem which he believed to have been "foisted in" by Milton's "editor," he
had put "between two Hooks." Cf. *Ep.* ii i 104*n.*—In making a particular
exception of Christ Church, Pope is thinking, no doubt, of the group of wits—
Atterbury, Freind, Alsop—who baited Bentley in the controversy following
on the publication of Boyle's *Letters of Phalaris.*—Warburton, however, had too
many friends in Oxford to allow the satire on the University to stand without
the small modification with which the note concludes.⟩

  196. *still expelling* Locke] In the year 1703 there was a meeting of the heads
of the University of Oxford to censure Mr. Locke's Essay on Human Understanding, and to forbid the reading it ⟨*1742*⟩. See his Letters in the last Edit.
⟨*1743*⟩.

  197. *thin and thick* ⟨Cf. A ii 264*n.*⟩

  198. *On German* Crouzaz *and Dutch* Burgersdyck] There seems to be an im-
probability that the Doctors and Heads of Houses should ride on horseback,
who of late days, being gouty or unweildy, have kept their coaches. But these

As many quit the streams that murm'ring fall
To lull the sons of Marg'ret and Clare-hall,   200
Where Bentley late tempestuous wont to sport
In troubled waters, but now sleeps in Port.
Before them march'd that awful Aristarch;
Plow'd was his front with many a deep Remark:
His Hat, which never vail'd to human pride,   205

201 Bentley] B—tl—y *1742a–e.*

are horses of great strength, and fit to carry any weight, as their German and
Dutch extraction may manifest; and very famous we may conclude, being
honour'd with *Names,* as were the horses Pegasus and Bucephalus. SCRIBL.
P.W. ⟨For Jean Pierre de Crousaz, see Biog. App. Francis Burgersdyck (1590–
1629) was a Dutchman, Professor of Logic and Philosophy at Leyden.⟩

199. *the streams*] The River Cam, running by the walls of these Colleges,
which are particularly famous for their skill in Disputation. P.W. ⟨EC's comment (iv 357) is that "the authorities of these colleges were prominent in the
quarrel between Bentley and the University." "Marg'ret" is St John's College,
Cambridge, founded by the will of Lady Margaret Beaufort.⟩

202. *sleeps in Port*] viz. "now retired into harbour, after the tempests that had
long agitated his society." ⟨i.e. Trinity College, Cambridge. Bentley's long
quarrel with the Fellows ended in 1738. See Biog. App., Bentley.⟩ So *Scriblerus.*
But the learned *Scipio Maffei* understands it of a certain Wine called *Port,* from
Oporto a city of Portugal, of which this Professor invited him to drink abundantly. SCIP. MAFF. *de Compotationibus Academicis.* P.W. ⟨Port was, in fact,
Bentley's favourite wine. His comment on claret was that it "would be Port if
it could."—Monk, ii 401. For Scipio Maffei, see Biog. App. The *De Compotationibus Academicis* is, of course, a Pope-Warburton joke, and may possibly refer
to some occasion at Cambridge when Maffei was too hospitably entertained by
Bentley.⟩

204. *Remark* ⟨EC is probably right in suggesting that this word is used with
special reference to such titles as Bentley's *Remarks upon a late Discourse of Free
Thinking,* 1713.⟩

205–8. *His Hat, &c.*] The Hat-worship, as the Quakers call it, is an abomina-
tion to that sect: yet, where it is necessary to pay that respect to man (as in the
Courts of Justice and Houses of Parliament) they have, to avoid offence, and
yet not violate their conscience, permitted other people to uncover them.
⟨contrived to hire people to uncover them with the appearance of force.—*1742.*⟩
P.W. ⟨"Bentley generally wore, while sitting in his study, a hat with an enormous brim, as a shade to protect his eyes."—Monk, ii 401. He had another
characteristic of the Quaker: he was in the habit of using "thou" and "thee"
in conversation. Op. cit. ii 403.⟩

Walker with rev'rence took, and lay'd aside.
Low bow'd the rest: He, kingly, did but nod;
So upright Quakers please both Man and God.
"Mistress! dismiss that rabble from your throne:
Avaunt——is Aristarchus yet unknown?   210
Thy mighty Scholiast, whose unweary'd pains
Made Horace dull, and humbled Milton's strains.
Turn what they will to Verse, their toil is vain,
Critics like me shall make it Prose again.
Roman and Greek Grammarians! know your Better: 215
Author of something yet more great than Letter;
While tow'ring o'er your Alphabet, like Saul,

211–12 *Om. 1742a–f, 1743b.*

206. *Walker* ⟨Dr Richard Walker, Vice-Master of Trinity College. See iv 273, and Biog. App.⟩

207. — *He, kingly, did but nod*] Milton ⟨*Par. Lost*, xi 249–50⟩,
> — *He, kingly, from his State*
> *Declin'd not* ——

208. *upright* ⟨Pope is apparently punning on this word.⟩

210. — *is* Aristarchus *yet unknown?*]
> —— *Sic notus* Ulysses? Virg. ⟨*Aeneid*, ii 44⟩.
> *Dost thou not feel me,* Rome? Ben. Johnson ⟨*Catiline*, 1 i 1⟩.

210. *Aristarchus*] A famous Commentator, and Corrector of Homer, whose name has been frequently used to signify a complete ⟨severe — *1742*⟩ Critic ⟨*1742*⟩. The Compliment paid by our author to this eminent Professor, in applying to him so great a Name, was the reason that he hath omitted to comment on this part which contains his own praises. We shall therefore supply that loss to our best ability. SCRIBL. P.W. ⟨*1743.*—For the name Aristarchus as applied to Bentley, see Monk, vol. 1, p. 310.⟩

212. *Made Horace dull, &c.* ⟨In his edition of Horace, 1711, and of *Paradise Lost*, 1732. Cf. Swift, *Tale of a Tub*, ed. A. C. Guthkelch and D. Nichol Smith, p. 96*n.*: "These [i.e. the Moderns] have with unwearied Pains made many useful Searches into the weak sides of the Antients."⟩

215. *Roman and Greek* Grammarians, *&c.*] Imitated from Propertius ⟨Bk. II, Eleg. xxv 65–6⟩ speaking of the Æneid.
> *Cedite,* Romani *scriptores, cedite* Graii!
> Nescio quid majus *nascitur Iliade.*

217. *like Saul* ⟨"And he had a son, whose name was Saul,. . . and there was not among the children of Israel a goodlier person than he: from his shoulders and upward he was higher than any of the people."—I Samuel, ix 2.⟩

217, 218. *While tow'ring o'er your Alphabet, &c.*] Alludes to the boasted restora-

Stands our Digamma, and o'er-tops them all.
'Tis true, on Words is still our whole debate,
Disputes of *Me* or *Te*, of *aut* or *at*,   220
To sound or sink in *cano*, O or A,
Or give up Cicero to C or K.
Let Freind affect to speak as Terence spoke,

221 A,] A? *1742a–e*.   222 K.] K? *1742a–e*.

tion of the Æolic Digamma, in his long projected Edition of Homer. He calls it *something more than Letter*, from the enormous figure it would make among the other letters, being one Gamma set upon the shoulders of another. P.W. ⟨Bentley appears to have reached his conclusions about the Digamma as early as 1713, but they were not made public till 1732.—The two lines echo the Rev. Thomas Newcomb's translation of Addison's Latin poem, *Pygmæo-Geranomachia*, l. 90:
    Towers o'er his subjects, and o'erlooks them all.⟩

220. *of* Me *or* Te] It was a serious dispute, about which the learned were much divided, and some treatises written: Had it been about *Meum* or *Tuum* it could not be more contested, than whether at the end of the first Ode of Horace, to read, Me *doctarum hederæ præmia frontium*, or, Te *doctarum hederæ*—W. ⟨According to a MS. note in a copy of *The New Dunciad* in the Victoria and Albert Museum (Dyce 7747), "Dr Douglas was preparing a treatise on this subject, but was prevented by his death." Cf. iv 394.⟩

222. *Or give up* Cicero *to* C *or* K] Grammatical disputes about the manner of pronouncing Cicero's name in Greek ⟨*1742*⟩. It is a dispute whether in Latin the name of Hermagoras should end in *as* or *a*. Quintilian quotes Cicero as writing it *Hermagora*, which Bentley rejects, and says Quintilian must be mistaken, Cicero could not write it so, and that in this case he would not believe Cicero himself. These are his very words: *Ego vero Ciceronem ita scripsisse ne Ciceroni quidem affirmanti crediderim.*—*Epist. ad Mill. in fin. Frag. Menand. et Phil.* W. ⟨*1743*.—Pope was basing his satire here on personal experience. According to Warburton, "Lord Granville had long wanted to pass an evening with Mr. Pope: when he at last did so, Mr. P. said that the two hours were wholly taken up by his lordship, in debating and settling, how the first verse in the Aeneid was to be pronounced: and whether we should say Cicero or Kikero! This is what is meant in the two lines inserted in the Dunciad, on those learned topics."—Spence, p. 376.⟩

223, 224. *Freind,* — *Alsop*] Dr Robert Freind, master of Westminster-school, and canon of Christ-church—Dr. Anthony Alsop, a happy imitator of the Horatian style. P.W. ⟨*1743*.—"Those two lines on Alsop and Freind have more of satire than of compliment in them: . . . though I find they are generally mistaken for the latter only. They go on Horace's old method of telling a friend some less fault, while you are commending him . . . I scarce meet with any body that understands delicacy."—Pope to Spence, p. 265. If Freind is being rebuked,

And Alsop never but like Horace joke:
For me, what Virgil, Pliny may deny,　　　　225
Manilius or Solinus shall supply:
For Attic Phrase in Plato let them seek,
I poach in Suidas for unlicens'd Greek.
In ancient Sense if any needs will deal,
Be sure I give them Fragments, not a Meal;　　　230
What Gellius or Stobæus hash'd before,
Or chew'd by blind old Scholiasts o'er and o'er.
The critic Eye, that microscope of Wit,

231 hash'd] cook'd *1742a–e*.

it is presumably because he was too much concerned with mere expression, or too conscious of his fine style. Alsop's jokes were not always decorous. Bentley had been attacked by both scholars; it is natural that the words which Pope here puts in his mouth should be sarcastic. For Freind and Alsop, see Biog. App.⟩

226. *Manilius or Solinus*] Some Critics having had it in their choice to comment either on Virgil or Manilius, Pliny or Solinus, have chosen the worse author, the more freely to display their critical capacity. P.W. ⟨Bentley's edition of Manilius was published in 1739.—Gaius Julius Solinus was the compiler of a work entitled *Collectanea rerum memorabilium*, consisting mainly of historical and geographical observations. He owed a great deal to Pliny.⟩

228, *&c. Suidas, Gellius, Stobæus*] The first a Dictionary-writer, a collector of impertinent facts and barbarous words; the second a minute Critic; the third an author, who gave his Common-place book to the public, where we happen to find much Mince-meat of old books. P.W. ⟨Suidas flourished A.D. 1100. He was edited by Ludolph Küster (see iv 237), with the assistance of Bentley. Theobald contributed two papers on Suidas to John Jortin's *Miscellaneous Observations upon Authors, ancient and modern*, 1731, vol. i.—Aulus Gellius, the Roman grammarian, circa 130 A.D., compiled a work called *Noctes Atticae*, containing many fragments of ancient writers.—Stobæus, a Greek writer, circa 400 A.D., also preserved in his work valuable fragments of ancient literature.⟩

228. *I poach in Suidas* ⟨Cf. J. Oldham, *A Satire*, 222–3:
　　　　　Turn o'er dull *Horace*, and the Classick Fools,
　　　　　To poach for Sense . . .⟩

230. *Fragments* ⟨Probably a reference to Bentley's work on the fragments of Callimachus and Menander; but Bentley was constantly citing fragments from obscure Greek authors in his various works.⟩

232. *Or chew'd by blind old Scholiasts*] These taking the same things eternally from the mouth of one another. P.W.

233–5. *The critic Eye, &c.* ⟨In his "Thoughts on Various Subjects" Pope noted that "the eye of a critick is often like a microscope, made so very fine and

Sees hairs and pores, examines bit by bit:
How parts relate to parts, or they to whole,   235
The body's harmony, the beaming soul,
Are things which Kuster, Burman, Wasse shall see,
When Man's whole frame is obvious to a *Flea*.
    "Ah, think not, Mistress! more true Dulness lies
In Folly's Cap, than Wisdom's grave disguise.   240
Like buoys, that never sink into the flood,
On Learning's surface we but lie and nod.

---

nice, that it discovers the atoms, grains, and minutest particles, without ever comprehending the whole, comparing the parts, or seeing all at once the harmony." The thought has some resemblance to one in *Ep. to Arbuthnot*, 169–70. Cf. also *E. on C.*, 243 ff., and *Essay on Man*, i 193 ff.⟩

237. *Kuster, Burman, Wasse* ⟨For these three scholars, see Biog. App.⟩

239, 240. *Ah, think not, Mistress, &c.—In Folly's Cap, &c.*] By this it would seem the Dunces and Fops mentioned ver. 139, 140. had a contention of rivalship for the Goddess's favour on this great day. Those got the start, but these make it up by their Spokesmen in the next speech. It seems as if Aristarchus here first saw him advancing with his fair Pupil. SCRIBL. W. ⟨*1743*⟩.

241, 242. *Like buoys, &c.—On Learning's surface, &c.*] So that the station of a *Professor* is only a kind of legal Noticer to inform us where the *shatter'd hulk* of Learning lies at anchor; which after so long unhappy navigation, and now without either Master or Patron, we may wish, with Horace, may *lie there still*.

> —— *Nonne vides, ut*
> *Nudum remigio latus?*
> —— *non tibi sunt integra lintea;*
> *Non Dî, quos iterum pressa voces malo.*
> *Quamvis pontica pinus,*
> *Sylvæ filia nobilis,*
> *Jactes & genus, & nomen inutile.* Hor. ⟨*Od.* i xiv 3–4, 9–13⟩.

SCRIBL. W. ⟨*1742f.* Warburton's witticism is far from clear. The "shatter'd hulk of Learning" may be Bentley, but is more probably Trinity College, which offers a better parallel to the Ship of State referred to in the quotation from Horace. To those who considered that the sentence of deprivation passed on Bentley in 1734 by the Bishop of Ely had in fact deprived Bentley of his mastership, Trinity College could be said, for the rest of Bentley's life, to be "without a Master." He remained, however, Professor of Divinity, and that is presumably the point of Warburton's reference to "the station of a *Professor*." On "Patron" in this context I can throw no light at all. It should be added that Warburton's note first appeared in *1742f*, some time after Bentley's death (July 14, 1742);

Thine is the genuine head of many a house,
And much Divinity without a *Noûs*.
Nor could a B A R R O W work on ev'ry block,   245
Nor has one A T T E R B U R Y spoil'd the flock.
See! still thy own, the heavy Canon roll,

but it was no doubt written during his lifetime, and never revised to meet the altered circumstances. The college was certainly not without a Master long, Dr. Robert Smith having succeeded Bentley on July 20, 1742.⟩

243–4. *Thine is the genuine head, &c.* ⟨"It has been suggested that Dr. Warburton inserted some lines of his own composition in this fourth book of the Dunciad, which the poet wrote at his earnest request; and these two verses, as containing some common cant words peculiar to the university, are mentioned as some of them: as also the following,

           As erst Medea, cruel so to save,
           A new Edition of old Æson gave.

And the calling the members of the University of Oxford,

           Apollo's May'r and Aldermen,

is said to be one of Dr. Warburton's witticisms. For the truth of this assertion I cannot vouch."—Warton.—The word "genuine" is probably meant to refer to the quarrel at Trinity College as to whether Bentley was, or was not, the rightful Master.⟩

244. *And much Divinity without a Noûs*] A word much affected by the learned Aristarchus ⟨i.e. Bentley⟩ in common conversation, to signify *Genius* or natural *acumen*. But this passage has a farther view: *Noûs* was the Platonic term for *Mind*, or the *first Cause*, and that system of Divinity is here hinted at which terminates in blind Nature without a *Noûs*: such as the Poet afterwards describes (speaking of the dreams of one of these later Platonists)

         Or that bright Image *to our Fancy draw,*
         Which Theocles *in raptur'd Vision saw,*
         That Nature — *&c.* P.W.

⟨See below, iv 486.⟩

245, 246. *Barrow, Atterbury*] Isaac Barrow ⟨1630–77⟩ Master of Trinity, Francis Atterbury Dean of Christ-church, both great Genius's and eloquent Preachers; one more conversant in the sublime Geometry, the other in classical Learning; but who equally made it their care to advance the polite Arts in their several Societies. P.W. ⟨For Pope's friend, Bishop Atterbury (1662–1732), see vol. iv, Biog. App.⟩

245. *block* ⟨In the double sense of a block of stone waiting to be worked by the sculptor, and a blockhead. Cf. l. 270. Wakefield points out the allusion to the Latin proverb: "Non ex quovis ligno fit Mercurius."⟩

247. *the heavy Canon*] Canon here, if spoken of *Artillery*, is in the plural number; if of the *Canons of the House*, in the singular, and meant only of *one:* in which case I

14*

And Metaphysic smokes involve the Pole.
For thee we dim the eyes, and stuff the head
With all such reading as was never read: 250

248 Pole] Poll *1742e*.
249–54 *Om. 1742a–f. Four lines of asterisks are substituted.*
249 For thee they dim their eyes and stuff their head. *1743b*.

---

suspect the *Pole* to be a false reading, and that it should be the *Poll*, or *Head* of
that Canon ⟨*1742*⟩. It may be objected, that this is a mere *Paranomasia* or *Pun*. But
what of that? Is any figure of Speech more apposite to our gentle Goddess, or
more frequently used by her, and her Children, especially of the University?
Doubtless it better suits the Character of Dulness, yea of a Doctor, than that of an
Angel; yet *Milton* fear'd not to put a considerable quantity into the mouths of
his. It hath indeed been observed, that they were the Devil's Angels, as if he did
it to suggest the Devil was the Author as well of false Wit, as of false Religion,
and that the Father of Lies was also the Father of Puns. But this is idle: It must be
own'd a Christian practice, used in the primitive times by some of the Fathers,
and in later by most of the Sons of the Church; till the debauch'd reign of Charles
the second, when the shameful Passion for *Wit* overthrew every thing: and even
then the best Writers admitted it, provided it was obscene, under the name of
the *Double entendre*. SCRIBL. P.W. ⟨*1743*.—In the Dyce copy of *The New Dunciad*
the Canon to whom this note points is said to be "Dr. G–g–y of C.C. Ox.," i.e.
Dr David Gregory, a son-in-law of the Duke of Kent, who was appointed Canon
in 1736. Gregory had qualified for the *Dunciad* by writing a Latin poem on the
death of George I, and another on the accession of George II. Since Christ
Church is known as "the House," the phrase, "Canons of the House," takes on a
particular significance. Another canon of Christ Church whom Pope was willing
to satirize was Dr John Gilbert, the "leaden Gilbert" of l. 608.⟩

248. *And Metaphysic smokes, &c.*] Here the learned Aristarchus ending the first
member of his harangue in behalf of *Words*; and entering on the other half, which
regards the teaching of *Things*; very artfully connects the two parts in an encomium on M E T A P H Y S I C S, a kind of *Middle nature* between words and things:
communicating, in its obscurity with *Substance*, and in its emptiness with *Names*.
SCRIBL. W. ⟨*1743*⟩.

248. *Pole* ⟨In the classical sense of "sky." Cf. Pope's *Iliad*, viii 692:
          And Stars unnumber'd gild the glowing pole.
—In the Dyce copy of *The New Dunciad* the annotator has written in the margin
of l. 248 "Dr. C–n–b–re," i.e. John Conybeare, 1692–1755, who had been Dean
of Christ Church, Oxford, since 1733. But Conybeare was a friend of Warburton's: the annotator is probably only guessing.⟩

249–54. ⟨After the four lines of asterisks, *1742* has a note: "*Hiatus*, but not
valdè deflendus, since the learned Aristarchus loves a Fragment." Cf. l. 230.⟩

For thee explain a thing till all men doubt it,
And write about it, Goddess, and about it:
So spins the silk-worm small its slender store,
And labours till it clouds itself all o'er.

   "What tho' we let some better sort of fool   255
Thrid ev'ry science, run thro' ev'ry school?
Never by tumbler thro' the hoops was shown
Such skill in passing all, and touching none.
He may indeed (if sober all this time)
Plague with Dispute, or persecute with Rhyme.   260
We only furnish what he cannot use,
Or wed to what he must divorce, a Muse:
Full in the midst of Euclid dip at once,

---

255 to 271. *What tho' we let some better sort of fool, &c.*] Hitherto Aristarchus hath displayed the art of teaching his Pupils words, without things. He shews greater skill in what follows, which is to teach things, without profit. For with the *better sort of fool* the first expedient is, ver. 254 to 258, to run him so swiftly through the circle of the Sciences that he shall stick at nothing, nor nothing stick with him; and though some little, both of words and things, should by chance be gathered up in his passage, yet he shews, ver. 255 to 260, that it is never more of the one than just to enable him to *persecute with Rhyme*, or of the other than to *plague with Dispute.* But, if after all, the Pupil will needs *learn* a Science, it is then provided by his careful directors, ver. 261, 262, that it shall either be such as he can never *enjoy* when he comes out into life, or such as he will be obliged to *divorce*. And to make all sure, ver. 263 to 268, the useless or pernicious Sciences, thus taught, are still applied perversely; the man of Wit *petrified* in Euclid, or *trammelled* in Metaphysics; and the man of Judgment *married*, without his parents' consent, to a *Muse*. Thus far the particular arts of modern Education, used partially, and diversified according to the Subject and the Occasion: But there is one general Method, with the encomium of which the great Aristarchus ends his speech, ver. 266 to 268, and that is A U T H O R I T Y, the universal *Cement*, which fills all the cracks and chasms of *lifeless* matter, shuts up all the pores of *living* substance, and brings all human minds to *one dead level*. For if Nature should chance to struggle through all the entanglements of the foregoing ingenious expedients to *bind rebel wit*, this claps upon her one sure and entire cover. So that well may Aristarchus defy all human power to *get the Man out* again from under so impenetrable a crust. The Poet alludes to this Master-piece of the Schools in ver. 501, where he speaks of *Vassals to a name.* W. ⟨*1743*⟩.

257–8. *Never by tumbler, &c.* ⟨"These two verses are verbatim from an epigram of Dr. Evans, of St. John's College, Oxford; given to my father twenty years before the Dunciad was written."—Warton.⟩

And petrify a Genius to a Dunce:
Or set on Metaphysic ground to prance,   265
Show all his paces, not a step advance.
With the same Cement, ever sure to bind,
We bring to one dead level ev'ry mind.
Then take him to devellop, if you can,
And hew the Block off, and get out the Man.   270
But wherefore waste I words? I see advance
Whore, Pupil, and lac'd Governor from France.

264. *petrify a Genius*] Those who have no Genius, employ'd in works of imagination; those who have, in abstract sciences. P.W.

265–6. ⟨Warton notes a debt to Lord Hervey here. In *Some Remarks on the Minute Philosopher*, 1732, pp. 32–3, Hervey had compared metaphysical writers to horsemen in a "manage" (i.e. a riding school). "The Horsemen of this Class show their Address, their Skill, and their Dexterity, only by making their Horse go backwards, or side-ways, or round . . . The Standers-by cry, *It is very fine;* and these *Metaphysical Jockies* get down just where they got up. It is impossible to help seeing the *Minute Philosopher*, in his *prancing* Performance, in this Light."⟩

270. *And hew the Block off*] A notion of Aristotle, that there was originally in every block of marble, a Statue, which would appear on the removal of the superfluous parts. P.W. ⟨This notion is usually credited to Michelangelo. I have failed to trace it in Aristotle.⟩

272. *lac'd Governor*] Why *lac'd*? Because Gold and Silver are necessary trimming to denote the dress of a person of rank, and the Governor must be supposed so in foreign countries, to be admitted into Courts and other places of fair reception. But how comes Aristarchus to know by sight that this Governor came from France? Why, by the laced coat. SCRIBL. P.W. ⟨See l. 281*n*.⟩

Ibid. *Whore, Pupil, and lac'd Governor*] Some Critics have objected to the order here, being of opinion that the Governor should have the precedence before the Whore, if not before the Pupil. But were he so placed, it might be thought to insinuate that the Governor led the Pupil to the Whore: and were the Pupil placed first, he might be supposed to lead the Governor to her. But our impartial Poet, as he is drawing their Picture, represents them in the order in which they are generally seen; namely, the Pupil between the Whore and the Governor; but placeth the Whore first, as she usually governs both the other. P.W.

272. *Whore, Pupil* ⟨"Meaning the late Duke of Kingston, and his celebrated mistress, Mad. de la Touche."—Warton. But Croker had in his possession a MS. in Pope's handwriting in which ll. 329–30 read:

> See to my country happy I restore
> Another Grace, and add one Venus more.

To this was appended a note: "N.B. There are three Graces already, by which

Walker! our hat"—nor more he deign'd to say,
But, stern as Ajax' spectre, strode away.
    In flow'd at once a gay embroider'd race,   275
And titt'ring push'd the Pedants off the place:
Some would have spoken, but the voice was drown'd
By the French horn, or by the op'ning hound.
The first came forwards, with as easy mien,
As if he saw St. James's and the Queen.   280

279 forwards,] forward, *1742a–f, 1743b.*
280 *After 280 add:*
    Dulness delighted ey'd the lively Dunce,
    Rememb'ring she herself was Pertness once. *1742a–f.*   [*Cf.* I
    111–12. Here *1742e* has a note of 13 lines.]

---

were meant the Duke of Rut–d, D. of King–n, D. of Bol–n." It therefore seems
impossible, as Croker pointed out, to identify this "other Grace" with the Duke
of Kingston, since he is separately accounted for in the note.—EC iv 360.⟩

273. *Walker! our hat* ⟨"Philip Miller, the celebrated botanist, and author of
the 'Gardener's Dictionary,' went on an embassy to Cambridge to consult
Aristarchus upon some classical subject for the advantage of a foreign scholar. He
was hospitably received at Trinity Lodge, and after dinner propounded his question, when Bentley, perhaps not approving this style of consultation, recommended him to drink his wine. Miller, however, took three opportunities of recurring to the object of his mission, when Bentley, offended, called to his faithful
companion, 'Walker, my hat!' and quitted the room in a manner not unlike that
described by the poet."—Monk, ii 406-7. ⟩

274. *stern as* Ajax' *spectre*] See Homer Odyss. xi. where the Ghost of Ajax turns
sullenly from Ulysses ⟨*1742*⟩. A Passage extremely admired by Longinus. W.
⟨*1743*⟩.

276. *And titt'ring push'd, &c.*] Hor. ⟨*Ep.* II ii 216⟩.
              Rideat & pulset lasciva decentius ætas.
P.W. ⟨Cf. *Ep.* II ii 324–5. In his imitation of this passage Pope had already used
the word "titt'ring." See vol. iv, p. 187⟩.

278. *op'ning* ⟨i.e. giving tongue. There is an almost identical usage at l. 403.⟩

279. *The first came forwards, &c.*] This Forwardness or Pertness is the certain
consequence, when the Children of Dulness are spoiled by too great fondness of
their Parent. W. ⟨*1743*⟩.

280. *As if he saw St.* James's] Reflecting on the disrespectful and indecent Behaviour of several forward young Persons in the Presence, so offensive to all serious
men, and to none more than the good Scriblerus. P.W. ⟨This ironical note may
have been intended to refer to the behaviour of Frederick, Prince of Wales, who

When thus th'attendant Orator begun.
"Receive, great Empress! thy accomplish'd Son:
Thine from the birth, and sacred from the rod,
A dauntless infant! never scar'd with God.
The Sire saw, one by one, his Virtues wake: 285
The Mother begg'd the blessing of a Rake.
Thou gav'st that Ripeness, which so soon began,
And ceas'd so soon, he ne'er was Boy, nor Man.
Thro' School and College, thy kind cloud o'ercast,

285 one by one, his] smiling, his own *1742a–d.*

---

was frequently at loggerheads with his father. After a prolonged banishment from the Court, he had returned to pay his respects on Feb. 18, 1742.⟩

281. *th'attendant Orator*] The Governor abovesaid. The Poet gives him no particular name; being unwilling, I presume, to offend or do injustice to any, by celebrating one only with whom this character agrees, in preference to so many who equally deserve it. SCRIBL. P.W. ⟨The note suggests that the Governor, though not named, is drawn from a particular individual. He may have been Pope's old enemy, J. D. Breval. See below, 327n. This ascription is perhaps strengthened by Pope's note to l. 272, where it is asked how Aristarchus (i.e. Bentley) comes "to know by sight that this Governor came from France." Bentley certainly knew Breval by sight: he was not likely to forget him, having been compelled to dismiss him in 1708 from his fellowship at Trinity College for a misdemeanour.⟩

282–334. *Receive, great Empress! &c.* ⟨"If I may judge myself, I think the travelling Governor's Speech one of the best things in my new editions [i.e. additions?] to the Dunciad."—Pope to Spence, *Anecdotes*, p. 264.⟩

284. *A dauntless Infant! &c.* Hor. ⟨Bk. III, Ode iv 20⟩.
          — ⟨*Non*⟩ *sine Dis Animosus Infans.*
⟨The infant is never frightened by being told that there is a God: he has no education in religion.⟩

286. *the blessing of a Rake* ⟨i.e. that she might be blessed by her son becoming a rake.⟩

288. *he ne'er was Boy, nor Man*] Nature hath bestowed on the human species two states or conditions, *Infancy* and *Manhood*. Wit sometimes makes the *first* disappear, and Folly the *latter*; but true Dulness annihilates *both*. For, want of *apprehension* in Boys, not suffering that conscious ignorance and inexperience which produce the awkward bashfulness of youth, makes them *assured*; and want of *imagination* makes them *grave*. But this *gravity* and *assurance*, which is beyond *boyhood*, being neither wisdom nor knowledge, do never reach to *manhood*. SCRIBL. W. ⟨*1743*⟩.

Safe and unseen the young Æneas past: 290
Thence bursting glorious, all at once let down,
Stunn'd with his giddy Larum half the town.
Intrepid then, o'er seas and lands he flew:
Europe he saw, and Europe saw him too.
There all thy gifts and graces we display,   295
Thou, only thou, directing all our way!
To where the Seine, obsequious as she runs,
Pours at great Bourbon's feet her silken sons;
Or Tyber, now no longer Roman, rolls,
Vain of Italian Arts, Italian Souls: 300
To happy Convents, bosom'd deep in vines,
Where slumber Abbots, purple as their wines:

290. *unseen the young Æneas past: Thence bursting glorious*] See Virg. Æn. 1 ⟨411–14⟩,

> *At Venus obscuro gradientes aëre sepsit,*
> *Et multo nebulæ circum Dea fudit amictu,*
> *Cernere ne quis eos;—*1. *neu quis contingere possit;*
> 2. *Molirive moram;—aut* 3. *veniendi poscere causas.*

Where he enumerates the causes why his mother took this care of him: to wit, 1. that no-body might touch or correct him: 2. might stop or detain him: 3. examine him about the progress he had made, or so much as guess why he came there. P. W.

293–326. *Intrepid then, &c.* ⟨The description of the young rake on his foreign travels bears a general resemblance to a similar passage in James Miller's *Of Politeness*, 1738, 211–50. Locke had criticized the Grand Tour in *Some Thoughts Concerning Education*. See also *Spectator*, No. 364, April 28, 1712.⟩

294. *Europe he saw, &c.* ⟨"Sir John Barnard's son desiring an Allowance to travel and see the world, he replied, He would give double the Summ to have the world not see him."—Walpole. A fragment by Pope on Education, with a similar turn of thought, is printed in Sir James Prior's *Life of Edmund Malone*, 1860, p. 367:

> Desirous all to see the world they seem,
> And ne'er consider that the world sees them.⟩

300. ⟨i.e. the Tiber is no longer Roman, and is now (so far have things degenerated) proud of *Italian* arts and *Italian* souls.⟩

302. *Abbots* ⟨"Abbots, purple as their wines, is from Rousseau the Poet."—Warton.⟩

To Isles of fragrance, lilly-silver'd vales,
Diffusing languor in the panting gales:
To lands of singing, or of dancing slaves,   305
Love-whisp'ring woods, and lute-resounding waves.
But chief her shrine where naked Venus keeps,
And Cupids ride the Lyon of the Deeps;
Where, eas'd of Fleets, the Adriatic main
Wafts the smooth Eunuch and enamour'd swain.   310
Led by my hand, he saunter'd Europe round,
And gather'd ev'ry Vice on Christian ground;
Saw ev'ry Court, heard ev'ry King declare
His royal Sense, of Op'ra's or the Fair;
The Stews and Palace equally explor'd,   315
Intrigu'd with glory, and with spirit whor'd;
Try'd all *hors-d'œuvres*, all *liqueurs* defin'd,
Judicious drank, and greatly-daring din'd;
Dropt the dull lumber of the Latin store,
Spoil'd his own language, and acquir'd no more;   320
All Classic learning lost on Classic ground;
And last turn'd *Air*, the Echo of a Sound!

320 Spoil'd] Left *1742a–f, 1743b*.

303. *Lilly-silver'd vales*] Tuberoses.

308. *the Lyon of the Deeps*] The winged Lyon, the Arms of Venice. This Republic heretofore the most considerable in Europe, for her Naval Force and the extent of her Commerce; now illustrious for her *Carnivals*. P.W. ⟨Venice at this time "had an unenviable pre-eminence as the brothel of Europe."—W. E. Mead, *The Grand Tour in the Eighteenth Century*, 1914, pp. 294–5.⟩

314. *Op'ra's or the Fair* ⟨No doubt a sneer at George II, two of whose chief interests in life are here named.⟩

317. *hors-d'œuvres* ⟨The earliest instance recorded by OED of the word used in this sense.⟩

318. *greatly-daring din'd*] It being indeed no small risque to eat thro' those extraordinary compositions, whose disguis'd ingredients are generally unknown to the guests, and highly inflammatory and unwholesome. P.W. ⟨Cf. ll. 553–4.⟩

322. *And last turn'd* Air, *the Echo of a Sound*] Yet less a Body than Echo itself; for Echo reflects *Sense* or *Words* at least, this Gentleman only *Airs and Tunes*:

— Sonus *est, qui vivit in* illo. Ovid. Met. ⟨iii 401.—*1742*⟩.

So that this was not a Metamorphosis either in one or the other, but only a Reso-

See now, half-cur'd, and perfectly well-bred,
With nothing but a Solo in his head;
As much Estate, and Principle, and Wit,   325
As Jansen, Fleetwood, Cibber shall think fit;
Stol'n from a Duel, follow'd by a Nun,
And, if a Borough chuse him, not undone;
See, to my country happy I restore
This glorious Youth, and add one Venus more.   330
Her too receive (for her my soul adores)

326 Ja—s—n, Fl—tw—d, C—b—r, *1742a–e.*
330 This] The *1742a–d.*

lution of the Soul into its true Principles, its real Essence being Harmony; according to the Doctrine of Orpheus, the Inventor of Opera, who first perform'd to a
choice assembly of Beasts. SCRIBL. W. ⟨*1743*⟩.

324. *With nothing but a* Solo *in his head*] With nothing but a *Solo?* Why, if it be a
Solo, how should there be any thing else? Palpable Tautology! Read boldly an
Opera, which is enough of conscience for such a head as has lost all its Latin.
BENTL. P.W.

326. *Jansen, Fleetwood, Cibber*] Three very eminent persons, all Managers of
Plays; who, tho' not Governors by profession, had, each in his way, concern'd
themselves in the Education of Youth; and regulated their Wits, their Morals, or
their Finances, at that period of their age which is the most important, their entrance into the polite world ⟨*1742*⟩. Of the last of these, and his Talents for this
end, see Book I. ver. 199, *&c.* P.W. ⟨*1743.*—The note is ironical throughout. Cibber and Fleetwood were "managers of plays" at Drury Lane, and were also notorious gamblers. Sir Henry Jansen (d. 1766) managed his play at gaming-tables.
See *Donne* ii 88*n.*, and Biog. App., vol. iv, Jansen. For Charles Fleetwood, see
Biog. App.⟩

327. *Stol'n from a Duel, &c* ⟨"Capt. Breval a travelling Governor had a nun
escap'd to him from a Convent at Milan, where she had been plac'd against her
will; and afterwards went to Rome and pleaded her cause & was acquitted there
and married Breval."—Walpole.—The likelihood that Breval or some other
individual was intended is increased by a similar statement in Savage's *An Author
to be Let*, p. 9: "I shou'd have made a very fashionable Tutor, I wou'd have spirit-
ed up my Pupil to run away with a Nun." Cf. 331*n.*⟩

328. *And, if a Borough, &c.* ⟨Members of Parliament were immune from arrest
for debt.⟩

331. *Her too receive, &c.*] This confirms what the learned Scriblerus advanced
in his Note on ver. 272, that the Governor, as well as the Pupil, had a particular
interest in this lady. P.W.

So may the sons of sons of sons of whores,
Prop thine, O Empress! like each neighbour Throne,
And make a long Posterity thy own."
    Pleas'd, she accepts the Hero, and the Dame,   335
Wraps in her Veil, and frees from sense of Shame.
    Then look'd, and saw a lazy, lolling sort,
Unseen at Church, at Senate, or at Court,
Of ever-listless Loit'rers, that attend
No cause, no Trust, no Duty, and no Friend.   340
Thee too, my Paridel! she mark'd thee there,

---

332. *So may the sons of sons, &c.*] Virg.

      Et nati natorum, et qui nascentur ab illis. Æn. iii ⟨98⟩.

Ibid. *sons of whores*] For such have been always esteemed the ablest supports of the Throne of *Dulness*, even by the confession of those her most *legitimate* Sons, who have unfortunately wanted that advantage. The illustrious *Vanini* in his divine encomium on our Goddess, intitled *De Admirandis Naturæ Reginæ Deæque mortalium Arcanis*, laments that he was not born a Bastard: *O utinam extra legitimum ac connubialem thorum essem procreatus! &c.* He expatiates on the prerogatives of a *free birth*, and on what he would have done for the *Great Mother* with those advantages; and then sorrowfully concludes, *At quia Conjugatorum sum soboles his orbatus sum bonis.* W. ⟨*1743.*—Lucilio (or, as he styled himself, Giulio Cesare) Vanini, 1585–1619, was an Italian freethinker. In 1618 he was condemned as an atheist at Toulouse, and sentenced to have his tongue cut out, to be strangled at the stake, and burnt. This ghastly sentence was carried out in February, 1619. The work which Warburton refers to was published in 1616; it, too, was condemned and burnt.—The "sons of whores" of l. 332 may possibly be a thrust at the Duke of Grafton, who, as Lord Chamberlain, had given Cibber the laureateship in 1730 and so had "propped the throne" of dullness. His father, the first Duke, as the natural son of Barbara Villiers, Duchess of Cleveland, qualified for Pope's contemptuous phrase; the second Duke was accordingly one of the "sons of sons of whores."⟩

341. *Thee too, my* Paridel!] The Poet seems to speak of this young gentleman with great affection. The name is taken from Spenser, who gives it to a *wandering Courtly 'Squire,* that travell'd about for the same reason, for which many young Squires are now fond of travelling, and especially to *Paris.* P.W. ⟨Faery Queen. Lib. |III], Can. 9.—*1742.*—"I believe Paridel means Rd. Arundel Esqr. not only from the likeness of the sound and character, but as his particular Friends Sr. Andrew Fountain and Ld. Burlington follow immediately, under the names of Annius and Pollio."—Walpole. The annotator of the Dyce copy of *The New Dunciad* hazards "Ld. C–rnb–y," i.e. Lord Cornbury. Cf. *1740. A Poem,* l. 18, and Biog. App., vol. iv; but see also *Ep.* i vi 60 ff.⟩

Stretch'd on the rack of a too easy chair,
And heard thy everlasting yawn confess
The Pains and Penalties of Idleness.
She pity'd! but her Pity only shed   345
Benigner influence on thy nodding head.
    But Annius, crafty Seer, with ebon wand,
And well dissembled em'rald on his hand,
False as his Gems, and canker'd as his Coins,
Came, cramm'd with capon, from where Pollio dines.
Soft, as the wily Fox is seen to creep,   351
Where bask on sunny banks the simple sheep,
Walk round and round, now prying here, now there;
So he; but pious, whisper'd first his pray'r.
    "Grant, gracious Goddess! grant me still to cheat, 355

342, *&c. Stretch'd on the rack &c.*] Virg. Æn. vi ⟨617⟩.

> *Sedet*, æternumque sedebit,
> *Infelix Theseus, Phlegyasque* miserrimus *omnes*
> *Admonet—*

344. *The Pains and Penalties, &c.* ⟨EC notes the resemblance to Boileau, *Epistle* xi 86:

> Le pénible fardeau de n'avoir rien à faire.⟩

347. *Annius*] The name taken from Annius the Monk of Viterbo, famous for many Impositions and Forgeries of ancient manuscripts and inscriptions, which he was prompted to by mere Vanity, but our Annius had a more substantial motive. P.W. ⟨If Annius, as Walpole suggested, is Sir Andrew Fountaine, the "ebon wand" would be a reference to the rod he carried as Vice-Chamberlain to Queen Caroline. In a note to l. 348 in his edition of 1751, Warburton supposes that Annius was "A Factor between the poor and rich, to supply these with their imaginary wants, and to relieve those from their real ones." Sir Andrew was a purchaser of antiques for the museums of the wealthy. See Biog. App., Annius.— Annius (or John Nannius), 1432?–1502, was a learned friar who published, in 1498, *Antiquitatum variarum volumina xvii . . .*, which contains various writings claimed to be the work of ancient historians, but now known to be spurious. See Bayle, Art. "Nannius."⟩

350. *Pollio* ⟨Walpole's guess is the Earl of Burlington; but more probable is Henry Herbert, ninth Earl of Pembroke. See Biog. App., Pollio.⟩

355. *grant me still to cheat! &c.*] Hor. ⟨Bk. 1, Ep. xvi 60–2⟩.

> —— *Da, pulchra Laverna,*
> *Da mihi fallere* ——

O may thy cloud still cover the deceit!
Thy choicer mists on this assembly shed,
But pour them thickest on the noble head.
So shall each youth, assisted by our eyes,
See other Cæsars, other Homers rise;   360
Thro' twilight ages hunt th' Athenian fowl,
Which Chalcis Gods, and mortals call an Owl,
Now see an Attys, now a Cecrops clear,
Nay, Mahomet! the Pigeon at thine ear;
Be rich in ancient brass, tho' not in gold,   365
And keep his Lares, tho' his house be sold;
To headless Phœbe his fair bride postpone,
Honour a Syrian Prince above his own;

Noctem peccatis & fraudibus objice nubem.

⟨In *A Compleat Key to the Non-Juror* (1718), p. 24, these lines are translated:

Goddess of Deceit,
Grant me the happy Privilege to Cheat.⟩

Ibid. *still to cheat*] Some read *skill*, but that is frivolous, for Annius hath that skill already; or if he had not, *skill* were not wanting to cheat such persons. BENTL. P.W.

361. *hunt th' Athenian fowl*] The Owl stamp'd on the reverse of the ancient money of Athens.

Which Chalcis *Gods, and Mortals call an* Owl

is the verse by which Hobbes renders that of Homer ⟨*Iliad*, xiv 291⟩,

Χαλκίδα κικλήσκουσι θεοὶ, ἄνδρες δε Κύμινδιν.   P.W.

363. *Cecrops*] The first King ⟨Kings—*1743*⟩ of Athens, of whom it is hard to suppose any Coins are extant; but not so improbable as what follows, that there should be any of Mahomet, who forbad all Images. Nevertheless one of these Annius's made a counterfeit one, now in the collection of a learned Nobleman. P.W. ⟨Atys was an ancient King of Lydia. Cecrops, who is credited with being the founder of Athens, came from Egypt.—Mahomet "made his friends believe, that . . . a white pigeon, which came to pick grains of corn in his ear, was the Angel Gabriel, who came to declare to him, in the name of the same God, what he was to do."—Bayle, Art. "Mahomet."⟩

367. *To headless Phœbe, &c.* ⟨Cf. Pope's *Epistle to Addison*, ll. 43–4:

And Curio, restless by the fair one's side,
Sighs for an Otho, and neglects his bride.

Pope had already ridiculed the collecting of mutilated pieces of sculpture in *Peri Bathous*, ch. xi, and again in *Ep. to Arbuthnot*, l. 236.⟩

Lord of an Otho, if I vouch it true;
Blest in one Niger, till he knows of two."   370
    Mummius o'erheard him; Mummius, Fool-renown'd,
Who like his Cheops stinks above the ground,
Fierce as a startled Adder, swell'd, and said,
Rattling an ancient Sistrum at his head.
    "Speak'st thou of Syrian Princes? Traitor base!   375

369, 370. *Otho . . . Niger* ⟨M. Salvius Otho, a Roman emperor who ruled for a few months in 69 A.D. C. Pescennius Niger, a Roman emperor who reigned for about a year, and was killed in 194 A.D. Owing to the shortness of those two reigns, coins of Otho and Niger are excessively rare.⟩

371. *Mummius*] This name is not merely an allusion to the Mummies he was so fond of, but probably referred to the Roman General of that name, who burn'd Corinth, and committed the curious Statues to the Captain of a Ship, assuring him, "that if any were lost or broken, he should procure others to be made in their stead:" by which it should seem (whatever may be pretended) that Mummius was no Virtuoso. P.W. ⟨*1743*.—Walpole and Warton both identify Mummius as Dr Mead, the celebrated physician and collector: EC suggests Woodward. For a discussion of the various antiquaries who fit the context, see Biog. App., Mummius. In *Henry and Minerva: A Poem*, by J. B. Esq. 1729 (bound up in a volume at South Kensington that belonged to Pope—Dyce 616), Mummius appears on p. 57, together with a note that bears some resemblance to Pope's note here.⟩

371. *Fool-renown'd* ⟨"A compound epithet in the Greek manner, *renown'd by fools*, or *renown'd for making Fools*."—P. *1751*.⟩

372. *Cheops*] A King of Egypt, whose body was certainly to be known, as being buried alone in his Pyramid, and is therefore more genuine than any of the Cleopatra's. This Royal Mummy, being stolen by a wild Arab, was purchas'd by the Consul of Alexandria, and transmitted to the Museum of Mummius; for proof of which he brings a passage in Sandys's Travels ⟨*A Relation of a Journey . . .* George Sandys, 1615, pp. 130–1⟩, where that accurate and learned Voyager assures us that he saw the Sepulchre empty, which agrees exactly (saith he) with the time of the theft above mention'd. But he omits to observe that Herodotus tells the same thing of it in his time. P.W. ⟨See Biog. App., Mummius.⟩

374. *Sistrum* ⟨A musical instrument consisting of a thin oval metal frame furnished with transverse metal rods loosely fixed in it and a handle by which it was shaken. Originally peculiar to Egypt and the worship of Isis (OED).—At meetings of the Egyptian Club, founded about 1740, a sistrum was laid before the President, and Pope may have had that fact in mind. The first president was the Earl of Sandwich.—Nichols, *Lit. Anec.*, v 334.⟩

375. *Speak'st thou of Syrian Princes? &c.*] The strange story following which may be taken for a fiction of the Poet, is justified by a true relation in Spon's Voyages

Mine, Goddess! mine is all the horned race.
True, he had wit, to make their value rise;
From foolish Greeks to steal them, was as wise;
More glorious yet, from barb'rous hands to keep,
When Sallee Rovers chac'd him on the deep.   380
Then taught by Hermes, and divinely bold,
Down his own throat he risqu'd the Grecian gold;
Receiv'd each Demi-God, with pious care,
Deep in his Entrails—I rever'd them there,
I bought them, shrouded in that living shrine,   385
And, at their second birth, they issue mine."
    "Witness great Ammon! by whose horns I swore,
(Reply'd soft Annius) this our paunch before
Still bears them, faithful; and that thus I eat,
Is to refund the Medals with the meat.   390
To prove me, Goddess! clear of all design,
Bid me with Pollio sup, as well as dine:
There all the Learn'd shall at the labour stand,
And Douglas lend his soft, obstetric hand."

394 Douglas] D—gl—s *1742a–e.*

⟨ed. 1678, Tom. i 17–22⟩. Vaillant (who wrote the History of the Syrian Kings as it is to be found on medals) coming from the Levant, where he had been collecting various Coins, and being pursued by a Corsaire of Sallee, swallowed down twenty gold medals. A sudden Bourasque freed him from the Rover, and he got to land with them in his belly. On his road to Avignon he met two Physicians, of whom he demanded assistance. One advis'd Purgations, the other Vomits. In this uncertainty he took neither, but pursued his way to Lyons, where he found his ancient friend, the famous Physician and Antiquary Dufour, to whom he related his adventures. Dufour first ask'd him *whether the Medals were of the higher Empire?* He assur'd him they were. Dufour was ravish'd with the hope of possessing such a treasure, he bargain'd with him on the spot for the most curious of them, and was to recover them at his own expence. P.W.

    376. *horned race* ⟨See 387n.⟩

    383. *each* Demi-God] They are called Θεῖοι on their Coins. P.W.

    387. *Witness great* Ammon!] Jupiter Ammon is call'd to witness, as the father of Alexander, to whom those Kings succeeded in the division of the Macedonian Empire, and whose *Horns* they wore on their Medals.

    394. *Douglas*] A Physician of great Learning and no less Taste; above all curious in what related to *Horace,* of whom he collected every Edition, Transla-

The Goddess smiling seem'd to give consent;   395
So back to Pollio, hand in hand, they went.
    Then thick as Locusts black'ning all the ground,
A tribe, with weeds and shells fantastic crown'd,
Each with some wond'rous gift approach'd the Pow'r,
A Nest, a Toad, a Fungus, or a Flow'r.   400
But far the foremost, two, with earnest zeal,
And aspect ardent to the Throne appeal.
    The first thus open'd: "Hear thy suppliant's call,
Great Queen, and common Mother of us all!
Fair from its humble bed I rear'd this Flow'r,   405
Suckled, and chear'd, with air, and sun, and show'r,

---

tion, and Comment, to the number of several hundred volumes. P.W. ⟨For
James Douglas, M.D., 1675-1742, a celebrated obstetrician, see Biog. App.⟩

   397. *Then thick as locusts black'ning all the ground*] The similitude of *Locusts* does
not refer more to the numbers than to the qualities of the *Virtuosi*: who not only
devour and lay waste every tree, shrub, and green leaf in their *Course*, i.e. of ex-
periments; but suffer neither a moss nor fungus to escape untouched. SCRIBL.
W. ⟨*1743*⟩.

   400. *A Nest, a Toad, &c.* ⟨Cf. the Virtuoso's will in *Tatler*, No. 216, Aug. 26,
1710.⟩

   404. *Great Queen* ⟨This appeal to the Great Queen (i.e. the goddess of Dullness)
may be intended to have a secondary reference to Queen Caroline, whose interest in gardening made her a suitable arbitress of such a dispute. In a satirical
poem on Virtuosi in *The Grub-Street Journal*, No. 76, June 17, 1731, her taste in
gardening is noted:

> And for the Queen, outlandish shoots
> To keep in pots at Kensington.

Cf. also Egmont, ii 138.⟩

   405, &c.   *Fair from its humble bed, &c.—nam'd it* Caroline:
           Each Maid cry'd, charming! *and each Youth,* divine!
           Now prostrate! dead! behold that Caroline
           No Maid cries, charming! *and no Youth,* divine!

These Verses are translated from Catullus, Epith. ⟨42-7⟩.

> *Ut flos in septis secretus nascitur hortis,*
> *Quem mulcent auræ, firmat Sol, educat imber,*
> *Multi illum pueri, multæ optavere puellæ:*
> *Idem quum tenui carptus defloruit ungui,*
> *Nulli illum pueri, nullæ optavere puellæ, &c.*

Soft on the paper ruff its leaves I spread,
Bright with the gilded button tipt its head,
Then thron'd in glass, and nam'd it C A R O L I N E :
Each Maid cry'd, charming! and each Youth, divine!
Did Nature's pencil ever blend such rays,   411
Such vary'd light in one promiscuous blaze?
Now prostrate! dead! behold that Caroline:
No Maid cries, charming! and no Youth, divine!
And lo the wretch! whose vile, whose insect lust   415
Lay'd this gay daughter of the Spring in dust.
Oh punish him, or to th' Elysian shades
Dismiss my soul, where no Carnation fades."
        He ceas'd, and wept. With innocence of mien,
Th' Accus'd stood forth, and thus address'd the Queen.

407–9. *Soft on the paper ruff, &c.* ⟨Pope is here referring to some of the mea-
sures taken by the eighteenth-century gardener to produce the perfect carnation.
In Philip Miller's *The Gardener's Dictionary*, 3rd ed., 1737, Art. "Caryophyllus,"
full instructions are given: "You must therefore be provided with some square
Deal Sticks about four Feet and a half long . . . These Sticks should be carefully
stuck into the Pots . . . In a few Days after the Flowers begin to open, you must
cover them with Glasses which are made for that Purpose, in the following
manner: Upon the Top of the Glass, exactly in the Center, is a Tin Collar or
Socket about three Fourth of an Inch square, (this is for the Flower-stick to come
through) . . . At this time also, or a few Days after, as you shall judge necessary,
you should cut some stiff Paper, Cards, or some such Thing, into Collars about
four Inches over, and exactly round, cutting a Hole in the Middle of it about
three Fourths of an Inch Diameter, for the Bottom of the Flower to be let through;
then place these Collars about them to support the Petals . . ." Miller requires
four double-column folio pages to deal with the carnation. The "leaves" of l. 407
are petals.⟩

409. *and nam'd it* Caroline] It is a compliment which the Florists usually pay
to Princes and great persons, to give their names to the most curious Flowers of
their raising: Some have been very jealous of vindicating this honour, but none
more than that ambitious Gardiner at Hammersmith, who caused his Favourite
to be painted on his Sign, with this inscription, *This is* My *Queen Caroline*. P.W.

418. *where no Carnation fades* ⟨" . . . Our modest Votary warms his imagination only with Carnations always in bloom; which, alluding, at the same time,
to the perpetual spring of the old Elysian fields, give an inimitable pleasantry
as well as decorum, to the conclusion of his Prayer."—Warburton, *1751*.⟩

"Of all th' enamel'd race, whose silv'ry wing　　421
Waves to the tepid Zephyrs of the spring,
Or swims along the fluid atmosphere,
Once brightest shin'd this child of Heat and Air.
I saw, and started from its vernal bow'r　　425
The rising game, and chac'd from flow'r to flow'r.
It fled, I follow'd; now in hope, now pain;
It stopt, I stopt; it mov'd, I mov'd again.
At last it fix'd, 'twas on what plant it pleas'd,
And where it fix'd, the beauteous bird I seiz'd:　　430
Rose or Carnation was below my care;
I meddle, Goddess! only in my sphere.
I tell the naked fact without disguise,
And, to excuse it, need but shew the prize;
Whose spoils this paper offers to your eye,　　435
Fair ev'n in death! this peerless *Butterfly*."

"My sons! (she answer'd) both have done your parts:
Live happy both, and long promote our arts.
But hear a Mother, when she recommends
To your fraternal care, our sleeping friends.　　440
The common Soul, of Heav'n's more frugal make,
Serves but to keep fools pert, and knaves awake:

441 Of Souls the greater Part, Heav'ns common make, *1742a–d.*
442 Serves] Serve *1742a–d.*

---

421. *Of all th'enamel'd race*] The poet seems to have an eye to Spenser, Muio-
potmos ⟨ll. 17–18⟩.
　　　　　Of all the race of silver-winged Flies
　　　　　Which do possess the Empire of the Air.
427, 428. *It fled, I follow'd, &c.*]
　　　　　—I started back,
　　　　It started back; but pleas'd I soon return'd,
　　　Pleas'd it return'd as soon—Milton ⟨*Par. Lost*, iv 402–3⟩.
430. *bird* ⟨An unusually bold extension of meaning for Pope; but the use of the
Latin "volucris" for any winged thing, bird or insect, probably accounts for, if
it does not justify, a similar usage here.⟩
435. *this paper* ⟨The dead butterfly was presumably mounted on paper or
paste-board.⟩
440. *our sleeping friends*] Of whom see ver. 345 above.

A drowzy Watchman, that just gives a knock,
And breaks our rest, to tell us what's a clock.
Yet by some object ev'ry brain is stirr'd;   445
The dull may waken to a Humming-bird;
The most recluse, discreetly open'd, find
Congenial matter in the Cockle-kind;
The mind, in Metaphysics at a loss,
May wander in a wilderness of Moss;   450
The head that turns at super-lunar things,
Poiz'd with a tail, may steer on Wilkins' wings.

443-4 And most but find that Centinel of God
    A drowzy Watchman in the land of Nod. *1742a–d.*
445 And yet the dullest brain, if gently stir'd, *1742a–d.*
446 The dull] Perhaps *1742a–d.*
448 matter] object *1742a–d.*

443. ⟨To the reading of *1742,* "A drowzy Watchman in the land of Nod," the following note was added: "Beware Reader, not to mistake this for a mere idle Paranomasia: It was the Land to which Cain retreated with his family, when they had lay'd *Reason* (this *Centinel* of God) asleep, and follow'd only the guidance of their Passions.—Scrib." With the revision of the poem this laboured jest (of Warburton's?) was quietly suppressed.⟩

444. *And breaks our rest, &c* ⟨"i.e. When the feast of life is just over, calls us to think of breaking up; but never watches to prevent the disorders that happen in the heat of the entertainment."—W.*1751.*⟩

446-50. *a Humming-bird, &c.* ⟨Pope is here drawing upon a long-established source of ridicule. For satire on the collectors of humming-birds, cockle-shells, moss, &c., see *Tatler,* No. 216, No. 221, where the wit's attitude to such interests is clearly stated: "It is, methinks, the Mark of a little Genius to be wholly conversant among Insects, Reptiles, Animalcules, and those trifling Rarities, that furnish out the Apartment of a Virtuoso." The virtuoso was not sufficiently "philosophical": he merely collected. "Sir Isaac Newton, though he scarce ever spoke ill of any man, could hardly avoid showing his contempt for your virtuoso collectors and antiquarians. Speaking of Lord Pembroke once, he said, 'let him have but a stone doll and he is satisfied. I can't imagine the utility of such studies: all their pursuits are below nature.' "—Spence, p. 325.⟩

450. *a wilderness of Moss*] Of which the Naturalists count I can't tell how many hundred ⟨above three hundred—*1742*⟩ species. P.W. ⟨Cf. *Moral Es.* i 18*n.* In *A Plan of Mr Pope's Garden,* J. Searle, 1745, "Moss of many sorts," both living and petrified, is several times mentioned.⟩

452. Wilkins' *wings*] One of the first Projectors of the Royal Society, who, among many enlarged and useful notions, entertain'd the extravagant hope of a

"O! would the Sons of Men once think their Eyes
And Reason giv'n them but to study *Flies!*
See Nature in some partial narrow shape,　　　455
And let the Author of the Whole escape:
Learn but to trifle; or, who most observe,
To wonder at their Maker, not to serve."
　　"Be that my task (replies a gloomy Clerk,
Sworn foe to Myst'ry, yet divinely dark;　　　460
Whose pious hope aspires to see the day

possibility to fly to the Moon; which has put some volatile Genius's upon making wings for that purpose. P.W. ⟨" 'Tis not perhaps impossible, that a Man may be able to Fly, by the Application of Wings to his own Body."—John Wilkins, *The Discovery of a World in the Moone*, 4th ed., 1684, p. 183. Wilkins (1614–72), was Bishop of Chester, one of the founders of the Royal Society, and its first secretary.⟩

453. *O! would the Sons of men, &c.*] This is the third speech of the Goddess to her Supplicants, and completes the whole of what she had to give in instruction on this important occasion, concerning Learning, Civil Society, and Religion. In the first speech, ver. 119, to her Editors and conceited Critics, she directs how to deprave Wit and discredit fine Writers. In her second, ver. 175, to the Educators of Youth, she shews them how all Civil Duties may be extinguish'd, in that one doctrine of divine Hereditary Right. And in this third, she charges the Investigators of Nature to amuse themselves in Trifles, and rest in Second causes, with a total disregard of the First. This being all that Dulness can wish, is all she needs to say; and we may apply to her (as the Poet hath manag'd it) what hath been said of true Wit, that *She neither says too little, nor too much.* P.W. ⟨The author of this last observation has not been identified.⟩

455–6. ⟨Cf. ll. 233–8.⟩

459. *a gloomy Clerk*] The Epithet gloomy in this line may seem the same with that of dark in the next. But *gloomy* relates to the uncomfortable and disastrous condition of an irreligious Sceptic, whereas *dark* alludes only to his puzzled and embroiled Systems. P.W. ⟨Pope may be punning on the word "Clerk." The "sworn foe to Myst'ry" is perhaps Dr Samuel Clarke (1675–1729). See 471*n*. By "Myst'ry" is meant religious truth known only through divine revelation. Cf. the title of Toland's work, *Christianity not Mysterious*, and A iii 353*n*. If Clarke is, in fact, the gloomy spokesman of the freethinkers, he probably owes this distinction to the hostility of Bolingbroke, whose influence upon this whole passage is obvious. But the speech put into his mouth does not fairly represent the views expressed in the famous *Demonstration of the Being and Attributes of God* (1704–5). Clarke certainly used the *a priori* method to demonstrate the existence of a God, but he also argues from Nature to Nature's cause. Nor do his *a priori* arguments lead him to "doubt of God" (l. 472).⟩

When Moral Evidence shall quite decay,
And damns implicit faith, and holy lies,
Prompt to impose, and fond to dogmatize:)
Let others creep by timid steps, and slow,   465
On plain Experience lay foundations low,
By common sense to common knowledge bred,
And last, to Nature's Cause thro' Nature led.
All-seeing in thy mists, we want no guide,
Mother of Arrogance, and Source of Pride!   470
We nobly take the high Priori Road,

462. *When Moral Evidence shall quite decay*] Alluding to a ridiculous and absurd way of some Mathematicians, in calculating the gradual decay of Moral Evidence by mathematical proportions: according to which calculation, in about fifty years it will be no longer probable that Julius Cæsar was in Gaul, or died in the Senate House. See *Craig's Theologiæ Christianæ Principia Mathematica*. But as it seems evident, that facts of a thousand years old, for instance, are now as probable as they were five hundred years ago; it is plain that if in fifty more they quite disappear, it must be owing, not to their Arguments, but to the extraordinary Power of our Goddess; for whose help therefore they have reason to pray. P.W. ⟨John Craig, d. 1731, Scots mathematician, was a friend of Bishop Burnet, and may be suffering for that fact here. The curious work referred to was published in 1699.—-The freethinkers for whom the "gloomy Clerk" is speaking would naturally welcome any weakening of the historical evidences of Christianity.⟩

465-68. *Let others creep—thro' Nature led*] In these lines are described the *Disposition* of the rational *Inquirer*, and the *means* and *end* of *Knowledge*. With regard to his *disposition*, the contemplation of the works of God with human faculties, must needs make a modest and sensible man timorous and fearful; and that will naturally direct him to the right *means* of acquiring the little knowledge his faculties are capable of, namely *plain and sure experience*; which tho' supporting only an humble *foundation*, and permitting only a very slow progress, yet leads, surely, to the *end*, the discovery of the *God of nature*. W. ⟨*1743*⟩.

468. *to Nature's Cause, &c.* ⟨EC notes the resemblance to *Essay on Man*, iv 332:
          But looks thro' *Nature* up to *Nature's* God.⟩

471. *the high Priori Road*] Those who, from the effects in this Visible world, deduce the Eternal Power and Godhead of the First Cause tho' they cannot attain to an adequate idea of the Deity, yet discover so much of him, as enables them to see the End of their Creation, and the Means of their Happiness: whereas they who take this high Priori Road (such as Hobbs, Spinoza, Des Cartes, and some better Reasoners) for one that goes right, ten lose themselves in Mists, or ramble after Visions which deprive them of all sight of their End, and mislead them in the choice of wrong means. P.W. ⟨"He alludes to Dr Clarke's famous Demonstrations of the Attributes of God, a book which Bolingbroke, who hated

And reason downward, till we doubt of God:
Make Nature still incroach upon his plan;
And shove him off as far as e'er we can:
Thrust some Mechanic Cause into his place;　　　　475

Clarke because he was a favourite of Queen Caroline, impotently attacked."—
Warton. Wakefield, who agrees, quotes from a letter of Bolingbroke to Pope:
"Rather than creep up slowly, *à posteriori*, to a little general knowledge, they
soar at once as far, and as high, as imagination can carry them. From thence they
descend again armed with systems and arguments *à priori*, and regardless how
these agree, or clash with the phænomena of Nature, they impose them on mankind."—Bolingbroke, *Works*, vol. iii, p. 327.⟩

472. *And reason downward, till we doubt of God*] This was in fact the case of those
who, instead of reasoning from a *visible World* to an *invisible God*, took the other
road; and from an *invisible God* (to whom they had given attributes agreeable to
certain metaphysical principles formed out of their own imaginations) reason-
ed *downwards* to a *visible world* in theory, of Man's Creation; which not agreeing,
as might be expected, to that of God's, they began, from their inability to account
for *evil* which they saw in his world, to doubt of that God, whose being they had
admitted, and whose attributes they had deduced *a priori*, on weak and mistaken
principles. W. ⟨*1743*⟩.

473. *Make Nature still*] This relates to such as being ashamed to assert a mere
Mechanic Cause, and yet unwilling to forsake it intirely, have had recourse to
a certain *Plastic Nature, Elastic Fluid, Subtile Matter, &c.* P.W. ⟨"Plastic nature"—
Cudworth's phrase for a life-force which, he held, accounted for natural pro-
cesses without the interference of God. Berkeley scoffs at it in *Alciphron*, iii 14:
"He is positive as to the being of God; and that not merely as a plastic nature, or
soul of the world . . ."—"Subtile matter" [materia subtilis] was a term coined
by Descartes to describe a material which he supposed to fill the whole of space.
It was by such philosophical refinements that God was "shoved off": the Creator
of the Book of Genesis was deprived of His creative acts.⟩

475-6.　　　　*Thrust some* Mechanic Cause *into his place,*
　　　　　　　　Or bind in Matter, *or diffuse in* Space.]
The first of these Follies is that of Des Cartes, the second of Hobbs, the third of
some succeeding Philosophers. P.W. ⟨The "folly" of Descartes was his explanation of celestial motions by his hypothesis of vortices. Hobbes had suggested that
God might be composed of a subtle or refined matter: he would not admit existence to anything immaterial. The philosophers who "diffuse God in space" may
include Henry More who, in his anxiety to rescue spirit from being a mere ab-
straction, claimed extension for it while distinguishing it still from matter. (Cf.
Basil Willey, *The Seventeenth Century Background*, 1934, pp. 164-7.) Perhaps Newton is glanced at: he had called space "the Sensorium of the Godhead" (*Spectator*,
No. 565). In this he was followed by Clarke.⟩

475. *Thrust some Mechanic Cause, &c.* ⟨This was the error of Martinus Scrible-

> Or bind in Matter, or diffuse in Space.
> Or, at one bound o'er-leaping all his laws,
> Make God Man's Image, Man the final Cause,

rus, who "having run through all Universal System of Phylosophy, and traced Nature in all her Intricacies, was so familiar with every Operation she was Mistress of, knew the Necessity of her acting in the regular manner she does, that he convinc'd himself there was no Occasion for a superior Power."—*Memoirs of the Life of Scriblerus*, 1723 (*Satires and Personal Writings by Jonathan Swift*, ed. W. A. Eddy, p. 152.)⟩

477. *Or, at one* bound, *&c.*] These words are very significant: In their Physical and Metaphysical reasonings it was a *Chain* of pretended *Demonstrations* that drew them into all these absurd conclusions. But their errors in Morals rest only on bold and impudent *Assertions*, without the least shadow of proof, in which they *o'er-leap* all the laws of Argument as well as Truth. W. ⟨*1743.*—Bowles notes the resemblance to *Paradise Lost*, iv 181:

> At one slight bound high overleap'd . . .⟩

478, *&c. Make God Man's Image, Man the final Cause,*
> *Find* Virtue local, *all* Relation *scorn,*
> *See all in* Self—

Here the Poet, from the errors relating to a Deity in Natural Philosophy, descends to those in Moral. Man was made according to *God's Image*; this false Theology, measuring his Attributes by ours, makes God after *Man's Image*. This proceeds from the imperfection of his *Reason.* The next, of imagining himself the Final Cause, is the effect of his *Pride:* as the making Virtue and Vice arbitrary, and Morality the imposition of the Magistrate, is of the *Corruption* of his *heart.* Hence he centers every thing in *himself.* The Progress of Dulness herein differing from that of Madness; one ends in *seeing all in God*, the other in *seeing all in Self.* P.W. ⟨Bolingbroke had ridiculed those anthropomorphic divines who made God after man's image, whose God was "in their notion of him, nothing but an infinite man" (*Works*, v 310; quoted by Leslie Stephen, *History of English Thought in the Eighteenth Century*, 3rd ed., 1902, i 182).—Hobbes may fairly be said to be among those philosophers who "find Virtue local." Cf. *Leviathan*, pt. i, ch. 15: "For Morall Philosophy is nothing else but the Science of what is *Good*, and *Evill*, in the conversation, and Society of man-kind. *Good*, and *Evill*, are names that signifie our Appetites, and Aversions; which in different tempers, customes, and doctrines of men, are different . . . " He, too, might be said to "see all in *Self*"; but perhaps Mandeville is the writer in Pope's mind here. By "all Relation scorn," Pope, who believed in "self-love . . . push'd to social" (*Essay on Man*, iv 353), seems to refer to conduct which is based on self-interest alone. Those who make "Man the final Cause"—if the phrase is not merely rhetorical—are presumably the atheists, or those, at least, who place man on so high a pinnacle that they forget to ascribe all his works to God.⟩

Find Virtue local, all Relation scorn,
See all in *Self*, and but for self be born: 480
Of nought so certain as our *Reason* still,
Of nought so doubtful as of *Soul* and *Will*.
Oh hide the God still more! and make us see
Such as Lucretius drew, a God like Thee:
Wrapt up in Self, a God without a Thought,   485
Regardless of our merit or default.
Or that bright Image to our fancy draw,
Which Theocles in raptur'd vision saw,

483 and] or *1742a–e*.

481. *Of nought so certain as our* Reason *still*] Of which we have most cause to be
diffident. ⟨Cf. Bolingbroke, *Works*, iii 328, 329: " . . . that primitive error which
encourages our curiosity, sustains our pride . . . consists in the high opinion we
are apt to entertain of the human mind . . . To be contented to know things, as
God has made us capable of knowing them, is the first principle necessary to
secure us from falling into this error." Cf. also 465 ff.⟩ *Of nought so doubtful as of*
Soul *and* Will: two things the most self-evident, the Existence of our Soul, and the
Freedom of our Will. P.W.

484. *Such as Lucretius drew*] Lib. I ver. 57.

> *Omnis enim per se Divom natura necesse'st*
> *Immortali ævo summa cum pace fruatur,*
> *Semota ab nostris rebus, summotaque longe—*
> *Nec bene pro meritis capitur, nec tangitur ira.*

From whence the two verses following are translated, and wonderfully agree with
the character of our Goddess. SCRIBL. P.W.

485–6. *a God without a Thought, &c.* ⟨Pope here seems to be at some pains to
undo what some of his critics thought he had done in the *Essay on Man*, and to
dissociate himself clearly from Deism.⟩

487. *Or that* bright Image] *Bright Image* was the Title given by the later Platonists to that Idea of *Nature*, which they had form'd in their fancy, so bright, that
they call'd it αὐτοπτον ἀγαλμα or the *Self-seen Image* ⟨*1742*⟩, i.e. seen by its own
light. W. ⟨*1743*⟩.

488. *Which* Theocles *in raptur'd Vision saw*] Thus this Philosopher ⟨Theocles,
in Shaftesbury's dialogue, *The Moralists, a Philosophical Rhapsody*⟩ calls upon his
Friend, to partake with him in these Visions:

> "To-morrow, when the Eastern Sun
> "With his first Beams adorns the front
> "Of yonder Hill, if you're content
> "To wander with me in the Woods you see,
> "We will pursue those Loves of ours,
> "By favour of the Sylvan Nymphs:

While thro' Poetic scenes the Genius roves,
Or wanders wild in Academic Groves;   490
That N A T U R E our Society adores,
Where Tindal dictates, and Silenus snores."
Rous'd at his name, up rose the bowzy Sire,

"and invoking first the *Genius* of the *Place*, we'll try to obtain at least some faint
"and distant view of the *Sovereign Genius* and *first Beauty*." *Charact.* Vol. 2. pag. 245.
This *Genius* is thus apostrophized (pag. 345.) by the same Philosopher:

> "—O glorious *Nature!*
> "Supremely fair, and sovereignly good!
> "All-loving, and all-lovely! all divine!
> "Wise Substitute of Providence! *impower'd*
> "*Creatress!* or *impow'ring Deity,*
> "*Supreme Creator!*
> "Thee I invoke, and thee alone adore."

Sir *Isaac Newton* distinguishes between these two in a very different manner.
[Princ. Schol. gen. sub fin.]—*Hunc cognoscimus solummodo per proprietates suas &*
attributa, & per sapientissimas & optimas rerum structuras, & causas finales; veneramur
autem & colimus ob dominium. Deus etenim sine dominio, providentia, & causis finalibus,
nihil aliud est quam Fatum & Natura. P.W. ⟨The joke of printing Shaftesbury's
prose as verse had already been played by Bishop Berkeley in his *Alciphron*,
1732, Dial. 5.⟩

489. *roves,—Or wanders wild in Academic Groves*] "Above all things I lov'd *Ease*,
"and of all Philosophers those who reason'd most *at their Ease*, and were never
"angry or disturb'd, as those call'd *Sceptics* never were. I look'd upon this kind of
"Philosophy as the *prettiest, agreeablest, roving Exercise of the Mind*, possible to be
"imagined." ⟨*Characteristics*⟩ Vol. 2. p. 206. P.W.

491. *That Nature our Society adores* ⟨"See the *Pantheisticon*, with its liturgy and
rubrics, composed by Toland."—Warburton, *1751*. This odd work of Toland's
was published in 1720 in Latin; the English translation did not appear until 1751,
and perhaps Warburton had been reading it for the first time when he wrote his
note. It is doubtful whether Pope intended a reference to Toland's book, which
supplies a kind of liturgy for celebrating "the Socratic-Society." In Part i the
brotherhood is invited to repeat the words: "And let us detest all Priest-craft."⟩

492. *Silenus*] Silenus was an Epicurean Philosopher, as appears from Virgil,
Eclog. 6. where he sings the Principles of that Philosophy in his drink. P.W.
⟨Silenus is clearly intended for Thomas Gordon, the translator of Tacitus. For
many years before these lines appeared, he had been one of Walpole's men. He
is called Silenus because he was a Commissioner of the Wine Licences, an appointment which was made in recognition of his journalistic services to the government. See Biog. App., Gordon.⟩

And shook from out his Pipe the seeds of fire;
Then snapt his box, and strok'd his belly down: 495
Rosy and rev'rend, tho' without a Gown.
Bland and familiar to the throne he came,
Led up the Youth, and call'd the Goddess *Dame*.
Then thus. "From Priest-craft happily set free,
Lo! ev'ry finish'd Son returns to thee: 500
First slave to Words, then vassal to a Name,
Then dupe to Party; child and man the same;

494. *seeds of Fire*] The Epicurean language, *Semina rerum*, or Atoms. Virg.
Eclog. 6 ⟨31 ff.⟩, *Semina ignis—semina flammæ*—P.W.

495. *his belly* ⟨Gordon was described by one who knew him as "a very large
man, and corpulent."—Nichols, *Lit. Anec.*, i 709. The "box" is a snuff-box.⟩

497–8. *Bland and familiar, &c.* ⟨Possibly in allusion to the familiar style in
which Gordon had translated Tacitus, which Pope had already noticed in *Peri
Bathous*, ch. xii. Tacitus, Pope held, had been made by Gordon to talk "like a
coffee house politician." The same two adjectives, however, are applied to
Settle, B iii 41.⟩

499, 500.—*From* Priest-craft *happily set free, &c.*]The learned Scriblerus is here
very whimsical. It would seem, says he, by this, as if the *Priests* (who are always
plotting and contriving mischief against the *Law of Nature*) had inveigled these
harmless Youths from the bosom of their Mother, and kept them in open
Rebellion to her, till Silenus broke the charm, and restored them to her indulgent
arms. But this is so singular a fancy, and at the same time so unsupported by
proof, that we must in justice acquit them of all suspicions of this kind. W.
⟨*1743.*—In Gordon's *Independent Whig* the word "priestcraft" is frequently used.
He was a severe critic of the clergy. For his general attitude, see his Dedication to
The Independent Whig, 1721: "Can you deny, Gentlemen, that the more Power
the Priest possesses, just so much the more Men suffer in their souls and Bodies?"⟩

501. *First slave to Words, &c.*] A Recapitulation of the whole Course of Modern
Education describ'd in this book, which confines Youth to the study of *Words*
only in Schools, subjects them to the authority of *Systems* in the Universities, and
deludes them with the names of *Party-distinctions* in the World. All equally concurring to narrow the Understanding, and establish Slavery and Error in Literature, Philosophy, and Politics. The whole finished in modern Free-thinking; the
completion of whatever is vain, wrong, and destructive to the happiness of mankind, as it establishes *Self-love* for the sole Principle of Action. P.W. ⟨Cf. 255–71*n.*
The last sentence—though it seems to have little reference to the context—may
be intended to glance at the influence of Mandeville. Cf. *The Fable of the Bees*, ed.
F. B. Kaye, ii 178: "Man centers every thing in himself, and neither loves nor
hates, but for his own Sake. Every Individual is a little World by itself, and all
Creatures, as far as their Understanding and Abilities will let them, endeavour

Bounded by Nature, narrow'd still by Art,
A trifling head, and a contracted heart.
Thus bred, thus taught, how many have I seen,   505
Smiling on all, and smil'd on by a Queen.
Mark'd out for Honours, honour'd for their Birth,
To thee the most rebellious things on earth:
Now to thy gentle shadow all are shrunk,
All melted down, in Pension, or in Punk!   510
So K * so B * * sneak'd into the grave,
A Monarch's half, and half a Harlot's slave.
Poor W * * nipt in Folly's broadest bloom,

509 Now, to thy shade from all their glory shrunk; *1742a–f, 1743b*.
511 K* . . . B**] * . . . * * *1742a–f, 1743b*.

---

to make that Self happy."—Pope may have taken a hint from Oldham for l. 501.
Cf. *A Satire Addressed to a Friend*, l. 91:
    Slaves to an Hour, and Vassals to a Bell.⟩
    504. *A trifling head* ⟨Cf. *Ep. to Arb: thnot*, l. 327:
        The trifling Head, or the corrupted Heart!
In the first edition the resemblance was even closer. See vol. iv, p. 119.⟩
    506. *smil'd on by a Queen* ⟨There is probably a gibe here at Queen Caroline,
whose patronage of freethinkers was a matter of public comment. Warburton's
note to *1751*—"i.e. This Queen or Goddess of Dulness"—only shows that he was
conscious of the *double entendre*.⟩
    510. *Punk* ⟨whore.⟩
    511. *So K* so B** ⟨EC, following Carruthers, supplies the blanks with "Kent"
and "Berkeley"; i.e. Henry de Grey, Duke of Kent (1671–1740), and James,
third Earl of Berkeley (1680–1736). Pope had already written disrespectfully
of the former in *Ep. i* 88, where, as "Bug," he is cited as one who has a pension.
See Biog. App., vol. iv. Berkeley had been First Lord of the Admiralty under
George I. Both men were Knights of the Garter. EC suggests that the reference
to a "Harlot's slave" indicates that they must have owed their places to the influence of one of George I's mistresses, perhaps the Duchess of Kendal, "and
that they were obliged to share their spoils with her." For B**, cf. a MS. addition to *Essay on Man* ii 194 (EC iii 390):
        For right or wrong have mortals suffered more?
        B[lount] for his prince, or B** for his whore?⟩
    513. *Poor W** ⟨Walpole thought this must be Philip, Duke of Wharton (1698–
1731); and EC explained the line that follows as an allusion to the prefatory
memoir, supposed to be written by the poet Young, for the edition of Wharton's
Works. This seems to strain unduly the meaning of "Tomb"; nor is Wharton,
who took a remarkably independent line in politics, well-suited to the context.

> Who praises now? his Chaplain on his Tomb.
> Then take them all, oh take them to thy breast!   515
> Thy *Magus*, Goddess! shall perform the rest."
>   With that, a W I Z A R D O L D his *Cup* extends;

He had, however, given offence to Pope by attacking him in a satire. (See *The Letters and Works of Lady Mary Wortley Montagu*, ed. Lord Wharncliffe, i 30.)— Perhaps W* stands for the dissipated young Earl of Warwick, an early acquaintance of Pope's, who died, in 1721, "in Folly's broadest bloom." He was buried in Kensington Church, and an elaborate Latin epitaph was inscribed on his tomb.⟩

   517. *With that a Wizard old, &c.*] Here beginneth the celebration of the *greater Mysteries* of the Goddess, which the Poet in his Invocation ver. 5. promised to sing. For when now each Aspirant, as was the custom, had proved his qualification and claim to a participation, the High-Priest of Dulness first initiateth the Assembly by the usual way of *Libation*. And then each of the Initiated, as was always required, putteth on a *new Nature*, described from ver. 518 to 529. When the High-Priest and Goddess have thus done their parts, each of them is delivered into the hands of his Conductor, an inferior Minister or *Hierophant*, whose names are *Impudence, Stupefaction, Self-conceit, Self-interest, Pleasure, Epicurism, &c.* to lead them thro' the several apartments of her Mystic Dome or Palace. When all this is over, the sovereign Goddess, from ver 565 to 600 conferreth her *Titles* and *Degrees*; rewards inseparably attendant on the *participation* of the *Mysteries*; which made the ancient *Theon* say of them—κάλλιστα μὲν οὖν, καὶ τῶν μεγίστων ἀγαθῶν, τὸ Μυστηρίων μετέχειν. Hence being enriched with so many various Gifts and Graces, *Initiation* into the Mysteries was anciently, as well as in these our times, esteemed a necessary qualification for every high office and employment, whether in Church or State. Lastly the great Mother shutteth up the Solemnity with her gracious benediction, which concludeth in drawing the Curtain, and laying all her Children to rest. It is to be observed that Dulness, before this her Restoration, had her Pontiffs *in Partibus*; who from time to time held her Mysteries in secret, and with great privacy. But now, on her Re-establishment, she celebrateth them, like those of the *Cretans* (the most ancient of all Mysteries) in open day, and offereth them to the inspection of all men. SCRIBL. W. ⟨*1743*.—The Wizard, as EC suggests, is almost certainly Walpole. In the lines that follow, Pope is probably thinking in particular of William Pulteney. Though he was not made Earl of Bath till 1742, Pulteney had been growing steadily more lukewarm in opposition, and rumours that he was willing to be silenced by a peerage had been circulating for some years. The concluding sentence of Warburton's note seems to suggest that the dull are no longer confined to particular societies (e.g. Freemasons): they have now overflowed into public life.⟩

   517. *his Cup, &c.*] The *Cup* of *Self-love*, which causes a total oblivion of the obligations of Friendship, or Honour, and of the Service of God or our Country; all sacrificed to Vain-glory, Court-worship, or yet meaner considerations of Lucre and brutal Pleasures. From ver. 520 to 528. P.W.

Which whoso tastes, forgets his former friends,
Sire, Ancestors, Himself. One casts his eyes
Up to a *Star*, and like Endymion dies: 520
A *Feather* shooting from another's head,
Extracts his brain, and Principle is fled,
Lost is his God, his Country, ev'ry thing;
And nothing left but Homage to a King!
The vulgar herd turn off to roll with Hogs,   525
To run with Horses, or to hunt with Dogs;
But, sad example! never to escape
Their Infamy, still keep the human shape.
    But she, good Goddess, sent to ev'ry child
Firm Impudence, or Stupefaction mild;   530
And strait succeeded, leaving shame no room,
Cibberian forehead, or Cimmerian gloom.
    Kind Self-conceit to some her glass applies,
Which no one looks in with another's eyes:

---

518. *Which whoso tastes, forgets his former friends,—Sire, &c.*] Homer of the
Nepenthe, Odyss. 4 ⟨220–1⟩.

Αὐτίκ' ἄρ' εἰς οἶνον βάλε φάρμακον, ἔνθεν ἔπινον
Νηπενθές τ' ἄχολόν τε, κακῶν ἐπίληθον ἁπάντων.

520. *a Star* ⟨The "Star" is that worn by Knights of the Garter or Knights of
the Bath. Cf. vol. iv, p. 15, l. 108; p. 237, l. 14.⟩

521. *Feather* ⟨i.e. the feathers worn by Knights of the Garter in their caps.⟩

523, 524. *Lost is his God, &c.*] So strange as this must seem to a mere English
reader, the famous Mons. de la Bruyere declares it to be the character of every
good Subject in a Monarchy: "Where (says he) *there is no such thing as Love of our*
"*Country*, the Interest, the Glory and Service of the *Prince* supply its place." *De la
Republique*, Chap. 10. P.W.

525–6. *The vulgar herd, &c.* ⟨i.e. they eat and drink like hogs, they patronize
horse-racing, they ride to hounds.⟩

528. *still keep the human shape*] The Effects of the Magus's Cup are just contrary
to that of Circe. Hers took away the shape, and left the human mind: This takes
away the mind, and leaves the human shape. W.

529. *But she, good Goddess, &c.*] The only comfort such people can receive,
must be owing in some shape or other to Dulness; which makes some stupid,
others impudent, gives Self-conceit to some, upon the Flatteries of their depend-
ants, presents the false colours of Interest to others, and busies or amuses the rest
with idle Pleasures or Sensuality, till they become easy under any infamy. Each
of which species is here shadowed under Allegorical persons. P.W.

But as the Flatt'rer or Dependant paint,   535
Beholds himself a Patriot, Chief, or Saint.
  On others Int'rest her gay liv'ry flings,
Int'rest, that waves on Party-colour'd wings:
Turn'd to the Sun, she casts a thousand dyes,
And, as she turns, the colours fall or rise.   540
  Others the Syren Sisters warble round,
And empty heads console with empty sound.
No more, alas! the voice of Fame they hear,
The balm of Dulness trickling in their ear.
Great C * *, H * *, P * *, R * *, K *,   545

541 warble] compass *1742a–d.*
545 Great Shades of **, **, **, *, *1742a–f, 1743b.*

---

538. *Party-colour'd* ⟨Pope is playing on the word "party."⟩

541. *the Syren Sisters* ⟨The Muses of Opera⟩.

544. *The balm of Dulness*] The true *Balm of Dulness,* called by the Greek Physicians κολακεία, is a *Sovereign* remedy, and has its name from the Goddess herself. ⟨κολακεία : fawning, flattery. By printing "Sovereign" in italics Warburton appears to intend a piece of sarcasm at the expense of George II.⟩ Its ancient Dispensators were *her Poets;* but it is now got into as many hands as Goddard's Drops or Daffy's Elixir. It is prepared by the *Clergy,* as appears from several places of this poem: And by ver. 534, 535, it seems as if the *Nobility* had it made up in their own houses. This, which *Opera* is here said to administer, is but a spurious sort. See my Dissertation on the *Silphium* of the *Antients.* Bent. W. ⟨1743. —Rev. Thomas Daffy (d. 1680) invented the famous "elixir salutis," one of the most popular of all English nostrums. Jonathan Goddard (1617–75), Gresham professor of physic, was the inventor of the "drops" that bear his name.—Mr E. H. Blakeney has pointed out to me that Bentley discussed the Silphium in a letter to the Rev. J. Lawrence (*The Correspondence of Richard Bentley,* ed. C. Wordsworth, 1842, vol. ii, pp. 620 ff.). John Evelyn had suggested that silphium was assafoetida, and Bentley agrees.⟩

545. *Great C** &c.* ⟨Walpole filled in four of these blanks with Cowper, Raymond, Harcourt, King. The annotator of the Dyce copy of *The New Dunciad* agrees, except that he adds Parker and omits Harcourt. Wilkes, annotating the line as it appeared in the quarto of 1743, gives all five. Croker, in support of Wilkes, points out that the five men named were all the sons of peers, and that those peers had been ennobled through their "toils" (EC iv 365). William Cowper, first Earl Cowper, Simon Harcourt, first Viscount Harcourt, Thomas Parker, first Earl of Macclesfield, and Peter King, first Baron King of Ockham, were at different times Lord Chancellor; Sir Robert Raymond, first Baron Raymond,

Why all your Toils? your Sons have learn'd to sing.
How quick Ambition hastes to ridicule!
The Sire is made a Peer, the Son a Fool.
   On some, a Priest succinct in amice white
Attends; all flesh is nothing in his sight!   550
Beeves, at his touch, at once to jelly turn,
And the huge Boar is shrunk into an Urn:
The board with specious miracles he loads,

was Lord Chief Justice. Their sons (in Harcourt's case, grandson) were un-
distinguished, and, as Pope's line implies, patrons of the opera. See Biog. App.⟩

549. *amice* ⟨An oblong piece of white linen, used in the Western Church in
conjunction with the alb, originally enveloping the head and neck, now generally
folded so as to lie round the neck and shoulders (OED). Pope's priest is, however,
a chef; the amice is presumably his cap.⟩

553. *The board with* specious Miracles *he loads, &c*] Scriblerus seems at a loss
in this place. *Speciosa miracula* (says he) according to Horace ⟨*Ars Poetica*, 144–5⟩,
were the monstrous Fables of the Cyclops, Læstrygons, Scylla, *&c*. What relation have these to the transformation of Hares into Larks, or of Pigeons into
Toads? I shall tell thee. The Læstrygons spitted Men upon Spears, as we do Larks
upon Skewers: and the fair Pigeon turn'd to a Toad is similar to the fair Virgin
Scylla ending in a filthy beast. But here is the difficulty, why Pigeons in so shock-
ing a shape should be brought to a Table. Hares indeed might be cut into Larks
at a second dressing, out of frugality: Yet that seems no probable motive, when
we consider the extravagance before mention'd, of dissolving whole Oxen and
Boars into a small vial of Jelly; nay it is expresly said, that *all Flesh is nothing in his
sight*. I have searched in Apicius, Pliny, and the Feast of Trimalchio, in vain: I
can only resolve it into some mysterious superstitious Rite, as it is said to be done
by a *Priest*, and soon after called a *Sacrifice*, attended (as all ancient sacrifices
were) with *Libation* and *Song*. SCRIBL.

This good Scholiast, not being acquainted with modern Luxury, was ignorant
that these were only the miracles of *French Cookery*, and that particularly *Pigeons
en crapeau* were a common dish. P.W. ⟨Those "miracles of French Cookery" had
already been noted by James Miller in *Of Politeness: An Epistle*, 1738:

        So strange each Viand, and so strangely dress'd,
        If Fish, Flesh, Fowl, roast, boil'd can ne'er be guess'd:
        Here hid in Peacock's Brains a Squirrel lies,
        With Gravy drawn from twice twelve Woodcock's Thighs.

Cf. also *The Diseases of Bath. A Satire*, 1737, l. 406, in which the author similarly
remarks upon how
        A *Norway* Rat assumes a Rabbit's Shape.
Satire on French luxury seems to have been particularly popular about this
time. Cf. 595–6.⟩

Turns Hares to Larks, and Pigeons into Toads.
Another (for in all what one can shine?)   555
Explains the *Seve* and *Verdeur* of the Vine.
What cannot copious Sacrifice attone?
Thy Treufles, Perigord! thy Hams, Bayonne!
With French Libation, and Italian Strain,
Wash Bladen white, and expiate Hays's stain.   560
Knight lifts the head, for what are crowds undone
To three essential Partriges in one?

556 *Verdeur*] Verdure *1742cd.* the Vine] each Vine. *1742a–f, 1743b.*
560 Bladen] Bla* *1742a–f, 1743b.*   Hays's] Ha**'s *1742a–e.*
561 Knight] Kn - - - - t *1742a–d.*

555. *in all what one can shine?*] Alludes to that of Virgil, Ecl. 8. ⟨63⟩
———*non omnia possumus omnes.*

556. Seve *and* Verdeur] French Terms relating to Wines. ⟨Seve: the fineness and strength of flavour proper to any particular wine (OED). Verdeur: briskness. Cf. Verdour in OED.⟩ St. Evremont has a very pathetic Letter to a *Nobleman in disgrace*, advising him to seek Comfort in a *good Table*, and particularly to be attentive to *these Qualities* in his Champaigne. P.W.

560. *Bladen—Hays*] Names of Gamesters. Bladen is a black man. Robert Knight Cashier of the South-sea Company, who fled from England in 1720, (afterwards pardoned in 1742.)—These lived with the utmost magnificence at Paris, and kept open Tables frequented by persons of the first Quality of England, and even by Princes of the Blood of France. P.W. ⟨The words in parenthesis were added in *1743a*. The Bladen mentioned here is almost certainly Thomas Bladen, a gamester, not Col. Martin Bladen as Warton supposed. In the EC MS., i 230 ran: "Can make a Cibber, Bladen, or Ozell," where Col. Bladen (1680–1746), who demonstrated his dullness by writing a tragi-comedy, *Solon, or Philosophy no Defence against Love*, is clearly intended. Hays has not been indentified. For Bladen and Knight, see Biog. App., and for Knight, cf. *Ep.* ii i 195*n.*⟩

Ibid. *Bladen, &c.*] The former Note of *Bladen is a black man*, is very absurd. The Manuscript here is partly obliterated, and doubtless could only have been, *Wash Blackmoors white*, alluding to a known Proverb. SCRIBL. P.W. ⟨A "black man" at this period was often no more than a man with a dark complexion, or with black hair.⟩

562. *three essential Partriges in one*] i.e. two dissolved into Quintessence to make sauce for the third. The honour of this invention belongs to France, yet has it been excell'd by our native luxury, an hundred squab Turkeys being not unfrequently deposited in one Pye in the Bishopric of Durham: to which our Author alludes in ver. 593 of this work. ⟨This note, presumably by Pope, was omitted in Warburton's 1751 edition. The Bishop who was so fond of turkey pie was Dr

Gone ev'ry blush, and silent all reproach,
Contending Princes mount them in their Coach.
   Next bidding all draw near on bended knees,   565
The Queen confers her *Titles* and *Degrees*.
Her children first of more distinguish'd sort,
Who study Shakespeare at the Inns of Court,
Impale a Glow-worm, or Vertù profess,
Shine in the dignity of F. R. S.   570
Some, deep Free-Masons, join the silent race

564 mount] take *1742a–f, 1743b*.

William Talbot, 1659–1731. See below, 593–4, and Biog. App.—In a poem dated 1739, *A Panegyric on a Court*, mention is made of partridge pie, and a note is added: "An elegant Dish made in France, and sold in Town to your Conoisseurs in Luxury at the small Price of twenty Guineas." See also vol. iv, p. 8, l. 46*n*.⟩

   565. *on bended knees* ⟨In conformity with the custom in universities of kneeling before the Vice-Chancellor when receiving a degree.⟩

   568. *Who study Shakespeare* ⟨Warburton's note, applying this line to Thomas Edwards, whose *Canons of Criticism* appeared in 1748, is characteristically misleading. If the line had any particular reference in 1742, it could hardly have been to Edwards. Pope was probably thinking generally of legal dabblers in Shakespearian criticism, the literary lawyers who studied Shakespeare rather than Coke upon Littleton. Cf. the Templar in the *Spectator* club, who was placed in the Inner Temple by his father "to study the laws of the land, and is the most learned of any of the house in those of the stage."—*Spectator*, No. 2.⟩

   570. *the dignity of F.R.S.* ⟨Warton notes a debt to James Bramston's *The Man of Taste*, 1733:

        Next lodge I'll be Free-mason, nothing less,
        Unless I happen to be F.R.S.

Bramston here and elsewhere in his poem covers much the same ground as Pope in *The New Dunciad*.—Gibes at the Royal Society were frequent among the wits. Cf. *Tatler*, No. 236, Oct. 12, 1710, and *The Champion*, April 29, 1740, where mention is made of "such as we generally say can hardly write or read, or in other Words, a Man *barely* qualified to be a Member of the R— S—y." At this period peers and gentlemen with little or no scientific knowledge were frequently elected to the Society. Among the Fellows in 1741 were Richard Arundel (cf. l. 341*n*.) and William, Earl Cowper (cf. 545*n*.).⟩

   571. *Some, deep Free-Masons, join the silent race*] The Poet all along expresses a very particular concern for this silent Race: He has here provided, that in case they will not waken or open (as was before proposed) to a *Humming-Bird* or *Cockle*, yet at worst they may be made Free-Masons; where *Taciturnity* is the *only* essential Qualification, as it was the *chief* of the disciples of Pythagoras. P.W. ⟨The Free-

Worthy to fill Pythagoras's place:
Some Botanists, or Florists at the least,
Or issue Members of an Annual feast.
Nor past the meanest unregarded, one   575
Rose a Gregorian, one a Gormogon.
The last, not least in honour or applause,
Isis and Cam made Doctors of her Laws.
    Then blessing all, "Go Children of my care!
To Practice now from Theory repair.   580
All my commands are easy, short, and full:

masons had been much in the news about the time that *The New Dunciad* was
written. On March 9, 1741, a mock Masonic procession, organized by Paul
Whitehead and Henry Carey, paraded along the Strand. A print of this spurious
procession, *Mock Masonry: Or the Grand Procession*, was advertised in *The Daily
Gazetteer*, Mar. 28, 1741. The joke was repeated in the following year. As a Catholic, Pope might be expected to disapprove of freemasonry. But see p. 467.⟩

574. *an Annual feast* ⟨The annual Old Boys' dinner was already well established
by this time, and learned societies, such as the Royal Society, also held an annual
feast. So, too, did the Freemasons. Cf. *London Daily Post*, Mar. 20, 1741: "Yester-
day the Antient and Honourable Society of FREE AND ACCEPTED MASONS
had their Grand Annual Feast at Haberdashers-Hall. The Cavalcade was very
Grand (more Noblemen and Gentlemen than has been known for some Years)
. . . "⟩

576. *a Gregorian, one a Gormogon*] A sort of Lay-brothers, *Slips* from the Root
of the Free-Masons. P.W. ⟨The Gregorians and Gormogons were both founded
in the early eighteenth century in ridicule of the Freemasons. "The Gormogons
made much noise during their brief existence, but perished ignominiously."—
The Royal Masonic Cyclopædia, ed. K. H. R. Mackenzie, 1877, p. 280. See also EC,
iv 367.⟩

578. *Isis and Cam, &c.* ⟨For Pope's quarrel with the University of Oxford,
see iv 116n.—Among those at whom this sneer may have been directed was the
Rev. William Broome, who had been made an LL.D. of Cambridge.⟩

581-2. *All my commands, &c.*] We should be unjust to the reign of *Dulness* not
to confess that her's has one advantage in it rarely to be met with in Modern
Governments, which is, that the public *Education* of her Youth fits and prepares
them for the observance of her *Laws*, and the exertion of those Virtues she recommends. For what makes men *prouder* than the empty *knowledge of Words*; more
selfish than the Free-thinker's *System of Morals*; or *duller* than the profession of true
Virtuosoship? Nor are her *Institutions* less admirable in themselves than in the fitness
of these their several relations, to promote the harmony of the whole. For she tells
her Sons, and with great truth, that "all her commands are *easy, short, and full.*"
For is any thing in nature more *easy* than the exertion of *Pride*, more *short* and

15*

My Sons! be proud, be selfish, and be dull.
Guard my Prerogative, assert my Throne:
This Nod confirms each Privilege your own.
The Cap and Switch be sacred to his Grace;   585
With Staff and Pumps the Marquis lead the Race;

---

simple than the principle of *Selfishness*, or more full and ample than the sphere of *Dulness?* Thus Birth, Education, and wise Policy all concurring to support the throne of our Goddess, great must be the strength thereof. W. ⟨*1743.*⟩

584. *each* Privilege *your own, &c.*] This speech of Dulness to her Sons at parting may possibly fall short of the Reader's expectation; who may imagine the Goddess might give them a Charge of more consequence, and, from such a Theory as is before delivered, incite them to the practice of something more extraordinary, than to personate Running-Footmen, Jockeys, Stage Coachmen, *&c.*

But if it be well consider'd, that whatever inclination they might have to do mischief, her sons are generally render'd harmless by their Inability; and that it is the common effect of Dulness (even in her greatest efforts) to defeat her own design; the Poet, I am persuaded, will be justified, and it will be allow'd that these worthy persons, in their several ranks, do as much as can be expected from them. P.W. ⟨*1742–51*⟩. And we see he was aware of this, by singling out one or two who aimed higher, but at the same time tells us that their aims must be unsuccessful. ⟨*1742.*—This last sentence, suppressed in *1743a*, refers to ll. 589–94 of *The New Dunciad* for which see below, p. 403.⟩

585. *The Cap and Switch, &c.* ⟨i.e. the cap and switch of a jockey. EC suggests that "his Grace" here is William, third Duke of Devonshire, the "most dirty D——" of *Ep.* II ii 222. (See vol. iv, Biog. App.) His interest in horse-racing was well known: Lord Hervey summed him up as "a much better jockey than he was a politician."—*Hervey Memoirs*, i 24.⟩

586. *With Staff and Pumps, &c.* ⟨Running-footmen wore "pumps" (a sort of shoe without heels), and carried a long staff, when accompanying their master's coach. Apparently it was a fashionable affectation about 1738–9 for young gentlemen to appear in public dressed like grooms, coachmen, &c. Cf. *London Evening-Post*, Dec. 26/28, 1738, where a female correspondent complains of the behaviour of several young noblemen at the theatre: "Some of 'em had those loose kind of great Coats on, which I have heard call'd Wrap-Rascals, with Gold Lac'd Hats slouch'd, in humble Imitation of Stage Coachmen; others aspir'd at being Grooms, and had dirty Boots and Spurs, with black Caps on, and long Whips in their Hands . . ." It may be this that Pope has in mind; or he may be alluding to the common practice among noblemen of matching their running-footmen in races. (See *Grub-Street Journal*, Jan. 2, 1735.) Here, however, the Marquis appears to be running himself. He may, as EC suggests, be the Marquis of Hartington, the son of the Duke of Devonshire.⟩

From Stage to Stage the licens'd Earl may run,
Pair'd with his Fellow-Charioteer the Sun;
The learned Baron Butterflies design,
Or draw to silk Arachne's subtile line;   590
The Judge to dance his brother Sergeant call;

587–8. *the licens'd Earl* ⟨"Earl of Salisbury [i.e. James, sixth Earl, 1713–80] who took the property of a Stage Coach and drove it himself."—Walpole. EC quotes from one of Walpole's letters: "If Lord Burleigh could rise and view his representative driving the Hatfield stage, he would feel as I feel now" (H. Walpole, *Letters*, ed. Mrs Paget Toynbee, vol. v, p. 43). "Licens'd" is an allusion to the licence which had to be paid by the owner of a stage-coach or hackney-carriage; but Pope no doubt intends to suggest the further meaning of "privileged," as in "a licensed fool."—By l. 588 Pope probably means that the Earl drove so furiously that his coach kept pace with the chariot of the sun. Writing to William Fortescue (EC ix 97), Pope had already remarked:"... like your fellow-circuiteer, the sun, you travel the round of the earth."⟩

589. *The learned Baron* ⟨"Baron Charles de Geer, a friend and pupil of Linnæus, and a celebrated entomologist, whose observations were communicated in a series of papers to the Royal Society, and were afterwards published in seven quarto volumes with illustrations."—EC.⟩

590. *Arachne's subtile line*] This is one of the most ingenious employments assign'd, and therefore recommended only to Peers of Learning. Of weaving Stockings of the Webs of Spiders, see the Phil. Trans. P.W. ⟨In 1709 M. Bon of Montpelier gave an account to the Royal Society of "The Usefulness of the Silk of Spiders" (*Philosophical Transactions*, vol. xxvii, No. 325). In the course of his observations he remarks: "The ingenious fable of Arachne shows us, that it is to the spider we owe the first hints of the weaving of cloth." In *A Voyage to Laputa*, ch. v, Swift had already satirized the attempts to obtain silk from spiders.—The phrase "Arachne's line" occurs in Denham's *The Progress of Learning*, l. 195.⟩

591. *The Judge to dance his brother Serjeant call*] Alluding perhaps to that ancient and solemn *Dance* intitled *A Call of Sergeants*. P.W. ⟨*1743.*—At a call of sergeants certain ancient ceremonies were observed which had some resemblance to a country dance. Pope's old enemy, Thomas Burnet, had been made one of the King's Sergeants in 1736. EC, however, quotes Edward Wynne (*Eunomus*, vol. iv, p. 108), who states that in this passage Pope intended to ridicule the Revels at the Inns of Court. At the Revel held in 1735 in honour of Lord Talbot's elevation to the Lord Chancellorship, "the Master of the Revels who went first, took the Lord Chancellor by the right hand, and he by his left took Mr. J[ustice] Page, who, joined to the other Judges, Sergeants and Benchers present, danced, or rather walked 'round about the coal fire,' according to old ceremony three times." op. cit., p. 106.⟩

The Senator at Cricket urge the Ball;
The Bishop stow (Pontific Luxury!)
An hundred Souls of Turkeys in a pye;
The sturdy Squire to Gallic masters stoop,   595
And drown his Lands and Manors in a Soupe.
Others import yet nobler arts from France,
Teach Kings to fiddle, and make Senates dance.
Perhaps more high some daring son may soar,

592. *The Senator at Cricket, &c.* ⟨Several peers were noted at this time (circa 1740) for their interest in cricket; notably the two sons of the first Duke of Dorset, viz. the Earl of Middlesex and Lord John Sackville. The Earl of Sandwich and the Duke of Bedford were also enthusiastic supporters of the game. *The General Evening Post*, Aug. 2, 1737, announced a match to be played by the Prince of Wales and ten noblemen against the London Club. Cricket gave offence to many because it encouraged lords and gentlemen to associate with "butchers and cobblers."⟩

593-4. *The Bishop stow, &c.* ⟨See iv 562n.⟩

596. *And drown his Lands, &c.* ⟨Cf. *Sober Advice*, l. 14:

    And Lands and Tenements go down her Throat,

and James Miller's *Of Politeness: an Epistle* (1738):

    Then swallows down whole Manors at a meal.

EC thinks that the satire may reflect particularly on Richard Oldfield, for whom see *Ep.* ii ii 87, *Sat.* ii ii 25n. in vol. iv.⟩

598. *Teach Kings to fiddle*] An ancient amusement of Sovereign Princes, (viz.) Achilles, Alexander, Nero; tho' despised by Themistocles, who was a Republican. —*Make Senates dance*, either after their Prince, or to Pontoise, or Siberia. P.W. ⟨In *Moral Es.*, iii 44 Pope had already written:

    Or ship off Senates to a distant Shore.

In his note on that line he made it clear that he was thinking of "several Ministers, Counsellors, and Patriots banished in our times to Siberia," and to the banishment of the Parliament of Paris by Dubois to Pontoise, 1720.—The reference to fiddling is possibly a thrust at Prince Frederick, who, according to Lord Hervey, was "fond of his violoncello, as Nero of his harp." Hervey had seen and heard him once or twice a week during a whole summer "seated close to an open window of his apartment, with his violoncello between his legs, singing French and Italian songs to his own playing for an hour or two together."—*Hervey Memoirs*, iii 868. Rolli (B ii 203) had instructed the Prince's sisters, and possibly Frederick himself.⟩

599-604. *Perhaps more high, &c.* ⟨In these daring lines Pope is attacking Walpole's long ascendancy as First Minister. He had been virtual ruler of the country since 1721. He fell at last in Jan. 1742—two months before this attack

Proud to my list to add one Monarch more;   600
And nobly conscious, Princes are but things
Born for First Ministers, as Slaves for Kings,
Tyrant supreme! shall three Estates command,
And MAKE ONE MIGHTY DUNCIAD OF THE LAND!"
    More she had spoke, but yawn'd—All Nature nods:
What Mortal can resist the Yawn of Gods?   606
Churches and Chapels instantly it reach'd;

600 Proud] Strive *1742a–e*.
601–4 But here, vain Icarus! thy flight confine,
     Forbear! nor hope to make that Monarch thine:
     Blind with Ambition! to think Princes things
     Made just for thee, as all beside for Kings. – – –
       1742a–d.
     Perhaps ——   *   *   *   *
     [*followed by three lines of asterisks*.] *1742ef*.
605 spoke,] said, *1742a–d*.
     — but here she stops, she yawns, she nods; — *1742ef*.

was made upon him in *The New Dunciad*, but probably not before the lines were written. In *The New Dunciad* there is a note to l. 589 (i.e. l. 599 in this text): "Ver. 589 contains a wise advice to all first Ministers, but especially to any unable one." This note was probably written after Walpole's fall as a gibe at the incompetent Spencer Compton, Earl of Wilmington, who succeeded him as First Lord of the Treasury.⟩

606. *What Mortal can resist the Yawn of Gods*] This verse is truly Homerical; as is the conclusion of the Action, where the great Mother composes all, in the same manner as Minerva at the period of the Odyssey.—It may indeed seem a very singular Epitasis of a Poem, to end as this does, with a *Great Yawn*; but we must consider it as the *Yawn of a God*, and of powerful effects. It is not out of Nature, most long and grave counsels concluding in this very manner: Nor without Authority, the incomparable Spencer having ended one of the most considerable of his works with a *Roar*, but then it is the *Roar of a Lion*, the effects whereof are described as the Catastrophe of his Poem. P.W. ⟨See *Mother Hubberds Tale*, ll. 1337 ff.⟩

607–18. *Churches and Chapels, &c.* ⟨These lines seem to owe something to Paul Whitehead's *The State Dunces*, ll. 116–22, 169–72.⟩

607. *Churches and Chapels, &c.*] The Progress of this Yawn is judicious, natural, and worthy to be noted. First it seizeth the Churches and Chapels; then catcheth the Schools, where, tho' the boys be unwilling to sleep, the Masters are not: Next Westminster-hall, much more hard indeed to subdue, and not totally put to

(St. James's first, for leaden Gilbert preach'd)
Then catch'd the Schools; the Hall scarce kept awake;
The Convocation gap'd, but could not speak: 610
Lost was the Nation's Sense, nor could be found,

608 Gilbert] G—lb—t *1742a–e*. G —— *1751*.

silence even by the Goddess: Then the Convocation, which tho' extremely desir-
ous to speak, yet cannot: Even the House of Commons, justly called the Sense
of the Nation ⟨cf. vol. iv, p. 304, l. 78*n*.⟩, is *lost* (that is to say *suspended*) during
the Yawn (far be it from our Author to suggest it could be lost any longer!) but
it spreadeth at large over all the rest of the Kingdom, to such a degree, that
Palinurus himself (tho' as incapable of sleeping as Jupiter) yet noddeth for a
moment: the effect of which, tho' ever so momentary, could not but cause some
Relaxation, for the time, in all public affairs. SCRIBL. P.W.

608. *leaden*] An Epithet from the *Age* she had just then restored, according to
that sublime custom of the Easterns, in calling new-born Princes after some great
and recent Event. SCRIBL. ⟨*1743*.—The preacher is Dr John Gilbert, afterwards
Archbishop of York, and at this time Dean of Exeter. The word "leaden" may
be intended by Pope to characterize Gilbert's matter; it does not do justice to his
manner, for he is said to have wept in the pulpit while preaching a funeral sermon
on Queen Caroline, Dec. 25, 1737.—Egmont, ii 458. Cf. *Dia*. i 69*n*. Bowles was
informed on excellent authority that "there never was an expression applied with
such injustice, as 'leaden' to Dr Gilbert, who was in fact an eloquent and impressive preacher." See Biog. App.⟩

610. *The Convocation gap'd, but could not speak*] Implying a great desire so to do,
as the learned Scholiast on the place rightly observes. Therefore beware Reader
lest thou take this *Gape* for a *Yawn*, which is attended with no desire but to go to
rest: by no means the disposition of the Convocation; whose melancholy case in
short is this: She was, it is *reported*, infected with the general influence of the
Goddess, and while she was yawning at her ease, a wanton Courtier took her at
this advantage, and in the very nick clap'd a *Gag* into her mouth. Well therefore
may she be distinguished by her *gaping*; and this distressful posture it is our poet
would describe, just as she stands at this day, a sad example of the effects of Dulness and Malice unchecked and despised. BENT. W. ⟨*1743*.—The Lower House
of Convocation had been prorogued in 1717, following upon its remonstrance
against Hoadly's famous sermon, and did not again receive the royal licence to
transact business till 1861. "Upon several occasions during the Hanoverian
period the question of venturing again upon the experiment of sitting convocations was discussed; and in 1741, in consequence of the strong representations of
Archbishop Potte; and Bishop Gibson, the convocations were allowed to meet for
business, only to provoke a hasty prorogation when the lower house reasserted
its independence of the upper" (N. Sykes, *Church and State in England in the xviiith
Century*, 1934, p. 313). It is probably to this situation in 1741 that Pope refers.⟩

While the long solemn Unison went round:
Wide, and more wide, it spread o'er all the realm;
Ev'n Palinurus nodded at the Helm:
The Vapour mild o'er each Committee crept;   615
Unfinish'd Treaties in each Office slept;
And Chiefless Armies doz'd out the Campaign;
And Navies yawn'd for Orders on the Main.
    O Muse! relate (for you can tell alone,

614. *Ev'n Palinurus nodded, &c.* ⟨Palinurus is here Walpole, the pilot of the
Ship of State. Wakefield points out that the comparison had already been made
by Edward Young, *Sat.* vii 225:

> What felt thy Walpole, pilot of the realm!
> Our Palinurus slept not at the helm.⟩

615–8.] These Verses were written many years ago, and may be found in the
State Poems of that time. So that Scriblerus is mistaken, or whoever else have
imagined this Poem of a fresher date. P.W. ⟨In *1742* this note concluded: "or
whoever else wrote the Argument prefixt to this Book, where it is said 'the effects
of the Yawn are not unfelt at this day.' " In *Orpheus and Margarita* (*Poems on
Affairs of State*, 1704, vol. iii, p. 407), Pope found the following lines:

> And since the tawny Tuscan rais'd her Strain,
> R[oo]k furls his Sails, and dozes on the Main;
> Treaties unfinish'd in the Office sleep,
> And Sh[ov]el yawns for Orders on the Deep.

But he seems also to have taken a hint from James Miller's *Are these Things So?*
(1740):

> Whilst the vast *Navies* rais'd for her Support
> *Nod* on the *Main*, or *rot* before the *Port*.

Pope is referring to the delay in fitting out two expeditions to Spanish America
in 1740. One, under the command of Sir Charles Ogle, sailed at the end of October to join Admiral Vernon at Jamaica; the other, after considerable misman-
agement, had sailed under Anson for Peru on Sept. 18. The Opposition made
great play in debate with the lack of enterprise shown by the government in
prosecuting the war with Spain; and Pope is only one of several men of letters
who satirized their delay. The reference to "unfinish'd Treaties" may be intended to glance at the Convention which was signed by England and Spain
on Jan. 14, 1739. It was "unfinished" in the sense that it was inconclusive, and
left several important points unsettled. By "chiefless Armies" Pope may be alluding to the troops sent out to the West Indies under Lord Cathcart, who died
from the effects of the climate. His successor, General Wentworth, was neither
very active nor very competent.⟩

Wits have short Memories, and Dunces none)   620
Relate, who first, who last resign'd to rest;
Whose Heads she partly, whose completely blest;
What Charms could Faction, what Ambition lull,
The Venal quiet, and intrance the Dull;
'Till drown'd was Sense, and Shame, and Right, and
    Wrong—   625
O sing, and hush the Nations with thy Song!

*   *   *   *   *   *

620 Dunces] Dulness *1742f, 1743b* [*corrected in Errata*].

---

620. *Wits have short Memories*] This seems to be the reason why the Poets, whenever they give us a Catalogue, constantly call for help on the Muses, who, as the Daughters of *Memory*, are obliged not to forget any thing. So Homer, Iliad 2 ⟨488, 491–2⟩,

> Πληθὺν δ' οὐκ ἂν ἐγὼ μυθήσομαι, οὐδ' ὀνομήνω,
> Εἰ μὴ 'Ολυμπιάδες Μοῦσαι, Διὸς αἰγιόχοιο
> Θυγατέρες, μνησαίαθ' —

And Virgil, Æn. 7 ⟨645–6⟩,

> Et meministis enim, Divæ, & memorare potestis:
> Ad nos vix tenuis famæ perlabitur aura.

But our Poet had yet another reason for putting this Task upon the Muse, that all besides being *asleep*, she only could relate what passed. SCRIBL. P.W.

624. *The Venal quiet, and intrance the Dull*] It would be a Problem worthy the solution of *Aristarchus* himself, (and perhaps not of less importance than some of those weighty questions so long and warmly disputed amongst Homer's Scholiasts, as, *in which hand Venus was wounded*, and *what Jupiter whisper'd in the ear of Juno*) to inform us, which required the greatest effort of our Goddess's power, to *intrance the Dull*, or to *quiet the Venal*. For tho' the *Venal* may be more unruly than the *Dull*, yet, on the other hand, it demands a much greater expence of her Virtue to *intrance* than barely to *quiet*. SCRIBL. W. ⟨1743⟩.

626. ⟨To the couplet with which Pope closed *The New Dunciad* of 1742 the following note was added:

o'er the Land and Deep] It was but necessary for the Poet to say this expressly, that Britain might not be suppos'd to be in this condition alone, but in company with all other Nations of Europe. It had been a monstrous impropriety, in such a case, to have made any Nation keep awake, except *France*. But our Poet, tho' a Satyrist, is an utter enemy to all National Reflections. SCRIBL.

It is impossible to lament sufficiently the loss of the rest of this Poem, just at the opening of so fair a scene as the Invocation seems to promise. It is to be hop'd however that the Poet compleated it, and that it will not be lost to posterity, if

> In vain, in vain,—the all-composing Hour
> Resistless falls: The Muse obeys the Pow'r.
> She comes! she comes! the sable Throne behold
> Of *Night* Primæval, and of *Chaos* old!   630
> Before her, *Fancy's* gilded clouds decay,
> And all its varying Rain-bows die away.
> *Wit* shoots in vain its momentary fires,
> The meteor drops, and in a flash expires.
> As one by one, at dread Medea's strain,   635
> The sick'ning stars fade off th'ethereal plain;
> As Argus' eyes by Hermes' wand opprest,
> Clos'd one by one to everlasting rest;
> Thus at her felt approach, and secret might,
> *Art* after *Art* goes out, and all is Night.   640
> See skulking *Truth* to her old Cavern fled,

627–56 *Om. 1742a–f. Add, after 626*:
    While the Great Mother bids Britannia sleep,
    And pours her Spirit o'er the Land and Deep.
    [*This is followed by two rows of asterisks, and the words,*
    "*De-est FINIS*".] *1742a–f.*
629 She comes! she comes!] The Gloom rolls on, *1743b.*
631 her] them *1743b.*   632 its] her *1743b.*

we may trust to a Hint given in one of his Satires [*Sat.* II i 59].
            Publish the present Age, but where the Text
            Is Vice too high, reserve it for the next.⟩

629. *the sable Throne behold*] The sable Thrones of Night and Chaos, here represented as advancing to extinguish the light of the Sciences, in the first place
blot out the Colours of *Fancy*, and damp the Fire of *Wit*, before they proceed to
their greater work. W. ⟨*1743*⟩.

637. *As Argus eyes, &c.* ⟨A iii 343.⟩

641. Truth *to her old Cavern fled*] Alluding to the saying of Democritus, That
Truth lay at the bottom of a deep well ⟨*1729*⟩, from whence he had drawn her:
Though Butler says, *He first put her in, before he drew her out.* W. ⟨*1743.—Hudibras,*
pt. II, canto iii, ll. 665–6:
                'Twas he that put her in the pit,
                Before he pull'd her out of it.
Warburton claims this note on the strength of the reference to Butler; but the
rest of the note had appeared in *1729a*. See A iii 347*n.*⟩

Mountains of Casuistry heap'd o'er her head!
Philosophy, that lean'd on Heav'n before,
Shrinks to her second cause, and is no more.
Physic of *Metaphysic* begs defence,   645
And *Metaphysic* calls for aid on *Sense!*
See *Mystery* to *Mathematics* fly!

---

643. Philosophy, *that lean'd on Heav'n*] Philosophy has at length brought things
to that pass, as to have it esteemed unphilosophical to rest in the *first cause*; as if
its ends were an endless indagation of cause after cause, without ever coming to
the first. So that to avoid this unlearned disgrace, some of the propagators of our
best philosophy have had recourse to the contrivance here hinted at. For this
Philosophy, which is founded in the principle of *Gravitation*, first considered that
property in matter, as something extrinsical to it, and impressed immediately
by God upon it. Which fairly and modestly coming up to the first Cause, was
pushing natural enquiries as far as they should go. But this stopping, though at
the extent of our ideas, was mistaken by foreign Philosophers as recurring to the
occult qualities of the Peripatetics. To avoid which imaginary discredit to the new
theory, it was thought proper to seek for the *cause* of *gravitation* in a certain *elastic
fluid*, which pervaded all body. By this means, instead of really advancing in
natural enquiries, we were brought back again by this ingenious expedient to
an unsatisfactory *second cause*: For it might still, by the same kind of objection, be
asked, what was the *cause* of that *elasticity*? See this folly censured, ver. 475. W.
⟨*1743*.—Cf. A iii 349–50*n*.⟩

645, 646. Physic *of* Metaphysic, *&c.—And* Metaphysic *calls*, *&c.*] Certain
writers, as Malbranch, Norris, and others, have thought it of importance, in order
to secure the existence of the *soul*, to bring in question the reality of *body*; which
they have attempted to do by a very refined *metaphysical* reasoning: While others
of the same party, in order to persuade us of the necessity of a Revelation which
promises immortality, have been as anxious to prove that those qualities which
are commonly supposed to belong only to an immaterial Being, are but the
result from the sensations of matter, and the soul naturally mortal. Thus between these different reasonings, they have left us neither Soul nor Body: nor
the Sciences of Physics and Metaphysics the least support, by making them depend upon and go a begging to one another. W. ⟨*1743*⟩.

647. *See* Mystery *to* Mathematics *fly*] A sort of men (who make human Reason
the adequate measure of all Truth) having pretended that whatsoever is not
fully comprehended by it, is contrary to it; certain defenders of Religion, who
would not be outdone in a paradox, have gone as far in the opposite folly, and
attempted to shew that the mysteries of Religion may be mathematically demonstrated; as the authors of Philosophic, or Astronomic Principles, natural and
reveal'd. W. ⟨*1743*.—To this Warburton added in *1751*: "who have much prided
themselves on reflecting a fantastic light upon religion from the frigid subtilty of
school moonshine." Warburton's note is directed against the Deists in general,

In vain! they gaze, turn giddy, rave, and die.
Religion blushing veils her sacred fires,
And unawares *Morality* expires.   650
Nor *public* Flame, nor *private*, dares to shine;
Nor *human* Spark is left, nor Glimpse *divine!*
Lo! thy dread Empire, C H A O s! is restor'd;
Light dies before thy uncreating word:
Thy hand, great Anarch! lets the curtain fall;   655
And Universal Darkness buries All.

656 Darkness] Dulness *1743b*.

but also, no doubt, against such philosophers as Descartes, Leibnitz, and Samuel Clarke who "attempted to shew that the mysteries of Religion may be mathematically demonstrated." In 1714 William Derham published his *Astro-Theology*, which he intended to be "a demonstration of the being and attributes of God from a survey of the heavens." It is just possible that Warburton is sneering at this innocent work.⟩

649. Religion *blushing veils her sacred fires*] *Blushing*, not only at the view of these her false supports in the *present* overflow of dulness, but at the memory of the *past*; when the barbarous learning of so many ages was solely employed in corrupting the simplicity, and defiling the purity of Religion. Amidst the extinction of all other Lights, she is said only to withdraw hers; as hers alone in its own nature is unextinguishable and eternal. W. ⟨*1743*.—This note was read, and presumably approved by Pope; but the first part of it seems to offer a fair example of his commentator's irrelevance. The whole of the concluding passage (ll. 627–56) refers to the present or to the immediate future; it is unlikely, therefore, that the poet was thinking of religion blushing "at the memory of the past." The decay of religion was only one aspect of the national degeneration which Pope saw, or thought he saw, in *contemporary* England.⟩

650. *And unawares* Morality *expires*] It appears from hence that our Poet was of very different sentiments from the Author of the Characteristics, who has written a formal treatise on Virtue, to prove it not only real but durable, without the support of Religion ⟨*An Enquiry concerning Virtue, or Merit*, by the Earl of Shaftesbury⟩. The word *unawares* alludes to the confidence of those men who suppose that Morality would flourish best without it, and consequently to the surprize such would be in (if any such there are) who indeed love Virtue, and yet do all they can to root out the Religion of their Country. W. ⟨*1743*⟩.

656. *Darkness buries all* ⟨Cf. *2 Henry IV*, I i 154, 160:

> Let Order die . . .
> And darknesse be the burier of the dead.⟩

F I N I S .

APPENDIX.

I.
PREFACE
Prefixed to the five first imperfect Editions of the DUNCIAD, in three books, printed at DUBLIN and LONDON, in octavo and duodecimo, 1727.

⟨See p. 201.⟩

II.
A LIST of
BOOKS, PAPERS, and VERSES,
In which our Author was abused, before the Publication of the DUNCIAD; with the true Names of the Authors.

⟨See p. 207.⟩

III.
ADVERTISEMENT
To the FIRST EDITION with Notes, in Quarto, 1729.

⟨See p. 8.⟩

IV.
ADVERTISEMENT
To the FIRST EDITION, separate, of
The FOURTH BOOK of the DUNCIAD.

WE apprehend it can be deemed no injury to the author of the three first books of the Dunciad, that we publish this Fourth. It was found merely by accident, in taking a survey of the *Library* of a late eminent nobleman; but in so blotted a condition, and in so many detach'd pieces, as plainly   5

---

4. *a late eminent nobleman* ⟨Pope almost certainly intended the reader to think that Edward Harley, second Earl of Oxford, was the nobleman in question. The Earl had died on June 16, 1741. In the preface to his *Letters of Mr. Alexander Pope and Several of his Friends*, 1737, Pope had sought to persuade the public that the collection of his letters published by Curll in 1735 had been stolen from Lord Oxford's library. See C. W. Dilke, *The Papers of a Critic*, 1875, i 287 ff.⟩

shewed it to be not only *incorrect,* but *unfinished.* That the author of the three first books had a design to extend and complete his poem in this manner, appears from the dissertation prefixt to it, where it is said, that *the design is more extensive, and that we may expect other episodes to complete it:* And from the declara- 5 tion in the argument to the third book, that *the accomplishment of the prophecies therein, would be the theme hereafter of a greater Dunciad.* But whether or no he be the author of this, we declare ourselves ignorant. If he be, we are no more to be blamed for the publication of it, than Tucca and Varius for that of 10 the last six books of the Æneid, tho' perhaps inferior to the former.

If any person be possessed of a more perfect copy of this work, or of any other fragments of it, and will communicate them to the publisher, we shall make the next edition more 15 complete: In which, we also promise to insert any *Criticisms* that shall be published (if at all to the purpose) with the *Names* of the *Authors;* or any letters sent us (tho' not to the purpose) shall yet be printed under the title of *Epistolæ Obscurorum Virorum;* which, together with some others of the 20 same kind formerly laid by for that end, may make no un- pleasant addition to the future impressions of this poem.

The text is that of *1743a* collated with the first edition, *1742a.*
21 end] purpose

5. *complete it.* ⟨The publisher of 1728 had been "well inform'd" that the author had spent six years on the poem, and intended to bestow six years more upon it. See pp. 204–5.⟩

7–8. *greater Dunciad.* ⟨See p. 56.⟩

10. *Tucca and Varius* ⟨Tucca Plautius and Lucius Varius, or Varus, friends of Virgil and his literary executors. They are said to have published the *Aeneid* by order of Augustus, though Virgil, who had left it uncompleted, had asked that it should be burnt.⟩

22. *this poem* ⟨This paragraph was no doubt intended to satirize Curll's methods of publication. Curll was always ready to fill out a pamphlet with letters sent to him "tho' not to the purpose," and to publish as Pope's work anything that was "communicated" to him. Cf. Pope's complaint about the advertisement in *The Craftsman,* which promised that "*any thing* which *any body* shou'd send as Mr. *Pope's* or Dr. *Swift's,* shou'd be inserted and publish'd as theirs." (Appendix II, p. 212.)⟩

V.

THE

GUARDIAN.

Being a continuation of some former Papers on the subject of
PASTORALS.

⟨See p. 222.⟩

VI.

OF THE

POET LAUREATE[1]

November 19, 1729.

THE time of the election of a Poet Laureate being now at
hand, it may be proper to give some account of the
rites and *ceremonies* anciently used at that Solemnity,
and only discontinued through the neglect and degeneracy
of later times. These we have extracted from an historian of   5
undoubted credit, a reverend bishop, the learned Paulus
Jovius; and are the same that were practised under the
pontificate of Leo X, the great restorer of learning.

As we now see an *age* and a *court*, that for the encouragement
of poetry rivals, if not exceeds, that of this famous Pope, we   10
cannot but wish a restoration of all its *honours* to *poesy*; the
rather, since there are so many parallel circumstances in the
person who was then honoured with the laurel, and in *him*,
who (in all probability) is now to wear it.

I shall translate my author exactly as I find it in the 82d   15

The text is that of *1743a* collated with *The Grub-Street Journal*,
Nov. 19, 1730. *The Grub-Street Journal* opens with a quotation
from Virgil, *Eclogue* viii, 55: *Sit Tityrus Orpheus.*

1–2 at hand,] *57 lines are here omitted: the* it may be proper *which
follows belongs to another sentence.*
6 a reverend] and a Reverend

---

[1] ⟨This piece first appeared as an Appendix to the *Dunciad* in *1743a*. It was
originally published in *The Grub-Street Journal*, Nov. 19, 1730.⟩

chapter of his Elogia Vir. Doct. He begins with the character
of the poet himself, who was the original and father of all
Laureates, and called Camillo. He was a plain country-man
of Apulia, whether a *shepherd* or *thresher*, is not material. "This
"man (says Jovius) excited by the fame of the great encourage-   5
"ment given to poets at court, and the high honour in which
"they were held, came to the city, bringing with him a
"strange kind of lyre in his hand, and at least some *twenty*
"*thousand of verses*. All the wits and critics of the court flock'd
"about him, delighted to see a *clown*, with a ruddy, hale   10
"complexion, and in his own long hair, so top full of poetry;
"and at the first sight of him all agreed he was born to be
"*Poet Laureate*[a]. He had a most hearty welcome in an *island*
"of the river Tiber (an agreeable place, not unlike our Rich-
"mond) where he was first made to *eat* and *drink plentifully*,   15
"and *to repeat his verses to every body*. Then they adorn'd him
"with a new and elegant garland, composed of *vine-leaves*,
"*laurel*, and *brassica* (a sort of cabbage) so composed, says
"my author, emblematically, *ut tam sales, quam lepide ejus*
"*temulentia, Brassicæ remedio cohibenda, notaretur*. He was then   20
"saluted by common consent with the title of *archi-poeta*, or
"*arch-poet*, in the style of those days, in ours, *Poet Laureate*. This
"honour the poor man received with the most sensible
"demonstrations of joy, his eyes drunk with tears and glad-
"ness[b]. Next the public acclamation was expressed in a   25
"*canticle*, which is transmitted to us, as follows:

26 transmitted] yet transmitted

---

1. *Doct.* ⟨*Elogia Doctorum Virorum* . . . 1557, pp. 178–80. The quotation is
from the 72nd chapter.⟩

4. *thresher* ⟨The satire which follows is directed against Stephen Duck
(1705–56), the agricultural labourer and poet patronized by Queen Caroline.
On Nov. 19, 1730, Swift told Gay that he heard Duck was to be the new laureate,
in succession to Eusden.⟩

[a]Apulus præpingui vultu alacer, & prolixe comatus, omnino dignus festa laurea
videretur.

14–15. *Richmond* ⟨Among Queen Caroline's gifts to Duck was "a Small House
at Richmond in Surrey." This is mentioned on the title-page of his *Poems on
Several Subjects*, 1730.⟩

[b]Manantibus præ gaudio oculis.

> *"Salve, brassicea virens corona,*
> *"Et lauro, archipoeta, pampinoque!*
> *"Dignus principis auribus Leonis."*

> *All hail, arch-poet without peer!*
> *Vine, bay, or cabbage fit to wear,*   5
> *And worthy of the* prince's ear.

From hence he was conducted in pomp to the *Capitol* of Rome, mounted on an *elephant*, thro' the shouts of the populace, where the ceremony ended.

The historian tells us farther, "That at his introduction to   10 "Leo, he not only poured forth verses innumerable, like a "torrent, but also *sung* them with *open mouth*. Nor was he only "*once* introduced, or on *stated* days (like our Laureates) but "made a *companion* to his *master*, and entertained as one of the "instruments of his *most elegant pleasures*. When the prince   15 "was at table, the poet had his place at the window. When "the prince had[c] half eaten his meat, he gave with his own "hands the rest to the poet. When the poet drank, it was out "of the prince's own flaggon, insomuch (says the historian) "that thro' so great good eating and drinking he contracted   20 "a most terrible gout." Sorry I am to relate what follows, but that I cannot leave my reader's curiosity unsatisfied in the catastrophe of this extraordinary man. To use my author's words, which are remarkable, *mortuo Leone, profligatisque poetis, &c.* "When Leo died, and poets were no more" (for I would   25 not understand *profligatis* literally, as if poets then were *profligate*) this unhappy Laureate was forthwith reduced to return to his country, where, oppress'd with *old age* and *want*, he miserably perish'd in a *common hospital*.

We see from this sad conclusion (which may be of example   30 to the poets of our time) that it were happier to meet with no encouragement at all, to remain at the plough, or other lawful occupation, than to be elevated above their condition, and taken out of the common means of life, without a surer

5 *bay, or*] Laurel,   6 *the*] thy   18 the poet] his poet

---

[c]Semesis opsoniis.

support than the *temporary*, or, at best, *mortal* favours of the great. It was doubtless for this consideration, that when the Royal Bounty was lately extended to a *rural genius*, care was taken to *settle it upon him for life*. And it hath been the practice of our Princes, never to remove from the station of Poet 5 Laureate any man who hath once been chosen, tho' never so much greater Genius's might arise in his time. A noble instance, how much the *charity* of our monarchs hath exceeded their *love of fame*.

To come now to the intent of this paper. We have here the 10 whole ancient *ceremonial* of the Laureate. In the first place the crown is to be mix'd with *vine-leaves*, as the vine is the plant of Bacchus, and full as essential to the honour, as the *butt of sack* to the salary.

Secondly, the *brassica* must be made use of as a qualifier of 15 the former. It seems the *cabbage* was anciently accounted a remedy for *drunkenness*; a power the French now ascribe to the onion, and style a soupe made of it, *soupe d'Yvronge*. I would recommend a large mixture of the *brassica* if Mr. Dennis be chosen; but if Mr. Tibbald, it is not so necessary, 20 unless the cabbage be supposed to signify the same thing with respect to *poets* as to *taylors*, viz. *stealing*. I should judge it not amiss to add another plant to this garland, to wit, *ivy:* Not only as it anciently belonged to poets in general; but as it is emblematical of the three virtues of a court poet in 25 particular; it is *creeping*, *dirty*, and *dangling*.

In the next place, a *canticle* must be composed and sung in laud and praise of the new poet. If Mr. C I B B E R be laureated, it is my opinion no man can *write* this but himself: And no

20 Dennis] *D—s*   28 CIBBER] *C—r*

3. *Royal Bounty* ⟨Queen Caroline allowed Duck a salary of £30 per annum, which was later raised to £80.⟩

20. *be chosen* ⟨The gibe here is directed at the poetical intoxication of Dennis. There is no reason to suppose that Dennis was an intemperate drinker.⟩

22. *stealing* ⟨"Cabbage: Shreds (or larger pieces) of cloth cut off by tailors in the process of cutting out clothes, and appropriated by them as a perquisite" (OED).—Theobald requires no remedy for poetical intoxication; he is only too sober already.⟩

26. *dangling* ⟨Cf. B i 304.⟩

man, I am sure, can *sing* it so affectingly. But what this canticle should be, either in his or the other candidates' case, I shall not pretend to determine.

Thirdly, there ought to be a *public show*, or entry of the poet: To settle the order or procession of which, Mr. Anstis and Mr. DENNIS ought to have a conference. I apprehend here two difficulties: One, of procuring an *elephant*; the other of teaching the poet to ride him: Therefore I should imagine the next animal in size or dignity would do best; either a *mule* or a large *ass*; particularly if that noble one could be had, whose portraiture makes so great an ornament of the *Dunciad*, and which (unless I am misinform'd) is yet in the park of a nobleman near this city:——Unless Mr. CIBBER be the man; who may, with great propriety and beauty, ride on a *dragon*, if he goes by land; or if he chuse the water, upon one of his own *swans* from *Cæsar in Egypt*.

We have spoken sufficiently of the *ceremony*; let us now speak of the *qualifications* and *privileges* of the Laureate. First, we see he must be able to make verses *extempore*, and to pour forth innumerable, if requir'd. In this I doubt Mr. TIBBALD. Secondly, he ought to *sing*, and intrepidly, *patulo ore:* Here, I confess the excellency of Mr. CIBBER. Thirdly, he ought to carry a *lyre* about with him: If a large one be thought too cumbersome, a small one may be contrived to hang about the

6 DENNIS] D—s

8 ride him:] *Add 1730:* none that I know (except Mr. *Bud*— who is no Candidate) having been used to the *menage*, and the rest never sat even on horseback. ⟨*Bud=Budgell.*⟩

13 CIBBER] C—r   22 CIBBER] C—r

1. *affectingly* ⟨For Cibber's squeaky voice, cf. B iii 306*n*.⟩

5. *Anstis* ⟨John Anstis (1669–1744), Garter King-of-Arms, and author of several heraldic works. One of the duties of his office was to regulate public processions.⟩

13. *city* ⟨The nobleman is perhaps Lord Hervey, whose regimen of ass's milk was well known. Cf. *Ep. to Arbuthnot*, 306*n*.⟩

16. *Egypt* ⟨For his *Caesar in Egypt* (1724) the stage carpenter had made pasteboard swans to swim on an imaginary Nile. When drawn across the stage, they occasioned some ridicule among the audience. See B. Victor, *History of the Theatres of London and Dublin*, 1817, vol. ii, p. 164.⟩

neck, like an order, and be very much a grace to the person. Fourthly, he ought to have a good *stomach*, to eat and drink whatever his betters think fit; and therefore it is in this high office as in many others, no puny constitution can discharge it. 5
I do not think CIBBER or TIBBALD here so happy: but rather a stanch, vigorous, season'd, and dry *old gentleman*, whom I have in my eye.

I could also wish at this juncture, such a person as is truly jealous of the *honour* and *dignity* of *poetry*; no joker, or trifler; 10
but a bard in *good earnest*; nay, not amiss if a critic, and the better if a little *obstinate*. For when we consider what great privileges have been lost from this office (as we see from the forecited authentic record of Jovius) namely those of *feeding* from the *prince's table*, *drinking* out of his *own flaggon*, becoming 15
even his *domestic* and *companion*; it requires a man warm and resolute, to be able to claim and obtain the restoring of these high honours. I have cause to fear the most of the candidates would be liable, either through the influence of ministers, or for rewards or favours, to give up the glorious rights of the 20
Laureate: Yet I am not without hopes, there is *one*, from whom a *serious* and *steddy* assertion of these privileges may be expected; and, if there be such a one, I must do him the justice to say, it is Mr. DENNIS the worthy president of our society. 25

6 CIBBER] *C—r*
24 DENNIS] *D—s*

7. *gentleman* ⟨Dennis, at this time over seventy, is intended.⟩
25. *society* ⟨i.e. the Grub-Street Society.⟩

VII.

ADVERTISEMENT

Printed in the JOURNALS, 1730.

WHEREAS, upon occasion of certain Pieces relating to the Gentlemen of the Dunciad, some have been willing to suggest, as if they looked upon them as an *abuse:* we can do no less than own, it is our opinion, that to call these Gentlemen *bad authors* is no sort of *abuse*, but a great   5
truth. We cannot alter this opinion without some reason; but we promise to do it in respect to every person who thinks it an injury to be represented as no *Wit*, or *Poet*, provided he procures a Certificate of his being really such, from any *three of his companions* in the Dunciad, or from Mr. *Dennis singly*, who is   10
esteemed equal to any three of the number.

VIII.

A
PARALLEL
OF THE
CHARACTERS
OF
Mr. DRYDEN and Mr. POPE.
As drawn by certain of their Contemporaries.
⟨See p. 230.⟩

By the AUTHOR
A DECLARATION.
⟨See p. 237.⟩

Advertisement ⟨This appeared in *A Collection of Pieces in Verse and Prose* . . . MDCCXXXII. (See Griffith, pp. 202–3.) It was presumably reprinted from some newspaper of 1730, but the newspaper has not been traced. It first appeared as an Appendix to the *Dunciad* in *1742e*.⟩

I N D E X

OF

M A T T E R S

Contained in this

POEM and NOTES.

[The first Number denotes the BOOK, the second the VERSE and
NOTE on it. *Test.* Testimonies. *Ap.* Appendix.]

419

16

⟨In this Index, and in the one on pp. 239–45, a few inaccurate line references have been silently corrected, and page references have been adjusted to the pagination of this edition.⟩

F I N I S.

BIOGRAPHICAL APPENDIX

The following biographical notes should be read in conjunction with Pope's own notes on the dunces, since repetition has been avoided here as much as possible. An asterisk denotes that the name in question does not appear in the text of *1729a* or *1743a*, but does appear in the text of some other edition, or in the EC MS. Pope's reasons for including his various dunces in the poem have been indicated wherever possible; but it is not suggested he had invariably a personal quarrel to settle. As the information supplied here is intended mainly to throw light on the careers of the dunces as known to Pope, biographical facts falling beyond 1743 have for the most part been omitted.

★　　　★　　　★

ALSOP, Anthony (d. 1726). B iv 224. Poet and scholar. He published in 1698 a volume of selections from Aesop in Latin verse, *Fabularum Aesopicarum Delectus*, in which he referred to Bentley as "quendam Bentleium virum in volvendis Lexicis satis diligentem". He also collaborated in *Dr. Bentley's Dissertations on the Epistles of Phalaris . . . Examin'd*. He left behind him many Latin odes in manuscript, which were published in 1752. Alsop's jokes, to which Pope refers, were not always decorous; but his Latinity was much admired by his contemporaries.

ANNIUS. B iv 347. This collector of coins has generally been identified with Sir Andrew Fountaine (1676-1753), a famous virtuoso. There were other amateurs of coins, of course, such as Roger Gale (1672-1744), and Martin Folkes (1690-1754). Folkes had assisted Theobald with notes for his Shakespeare. The "ebon wand," however, points almost certainly to Fountaine being the man. (Cf. iv 374 *n*.) It is true that he was an old friend of Swift, but by 1742 Swift's mind was hopelessly deranged, and he was beyond noticing such trifles as *The Dunciad*. Pope here seems to have been " willing to wound, and yet afraid to strike." If pressed, he could claim that the satire was general. A story relating to Fountaine's dealings in Italy (J. Nichols, *Lit. Anec.*, ix 603) suggests that he was not always scrupulous in his transactions. His *Numismata Anglo-Saxonica et Anglo-Danica breviter illustrata* appeared in Hickes's *Thesaurus*, 1705. In 1727 he had succeeded Sir Isaac Newton as Warden of the Mint. Pope—and, for that matter, Swift—probably looked with displeasure on Sir Andrew's friendly relations with the Hanoverian court.

ARCHER, Thomas (*c.* 1668–1743). B i 309. Architect. He matriculated at Oxford in 1686, and after spending three years at the university he travelled abroad for the next four years. He became groom-porter in 1705, and held that office till his death. As an architect Archer followed the style of Vanbrugh

427

and Hawksmoor. He built a number of churches and private houses, and designed the colonnades at Cliefden, Bucks. For information supplementing the account of him in D.N.B., see *Institute of Historical Research* (University of London) *Bulletin*, Nov. 1941.

ARNALL (or ARNOLD), William (1700?-1736). A ii 293n.; B ii 315. Political journalist. In *A Letter to Richard Arnold* (1731), he is described as "a run-away pettyfogging Attorney's Clerk". (Cf. E. Budgell, *A Letter to . . . Mr. Ulrick D'Ypres*, 1731, p. 49.) A protégé of Sir William Yonge, he was taken into Walpole's pay, and by 1729 was writing as "Roger Manly of Lincoln's Inn, Esq." in *The British Journal*. In December of that year he became "Francis Walsingham" in the newly-founded *Free Briton* (1729-35). A signed account of Arnall's, dated January 13, 1732, is reproduced in facsimile in L. Hanson, *Government and the Press*, 1936: his bill to the government from October 14, 1731, to January 13, 1732, for writing and printing *Free Britons* and for writing some miscellaneous pamphlets is £568 16s. 8d. When the government launched *The Daily Gazetteer* Arnall continued to write his political essays there until his death in May, 1736 (Hanson, p. 115). He seems to have been the most highly rewarded of all Walpole's hacks.

*BAKER, Henry (1698-1774). A iii 188n. Naturalist and poet, son-in-law of Daniel Defoe, whose daughter Sophia he married in 1729. A letter from Baker to Pope, undated but apparently written to accompany a presentation copy of his poem, *The Invocation of Health*, is preserved in the Victoria and Albert Museum (Forster 23). He was thus one of those who had seen fit to " . . . fly to Twit'nam, and in humble strain, Apply to me, to keep them mad or vain." See also G. R. Potter, "Henry Baker, F.R.S.," *Modern Philology*, vol. xxix, pp. 301 ff. In October, 1728, he started a successful weekly journal, *The Universal Spectator*.

BARBER, John (1675-1740). B iv 131. Printer. He was elected alderman, 1722, and Lord Mayor, 1732. His monument to Samuel Butler was erected in Westminster Abbey in 1721. Barber was Swift's printer during his London period, and Swift remained his friend. He was well known to Pope, to whom he left a small legacy. It was said of him that he would have given three or four thousand pounds for a compliment to himself in Pope's works, but Pope never gratified him (Spence, p. 308; *Ep. to the Satires*, ii 112 n.). Instead, Pope is said to have written a satirical couplet "which he proposed should be placed on the vacant scroll under Shakespeare's bust:

> Thus Britain lov'd me, and preserv'd my fame,
> Safe from a Barber's or a Benson's name."

(J. Nichols, *Lit. Anec.*, i 73 n.; *Additions to the Works of Alexander Pope*, i 13.)

BENSON, William (1682-1754). A iii 321; B iii 325, iv 110. Whig politician. He succeeded Sir Christopher Wren as Surveyor-General, but was suspended for the fault mentioned in Pope's note to A iii 321. Later he became Auditor of the Imprest. There are some mild criticisms of Pope in Benson's *Letters Concerning Poetical Translations* (1739); but he is complimented in Letter x, p. 80. Pope had some slight grounds for annoyance on another account: William Dobson of New College was going to translate the *Essay on Man* into Latin verse, but abandoned the project on being offered £1,000 by Benson to translate *Paradise Lost* (Spence, p. 179).

BENTLEY, Richard (1662–1742). B ii 205(?), iv 201 ff. Scholar and theologian; Master of Trinity College, Cambridge, 1700–1742. In 1697 Bentley (who was then Keeper of the Royal Libraries) fell foul of the Wits by contributing to the second (1697) edition of Wotton's *Reflections on Ancient and Modern Learning* an essay proving that the Epistles of Phalaris, recently edited by the Hon. Charles Boyle, were not genuine. The Wits rallied to Boyle's defence, and for the rest of his life Bentley was subjected to ridicule by men far inferior to him in scholarship—the yapping of dogs about a bear. Pope had thus inherited a satirical tradition from his friends, Swift, Atterbury, etc.; but he may have had some more personal reasons for joining in the attack on the great scholar. (See Biog. App., vol. iv.) In any case, to ridicule verbal critics like Bentley and Theobald was to ridicule that sort of scholarship in which he himself had conspicuously failed. Bentley's long term of office as Master of Trinity was enlivened by a prolonged quarrel with the Fellows, who did their utmost to have him removed: Bentley, however, succeeded by a series of stratagems in retaining office till his death.

BENTLEY, Thomas (1693?–1742). B ii 205. Nephew of Dr Richard Bentley, and himself a classical scholar. His "small Horace" (1713) was an annotated edition of his uncle's text, and he published editions of several other classical texts. Pope's *Sober Advice* with the mock notes attributed to Bentley annoyed his nephew, who replied in *A Letter to Mr. Pope . . .* (1735). He is even said to have sent a challenge to Pope as a result of that satire. See also Johnson, *Lives*, iii 276.

BLACKMORE, Sir Richard (1655?–1729). A i 102, ii 247, 256n.; B i 104, ii 259. See Biog. App., vol. iv. In addition to his attack on Pope, he had characterized Swift as "an impious buffoon" (*Essays*, vol. i, p. 217). In *A Full and True Account of . . . Mr. Edmund Curll*, 1716, and again in *A Further Account . . .*, 1716 (*Pope's Prose*, pp. 259, 275) Blackmore had come in for some amusing ridicule as one of Curll's authors. Apart from personal grounds, Blackmore earned his place in the *Dunciad* on his merits as a writer, and he had been a butt of the wits since his attack on Dryden in *Prince Arthur* (1695). The author of *Characters of the Times* (1728), p. 25, points out that, like Ward, Durfey, etc., ". . . he is not mention'd for his own Sake, but only to fix the Abuse strongly on others".—i.e., mere proximity to Blackmore was a form of ridicule.

BLADEN, Thomas(?). B iv 560. Sir Theodore Jansen (d. 1748) had a son-in-law, Thomas Bladen (Nichols, *Lit. Anec.*, iii 408), who may have been the gamester of the context. Under the date, Nov. 6, 1731, the Earl of Egmont noted in his Diary (i 207): "I had an account this day that the Duke of Bedford lost this day sennit at Newmarket 3800 l. to Captain Johnson [Jansen?], Captain Bladon, and other professed gamesters."

BLAND, Henry (d. 1746). B i 231. See Biog. App., vol. iv. He became Dean of Durham in March, 1728 (*London Evening-Post*, March 9-12, 1728). Bland, a schoolfellow of Walpole's, was one of the chief government writers in *The Daily Courant* (Ralph, p. 517; E. Budgell, *The Bee*, vol. i, p. 11).

BOND, William (d. 1735). A ii 118, iii 151; B ii 126. Journalist and dramatist. According to a writer in *The Thursday's Journal*, Oct. 1-8, 1719, Bond was author of *The Weekly Medley*, which ran from 1718-20. Later he collaborated with Aaron Hill in writing *The Plain Dealer*, 1724-5, a periodical in which Pope was sometimes praised and sometimes mildly criticized. Savage called Hill and Bond "the two contending powers of light and darkness" because "the work was observed regularly to rise in Mr. Hill's weeks, and fall in Mr. Bond's" (Johnson, *Lives*, ii 341*n*.). Bond can hardly have improved his relations with Pope by dedicating the collected edition (1734) of this periodical in flattering terms to Lord Hervey. In the anti-Pope pamphlet, *The Progress of Dulness* (1728), there is a poem with that title, dated June 6, 1720, and ascribed to "H. Stanhope." From a statement in *The Curliad*, pp. 24-5, it looks as if Stanhope was a pseudonym for Bond. He may have annoyed Pope by securing the patronage, and apparently the admiration, of the Duke of Buckingham. According to an advertisement of Curll's in *The St. James's Evening-Post*, Feb. 3-6, 1728: "Mr. Bond's Poem on Buckingham-House in St. James's Park, the late Duke used to say, would last much longer than the Building."

BOYER, Abel (1667-1729). A ii 381; B ii 413. Historian, newswriter, compiler of a French-English dictionary, and author of *The Political State of Great Britain*, a monthly review of current events which ran from 1711 till his death. He was a confirmed Whig, and as such aroused the contempt of Swift, who called him "a little whiffling Frenchman" (*Examiner*, No. 41, May 17, 1711). Boyer frequently retaliated on Swift, and in 1726, while incorporating large extracts from *Gulliver's Travels* in his *Political State*, he sneered at Swift's book as "extremely diverting to all Nurses, Chamber Maids, School-Boys. . ." (vol. xxxii, p. 477). He also attacked other friends of Pope, e.g. Bolingbroke (op. cit., vol. xxxiii, pp. 155-6). The mild reference to him in the *Dunciad* hardly suggests that Pope had any personal grievance; Boyer was merely an arrant Whig.

BREVAL, John Durant (1680?-1738). A ii 118; B ii 126. Poet, dramatist, and miscellaneous writer. Deprived of a fellowship at Trinity College, Cambridge, he enlisted in the army, and fought in France, where he obtained a commission in Pearce's 5th Regiment of Foot (C. Dalton, *English Army Lists*, vol. v, pp. 231, 232). Later he became one of Curll's authors. "The first Poem Captain *Breval* ever published was, *The Art of Dress*, which I am well assured, Mr. *Pope* read over in Manuscript, and approv'd" (*Curliad*, p. 26). In 1717 Breval ridiculed *Three Hours after Marriage* and its authors in a farce called *The Confederates*, one of several works attributed to "Joseph Gay", and so earned a place in the *Dunciad*. The Prologue must have been particularly offensive to Pope: he is there said to be "in Form a Monkey, but for Spite, a Toad". About 1720 Breval went abroad as travelling tutor to the young Viscount Malpas. On the tour, a nun fell in love with Breval at Milan, and ran away to him (B iv 327*n*.).

BROOME, William (1689–1745). A iii 328; B i 146(?). Poet and clergyman. He collaborated with Oldisworth and Ozell in a prose translation of Homer, 1712, and published a volume of *Poems on Several Occasions*, 1727. When Pope was translating the *Iliad* Broome read for him the commentary of Eustathius. With Elijah Fenton he assisted Pope in his translation of the *Odyssey*, Broome's share amounting to eight books (ii, vi, viii, xi, xii, xvi, xviii, and xxiii). Pope misled the public as to the help he had received, and apparently prevailed upon Broome to give support to this deception. (See Sherburn, pp. 259–60.) As early as Dec. 1, 1725, Broome suspected that Pope might prove unwilling to give him due credit for his share in the *Odyssey*. "He is a Caesar in poetry," he wrote to Fenton, "and will bear no equal." Delay in coming to a financial settlement for the work done seems to have been partly due to Broome's timidity in dealing with Pope. Later the two men drifted into more or less open hostility, and Pope ridiculed some of Broome's verses in the *Peri Bathous*, and classed him with the Parrots and Tortoises. On May 3, 1728, Broome was telling Fenton that he no longer corresponded with Pope. "He has used me ill, he is ungrateful. . . I often resemble him to an hedgehog; he wraps himself up in his down, lies snug and warm, and sets his bristles out against all mankind." The slighting reference in the *Dunciad*, with its disingenuous note, remained till 1736, when Pope brought himself "to cancel an impression of a thousand leaves" (EC iii 181) to substitute a couplet in which no mention of Broome was made. The substitution of "Broome" for "Blome" in 1743 may have been Pope's way of reintroducing Broome into the *Dunciad*. Cf. B i 146*n*.

BROWN. A iii 20; B iii 28. Either Daniel Browne, or Jonas Browne, both of whom were publishing from "the Black Swan without Temple Bar" in the 1720's. Daniel Browne, Junior (d. 1762), was responsible with Samuel Chapman for publishing Mrs Haywood's *Works* (1724). J. Browne published Theobald's *Censor*, his *Cave of Poverty*, and his *Perfidious Brother*. As he sometimes worked in partnership with W. Mears, he may be the one intended by Pope.

BUDGELL, Eustace (1686–1737). A ii 365; B ii 397. A cousin of Addison's, who gained a considerable reputation in his earlier life as a writer of real talent and as an administrator in Ireland. In addition to the celebrated epilogue men-

16*

tioned in Pope's note, he wrote some thirty essays for the *Spectator*, and produced an admired translation of Theophrastus. Personal difficulties in Ireland with the Duke of Bolton, and severe losses in the South Sea year seem to have unsettled Budgell, and from 1721 onwards he became more and more irresponsible in his behaviour. In April, 1728, not long before Pope's note on him was written, he stopped the King as he was on his way to Cambridge, and invited him to partake of a cold collation by the roadside (*The Craftsman*, April 27, 1728). A long-standing enmity against Walpole culminated on April 21, 1730, in his kneeling at Court and presenting the King with a petition in which he set forth "the wrong and injustice done to him by Walpole" (Egmont, i 96). Pope's reference to "Courts of Law" in the later editions probably alludes to Budgell's troubles in 1733 over the will of Matthew Tindal, though he was never called upon to face a charge in court (cf. *Ep. to Arbuthnot*, 378-9); but his later life was one long litigation. In 1737, overwhelmed by his various troubles, he ended his life by jumping into the Thames. Egmont recorded in his Diary (ii 407) that "he was the most conceited pragmatical cur I ever knew, but he was a good scholar and wrote well." See also vol. iv, Biog. App., and pp. 124n., 125n.

BURMANN, Peter (1668-1741). B iv 237. A Dutch scholar who published Bentley's emendations to the fragments of Menander and Philemon, with the title of *Phileleutherus Lipsiensis* (1710).

BURNET, Sir Thomas (1694-1753). A iii 175; B iii 179. The youngest son of Gilbert Burnet, Bishop of Salisbury. As a young man (circa 1715) he was one of Addison's circle at Button's. He wrote a number of political pamphlets about this time—he was a keen Whig—and in 1715 attacked Pope in a periodical called *The Grumbler*. He collaborated with his friend Duckett (*q.v.*) in two separate pamphlets called *Homerides* (1715, 1716) attacking Pope and his *Homer*. Pope's first retort may have been made in a pamphlet, *The Dignity, Use and Abuse of Glass-Bottles* (*Pope's Prose*, i, lxxv). He retaliated on Burnet, though not very sharply, in "Sandys' Ghost" (1727). In 1729 appeared *Pope Alexander's Supremacy . . . examin'd*, a pamphlet which Pope thought was "writ by Burnet, and a person who has great obligations to me" (EC viii 255), but which in editions of the *Dunciad* from *1735a* he attributed to Duckett and Dennis. It is unlikely that Burnet had any part in it (*The Letters of Thomas Burnet to George Duckett*, ed. D. Nichol Smith, p. xixn.). Pope probably glanced at Burnet again in the *Ep. to Arbuthnot*, l. 146. In 1741 Burnet became a judge; in *Dunciad B* he is not actually named, the offensive epigram of 1729 is removed, and the note in which it appeared has been toned down.

CENTLIVRE, Susanna (1667?-1723). A ii 379, iii 145; B 411. The most prolific comic dramatist of Queen Anne's reign. *The Busy Body* (1709), *The Wonder: or A Woman Keeps a Secret* (1714), and *A Bold Stroke for a Wife* (1718) kept their place in eighteenth-century repertory owing to their liveliness and humour rather than to their wit. Her biographers differ as to the number of her husbands; but on April 23, 1707, she married Joseph Centlivre, Yeoman of the Mouth to Queen Anne, giving her name as Susanna Carollalies Rawkins (*Registers of St Bene't and St Peter Paul's Wharf, London*: vol. ii, p. 67). She was an ardent Whig, a friend of Farquhar, Steele, Rowe, Cibber, Philips, Charles Johnson, William Bond, and Budgell, and an outspoken enemy of Popery. In *A Wife Well Managed* (1715) and in *The Artifice* (1722) she had ridiculed priests in a highly offensive way. She may possibly be the Phoebe Clinket of *Three Hours after Marriage* (Sherburn, p. 194). Pope referred to her in *A Full and True Account* as one of Curll's favourite authors, and in *A Further Account* as "the Cook's Wife in Buckingham Court" (*Pope's Prose*, pp. 265, 279).

*CHAPMAN, Samuel. (fl. 1728). A ii 159. Bookseller, at The Angel, Pall Mall, 1723–8. With D. Browne he published Mrs Haywood's *Works* in 1724, but his crowning offence in Pope's eyes was probably the fact that he was one of the four booksellers who published *Shakespeare Restored* in 1726.[1]

CHETWOOD, William Rufus (d. 1766). A ii 159. Bookseller, dramatist, and miscellaneous writer. He earned his place in the *Dunciad* as the publisher of many of Mrs Haywood's works, but possibly, too, on account of an incident recorded by Curll. (See A ii 182*n*.) He was for many years prompter at Drury Lane; but in later life he was in distressed circumstances, and in Jan. 1741, when *The Old Bachelor* was played for his benefit, a prisoner in the King's Bench. In addition to some dramatic pieces and novels, he compiled *A General History of the Stage*, 1749, and *The British Theatre*, 1750.

CIBBER, Colley (1671–1757). A i 240, iii 134, 262, 289, 320; B *passim*. For a brief sketch of Cibber's career, see Biog. App., vol. iv. The best accounts of his life are his own *Apology* (1740), and R. H. Barker's *Mr. Cibber of Drury Lane* (1939). The quarrel between Pope and Cibber appears to have begun in 1717, when Cibber, who had accepted *Three Hours after Marriage* for Drury Lane, and had himself played the part of Plotwell, withdrew it, after a stormy week, on the seventh night. Two weeks later, when he was playing Bayes in a revival of *The Rehearsal*, he slipped in a satirical gag about *Three Hours after Marriage*, and Pope, who was present in the theatre, went behind the scenes, "his lips pale and his voice trembling, to call me to account for the insult" (*A Letter from Mr. Cibber to Mr. Pope* . . . 1742, p. 19). Pope's earliest retort in print may have been the anonymous pamphlet, *The Plot Discover'd; or A Clue to the Comedy of the Non-*

---

1. A copy in the British Museum (644 l. 8) is "Printed for R. Franklin and T. Woodman in Russell-Street, Covent-Garden, Charles Davis in Hatton-Garden, and S. Chapman in Pall-Mall, MDCCXXVI." The copy in the library of Birkbeck College, University of London, also dated 1726, was published by Franklin, Woodman and D. Lyon, and C. Davis. R. F. Jones (*Lewis Theobald*, p. 351) had not apparently seen a copy with the Chapman title-page.

Juror 1718 (*Pope's Prose*, pp. cxvii ff.; Barker, pp. 205–6). In the *Peri Bathous* Cibber was placed among the parrots, who repeat other men's words and pass them off as their own. After appearing in the *Dunciad*, he was mentioned several times with derision in Pope's satires, but he took it all in good part. In his *Apology* he took note of Pope's frequent attacks, but his protest is "almost an offer of reconciliation" (Barker, p. 209). Subsequent developments are dealt with in the Introduction (pp. xxxiii ff.). In addition to the various pamphlets there mentioned, Cibber was probably the author of *The Egoist, or Colley upon Cibber*, 1743 (Barker, pp. 215, 265). The last shot fired in the quarrel was Cibber's *Another Occasional Letter* . . , 1744. Pope died a few months later. Though far from a fool, Cibber was a natural butt for satire; his life and his actions invited satirical comment, and he himself seems to have preferred the notoriety of ridicule to the distress of being ignored. Cibber was not a gentleman, but he was the friend and companion of gentlemen; he was not an educated man, but he had succeeded as an author. No doubt Pope genuinely despised him; but his contempt was perhaps mixed with a certain amount of envy.

CIBBER, Theophilus (1703–58). A iii 134; B iii 142. Actor, dramatist, and pamphleteer. The son of Colley Cibber, he was an unattractive replica of his father, with the shrill voice, the impudence, and something of the vivacity of the old man. He even followed his father in issuing proposals for publishing his autobiography; but this work (which never appeared) was anticipated by *An Apology for the Life of Mr. T— C—*, sometimes attributed to Fielding. *The Lives of the Poets . . . By Mr. Cibber and other Hands*, 1753, was mainly the work of Robert Shiels. (See D. Nichol Smith's note in W. Raleigh, *Six Essays on Johnson*, 1910, pp. 120ff.) Theophilus Cibber is not known to have attacked Pope before the *Dunciad* appeared, but his life and character made him fair game for the satirist. "A Letter from T—ph—s C—r, at —, to Mr. POPE, at Twickenham," in *The Universal Spectator*, Oct. 16 and 23, 1742, is probably not by Cibber at all. It states that he had defended Sir Robert Walpole, *totis viribus*, apparently in *The Daily Gazetteer*.

CLELAND, William (1674?–1741). Friend of Pope. There was a Captain William Cleland in Lord Mark Kerr's Regiment of Foot. His commission is dated Jan. 1, 1706, and he was promoted Major before 1710. The regiment fought at Almanza, and was badly cut up. It was re-formed in 1708, and disbanded in 1712 (C. Dalton, *English Army Lists*, 1661–1714, v 225). A William Cleland—possibly the same man—was gazetted Captain in Major-General Robert Killigrew's Regiment of Dragoons, Jan. 23, 1712 (C. Dalton, op. cit., v 40–41). Cleland became a commissioner of customs in Scotland, and from 1724 to 1738 he was a commissioner of the land tax and house duties in England.

CONCANEN, Matthew (1701–49). A ii 130, 287; B ii 138, 299. Irish poet and miscellaneous writer, who employed his pen in defending Walpole's government. In his youthful volume of *Poems upon Several Occasions* (1722), there is some praise of Pope. Some later verses were published in Savage's *Miscellaneous Poems and Translations* (1726). In 1730 he collected a number of the essays he had written for *The London Journal* and *The British Journal* from 1725-7, and published them in a volume called *The Speculatist*. For attacks on Pope, see *The Speculatist* (2nd ed. 1732), pp. 14, 40, 185, 260-1. Concanen's circle included Theobald, Roome, and Warburton, and he was one of a kind of club of writers who, about 1725-6, were attacking Pope's *Shakespeare* in *Mist's Journal*. (See Sherburn, p. 243.) He also contributed letters of Theobald's on Pope's *Shakespeare* to *The London Journal* and *The Daily Journal* (J. Nichols, *Lit. Ill.*, ii 189, 214). His Preface to *A Collection of all the Verses . . .* 1728, and his *Supplement to the Profund* are noted by Pope in *Dunciad A*, Appendix ii.

COOKE, Thomas (1703-56). A ii 130; B ii 138. Poet, pamphleteer, and translator. Cooke was one of Curll's authors: he was paid £5 by Curll "for writing Mr. Marvell's Life, procuring some of his Letters, and Publishing his Works" (B.M. Add. MSS. 38, 728, f. 52). For his various collisions with Pope see Biog. App., vol. iv. In the later version of his *Battle of the Poets* (1729) Moore Smythe is quite extravagantly praised ("Another Dryden shall arise in Thee" etc.), and Philips and Welsted are honoured highly. Cooke's literary judgments, in fact, were often singularly wrong-headed: in spite of some ability he had a good deal of the dunce in him, and some of his verses were justly ridiculed by Pope in *Peri Bathous*. To his attacks on Pope mentioned in Biog. App., vol. iv may be added his "Letter in Prose to Mr. Alexander Pope" (occasioned by Pope's "Epistle to Burlington"), which appeared in *The Comedian*, 1732, pp. 13-24. He may have been the author of an anonymous *Key* to the *Dunciad* (Introduction, p. xxivn.). He was a friend of Moore Smythe, Concanen, Theobald, etc., who "held constantly weekly meetings"—if Pope's statement (Appendix ii) is to be taken seriously—for the purpose of abusing him in print. See also Carter R. Bishop, "Alexander Pope and 'The Battle of the Poets' ", *West Virginia Univ. Studies: 1. Philological Papers*, 1936, pp. 19ff.

COWPER, William, 2nd Earl Cowper (1709-64). B iv 545. Son of William, first Earl Cowper (for whom see Biog. App. vol. iv). Paul Whitehead in his *Manners* (1738) had already remarked on the second Earl's tastes for opera and opera-singers:

> Who blushes not to see a C—— Heir
> Turn slave to sound, and languish for a Play'r?

A note to this couplet indicates that the object of the Earl's passion was Farinelli. For some time Cowper was the principal manager of the opera at Haymarket (C. Burney, *A General History of Music*, iv, 380).

CROUSAZ, Jean Pierre de (1663-1748). B iv 198. Swiss philosopher and mathematician. He was an unsparing critic of Bayle and Leibnitz. In 1737, after reading the *Essay on Man* in the Abbé du Resnel's French translation, he published what he intended to be a confutation of the religious ideas implicit in the *Essay*. This *Examen de l'Essai de M. Pope sur L'Homme* and his *Commentaire sur la Traduction . . . de l'Essai sur l'Homme* were both translated into English, the latter by Dr. Johnson. (See Boswell, *Life*, iv 494–6.) For Warburton's subsequent defence of Pope's orthodoxy, see vol. iii.

CURLL, Edmund (1675–1747), *passim*. Bookseller. Curll was an unscrupulous, persistent, and adroit publisher, who realized the commercial value of scandal and impudence. He published a number of useful works, but he concentrated rather on poetical miscellanies, hastily-compiled biographies (in Arbuthnot's phrase "one of the new terrors of death"), and pornographical pamphlets. He succeeded in selling his books partly on their own demerits, but partly also by finding attractive titles for them and by pushing them in frequent and highly personal advertisements. (See a long letter signed "Kirleus", *Grub-Street Journal*, Jan. 29, 1730.) Since neither Swift nor Pope would deal with him, and he was determined to publish their works, he did so without their permission, and with little regard for the authenticity of what he was publishing. With Pope he began modestly enough in 1714 by publishing an obscene epigram in one of his Miscellanies (Sherburn, pp. 164–5). In 1716 came the more serious offence of publishing *Court Poems*, "found" (so he claimed) "in a Pocket-Book". The upshot was the emetic administered by Pope to Curll, and the pamphlets in which he describes the whole unsavoury business (Sherburn, pp. 167ff.). From now on the two men were at war, and Curll published one attack after another on the poet, besides issuing unauthorized editions of his poems and letters. The *Dunciad* was a gold mine to Curll, and he worked the vein thoroughly for several years with his *Key's, Popiad, Female Dunciad, Dunciad Dissected, Curliad,* and so on. A collection of anti-Pope pieces was advertised by Curll in *The Daily Journal*, July 19, 1728, as "The Whole Pope-ish Controversy". Besides ridiculing Curll in the *Dunciad*, Pope tricked him into publishing another collection of his letters in 1735, and then succeeded in having him brought to the Bar of the House of Lords to answer a charge of having published matters reflecting on certain members of that House. Pope had good reason for putting Curll in the *Dunciad*, but he also wished to pillory Curll's authors, who were almost all hostile to him. Curll was buried in St Paul's, Covent Garden, on Dec. 13, 1747 (*Registers of St Paul's, Covent Garden*, iv 430). For a detailed account of the Pope-Curll quarrel up to 1720, see N. Ault, *Pope's Prose*, pp. xciv ff.

CURLL, Henry (fl.1728). A ii 159. Bookseller, son of Edmund Curll. In 1726, when his father was in trouble, Henry Curll seems to have run the business. His name appears on the title-page of several books published in that year, and it turns up again from time to time for the next ten years; but as a publisher he was of little account, and perhaps never wholly independent of his far more lively father. He was married on Feb. 9, 1729 (*Registers of St Bene't and St Peter Paul's Wharf*, ii 359). In 1742 E. Curll added a rhyming codicil to his will, in which he stated: "I have no relatives, my son is dead. . ."

DEFOE, Benjamin Norton (fl.1720). A ii 383; B ii 415. In the Preface to Savage's *Author to be Let*, the statement about Norton Defoe's origin is repeated —"Daniel de Foe's Son of Love, by a lady who vended Oysters." He was writing for *The London Journal* in 1722, when it was bought by the government, and he appears to have been taken into their pay at the same time (*The Library*, June 1934, pp. 116–17). He was still alive in 1739 when he addressed several desperate letters to the Duke of Newcastle complaining of his poverty and misfortunes (B.M. Add. MSS. 32,691, ff. 390, 409; 32,692, ff. 454, 480).

DEFOE, Daniel (1660?–1731). A i 101, ii 139; B i 103, ii 147. As one of the most frequently abused authors of his generation, Defoe takes his place naturally in a satirical portrait gallery; it would have been surprising if Pope had left him out, or failed to mention the pillory. If Pope knew that Defoe was writing for John Applebee, he may have credited him with the long attack on his *Homer* which appeared in Applebee's *Weekly Journal*, Aug. 7, 1725. Defoe, however, joins the dunces as a notorious political writer—his connection with *Mist's Journal* was common knowledge—and also as the type of popular author who wrote for "porters and oyster wenches". Pope's real opinion of Defoe was given to Spence (p. 258): "The first part of Robinson Crusoe is very good. De Foe wrote a vast many things; and none bad, though none excellent, except this. There is something good in all he has written." In the *Peri Bathous* he had been placed—perhaps on account of his *Jure Divino*—among the Ostriches, "whose heaviness rarely permits them to raise themselves from the ground".

DENNIS, John (1657–1734) A i 104, ii 231, 271, iii 167; B i 106, ii 239, iii 173. Critic and dramatist. An unguarded comment by Pope (*Essay on Criticism*, ll. 582–7) on one of his tragedies enraged Dennis, who was never difficult to provoke. He replied almost at once in his abusive *Reflections . . . upon a late Rhapsody call'd, An Essay upon Criticism*, 1709. If Pope is author of the anonymous *Critical Specimen* (1711) this was his first prose reply to Dennis (Sherburn, p. 93; *Pope's Prose*, pp. xi ff.). More effective was *The Narrative of Dr. Robert Norris* (1713), which appeared soon after Dennis had belaboured Addison's *Cato*. Dennis, determined to see nothing good in Pope's poetry except his "knack at smooth verse", returned to the attack in *A True Character of Mr. Pope and his Writings*, 1716. The following year he published his fault-finding *Remarks upon Mr. Pope's Homer*. Pope took a mild revenge in 1717 when, with Gay and Arbuthnot, he caricatured the critic as Sir Tremendous in *Three Hours after Marriage*. In 1721 Pope made peace with Dennis, but in the *Peri Bathous* (1728) he again ridiculed him. Dennis responded with *Remarks on Mr. Pope's Rape of the Lock*, written in 1714, but for some reason left unpublished. After the *Dunciad* Dennis wrote *Remarks upon Mr. Pope's Dunciad* (1729) in the old violent strain, and, if Pope was well informed, collaborated with Duckett in *Pope Alexander's Supremacy . . .* (1729), a pamphlet containing much personal abuse. Just before the old critic's death *The Provoked Husband* was acted for his benefit, and Pope wrote a prologue for the occasion. Even here, however, Pope could not refrain from a reference to Dennis's famous thunder, and from various other satirical thrusts at his old enemy. Where Pope was concerned, Dennis was hopelessly prejudiced. There is much truth, too, in Plotwell's gibe at him in *Three Hours after Marriage* as "a gentleman who can instruct the Town to dislike what has pleased them, and to be pleased with what they disliked". Dennis had all the intellectual's suspicion of what was popular, and Pope had succeeded with the Town.

DODD, Anne (d. circa 1750?). Wife of Nathaniel Dodd, Stationer. In her husband's life time she kept a pamphlet shop at the Peacock without Temple Bar, and dealt largely in newspapers, which she distributed to retailers. She was in trouble in Aug. 1714 for distributing the *Post Boy* (P.R.O. S.P. 35/1/28). If, as seems almost certain, she was the widow Dodd whose business Thomas Gent managed for some time, her husband had died about 1721 (T. Gent, *The Life of Mr. Thomas Gent, Printer, of York*, 1832, p. 145). Gent describes her as "a most agreeable person. . . There never could be a finer economist, or sweeter mother to her dear children, whom she kept exceedingly decent" (op. cit., p. 146). She carried on her husband's business for many years, publishing trivial poems, tales, and miscellaneous pieces, either separately or (more frequently) in collaboration with other publishers, such as Curll. In the weeks following the publication of the *Dunciad* she was selling many of the attacks upon Pope, including Curll's *Key*. It is perhaps significant that from 1706 to 1709 Curll had been publishing from the Peacock in the Strand. Mrs Dodd was in trouble in 1727 (P.R.O. S.P.44/80); and again in 1731 for publishing the *Craftsman* (*Calendar of Treasury Books and Papers, 1731-4*, p. 51). She lived to publish *The Last Will and Testament of Alexander Pope, of Twickenham, Esq.*, 1744.

*DOUGLAS, Charles, 2nd Earl of Selkirk (1663-1739). A ii 382*n*. One of the Lords of the Bedchamber. See Biog. App., vol. iv. In February, 1728, he "was seiz'd with an Apoplectick Fit in his Bed, but being immediately Blooded, his Lordship is likely to recover it" (*Evening Post*, Feb. 17/20, 1728). Pope may have had this circumstance in mind when he wrote, "Nor Selkirk whisper'd more."

DOUGLAS, James (1675-1742). B iv 394. Physician to Queen Caroline, and a celebrated anatomist and obstetrician. The part he played in the exposure of Mary Tofts (1726) may account for his appearance in this ludicrous episode of Annius. He was a F.R.S., contributed some papers to the *Philosophical Transactions*, and published some useful medical works. His interest in Horace was shown by his *Catalogus editionum Horatii*, 1739. "Mr. Jones, Rector of Uppingham . . . thinks our friend Dr. Douglas's life was shortened by Pope putting him into his *Dunciad*."—*Family Memoirs of the Rev. W. Stukeley*, 1882-7, ii 352.

DUCKETT, George (1684-1732). A iii 176; B iii 179. Politician and author. He collaborated with his friend Tom Burnet in the two *Homerides* (1715, 1716), and probably wrote two numbers of *Pasquin* which annoyed Pope (Nos. 12 and 13). Pope retaliated in 1728 by placing him among the didappers in the *Peri Bathous*. Dennis dedicated his *Remarks on Mr. Pope's Rape of the Lock* to him. Pope attributed the clever but cruel caricature of himself in *Pope Alexander's Supremacy* to Duckett; he may have been right, for it was signed "G.D." (EC viii 255). Duckett is said to have demanded and obtained satisfaction from Pope for "a scandalous imputation on his moral character"—presumably that made in *Dunciad A* iii 176 (Chalmers, *Biographical Dictionary*, xxv, 170). See also *The Letters of Thomas Burnet to George Duckett*, ed. D. Nichol Smith, *passim*.

DUNTON, John (1659–1733). A i 104*n*., ii 136; B ii 144. Bookseller and author. His *Life and Errors of John Dunton* (1705) had marked him out as an eccentric character; his later writings and behaviour seem to have convinced many of his contemporaries that he was mad. Dunton was a violent Whig and Hanoverian, but obtained little reward for all his zeal. He had attacked Pope's friends, Oxford and Bolingbroke, in *Neck or Nothing* (1713), and again in *Ox and Bull* (1715). In *Frank Scammony* (1720) he attacked Atterbury.

D'URFEY or DURFEY, Tom (1653–1723). A iii 138; B iii 146. Poet and dramatist. Durfey had been a recognized butt of the wits from Dryden's day, and was no doubt introduced into the *Dunciad* for that reason alone. The author of *Characters of the Times* (1728), p. 27, observes that "for many Years past, it has been the constant Practice of every little Author, to fall foul upon him, in order to get a Reputation for Wit". Pope had mentioned him with good-natured contempt in his letters (EC vi 92) as the laureate of the country squires, among whom Durfey's songs enjoyed great popularity. He glanced at him in the *Essay on Criticism* (l. 617), he wrote a faintly satirical "Prologue Designed for Mr. D'Urfey's Last Play" (see vol. vi), and he introduced him into the *Peri Bathous* as one of the Frogs who "can neither walk nor fly, but can leap and bound to admiration". Durfey had attacked Popery, and had satirized Oxford and Bolingbroke; but Pope is not likely to have borne him a grudge on either score.

EVANS, Abel (1679–1737). A i 108; B i 116. An Oxford wit and Doctor of Divinity who gained a considerable reputation from various short satirical pieces of verse. "Evans with laugh jocose" is one of those who greet Pope in Gay's *Welcome from Greece*. A letter from Young to Tickell, April 20, 1727, gives a characteristic glimpse of Evans: "Our Friend Evans has a pleasant Parsonage in Surrey, but is at odds with all his Parish and talks of Law, but is yet got no farther than Epigrams."—R. E. Tickell, *Thomas Tickell and the Eighteenth Century Poets*, p. 129.

FLEETWOOD, Charles (d. 1747?). B iv 326. Manager of the Drury Lane theatre from 1734, when he purchased five-sixths of the patent, until 1745. At the age of twenty-one he came into possession of a landed estate worth

£5,000 per annum. Losing his fortune, he turned sharper. His management of Drury Lane gave much offence to the dramatists, who complained that he put on worthless entertainments instead of their plays. About the year 1738 Johnson, Thomson, Mallet, and Hill were all experiencing great difficulty in their dealings with Fleetwood. Writing to Hill, Feb. 12, 1739, Pope expressed his contempt for this "man of the stage" who had recently refused to produce Hill's tragedy of *Caesar*. Paul Whitehead was one of the young men who suffered from his acquaintance with Fleetwood. Having persuaded Whitehead to stand as surety for a debt of £3,000 Fleetwood left him to face his creditors, and Whitehead, unable to raise this sum, was confined for some years in the Fleet prison. His will was proved on April 22, 1748 (R. W. Buss, *Charles Fleetwood*, 1915, p. 4).

FOXTON, Thomas (fl. 1728). A iii 151. Poet and literary hack. Curll gave him one guinea "and several books" for his poem, *The Tower*, but paid him rather more generously for translating various works from the Latin, such as *Laus Ululae* £3), and Burnet's *De Futura Judorum Restauratione* (£2 17s. 6d.). See B.M. Add. MSS. 38,728. Even among literary fleas he must be reckoned a small flea. He was so insignificant, indeed, that he failed to appear at all in *Dunciad B*, being perhaps dead and quite forgotten by 1743.

FREIND, Robert (1667–1751). B iv 223. Headmaster of Westminster School, 1711–33. Like Alsop, with whom Pope couples him, he was a Christ Church man, and joined in the attack on Bentley in defence of Boyle. Two of his Latin poems were printed in *Musarum Anglicanarum Delectus Alter*, 1698. A Latin ode to the Duke of Newcastle, 1737 (*Gent. Mag.*, vii 631) may have had something to do with Pope's double-edged compliment to Freind in the *Dunciad*. Pope has also been credited (J. Nichols, *Select Collection of Poems*, v 316) with an epigram on Freind's flattering epitaphs.

GILBERT, John (1693–1761). B iv 608. Bishop of Llandaff 1740, and of Salisbury 1749; Archbishop of York from 1757 till his death. "He had never given Pope any particular offence; but he had attacked Dr. King of Oxford, whom Pope much respected. And this attack was made in a rough and rude manner" (Warton). Most probably Gilbert was introduced to enable Pope to glance back ironically at his celebrated funeral sermon on Queen Caroline. Cf. *Dia.* i 69n., ii 164n.

GILDON, Charles (1665–1724). A i 250, iii 167; B i 296, iii 173. Critic and dramatist. His principal attacks on Pope are listed in the note to A i 250. See also Biog. App., vol. iv. He is apparently the person characterized in a letter from Pope to H. Cromwell, Oct. 19, 1709, as "every way a scoundrel, but that he has the luck to be born a gentleman". According to Welsted (*One Epistle . . .* 1730, p. 22n.) Gildon was dismissed from the Duke of Buckingham's favour "on Account of his Obstinacy in refusing to take the Oaths to P——pe's Supremacy". If this is true, it would account for the bitter tone of Gildon's references to Pope.

See also Sherburn, p. 164. By 1718 Gildon was blind, and living in a garret in Chancery Lane (*Robinson Crusoe Examin'd and Criticis'd*, ed. P. Dottin, p. 31). On Nov. 24, 1721, he was awarded £100 "as of Royal Bounty," presumably for services rendered to the government by his "venal quill" (P.R.O. T.38/225). For a detailed review of the Pope-Gildon quarrel, see N. Ault, "Pope and Addison," *R.E.S.*, 1941, xvii 436 ff.

GOODE, Barnham (1674–1739). A iii 147; B iii 153. Master at Eton College for thirty years, and one of Walpole's writers in *The Daily Courant* (Ralph, p. 517; E. Budgell's *Bee*, i 11). Goode was a friend of Theobald (*The Curliad*, p. 35), and of Giles Jacob, who addressed a letter to him in *The Mirrour*, 1733. From the fact that he spoke to Walpole on Curll's behalf (1724) about "something in the Post Office" (*Gent. Mag.*, vol. lxviii, Pt. i, p. 190), it appears that he and Walpole were on terms of some intimacy: they had been schoolfellows at Eton. See also *Gent. Mag.*, vol. ix. p. 383. For Goode's solemn denial that he wrote *The Mock Aesop*, see "Errata," p. 199.

GORDON, Thomas (d. 1750). B iv 492 ("Silenus"). Journalist, pamphleteer, and translator of Tacitus and Sallust. Gordon, a Scot, collaborated in 1721 with John Trenchard in criticizing the government in the so-called "Cato's Letters", which appeared in *The London Journal*. When in 1722 this paper was bought out by the government, the two men carried on their attack for some time in *The British Journal*. By 1727 Gordon had made his peace with Walpole, to whom he now dedicated his *Tacitus*. In an unpublished couplet in the *Epilogue to the Satires* Pope sneered at this change of front (EC iii 459). Gordon served Walpole by maintaining "a general supervision over the whole of the government press" (Hanson, p. 114), and was rewarded by being made a Commissioner for Wine Licences. He appears in the *Dunciad* as a "pensioner", and as an unsparing critic of the priesthood. See also the *Peri Bathous*, Ch. xii.

HAMMOND, James (1710–42). "Testimonies of Authors," p. 37. Poet. His *Love Elegies* (1743) went through numerous editions in the eighteenth century; but Johnson found in them "neither nature, passion, nor manners", and only a "frigid pedantry" (*Lives*, ii 315). He was a friend of Chesterfield, Cobham, Lyttleton, and other members of the Opposition.

HANDEL, Georg Friedrich (1685–1759). B iv 65. Composer, and conductor of the opera in Hamburg. He came to England in the winter of 1710, and his opera *Rinaldo* was performed at the Haymarket theatre in 1711. After a brief return to Hanover, Handel settled permanently in England in 1712. His coming to England had annoyed George, Elector of Hanover; but some months after George became King of England he was reconciled to Handel. In England Handel was patronized by Pope's friend, the Earl of Burlington, at whose house he stayed for three years, and later by the Duke of Chandos, with whom he stayed at Cannons. Handel composed numerous operas and oratorios, and much incidental music for the Court. From 1720–28 he was Director of the Royal Academy of Music; and from 1735–7 he was producing operas at Covent Garden. His *Esther*, for which Pope wrote the book, was composed for performance at Cannons in 1720; it was publicly performed in 1732. In 1743 Handel acknowledged Pope's complimentary lines in the *Dunciad* by inserting his setting of Pope's "Where e'er you walk" in his *Semele* (G. Sherburn, " 'Timon's Villa' and Cannons," *Huntington Library Bulletin*, No. 8, Oct. 1935, pp. 144ff.). Pope, who had no ear for music, once explained that he had gone out of his way to praise Handel for the reason that "merit in every branch of science ought to be encouraged; that the extreme illiberality with which many persons had joined to ruin Handel, in opposing his operas, had called forth his indignation; and though nature had denied his being gratified by Handel's uncommon talents in the musical line, yet when his powers were generally acknowledged, he thought it incumbent on him to pay a tribute due to genius" (W. Coxe, *Anecdotes of . . . Handel*, 1799, p. 40). In musical matters Pope relied upon the judgment of his friends, Arbuthnot and Burlington. His praise of Handel, however, may have been in part political; in 1736 Handel (who had hitherto enjoyed the patronage of George II) wrote an anthem for the marriage of the Prince of Wales, and the King was offended. Praise of Handel was thereafter an indirect censure of the King.

HANMER, Sir Thomas (1677–1746). B iv 105 ("Montalto"). Fourth baronet, Speaker of the House of Commons, and editor of Shakespeare. As a pompous and rather dull celebrity, Hanmer is not out of place in the *Dunciad*; but he owes his inclusion to his quarrel with Warburton over his edition of Shakespeare. The details of this misunderstanding will be found in Evans, pp. 147–58. If Hanmer was the author of *Remarks on the Tragedy of Hamlet* (1736), Pope may have had a more personal score to pay off. The critic explains that he has decided to "make use of the edition of this poet given us by Mr. Theobald, because he is generally thought to have understood our Author best. . . I would not have Mr. Pope offended at what I say, for I look upon him as the greatest genius in England; but the province of an editor and a commentator is quite foreign to that of a poet." The praise could scarcely be more handsome, but the unfavourable comparison with Theobald may have left a scar.

HARCOURT, Simon, first Earl Harcourt (1714–77). B iv 545. Son of Pope's friend, the Hon. Simon Harcourt (1684–1720), whose epitaph he composed. (See Vol. vi.) He turned out to be a more useful patrician than Pope's reference would suggest. He was present at the battle of Dettingen (1743), and ended up, after holding various offices, as Viceroy of Ireland. His fondness for opera is confirmed by a letter which he wrote from Italy about the Italian singers (*Harcourt Papers*, ed. E. W. Harcourt, vol. iii, p. 27).

HARE, Francis (1671–1740). B iii 204. See Biog. App., Vol. iv. Pope's praise of Hare's preaching may be ironical. Hare had his eyes eagerly fixed on Lambeth, and a sermon which he preached on Jan. 30, 1733, on the text, "Woe be unto them that are given to change", provoked much satirical comment. Paul Whitehead refers to it in his *State Dunces* in a passage which begins:

> Lo! o'er yon flood H——e casts his low'ring eyes,
> And wishful sees the rev'rend turrets rise. . .

(250 ff.). Hare may also have qualified for the *Dunciad* as one of the government's supporters in *The Daily Courant* (Ralph, p. 517).

HARTE, Walter (1709–74). "Testimonies of Authors," p. 36. A friend and admirer of Pope. His *Essay on Satire*, 1730, and *Essay on Reason*, 1735, were inspired by the *Dunciad* and the *Essay on Man* respectively. Pope, who touched up his verses, told Caryll that he was "a very valuable young man" (EC vi 327). Harte, who took orders, became Vice-Principal of St Mary's Hall, Oxford, and a Canon of Windsor. He published a *History of the Life of Gustavus Adolphus* in 1759.

HAYWOOD, Mrs Eliza (1693?–1756). A ii 149; B ii 157. Novelist, dramatist, and writer of scandalous memoirs. She had attacked the character of Martha Blount in her *Memoirs of a certain Island adjacent to the Kingdom of Utopia*, 1724 (Sherburn, pp. 295–6). Her *Secret History of . . . the Court of Caramania* followed in 1727. She was a friend of Theobald, who inscribed a copy of *The Dunciad* to her "as a testimony of his esteem"—a strange gift in the circumstances (*Notes and Queries*, 1 x 110). Swift called her "a stupid, infamous, scribbling woman" (Oct. 26, 1731). Pope's satire was merciless, but not undeserved. "More pity has been wasted on Mrs. Haywood than her character warrants" (Sherburn, p. 296. See also G. F. Whicher, *The Life and Romances of Mrs. Eliza Haywood*, 1915).

HEARNE, Thomas (1678–1735). A iii 181; B iii 185. Antiquary, and editor of Leland, Camden, and many English chronicles. On Humfrey Wanley's death in 1726 the Earl of Oxford tried to induce Hearne to become his librarian. Like most of his generation, Pope failed to appreciate the value of Hearne's antiquarian researches, and in the *Dunciad* he laughs, good-naturedly enough, at a man whom he considered to be a mere pedant. Pope's bantering letters to Wanley (EC x 115-16), phrased in a pseudo-archaic diction, provide another instance of the wit smiling at the labours of the antiquarian. Long before he knew Pope, Warburton had expressed his contempt for Hearne. Cf. *A Critical and Philosophical Enquiry into . . . Miracles* (1727), p. 63: "Every Monkish Tale, and Lye, and Miracle, and Ballad, are rescued from their Dust and Worms, to proclaim the Poverty of our Forefathers . . . For of all those Writings given us by the *Learned Oxford Antiquary*, there is not one that is not a Disgrace to Letters." See also David Douglas, *English Scholars*, 1939, pp. 226 ff.

HEIDEGGER, John James (1659?–1749). A i 244; B i 290. A Swiss, whose activity in promoting masquerades and other fashionable entertainments in

London earned him the title of "surintendant des plaisirs d'Angleterre"—a French equivalent for "Master of the Revels", an office which he actually held under George II. (See James Bramston, *The Art of Politicks*, l. 44*n*.) In 1720 he collaborated with Handel in producing operas for the Royal Academy of Music, and from 1728–34 the two men were again working in an operatic partnership. Heidegger's ugliness was the subject of several anecdotes and of much contemporary comment, and is the main reason for his being brought into the *Dunciad*.

HENLEY, John (1692–1756). A ii 2, 338, iii 195; B ii 2, 370, iii 199. See Biog. App., vol. iv. Henley had given Pope some offence by associating himself with Gildon and Theobald in the preparation of Curll's edition of the Duke of Buckingham's *Works*, for which he wrote a dedicatory poem. He is credited, too, with a neat couplet on Pope's *Homer*:

> Pope came off clean with Homer; but they say
> Broome went before, and kindly swept the way.

(D.N.B. Art. Broome.) Henley was in Walpole's pay as early as 1724, when he appears to have been acting with Curll as an informer (*Gent. Mag.*, vol. lxviii, Pt. i, p. 190). His *Hyp-Doctor* (1735–41) frequently attacked Pope; and he also published in 1736 his vituperative pamphlet *Why How now, Gossip Pope?* After the appearance of the *Dunciad*, the newspaper advertisements for Henley's Oratory are frequently abusive of Pope: e.g. *The Daily Post*, April 29, 1729: "Tomorrow, at Seven o' Clock, will be held forth Tom o' Bedlam's Dunciad; or a Wager, who makes the best Hurlothrumbo, I, or Pope Alexander the Pig?" Henley was a mountebank and a buffoon, who went steadily from bad to worse, and his inclusion in the *Dunciad* was fully justified; but he had considerable ability, and scattered through the pages of the *Hyp-Doctor* and his other writings there is a good deal of misplaced wit.

HILL, Aaron (1683–1750). A ii 283; B ii 295. Dramatist, poet, essayist, and projector. Hill's troubled relations with Pope began in 1718, when Lintot showed Pope his poem, *The Northern Star*, and tactlessly reported Pope's not very enthusiastic comment. In his preface to the poem (1720) Hill showed his resentment. Repenting some time later, he wrote to ask Pope's pardon (EC x 3), and published in 1720 another poem, *The Creation*, in the preface to which he publicly owned his mistake. In his periodical, *The Plain Dealer*, however, Hill printed some disparaging remarks on Pope's *Shakespeare* (No. 116, May 3, 1725); and Nos. 54 and 82 may also have annoyed Pope, if he read them. When the *Peri Bathous* appeared in March, 1728, "A. H." was among the flying-fish, and Hill assumed, no doubt correctly, that he was the person meant, and retaliated with an epigram on Pope in the *Daily Journal*, April 16. When the *Dunciad* appeared in May, "H——" was among those dark and dirty writers who took part in the diving match; if there was any doubt in Hill's mind as to who was intended, a note to the quarto of 1729 must have removed it. Hill replied, more in sorrow than in anger, in *The Progress of Wit, a Caveat,*

1730; but in a letter dated Jan. 18, 1731, he complained to Pope about the note in the *Dunciad*. For Pope's evasive response to this, and Hill's shattering retort, see their correspondence in EC x, pp. 8–23. A new note was substituted in 1735; but the two men seem to have fallen out again, for Pope was attacked several times in Hill's periodical, *The Prompter*, 1735–6. (See Biog. App., Popple.) In 1738 Hill re-opened their correspondence, and took a long-drawn-out revenge on Pope by sending him a succession of his poems and plays to read in manuscript. Hill was no fool, but he was something of a bore: Pope had to pay dearly for his enmity, but still more for his friendship. Perhaps it was of Hill that he was thinking in *Ep. to Arbuthnot*, 107–8:

> A Fool quite angry is quite innocent;
> Alas! 'tis ten times worse when they *repent*.

HOADLY, Benjamin (1676–1761). A ii 368*n*.; B ii 400*n*. See Biog. App., vol. iv. As a Whig and a Low Churchman, Hoadly had consistently opposed Pope's friend, Bishop Atterbury. As "Britannicus" he wrote against him in 1721 in *The London Journal*, and he published the speech which he had delivered at Atterbury's trial in 1723. Swift, writing to Archbishop King, Sept. 28, 1719, calls him "that wretch of Bangor"; but he was one of the ablest of the Whig bishops.

HORNECK, Philip (d. 1728). A iii 146; B iii 152. Son of the Rev. Anthony Horneck (1641–97); Solicitor to the Treasury from 1716 to his death, and author of *The High-German Doctor*, 1714–15. Besides attacking Pope's *Iliad* in No. 14, Horneck abused his friends Oxford, Bolingbroke, and Atterbury throughout; and Gay, writing to Parnell on March 18, 1715, complained of an attack on his *What D'ye Call It?* Pope's first published reply to Horneck may have been in *The Use and Abuse of Glass-Bottles*, 1715. (See N. Ault, *Pope's Prose*, vol. i, pp. lxxxviii f.) In the *Memoirs of . . . Martinus Scriblerus* Horneck is mentioned in Chapter vi as one whom it is impossible to bring "to common civility". The second Earl of Oxford called him "a special rascal" (*Notes and Queries*, 2 Ser. ix 419).

JACOB, Giles (1686–1744). A iii 149; B iii 149. Compiler of various law dictionaries and other works of reference, including *The Poetical Register*, 1719–20. The latter contains an account of Pope and his writings, which Jacob subsequently claimed had been corrected and amplified by Pope while it was in proof, to such an extent that "by his Alterations and Additions therein, he entirely made the Compliment his own" (*Remarks upon the Dunciad*, pp. 48–9). In a letter to Dennis on "Mr. Pope and his Poetry" (*The Mirrour*, 1733, p. 5), Jacob declared that he had never written against Pope until after the publication of the *Dunciad*; but in his preface to *The Rape of the Smock* (1717) he referred to "that stupid Farce, called *Three Hours after Marriage*", and in *The Poetical Register* he repeated his attack on this unhappy play. Jacob's own explanation of Pope's enmity is inadequate, but it may contain a part of the truth: "It seems the envious little Gentleman is angry with me for presuming to say any thing in Favour of others. Here's the Center and Fountain of his Malice" (*Remarks upon the Dunciad*, p. 46). His

Poetical Register is, in fact, full of polite tributes to contemporary scribblers whose writings Pope quite justifiably despised. "The Law of Liberty and Property: or a New Year's Gift for Mr Pope . . . By Giles Jacob, Gent." (an attack on Pope?) was advertised in *The London Evening Post*, May 20, 1736.

JOHNSON, Charles (1679–1748). A i 240. Dramatist; the "fat Johnson" of Pope's *Farewell to London* (vol. vi), and a faithful member of the Button's group of Whig writers who paid court to Addison. He was a prolific dramatist, but his plots were mostly borrowed: it is as a plagiary that he is cited in the *Dunciad*. Johnson's sneering lines about *Three Hours After Marriage* in his *Sultaness* (cf. A i 240n.) were not very damaging; but any reference to this unhappy farce seems to have goaded Pope to a kind of fury. Johnson in the Preface to his *Medea* (1731) took note of Pope's satirical references to himself : the "little Gentleman" had taken it into his head that "he was really and truly the King of *Parnassus*, and that all People, who pretended to oppose this his Title to poetical Royalty or to make Verses without his Patent and Authority, were Rebels". For further references to him, see vol. iv, vol vi, and EC iii 260.

KENNETT, White (1660–1728). A iii 200. Dean of Peterborough, 1708; Bishop of Peterborough, 1718. He published many sermons, including some against Popery. The sermon he preached at the funeral of the Duke of Devonshire in September, 1707, occasioned the charge that he was encouraging a death-bed repentance. Pope's praise of Kennett's preaching may be ironical.

KING, Peter, Baron King of Ockham in Surrey (1669–1734). B iv 545. A distinguished judge, who became Lord Chancellor in 1725. Each of his four sons succeeded to the title in turn. Of John, second Lord King, who died in 1740, nothing of interest seems to be known.

KNIGHT, Robert (d. 1744). B iv 561. Cashier to the South Sea Company. In 1721, when the affairs of the company were in a state of chaos, he fled to France. His son told the Earl of Egmont that before his father "withdrew" he delivered to the company "all the money and bonds in his hands, as Cashier, amounting to above 200,000 l., but by reason of his flight (which was to save the reputation of the then Ministry who promised he should be speedily recalled) the Parliament forfeited that sum to the Company, which was not public money but his own property, though he had no hand in the corruption of that time" (Egmont iii 269). Pope told Swift (Nov. 28, 1729) that Knight had recently sent a rich present to the Queen with a view to securing his pardon. Knight, who had been obliged to remain abroad ever since his flight, was pardoned at length on Aug. 17, 1742—a circumstance which Pope noted with disapproval in a letter to the Earl of Orrery, Aug. 27, 1742. See also *Ep.* ii i 195n., and EC iii 48, 128.

KUSTER, Ludolph (1670–1716). B iv 237. A Westphalian scholar whom Bentley assisted with an edition of the lexicographer Suidas, and later with an edition of Aristophanes. The Suidas was published by the University of Cambridge through the influence of Bentley.

LAW, William (1686–1761). A ii 381; B ii 413. High Church clergyman, author of *A Serious Call to a Devout and Holy Life*, 1728. His attack on the stage, *The Absolute Unlawfulness of the Stage Entertainment fully demonstrated*, was published in 1726. In later life Law was a disciple of Jacob Behmen.

MAFFEI, Francisco Scipio (1675–1755). B iv 202*n*. Marquis of Verona; author of *Merope*, and a learned scholar. He visited Pope in 1736, and found him "in the gesture of translating *Merope* from the Italian" (Sherburn, p. 41). It is hard to see why Maffei should be ridiculed in the commentary unless Pope is alluding to some drinking episode. He was, it is true, a D.C.L. of Oxford (1736) and a F.R.S., both of which distinctions afforded, when Pope or Warburton chose to think so, presumptive evidence of dullness.

MALLET (*alias* Malloch), David (1705?–1765). "Testimonies of Authors," p. 36. Poet and dramatist, author of the ballad, *William and Margaret*. He published the poem from which Pope quotes, *Of Verbal Criticism; an Epistle to Mr. Pope*, in 1733, as "a public testimony of his inviolable esteem for Mr. Pope". Dr. Johnson took a more realistic view of Mallet's motives, and remarked that the poem was "written to pay court to Pope" on a subject which Mallet "either did not understand, or willingly misrepresented" (Johnson, *Lives*, iii 401–2). Mallet, who wrote some other poems and plays, enjoyed the friendship of Pope, Hill, and Thomson, and later of Bolingbroke, whose Works he published in 1754. Johnson, who despised Mallet, handed on the cutting remark that "he was the only Scot whom Scotchmen did not commend".

MEARS, William (fl. 1720). A ii 117, iii 20; B ii 125, iii 28. Publisher "at the Lamb, without Temple Bar" until 1727, and perhaps later. His authors include many of Pope's dunces—Defoe, Dennis, Philips, Mrs Centlivre, etc. In 1721 he published *The Grove*, a poetical miscellany to which Theobald, Moore Smythe, and Barnham Goode contributed a number of pieces. For some reason still unexplained—was he, too, a contributor?—Pope took four copies on royal paper. Mears sometimes published in partnership with Jonas Browne "at the Black Swan without Temple Bar"—no doubt the "Brown" with whom Pope has coupled his name.

MILBOURNE, Rev. Luke (1649–1720). A ii 325; B ii 349. Poet and High Church divine. In 1698 he attacked Dryden in *Notes on Dryden's Virgil:* Dryden retorted with good-humoured contempt in the Preface to his *Fables* (1700). In 1711 Pope coupled him with Blackmore in the *Essay on Criticism*, l. 463. For some specimens of Milbourne's abuse of Dryden, see Appendix vi. Milbourne was brought into the *Dunciad* mainly to press home the parallel which Pope sought to establish between himself and Dryden.

MIST, Nathaniel (d. 1737). A i 194, iii 286; B i 208. Printer and publisher, owner of the popular Tory newspaper, *The Weekly journal; or Saturday's post*, 1716-28, one of the most formidable of the anti-ministerial journals. According to *The Daily Gazetteer*, July 31, 1741, "Mist's treasonable Papers were sold sometimes for Half a Guinea a-piece". Mist sailed very near the wind on several occasions, and was more than once fined and imprisoned for his indiscretions. His contributors included Theobald, Bezaleel Morrice, and even the Whig Concanen. Defoe was his leading author from 1717 to 1724. In September, 1728, Mist went too far once too often, and fled to Paris (*Universal Spectator*, Dec. 14, 1728), but his paper was carried on as *Fog's Journal*, which was advertised as springing "from the Ashes of the late Mr. Mist" (*Daily Journal*, Oct. 4, 1728). From 1725 onwards Pope was frequently abused in Mist's paper, which made a particular point of gibing at his *Shakespeare*. Pope agreed, no doubt, with the correspondent in the *St. James's Journal*, Aug. 2, 1722, who sneered at Mist's vulgar appeal, and said that he catered "only for Porters and Coblers, and such dirty Customers as are his greatest Patrons". Yet, according to another witness, "The Two famous Universities of this Land are the grand Centers of it: Men and Horses are employed to convey it in large Quantities to *Oxford* and *Cambridge*; where, senseless as it is, it is constantly read and applauded." (*The Commentator*, April 1, 1720.)

*MITCHELL, Joseph (1684-1738). A iii 146*n*. Dramatist and minor poet. The son of a stone-cutter in Scotland, he came to England and addressed his verses in so servile a strain to Walpole that he became known as "Sir Robert Walpole's poet". In "An Anacreontique to the . . . Earl of Stair", 1727, he reflected stupidly on the diminutive size of "little Pope". He may also have annoyed the poet by his indiscriminate way of coupling his name with that of Philips and of Aaron Hill. Pope, however, got the better of his resentment and subscribed for Mitchell's sumptuous *Poems on Several Occasions* in two volumes, 1729. The quarrel, such as it was, may have been composed by Arbuthnot, a brother Scot, who paid for two sets of Mitchell's wretched poems himself, and who probably persuaded Swift, whose name also appears in the list of subscribers, to take another.

MOLLOY, Charles (d. 1767). A ii 268*n*. Journalist and dramatist. He wrote for *Mist's Journal* (W. T. Laprade, *Public Opinion in Eighteenth Century England*, p. 248), *Fog's Journal* (Ralph, p. 516), and, from 1737-9, for *Common Sense*. In 1718 Curll paid Molloy five guineas for his comedy, *The Coquet*, and "his Note of hand for the Same Summe made conditionally payable upon the Sale of Nine Hundred" (B.M. Add. MSS. 38,728, f. 157).

MORGAN, Thomas (d. 1743). B ii 414. Deist, and Doctor of Medicine. His best-known work, *The Moral Philosopher*, was published in 1737; a second volume followed in 1739, and a third in 1740. Writing to the Rev. Thomas Birch, Aug. 17, 1737, Warburton stated that it was "composed principally of scraps ill put together from 'Christianity as old as the Creation' larded with some of the most stupid fancies of his own''. If he is the author of an attack on Warburton's *Divine Legation of Moses* (Evans, pp. 116–17), his appearance in the *Dunciad* of 1743 is sufficiently explained.

MORRICE, Bezaleel (1675?–1749). A ii 118; B ii 126, iii 168. Poet. Third son of Capt. William Morys (W. C. Morice, *A Collection of Morice and Morrice Biographies*, p. 24). In what is probably his first book, *The Muse's Treat*, 1702, it appears that, though born in England, Morrice had spent his childhood and early manhood in the East Indies. In later life he scribbled verses persistently. In *A Satyre on the English Translations of Homer* (1721), and again in *The Present State of Poetry. A Satyr* (1721) he joined in the attack on Pope's *Homer*. His *Poetical Descriptions*, 1722, was dedicated to Aaron Hill. Morrice was a regular contributor of verse to *Mist's Journal* (*A Collection of Miscellany Letters Selected out of Mist's Weekly Journal*, Part I, Preface). Later some of his pieces appeared in Budgell's *Bee* (vol. iii, pp. 1589, 1708). A letter abusing Pope, signed "B.M.", in *The Daily Journal*, July 27, 1728, is almost certainly his. In 1730 appeared his *Dissectio Mentis Humanae*, in which he writes satirically of "modern critics, stage and epic poets, translators, drolls, etc.", and some years later *The Present Corruption of Britons, being a Paraphrase of the latter part of Mr P——e's Dialogue, entitled, One Thousand Seven Hundred and Thirty-eight*. Yet another attack on Pope followed in 1742: *To the Falsely Celebrated British Homer*. See also Appendix ii, and *Gent. Mag.*, vol. xcvii, Pt. I, p. 29.

MUMMIUS. B iv 371. "I have been lately informed that by Mummius was meant Dr. Mead" (Warton). Warton was almost certainly misinformed: at the time the Mummius passage was published Pope was on friendly terms with that physician, and had recently been his patient. Pope's note is sufficiently precise for the person aimed at to recognize himself immediately as the antiquary ridiculed. At the same time, Pope must have realized that as the possessor of two celebrated mummies Mead was almost sure to be taken for Mummius by many readers. One of his mummies was found "in the Catacombs of Sakara near *Cairo*, and sent from thence by Consul *Barton*, and Mr. *Lile*, to England, together with another, which Dr. *Mead* gave as a Present to the College of Physicians in *London*, both which arrived there about the Year 1734" (Alexander Gordon, *An Essay towards Explaining the . . . Egyptian Mummy in the Museum of Dr. Mead*, 1737, p. 1). There were, however, several other English owners of mummies, *e.g.* William Lethieullier, the Earl of Sandwich (who returned from his travels in 1739 with two mummies from Memphis), Joshua Locke, Edward Lisle. (See Alexander Gordon, *Twenty-five Plates of all the Egyptian Mummies . . . 1739*.) Charles Perry sent a mummy home to England in 1741 from the Arabs: a plate of it will be found in his *View of the Levant*, 1743. E.C.'s suggestion that Mummius was Dr John Woodward (1665–1728) seems to be ill-founded: Woodward had been dead almost fifteen years when *The New Dunciad* was published. Perhaps the likeliest candidate is John Montagu, fourth Earl of Sandwich (1718–92) mentioned above. In addition to being a virtuoso, he had been elected (1740) a Fellow of the Royal Society. As President of the Egyptian Club he was the person who might most appropriately be described as "rattling an ancient sistrum". (Cf. B iv 374n.) For a list of other members of this club, see Nichols, *Lit. Anec.*, v 334.

OLDMIXON, John (1673–1742). A ii 199; B ii 283. Miscellaneous writer. Trouble with Pope probably started with the publication in 1714 of Oldmixon's Miscellany, *Poems and Translations*, in which he included Pope's "Receipt to make a Cuckold", and went out of his way to apologize for its indecency. Subsequent offences are noted in Biog. App., vol. iv. See also Appendix ii. Oldmixon was a frequent contributor to *The Flying-Post*, part-author of *The Medley* (1710–11), and author of the ultra-Whig periodical, *The Protestant Packet* ("A Full and True Account," *Pope's Prose*, p. 265). Apart from his personal attacks on Pope, he qualified for the *Dunciad* by his virulent party-writing, his association with Curll, and the violence of his anti-Catholicism. He was one of "the hireling class, who had no personal acquaintance with Pope and who wrote simply for their daily bread" (Sherburn, p. 184). He appears with Gildon and Dennis in the *Peri Bathous* among the porpoises.

OSBORNE, Thomas (d. 1767). B ii 167ff. Son of Thomas Osborne (d. 1743), and one of the leading booksellers of the mid-eighteenth century. In so far as he is still remembered, it is mainly because Dr Johnson knocked him down on account of his impudence (Boswell, *Life*, i 154). He bought the Earl of Oxford's library in 1742, and employed Johnson in cataloguing it, and he published a number of notable books, including Richardson's *Pamela*. According to Johnson, "Osborne was a man entirely destitute of shame, without sense of any disgrace but that of poverty. He told me, when he was doing that which raised Pope's resentment, that he should be put into *The Dunciad*" (*Lives*, iii 187).

OZELL, John (d. 1743). A i 240; B i 286. An industrious and voluminous translator, to whom the gibe "less reading than makes felons 'scape" was singularly inapplicable. With Oldisworth and Broome he produced a prosy version of the *Iliad* (from the French of Madame Dacier), 1712, and his earlier verse translation of *Le Lutrin*, 1708, occasioned Pope's epigram, *The Translator*. (See vol. vi.) In 1713 he did a verse translation for Curll of Tassoni's *La Secchia Rapita* ("The Rape of the Bucket"). For Pope's annoyance when Jacob mentioned this poem along with *The Rape of the Lock*, see "Errata," p. 190. The "J.O." who is placed among the porpoises in the *Peri Bathous* is probably Oldmixon, but the initials and the definition fit Ozell too. On finding himself in the *Dunciad*, Ozell—who seems to have been a highly irritable man—lost his temper completely, and referred to the *Dunciad* as "that beastly and rascally Book", and to Pope as "that second CAIN, *whose Hand is against every Body*" (*The Weekly Medley*, No. 51, Sept. 20, 1729). He attacked Pope again in *The Herculean Labour*, 1729, No. 1, p. 2, as "a certain Monkey." His religious views were, on his own confession, illiberal: "I can no more help Buffooning when Popery comes in my way, than that Zany when Scripture comes in his" (*The Henriade*, p. 12). Ozell accented his name on the first syllable (*The Weekly Medley*, No. 51).

PAGE, Sir Francis (1661?–1741). B iv 30. See Biog. App., vol. iv. Pope may have met this notorious judge in 1739. Writing to Fortescue, July 26, he stated: "I am within a mile of your brother Page, who threatens to come hither: and it is very probable I may see him at dinner tomorrow."

PARKER, Sir Thomas, Earl of Macclesfield (1666?–1732). B iv 545. Lord Chancellor, 1718–25, when he resigned the seals after a report by a committee of the Privy Council that he had been guilty of financial misdemeanours in the execution of his office. In May, 1725, he was impeached, found guilty, and fined £30,000. His son George, second Earl of Macclesfield (1697–1764) was not the degenerate that Pope's reference to him suggests. He had scientific tastes, and was particularly interested in astronomy. He became a Fellow of the Royal Society in 1722, and its president in 1752. He took a leading part in the passing of the bill for the Reform of the Calendar.

PITT, James (1679–1763). A ii 380; B ii 312. See Biog. App., vol. iv. Originally a schoolmaster in Norwich, Pitt was given "a small Place in the Revenue", and later a post in the Customs House as a reward for his party writing (E. Budgell, *The Bee*, i 14; Ralph, p. 517). He wrote for *The London Journal* and *The Daily Gazetteer* under several different names, viz.: "Publicola" (P.R.O. *S.P.D.* 36/11/85, and *The Universal Spectator*, May 3, 1729); "Socrates" (*Bee*, i 14); and— the name by which he was best known—"Francis Osborne." Pitt was for some time "the oracle of a political circle, in George's Coffee-house, Temple-bar, 'giving his little Senate laws' " (J. Nichols, *Lit. Ill.*, iⁱ 619n.). The nickname "Mother Osborne" was given him by *The Craftsman* (March 13, 1742).

PHILIPS, Ambrose (1675?–1749). A i 103, iii 322, Appendix v; B i 105, iii 326, Appendix v. See Biog. App., vol. iv. Pope believed that Philips had been encouraged to abuse him "in coffee-houses and conversations" (Spence, p. 148). After Pope's joke at Philips's expense in the *Guardian*, a petty warfare broke out between the two men, and Philips, who was Secretary to the Hanover Club, held up subscriptions for the *Homer* paid to him by some of the members (EC vi 210). In the *What D'ye Call It* (1715), in which Pope was thought to have a hand, Philips's *Distrest Mother* came in for some burlesque, and he was listed among Curll's authors in *A Further Account* (1716) as "a Pindarick Writer in red Stockings," and in the *Peri Bathous* as a tortoise. For further flippancies at his expense, see Index to vol. vi. Pope, however, genuinely admired some of Philips's poetry. See his letter to H. Cromwell, Oct. 28, 1710, where he gave it as his opinion that Philips was "capable of writing very nobly".

*PIX, Mrs Mary (1666–1709). A iii 141n. Dramatist. Her tragedy of *Ibrahim*, produced in 1696, was followed by a number of other plays. She was notorious for her fatness. Tom Brown, searching for a comparison that would indicate extreme bulk, remembered Mrs Pix, and wrote: " . . . she was . . . three times as thick and bulky as Mrs. *Pix* the Poetress" (*Letters from the Dead to the Living*, 1702, p. 9). Pope may have seen her, though she died when he was still a young man. The D.N.B. conjectures 1720 as the date of her death; but the *Post Boy*, May 26-28, 1709, advertises a performance of Mrs Centlivre's *Busy Body* "for the Benefit of the Family of Mrs. Mary Pix, deceas'd . . . the greatest part of which said Comedy, and also of that of the Gamester, was wrote by the said Mrs. Pix".

POLLIO. B iv 350. Most probably Henry Herbert, ninth Earl of Pembroke, "the architect earl", for whom "Statues, dirty Gods, and Coins" were bought in *Moral Es.* iv 8. If Annius (q.v.) is Sir Andrew Fountaine, this identification is strengthened; for the Pembroke family were apparently on terms of friendship with the antiquary, and possessed both a portrait and a bust of him. (See James Kennedy, *A Description of the Antiquities . . . in Wilton House*, 1769, pp. 33, 43.) It is unlikely, in view of B iii 328, that Richard Boyle, Earl of Burlington (Walpole's guess) is Pollio.

POPPLE, William (1701–64). B iii 151. Dramatist, Solicitor, and Clerk of the Reports to the Commissioners of Trade and Plantations (1737); Governor of Bermuda (1745). His plays include *The Lady's Revenge* (1734), and *The Double Deceit* (1735). Popple collaborated with Aaron Hill in *The Prompter*: Pope was attacked in the numbers for Nov. 18, 21, Dec. 2, 1735, and Jan. 2, 1736, and retaliated in 1743 with the reference to Popple's "brow, tremendous to the town." Popple's political views resulted in *The Lady's Revenge* being interrupted on the fourth night. In the Preface he explains that a report had been spread that it was a party play, and supported by the Court.

RALPH, James (1705?–1762). A iii 159; B i 216, iii 165. Miscellaneous writer. Born in Pennsylvania, he came to England in 1724 with Benjamin Franklin. His rash attack on Pope in his *Sawney* (1728) was probably a deliberate attempt to push his name before the public. Pope's ridicule of him in later editions of the *Dunciad* may have had the contrary effect. (See G. Jacob, *The Mirrour*, 1733, pp. 77–8, where his reputation is said to have "greatly suffer'd with his Booksellers, Printers and Hawkers" as a result of Pope's devastating reply.) Ralph published *Miscellaneous Poems, By Several Hands* (1729), and a number of almost worthless plays and poems of his own. More interesting are his *Critical History of the Administration of Sir Robert Walpole*, 1743, and *The Case of Authors by Profession or Trade Stated*, 1758, both issued anonymously. According to Nichols (*Lit. Anec.*, ix 590) Ralph had a hand in *The Universal Spectator*, and may have written for Aaron Hill's *Prompter*. He assisted Fielding in *The Champion*, and afterwards was in sole charge of it. Later he found a patron in Bubb

Dodington, and attacked the government in *The Remembrancer* (1748). Later still (1751), when the Duke of Bedford founded his anti-ministerial paper, *The Protester*, Ralph was persuaded to edit it. He was finally silenced by the government with a pension of £300 a year (Hanson, pp. 120–1).

RAYMOND, Robert, 2nd Lord Raymond (1717?–1756). B iv 545. The son of Sir Robert Raymond, Baron Raymond (1673–1733), who became Lord Chief Justice in 1725. Little is known of this peer, but EC quotes from a letter of Lord Barrington to Mallet, June 7, 1737: "Lord Raymond plays much the same game with the —— at Venice, that he played with the singing women at Florence." This hardly confirms Lord Raymond's fondness for music, but it sufficiently indicates his character. With his death the peerage became extinct.

RICH, John (1682?–1761). A iii 257; B iii 261. Theatrical manager, and the creator of numerous pantomimes. See Biog. App., vol. iv. Pope was not likely to forget that it was to Rich that Theobald dedicated his *Shakespeare Restored*; but he appears in the *Dunciad* as one of those most directly responsible for the decay of the regular drama. In spite of his ridicule of Rich, Pope seems to have remained on speaking terms, for in 1733 he successfully recommended to him Dodsley's play, *The Toy-Shop* (EC ix 535–6).

RIDPATH, George (d. 1726). A ii 141, 286; B i 208, ii 149. Whig journalist, and author for some years of *The Flying-Post*. In 1712 he was committed to Newgate for libel, but escaped to Holland in May, 1713, after being convicted. On Nov. 8, 1712, Pope was complaining that "the rascally scribbler, the Flying Post" had maliciously reflected on his friend Caryll, and he offered his services "in reply to, or raillery upon, that scoundrel".

ROLLI, Paolo Antonio (1687–1767). A ii 195; B ii 203. A Florentine who came to England about 1718, and became Secretary to the Royal Academy of Music. He wrote the libretto of numerous Italian operas performed under the direction of the Academy, translated a number of English books, including *Paradise Lost*, into Italian, and wrote in English *Remarks upon M. Voltaire's Essay on the Epick Poetry of the European Nations* (1728). He dedicated to George II and to many of the nobility, including the Dukes of Newcastle and Montagu, and the Earl of Burlington. In 1729 he became "preceptor to the princesses in Italian" (*The Flying-Post; or The Weekly Medley*, Jan. 11, 1729).

ROOME, Edward (d. 1729). A iii 146; B iii 152. Poet. With Concanen and Sir William Yonge he altered Brome's *A Joviall Crew* into a ballad-opera, and wrote some of the songs for it. He was a friend of Theobald and Warburton, and Theobald wrote feelingly of his death (J. Nichols, *Lit. Ill.*, ii 326). A very different picture of Roome from Pope's was given by Concanen, who praised

him for his easy and genteel humour, and his cheerful culture—
            "The learned hint, the ,pleasing tale,
            The wise remark, th' unwounding jest."
—*The Flower Piece* (1731), p. 43.

ROPER, Abel (1665–1726). A ii 141; B ii 149. Publisher of the Tory *Post Boy*, which he started in 1695. Tom Brown was one of those who fell foul of Roper (M. Noble, *Biographical History of England*, 1806, ii 309). In 1716, in a coffee-house, Roper was "decently chastiz'd by a worthy Gentleman, who he had aspersed in one of his late written News Letters" (*The Weekly Journal; or British Gazetteer*, Sept. 8, 1716).

SHADWELL, Thomas (1642?–92). A ii 324; B i 240, iii 22. Dramatist; poet laureate from 1689 till his death. Shadwell glanced at Dryden in the preface to his first play, *The Sullen Lovers* (1668), but the two men were on good enough terms in 1674 to join in an attack on Settle, viz. *Notes and Observations on the Empress of Morocco*. In 1682, however, appeared *The Medal of John Bayes*, in which Dryden was bitterly attacked. Narcissus Luttrell, who bought his copy on May 15, wrote in it: "By Thomas Shadwell. Ag^t Mr Dryden. very severe". On Oct. 4, 1682, Luttrell also purchased the (pirated?) first edition of *Mac Flecknoe*, in which Shadwell was unsparingly ridiculed. This poem was not, however, a reply to *The Medal*; it had been written probably as early as 1678, though it had remained unpublished. Dryden's answer to *The Medal* is in the second part of *Absalom and Achitophel* (Nov. 1682), and further shots were exchanged on both sides. It was this celebrated quarrel and, above all, the fame of *Mac Flecknoe*, that led to Shadwell's appearance in the *Dunciad*. In *Mac Flecknoe* Dryden had already dealt with the theme of dullness and dunces. For Shadwell's reputation in his own day and in the generation following, see A. S. Borgman, *Thomas Shadwell: His Life and Comedies*, 1928, pp. 95 ff.

SHERLOCK, Thomas (1678–1761). B iii 204, [ii 323]. Bishop of Bangor 1728, of Salisbury, 1734, of London 1748–61. As Master of the Temple (1704–53) he obtained a wide reputation as a preacher, and that is apparently why he is introduced at B iii 204. The concealed reference to him at B ii 323 is altogether less flattering. Pope had reason to dislike Sherlock as a consistent supporter of Walpole in the House of Lords. He had been severely satirized by Paul Whitehead in *The State Dunces* as "faithful to his Fee" and proving "Parliaments *dependent* to be free" (ll. 244–5), and in *Manners* the same author had suggested that "if the lawn'd *Levite*'s earthly vote be sold", then "*Henley*'s shop, and *Sherlock*'s are the same" (op. cit., ll. 63, 66).

SMEDLEY, Jonathan (b. 1671). A ii 279 ff.; B ii 291 ff. "That rascal Smedley" (Swift, *Correspondence*, ii 351) was Dean of Clogher, 1724–7. He wrote the notorious verses (*Gulliveriana*, p. 77) which were said to have been fixed to the door of St Patrick's Cathedral. Swift ridiculed Smedley's Epistle to the Duke of Grafton in *His Grace's Answer to Jonathan* (1724), and again in *A Letter from D. S — t to D. S — y* (1725). In 1728 Smedley published *The Metamorphosis* (an attack on Pope and Swift), and some time later the scurrilous *Gulliveriana*, in the Preface to which he made much play with Pope's deformity—"this same little crooked creature". Smedley wrote (puffing one of his own books) for *The London Journal* (April 6, April 26, 1728). He was one of Walpole's hacks, and carried on the subsidized *Baker's News; or, The Whitehall journal* (1722-3) on behalf of the government (Hanson, p. 106). In 1729 he sailed for Madras to improve his fortunes, and there he presumably died.

SMYTHE, James Moore (1702-34). A ii 46; B ii 50. See "Testimonies of Authors," and Biog. App., vol. iv. Moore Smythe died on Oct. 18, 1734 (*London Journal*, Oct. 26, 1734). He lived beyond his means, and he was vain and ostentatious; but those who had no interest in blackening his character speak of his "great Wit and Vivacity" (*Characters of the Times*, 1728, p. 13), and his "power of rendering his conversation agreeable by a facetious and gentleman-like manner" (T. Cibber, *Lives* iv 214). According to Young, the lengths to which he went to secure a full house for *The Rival Modes* disgusted the town (R. E. Tickell, *Thomas Tickell and the Eighteenth Century Poets*, p. 125). In giving £105 for this play (for which Theobald wrote the prologue) Lintot was paying a price well above the average. Pope no doubt resented the fuss that was being made about this superficial young man in certain quarters. Cooke's optimistic prophecy (*The Battle of the Poets*, 1729), "Another Dryden shall arise in Thee", was only one of the more absurd of several unduly respectful tributes.

TALBOT, William (1659?-1730). B iv 562n., 593. Bishop of Oxford, 1699; of Salisbury, 1715; of Durham, 1721-30. His interests appear to have been commercial rather than spiritual; and he extracted the maximum revenue from the very rich see of Durham. "He was of a magnificent taste and temper, which often run him into difficulties, his great revenue not being answerable to his expences, and his son was often then obliged to extricate him from his embarrassments" (J. Nichols, *Lit. Ill.*, i 419). The son just mentioned is presumably his eldest son, Charles Talbot, Baron Talbot, who became Lord Chancellor in 1733. See B iv 168, and Biog. App., vol. iv.

THEOBALD, Lewis (1688-1744). A i 105 ff., ii 5-10, iii 1 ff.; B i 133, 286. Besides his work on the text of Shakespeare, which brought him into conflict with Pope, Theobald wrote a considerable number of plays, pantomimes, essays, and poems, and translated various works from the Greek and Latin. If Theobald had a hand, as Pope asserted, in *A Complete Key to . . . The What D'ye Call It* (1715), he was the first to give provocation; but Pope may have been misinformed as to the authorship of this mild pamphlet. Theobald, at any rate, went out of his way to praise Pope's *Homer* in *The Censor*, Jan. 5, 1717. In 1722 Curll advertised the Duke of Buckinghamshire's Works "with his Life (compleated from a Plan drawn up by his Grace) by Mr. Theobald" (*Daily Journal*, Jan. 22, 1722; Sherburn, p. 222), but the project was brought to the notice of the House of Lords (perhaps by Pope), and Curll was forced to omit Theobald's Life from the volume which he eventually published. Theobald's hostility to Pope may date from this episode. He wrote the prologue for Moore Smythe's *Rival Modes*, 1727. In the *Peri Bathous* Theobald was classed by Pope among the eels and swallows; and in "A Fragment of a Satire," published in the same volume of *Miscellanies* as the *Peri Bathous*, there occurred a reference to "piddling *T*——s", one of the "word-catchers" who lived on syllables. Theobald may have taken his revenge for this in the anonymous "Essay on the Art of a Poet's Sinking in Reputation" which appeared in *Mist's Journal*, March 30, 1728. In 1728 Theobald edited a volume of Wycherley's posthumous pieces, and promised a second. Pope, however, who characterized him in a letter to Lord Oxford, Oct. 16, 1729, as "an unlicensed and presumptuous mercenary", brought out a second volume himself, and announced that nothing else of Wycherley's which was "fit for the press" now remained to be published. Theobald took notice of the *Dunciad* in a letter printed in *The Daily Journal*, April 17, 1729. Early in 1730 he wrote to Warburton, with whom he was corresponding regularly on Shakespeare, to say that he intended to bring out "An Essay upon Mr. Pope's Judgment" extracted from his works, but he seems to have abandoned this project (J. Nichols, *Lit. Ill.*, ii 551 ff., 566 ff.). Theobald, in fact, was always a dignified opponent, and even in *Shakespeare Restored* he made it clear that it was the editor, and not the poet, that he was criticizing. In December, 1730, on Eusden's death, he "put in for the withered laurel," and was warmly recommended by Walpole to the Lord Chamberlain, but found himself "supplanted by *Keyber*" (ibid., p. 617). His Shakespeare was published in 1734 (dated 1733): a second edition appeared in 1740.

*THOMAS, Elizabeth (1667–1731). A ii 66; B ii 70. "Curll's Corinna." The name had been given to her by Dryden, who corresponded with her in his old age. She became the mistress of Pope's friend, Henry Cromwell, who passed on to her some of Pope's letters which she sold to Curll for ten guineas. According to Ayre (i 192), she "pass'd whole Days, and often more than Days, with either Mr. *Cromwell* or Mr. *Pope*, or both". The suggestion, so far as Pope was concerned, is almost certainly false. Mrs Thomas retaliated feebly to Pope's disgraceful attack by compiling *The Dunciad Dissected* (Curll, *Key*, 2nd ed., p. 31). The story of her later amours and misfortunes is told in full in T. Cibber's *Lives of the Poets*, iv 158–60. From some details of her medical history given there, it seems possible that Pope's reference to Mrs Thomas is not only disgusting but also accurate.

TOLAND, John (1670–1722). A ii 367, iii 208; B ii 399, iii 212. Deist, and author of *Christianity not Mysterious* (1696), a work which provoked a considerable controversy and was presented by the Grand Jury of Middlesex. He wrote on political questions, not always on the same side, and was at one time on government service at the Court of Hanover. His religious opinions gave much scandal to the orthodox. On Toland's death, Defoe devoted one of his articles in Applebee's *Weekly Journal* (March 17, 1722) to a horrified disquisition on the atheism, blasphemy, and heresy of the age. Toland's unorthodox religious opinions probably account for his inclusion in the *Dunciad*; but he had given Pope some more personal grounds for disliking him by publicly declaring that Ozell's translation of Homer was superior to Pope's. See "Errata," p. 198.

*TRAPP, Rev. Joseph (1679–1747). A ii 381n. Poet, pamphleteer, and author of the tragedy of *Abra-Mule* (1704), which gained him some reputation. A punctilious commemorator of royal deaths, Trapp was from 1708–18 the first Professor of Poetry at Oxford. The wits laughed at his poetry, and Swift told Stella (March 17, 1712): "Trapp is a coxcomb." Just before the *Dunciad* was published, Trapp, who was a Tory and High Churchman, had been particularly active in denouncing the Catholic Church. His *Church of England defended against the Church of Rome* appeared in 1727, and was probably the occasion of Pope's ironical comment. On Feb. 1, 1728, as a reward, perhaps, for his zeal, Trapp was made a D.D. of Oxford. See also B i 33n.

TUTCHIN, John (1661?–1707). A ii 140; B ii 148. Whig pamphleteer. He ran his twice-weekly *Observator* (a dialogue between the Observator and a Countryman) from 1702 till his death. More than once prosecuted and often threatened on account of his violently Whig views, Tutchin was at length set upon by ruffians in September, 1707, and died a few days later. The article in the D.N.B. suggests that the manner of his death is in doubt, but it seems to be sufficiently documented by the accounts given in his *Observator*, Sept. 20–24, Sept. 27–Oct. 1, 1707.

WALKER, Richard (1679–1764). B iv 206, 273. "Hat-bearer to Bentley", he was Vice-Master of Trinity College, Cambridge, from 1734, a friend of Bentley, and one of his chief allies in the long struggle with the fellows of the College. He was a Doctor of Divinity, and became Professor of Moral Philosophy in 1744.

WARD, Edward (1667–1731). A i 200, iii 138; B i 233, iii 34. A lively writer of miscellaneous pieces in verse and prose. As a verse-writer he was fond of imitating Samuel Butler; his *Hudibras Redivivus* (1705), an attack on the Whigs and Low Church, landed him in the pillory. His raciest work was a monthly periodical, *The London Spy*. From about 1717 to 1730 Ward kept the Bacchus Tavern in Moorfields. Pope, who had put him in the *Peri Bathous* without (so far as is known) any personal provocation from Ward, included him in the *Dunciad* as a writer whose work appealed to the uneducated reader. Not till then did Ward attack Pope in *Durgen*, and in *Apollo's Maggot in his Cups*.

WARNER, Thomas (fl. 1728). A ii 117; B ii 125. Bookseller, at The Black Boy in Pater-Noster-Row, from which in 1717 he published *A Collection of the*

Best English Poetry in two volumes. He was publisher at different times of *The St. James's Post, The Daily Journal* (in which Pope was frequently attacked), and *The Flying-Post*. On quarrelling with the proprietor of the last-named newspaper, he continued for some time to publish a spurious one with the same title. (See *The Daily Journal*, Jan. 1, 1728.) As he is cited in Pope's note as a printer of "much anonymous stuff", it is probably on account of his newspapers that he appears in the *Dunciad*; but in 1725 he had published *A New Miscellany: Being a Collection of Pieces of Poetry, from Bath, Tunbridge, Oxford, Epsom . . . Written chiefly by Persons of Quality.*

WASSE, Joseph (1672–1738). B iv 237. Classical scholar. Bentley is reported to have said: "When I am dead, Wasse will be the most learned man in England." In No. vi of *Bibliotheca Literaria* there is a Latin elegy of his addressed to Bentley. His edition of Sallust was published in 1710; and he helped Kuster —with whom Pope couples his name—in his edition of Suidas (J. Nichols, *Lit. Anec.*, i 259, 263).

WEBSTER, Edward (fl. 1718–1729). A ii 205ff.; B ii 213ff. Chief Secretary to the Duke of Bolton (1718), who was then Lord Lieutenant of Ireland. Later he was one of the twelve Clerks to the Treasury (*The True State of England*, 1729, p. 72). When Eustace Budgell returned from Ireland in 1719 he wrote *A Letter to the Lord * * * ***, full of complaints and scandal, which ran through numerous editions. Budgell had quarrelled with Webster, and he purported to give the true explanation of Webster's sudden rise, and his own dismissal. He had been "one of the *Under-copying* Clerks of the Treasury, sat at a *little Desk* in the *Outer Room*", and maintained on a salary of £200 "a *Wife, two Sons,* and a *Daughter,* who is generally said to be a *very pretty young Woman*" (op. cit., 5th ed., pp. 11–12). "*Common Fame*", he adds, "gives a Reason for his Preferment, which is so little for his own Reputation, or for the *Honour of his Majesty's Affairs* committed to his Charge, that I am sure he will have *good Nature* enough to excuse my not mentioning of it" (pp. 13–14). In short, Webster's daughter had become the Duke's mistress, and her father had been promoted as a reward for his parenthood rather than for his executive abilities. The story may have been true; but how many people would be likely to remember the facts ten years later, or even to realize from Pope's veiled allusions that Webster was "the youth unknown to Phœbus", whose sister's (*i.e.*, daughter's) easy morals had procured his promotion?

WEBSTER, William (1689–1758). B ii 258. A clergyman who wrote *The Weekly Miscellany*, 1732–41, under the pseudonym of "Richard Hooker of the Temple, Esq." He was almost certainly brought into the *Dunciad* to please Warburton, whose *Divine Legation of Moses* he had attacked in a series of articles which were afterwards reprinted with the title, *Remarks on the Divine Legation*. Warburton had replied to him in 1738 in *A Vindication of the Author of the Divine Legation . . .*, and again, in 1741, in the preface to the second volume of that work. See also Egmont i. 406, 412, 435.

*WHATLEY, Stephen (fl. 1720). A i 104n. Whig journalist. He carried on *The Flying-Post* in 1713 after George Ridpath had fled to Holland. He received a certain amount of government bounty (Hanson, p. 114). Whatley was mentioned as a government writer as late as 1739 in Henley's *Hyp Doctor*, July 10.

WHITEFIELD, George (1714–70). B ii 258. Leader of the Calvinistic Methodists, and a famous preacher. About the time (1741?) that Pope was sneering at Whitefield in the *Dunciad* he had returned from a highly successful missionary visit to America. In 1741 he opened in London the Moorfields tabernacle. Whitefield made several later visits to America, and also preached in Ireland and Scotland. He died at Newburyport, Massachusetts. Whitefield had probably Warburton to thank for his inclusion in the *Dunciad*. Warburton criticized the leaders of the Methodists in the second (1742) edition of his *Divine Legation*. His opinion of Whitefield in particular may be seen in a letter to Des Maizeaux: "I have seen Whitefield's Journal; and he appears to me to be as mad as ever George Fox the Quaker was" (Nichols, *Lit. Anec.*, v 578).

WILKINS, William (d. 1756). A ii 117; B ii 125. Printer and publisher. Wilkins was a staunch Whig, and printer of *The Whitehall Evening-Post*, *The Whitehall Journal*, *The London Journal*, and other Whig periodicals, in which much of the "anonymous stuff" appeared of which Pope's note complains. Not long before the *Dunciad* was published Wilkins had been in the public eye. He had published a series of mock advertisements mainly directed against "Harry Gambol" (*i.e.*, Lord Bolingbroke), and as a result he was savagely beaten up in the Crown Tavern, Smithfield. (See *The Evening Post*, Feb. 1/3, 1728; and *As much as may be publish'd of A Letter from the late B — of R — ch — r to Mr. P ——*, 1728.) He was also the publisher of *Homerides*, 1715.

WOOLSTON, Thomas (1670–1733). A iii 209; B iii 212. Freethinker, and a prolific writer of controversial pamphlets. He was indicted in November, 1725, for blasphemy, but the charge was dropped. Between 1727 and 1729, however, he published six *Discourses on the Miracles of our Saviour*, dedicated to Bishops Gibson, Potter, Hare, etc. He was tried on March 4, 1729, by L. C. J. Raymond, found guilty on four charges of blasphemy, and sentenced to one year's imprisonment and fined £100. He died in the liberty of the King's Bench, being unable to pay his fine and find a recognizance of £3,000. Woolston was an able man, but was generally reckoned mad.

ADDITIONAL NOTES
To The Second and Third Editions

[The following pages present a conflation of the notes added to the second edition (1953), together with those now added to the third. The following abbreviations have been used to indicate the sources of various notes:

R.A.B.   Reuben Arthur Brower, *Alexander Pope: The Poetry of Allusion*, 1959.
N.W.B.   N. W. Bawcutt, "More Echoes in Pope's Poetry," *Notes and Queries*, 1958, cciii 220–1.
F.E.H.   The late Canon F. E. Hutchinson (privately communicated).
G.G.L.   The late George G. Loane, *Notes and Queries*, 1944, clxxxvi 36–7.
J.C.M.   J. C. Maxwell (privately communicated).
A.L.W.   Aubrey L. Williams, *Pope's Dunciad. A Study of its Meaning*, 1955.]

Notes to Introduction

pp. xvii–xxix. In my account of the publication of the *Dunciad* I referred perhaps too often to an article which I had written some years earlier, "The *Dunciad* of 1729" (M.L.R., 1936, xxxi 347–53), and so left the reader in some doubt about the evidence on which my statements were based. The evidence, too, is open to different interpretations, and any interpretation must proceed on the understanding that some of the facts are missing, and that some of the evidence appears to be false. Through the kindness of Professor George Sherburn, who allowed me to see a number of unpublished letters which have since appeared in his edition of the Correspondence, I am now in possession of some facts that I did not have in 1943. If this new information does not remove all the difficulties, it makes it a little easier to reconstruct the events preceding and following the publication of the *Dunciad* of 1729. Of the facts still missing, the most important concern, in the first place, the date on which the poem was assigned by Pope to the three noble lords, and, in the second place, the date on which Lawton Gilliver first appeared on the scene, the extent to which he was involved in 1729 in the publication of the poem, and the precise nature of his understanding with Pope.

As to the three lords, we begin to hear of them about the second week of March 1729. On March 12 a copy of the poem in its new annotated form in quarto had been presented to the king by Sir Robert Walpole (Introduction, p. xxviii). The following day Pope wrote to Lord Oxford: "You are now at full liberty to publish all my faults and enormities" (EC viii 250). March 13 was therefore D-day for *The Dunciad Variorum*. On March 27 Pope wrote to the Earl again, asking him to "send about twenty books to Cambridge, but by no means to be given to any bookseller, but disposed of as by your own order at six shillings by any honest gentleman or head of a house" (EC viii 252). Publication was now in progress, but the book had not yet been released to the trade. This secret method of dispersing the poem must have given it a wonderful advertisement. What had been happening is made a little clearer in a letter from Pope to Caryll, April 8 (EC vi 304–5). The *Dunciad*, he says,

> would have been a sort of curiosity, had it reached your hands a week ago, for the publishers had not then permitted any to be sold, but only dispersed by some lords of theirs and my acquaintance, of whom I procured yours. But I understand that now the booksellers have got them by consent of Lord Bathurst.

Who are the "publishers" to whom Pope refers? At this stage, in all probability, they are no more than a myth of Pope's invention. The real publishers in March were Pope's three noble friends, Burlington, Oxford, and Bathurst, who published the poem by distributing copies on their own account, and also, as a letter of April 18 seems to indicate, by persuading some of their noble friends to do the same. (See EC viii 253–4.) But in view of later developments it seems unlikely that the three lords were, as yet, the legal owners of the copyright.

It is about this time that Gilliver comes upon the scene, and he too becomes a publisher of the *Dunciad* before he has any legal right to the copyright. On April 10 he advertised the *Dunciad* as "Printed for Lawton Gilliver . . . and A. Dodd" (Introduction, p. xxviii). On April 12 he entered his title for the poem in the Stationers' Register, at the same time depositing nine copies of the book, as the Act of Anne 8 stipulated (EC iv 309). As events were to prove, he had no right to claim copyright at all, and yet he was acting for Pope. On what terms, then, did Gilliver come to be employed by Pope in the publication of the poem? The obvious answer is that if Pope was not to give endless trouble to his three noble friends he had to find some one in the book trade willing to act as publisher of his poem. Until he knew how it was received, however, Pope preferred to work in the dark: at this stage he was not prepared to acknowledge that he was the author of the *Dunciad*. To the poem of 1728 he had now added a lengthy commentary, containing a good deal of personal reference to the authors he had satirized, and he had set out the names of most of them in full. That he was genuinely alarmed about the extent to which he might have laid himself open to legal reprisals may be seen from several revealing letters written in the winter of 1728–9 to the Earl of Burlington. Pope had asked, or the Earl had offered, to have the proof sheets shown to Burlington's lawyer, N. Fazakerley, for an opinion as to whether there were any passages on which an action for libel could be grounded. In one of those letters (dated conjecturally by Professor Sherburn January 1729) Pope suggests to Burlington that there is no need to mention his name to Fazakerley as being in any way concerned in the publication, and expresses his belief that the way in which the poem is going to be published should be enough to safeguard the author. (*The Dunciad Variorum* was published, like the editions of 1728, without Pope's name on the title-page, and he nowhere acknowledges his authorship. On the other hand, in "A Letter to the Publisher", p. 12, W. Cleland does, in fact, attribute the poem to Pope:

"He has laugh'd and written the DUNCIAD." But that, no doubt, would not constitute proof of his authorship in a court of law, and still less that he had authorized the publication of the poem.) What Pope is worrying about, or says he is worrying about, is the position of the printer and publisher. Would any action lie against them? Apparently his fears were well grounded. On April 18 he was writing to the Earl of Oxford (EC viii 253–4):

> the gentlemen of the Dunciad intend to be vexatious to the bookseller and threaten to bring an action of I cannot tell how many thousands against him.

In this crisis Pope suggested that if the three lords would put their names to a certificate admitting that *they* had been the publishers and dispersers of the poem, Gilliver would be adequately protected. So far as is known, the three lords took no action of the kind suggested in Pope's letter.

Behind Pope's suggestion to Lord Oxford there probably lay some protest from Gilliver, or even a threat that he would wash his hands of the *Dunciad* unless he could be made secure from prosecution. As Professor R. H. Griffith has pointed out (P.Q., 1945, xxiv 154–5) Gilliver was at this time a young man, who had set up as a bookseller only a few days before the *Dunciad* was first published. As such, he could probably be more easily managed than a well-established bookseller, but he was probably easier to frighten. On what date Gilliver was first approached it is impossible now to say—perhaps late in 1728, but more probably early in 1729. What Pope said to the young publisher can only be conjectured; but at this stage Gilliver had probably to be content with verbal promises. In view of Gilliver's advertising of the poem on April 10, and his entry in the Register on April 12, we may fairly assume that he had entered into a gentleman's agreement with Pope that he should be allowed to purchase the copyright of the poem as soon as it was safe for him to own it and it suited Pope to acknowledge his authorship. That this is a correct reading of the evidence is suggested by an affidavit sworn by Thomas Wooton, bookseller, on June 2, 1729. "Being in company of Gilliver on or about 26 April," Wooton found him complaining about the publication of two octavo editions of the *Dunciad*. On his asking Gilliver "why he made such a rout about the publishing of the said octavo editions, as he had no right to the copy," Gilliver replied "that he had then no assignment of the said copy but should have it in a little time" (M.L.R. xxxi 349). Gilliver's concern over the "Dob" piracy (Introduction, p. xxix) was therefore due to the fact that by April 1729 he knew that, accidents excepted, he would be the eventual owner of the copyright. Until then, he could only try to bluff the London booksellers into believing that he was already in possession of it. (The entry in the Stationers' Register of April 12 was part of that bluff.) But the bluff failed. In the suit which he had brought against James Watson and others to restrain them from publishing the "Dob" piracy, Gilliver claimed that on or about March 31 he legally purchased or acquired the copy of the *Dunciad*, and that some time in April he caused it to be printed. But the four defendants answered that his name was not mentioned on the title-page of the 1729 quarto; and one of the four, John Stagg, made oath that on either April 7 or 8 he had bought a number of copies at five shillings apiece, and that Gilliver had admitted to him that he also had bought some at the same price, and had begged Stagg not to sell them to any bookseller at less than six shillings (M.L.R. xxxi 350–1). So much for Gilliver as a secret agent. It is true that on May 19 he obtained his injunction to stop further publication of the "Dob" edition (*ibid.*, p. 349), but the injunction was subsequently dissolved (*ibid.*, p. 353) on the grounds that though he had purchased or legally acquired the copy of the *Dunciad*, he had not said *of the author*, nor had he stated *who was the author*. In all probability the injunction might equally well have been dissolved at this stage on the ground that Gilliver had *not* purchased or legally acquired the copy. If he had, then we must suppose that Pope had made him promise not to divulge his name, and that Gilliver had loyally kept silence, even though that meant exposing his literary property to further piracy. In that case, what happened "on or about March 31" between Gilliver and Pope I cannot say. There should have been a legal document assigning the poem to Gilliver, and bearing Pope's signature: in view of later events there almost certainly was not.

Until Pope was willing to acknowledge his authorship the danger of piracy remained. It is here that we return to the three lords. Some time in 1729—and the most likely time would be shortly after Gilliver's injunction had been dissolved, and the poem was again unprotected from piracy—Pope assigned the *Dunciad* to Burlington, Oxford, and Bathurst. We do not have this document. But on November 21, 1729, Gilliver made an entry in the Stationers' Register which stated that "the author of a book entitled *The Dunciad, an Heroick Poem*" had "by writing under his hand and seal" assigned it to the three lords, who now reassigned it to him (EC iv 309). Gilliver, therefore, had no legal claim to the copyright of the *Dunciad* until it was reassigned to him by the three lords. I am indebted to Professor Robert W. Rogers for telling me what in 1943 I did not know, viz. that this assignment is preserved in the British Museum (Egerton MS. 1951 f 7), that it was drawn on October 16, 1729, and that Gilliver agreed to pay the three noblemen "the sum of £100 of lawful money", which they presumably handed over to Pope. An unpublished letter from Pope to Burlington makes it clear that Burlington, who had been out of town, did not sign the document until on or after November 2. Gilliver then—but not till then—could go ahead without fear of further piracy. On November 24, three days after he had made his entry in the Stationers' Register, he published his so-called "Second Edition, with some Additional Notes".

One final complication must be faced. In 1742 Pope was already planning to publish the *Dunciad* in its final four-book form; he had sent copy to the printer in April of that year (EC ix 223). In the Chancery suit which he brought against Lintot in 1743 he claimed that Gilliver's copyright in the poem expired in December 1742. Copyright was for fourteen years, and it was generally secured by entering a claim for it in the Stationers' Register. But no such entry is to be found for any day in December 1742; and in fact the poem had been published by May 18, 1728, and Bettenham had made his entry for the copyright on May 30. Bettenham's entry was insufficient to secure copyright, since he had not mentioned the author's name, nor proved that he had legally acquired the copy. What, then, had happened in December 1728 to justify Pope's claim that the copyright ran from that date? It is just possible that it was then, and not in 1729, that he assigned the poem "under his hand and seal" to the three lords, and that Pope's lawyers were prepared to argue that all the 1728 editions of the poem were "unauthorized". But in that case Bettenham's entry in the Register would also, presumably, have to be reckoned unauthorized, and they could not claim that it satisfied the provision that copyright must be entered in the books of the Company. It is altogether more likely that the statement in Pope's bill is a false statement—unintentionally false because after so many years he simply forgot the proper sequence of events, or deliberately false because it suited Pope to have it so. We do not have the Lord Chancellor's judgment. But in view of subsequent events he almost certainly took the view that copyright ran from October 16, 1729—the date of the document in which the three lords assigned the copyright to Gilliver—and that it therefore expired on October 16, 1743. It was, at any rate, exactly twelve days later, on October 28, 1743, that Mary Cooper entered her claim for the copyright of *The Dunciad, in Four Books* in the Stationers' Register. It was published on the following day.

p. xli. My contention that the *Dunciad* suffers from a lack of action has been characterized by Professor Griffith as "beside the mark" (P.Q., 1945, xxiv 155). Pope, he believes, "chose a structure that was typical from *Cooper's Hill* to *The Task*, a sequence of 'characters' linked together by a thin thread of 'plot'." This argument would scarcely dispose of my view that the reader of the poem has no clear idea of what is going on. But Pope, of course, was doing no such thing as Professor Griffith suggests. What the public of 1728 bought from the booksellers was *The Dunciad. An Heroic Poem*. The Arguments to the Books (parodying those of *Paradise Lost*) with their reminder of the epic structure of the poem, and the ample discussion in "Martinus Scriblerus, Of the Poem" of its hero, fable, episodes, characters, narration, etc. are alone sufficient to disprove Professor Griffith's statement. This is, in fact, a narrative poem; and Pope allows the narrative to be swamped occasionally by the satire.

An interesting and ingenious defence of the structure of Book IV has been made by Professor Sherburn (*Studies in English*, The University of Texas, 1944, No. 24, pp. 174-8). He contends that "the structural pattern of the last *Dunciad* had been made familiar to the world of fashion by Fielding's popular farces". He instances the *Author's Farce* of 1730, with the drawing-room of Queen Nonsense, *Pasquin* (1736), and *The Historical Register for 1736*, in all of which there were "royal levees crammed with incongruous episodes that followed each other kaleidoscopically much as do the passages of Book IV". All this, it is true, may have helped at least some readers in 1743 to find their bearings in Book IV more easily. The reader of today is hardly likely to have that advantage.

The action and structure of the *Dunciad* are very much the concern of Professor Aubrey L. Williams in his detailed and valuable elucidation of the poem, *Pope's* Dunciad. *A Study of its Meaning*, 1955, the first critical book to be entirely devoted to the poem. Among the points which he has brought out clearly for the first time, or to which he has given new prominence, I summarize briefly the following:

(1) The poem is more closely linked to the *Æneid* than has been generally realized; it is not "an attempt to imitate classical epic *in general*," but "a foreshortened imitation of one particular epic, the *Æneid*". Since the action of Pope's poem "is the removal of the empire of Dulness from the City of London to the polite world, Westminster, just as the action of the '*Æneid* is the Removal of the empire of *Troy* to *Latium*' ", we have, in Pope's poem as in Virgil's, "the destruction of one empire . . . and the establishment of another" (pp. 17–18). In the *Dunciad* the "City" figures metaphorically as Troy, and "since London town was traditionally known as Troy-novant, Pope was able to make this imaginative relationship with a good deal of aptness and ease" (p. 18). Professor Williams is careful to add (p. 19) that although this constitutes the action of the poem, "it is not rigidly schematized"; and while, for example, Theobald is the Æneas of the *Dunciad*, Settle may be equivalent to Hector in Book I and to Anchises in Book III. Again, it is only the *action* of the *Æneid* that Pope professes to be imitating, not the entire epic poem with its various episodes.

(2) The *Dunciad* is a "progress piece". In Book I (however hazily), and more clearly in Book II, we have "the idea of a progress from one area of London to another" (p. 29. The route taken by the Lord Mayor is followed in detail. See pp. 38 ff.). But it is also a progress piece in the sense that it offers "a historical survey of the past" (p. 42); and we are reminded that the original title of the *Dunciad* may have been "The Progress of Dulness". (See above, pp. xvii, xxi f.) "It is the historic consciousness of his place at the end of a long chronicle of events that underlies Pope's use of the convention, an awareness of a great cultural stream which has transmitted to the present the learning of the past" (pp. 43–4). Professor Williams draws attention to the idea of the *translatio studii* (pp. 44 ff.) which informs much of Book III.

(3) In his discussion of Book IV Professor Williams makes the point that Pope gives us here a "more dramatic presentation of the dunces' folly. The dunces reveal more in action and in speech their follies: Pope validates, in more immediate and dramatic fashion, his criticism of the dunces *in the poem*" (p. 88). He also touches on the debt that the poem may owe to "the 'session' poem, a genre marked by assemblies of poets, musicians, critics, and the like, before the throne of Apollo"; and he finds, too, some debt to "the 'Tablet of Cebes', a work in which appear various female personages of allegorical significance who are flanked in statuesque fashion by symbolic attendants" (p. 89. See also his more extended discussion of those two points in his "Literary Backgrounds to Book Four of the *Dunciad*", P.M.L.A., 1953, pp. 806–13).

(4) His fourth chapter deals with the humanistic standpoint from which the poem was written, and the rhetorical tradition in which Pope believed. For Pope "a corrupt literature may be considered an index, a sign (or a metaphor, as in the *Dunciad*), pointing to more fundamental disorders. . . . Such, at any rate, is the rationale of Pope's thesis in the *Dunciad* that a reign of literary dulness portends a cultural breakdown."

(5) In his final chapter, "The Anti-Christ of Wit", Professor Williams deals with the religious overtones of the poem, and emphasizes its Christian symbolism, and the extent to which Pope drew upon the Bible and *Paradise Lost*. I have incorporated some of his particular insights in the notes that follow.

Note to Testimonies of Authors

pp. 45–6, *n.g.* What is in Wagstaffe's *Works* (1726) is a different pamphlet: *A Letter from the Facetious Dr. Andrew Tripe, at Bath, to His Loving Brother the Profound Greshamite* (1719). See *The Critical Works of John Dennis*, ed. E. N. Hooker, ii 459.

Notes to the Poem

A i 23*n*. Dryden in his "Life of Plutarch" (*Works*, ed. W. Scott, 1807, xvii, 19) had already noted this fact. "Yet this foggy air . . . produced three wits, which were comparable to any three Athenians; Pindar, Epaminondas, and our Plutarch . . ."

A i 33. *The Great Mother*] For a discussion of *Magna Mater*, "the maternal deity whose cult was popular in Rome", see Williams, *op. cit.*, pp. 26 ff.

A i 37. *each weekly Muse*] I take this to refer to the frequency with which Curll and Lintot published volumes of verse (cf. the reading of B i 39: "Hence Miscellanies spring"). In the following line, "living" appears to mean "while they are still alive", i.e. for the week in which they were first published.

A i 56. *mass*] as in *OED* 1d: "a kind of matter capable of being fashioned; a plastic substance".

A i 75. *On cold December fragrant chaplets*] Mr. Basil Greenslade has drawn my attention to Shakespeare, M.N.D., ii i 107 ff.:

> The seasons alter: hoary-headed frosts
> Fall in the fresh lap of the crimson rose,
> And on old Hiems' thin and icy crown
> An odorous chaplet of sweet summer buds
> Is, as in mockery, set.

A i 81 ff. *She, tinsel'd o'er*] Mr. Thomas R. Edwards Jr. ("The Colors of Fancy: an Image Cluster in Pope", M.L.N., 1958, lxxiii 485 ff.) calls attention to a recurring image cluster in Pope's poetry of "fancy-dream-colour-various-gold-cloud-decay". Cf. B iv 537 ff., 629 ff.

A i 101. For the reading of *1728a–c*, cf. Milton, *P.L.*, iii 139: "in him all his Father shone", and Seneca, *Hippolytus*, 657–8:

> in te magis refulget incomptus decor;
> est genitor in te totus. . . .   (G.G.L.)

A i 119 f. *Or where by sculpture*] cf. Matthew Prior's lines on John Ogilby in "A Satyr on the Modern Translators":

> Had not the first the Town with Cutts appeas'd,
> And where the Poem fail'd the Picture pleas'd.

(*The Literary Works of Matthew Prior*, ed. H. Bunker Wright and Monroe K. Spears, 1959, i 23. (N.W.B.)

A i 241 ff. *The Goddess then*] As Professor Williams observes (*op. cit.*, p. 148), "this fantastic incident derives from Matthew iii", 16, 17.

A i 249. *Safe, where no . . . duns molest*] Joseph Warton (*The Adventurer*, 29 May, 1753, No. 59) noted the resemblance to l. 26 of Boileau's first satire:

> D'ou jamais ni l'huissier ni le sergent n'approche.

(Arthur Sherbo, "Pope and Boileau", *Notes and Queries*, 1951, cxcvi 495.)

A i 251 f. An obvious reference to the Chosen People and the land flowing with milk and honey that was promised them. (G.G.L.)

A i 259. *Loud Thunder*] Milton, *P.L.*, ii 882 f:

> Harsh Thunder, that the lowest bottom shook
> Of *Erebus*. (A.L.W.)

A ii 127 f. *Duchesses and Lady Mary's*] In "Pope's Duchesses and Lady Mary's" (R.E.S., 1953, New Ser. iv 359 ff.) Professor Williams showed that it was a common practice for Drury-Lane prostitutes to be introduced, or to pass themselves off, as actual ladies of title. The word "Duchesses", therefore, "merely suggests the false titles adopted by ladies of the evening, and the gullible acceptance of such titles by romantic French gentlemen". This does not, of course, alter the fact that by "hapless Monsieur" and "Lady Mary's" Pope meant to allude to one particular French gentleman and one particular titled lady; but, as Professor Williams has now shown, he could claim that his words *were* meant in general of "all whores and cheats under the name of ladies". The note, in fact, provides him with a means of escape, and at the same time ("whores and cheats") heightens the abuse of Lady Mary Wortley Montagu. Still more convincing evidence for the above interpretation of "Duchesses" is offered by N. W. Bawcutt (*Notes and Queries*, 1961, ccvi 253 f.), citing a passage from *The Spectator*, 25 Oct. 1711, No. 205. For further light on Toussaint Rémond de Saint-Mard, see Robert Halsband, *The Life of Lady Mary Wortley Montagu*, 1956, pp. 102 ff. (and elsewhere).

A ii 188. *this Patron*] In the papers of the Marquess of Downshire deposited in the Berkshire County Record Office are some manuscript notes on the *Dunciad* (MS. d. 59). The "Patron" of this line is identified, rightly or wrongly, with the Duke of Bolton. (George Sherburn, "New Anecdotes about Alexander Pope", *Notes and Queries*, 1958, cciii 348.)

A ii 216. *With Shakespear's nature*] Cf. *Ep.* ii i 82 f.:

> Not one but nods, and talks of Jonson's art,
> Of Shakespear's nature. . . . (G.G.L.)

A ii 218n. For further information on Dennis's thunder, see A. N. Wilkins, "John Dennis' Stolen Thunder", *Notes and Queries*, 1956, ccxxi 425 ff.

A ii 246. *attemper'd*] Cf. Pope, *Od.* i iv 24:

> High airs, attemper'd to the vocal strings.

Mr. George G. Loane and Mr. Esmond De Beer both suggest, independently, a debt to Milton, "Lycidas", 33: "Temper'd to the oaten flute."

A ii 249n. In remarking that an earlier reading for "Tot'nam fields" was

"Tothill fields", I said that the reason for Pope's alteration is not clear. Professor Williams suggests (*op. cit.*, p. 38) that "with the southern limit already set by Westminster Hall, Pope needed a northern boundary".

A ii 251. *retentive*] I had taken this word in *OED*'s sense 4, viz. "having the property of, tending or inclined to, the retention or keeping of something". But Mr. J. C. Maxwell has pointed out to me that "retentive" is also given a separate entry by *OED*, with the meaning, "that reverberates or resounds", derived from an obsolete verb "retent" (Fr. *retentir*) = "resound". For the word in this sense the only example offered is this from the *Dunciad*. Pope's note hardly seems to support this interpretation.

A ii 258. *As morning-pray'r*] Pope points out in his note that "it is between eleven and twelve . . . that the criminals are whipp'd in Bridewell". Professor Williams (*op. cit.*, p. 39) cites evidence to show that it was "between eleven and twelve" that the Lord Mayor customarily journeyed to the Thames on Lord-Mayor's day.

A ii 271. *In naked majesty*] Milton, *P.L.* iv 290:
> In naked majesty seemed lords of all.   (G.G.L.)

A ii 278. *Who but to sink the deeper, rose the higher*] I now think that this may be another allusion to that "divine madness . . . that poetical rage and enthusiasm" with which Dennis is credited in Pope's note to A i 104 (p. 72). As a critic Dennis talked a good deal about the sublime, and tried to achieve it in his pindaric odes, etc. When he failed to do so, he "sank the deeper".

A ii 303. *the horrors of his . . . brows*] A comical perversion of the phrase "the honours of his head", for hair.   (G.G.L.)   But cf. also *Comus*, 38:
> The nodding horror of whose shady brows.   (J.C.M.)

A ii 313. *nutbrown maids*] A similar perversion of the title of the old ballad, well known in the early eighteenth century from Prior's modernization of it in *Henry and Emma*.

A ii 359 f. *As to soft gales etc.*] Cf. Statius, *Thebaid*, vi 854 ff.:
> ille autem, Alpini veluti regina cupressus
> verticis urgenti cervicem inclinat in Austro,
> vis sese radice tenens, terraeque propinquat,
> iamdudum aetherias eadem reditura sub auras.

and Lucan, *De Bello Civili*, i 388:
> it tantus ad aethera clamor,
> quantus, piniferae Boreas cum Thracius Ossae
> rupibus incubuit, curvato robore pressae
> fit sonus aut rursus redeuntis in aethera silvae.   (G.G.L.)

A ii 389 f. *Why should I sing etc.*] Cf. Milton, *P.L.*, viii 29 (of Urania):
> yet not alone, while thou
> Visit'st my slumber nightly.   (G.G.L.)

A iii 10. *the golden Dream*] Taken in proximity to "the Statesman's scheme" of the previous line, these words could refer to the South Sea Bubble. The statesman with whom the South Sea scheme originated was Pope's friend, Robert Harley, but he had no responsibility for the disastrous crash of 1721.

A iii 23 f. *Millions and millions etc.*] Cf. Milton, *P.L.*, v 743 ff.:

> Satan with his Powers
> Far was advanc't on winged speed, an Host
> Innumerable as the Starrs of Night,
> Or Starrs of Morning, Dew-drops.   (A.L.W.)

A iii 47 f. *As man's maeanders etc.*] Cf. Cowley, *Poems*, ed. A. R. Waller, 1905, p. 416 (of Nature):

> She leap't at last into the winding streams of blood;
> Of man's Meander all the purple reaches made,
> Till at the heart she stay'd. . . .   (G.G.L.)

A iii 110. *had Easter never been*] Pope had perhaps more particularly in mind the disputes between Celtic and Roman-bred clergy, settled at the Synod of Whitby, A.D. 664.   (F.E.H.) Cf. Dryden's translation of Virgil, *Ecl.* vi 45, to which Pope refers the reader:

> Happy for her if Herds had never been.

A iii 114. *Influence . . . Rage*] The kindly and the unkind control of the stars, as in Jonson's lines on Shakespeare (18 ff.):

> Shine forth, thou Starre of Poets, and with rage,
> Or influence, chide, or cheere, the drooping Stage.   (G.G.L.)

A iii 149. *Jacob, the Scourge of Grammar*] There seems to be no good reason for calling Jacob's style ungrammatical. When Pope substituted him for "Woolston, the scourge of Scripture" (*1728a–e:* "the scourge of Gospel", *1728f*) he had to find an equivalent charge, and "grammar" was, no doubt, an easy way out.

A iii 159. *Ralph*] Ralph was said by a contemporary to have complained that he was "near being famished by this Line. None of the Booksellers would employ him." See George Sherburn, "New Anecdotes about Alexander Pope", *loc. cit.*, p. 348.

A iii 161. *speech*] The faculty or power of expressing thoughts (*OED* 5).

A iii 192. *Hist'ry her Pot*] Cf. Sir George Etherege, *The Man of Mode* (1676) 1 i: "You know the old proverb—ale and history." No one today, however, appears to know just what this proverb was, though G. L. Apperson, *English Proverbs and Proverbial Phrases*, s.v. "ale", gives some other allusions to it.

A iii 245–7, 269–70. *Joy fills his soul. . . . And are these wonders*] Cf. Satan, viewing the "stupendious bridge" created by Sin and Death, Milton, *P.L.*, x 350 ff.:

> Great joy was at thir meeting, and at sight
> Of that stupendious Bridge his joy encreas'd.
> Long he admiring stood, till Sin, his faire
> Inchanting Daughter, thus the silence broke.
> O Parent, these are thy magnific deeds,
> Thy Trophies, which thou view'st as not thine own . . .   (A.L.W.)

A iii 249 ff. *In yonder cloud etc.*] Professor Williams (*op. cit.*, p. 95) refers here to *Spectator* 592, 10 Sept. 1714, where Addison mentions theatrical meteors, thunder ("They have a Salmoneus behind the scenes, who plays it off with great success"—cf. Pope's reference to Salmoneus, 252*n.*), lightnings, clouds "better furbelowed, and more voluminous", a violent storm "locked up in a great chest", and "above a dozen showers of snow". This essay, as he suggests, may well have been in Pope's mind.

A iii 252. *Wings the red lightning*] Cf. Milton, *P.L.*, i 175:
> Wing'd with red Lightning.   (E. S. De Beer)

A iii 261. *to dark encounter*] Cf. Milton, *P.L.*, ii 718, where Satan and Death prepare
> To joyn thir dark Encounter in mid air.   (A.L.W.)

A iii 272*n*. (foot of p. 181). "Caparisons" was Pope's emendation to the First Folio's "Comparisons" in *Antony and Cleopatra*, iii xi 26.   (J.C.M.)

A iii 325. *Wren with sorrow*] He lost his post as Surveyor-General in 1718, at the age of eighty-six.

A iii 335. *Signs . . . year*] Cf. Virgil, *Ecl.*, iv 5:
> magnus ab integro saeclorum nascitur ordo   (R.A.B.)

A iii 339. *Anarch's*] Milton also uses "Anarch" of Chaos, *P.L.* ii 988.   (G.G.L.)

A iii 342. *th'æthereal plain*] Cf. Pope's translation of Homer, *Iliad*, x 252:
> The stars shine fainter on th'æthereal plains.   (Norman Callan)

A iii 358. For an interesting comment on the "ivory gate" and on Pope's note to A iii 337, see Daniel P. Deneau, M.L.N., 1959, lxxiv 208 ff.

Ricardus Aristarchus Of the Hero of the Poem, p. 260, l. 20] "look" is used here in *OED*'s sense 4b. Since this is a considerably later example of this use of the word than any recorded in *OED*, it may be intended as a parody of Bentley's rather antiquated style.   (J.C.M.)

B i 15*n*. The quotation with which this note ends is apparently taken, without verification, from Dryden, *The Hind and the Panther*, ii 220 f.
> Where all the rounds like Jacob's ladder rise,
> The lowest hid in earth, the topmost in the skies.   (Ian Jack)

B i 27. *mighty wings out-spread*] Cf. Milton, *P.L.*, i 20 f.
> with mighty wings outspred
> Dove-like satst brooding. . . .

B i 321. *Familiar*] (1) known from constant association (*OED* 6); (2) affable, sociable (*OED* 7); (3) unceremonious, taking liberties with (*OED* 8).

B ii 11 f. Cf. Milton, *P.L.*, vii 364 ff.
> Hither, as to thir Fountain, other Starrs
> Repairing, in thir gold'n Urns draw Light;
> And hence the Morning Planet guilds her horns . . .   (Wakefield)

B ii 99 f. *List'ning delighted to the jest unclean*] Pope may be recalling White Kennet's account (*Register and Chronicle*, 1728, p. 320) of how Robert Burton would sometimes fall into such a state of despondency that he could get relief only by going to Folly Bridge at Oxford and listening to the bargemen swear at one another, "at which he would set his hands to his sides and laugh most profusely".   (F.E.H.)

p. 338. Argument to Book IV. *Minute Philosophers and Freethinkers*] The phrase "Minute Philosopher" was not invented by Bishop Berkeley, but (as Mr. J. C. Maxwell has suggested to me) it probably owed its currency at this period to

Berkeley's *Alciphron: Or, The Minute Philosopher*, 1732. It is difficult to assess Pope's debt to *Alciphron*, but at B iv 453–516 he goes over much the same ground as Berkeley had covered. In "The First Dialogue", Sect. x, Crito remarks that "the modern free-thinkers are the very same with those Cicero called minute philosophers, which name admirably suits them, they being a sort of sect which diminish all the most valuable things, the thoughts, views, and hopes of men; all the knowledge, notions, and theories of the mind they reduce to sense; human nature they contract and degrade to the narrow low standard of animal life, and assign us only a small pittance of time instead of immortality."

B iv 1n. Dr. Ian Jack (*Augustan Satire*, 1952, p. 124n.) remarks, fairly enough, that my comment on Warburton's note "contains only part of the truth: the main reason for the note was the shift of intention between 1728 and 1743".

B iv 4. *deep intent*] Cf. Satan's "dark intent", Milton, *P.L.*, ix 162. (A.L.W.)

B iv 6. *To whom Time . . . wing*] Cf. Milton's sonnet, "How soon hath Time . . .", 1–2, 12. (A.L.W.)

B iv 18n. Cf. *Exodus*, xxxiii 23: "And I will take away mine hand, and thou shalt see my back parts: but my face shall not be seen." (F.E.H.)

B iv 75 f. *by sure Attraction*] Professor Maynard Mack remarks (*Pope and his Contemporaries*, ed. James L. Clifford and Louis A. Landa, 1949, p. 29) on the resemblance between "the duntes irresistibly drawn into the gravitational field of Dulness" and "the feeling Sin has in Milton's poem, after the Fall, of being pulled toward earth by 'sympathy, or some connatural force'." Cf. *P.L.*, x 262 f.:

> so strongly drawn
> By this new-felt attraction and instinct.

B iv 104. *sunk beneath a show'r*] Cf. also Pope, *Iliad*, viii 371 ff.

B iv 162. *padlock on the mind*] Cf. Prior, "An English Padlock", *Works, ed. cit.*, i 229:

> Let all her Ways be unconfin'd:
> And clap your PADLOCK—on her Mind. (N.W.B.)

B iv 174n. Cf. Dryden, "Dedication of the Æneis", *Essays*, ed. W. P. Ker, ii 154: "A Heroic Poem, truly such, is admittedly the greatest work which the soul of man is capable to perform."

B iv 178. *war with words alone*] Probably an allusion to James I's proud boast of being "Pacificus". (F.E.H.)

Cf. Dryden, *MacFlecknoe*, 84:

> And *Panton* waging harmless war with words.

and Prior, "A Satyr on the Modern Translators", 118 (*Works, ed. cit.*, i 22):

> He shou'd be kept from waging War with words. (N.W.B.)

B iv 204. *Plow'd was his front*] Cf. Milton, *P.L.*, ii 301 ff.:

> rose and in his rising seem'd
> A Pillar of State; deep on his Front engraven
> Deliberation sat and public care;

and i 599 ff. (of Satan):

yet shon
Above them all th'Arch Angel: but his face
Deep scars of Thunder had intrencht . . .   (A.L.W.)

B iv 241 f. *Like buoys etc.*] In an endeavour to clear up the obscurities of Warburton's note on those lines I appealed to Mr. A. N. L. Munby, who enlisted the help of Dr. R. Robson of Trinity College, Cambridge. I had pointed out that the Bishop of Ely (who was also the Visitor of the College at the time of the war with the fellows) was Thomas Green, and that he had died on 18 May, 1738. I therefore asked if it was possible for Warburton's "without' . . . Patron" to refer to the death of Green, i.e. whether "Patron" here is equivalent to "Visitor". They think this is probably so, but cannot produce any parallel for the word "patron" being used in this sense.

B iv 294. *Europe he saw*] Cf. Virgil, *Ecl.*, iv 15 f.

divisque videbit
permixtos heroas et ipse videbitur illis.   (R.A.B.)

B iv 301. *bosom'd deep in vines*] Cf. Milton, "L'Allegro", 78.   (G.G.L.)

B iv 321. *on Classic ground*] Cf. note to A iii 254.

B iv 369. *Blest in one Niger*] When I originally annotated this passage I did not realize just how rare the Pescennius coinage is. In *An Essay on Medals* (1784) John Pinkerton noted (Appendix iv, *s.v.* "Pescennius") that the gold coin of Pescennius Niger was of the highest possible rarity, viz. "unique in the King of France's cabinet". In *Biographie Universelle, s.v.* "Pescennius", it is stated that the only known gold coin of Pescennius "a été placée dans le cabinet du Roi, en 1749, par de Boze, qui la tenait d'un missionnaire, arrivé récemment de l'Orient". If this coin was obtained from a missionary "récemment de l'Orient" in 1749, that is too late for Pope to have known about it. But M. Jacques Yvon, of the Cabinet des Médailles at the Bibliothèque Nationale, has kindly informed me of a communication made to the Académie Royale des Inscriptions by M. Gros de Boze in 1750, in which he refers to "un savant anglais", who, about 1736 or earlier, came from Montpellier, and told him "qu'il avait vu dans une collection peu nombreuse faite par M. Veissières . . . deux Pescennius d'or, dont l'un était visiblement faux et l'autre méritait d'être examiné . . ." (*Mémoires de littérature tirés des registres de l'Académie Royale des Inscriptions et Belles Lettres depuis l'année MDCCXLVIII jusques et compris l'année MDCCLI, tome* xxiv, 1756). If it were possible to identify the English scholar who was at Montpellier around 1736 and saw M. Veissières' coin collection (Sir Andrew Fountaine, Roger Gale, and Martin Folkes are possible candidates) he might turn out to be the source of Pope's knowledge of the gold Pescennius. At all events, I take "Blest in one Niger, till he knows of two" to indicate some awareness on Pope's part of the existence of a unique coin, true or false, of that reign. I wish to thank M. Jacques Yvon for his courtesy in answering my enquiries, and also Dr. C. H. V. Sutherland, Keeper of the Heberden Coin Room at the Ashmolean Museum, for introducing me to M. Yvon, and himself helping me with information. I can only regret that in spite of our joint efforts we have not quite succeeded in nailing the Pescennius to the right counter.

B iv 459 f. *a gloomy Clerk . . . divinely dark*] Cf. Prior, "The Conversation,"
35–6 (*Works, ed. cit.*, i 524):
> Thro' many Points divinely dark,
> And WATERLAND assaulting CLARK . . .   (N.W.B.)

I take it that Pope is punning on "divinely" = "like a divine".

B iv 459–92. A useful commentary on those lines will be found in Arthur
Friedman, "Pope and Deism", *Pope and his Contemporaries, ed. cit.*, 89 ff. Special
attention is given to Tindal's *Christianity as Old as Creation*, 1730.

B iv 477. *Or, at one bound*] Cf. Milton, *P.L.*, 180 f. (of Satan):
> and in contempt,
> At one slight bound high overleap'd all bound . . .   (A.L.W.)

B iv 549, *amice*] Mr. Max Bluestone ("Pope's Dunciad, iv 549", *The Explicator*,
1962, xx No. 5) thinks that the chef's amice must be "an apron *engirdling* him as
he performs his mystic rites".

Attention should perhaps be drawn to the sustained religious parody, or
blasphemy, in this passage, culminating in the "three . . . in one" of l. 562.

B iv 560n. The editorial note on "Bladen" may possibly do less than justice to
Pope's fondness for ambiguities. While the gamester alluded to is probably
Thomas Bladen (see Biog. App.), Pope may also be willing to involve Col.
Martin Bladen in his commentary. The latter had married a lady who had "a
great sugar estate" in the West Indies (see Frank Wesley Pitman, *The Develop-
ment of the British West Indies, 1700–1763*, 1917, p. 187). "Bladen is a black man"
may therefore be Pope's way of saying that he was a man who employed blacks,
or negroes, on his plantation. Bladen, a consistent supporter of Sir Robert
Walpole in parliament, was also one of the Commissioners to the Board of Trade
and Plantations, and had been active in trying to get protection for the sugar
trade (F. W. Pitman, *op. cit.*, pp. 260, 262). The otherwise rather pointless
allusion to the proverb "Wash Blackmoors white" tends to strengthen the probability that Pope means to glance at Col. Martin Bladen, whom he had
previously (A i 240n.) shown himself willing to wound.

B iv 571n. Since this note was written Professor Rae Blanchard has dis-
closed in her article, "Was Sir Richard Steele a Freemason?" (P.M.L.A., 1948,
lxiii 911) that Pope and Swift were apparently freemasons—unless the "Mr.
Alexʳ Pope and Mr. John Swift" mentioned in *The Minutes of the Grand Lodge
1723–39*, p. 156, were other persons bearing the same names. Mr. James Osborn
has informed me, however, that there was a close connection in the early
eighteenth century between the Roman Catholics and the Masonic Order: in
1729–30, for example, the Duke of Norfolk was Grand Master of the Grand
Lodge. The last sentence of my note is accordingly misleading.

B iv 629 f. *sable Throne . . . Night . . . Chaos*] Cf. Milton, *P.L.*, ii 959 ff.
> when strait behold the Throne
> Of *Chaos*, and his dark Pavilion spread
> Wide on the wasteful Deep; with him
> Sat Sable-vested Night, eldest of things.   (A.L.W.)

Professor Williams also suggests (*op. cit.*, p. 153) that "the 'sable Throne' inverts the 'great white throne' upon which Christ makes *His* Second Advent" (*Rev.* xx 11).

p. 416, *n.*16. Horace Walpole seems to suggest (*The World*, No. 6, February 8, 1753) that Cibber's swans were, in fact, real geese: "Mr. Cibber . . . attempted to introduce a taste for real nature in his *Caesar in Egypt*, and treated the audience with real—not swans indeed, for that would have been too bold an attempt in the dawn of truth, but very personable geese."

Note to Biographical Appendix

p. 457. WARD, Edward. Ward was proprietor of an ale-house near Clerkenwell-Green from 1712–17; the Bacchus Tavern in Moorfields from 1717–30; the British Coffee-House in Fullwood's Rents, near Gray's Inn, from 1730 till his death (H. W. Troyer, *Ned Ward of Grubstreet*, 1946, pp. 169, 175 ff., 202). Pope's statement that Ward's works had a large transatlantic sale is supported by a statement of Cotton Mather, *Manducto ad Ministerium* (Boston, 1726). p. 43: "How much do I wish that such Pestilences [plays], and indeed all those worse that Egyptian Toads (the Spawns of a Butler, and a Brown, and a Ward, and a Company whose name is legion!) might never crawl into your chamber" (*ibid.*, pp. 227–8).

INDEX

Italics have been used for entries from pp. 1 to 194, and from pp. 267 to 409, to indicate that the reference is to the text of the poem; references to the notes in these pages are given in ordinary type. Elsewhere in the volume references to the text are given in ordinary type, and to the notes in ordinary type followed by the letter *n*.

18